T0323574

Proprietary capitalism

Proprietary capitalism
The textile manufacture at Philadelphia, 1800–1885

PHILIP SCRANTON

CAMBRIDGE UNIVERSITY PRESS

Cambridge
London   New York   New Rochelle
Melbourne   Sydney

This publication was supported by a grant from the
Merrimack Valley Textile Museum.

PUBLISHED BY THE PRESS SYNDICATE OF THE UNIVERSITY OF CAMBRIDGE
The Pitt Building, Trumpington Street, Cambridge, United Kingdom

CAMBRIDGE UNIVERSITY PRESS
The Edinburgh Building, Cambridge CB2 2RU, UK
40 West 20th Street, New York NY 10011–4211, USA
477 Williamstown Road, Port Melbourne, VIC 3207, Australia
Ruiz de Alarcón 13, 28014 Madrid, Spain
Dock House, The Waterfront, Cape Town 8001, South Africa

http://www.cambridge.org

First published 1983
First paperback edition 2002

A catalogue record for this book is available from the British Library

Library of Congress Cataloguing in Publication data
Scranton, Philip.
Proprietary capitalism.
Includes index.
1. Textile industry – Pennsylvania – Philadelphia –
History – 19th century.   I. Title.
HD9858.P5S35   1983   338.4′7677′00974811   83-10155

ISBN 0 521 25245 8 hardback
ISBN 0 521 52135 1 paperback

For my parents, who taught me to love the past,
and for my son, who teaches me to live in the present

Contents

Maps and figures

Maps

Figures

Preface

Five years ago, as the centennial of the Philadelphia College of Textiles and Science approached, I undertook what appeared to be a customary research project, an attempt to document the circumstances surrounding the origins of the institution and its century of growth, crisis, and change. A summer spent pursuing traces of the founders, a cluster of local textile manufacturers, raised questions far broader. Despite the vast size of the city's textile industry, the secondary literature proved disappointing, focusing with rare exceptions on the New England manufacturing experience. Was this omission significant? Were the textile trades in Philadelphia an industrial backwater? Were the men who started a school for practical manufacturing instruction local oddities or educational innovators? As I began to appreciate the importance of textile work to the city's economy, as the largest sector of industrial employment, exploration of its structure and background beckoned, and comparison with the much-studied Lowell system seemed plausible. Seeing the creation of the Philadelphia Textile School in a larger context demanded basic research to reconstruct that context.

The Philadelphia Social History Project at the University of Pennsylvania provided the initial pool of raw materials for that effort, through its holdings of copies of both manufacturing and population census manuscripts, 1850–80. Both the center's staff and its director, Theodore Hershberg, offered support and timely criticism of my first feeble efforts to reconstruct the development of the textile trades in the generations surrounding the Civil War. When I swallowed the research hook, issues related to the launching of textile education were enveloped in an effort to understand the place of Philadelphia's textile industry in the larger process of American economic development. It gradually dawned upon me that Philadelphia differed from Lowell, Lawrence, and Manchester not just in detail but in structure. Collectively, its firms represented a different version of industrial development, followed a different path to profit, prominence, and accumulation than did the mass-production corporate giants.

To pursue these notions, to elaborate a conceptual framework within which to evaluate and present them would have been virtually impossible without the benevolence of the National Endowment for the Humanities, whose fellowship grant enabled me to take a year's leave from the diverse responsibilities that accompany teaching at a small technical college. Without the opportunity to read widely, travel to archives, stare (and occasionally glare) for hours at microfilmed documents, without the chance to write into the small hours, this book would not have been completed. The NEH fellowship took me to Brown University to join colleagues from other teaching colleges in a research and reading seminar, "The New Labor History," under the direction of Professor Joan Scott. There this project took root and was nourished. The regular, critical assistance of my "fellow workers" in the seminar helped me test first-cut formulations. However, the extension of this work from article scale to its final book length must be credited to Joan Scott, whose generous enthusiasm and sensitivity to argument, style, and nuance shaped both the research and the writing. No words of thanks can ever fully convey my appreciation for her concern and support, which has extended well beyond the close of my year in Providence.

Here in Philadelphia, my debts are many. In addition to its collection of primary sources, the Philadelphia Social History Project offered workspace, endless cups of coffee, and the valued assistance of fellow scholars, most particularly Mike Frisch, Henry Williams, Gretchen Condran, and Morris Vogel. Judy Goldberg, working on her dissertation on Philadelphia's Knights of Labor, shared with me her voluminous extracts from the *Public Ledger,* 1870–86. At the Philadelphia College of Textiles and Science, my home base, the encouragement I received from President Donald Partridge, Dean William Andrews, and my department chair, William Brown, was of tremendous importance. Far more basic was the cheering warmth of my colleague Natalie Allon, a scholar and teacher of sociology who was lost to us through a tragic accident in the fall of 1980.

The Rockefeller Library at Brown was a mine of priceless information, and its Government Documents and Interlibrary Loan divisions were constantly helpful. To the staffs of the Van Pelt Library at the University of Pennsylvania, the Pastore Library at Textile, the Baker Library at the Graduate School of Business, Harvard University, and the Historical Society of Pennsylvania, my thanks for their toleration of my incessant scrounging. At the Historical Society, special mention must be made of Peter Parker and John Platt, whose extraordinary knowledge of their collections led me to important sources. Similar virtuosity was in evidence at the National Archives, whose staff directed me to Quartermaster Corps records that shed light on Civil War contracting. R. R. Looney of the Free Library of Philadelphia, Prints and Photographs Division, searched diligently to unearth most of the illustrations that accompany the text.

For their careful reading of early drafts and for suggestions that improved the final manuscript immeasurably, my gratitude goes to Stanley Engerman, Alan Dawley, James Hassell, Judy Goldberg, and Joan Scott. At Cambridge University Press, Steve Fraser read the first few chapters and pressed me for more, providing a special stimulus to complete the writing process. His successor, Frank Smith, handled the knotty task of editing the result with professional skill. Judy Kovach and Donna Trieger typed the text and tables; and Donna, with her customary expertise, handled revisions serenely. My friends shared the whole experience, the frustrations and the breakthroughs. For keeping at least one of my feet planted in the present, I must acknowledge Ben Judkins, Charlie Roberts, Deb Sanford, Jeff Halpern, Mary Lyster, Walter Licht, and Ardis Cameron. Finally, for sharing her life, her wisdom, and her laughter with me, I offer my thanks and my love to Virginia McIntosh.

PART I

Pathways to textile industrialization

1

Introduction: the matrix of accumulation

The motive of business is pecuniary gain, the method is essentially purchase and sale. The aim and usual outcome is the accumulation of wealth. Men whose aim is not increase of possessions do not go into business, particularly not on an individual footing.

Thorstein Veblen, *The Theory of Business Enterprise*

In January 1880, a company of men, aimed at accumulation and in business on an "individual footing," gathered to banquet and plan the affairs of an association they had recently formed. They were the chief figures in a local industry that represented "seventy five millions" in invested capital and that provided the National Association of Manufacturers with its first two presidents. Their spokesman, Thomas Dolan, asserted proudly that their division of the nation's textile industry was "composed almost exclusively of individuals and individual firms, in the aggregate, 849, no corporations."[1] These were the textile manufacturers of Philadelphia. They had created the single greatest assemblage of textile mills in the nation, without recourse to the device of corporate ownership that keyed the development of New England's heavily capitalized mass-production mills. By the 1880s they and their 55,000 workers had erected a manufacturing system that stood as a fully realized alternative to the corporate industrial model. For historians who sought to trace the evolution of corporate America, the Philadelphia experience in textiles has been of little significance. But for those who would undertake to establish how capitalist industry functioned in the nineteenth-century context, who see some value in the reconstruction of industrial development as a moving totality, the documentation of a mature "small-business" alternative to industrial gigantism will add a missing dimension to economic history.

This study has three goals. It aims to detail the emergence of a vital and complex textile industry in Philadelphia, a manufacturing enclave characterized by the multiplication of small, separate, specialized firms. Second, in

[1] *Public Ledger*, January 28, 1980. Pennsylvania enacted a general incorporation statute in 1874, but textile manufacturers did not rush to secure the protections of limited liability.

3

contrasting this production format with the bulk staple system inaugurated at Lowell, it will demonstrate the historical coexistence of multiple successful paths to profit and accumulation. Recognition of these sharply different forms of textile capitalism, each productive of "pecuniary gain," lays the base for reconceptualizing the development of this industry in a more comprehensive fashion than previously attempted. Third, as a device to facilitate comparison of the several formats for textile manufacturing, the notion of an "accumulation matrix" will be introduced. The matrix is a catalogue of the broad range of social and economic factors that together constitute the total situation for production and profit faced by entrepreneurs. In stressing the interlocks between various factors and the sequential effects of decisions regarding them upon future firm options, the full complexity of the manufacturing environment will be revealed.

The matrix concept is introduced to allow alternative solutions to the problems of production and accumulation to be viewed on an equal footing. To assume that the productive systems established in the great New England firms were a form of industrial "best practice" and to chart variations from those forms would serve to prejudice the outcome of analysis, for on that model differences could subtly become deficiencies. Instead, by assembling the common set of factors that affect the success chances of all manufacturers, we introduce the possibility of multiple correct solutions, each fitted to a particular constellation of givens, choices, and responses to the dynamics of historical changes within the firm and in the external environment. "Matrix" here refers to an interrelated array of determinants bearing on behavior across time, a usage present in the social sciences from political studies to family therapy.[2] For manufacturing, the "accumulation matrix" designates the constituent elements of the historical situations within which accumulation originates, develops, and is constrained.

All industrial firms, whatever their form of organization or their output, are linked by the drive for profits, feasible only through the mobilization and exploitation of productive labor, a process solidified by the extension of the base from which it is mounted through accumulation. Whereas profits are the short-term results of exchange, the accumulation of capital is the residue of longer-term profitability, that is, a surplus that may become embodied in simple additions to existing plant and machinery, in ventures toward innovative technology or marketing, or in the form of proprietors' personal funds, which when sufficient may allow them to cease operations and lead a life of

---

[2] See, for example, Frances Stewart, *Technology and Development*, London, 1977, chap. 1; Ivan Boszormenyi-Nagy and Geraldine Spark, *Invisible Loyalties: Reciprocity in Intergenerational Family Therapy*, New York, 1973, chap. 1; Donald Kingdon, *Matrix Organization: Managing Information Technologies*, London, 1973; and Joseph Berliner, *Factory and Manager in the USSR*, Cambridge, Mass., 1957, Foreword.

leisure or public service. The factors that bear on this accumulation project may be clustered in three groups: material, sociocultural, and external.

Eight material elements can be specified: raw materials, transport and communications, marketing, production processes and technology, labor (supply and skill use), firm structure and organization, space (land and the built environment), and finance (capital and credit). Over them, businessmen can reasonably hope to exercise a measure of control or influence; they are the subject of customary decision making. Moreover, given their openness to manipulation by firm directors, they will, in particular, divergent combinations, illustrate alternative paths to accumulation. Decisions about these material elements cannot be abstracted from the sociocultural context within which the firm seeks to function. A range of institutions, values, and practices fundamentally condition capitalist manufacture, creating both opportunities and impediments to accumulation, for it is amid a concrete social thicket that the firm must establish the mechanics of production. Manufacturers are rarely in a position to control the social context of production with anything like the same decisiveness with which they may contract for new equipment or construct an addition to their facilities.

Most visible among the contextual elements are the several levels of state structure whose laws, taxes, tariffs, police, and educational and other services all impinge on the capacity of the firm to accumulate. Likewise operating continually as elements in the social relations of production are religious beliefs and culturally derived notions of time, hierarchy, justice, and labor, along with the rhetoric and rituals embodying them (from riots to parades, from St. Monday to testimonials for manufacturers). These intersect and overlap with patterns of family and community organization and action to flesh out the sociocultural elements. Communities, composed of families in many configurations, elites and immigrants, literary societies, pool halls and sodalities, form networks of authority and action of which the firm and the mill are but a part, more or less dominant but hardly omnipotent, outside the pure and unstable case of the company town. Finally, the quality and cost of housing and provisions and the related issue of public health are physical elements in the social context of industrial operations.

The external elements influencing a firm's capacity to accumulate are the events and processes utterly beyond the control of businessmen that have a fortuitous or catastrophic impact on them – disasters, fires, and floods, as well as wars and commercial panics and depressions. Yet the often double-edged quality of such events becomes evident when we ask for whom they are disastrous. A flood at Fall River may immobilize the city's mills, providing a rash of orders for rivals at Lowell or Philadelphia. Wars may imperil firms dependent on embattled areas for supplies or markets, yet may benefit others who can meet military demands for tents or blankets. More processual are the effects of immigration, internal migration, and altered patterns of fertility, life-span, and infant mortality. In addition to these demographic issues, the collective results of individual decisions that urban agglomeration represents can have a substantial effect on manufacturers, whether in increased competition for labor and markets or in providing multiple possible sources for inputs and services.

Decisions manufacturers make about the particular configuration of material factors reflect the links among these elements at a particular time and place. Raw materials must be selected so as to match the capacities of the technology at hand, whose choice must in turn be in part based on an appraisal of the availability of workers with sufficient skill to run the machinery effectively. The presence of numerous firms already producing yarns appropriate to the fabrics entrepreneurs seek to manufacture may permit the saving of capital on spinning equipment and the purchase of a larger complement of looms for a single-function weave shed. The adoption of a standardized output may simplify production processes so that lower-skill, cheaper, and readily replaceable labor can be employed by the firm. Handing over marketing tasks to a commission agency may free proprietors, allowing them to become more directly involved in production and thus lead to better quality goods.

Yet once the format for production is established, and initial risks have been taken and surmounted, contingency resurfaces again and again. Naturally, once a firm has exercised certain options and forgone others, it proves difficult and costly to redirect its productive strategy. A decision to secure technology that is fast but of limited flexibility may prove problematic as other firms follow the same path and glut the market with nearly identical goods. Moreover, should demand develop for sophisticated weaves, none of these firms will be able to respond without massive alterations and concomitant capital spending. The firm relying on skilled workers to manufacture a wide range of fancy knits will be ill placed to profit from an influx of immigrant peasants who would be welcomed by a mass-production enterprise seeking to cut costs in its routinized operations. Examples could be multiplied indefinitely, but the core point is that necessary initial decisions about the configuration of production entail constraints on future decision making. There is no permanent solution to the manufacturer's problems, for the material and social elements bearing on accumulation are ever in motion, creating new dimensions of risk for the firm.

To be sure, an emphasis on contingencies does not imply boundless chaos, just as the sequential actions that structure and revise manufacturing processes cannot be reduced to the formulas of economic determinism. Yet if the matrix notion is at all useful, it should help us realize that focus on one or several of the elements in accounts of industrial development to the exclusion of others will lead to "histories" that are fragmentary and distorted. Keeping in mind the tentative conceptual framework just described, we can proceed to question historical materials in search of the patterns and clusters of factors and actions that brought forth quite different trajectories of textile industrialization. Until recently, most research on nineteenth-century textiles centered on the New England experience, viewed along two dimensions. For early scholars, the developmental track of the cotton trades, from handwork to Slater's spinning mill with outwork weaving to the Waltham-Lowell integrated model, seemed to chart the course for industrial development in America, a course repeated in the experience of other trades. Primitive early forms were superseded by a more modern corporate system, whose competition eradicated its predecessors. This simplified and linear "textile paradigm" has been largely rejected, for other industries departed from this neat pattern as they matured.[3] It is my contention that the imagined paradigm fails as well to account for the development of the industry it initially treated, once elements omitted from its chronicle are included.

A second focal point for research on New England textile firms has been the pioneering role of the Lowell corporations as modern mass-production firms. Though Alfred Chandler has offered a substantial corrective to this view,[4] his recent work continues the traditional emphasis on the evolving corporation as the unifying thread in American business history. Consistent with the search for the roots of contemporary corporate practice, nineteenth-century joint-stock companies have claimed by far the greatest share of historians' attention, with their wide dispersal of ownership and fascinating gap between stockholders and operating personnel. Meanwhile, the closely held corporation, in textiles or elsewhere, and the incorporated proprietorship have gone largely unexamined, much less analyzed, partly, to be sure, a result of the privacy prized by their owners. The array of unincorporated formats for capitalist production (partnerships, family firms) has been quietly passed over. What harm does this do to historical analysis? Are the uninterrogated merely unimportant?

Part of the answer may be drawn from the shortcomings of the textile paradigm. The corporate focus underlying its creation thoroughly blocked perceptions of the persistent alternatives that capitalist inventiveness sustained in textiles and in other productive arenas. The result of historians'

---

[3] Ralph Samuel, "The Workshop of the World: Steam Power and Hand Technology in Mid-Victorian Britain," *History Workshop Journal* 3:6–72; Bruce Laurie and Mark Schmitz, "Manufacture and Productivity: The Making of an Industrial Base, Philadelphia, 1850–1880," in Theodore Hershberg, ed., *Philadelphia: Work, Space, Family and Group Experience in the 19th Century*, New York, 1981, pp. 43–92.

[4] Alfred Chandler, *The Visible Hand: The Managerial Revolution in American Business*, Cambridge, Mass., 1977.

acceptance of the joint-stock company as the agent of economic dynamism is a remarkably one-dimensional account of nineteenth-century industrialism.[5] The twentieth-century prominence of giant manufacturing corporations has given rise to business histories that probe the past for their antecedents. This effort reflects an implicit teleology in which the essential and inherent superiority of corporate structures is assumed.

Three things are troubling about such approaches. First, given that the triumph of mass production and the efficiency of corporate forms are "known" in advance, inquiry and explanation may take place largely in technological and organizational terms. The broader material and sociocultural context of corporate development remains external to the analysis, presumably "held constant." Second, such shrunken boundaries of inquiry prevent our comprehending in anything like their totality the historical relationships through which corporate and proprietary capitalist manufacturing shaped our society and were in turn shaped in the struggles for profit and power that industrialization sparked. If corporate economic dominance was necessary but merely latent until its potentials were exploited by enterprising technicians and executives, contingency drops from industrial history, and economic development can be described through a chronicle of discoveries and discoverers (from the power-loom and steam-engine versions of technological determinism to the biographical tradition encompassing Rockefeller, Carnegie, Steinmetz, and Ford). Not only is there a reductionist and determinist core to this method, it also generates a history ironically depopulated of both capitalists and workers. Manufacturers outside the main line of development seem peculiar, anachronistic, and doomed, and workers become ciphers. Culture, family, and religion are viewed through a filter that merely assesses their acquiescence, resistance, or indifference to the inevitable. Such history is again "idealist" in the sense that we are called upon to witness Progress or Modernity unfolding themselves through the great men and great firms of the last century. Third, within this perspective, the corporation becomes concretized as a "thing" rather than seen as a set of relationships more or less adequate for dealing with the challenges of production, realization, and accumulation. Just as the concept of class becomes frozen and lifeless when regarded as an entity, so too does the firm lose its dynamic, open, and problem-solving profile when it is similarly objectified as an institution through which the agency of historical progress materializes.

What seems to me to be needed is a more inclusive empirical investigation

---

5 Chandler's *Visible Hand* is particularly valuable in documenting substantial variations from a simpler linear "progress" account and in tying these variations to concrete differences in productive arrays and organizational forms.

into the socioeconomic relationships that constituted capitalist manufacturing a century or more ago, a specification of the ways in which a variety of firms sought to "create" and appropriate value, the blocks to that end they had to overcome, and the range of strategies that emerged under different concrete conditions. The goal of this effort would be to document the accumulation process in motion, as a contingent phenomenon that men and women activated, opposed, and shaped. It is the process, the uncertainty, and the variation that are ignored by idealist tales of corporate deployment. In recovering these aspects of economic history, we may come to understand that the boundaries of possibility in both the past and the present are wider than we had imagined. To restore the integrity and complexity of the past is simultaneously to liberate our imagination in the present.

A second broad rationale for reexamining the unfolding relationships of capitalist manufacturing stems from the flood of recent scholarship in labor history. For if E. P. Thompson, Herbert Gutman, and David Montgomery have rightly stressed the richly varied initiatives and relatively autonomous cultures of workers in the social and economic struggles accompanying industrialization, the bald fact of capitalist power remains. As historians have reconstructed the interacting moments of religion, politics, family, and community that informed workers' resistance or accommodation, it seems timely to ask similar questions of the capitalists and their institutions and to explore the variety of paths to accumulation they followed. This is the main theoretical question that triggered the present study: given a heterogeneity of material and sociocultural conditions under which capitalist production proceeded in the nineteenth century, what variety of strategies and formats for accumulation can be specified? What are the relations conditioning success for each? How do various structures of production, finance, marketing, labor relations, and so forth relate to historical conditions of regions and communities and their situation within a national political entity and an international marketplace? Ultimately, if various roads to profitability can be documented and their persistence be allowed to imply a measure of success over time, how are we to revise our accounts of capitalist development in a fashion that accommodates historical experiences that to this point have been ignored or dismissed?

It is toward beginning to respond to such questions that this work is presented. The central focus will be on Philadelphia, but through the depiction of the characteristics of textile production in a corporate mill city and rural seat in Chapter 2, a base of reference will be offered for the contrasting patterns established in the main body of the text. Moving to Philadelphia, Chapter 3 will present two case studies for comparison with the formats described in Chapter 2, rounding out Part I and setting the scene for a more detailed exposition of textile capitalism's development in the Quaker City. In

Part II, Chapters 4–7 will portray the emergence of the city's textile trades during the period 1800–60.

Through these chapters it will become clear that by 1860 there existed in Philadelphia a complex of specialized and flexible manufacturing enterprises of all sizes, employing labor of recognized skill in the production of wools, cottons, blends, hosiery, carpets, silks, and trimmings. There were connections among the firms of both a productive and a cultural character. The form of ownership was private, in proprietorships and partnerships, and often a manufacturer's family was welded to the relations of production. Capitalists ran their enterprises directly, ranging from small-scale shop-floor labor to sophisticated marketing postures. The city provided transportation and communication systems and a central sales district that facilitated flows of information and goods for those sufficiently well fixed to locate their agencies there. Artisanal and paternalist cultural elements merged profitably with market rationalizing. Immigrants played a major role in the development of the local industry, their strategies and actions perhaps significantly different from those of native-stock manufacturers and certainly at broad variance from their colleagues in New England. Mills were shared, older and newer technologies combined, and on occasion factory, outwork, and artisanal relations of production were mixed in the same firm. The first families of Philadelphia and their financial institutions, indifferent to all this hubbub, were nowhere on the stage.

With this much established, in Chapter 8 the Civil War's dramatic impact on Philadelphia textile maufacturing will be assessed and contrasted with the near catastrophe that the war brought to Lowell. The twenty-year period following the war, an era of enormous growth, will be reviewed in Chapters 9 and 10, ending with the crisis events of the mid-1880s. The conclusion will summarize the main themes and will suggest directions for additional research.

In the preparation of this book both traditional and "quantifiable" sources provided crucial production-centered information, and the secondary literature provided the evolving scenic background against which the accumulation process unfolds and with which elements of it interact. Primary data on textile manufacturing appeared in the manuscript schedules from four federal censuses of manufacture (1820, 1850, 1860, 1870), the *McLane Report* (1832), and one city manufacturing census (1882). Business and industrial directories provided useful additional information, principally for the postwar period. Population census linkages for many manufacturers in the 1850 and 1880 counts (compiled by the Philadelphia Social History Project) profiled household composition and ethnicity. The Hexamer Insurance Survey, preserved at the Free Library of Philadelphia, yielded a glimpse of the physical facilities for manufacturing from the late sixties, documenting the role of tenancy. Judy Goldberg's meticulous review of the daily *Public Ledger* exposed the quotidian activity of an emerging working class in the seventies and eighties. Some neighborhood newspapers have also survived, and for the 1830s *Hazard's Register of Pennsylvania* was often valuable. It is from these and other raw materials that I have assembled this portrait of proprietary textile capitalism.

2

The textile manufacture in corporate Lowell and rural Rockdale

The capitalists, mill agents, overseers, and mill girls of Lowell have long formed the cast of a mythic drama of New England industrialization. Whether portrayed in a heroic or tragic mode, the story of early Lowell is familiar enough to need only the briefest recapitulation. The mercantile group known as the Boston Associates, fresh from their first manufacturing success at Waltham, determined rather grandly about 1820 to create a manufacturing center along the Merrimack River. They purchased all the shares in the Locks and Canals company, a venture of the 1790s that had dug the ill-fated Pawtucket Canal at East Chelmsford as a bypass to the Falls of the Merrimack.[1] Proceeding systematically, over the next four years the associates purchased farms covering nearly 400 acres above and below the falls. The first mill, that of the Merrimack Manufacturing Company, was erected while the land transactions were still in process. By the fall of 1823, the first cloth had been produced.[2]

Both the canals and the subsequent textile firms were organized as corporations, the vast capital in the hands of the associates quickly ranking them among the largest manufacturing institutions in the nation. In the *McLane Report* of 1832, of the 106 manufactories in the nation valued at more than $100,000, 88 were textile companies. Eight of these were Lowell firms, none of whose capitalization was less than $600,000.[3] Seven of the mills turned out staple cottons, one (Middlesex) wool broadcloths and cassimeres. Cotton's dominance of the Lowell scene would continue throughout the century. The two later mills, Boott (1835) and Massachusetts (1839), produced yet more millions of yards of sheetings and drills, all cotton.

---

[1] Henry Miles, *Lowell As It Is, and As It Was*, Lowell, 1846, pp. 13–16, 24–5. If Miles is to be believed, the scattered 500 shares were purchased below their par value, so dormant was the original Locks and Canals company.

[2] Louis Hunter, *A History of Industrial Power in the United States, Volume I: Waterpower*, Charlottesville, Va., 1979, p. 212.

[3] Alfred Chandler, *The Visible Hand: The Managerial Revolution in American Business*, Cambridge, Mass., 1977, p. 60; Miles, *Lowell*, pp. 48–55.

Initially, all the Lowell factories were powered by water channeled through a regularly refined and expanded system of canals to breast wheels at each millsite. By midcentury, 9,000 horsepower were available to drive machines of the ten mills and the related Lowell Machine Shop. Technical refinements would increase the waterpower to nearly 12,000 horsepower by the early 1880s. The Locks and Canals company denied use of Lowell's power resource to small firms, from whom there were frequent applications. Given that steam cost from two to three times as much per unit at midcentury, the effect was virtually to prevent creation of any small manufactories, even of such industries as could "service and supply" the textile giants. Louis Hunter observes: "The more obvious solutions [powered buildings in which space was rented] were either ignored, considered and rejected, or determinedly opposed by the Locks and Canals, the controlling authority in what was in basic respects a 'company town.' "[4] To be sure, the "controlling authority" in Locks and Canals remained the same group who owned the Lowell mills. Their profits from the "natural monopoly" of land and water averaged 24% per year during the twenty years of the company's existence, far surpassing the returns (estimated by McGouldrick) from the mills.[5] In 1845, the Locks and Canals company was liquidated as a partially autonomous corporation, its remaining lands, buildings, and the machine shop realizing nearly a half million dollars. Given the estimated initial share cost ($40,000–50,000 for the 500 original shares),[6] the final balance sheet must fairly have glowed.

During its lifetime, the Locks and Canals company had been an effective instrument for both accumulation and mystification. When markets for cotton goods weakened, or the price of raw materials skyrocketed, the proprietors of the Locks continued to draw the standard rates for power and thus generate striking profits. It was to the workers that the individual mills turned in such times, cutting piece rates or increasing board charges in corporate housing to balance the ledgers at Boott or Suffolk. While the ownership of the mills and the Locks was marvelously intertwined, the structural independence of the manufacturing firms "necessitated" the squeeze on workers, especially women workers, as Thomas Dublin demon-

4 Hunter, *History of Industrial Power*, p. 218.
5 Thomas Dublin, *Women at Work*, New York, 1979, p. 20; Paul McGouldrick, *New England Textiles in the Nineteenth Century: Profits and Investments*, Cambridge, Mass., 1968, p. 85. For the period 1836–42, the five Lowell firms in McGouldrick's Baker sample averaged 9.3% profits (to standard net worth). For the whole group (8 firms), for the period 1836–46, the mean profits were 14.4% per year, with a range from 6.0% (1838) to 31.2% (1845).
6 Miles, *Lowell*, p. 25.

strates.[7] Though primitive, the process foreshadowed the financial and organizational strategies that "big businesses" would employ in a later era. The Lowell mills were from the outset controlled by absentee owners. The principal shareholders were centered in Boston, as were the mill treasurers, though the latter visited the mills with regularity.[8] Treasurers functioned as the chief executive officers, meeting with the boards of directors, relaying their mandates to resident agents at the mills, supervising marketing as well as production, and securing raw materials through cotton and wool brokers. At Lowell there were linkages between the companies beyond the level of Locks and Canals and overlapping shareholding. Treasurers at times served more than one corporation; Henry Hall in the 1830s handled the task simultaneously for the Lawrence, Tremont, and Suffolk firms.[9] Resident agents (or superintendents) likewise shared information, not only to identify fractious workers through circulated lists but also, through conferences, to establish citywide movements in piece rates.

What emerges gradually is a picture of a widely integrated network of self-conscious capitalists who, as Adam Smith suggested, scarcely ever gathered but to conspire against the public. To strengthen their position and national market competition, the Lowell firms sought collective control of the relations of production through common policies toward labor. Uniformity among the mills helped maximize the surplus value in every yard of product. So long as markets were favorable, the realization of the surplus could be had by all (e.g., 1825–32, 1836–37, 1839, 1844–48).[10] When the tides turned (1834, 1838, and the early and late forties), the same linkages made it possible to force workers to absorb the effects of contraction, through rate cuts, increases in lodging charges, stretch-outs, and the like.

Two additional features of this capitalist network will suggest its intricacy in greater depth. The Lowell mills were incorporated in a steady sequence; Merrimack in 1822, Hamilton in 1825, two more in 1828, and four in 1830. With integrated ownership of the first mills and the Locks and Canals, "the first investment at Lowell was seldom the last. . . . The dividends from one company were restored to the industry by the formation of another."[11] Thus, the Boston Associates engendered a cycle of profit and reinvestment sufficiently powerful not only to permit the regular expansion of existing

---

7 Dublin, *Women at Work*, chap. 6.
8 Chandler, *Visible Hand*, p. 70.
9 Dublin, *Women at Work*, p. 90.
10 Caroline Ware, *The Early New England Cotton Manufacture*, New York, 1931 (rpt., 1966), pp. 140–3; McGouldrick, *New England Textiles*, p. 99. Ware notes that capital was easily raised by 1830 and that profits in 1830–1 were "immense," hovering near 20%.
11 Ware, *Early New England Cotton Manufacture*, p. 142.

facilities but also to spawn new Lowell corporations through the "plowing sideways" of dividends. To be sure, the dividends gathered by members of the dozen or so associates' families were not by themselves sufficient to fully capitalize the 1828 and 1830 ventures. Yet the aura of success that surrounded first Waltham and then the Merrimack and Hamilton companies, combined with the contemporary scarcity of investment opportunities for mercantile capital, led men of substance to "subscribe . . . to shares in one or more Lowell corporations in blocks of twenty-five, fifty and one hundred thousand dollars."[12] Over the next generation, these large blocks themselves were gradually sold off, somewhat dispersing ownership.

The uncertainties of textile marketing were a source of constant anxiety for cloth and yarn manufacturers. Though Slater, Almy and Brown may have pioneered the factory system in Rhode Island, they never mastered the market end of their business, delivering goods to a score of commission agents, haggling over rates, complaining of curious currencies, and even accepting goods exchanges when pressed. The venerable Nathan Appleton, in the prototype Boston Manufacturing Company (Waltham), devised a more reliable scheme. The entire output of the mills was placed in the hands of a single general commission house, in which Appleton, in Caroline Ware's phrase, was "largely interested," where he was charged two-thirds less than rates paid by Almy and Brown. The Lowell capitalists improved doubly upon this innovation. In 1828 they formed their own selling house (J. W. Paige & Co.), specializing only in textiles, which took to market at minimal commission rates all the goods of the four factories then in operation. Moreover, this and other selling houses in turn bought stock in the current and later ventures and provided members to boards of directors. As a final complementary gesture, the firms paid out to stockholders "virtually all earnings net of standard depreciation" over the half century that followed. Thus was the network of investment, production, realization, and accumulation neatly laced together.[13]

The laces stayed tied. McGouldrick puts it best: "For the rest of the nineteenth century [after 1830], structural characteristics of the New England industry remained substantially unchanged." Financially, expansion and retooling expenses never threatened a healthy asset–debt ratio.[14] New issues of stock were infrequent. Six of the ten Lowell companies had the same capital stock outstanding in 1885 as they had had in 1845.[15] The

12 Ibid., p. 141.
13 Ibid., pp. 142, 178–9; McGouldrick, *New England Textiles*, p. 28.
14 McGouldrick, *New England Textiles*, pp. 14–15.
15 Miles, *Lowell*, pp. 48–57; *Textile Manufacturers Directory of the United States*, New York, 1885, pp. 97–9, 341–3.

board-treasurer-agent structure remained intact, as did the responsibilities assigned to each. Commission houses continued to handle the mill product, though the shift to New York as the trading center is visible. In 1870, all the Lowell mills still sold through an exclusive agent, five of them employing the George C. Richardson house of Boston and New York. Fifteen years later, six of the ten were selling through Richardson, and one had engaged an additional house for access to the Philadelphia market.[16] Stockholders could rely on dividends and were generally well satisfied. McGouldrick again: "The operation of a textile mill had become so routine that a reasonably well capitalized business having competent supervisory personnel could perform satisfactorily without stockholder surveillance. . . . A lack of the need to make challenging decisions explains the passivity of stockholders."[17]

The Lowell mills initially seem to have sought to avoid direct competition by producing different products. The Merrimack plant offered printed cottons, Appleton, brown sheetings, and Middlesex, wools. However, by the mid-1830s overlaps were apparent with the increased numbers of mills whose equipment was virtually standardized. In an 1870 directory, seven of the ten firms were listed as producers of cotton sheetings, shirtings, and drills in one combination or another. The others ran wools, carpets, and prints.[18] To be sure, to the extent that the market expanded for these staple goods and to the extent that common selling houses apportioned the market, competition was mitigated for the Lowell firms. These qualifiers were not perfectly reliable, however, and mills outside Lowell produced competing goods as well. Increased total capacity would saturate markets, certainly after the 1850s, prices and margins would fall, and the heavenly profits of the middle forties would return only once, for a moment, amid the yawning demands of the Civil War. For New England as a whole, competition in textiles became "near-perfect" after the 1830s.[19]

Having surveyed the organization and management of textile manufacturing at Lowell, it is time to turn directly toward production itself – the physical structure of the mills, their equipment, products, siting, and, most critically, their work force. Finally, the environs surrounding the central corporations will be explored: the development of the town, housing, and local government and the emergence of other textile firms in Lowell in the later decades.

---

16 *Dockham's United States Cotton Woolen . . . Manufacturers' Report & Directory, 1870–71,* Boston, 1870, pp. 16–19; cited hereafter as *Dockham's Directory; Textile Manufacturers Directory,* pp. 97–9, 341–3, *Statistics of Lowell Manufactures, Jan. 1871,* Lowell, 1871.
17 McGouldrick, *New England Textiles,* p. 27.
18 *Dockham's Directory,* pp. 16–19.
19 McGouldrick, *New England Textiles,* pp. 34, 81.

Bricks, machines, and workers: the structure of production

Built of brick, four to six stories tall, the mills of Lowell stood as monuments to the ambitions of Boston merchants, to the magnetism of standardized machine production, and to the vision of economies of scale. They were, however, erected, outfitted, operated (and, on occasion, disrupted) by working people, in exchange for a wage, the essential transaction of industrial capitalism. Over the course of three generations, shares would change hands, machinery and buildings would be replaced, the work force would turn over innumerable times and its structure alter considerably, yet that essential relationship would remain. Producers would daily visit the means of production, expend labor power in a manner determined by others, depart into a city that for years resembled a total institution, and receive their wages once monthly in a paper packet. It is this, the process of capitalist production and realization, that structured Lowell and gave it lasting significance.

As physical structures, the Lowell mills illustrated the corporations' production strategy. Integrating preparation, spinning, weaving, dyeing and finishing, and printing within the same facility called for large-scale construction. Very likely copying contemporary English structures, the Lowell mills were both broader and longer than earlier American efforts. A description of the Merrimack mill complex in 1849 verifies this. Each of the company's five mills was five stories tall, having one enormous room on each floor, 40 by 151 feet, the ceilings 10 feet high.[20] Perhaps more significant than their sheer size was the extent to which the mills standardized their form. Views of the manufacturing district from the 1840s show a common layout pattern, varied to accommodate different placements along the canal system. Farm-bred women workers very probably had never seen structures on this scale, such rural mills as previously existed being both small and solitary. With the adjacent rows of mill-built boardinghouses, the Lowell factories presented to the in-migrant a spatially structured environment to whose constraints submission was necessary. The concentration of manufacturing and residence within this space should also be emphasized. Though the rough rectangle of land defined by the river and the canal measured about a mile by a mile and a half, until the 1850s nearly all manufacturing and most housing, along with the central commercial street, were located in the eastern third of that space on a few hundred acres of ground.[21]

---

20 Norman Ware, *The Industrial Worker, 1840–1860*, New York, 1924 (rpt., 1964), p. 98; Steve Dunwell, *Run of the Mill*, Boston, 1978, pp. 26–7.

21 Maps in Dublin, *Women at Work*, pp. 63–4; Miles, *Lowell*, facing title page, and Dunwell, *Run of the Mill*, pp. 26–7.

Within the mill buildings, space was allocated vertically along a functional sequence of production steps. On the lowest floor, cotton bales were opened and the raw material was fed into pickers and cards from which it emerged as "laps," or inch-thick sheets. Nearby, the laps were drawn down into soft cords, or "roving," which completed the preliminary operations. On the two higher stories, in open rooms, spinning frames stood arrayed, each holding a fairly standard 128 throstle spindles, which produced coarse counts of yarn. The filling yarn was loaded on elevators for the weaving floors above, but warp yarn, wound on three-foot beams for insertion in the back of the looms, had to be stiffened through the application of sizing. This work was an exacting hand process, intersecting mid-way in an otherwise machine-based production. (Ultimately, this potential bottleneck would be eliminated through the introduction of a dressing or sizing machine, commonly as a "slasher.") Power looms occupied the top floors, again in rows in huge open rooms, elevators linking the sections together. Finished beams of cloth traveled to a separate storehouse or at the Merrimack mills to the printworks.

The whole apparatus drew power from the waterwheel by means of a system of shafts and belts. The loss of power in turning the shafts, the inefficiencies of early belting, and the decrease in power transmitted over long distances functionally limited the size of the floor space on which machinery could be efficiently employed. With the replacement of wooden shafting by lighter and more durable metallic rods, with the advent of reliable gearing, and with progress in realizing more fully the hydraulic potential of the Merrimack, the transmission of more power over greater distances became feasible.[22] This facilitated increased machine speeds, which had been prohibited by vibration and rapid shaft and gear wear before the 1840s. Moreover, it made reasonable the erection of taller and longer structures within which each waterwheel could drive yet more machinery.

These considerations, supplemented by the considerable profits of the enterprises and declining construction and machinery costs, led the companies to build additional mills. Construction, though perhaps erratic, was a constant feature of the manufacturing environment. Miles noted in 1846 the completion of a new mill by the Lawrence company and work in progress on "an Extension of their works" by both Appleton and Hamilton, this at the close of several highly profitable seasons. Between 1836 and 1850, the number of mills in the city doubled (from 20 to 40), while looms and spindles increased two and a half times, suggesting an increase in mill size.[23]

---

[22] Dunwell, *Run of the Mill*, pp. 62–8; Hunter, *History of Industrial Power*, chap. 6.

[23] Miles, *Lowell*, pp. 60–1; Dublin, *Women at Work*, p. 133. As earlier mills were packed to the gills with machinery, it is unlikely that the largest proportion of the additional spindlage could have been located in these crowded confines.

Table 2.1. *Number of spindles on cotton
and wool, Lowell, 1836–85*

Year	No. of spindles
1836	130,000
1846	216,948
1850	320,000
1870	515,052
1875	580,500
1885	814,182

Source: 1836 and 1850, Thomas Dublin,
Women at Work (New York, 1978); 1846,
Henry Miles, *Lowell As It Is, and As It Was*
(Lowell, 1846); 1870, *Dockham's United
States Cotton Woolen . . . Manufacturers' Report & Directory, 1870–71* (Boston, 1870);
1875, *U.S. Textile Directory* (Washington,
D.C., 1875); and 1885, *Textile Manufacturers Directory of the United States* (Boston,
1885).

Similarly, after the Civil War, the original ten companies continued to construct and expand, as the increase in spindlage figures indicates (Table 2.1).
While the early replication of firms was seen as remarkable by contemporaries, the postwar expansion was no less so. Bursts of "net investment" in the early seventies and eighties brought into production a number of facilities, some of which continued to function well into the twentieth century.[24] Both in terms of capital and plant, Lowell textile manufacturing started big and stayed big.

Though, at any given moment, the built forms of the mills, their standard machinery and common products, and their unchanging management and production formats gave the impression of stasis, there was considerable movement over time, for beneath the surface swirled the rich dialectic of the quest to refine the means of accumulation. Had profits been high? Were market prospects favorable? Then expand, buy new looms, replace old equipment, turn the oldest mill into a storehouse, add a steam engine. Finance it out of retained earnings, with short-term borrowing at peak times.[25] Have to pay off those loans? Had the cloth margin dropped? Was

[24] McGouldrick, *New England Textiles*, chap. 7, esp. pp. 156, 162.
[25] Ibid., pp. 170–2.

there a market crisis? Well, stretch out weavers and spinners, cut the piece rate, speed up the machines now that the technology will handle it, or, in a crisis, lay off thousands and sell inventory for a time.[26] Did the new machines falter? Did the shafting need repair? Piece rates saved the company's accounts, at least. Did the workers turn out in reply? Denounce them, hire others, let them learn their place in the mechanism, inform your colleagues about the most ungrateful, take back the penitent.[27]

Yet within all these relations of power and production, there were constraints generated by the same historical processes that facilitated accumulation in the first place. Because they relied on waterpower, the Lowell mills were vulnerable to power shortfalls caused by low water. Responding to this and the conflict-producing interdependencies of the system, the millmen moved to control the source of waterpower in the New Hampshire lakes. This in turn yielded a cycle of interstate political conflicts and efforts by New Hampshire manufacturers to buy into the local Lake Winnepesaukee Cotton and Woolen Manufacturing Company, the joint offspring of Locks and Canals and the owners of the Lawrence (Mass.) mills. These tangles lasted well into the 1870s, when provisional accord was reached with both state and corporate rivals.[28] The issues were rendered less potent as steampower came first to supplement and then to supplant the central force of water flow. Thus did expansion generate imperatives of wider control, producing wider conflicts and contradictions, which were resolved in this case by the technical displacement of the central source of antagonism.

Other dilemmas that emerged from the structuring of Lowell manufacture proved more difficult to solve. The cotton production capable of machine manufacture in the early growth era (1822–45), employing a semiskilled force of tenders, was that of coarse sheetings and prints, using heavy yarns of standard counts. Fine spinning for fine cottons implied the use of mules, necessitating highly skilled mule spinners and a work force of children to assist them. Not only were mule spinners expensive, in short supply, and (then and later) notoriously uppity, but child labor under the family system was problematic in northern New England. Numbers of young women *were* available, as were throstle-spinning machines yielding coarser yarns for staple cloths. The tariffs on cheap cottons restrained import competition, and lower grade raw materials could be employed in production. All these and perhaps other factors induced the Boston Associates to embark on the standardized mass production of several simple cloths. These initial commit-

26 Dunwell, *Run of the Mill*, p. 104.
27 Dublin, *Women at Work*, pp. 79, 86–107.
28 Hunter, *History of Industrial Power*, pp. 279–81.

ments would carry with them subtle constraints, particularly as the replication of mills took hold in and out of Lowell. First, staple cloths brought a small price in the market and that price declined over time (brown sheetings fell from 7½¢ to 4¢ per yard between 1830 and 1849).[29] Caroline Ware notes appropriately: "Even tripled production did not make up for the slender return on each unit" by 1859.[30] And, indeed, increased production was each manufacturer's individual answer to the problem. Thus, in conformity with a classic capitalist contradiction, the individualist solution provoked a collective worsening of the situation.

There were attempts at varying the mill output but only within the limits imposed by the product of the spinning process. Mills used mountains of No. 14 yarn in different weaves but retained the bulk strategy with which they had commenced. To introduce a sharply flexible production, virtually every aspect of the industrial structure would have required modification. Various grades of cotton would have been needed as well as wools for use as filling in mixing goods, adding complexity to purchasing, storage, and supervision. A variety of yarn counts would have been necessary, their quantities determined by the anticipated production and markets for a wider variety of goods of higher quality and value. Mills would have needed workers of greater skill, machinery would have needed frequent resetting and adjustment, or whole new arrays of it purchased, and all of this with the risk of catastrophe should any key section of the more complex production process fail to perform fluidly. Should the anticipated markets be filled by others or simply not materialize, the whole enterprise might suffer severely. Born on staples, Lowell kept its focus on them through the Civil War era. Relatively rigid in their output and production mechanics, the mills sought to restore profitability through grinding the work force.

The impressive scale upon which this production was mounted entailed yet other limitations. Three dimensions of enterprise scale inhibited corporate response to competitive price declines.

First, one of the fixed investments of the first quarter century had been construction of housing for each mill's work force. With the squeeze of the 1840s, construction of mill boardinghouses did not keep pace with plant expansion, ceasing entirely after 1848. Sale of the lands once held by Locks and Canals delivered the housing problem into private hands.[31] These two steps signaled the abandonment of the last shreds of "benevolent" paternalism; it was replaced by chaotic market relations in housing and "thrown-up"

---

[29] Dublin, *Women at Work*, p. 136.
[30] Ware, *Early New England Cotton Manufacture*, p. 113.
[31] Dublin, *Women at Work*, pp. 134–5.

tenements crowded with workers. The constraint on expansion imposed by the construction of "proper" housing for additional workers simply vaporized after the late forties.

Second, because of high fixed costs (e.g., cotton was commonly purchased a year in advance), firms achieved what McGouldrick calls "minimum average total cost . . . at a scale of output very close to capacity."[32] Mills could not easily reduce production in times of uncertain markets. Should they close entirely, they risked turning their suspension into relief for their competition. Thus their scale and its attendant costs obliged the Lowell factories to continue to churn out goods, even though this collective overproduction threatened to slash every mill's individual profits.

Finally, the scale of Lowell's mills blocked a solution to product inflexibility that was valued elsewhere. Refusing power and land to small mills prevented the formation at Lowell of a group of contract spinning and dyeing and finishing firms that could have provided flexible skills that might have been integrated into the larger production process to vary the eventual output. Only one such company, the Lowell Bleachery, existed in 1846. Though small mills appeared in the sixties, their output suggests only the most incidental relationship with the giants.[33] Insofar as output variation was achieved at Lowell, it came through the installation of new machinery in newly erected buildings for the bulk production of a standardized output not previously manufactured (carpets first at the Lowell company, later flannels at Hamilton and hosiery at the Lawrence company).[34]

These interlocked limitations on the antebellum development of the textile manufacture eventually had to include the work force. The low-skill requirements of the initial manufacturing setup were designed to draw Yankee rural women to the mills. The bulk production of staple fabrics, which continued for two generations, did not demand or induce sophisticated skills among operatives, for they performed the same tasks year after year in a fashion mindful of stereotyped assembly-line workers.[35] Moreover, they were sped up and stretched out at these tasks, perhaps increasing their proficiency at narrow skills but certainly not broadening them. High labor

[32] McGouldrick, *New England Textiles*, pp. 29–30.

[33] *Dockham's Directory*, p. 56.

[34] McGouldrick, *New England Textiles*, pp. 29, 148–9; *Dockham's Directory*, p. 62; *U.S. Textile Manufacturers Directory* (1875), Boston, 1875, pp. 73–85; Arthur Cole and Harold Williamson, *The American Carpet Manufacture*, Cambridge, Mass., 1941, pp. 57–8.

[35] This is not to deny mobility within the factory, which Dublin documents. The point, however, is that operatives' tasks were sharply separated from the richly complex spinning and weaving skills needed in those mills where production was highly differentiated. Spinning a million pounds of No. 14 yarn is a world apart from spinning a dozen different counts each week in job lots, a common practice in contract spinning, or in integrated mills where varied production was the rule.

turnover justified and reinforced the imperatives of keeping production tasks standardized. Some few skilled veterans were required to supervise carding, to run the carpet looms and printworks at several mills, and for maintenance and repair. A small body of Scots and English immigrants filled many of these roles and occupied special mechanics' housing in recognition of their status. Yet prewar Lowell was no magnet for arriving British or German dyers, mule spinners, and the like. Their skills (and perhaps their values) led them toward the more diversified and flexible textile manufacturing of other regions.[36] Lowell workers could not easily manage any marked transition to more differentiated production, should an incentive for such a change activate the corporate directors.[37]

The sheer momentum of Lowell production kept each mill rolling proudly onward, short of a collective catastrophe. The Civil War provided catastrophe enough, magnified by the "blunders" of mill treasurers into a derailment of the whole accumulation process. The cotton famine is justly famous; its impact on Lowell caused one historian to credit it with "beginning the long decline of Lowell's textile industry."[38] Within weeks of the commencement of hostilities, the directors of the Merrimack Manufacturing Company resolved to cut production and suspended it entirely in August 1861.[39] With the price of raw cotton soaring, and the traditional supply of a year or more of stock on hand, the directors sold bales in the bull market, reaping windfall profits without manufacturing a yard of cloth. In their turn, other Lowell companies followed suit, "being accustomed to 'dress' on the Merrimack," as Charles Cowley crisply noted.[40] Moreover, the firms disposed of their existing inventories at high prices, multiplying the short-run gains. They all banked on a short struggle. This grave miscalculation fractured the system of manufacturing that had frozen in place over the previous four decades.

Thousands of workers, laid off indefinitely, left the city for other employment or, in smaller numbers, volunteered for the Union forces. Lowell volunteers were in such abundance that, even in the last stages of the war,

---

[36] Philadelphia and Fall River drew heavily on these groups. Mule spinning came to Lowell only at midcentury, other than in woolen manufacture, in which spinning jacks were the basic device. The jacks were a variation on the cotton mule, at best semiautomatic in this era. Nothing comparable to the standard cotton throstle frame was available for woolen yarn production. See A. H. Cole, *The American Wool Manufacture*, Cambridge, Mass., 1926, vol. I, pp. 113–16, 358–61.

[37] Working wools was not done simply by using the cotton template. Every step of manufacturing was either somewhat or vastly different. Skills needed for mixed-goods production, hosiery, or carpets were also not born overnight, not to speak of the skills needed to oversee machinery, supplies, and distribution.

[38] Fidelin Brown, "Decline & Fall," in A. Eno, ed., *Cotton Was King*, Lowell, 1976, p. 141.

[39] Ibid.

[40] Charles Cowley, *Illustrated History of Lowell*, Boston, 1868, p. 48.

only once was a draft call visited upon the city.[41] City records imply that single men and women emigrated, whereas family men enlisted. Here the mayor:

> Many of our manufactories, where were constantly heard the hum of the spindle and the clatter of the loom, are now silent. No lack of opportunity has prevented all able-bodied men, of suitable age, from serving their country, and by their earnings and the allowances from the state to their families, providing well for their wants.[42]

From the school Committee:

> The complete cessation, for so long a time, of the cotton manufacture, has driven many of our people elsewhere for employment, and though the exodus has been in large proportion of single persons, many families, with children, have also gone. . . . Probably, within no preceding six months has the emigration been larger than during the last [July-December 1863].[43]

By 1865 the city's population had declined to 30,990 from the 36,827 tallied in the 1860 census.[44]

The mills did not stay silent. Indeed, those already producing woolen goods (Middlesex and the carpet section of the Lowell company) never closed, keeping 2,000 operatives at work throughout the war. Further, the huge war-induced demand for woolens (uniforms, blankets, etc.) prompted the Suffolk, Tremont, and Hamilton companies to break with tradition and commence an entirely new production. The experiment, if Cowley is to be believed, was a disaster, something that the structural limitations argued earlier surely conditioned: "Several of [the cotton companies] made abortive experiments in other branches of manufacture, by which they incurred losses, direct and indirect, exceeding the amount of their entire capital."[45] By 1865 a number of cotton mills had reopened, buying foreign stock at the shocking average price of 87¢ a pound,[46] nearly seven times the 1860 domestic price of 13¼¢. Nonetheless, inflated prices for finished goods offered profits to manufacturers, sparking the cotton mills again to life. They too altered their production, perhaps experimentally, in a fashion that introduced variation and differentiation novel to Lowell manufacturing.

[41] Horum Hosford, "Mayor's Address," in *Lowell City Documents (1863)*, Lowell, Mass., 1864, p. 5; Arthur Eno, "The Civil War," in A. Eno, ed., *Cotton Was King*, Lowell, 1976, pp. 134–5.

[42] *Lowell City Documents (1863)*, p. 34.

[43] "School Committee Report," in *Lowell City Documents (1863)*, pp. 5–6.

[44] "Report of Births, Marriages & Deaths," in *Lowell City Documents (1870–71)*, p. 8.

[45] Cowley, *Illustrated History of Lowell*, p. 48, quoted in Cole, *American Wool Manufacture*, vol. I, p. 379.

[46] Oliver Warner, *Statistical Information Relating to Certain Branches of Industry in Massachusetts*, Boston, 1865, p. 363.

Several of the Civil War experiments appear to have been discarded by the early seventies: cotton cashmerettes (imitation cashmeres), mixed satinets (a sturdy but ugly blend), mousseline de laine (a cotton-wool muslin for women's wear), and all-wool blankets and repellents (coatings). Yet a few of the wartime innovations persisted, most notably the hosiery manufacture at the Lawrence company and worsted-yarn spinning at the Hamilton. Lowell's all-wool Middlesex company also changed its production, though immune from the cotton famine. The largest wool mill in the nation during the 1840s,[47] it was one of the last to give up the antiquated broadcloth manufacture.[48] By 1872 Middlesex added fashionable opera flannels and beaver coatings to its reliable cassimeres and shawls. The two new fabrics were simple to produce, flannels needing none of the elaborate finishing required for fine wools, beavers being traditionally made in solid dark colors. Overall, the effects of the sixties on Lowell production can be summarized as introducing variation within the system but not transforming the structural relations of production. Lowell mills widened the scope of standardized production but did not move toward highly flexible, fashionable products, other than those that could be integrated into a low-skill, mass-scale process.[49]

The impact of the Civil War on Lowell's workers cannot be overlooked. That the corporations held dominion over the city was never more clearly demonstrated than when they "unanimously, in cold blood, dismissed ten thousand operatives, penniless into the streets!"[50] Cowley, rhetoric notwithstanding, did not overstate the layoffs by much. The 1861 *Statistics of Lowell Manufactures* gives a total of 11,534 workers for the ten mills, whereas the total for 1865 was but 5,277.[51] Of this latter group, 2,797 were employed at the reopened cottonworks. If they are excluded, the difference between 1861 and the years of a full cotton shutdown mounts to more than 9,000. As suggested by the city documents, the largest proportion of those fired left Lowell.

The Civil War–era disjuncture not only provided the impetus for some differentiation of corporate production at Lowell. It also was the occasion for further development of the textile manufacture, beyond the confines of the founding corporations. The 1885 Massachusetts State Census provides a table of the "Dates of Establishment" of all manufacturers operating in that

[47] William Graham, *Statistics of the Woolen Manufacture in the United States*, New York, 1845, p. 117.

[48] See Cole, *American Wool Manufacture*, vol. I, pp. 300–6.

[49] Incidentally, of the ten Lowell corporations, only one (Appleton Company) manufactured the same product line (standard No. 14 sheetings, shirtings, and drills) in 1861 and 1872.

[50] Cowley, *Illustrated History of Lowell*, quoted in Brown, "Decline & Fall," p. 141.

[51] Warner, *Statistical Information*, p. 363.

year. Of thirty-seven textile firms surveyed, thirteen, including the ten major corporations, had been founded before 1860, ten during the war decade, and fourteen in the period 1870–85.[52] Six of those formed in the sixties were wool manufacturers, though none was on the scale of even the smallest of the original ten.[53]

In the seventies and early eighties, more small, specialized textile firms popped up at Lowell, diversifying the textile manufacture a bit more. By 1885, new manufacturers had undertaken production in areas that the majors failed to enter: elastic goods, suspenders, yarn for sale, felt, gauze, and especially worsteds, the fastest growing and most fashion-related sector of the wool trade. By 1885 five specialty firms were making worsted yarns, perhaps for sale to the two new worsted-cloth firms and the Middlesex Company.[54] Though several of the postwar firms sported six-figure capitalizations by 1885, it is doubtful that the twenty-five to thirty new companies employed more than 10% to 15% of the city's textile workers. Statistics are available for the ten majors (13,500 workers) and for all textile mills in 1875 (16,000), giving the smaller firms 15% of the city's textile work force. New firms in the next decade may have pushed the nonmajors' share above 15%. In all, the product variation by the Lowell corporations was modestly supplemented by postwar start-ups of specialty textile manufacturers. The new firms dispersed outside the central district, particularly to the south, a process necessitated by the majors' monopoly of downtown land and water-power and facilitated by the wider availability and diminishing cost of steampower.

These modifications took place in a wider context of textile expansion both in Massachusetts and on a national scale. Completion of a national rail network, the emergence of standardized and "mass-produced" clothing, huge urban populations, major retailing centers, and heightened fashion consciousness meant expanded demand for textiles along two dimensions. For staple goods, from shirtings to cassimeres, bulk production continued to afford profits, though Lowell experienced sharp competiton from the even-more-ruthless capitalists of Fall River and New Bedford.[55] For fine goods,

---

[52] *Census of Massachusetts, 1885, Vol. 3: Manufactures*, Boston, 1888, pp. 74–5.

[53] Three were corporations: U.S. Bunting Co. (1865), Wament Worsted Co. (1867), and Lowell Hosiery Co. (1869). Capitalization for the hosiery firm is given as $100,000 in 1870. See *Dockham's Directory*, p. 17.

[54] *Textile Manufacturers Directory*, pp. 97–9, 341–3. The Middlesex Company appears to be making worsted goods, but, unlike integrated worsted mills, it does not list worsted spinning machinery in the directory. It is possible that the city's largest woolen mill opted to contract out the spinning of worsted yarns but retain the spinning of its own woolen yarns for other goods.

[55] "Fall River, Lowell and Lawrence," in *Massachusetts Bureau of the Statistics of Labor 1882*, Boston, 1883, pp. 195–415; cited hereafter as *Mass. BSL*.

the consumption by the urban middle and upper strata of fancy cotton, silk, and worsted dress goods, draperies, carpetings, and so on called forth entrepreneurs in the specialty trades. Only the tip of this production emerges at Lowell; much more will be seen in Philadelphia. The imperatives of accumulation in specialty textiles, indeed the structure of production itself, depart markedly from the Lowell format, as I shall suggest later.

A sketch of the textile work force and its transformation (1825–85) will help flesh out this portrait of the social relations of production at Lowell. Production engaged skilled workers, overseers, and operatives at the large mills. Skilled jobs (dyers, engineers) were filled from the outset exclusively by men, some of whom were Scots and English immigrants. The introduction of mule spinning at several mills before the Civil War and the expansion of the wool manufacture brought more skilled male immigrants to Lowell, though never in the numbers experienced at Fall River.[56] British immigrants of all occupations, ages, and sexes comprised 4.7% of the Lowell population in 1875 but 8.8% of the textile workers three years later. (Comparable figures for the same years at Fall River are 19.2% of the population and 36.3% of the textile workers.)[57] Dublin found in his detailed study of the Hamilton Company 4.9% British workers in 1850 at the beginning of the company's mule-spinning era, rising to 8.3% by 1860.[58] The totals for both dates for the ten majors are likely lower, given the uneven introduction of mule spinning.

Overseers likewise were all men. Generally of long experience in textile manufacturing, they drew the highest wages in the mills and were responsible for maintaining efficient production. Though generally cordial in their relations with spinners and weavers in the early decades, they were transformed into "drivers" when the premium system was introduced in the forties and the labor process was intensified. Competiton among overseers for prizes that might reach $100 brought harsher conditons for shop-floor operatives.[59]

Most workers "on the Corporation" served as operatives, predominantly in jobs connected with spinning and weaving. Three broad groups of workers handled these routinized tasks in the Lowell mills: Yankee women, immigrant Irishwomen (and later men and children), and immigrant Quebecois. Initially the core of the operative force, Yankee women began leaving

---

[56] *Mass. BSL (1882)*, pp. 198–9.

[57] Ibid., pp. 198, 204. Of the immigrants working in the Lowell mills in 1878 (705 English, 178 Scots, and 2 Welsh), 293 were 20 years old or less, leaving a maximum of 602 skilled immigrant workers. Further, 286 of the over-20 group were women, reducing the final skill pool to 306 adult males (*Mass. BSL [1878]*, p. 238).

[58] Dublin, *Women at Work*, p. 139.

[59] Ibid., pp. 111–12; Ware, *Industrial Worker*, p. 124; Miles, *Lowell*, pp. 182–3.

Table 2.2. *Textile workers by nativity, Lowell, 1836–78*
(in percentage)

Nativity	Hamilton Company workers			Workers, all mills, 1878
	1836	1850	1860	
United States	96.3	61.4	38.2	48.6
Ireland	2.3	29.4	46.9	29.6
Britain	0.5	4.9	8.3	8.8
Canada	0.9	3.4	4.5	12.6
Other	—	1.0	2.1	0.4
Total	100.0	100.1	100.0	100.0

Source: For 1836–60, Thomas Dublin, *Women at Work* (New York, 1978), pp. 26, 139; for 1878, *Massachusetts Bureau of the Statistics of Labor, 1878* (Boston, 1879), pp. 237–8.

Lowell in the forties and were replaced by increasing numbers of Irish in-migrants. There was not a sudden or wholesale replacement, however. Conditioned by a continued decline in the rural reservoir, new opportunities for labor outside the mills, and the worsening conditions therein, the flow of Yankee daughters to Lowell dwindled to a trickle.[60] Mill recruiters contined to range into upper New England well after the Civil War, but their "catch" shifted to include ever larger numbers of Quebecois families by the seventies.[61]

Commencing in the forties, a wave of immigrant Irishwomen, participating in a variant of the family labor system, succeeded the much-chronicled Yankees, whose "independence" has often been stressed. Dublin discovered by the 1850s a high proportion of female-headed immigrant households whose teen-age children held mill jobs while the mother took in boarders or did outwork.[62] The absent fathers may well have been engaged in casual or construction labor. In any event, by 1860, more than 60% of the women workers at Hamilton were Irish wives and daughters.[63] In the next decade, as the Irish influx waned, the first sizable contingents of French Canadians surfaced at Lowell. By 1878 the ethnic and sexual configuration of the 1840s work force had been transformed (Table 2.2).[64]

[60] Dublin, *Women at Work*, chap. 8.
[61] For an 1870 recruiting poster in northern Vermont, see A. Eno, ed., *Cotton Was King*, Lowell, 1976, p. 104. For French recruitment, see "The Canadian French in New England," *Mass. BSL (1881)*, pp. 8, 17.
[62] Dublin, *Women at Work*, pp. 162–4.
[63] Ibid., pp. 184–5.
[64] *Mass. BSL (1878)*, pp. 237–8.

Table 2.3. *Textile workers by sex, Lowell, 1837–83*

Year	Male workers[a]	Female workers[a]	Total
1837	1,671 (21.2)	6,181	7,852
1861	3,169 (27.5)	8,345	11,534
1866	3,502 (28.7)	8,713	12,215
1872	3,546 (31.4)	8,514	12,060
1878	4,586 (33.4)	9,155	13,741
1883	5,366 (33.6)	10,587	15,956

Note: Figures in parentheses indicate percentages.
[a]At ten major Lowell corporations.
Source: Statistics of Lowell Manufactures (microfilm, Baker Library, Harvard University), various years.

The increase in U.S.-born workers by 1878 reflects the rising numbers of immigrant offspring at Lowell, as the proportion of residents of native-born parents declined to 20% of total population by the turn of the century.[65] The gradual rise of the percentage of male workers can be linked to several ongoing developments in the Lowell manufacture: the installation of mule spinning, establishment of the specialty worsted trade in which male workers predominated, and the intensification of the labor process, which called for more durable workers. As the stretch-out forced workers to tend four rather than two looms, as male immigrants could be had for the same piece rates paid women, and as concern for Lowell's role as a model manufacturing town dissipated (ending the need for sexual segregation on the job as an inducement to the migration of Yankee daughters), the "mixing" of men into the operative work force was accomplished. Moreover, the exploitation of child labor rose as well (in turn linked with mule spinning, the family labor pattern, and the drive to lower labor costs amid competition). Dublin found children under 15 to be but 6.6% of the Hamilton Company employees in 1850, 15.4% of males and 2.7% of female workers. By 1878, for all mills, children 15 and under formed 11.1% of textile workers, 14.6% of males and 9.4% of females.[66]

---

[65] Mary H. Blewett, "The Mills and the Multitudes," in A. Eno, ed., *Cotton Was King*, Lowell, 1976, p. 175.

[66] Dublin, *Women at Work*, p. 141; *Mass. BSL (1878)*, pp. 237–8. The two sources have slightly different boundaries for "children": the earlier one includes 15-year-olds, the later one does not. The significance of "15" derives from its being the legal age for "school-leaving" in Massachusetts. It is thus *possible* that no increase in child labor took place during this era. However, two factors argue against this, apart from contemporary observers (see "School Committee Report," *Lowell City Documents (1878–79)*, pp.

Wages, productivity, and the cost of living and housing at Lowell are all complementary fractions of the social relations of production within and without the mills. From the 1840s, the corporations added machinery and new buildings faster than they increased the total workforce. Wages remained stable or declined slightly, while productivity blossomed.[67] Piece rates, which enabled some single women to amass modest savings in the thirties, were cut in the forties and barely sufficed. By 1871, when the State Bureau of Labor calculated a family-of-four budget, the gap between textile wages and the cost of living was substantial. With $644 considered necessary for a minimum of essentials, Massachusetts males in cotton ($531) and wool ($458) fell well short, and women realized but $307 and $317 in the same trades for a year's work.[68] Under such conditions, families pyramided small incomes to meet their living expenses.[69]

Relations outside the mill underwent a parallel transformation, centered on housing and suggesting corporate directors' growing perception of the simple centrality of production in the accumulation process. In the same decades that the millmen tightened their control over work, they gradually withdrew from direct management of workers' lives outside the gates. Inside the factory, the heightened pace of production prevented the casual association of workers and ended the informal reading and rest periods remembered by veterans of the thirties.[70] Outside, the corporations ceased to construct boardinghouses to shelter operatives called to the expanding mills. Materially and ideologically necessary in the Yankee era, the boardinghouses had never brought returns comparable to those derived from manufacturing. Instead, directors invested in expanding production.[71] Combined with exacting regulations, compulsory church attendance, and the "moral police" informer system, boardinghouses exemplified a corporate dominion akin to that of the total institution. Discarding as much of this baggage as was practicable was consistent with the narrowed requirements of political econ-

---

12–15). First, to report as few underage workers as possible, the mills required substantiation of a child's age from parents; and second, parents in need of additional income gladly asserted, in turn, that underage children were 15 or older to secure them a place in the mill. The numbers, as ever in statistics, are suggestive rather than conclusive.

67 McGouldrick, *New England Textiles*, p. 147.

68 *Mass. BSL (1871)*, pp. 531–2. J. P. Harris-Gastrell gives similar figures for 1873 Lowell in "United States," *Reports by Her Majesty's Secretaries of Embassy and Legation Respecting Factories for the Spinning and Weaving of Textile Fabrics Abroad*, London, 1873, p. 278.

69 For an in-depth discussion of the origins of the family work unit in the fifties at Lowell, see Dublin, *Women at Work*, chap. 10.

70 Ware, *Industrial Worker*, pp. 120–2.

71 McGouldrick, *New England Textiles*, pp. 29, 41, 65–6, 243. McGouldrick cites 1831 and 1836 figures for cost of employee housing at $5.70 *per spindle* and up to 20% of total capital outlay. The shift away from company housing was no minor affair.

omy. Excesses of visible domination would infringe upon accumulation, class consciousness being sharpened by naked control (mining company towns, Pullman, etc.). Let other institutions handle untoward behavior (police), housing (speculators), and the rest; the task of the corporation was clear: to make money and to mystify the mechanics of that process as thoroughly as possible. It is not at all likely that corporate directors and agents were fully conscious manipulators. Rather, they simply learned to do that which would yield and protect the greatest return feasible under conditions of considerable uncertainty. As McGouldrick writes: "Even if [treasurers] did not consciously take long-run profit maximization as their guide to behavior, they acted as if they did."[72]

Housing conditions for Lowell operatives, particularly for the immigrant families among them, became sufficiently deplorable in the second half of the century to make the drab and puritanical boardinghouses of the thirties seem havens in a golden era. The conditions were not the responsibility of the corporations; management had neatly severed the prior linkage between "home" and work as situations whose problems had a common source. In the 1840s, Locks and Canals liquidated its landholdings near the manufacturing district to facilitate the upsurge of a "private" housing market, through which both tenements and comfortable bourgeois housing were constructed. In the sixties, the Locks offered sections of its remaining lands on sixteen-year leases to housing speculators, becoming the rentier behind the worst slums of the period. Landlords, whose business sense called for fast returns on potentially shaky leaseholds, threw up shabby buildings in what came to be known as "Little Canada," packing greenhorn Quebecois into facilities that were overcrowded from day one.[73] Ultimately, after the Civil War, Lowell's mills sold off their original boardinghouses to private operators, distancing themselves from the "housing question" once and for all.[74]

Throughout, skilled workers inhabited a separate sphere. The corporations erected neat row homes for dyers and others as early as the 1830s, likely as an incentive to draw them to Lowell and encourage permanent settlement. Earning double the wages the operatives commanded, linked by common craft skills, possessed of specialized knowledge critical to the production process, housed comfortably in sharp contrast to the common work-

[72] Ibid., p. 207.
[73] Peter Blewett, "The New People," in A. Eno, ed., *Cotton Was King*, Lowell, 1976, pp. 208–9. Blewett asserts that the landlords were "usually French-Canadians," in contrast to the list of names given in "The Canadian French in New England," *Mass. BSL (1881)*, p. 47: "Mr. Farrington, Mr. Thompson, Mr. Lombard, George W. Harris, – Harris owns two thirds of the place, and four-fifths are owned by Americans."
[74] Brown, "Decline & Fall," p. 142; also, McGouldrick, *New England Textiles*, p. 66.

ers, the skilled textile men at Lowell rarely acted in concert with the operatives. When piece rates were cut, they remained immune, for they worked at
a weekly rate. When women workers struck in the thirties, they were not
supported by the skilled men.[75] More positively, when machinists and overseers joined the ten-hour drive in the 1850s, the companies responded by
cutting the hours to eleven per day.[76] But for the most part, skilled workers
and overseers occupied a different social space from that of the operatives, a
fracture among wage earners that the housing and piece-work practices of
the corporations fostered.

Strikes in Lowell textile mills were infrequent, usually brief, and almost
always unsuccessful from the thirties through the eighties. The 1834 walkout, though spectacular in demonstrating the rejection of wage cuts by wom-
en workers, involved only a sixth of the Lowell work force and failed to stop
the reductions. The second strike, two years later, amid heavy demand for
cottons, managed to force a rollback of increased boardinghouse charges.
Twice as many workers participated, aided by the tactical sophistication and
the citywide organization of the Factory Girls Association. The struggles
over the ten-hour day in the 1840s exposed a second fissure in the Lowell
work force, that between "loyalists" and "rebel" operatives. The former
group, speaking through the *Lowell Offering*, avoided criticism of factory
conditions, seeking rather to augment their individual worthiness through
hard work and upright morality. Taking the critical offensive in the *Voice of
Industry*, the rebels participated in labor reform movements, attacking the
speedup, women's subservient social role, and the linked ideologies of "true
womanhood" and paternalism. Despite statewide agitation, they failed of
their object. The millmen's political clout, leavened by legislators' own interests and intrigues, blocked the ten-hour bill for three more decades in
Massachusetts.[77]

The introduction of immigrant Irishwomen to the factory work force,
supplemented later by Irishmen and Quebecois of both sexes, further fragmented the potential for worker resistance.[78] From 1836 to the Civil War,
there was but a single strike at Lowell (1859). The walkout involved 300 to
500 Irish workers who demanded higher wages. Although defeated by the
corporate recruitment of Yankee women to replace the strikers, the 1859
strike nevertheless demonstrated a quickening of immigrant activism. It
demonstrated as well the continuity of capitalist power.[79]

After the Civil War, Lowell experienced two strikes by combative mule

[75] Dublin, *Women at Work*, chap. 6.
[76] Ibid., p. 202.
[77] Ibid., pp. 112–28.
[78] Ibid., p. 199.
[79] Ibid., pp. 203–5.

spinners amid the resurgence of the labor movement nationwide. The corporate response was unequivocal. Strikers were considered dismissed; they were either replaced or the mills were closed until they relented, at which point activists were refused reemployment. When the mule spinners union "ordered a test strike at selected Lowell Mills" in 1875, the corporations unanimously discharged all their mule spinners, thereby breaking both the strike effort and the union.[80] When women at the Lowell Company struck against a reduction in 1878, this pattern of management response was reemphasized. The resisting group of warp-preparation workers was "at once discharged," and the strike was "quickly settled."[81] A later strike at the same mill was equally fruitless.

After the Civil War, led by the factious mule spinners, Lowell textile labor may have struggled more boldly than before but with no appreciable success. Intercorporate cooperation remained high, and the bonds among workers feeble. This brief chronicle of domination does not include reference to shop-floor conflicts, the daily counterpoint to factory exploitation, as documentation has not come to light. Whatever small concessions may have been won informally from time to time, when Lowell textile workers, divided along several dimensions, confronted unified and aggressive capital directly, they lost the fight on every occasion save one (1836) over a sixty-year span.[82]

Corporate power at Lowell was not confined within the walls of its factory complexes. Mill operators and agents served again and again as state legislators and local government officials throughout the six decades under consideration. Indeed, the creation of local government at Lowell was twice the product of corporate initiative, the second time an offshoot of corporate

---

[80] Brown, "Decline & Fall," pp. 146–8.

[81] *Mass. BSL (1880)*, p. 48.

[82] The first citywide strike was mounted only in 1903 and failed after more than two months. The single successful strike by Lowell textile workers between the Civil War and World War I was managed in 1912 by the IWW at the time of the famous Lawrence struggle. This effort merits some attention, though no study of it to date has been made, to the best of my knowledge. That there were but seven walkouts in as many decades at Lowell (1820s–80s) may imply that activist workers were motivated by the power of the corporations to migrate elsewhere. Lowell was distinctly rocky soil for textile unionists. Several other peripheral comments may be appended here. First, there is no recorded violence connected with any of the Lowell strikes, including that promoted by the IWW in 1912. This is in sharp contrast to both Philadelphia and Fall River and indeed to labor conflicts elsewhere in the nation in and out of textiles. Second, the continuity of corporate solidarity at Lowell can hardly be overemphasized, especially given the market competition that had developed nationally by the forties and fifties. Third, the collapse of the Lowell corporations came on the heels of World War I, though the precise mechanism of decline has not been specified for either Lowell or Philadelphia, both of whose textile sectors experienced crises before the onset of the Great Depression.

frustration at their lack of control over the institutions set up in the mid-twenties. Initially,

> in 1824, the Merrimack Manufacturing Company organized a commit-tee to prepare a petition to the state legislature for the incorporation of the area [surrounding the Locks and Canals land] as a town. . . . The mill management wished to exert more control over local taxation and school policy. It was unacceptable to them to have the property which they managed subject to taxation by a rural town government miles away which did not represent their interests.[83]

Kirk Boott, "the imperious agent of the Merrimack Company and the Locks and Canals," shepherded the request through the legislature, and the charter was approved early in 1826.

It was evident from the first elections "that the major issue of local politics in the new town was to be a struggle between the old residents and the new mill interests."[84] This antagonism surfaced in 1832 over the issue of school consolidation and construction. The town selectmen and school committee, led by Episcopal minister Theodore Edson, proposed the construction of two sizable buildings to replace six ungraded primaries then scattered about the town. This move was opposed by corporate leaders, including Boott, Luther Lawrence, and E. Appleton. The town meeting affirmed the plan and reaffirmed that decision at a second meeting at which two corporation lawyers protested the expense that "would fall upon the corporations, . . . and from which they could derive no benefit."[85] Twice defeated, the com-panies took a petty revenge by evicting Edson from his parsonage, which was owned by the Merrimack mills, thereby "precipitating a law suit." This secondary conflict was resolved only when his congregation purchased both the church and the residence from the corporation.[86]

The long-term fallout from the school controversy brought down the town-meeting form of direct democratic government at Lowell. The com-panies' 1832 defeat was soon followed by another in 1834, as the townsmen agreed to annex the district of Belvidere across the Merrimack. Though Boott opposed the annexation on grounds that the Belvidere folks had a "lawless nature," the addition of hundreds of "old settler" votes to Lowell meetings was perhaps at the back of his mind.[87]

---

83 Blewett, "The Mills and the Multitudes," p. 161.
84 Ibid., p. 162.
85 Theodore Edson, *An Address Delivered at the Opening of the Colburn Grammar School in Lowell, December 13, 1848,* Lowell, 1849, pp. 11–15, 20–32.
86 Cowley, *Illustrated History of Lowell,* p. 105.
87 Blewett, "The Mills and the Multitudes," p. 164.

Two years later corporate forces moved to dismantle the town meeting and replace it with a mayor-council system.

> The mill interests in Lowell found that the town meeting system of government with its annual appropriations voted by a majority of those present was uncontrollable and unresponsive to their needs. . . . At the February 17, 1836, town meeting a city charter committee chaired by corporation lawyer Luther Lawrence reported after two weeks' deliberations that a city charter was essential to order and progress. The report cited the principal defects of the town system to be "the want of executive power, and the loose and irresponsible manner in which money for municipal purposes is granted and expended." These concerns, of course, were primarily of interest to the mill owners.[88]

Bearing the standards of order and progress, the corporate spokesmen persuaded the townsmen in April to adopt the charter dutifully issued by the state legislature. Some evidence that the final arrangement was a compromise with the old system, in which selectmen were annually subject to dismissal, was the provision that elections of town officials would remain a yearly exercise. The new system, formalized, bureaucratized, and indeed run initially by either corporate retainers or "professional" politicians with whom they were comfortable, was more to the corporations' liking. For the next half century, the political clout of the Lowell corporations on their home turf was unquestionable if not unchallenged. Cotton Whigs and Republicans, "low mean-spirited creatures" in Cowley's acid phrase,[89] ran the city almost without interruption until Ben Butler's 1882 gubernatorial triumph brought Lowell an Irish-Catholic Democrat as mayor.[90] The influence of Lowell and other manufacturing interests at the state level helps account for the long blockade of the ten-hour bill. In addition, their congressional spokesmen secured early tariff protection for the cotton manufacture and were later allies of slave interests in antebellum political infighting.[91]

Finally, touching on other sociocultural factors in the matrix of accumulation, we may note the tremendous gap between the patrician elite who founded and defended the corporations and the farm girls and immigrants who labored there. This broadened into religious dimensions with the influx of Irish and Quebecois Catholic workers and was always overlaid with the stereotypical expectations of women and "girls" that became visible in the outrage triggered by female activism in the thirties and after. Education was

[88] Ibid.
[89] Cowley, *Illustrated History of Lowell*, p. 206.
[90] Blewett, "The Mills and the Multitudes," pp. 174–5.
[91] Ibid., p. 167; Dunwell, *Run of the Mill*, p. 103.

not a primary corporate goal, as the Edson controversy makes clear. That the School Committee was tamed under the charter government is suggested by an 1863 appeal by the committee for an exemption from a state law that prohibited factory work for children under 15 unless they had received "eleven weeks" schooling during the year. Schooling would interfere with production and necessitate the employment of a larger body of child workers to rotate in and out of the mills. The committee asked the state if it might be satisfactory to show that "children of this description should have a certain given amount of elementary knowledge, such as to be able to read correctly, work problems in the ground rules of arithmetic and write their names, in lieu of a prescribed term of schooling."[92] How this might benefit the children is not clear, but it certainly would simplify production scheduling for the corporations.

In examining the organization and development of the Lowell corporate form of textile production – its capacities and limitations, material success, marketing, and labor practices – its matrix of accumulation has taken shape. Focused on the bulk production of standardized goods, heavy investment in plant and power sources, and early and exclusive reliance on machine production in factory settings, the Lowell matrix of accumulation included as well low-skill demands for the largest portion of the work force, the exercise of unilateral corporate power in mill and city, cooperation and managerial linkages among the firms, access to and use of state power for corporate advantage, and the embeddedness of the founders and operators of the companies in an elite network distanced both culturally and physically (Boston) from the world of those at the point of production. Though pressed by regional and, after 1880, southern competition, this format for accumulation at Lowell endured until the second decade of the twentieth century.

The rural dimension: Rockdale

Review of manufacturing census schedules and industrial directories indicates that a significant proportion of the textile manufacturing carried on in nineteenth-century America took place in environs quite different from those of the New England mill cities. The rural mills that dotted the landscape from Maine to Ohio embody an alternative constellation of matrix elements to that detailed for Lowell, one that is also noticeably at variance with the Philadelphia developments. While no single case can stand for the whole, in Anthony Wallace's *Rockdale* a vast array of detail about one such rural manufacturing district opens a window into this rarely probed man-

---

[92] "School Committee Report," *Lowell City Documents (1863)*, pp. 6–7.

ufacturing situation. Although a fuller appreciation of the problems and patterns of rural textile industries must wait for additional research along these lines (encouraging work is being done by Jonathan Prude and Elizabeth Hitz, among others), through *Rockdale* we may examine closely one site, thereby enhancing the base from which Philadelphia's textile manufacture will be reviewed.

Between the early 1820s and the Civil War, more than a dozen firms undertook to produce textiles at mills situated in the Rockdale district of Delaware County, Pennsylvania. All were either proprietary or partnership ventures, most commencing with small capitals raised from the resources of immediate family or kinsmen.[93] The goods produced were marketed in Philadelphia through the services of commission agents; indeed, several of the early manufacturers had merchant experience and thus were operating through familiar channels.[94] Working capital was managed through the exchange of promissory notes, or acceptances, received for goods delivered to commission houses, commercial paper that was tendered to sellers of materials or converted to cash at a discount for payment of rent or wages.[95]

The cotton manufacture predominated, only one mill departing from that track. Each firm started with a single division of the production process, spinning coarse yarns in most cases. During the 1830s, all the factories gradually integrated, so that by "1842, the old system of partial process mills was entirely replaced by complete process mills, which took cotton in and sent out cloth."[96] Rockdale firms sold sturdy but undistinguished gray goods, printing cloths, and flannels, largely supplanted by 1850 by twilled tickings, drills, and denims. Invited to an exhibition in 1845, John P. Crozer, a durable proprietor, noted that local production "does not comprise any great variety of styles nor of a kind to make much display."[97] Staple production did not require highly complex machinery, but the rural location of the mills made maintenance and repair a central concern for the owners. Tools and advice were shared among the mills, and new machinery had to be assembled on site, often with the barest of instructions. In the first generation, most proprietors rented old, converted waterpowered mills. If they survived, firms would both purchase their buildings and expand through new construction financed by accumulated profits.

---

93 Anthony F. C. Wallace, *Rockdale*, New York, 1978, pp. 76, 79, 84, 121–3. In 1825 Daniel Lammot sought to form an incorporated company with initial capital of $150,000, a fraction of Lowell-scale financing, but the plan collapsed in bickering among the parties involved (ibid., pp. 121–2).

94 Ibid., pp. 75, 77, 87, 94, 183.

95 Ibid., pp. 100, 123, 163.

96 Ibid., p. 164.

97 Ibid., pp. 161, 184 (quote from 184).

Given that eight of the first ten Rockdale firms were headed by men without mill training, the search for managers to operate the factories was a chancy necessity. If the manager had overstated his credentials or if a lax or imperious manner disturbed the social relations of production, the firm was endangered.[98] Indeed, the early Rockdale mills failed with some regularity. Their bankruptcies, linked with the narrow resilience of thinly capitalized firms producing relatively low-profit staples amid an often shaky credit environment, were due as well to the proprietors' deficiency of manufacturing knowledge.

The labor requirements for the local textile manufacture involved a small core of mill-veteran mechanics, master spinners and loom bosses, and a much larger body of piecers, bobbin changers, and loom tenders, generally women and children. Male employees frequently sent their children to work in the factories, and, as elsewhere, widows seem to have migrated into the district to place their children at work.[99] Immigrants by 1850 comprised a quarter of the 2,000 district residents, overwhelmingly English and Northern Irish, presumably largely engaged in textile labor. Skilled workers were able to secure places for kinsmen, boarders, and offspring, but the workforce turnover was fairly high, a year's stay being about average.[100] Housing for the district's factory workers was in part provided by manufacturers' erection of short blocks of row houses near the mills. Occupancy of mill "tenements" depended on the ability of the resident family to supply several workers to the factory master. Other workers boarded with farmers, village tradesmen, or workers who lived in the rowhouses; homeownership is not evident. According to Wallace's calculations, skilled workers with family members in the mill (or boarders) could expect to live fairly well and save money, an outcome possible but more difficult for loom and frame tenders and in both cases dependent on steady work.[101]

The Rockdale manufacturers shared a fairly consistent political perspective. In the twenties and thirties, they were high-tariff and pro-bank Whigs, sponsoring petitions and memorials and a reception for Henry Clay. Testifying at the 1837 state hearings on child labor, two of them favored schooling for mill children and limited work hours, but only if other states acted in like manner. In later years, the more active held local offices, became Republicans, opposed the extension of slavery, and joined ultimately in the war effort, organizing militia companies and aid societies.[102]

[98] Ibid., pp. 78–100, 117–20.
[99] Ibid., pp. 38, 40, 171–7.
[100] Ibid., pp. 37, 60, 63.
[101] Ibid., pp. 14, 15, 39, 61–3.
[102] Ibid., pp. 412–29, 460–2.

Yet the labor conflicts of the same decades illustrated a real gap between the native merchant-farmer millowners and a crusty immigrant proprietor, Samuel Riddle, who leased a mill on Chester Creek in 1831 after nine years of work in Belfast mills and eight more in those of the Middle Atlantic states. Given a background in both the mechanics and the culture of the factory, Riddle "could identify with his workers."[103] The others, approaching the mill from "outside," sought both to appropriate the labor and save the souls of the "lower classes," people for whom they had stylized regard but not respect. The agents of Christian industrialism peddled salvation to their operatives and at the same time threatened them with dismissal should they vote against their masters' interests; they posted wage cuts unilaterally and fired individuals who voiced grievances, triggering walkouts on several occasions.[104] Riddle, learned in the ways of factory culture and a "nominal Presbyterian" with "a salty tongue," did not presume to teach his workers religion. He paid them straightforwardly for political support; in 1842, he put through a wage reduction by calling together his workers and explaining his action with an account of market conditions. He pledged as well revocation of the cut as soon as the economic situation brightened.[105] Riddle's workers, treated with some dignity by this honorable if rough-edged man, toiled on, but those of John Crozer and five others embarked on a bitter strike against a posted reduction. When the strike was eventually broken with the engagement of state power, eighteen were arrested and tried for conspiracy and riot. In the wake of this turmoil, one manufacturer's daughter grieved that the strikers had "made shipwreck of their faith," and Crozer was left hoping that "disaffection . . . will subside without . . . deep rooted hatred on the part of the employed."[106] Riddle's reflections on this dismal situation are not recorded, but he took no part in the trials of the accused workers.

These divergent paths suggest the existence of two "cultures" in the Rockdale mill district in the 1840s, one based on the experience and social relations of the shop floor and the other on an abstracted and sacralized notion of the relations between pecuniary gain and stewardship. Both workers and millmen participated in each, Riddle sharing the shop culture, whereas some of Crozer's believing workers testified against their fellows at the trials. Other than at Riddle's mill, betrayal had been the order of the day. If the workers betrayed the manufacturers' ideals of Christian obedience, defying those set over them, the millowners showed themselves to be dishonorable men, "lordly and aristocratic" in bearing yet wily and impersonal in their actions, springing the sheriff from behind a curtain to break the strike.

Had there not been the intervention of an external event the following year, the long-term impact of the 1842 conflicts might be visible through the rest of the decade at Rockdale. That event, a monstrous flood, savaged Crozer's holdings and barely grazed Riddle's, forcing a month-long closure of most of the factories for extensive repairs and a scattering of workers in search of employment. Crozer alone sustained about $45,000 in losses to dams, wheels, and machinery. That disaster, together with the abandonment of a rail project to link Chester and West Chester through Rockdale, encouraged Crozer to reinvest a portion of the "considerable fortune left" after the flood in a Chester mill adjacent to an existing rail line.[107] Thus did transport, spatial considerations, and a key external event intersect with matters of production and investment in the Rockdale matrix of the 1840s.

There is one final point of contrast between Rockdale's immigrant mill-bred manufacturers and the native farmer-merchant cluster. The only two operators who undertook specialized production were Riddle, "unique" in his "exclusive use of mules for spinning," and George Callaghan, also from Northern Ireland, who arrived about 1849 to produce "cotton counterpanes and figured tablecloths on . . . power looms and woolen carpets on draw [hand] looms." Callaghan's were the only "fancy goods" manufactured in the district, and "his mill required older, highly skilled male operatives."[108] Success in the Rockdale effort led George and his sons to rent a second mill, in Philadelphia, to which they removed entirely during the Civil War. The cotton-based Rockdale mills closed during the cotton famine accompanying this second major external event, as historically frozen on skill and output terms as were the great Lowell corporations. In Philadelphia, the Callaghan's flexible, skill-intensive capacity brought them wartime business sufficient to fund construction of the Angora Mills at 60th Street and Baltimore Avenue, where the sons continued operations after their father's death in 1865.[109]

Overall, the Rockdale configuration of antebellum textile manufacturing shared characteristics with both the Lowell and the Philadelphia formats for production. As at Lowell, the mills were planted at power sources in an old farming district, largely by native merchants and landowners. The millmen

107   Ibid., pp. 377–80.
108   Ibid., pp. 44, 171.
109   Ibid., p. 461; William Bagnall, "The Textile Industries of the United States," vol. II, typescript on microfiche, 1970, pp. 2654–62, Merrimack Valley Textile Museum, North Andover, Mass.; transcribed from the handwritten manuscript of Bagnall's classic study; pagination is that of the original manuscript.

constructed housing for their employees, became the chief figures of the place, relied on the production of staple cotton goods, and defended a high tariff. The manufacturers generally were distanced from workers' culture and, as at Lowell, shuttered their mills during the Civil War. Unlike Lowell, however, the Rockdale entrepreneurs suffered bankruptcies, experienced shortages of capital and credit, leased and converted old buildings, and reached integration after starting with single-function production. They did not form corporate organizations. These elements bring them closer to the Philadelphia pattern, for like the city manufacture, Rockdale production was proprietary and family-based, advanced, when successful, from mill rental to mill ownership, and relied on immigrant skills and family labor pools. The Riddle and Callaghan experiences suggest that the more that Rockdale firms shared the key characteristics of the Philadelphia format (mill experience, mutuality in factory social relations, productive flexibility), the more smoothly they weathered the crises created by depressed markets and the Civil War.

The matrix elements as constituted at Lowell and Rockdale have been presented in the hope that the outlines of the particular, patterned approaches to accumulation practiced along the Merrimack and Chester Creek will allow informed comparison with other capitalist efforts in the same industry at roughly the same time. A major center for such efforts was the city of Philadelphia, where we shall find the brethren of Riddle and the Callaghans by the score.

3

The proprietary alternative at Philadelphia

A prominent characteristic of the Philadelphia [textile] manufacture is the diffusion of the industry in small establishments. Philadelphia, with its cheap homes, its abundant and cheap market, and the faculty, which it seems to possess above all other cities, of appropriating the talents of the artisans which resort to it, is the paradise of the skilled workman.

> – John L. Hayes, "Wool Fabrics," in *The Awards and Claims of Exhibitors at the International Exhibition, 1876*

With these vivid lines, the Philadelphia textile manufacture moves to stage center. Two characteristics of the industry that grew to prominence in the city stand out immediately: that textile firms in Philadelphia remained small by Lowell standards late into the century and that skilled textile workers flocked to these mills, where their capacities were "appropriated" by the city's textile capitalists. At Lowell, skilled workers were the exception, handled with care in those areas where their skills were essential to production. High levels of flexibility and specialization in Philadelphia gave its hundreds of small mills a special character that stemmed from a network of material and sociocultural factors of accumulation markedly different from those arrayed at Lowell. By documenting the patterns of capitalist development in textiles in Philadelphia and comparing them with the Lowell experience, we can analyze the differences in productive scale and the labor process that raise yet more questions for theoretical reflection and empirical investigation. Philadelphia's textile manufacture was not primitive, underdeveloped, or unsophisticated. Neither was its organization, in partnership and family firms, a development in some blind alley of economic history. Philadelphia's mills still employed some 40,000 workers after World War II, when the Lowell monuments stood gaunt and empty, awaiting the wrecker's ball.[1]

What the textile capitalists of the Quaker City did was something hitherto little regarded by chroniclers of American economic development. They constructed an alternative pathway to accumulation, overcoming a score of obstacles with strategies that differed systematically from those employed by

---

[1] Gladys Palmer, *Philadelphia Workers in a Changing Economy*, Philadelphia, 1956, p. 35.

the Lowell corporations. The complexity of the industry and its productive relations can be untangled through patient application of the matrix formulations set forth in the Introduction. The significance of the mode of economic integration[2] employed in Philadelphia will be suggested throughout the narrative and restated in the conclusion, together with an assessment of its theoretical implications.

Historians well versed in the literature of business and labor scholarship know little of the nineteenth-century textile trades in Philadelphia. The contrast with Lowell is immediate, a historiographical imbalance. "Lowell": The very name carries with it an evocative power commensurate with the mass of perceptive investigations of its economic, social, and even symbolic significance. Its corporations were "pioneering," their founders eminent men whose stature was inadvertently confirmed in the doggerel of popular culture ("and the Cabots talk only to God"). Their political reach was national, their hegemony in the manufacturing city near absolute for a generation or more. The physical massiveness of Lowell calls forward the imagery of "satanic mills," "engines of progress," "the Manchester of America" as a cultural reflex. Nothing comparable is summoned up by "the mills of Philadelphia," given the historical silence that enveloped their development and attenuated decline. The labor-force studies produced at the University of Pennsylvania by social scientists like George Taylor and Gladys Palmer (ca. 1925–50) and occasional articles in regional historical journals constitute the bulk of the literature on the Philadelphia textile manufacture.[3] Textile workers are mentioned in a number of dissertations on manufacturing in the city, but both business and labor historians have generally found

---

[2] This term was coined by David Harvey to indicate any of a number of formats under which production might be carried out within a mode of production (see David Harvey, *Social Justice and the City,* Baltimore, 1973, chap. 6).

[3] A. H. Williams, M. A. Brumbaugh, and H. S. Davis, *An Analysis of the Production of Worsted Sales Yarn,* Philadelphia, 1929; George Taylor, *The Full Fashioned Hosiery Worker,* Philadelphia, 1931; Dorothy de Schwernitz, *How Workers Find Jobs,* Philadelphia, 1932; C. C. Balderston, Robert Brecht, Miriam Hassey, Gladys Palmer, and Edward Wright, *Philadelphia Upholstery Weaving Industry,* Philadelphia, 1932; Gladys Palmer, *Union Tactics and Economic Change,* Philadelphia, 1932; Gladys Palmer, *Philadelphia Workers in a Changing Economy,* Philadelphia, 1956; For more recent work that includes data on the Philadelphia textile industry, see David Jeremy, *Transatlantic Industrial Revolution,* Cambridge, Mass., 1981; Thomas Cochran, *Frontiers of Change,* New York, 1981; Bruce Laurie, *Working People of Philadelphia, 1800–1850,* Philadelphia, 1980; and Susan Levine, "Their Own Sphere: Women's Work, the Knights of Labor and the Transformation of the Carpet Trades, 1870–1890," Ph.D. diss., City University of New York 1979. The long-term research efforts of the Philadelphia Social History Project and the Eleutherian Mills-Hagley Foundation have generated renewed interest in the manufacturing in Philadelphia and the Middle Atlantic states. The occasional papers of both research groups are of considerable value.

other sectors of Philadelphia's economic system more manageable (Biddle and the Second Bank of the United States, Wanamaker's great emporium, Fredrick Taylor and Midvale Steel).

Perhaps more important, given the remarkable diversity of form and function that characterized it, the Philadelphia textile manufacture cannot be reduced to an image. Instead, its aspects will become clear through systematic comparison with the Lowell model along several lines, the points of comparison being drawn from the matrix notion detailed earlier. Starting at the level of the firm, two large Philadelphia mills will be examined to offer a provisional frame of reference for the use of "the Philadelphia textile manufacture" as a term describing a manufacturing array that operated in a manner distinct from the Lowell system. Seeking the origins of this pattern will entail a look backward to the early nineteenth century and outward to the analysis of the Philadelphia textile industry as a whole at that time. Focusing on the aggregate level, in turn, in the 1820s, the 1850s, and the 1880s will allow the developmental lines to emerge, with particularity and depth afforded by discussions of individual firms and mill districts that will link the aggregate snapshots. Background materials on manufacturers and workers, political and labor conflicts, and external influences (panics, the Civil War) will generate the full range of factors of accumulation indicated in the Introduction.

Philadelphia at midcentury

By the 1850s, Philadelphia had settled into position as the nation's second city, surpassed in population, commerce, and manufacturing only by New York. In the census of that year, the city reported more than 408,000 inhabitants in the scattered jurisdictions that soon would be consolidated politically into the present city and county limits (1854). Whereas New York had topped half a million, Philadelphia still represented the single largest concentration of native-born Americans in the land (286,000 vs. 277,000 in New York). Its immigrant population was half that of the northern metropolis (122,000), constituting about 30% of the whole. Of Philadelphia's native residents, 85% were Pennsylvania-born; its immigrants had come predominantly from Ireland (59%), Great Britain (17%), and Germany (19%).[4] Nearly 20,000 blacks also resided in midcentury Philadelphia, the largest total among northern cities, though in the South, smaller Baltimore held

---

[4] J. D. B. Debow, *Compendium of the Seventh Census* Washington, D.C., 1854, p. 399. The overall breakdown by ethnicity is: white native-born, 65%; black native-born, 5%; Irish, 18%; British and Scots, 5%; German, 6%; other immigrants, 1%.

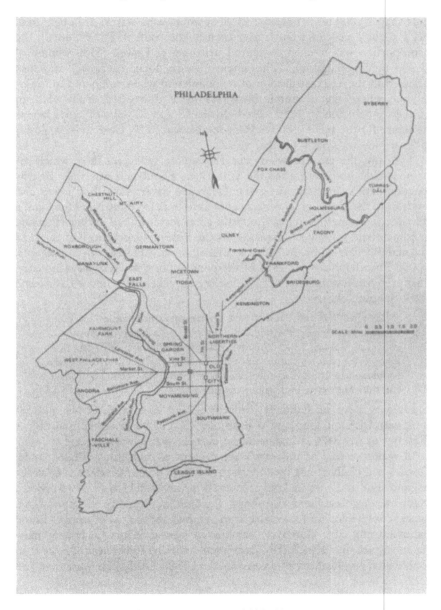

Map 1. Philadelphia and its neighborhoods, 1850–80. (Theodore Hershberg, ed., *Philadelphia: Work, Space, Family and Group Experience in the 19th Century*, New York 1981, p. 127.)

more than 28,000 black citizens, 3,000 of whom were slaves. Although there was a slight excess of women over men in the count (52% vs. 48%), the disproportion was modest compared with that at Lowell (61% women of 33,300 total population).[5] The single industry focus of Lowell was also reflected in the age distribution of its population when compared to Philadelphia, where the economic base was more diversified. Fully 45% of Lowell's inhabitants in 1850 were between 15 and 30 years of age, whereas the figure for the same group at Philadelphia was 32%, close to New York's 35% or Newark's 33% for that cluster.

Physically, the city sprawled over 128 square miles, much of which remained rural until well after the Civil War. Population was most heavily concentrated in an area along the Delaware River, spreading north and south from the old colonial center, a crescent perhaps three miles long and a mile deep. Though many of the city's great fortunes had earlier stemmed from merchant trading and banking, by the fifties Philadelphia had emerged as a manufacturing city. In 1850, according to the Census of Manufactures, 58,000 Philadelphians, or 14% of the population, worked in local industry. That proportion would rise to 20% in the next generation. Bruce Laurie and Mark Schmitz observe:

> By the Civil War only a few of New England's textile counties and Essex County, New Jersey, the home of Newark, had a higher proportion of industrial workers, and Philadelphians contributed more than their share to the nation's commodity pool. Making up about 2 percent of the population in 1850, they fabricated 6 percent of the national product, and they held their own in the ensuing years.[6]

Immigrants were substantially overrepresented in manufacturing occupations, with Irish and Germans constituting 23% of the general population in 1850 but nearly 38% of males in the manufacturing work force.[7]

All major sectors of industry were present in midcentury Philadelphia. Textiles and clothing engaged more than a third of all manufacturing workers, and shoe and boot making accounted for another 11% (6,249 workers). Ironwork, machinery and tool shops, shipbuilding, printing and publishing, construction, wood and furniture work, all had substantial presences in the manufacturing city. Moreover, virtually all were growing. Of twenty manufacturing sectors identified by Laurie and Schmitz, fifteen would more than double total employment between 1850 and 1880.[8] Although more than $32

---

[5] Ibid., pp. 395–7.
[6] Bruce Laurie and Mark Schmitz, "Manufacture and Productivity: The Making of an Industrial Base, Philadelphia, 1850–1880," in Theodore Hershberg, ed., *Philadelphia: Work, Space, Family and Group Experience in the 19th Century*, New York, 1981, pp. 44–5.
[7] Ibid., p. 54.
[8] Ibid., p. 45.

million was invested in industry, the average investment for the 4,542 enterprises tallied in the 1850 Manufacturing Census was about $7,000,[9] because of the prevalence of small firms.

The fifties were an important decade for manufacturing development at Philadelphia, as the returns from the 1860 census indicate. In ten years, manufacturing capital had leapt to $73 million and industrial employment to 99,000. Seventeen hundred more firms were in operation than in 1850 and their output surpassed $135 million in value. In this burst, the city kept pace with New York, which in 1860 (Kings County included) showed nearly $74 million invested in manufacturing and 102,000 workers generating output valued at about $193 million.[10] Within the manufacturing trades at Philadelphia, the textile sector was the largest, with 326 firms in 1850 accounting for 12,369 jobs (21.6% of the manufacturing total). By 1860, the textile sector numbered 464 firms with 18,521 employees, with the average firm size having changed little (38 employees vs. 40). More rapid growth and larger unit sizes in other sectors (iron and steel, locomotive and machinery works) brought a short-run drop in the textile proportion of total employment (to 18.7% in 1860). However, boom years during the Civil War and after would triple textile employment by the early 1880s, and textile work would total nearly a quarter of all industrial labor.[11]

All the components of the textile industry's nine rough divisions were active in midcentury Philadelphia: the three main fabric sectors, cotton, mixed goods, and wool; the specialties, silk, carpets, and knit goods; the services, spinning, dyeing and finishing, and miscellaneous mills (preparers of shoddy, cotton laps, braids, etc.). So that the reader may quickly grasp the distinctive character of these firms and their particular combination of the elements in the accumulation matrix, we will turn now to case studies of two mills that stood side by side in the Manayunk industrial district of northwest Philadelphia. Contemporaneous with the Lowell and Rockdale firms sketched in Chapter 2, and using similar raw materials, these two firms should provide an initial framework for appreciating the Philadelphia alternative at

[9] Ibid., pp. 65–6.

[10] *Manufactures of the United States in 1860*, Washington, D.C., 1865, pp. 374, 390, 527.

[11] Calculated from unpublished manuscript returns for the Census of Manufactures, Philadelphia County, 1850 and 1860, and from Lorin Blodget, *Census of Manufactures of Philadelphia (1882)*, Philadelphia, 1883. For the most part, the original textile data from the 1880 Manufacturing Census in Philadelphia have been lost. Fortunately, the subsequent 1882 city survey seems quite thorough, particularly when supplemented by reference to an 1880 report (*The Textile Industries of Philadelphia*) by Lorin Blodget, who also supervised the 1882 city industrial census and worked on the 1870 and 1880 federal manufacturing censuses; his meticulous reports lend credibility to his local efforts of 1880 and 1882.

midcentury. In later chapters, the larger structure of the Philadelphia industry and its development from the early nineteenth century through the crises of the 1880s will be presented in greater detail.

Manayunk emerged in the 1820s as the first powered-factory concentration in the region, as textile mills dotted the canal dug by the Schuylkill Navigation Company.[12] The Schuylkill Navigation Company bears an initial resemblance to Lowell's famous Locks and Canals. Chartered by the state, the SNC constructed its facility in the depressed conditions of 1819–20. Millsites were laid out and sold to entrepreneurs, and power was available for an annual charge, depending on the quantity used. Beyond these particulars, the differences are most striking. The waterpower provided by the Schuylkill fall was minuscule in comparison with that of the massive Merrimack. The mill operators neither owned nor influenced the canal company. The SNC proved far more concerned with exploitation of the anthracite coal regions, linking them to the Philadelphia market, than with its modest Manayunk division, where no manufacturing *corporation* appeared for half a century.

The limits to growth at Manayunk involved more than the full utilization of the available waterpower. Geography was a serious constraint. Only a hundred yards or so from riverside, the "Ridge" commences to rise toward Roxborough at its summit, the angle of ascent breathtaking and formidable to all but the most hardy prospective mill builder. As the first canal-bank mills were small and the sites relatively elongated (there being limits to how close waterwheels may be set), there was room for expansion for the lucky few. Rows of worker housing were built both up and along the slope, interspersed with churches, an occasional mansion, and a handful of small factories, which crowded about on all sides, spatially frozen. Upriver, the flatlands narrowed uselessly, and downstream the mills spilled outward toward the city center (they would be demolished before the Centennial to allow the construction of Fairmount Park).

Still, this manufacturing enclave was vital and robust, its own weekly newspapers taunting stuffy Germantown, its councilmen vocal in city affairs, its clubs, churches, and temperance societies awesomely busy, and several of its textile mills among the largest in the city. Yet Manayunk was not a microcosm of Philadelphia. It was rather an aspect, a dimension of the complexities of the "urban process" unfolding citywide. Similarly, its big mills, however fully described, cannot through some multiplier be totaled to

---

[12] Kensington, a center of handloom production, the second of the city's five textile manufacturing districts, developed simultaneously near the Delaware north of Old City. Germantown, Frankford, and Spring Garden completed the main concentrations by the 1870s as steampower and spreading rail networks facilitated "inland" locations.

represent the textile industry either at any moment or as an exemplar of the aggregate development. They can, however, be usefully set against the Lowell giants as a way of throwing into relief just how far from the Lowell paradigm was the capitalist project mounted by the few Philadelphia mills that operated on a comparable scale.

Archibald Campbell and Company: the path of productive flexibility

About 1825, Jerome Keating occupied one of the new waterpowered mills along the Manayunk Canal to undertake cotton production. Jerome Kempton took over the mill shortly before Keating's death in 1833 and continued the cotton manufacture. By 1850, Kempton was sole possessor of three factories, two on the original site and a third at nearby Roxborough, employing more than 600 workers. Half of them labored at the expanded old mill, renamed the Schuylkill Factory for the river whose waters powered its machinery. The new Manayunk mill, constructed in 1847 and named Blantyre, was steam powered and employed 133 workers at the time of the 1850 Manufacturing Census. All together, the mills represented a reported investment of $250,000.[13] The next year Kempton began his withdrawal from active manufacturing by leasing the Blantyre mill to Archibald Campbell and Company. As the Campbells also manufactured cottons, it seems likely that the machinery on hand went with the lease and not improbable that many of Kempton's workers stayed on.

Archibald Campbell and Company was a family partnership, with brothers John and William joining the "senior partner" in the venture. A fourth partner, William Somerset, like his three colleagues, was an immigrant Scots-Irish Presbyterian. When their leased facilities partially burned in 1854, Kempton rebuilt the mill and the Campbell firm resumed operations. By 1857 the partners had taken up residence at the Schuylkill factory as well and had expanded into a nearby converted paper mill, dubbed the Crompton Steam Mill. Kempton was by then fully retired and lived comfortably from his accumulated wealth until his death in 1862 and burial in St. James the Less Episcopal Cemetery.[14] The Campbell firm acquired the Schuylkill mill

---

13 Mildred Goshow, ed., "Mills and Mill Owners of Manayunk in the 19th Century," typescript, 1970, pp. 50, 54–7, 68, 86, 106, Roxborough Branch, Free Library of Philadelphia; 1850 Manufacturing Census Schedules, Philadelphia Co. p. 87; cited hereafter as MCS.

14 Goshow, "Mills and Mill Owners," esp. pp. 55 and 106; 1860 Population Census Schedules, Philadelphia Co. Ward 21, pp. 241–54, cited hereafter as PCS. Kempton was a longtime member of this church, and his family's births, marriages, and burials are inscribed in its records.

from the estate, and Sevill Schofield purchased the Blantyre building, leasing it back to Archibald Campbell and Company until 1869.

Several things are initially noteworthy. The firm replacement sequence forms an initial contrast with Lowell, reflecting both on firm organization and the spatial dimension of production. Partnerships and proprietary firms ceased to exist upon the death or retirement of the mill operators. (Term partnerships ended at the expiration of a set period, usually five years.) These forms of ownership characterize the textile manufacture at Philadelphia throughout the nineteenth century. The Lowell corporations, because of their formal structure, were invulnerable to individual mortality. For owner-operated mills, the reverse was true. Thus the constant in the Philadelphia industry, as often as not, is the *mill building* rather than the textile firm. Occupied in succession by entrepreneurs, expanded and modified by each in turn, the factory is a spatial element of continuity. Moreover, Kempton's withdrawal from manufacturing opened a physical and productive space for the Campbell firm, which could take advantage of this "built environment" with far less capital than would have been required had they started with a vacant lot. The succession process was orderly. As Archibald Campbell and Company accumulated profits, the partners evidently plowed them back into larger leased quarters and after a decade purchased one mill while continuing to lease the other. Finally, after the Civil War, they entered a third phase of these spatial relations of production by erecting additional buildings on the Schuylkill site. How different this is from Lowell, where the leasing of space to fledgling firms was unknown and the sale of a mill unthinkable,[15] where enormous capital funds and easy access to further borrowing made vast construction the first order of business.

The partnership organization of the Campbell firm facilitated this orderly accumulation and plow-back sequence, which was likely further reinforced by the family character of the partnership. The surplus realized by large-scale operations funneled into four sets of hands, rather than being dispersed among scores of shareholders. To be sure, serious disagreements could bring the partnership to an end at the insistence of any member. Indeed, such dissolutions litter Philadelphia's textile history. Yet the family tie operated as a brake on such fracturing, a cultural element in the accumulation process of considerable moment at Philadelphia. While individually disaffected Lowell stockholders could, at times, shout loudly at annual meetings and demand the heads of the directors, their ultimate weapon was merely to sell out and move their investment elsewhere, hardly a

---

[15] At least until the twentieth-century collapse, during which both phenomena occurred. See M. T. Parker, *Lowell: A Study of Industrial Development*, Port Washington, N.Y., 1970 (orginally published 1940).

threat to corporate survival. Family partners were located differently, responsible to no horde of querulous outsiders but bound by ties of blood and duty that should not go unappreciated. The family mill stood as a future *legacy* as well as a daily productive mechanism. On Archibald Campbell's death in 1874, the firm was reorganized as a "joint-stock company," closely held, I suspect, the principals being the surviving brothers, Archibald's two sons, and another partner admitted to the firm in 1868, William Stephens. Ten years later the sons withdrew and started a partnership on their own account at the Crompton Mill, and the original Archibald Campbell and Company continued operations until the Schuylkill mills were leveled by two disastrous fires about 1890.[16] As late as 1913, A. Wilson Campbell was producing hosiery in a cotton mill in Frankford, having moved crosstown from the Crompton mills.[17]

An 1868 account of the operations of Archibald Campbell and Company makes possible a sketch of the firm's output, marketing relationships, and technological sophistication.[18] Although the Campbell mills contrast developmentally along organizational and spatial lines with Lowell mills, we still might expect similarities in production and machine use. The scale of investment and employment was comparable at the level of the firm. Three Lowell mills – Appleton, Tremont, and Suffolk – were about the same size as the Campbell mill in 1860. In that year the Manayunk partnership reported invested capital of $330,000 and 765 workers (319 male and 446 female), steampower and waterpower totaling 350 horsepower, and wages paid of roughly $140,000 for the year.[19] Ten years later investment had reached $700,000 and wages paid to 900 workers totaled $295,000.[20] (Given the softness of such numerical data and the inflation of the sixties, these dramatic increases must be viewed with caution, suggestive only of the rough scale parallel previously mentioned.) Both the Manayunk and Lowell firms possessed integrated mills for cotton manufacture. Both were located close to rail systems, allowing reliable transport of materials and products and easy personal access to the metropolitan hub a few miles distant. Both

16 Goshow, "Mills and Mill Owners." This kind of joint-stock organization was quite rare in Philadelphia textiles until near the close of the century. Even then, proprietors seem to have retained almost all the shares in their own hands, over 90% in the two cases for which share registers have been examined (see Dearnley Worsted Yarn Papers, Paley House, Philadelphia College of Textiles and Science, Philadelphia, and William Grundy Papers, Grundy Library, Bristol, Pa.).

17 *Official American Textile Directory (1913)*, Boston, 1913, p. 264.

18 J. L. Bishop, *A History of American Manufactures from 1608 to 1860*, Philadelphia, 1868, vol. III, pp. 43–4. Volume III was completed after Bishop's death by Edwin Freedley, author of *Philadelphia and Its Manufactures (1857)*, cited elsewhere.

19 1860 MCS, Philadelphia Co., p. 474.

20 1870 MCS, Philadelphia Co., p. 600.

rented waterpower from a canal corporation from whom the original millsite was secured. Yet these formal parallels prove superficial, as would be analysis based on them alone, when the dynamics of Campbell's operations are closely examined.

First, the production process, as detailed by J. L. Bishop in *A History of American Manufactures from 1608 to 1860*:

> [Campbell's mills] are equipped, provided, and managed with reference especially to supplying temporary demands – whether it be for the highly colored negro goods sought from the South, or the more sombre and substantial fabrics demanded in the West, or the neater styles required by the merchants of the Middle States. In this respect, they differ essentially from the large mills of New England, which are generally provided with machinery for making only one class of goods – and consequently when demand for these ceases, they must suspend operations or accumulate stock. In Messrs. Campbell's factories, however, a change or rotation of fabric, according to the wants of the season, is so far from being an extraordinary circumstance, that it may be called an established rule.[21]

The sharp contrast in output strategies is made explicit in the text. Both Campbell and the New England cotton manufacturers reached for a national market, but they reached for different segments, making decisions about the selection of appropriate machinery that conditioned production and marketing activity. The mass production of staples at Lowell brought forth an accumulation matrix centered on standardized yarns, cloths, machines, and so on, engaging masses of modestly skilled operatives in production relations that became increasingly rigid and bureaucratically authoritarian by midcentury. Campbell and Company sought to "supply . . . temporary demands" and presumably to reap the high profits that rapid response to such demand might promise. This approach entailed the establishment of a high level of productive flexibility. Such flexibility did not mean having a variety of machines endlessly weaving fifteen or twenty different patterns. It meant being ever able to alter production "according to the wants of the *season*." This in turn necessitated the acquisition of machinery of sufficient sophistication to permit changes in yarn count, pattern (multiple-shuttle looms), and cotton-wool blend weaving (for winter sales). Central as well to this process was the presence of workers whose skill and experience was qualitatively richer than that of machine tenders on sheetings and drills. Spinners would be called upon to run yarns of many counts, dyers to use the full array of their talents, loomfixers to master the workings of both varied and complex machinery, and weavers to adjust to regularly changing setups and sharpen their some-

---

[21] Bishop, *History of American Manufactures*, vol. 3, pp. 43–4.

what narrower skills. Consider the contrast with the Lowell monotony – millions of yards of plain goods – and Philadelphia's position as "the paradise of the skilled workman" gains credibility. At Campbell and Company, workers' skills might develop rather than stagnate.

Bishop provided a summary of the plant and products:

> The mills mentioned consist of an aggregation of buildings, having . . . a floor surface of 144,000 square feet, . . . They contain 14,270 cotton spindles, 1560 wool spindles, and 1236 spindles for doubling and twisting – in all 17,000 spindles and 652 looms. The machinery is propelled by three Corliss engines – the firm being the first to adopt these engines, now so generally appreciated; and besides these there are two water wheels, to be used in cases of accident or other emergency. The average product of each loom being about 25 yards per day, the aggregate annual product is over five million yards – consisting principally of pantaloonery ginghams, striped and plaid osnaburghs, etc. The Cottonades made here include all grades of exclusively fast colors (the demand for very low-priced or fugitive colors having almost entirely ceased), and extend to the very best qualities, such as command a higher price than any in the market.[22]

This 1868 information can be assessed against the 1870 census data to yield a partial picture of the conditions on the shop floor at Campbell and Company. The firm reported 900 workers, 250 men, 450 women, and 200 youths, surely approximate figures. The men presumably were concentrated in skilled trades (spinners, dyers, fixers, carders, finishers, etc.) and as common labor in and about the mill. The boys and girls likely assumed the varied helper roles (piecing, runners in the weave shed), some few being apprenticed at dyeing and mechanical work. However the women were distributed among doffing, warping, weaving, inspection, and so on, there were but 652 looms to be run by this sizable work force. It thus appears that Campbell and Company ran a two-loom system in the weaving rooms, if we assume reasonably that only a third of the workers were weavers.[23] The four-loom pattern (installed at Lowell as a stretch-out measure in the 1840s) would place but 160 of the 900 workers in the weave sheds, an unlikely distribution. The two-loom system also makes sense in view of the production of higher quality goods and patterns (stripes and plaids) needing close attention to prevent damaging flaws. If plausible, the inference of a more labor-extensive production process at Campbell and Company than at Lowell does not

---

[22] Ibid.

[23] This was about the proportion at the Hamilton Company at Lowell in 1860. Tom Dublin gives 442 female weavers in the June 1860 Hamilton work force (*Women at Work*, p. 159). Total 1860 Hamilton employment reported in *Statistics of Lowell Manufactures, January 1861* (Lowell, Mass., 1861) was 1,250. Some Irish male weavers also were in place by this date, increasing the overall proportion somewhat.

indicate that the firm was backward, a case of arrested development along some ladder of capitalist rationalization. To the contrary, this format was consistent with the firm's effort to make goods "that command a higher price" in the market. This quality factor might well mean that the daily cottonade output of two looms was as profitable in terms of return per worker as four looms' worth of brown shirting were at Lowell.[24]

The installation of the Corliss engines in the 1860s at Campbell and Company indicates an appreciation of the special perils of low water and frozen millraces for their "temporary demand" trade. The preservation and upkeep of the waterwheels in the late sixties reinforces the same point, for engine breakdowns in the face of urgent demand meant profits forgone and potential customer shifts to other suppliers. Having reliable power sources introduced an element of stability into a productive strategy that was cluttered with risks and costs outside the experience of Lowell manufacturers. Misperceiving short-run demand could be catastrophic if mistakes were frequent. Frequent changes in setups meant considerable downtime on the looms. Too much success could be as troublesome as too little if orders exceeded productive capacity and delays ensued, angering buyers and jobbers as the "season" slid past.

How Campbell and Company dealt with some of these issues can be seen from the following passages, which bear particularly on marketing:

> In another particular, these mills are operated in a manner that must render them of great accommodation to merchants. Jobbers, for instance, desiring the control or exclusive sale of a certain quality or brand of goods, can have their orders executed by this firm and the monopoly of the brand secured to them. . . .
>
> The senior partner is a merchant, as well as a manufacturer, having charge of the firm's warehouse in Philadelphia, and thus has the advantage of obtaining more reliable and early information of the wants of the market, and the state of the trade, than manufacturers who are dependent for such facts upon the advice of agents or commission merchants.[25]

Satisfying temporary demands involved problems both of the timing and the extent of production of any fabric, problems quite different from those faced by other large firms weaving and stockpiling common sheetings. Hence, Campbell and Company reached forward into distribution with its own downtown warehouse and sales office, joining commission houses and other mills able to support similar sales arms in the wholesale district near the

---

24 The lack of company records for almost all the Philadelphia mills frustrates just the sort of detailed inquiry that these speculations should trigger.

25 Bishop, *History of American Manufactures*, vol. 3, pp. 43–4.

Delaware. Archibald Campbell's merchant experience and network of contacts enabled the Manayunk firm to bypass the time lags and favoritism in information flows that were implicit in having an outside agent interposed between the manufacturer and the market. Samples of the firm's prowess could be displayed to potential buyers in attractive surroundings that temporarily excluded the competition. Finally, the cost of the facilities could be set against the saving of commission-house charges that otherwise would have cut into production margins.

The brand monopoly gambit indicates that Campbell and Company's marketing practices correlated with their production flexibility. Jobbers who knew they were the only distributor of an attractive seasonal specialty would place larger orders and, if successful, repeat the cycle with new fabrics. This not only was a skillful mechanism for inducing some regularity into the short-run trade for the Campbells. It also offered the prospect of monopoly profits to the reseller of "fashionable" goods. Though not mentioned in the text, it is likely that samples of these brand monopoly goods were run at the mill for display in the showrooms, a practice common in Philadelphia woolens later in the century. This strategy had implications backward into production, for exclusive fabrics had to display some elements of novel design (often copied from European goods in this era) in order to be marketable at the premium prices called for by shorter production runs, higher setup costs, and market risks. The design component placed demands on work-force skills and on machine flexibility as well.

Timing in all this was crucial, as the need for "early information" indicates. Yet what was the firm to do if a flood of orders surpassed its capacity to turn them out in a timely fashion? A frequent problem, it was nevertheless not without a solution:

> [The] two factories . . . are occupied exclusively in the manufacture of colored cotton goods, sometimes known in the market as "Philadelphia goods"; but as these are often found inadequate to supply the demand for their fabrics, they call into service the machinery of other manufacturers.[26]

The Campbells depended with regularity on a network of other (smaller?) manufacturers to whom overflow orders might be subcontracted. This pattern reflects the financial strategy of the firm, its use of capital. The complexities of supplying fluctuating markets for variable goods made reasonable the operation of plant and machinery markedly smaller than that needed when demand peaked, optimal rather than maximum investment in capacity. This was possible without loss of customers in busy periods only because Campbell and Company functioned within a manufacturing environment

[26] Ibid.

itself sufficiently flexible to allow regular utilization of other mills and men to handle the excess orders. Campbell "rented" them, when needed, at no capital cost. It is possible, but unlikely, that these were reciprocal relationships among large manufacturers. A dozen small mills straddled the Manayunk hillside and others were but a mile farther east in Germantown. That small, flexible factories prospered alongside huge, flexible factories, making especially good profits from "rush" subcontracts, seems plausible. At a minimum, Campbell's manufacturer colleagues must have had machinery sophisticated enough to weave first-quality cloth of various designs. In this environment, capital investment in endless expansion of capacity (the Lowell experience) was neither necessary nor appropriate.

To this point, we have touched upon seven of the eight material factors of accumulation: transport, firm structure, space, technology, labor, marketing, and finance and upon a number of their intersections. Finally, Bishop makes an interesting reference to the role of raw materials.

> The proprietors of these mills, appreciating the fact that the present [1867] high price of cotton calls for a corresponding improvement in the quality of the articles fabricated, are now importing new and improved machinery, with a view of producing a higher and finer grade of goods than any they have heretofore manufactured.[27]

Consider the options the firm had in the face of "high cotton." One, maintain prices and cut wages. Two, pass along the increased costs. Three, maintain prices and wages and cut profits. Four, expend capital for fine-goods machinery, stretching each pound of cotton farther in producing higher-count yarns and high-priced cloths that would challenge British imports. It is this last and more creative strategy that is suggested by the text, and it is facilitated by material dynamics of accumulation that differ fundamentally from the Lowell pattern.

The domination of fine cottons by British producers is a commonplace of nineteenth-century industrial history: that Campbell and Company would *import* machinery, presumably from England, to enhance their already varied production output follows directly. What is more interesting is that the complex of material factors that informed the New England big-mill focus on coarse staples can now be contrasted with, to start, one example of a wholly alternative array of actions of which the Lowell mills *were not capable.* To the labor force at Campbell and Company, the production of finer goods would be but an incremental change in skill demands, not a leap into unknown territories; flexible output was the rule with marketing in the hands of the senior partner; a network of jobbers who were accustomed to dealing with new goods (and presumably appropriate margins) lay waiting; another

27 Ibid.

network of auxiliary manufacturers could carry part of the firm's "standard" production while the new machinery was installed and the bugs ironed out. This is the capitalism of skill, creativity, personal relations, and decisiveness that formed a rich alternative to the corporate system at Lowell, though not a whit less "rational" or "modern" for all its lack of corporate trappings and just as resolutely focused on profit and accumulation.

This assertion can be reinforced by examining the entrepreneurship of Sevill Schofield, a neighbor of Campbell and Company. Schofield's woolen establishment was the largest in the Manayunk complex during the post–Civil War era. Seven years after Edwin Freedley completed the final volume of Bishop's *History of American Manufactures*, from which the preceding quotes about Archibald Campbell and Company were extracted, Daniel Robson published a huge compendium (more than 500 double-columned pages) entitled *Manufactories and Manufacturers of Pennsylvania of the Nineteenth Century*. The work, which had taken three or more years to produce, was the result of direct contact with hundreds of capitalists, the largest proportion of whom operated in Philadelphia.[28] In lauding the virtues of his subjects, Robson provided as well a wealth of priceless detail on their families, mill layouts, firm histories and the like, plus more than a hundred engravings portraying the men and their factories. Included in this mass of material were "biographies" of fifty-nine Philadelphia textile firms, five textile machinery manufactories in the city, and sixteen mills located in outlying towns. Sevill Schofield occupied almost two full pages, accompanied by a pair of factory views. Supplemented by other sources and stripped of its ornamental praise to a "self-made man," Robson's account permits the construction of a companion piece to the Campbell case.

Sevill Schofield and the networks of family capitalism

Sevill Schofield was the third son born to a Lancashire textile district family (1832, at Lees near Oldham). Thirteen years later, at the tail end of the depression of the early forties,[29] Joseph and Malley Schofield emigrated with their six children to the United States. Joseph was about 45 years old and his wife was carrying their seventh child.[30] After disembarking at New

<hr/>

28 Daniel Robson, ed., *Manufactories and Manufacturers of Pennsylvania of the Nineteenth Century*, Philadelphia, 1875, Preface; cited hereafter as *M&MP*.

29 Ibid., p. 53.

30 *Bulletin of the Historical Society of Montgomery County, Pa.*, vol. XVI, p. 79. The 1850 Population Census entry for the Joseph Schofield household is here printed. Other children, of course, may not have survived; in 1850, eight Schofield children were present in the household.

York, they "proceeded directly to Manayunk, Philadelphia," where Joseph promptly undertook the business of "contracting to furnish the necessary labor to operate mills for other parties." From this it is clear that Joseph Schofield was familiar with the practices of textile manufacture. Moreover, some of those whose labor he furnished were his own offspring: "Sevill, in common with his four brothers and two sisters, contributed their labor, but received no wages."[31] The six oldest children in the late forties ranged from about 23 to 8 years of age. Here is a gesture toward a fascinating variation on the family economy, the family economy of a nascent capitalist. Whether their father worked on shares with the millmen, who "furnished machinery, materials, etc.," or simply appropriated the earnings of his offspring cannot be determined. But in either case, a tiny engine for accumulation was turning.[32]

After four years, Joseph Schofield entered a manufacturing partnership:

> [He] associated with James Lees, in 1849, and . . . operated mills upon Mill Creek, but in 1857 the partnership was dissolved and Sevill assumed full charge of the business. Having purchased a team, he himself did all the hauling, besides superintending indoor matters.

In business with Lees, whose name echoes Sevill's birthplace, Joseph likely kept his offspring active. Both sons John and Thomas appeared in the 1850 household, listed as "manufacturers," and later in the decade Sevill became responsible for local transport. The circumstances surrounding young Schofield's replacement of his father at the head of the family enterprise remain unclear, but the death of Joseph Schofield later in 1857 suggests that ill health may have provoked the transfer. The family base of capitalist manufacture is underscored by the relationships surrounding the Schofield's acquisition of a small Manayunk mill in the same year.

According to Daniel Robson, Sevill's

---

31 *M&MP*, p. 53. The reference to seven unpaid Schofield children was made in 1875, and includes as the seventh, Joseph Schofield (b. 1848), who would have worked for his father circa 1855–8.

32 Several questions arise from this tale. How did it happen that the Schofield family "proceeded directly" to Manayunk? Was this mill district already well known among Lancashire townsmen? Can Maldwyn Jones's conjecture be applied here? "It seems likely that what lured Britons across the Atlantic more frequently [than printed travelers' accounts] was the specific vision conjured up by an emigrant letter of a good job or a cheap farm in a locality where relatives or friends had settled earlier" (M. Jones, "The Background to Emigration From Great Britain," *Perspectives in American History* 7 (1973): 20). Moreover, in contracting for labor, did the elder Schofield recruit other kin and countrymen locally or did he send back to England for Oldhamites seeking a "place" in a new land? Questions such as these cannot be resolved at present, for no Manayunk mill records of this period have survived, local newspapers are incomplete, and no diaries or letter groups bear directly on this matter.

industry and energy were noticed by the proprietor of McFadden's Mill, who was on intimate terms with his father's family, and he one day proposed [that] Sevill purchase his mill. The offer was at first declined, on account of limited means, but, on the proposal of the owner, William McFadden, to sell for $10,000, one fifth to be paid in one year, and the balance in ten years, he resolved that the opportunity was not to be lost.[33]

Whether McFadden was motivated by personal financial troubles in the panic year or by a combination of friendship and respect for the Schofields' manufacturing talents, he repeated his initial offer on terms that were clearly generous. No cash was initially required, though realizing $2,000 at the close of the first year's operations would surely be quite a task for a new venture in a troubled economic environment. Sevill would either put his skills immediately to profitable use or the firm would fold in defaulting the year-end payment. Once that hurdle was cleared, generosity for the longer term was present. Rather than being tied to subsequent annual obligations, the firm would have nine years to reserve funds for the $8,000 balance, being thus able to plow back surpluses into equipment and plant.[34] This transaction illustrates an intersection between family and community networks and the economics of small manufacture. The sale was neither simply a favor to a friend nor purely a "free-market" exchange but a more subtle amalgam of the cultural and economic relations of a manufacturing district.

Though Sevill was to run the firm and had reached the age of 25 at that time, the papers were drawn up in his father's name. When six months later Joseph Schofield died "leaving a will providing that the property should not be divided during the lifetime of his widow," Sevell responded to the family obligations, "carrying on the business in his mother's name until 1859."[35] (This assertion is confirmed in part by the presence of "Schofield, M[alley], McFadden's Mill, Manayunk" in Freedley's 1857 list of city textile manufacturers.)[36] During these years, Schofield's tiny operation prospered. The firm spun cotton and carpet yarns, aiming their output toward the substantial handloom trades in crosstown Kensington. In two years Sevill's enterprise increased his mother's wealth "from $800 to $16,000."

---

[33] *M&MP*, p. 53 McFadden was a Scots-Irish Presbyterian, as were the Somersets. Schofield was later active in the Fourth Reform Church of Manayunk. See Goshow, "Mills and Mill Owners," p. 103; R. W. Givin, ed., *Manayunk, Roxborough, and Falls of Schuylkill Directory for 1883*, Philadelphia, 1883, p. 59.

[34] Were an alternate reading of this passage to presume nine payments of $900 over the rest of the ten years (plus interest, which is not mentioned), a similar initial test would remain, with skillful first-year performance leading to smaller payments thereafter.

[35] *M&MP*, p. 185.

[36] Edwin Freedley, *Philadelphia and Its Manufactures*, Philadelphia, 1857, p. 261.

This dramatic success was facilitated by at least three elements in the larger strategy for accumulation used widely in the city's textile trades. First, Schofield operated on but one floor of the small (40- by 60-foot), five-story factory, renting out "the remainder, from which the revenue was sufficient to cover all expenses." Both tenants, Lord, Ralston and Co. and Greenwood and Co., were spinners of carpet and woolen yarns, a fact that proved useful several years later. Second, local markets for yarn sales were readily available, as Kensington carpet firms were uniformly weave sheds without spinning capacity. Third, the M. Schofield firm evidently retained virtually all earnings, Sevill again drawing no wages. Given the expansion that followed in 1859–60, Malley likely banked the profits less a sum for running the family household, which then included her manufacturing son and three younger children.[37]

Given the two decades of filial duty here outlined, Sevill's relations with his widowed mother might be expected to alter only when he established his own family through marriage. On April 28, 1859, Mr. Culver, minister of the First Presbyterian Church, solemnized vows between the 28-year-old manufacturer and Miss Kate Somerset, then 23.[38] Both the Schofields and the Somersets lived on Mechanic Street in 1858, according to the city directory, and it is plausible that Kate had been the "girl next door." In the 1860 manuscript population census schedules Malley Schofield and her three youngest children were listed following the Somersets.[39] The young couple did not strike out on their own, for they and their 4-month-old son, William, made their home at the time of the 1860 census tally with the Somerset clan. Though Sevill had only moved next door, marriage and departure from his mother's house occasioned a major change in the social and economic arrangements through which manufacturing had been prosecuted to that point.

Robson reports that, "having married, he arranged to engage in business on his own account, and giving his mother the interest on her $16,000 associated with his brother Charles, as S. & C. Schofield, and commenced operating."[40] Though there was surely no break in production at the old McFadden Mill, this brief account indicates a substantial transformation of the economic relationships within the firm. Henceforth, such accumulation as was managed by the partner brothers would be theirs to enjoy or reinvest. Malley was guaranteed an income of perhaps a thousand a year (if 6% were

---

37 Ibid., pp. 259–60; *M&MP*, p. 186. The $16,000 figure likely represents equity in mill and machinery along with retained earnings.

38 *Manayunk Star and Roxborough Gazette*, April 30, 1859. The editor expressed thanks for the "excellent cake" that accompanied the notice of the wedding to the *Star*.

39 1860 PCS, Philadelphia Co., Ward 21, pt. 1, p. 241. *McElroy's Directory of Philadelphia for 1858*, Philadelphia, 1858, pp. 600, 641.

40 *M&MP*, p. 186.

the interest) but would no longer hold the entire capital. In a sense, Sevill came into his inheritance upon this agreement and drew his younger brother into the firm to share its potential. There was justice in this arrangement, for while three other brothers had married and departed,[41] Sevill had remained with the core family long after reaching his majority and had devoted his energies to his mother's welfare after his father's death. Sevill's offer of a partnership to Charles was both culturally sound and organizationally practical, anticipating division of production and office/marketing tasks as the business expanded. It was surely not a fund-raising effort, for in 1860 the two brothers reported almost identical property holdings to census marshals (Sevill: $3,750; Charles: $3,950).[42] The elder sons were excluded and never appeared in any connection with the firm's subsequent development.

If Sevill's marriage signaled a reformulation of economic, and by extension power, relations within the Schofield family, it also exemplified a variant of a wider phenomenon pertaining to proprietary manufacture, that linking of capitalist families through marriage, which is elsewhere termed "dynastic industrialism."[43] A well-documented practice for textile firms in Lancashire, dynastic marriages stemmed from a social context in which "the management function of the family is directly geared to the preservation of the estate." Daughters were useful in such an environment, insofar as they might be matched to locally powerful families or to "incomers," men of peculiar talent whose energy, rather than wealth or contacts, was prized. The Somerset–Schofield marriage falls in the latter category.

Kate Somerset Schofield's father, William, was the fourth partner in Archibald Campbell and Company. He possessed at the time of his daughter's marriage property worth more than $60,000. The Somersets' three children were Kate, her teen-age sister Eliza, and young William, who was 12 in 1859. The 1860 census property report recorded real estate valued at $6,000 and personal property for William, probably his interest in the Campbell firm, worth $37,000. Real and personal property valued at $20,000 was held by Catherine Schofield, a third of the Somerset holdings having likely been conferred upon her as a marriage settlement.[44] That these properties were not conveyed to her husband reflects not an early feminist consciousness on William Somerset's part but both an understanding of business law and the conservancy-of-the-estate element common to such marriages. Unincorporated businesses were vulnerable to the seizure of all

---

41 1860 PCS, Philadelphia, Co., Ward 21, pt. 1, p. 256. Charles, the younger brother, had married about 1855.

42 Ibid., pp. 241, 256.

43 Patrick Joyce, *Work, Society and Politics: The Culture of the Factory in Later Victorian England,* Brighton, England, 1980, pp. 22–5.

44 "Co-Partnership Directory," in *Boyd's Philadelphia City Business Directory for 1859–60,* Philadelphia, 1859, p. 359; 1860 PCS, Philadelphia Co., Ward 21, p. 241.

personal property of the principals should they default on their creditors, though this unlimited liability generally assured the close attention of partners to the firm's affairs. Were Schofield's promising but fledgling enterprise to go under, the Somerset estate would rest untouched, given the prudence of recording the marriage endowment in Kate's name. Had Sevill Schofield been a bit piqued by this caution, his grumbles should have been assuaged by reflection on the fact that two-thirds of the settlement was real estate, the remainder "personal" property (cash?). The income from this sizable holding, whether in rents or interest, would easily meet the new family's needs, with expenses lessened by their sharing of the Somersets' quarters. This in turn left Sevill financially free to funnel manufacturing profits into expansion, without having to draw off funds for his own household in addition to the sums guaranteed his mother.

Sevill Schofield had left one family only to join another, on terms that were clearly set by the Somersets but of tangible advantage to his own prospects as well. His father-in-law shared in the operations of one of Manayunk's largest mills (765 workers in 1860), opening a range of valuable trade contacts. Sevill no longer stood as the dependent child but nevertheless remained a dutiful son (and son-in-law, for the Schofields' firstborn was named after his wife's father).[45] Here was a young man of potential, upon whom had been conferred an opportunity to prove himself worthy of integration into an established clan. As a result, his situation involved substantial psychological pressures for performance, pressures that the birth of a grandson may have relieved to only a small degree. The aggressive business moves Sevill Schofield made over the next few years probably stemmed in part from a fundamental need to show his individual capacities, indeed to match or to best his palpably successful father-in-law. Surely the incorporation of new blood through dynastic marriage was intended to elicit just such entrepreneurial assertiveness, as the "incomer" sought both to demonstrate the wisdom of his selection and to transcend the personal shackles it carried.

The network of interfamily links among textile manufacturers is evident as well through the later years of the Schofield firm. After his brother withdrew from the partnership, Sevill Schofield carried on as sole proprietor until his son was of age to enter as a partner in the 1880s. In the same decade Sevill brought his young brother-in-law, William Somerset, into the firm as well, for after the death of Archibald Campbell, the fortunes of his company foundered.[46] More interesting is the relationship with the Dobson family. If marriage could inaugurate a manufacturing connection, it could also follow one.

---

[45] Charles's first two children, who were born in 1856 and 1858, were named for *his* parents, a frequently observed custom (1860 PCS, Philadelphia Co., Ward 21, p. 256).

[46] Goshow, "Mills and Mill Owners," p. 105.

James and John Dobson, brothers and partners in the Falls of Schuylkill woolen mills. Linked by marriage to the Schofield family of Manayunk, the brothers Dobson became the proprietors of Philadelphia's largest mill complex. (Free Library of Philadelphia)

James Dobson, who eventually became a partner in one of the nation's largest proprietary woolen mills, arrived in Philadelphia in 1854 from Oldham, England, with his brother John. Having "entered the mills at eight years of age," Jim Dobson was a textile veteran at 17.[47] He secured employment in the Schofields' Mill Creek plant, working alongside Sevill, who was five years his senior.[48] In a year's time, and with "$125 of his own," James induced his brother to join him in a venture on their own account at Manayunk. When the Civil War broke out, the Dobsons were already involved in blanket manufacturing. They soon secured a contract to supply the Union Army with woolen blankets and drew Sevill Schofield into the same trade. During the sixties, both firms made stunning profits, Sevill named his second son Dobson, and the Dobson brothers married two of Sevill's sisters. During the 1870s, Thomas Schofield, Seville's older brother, managed John Dobson's Rockhill Mill in West Manayunk. This lacework of ties extended into the next generation. When the Schofield mills were troubled in the 1890s, James Dobson took over two of the three family factories. They appear in the 1900 textile directory as the Imperial Woolen Company, James Dobson, president, Dobson Schofield, treasurer and buyer.[49] This linkage

---

[47] *M&MP*, p. 53.

[48] F. Childs, ed., *East Falls: Three Hundred Years of History*, Philadelphia, 1976, p. 10.

[49] *M&MP*, p. 53; *Textile World Official Directory of the Textile Mills and Buyers of Textile Fabrics, 1900*, Boston, 1900, p. 214.

continued at least until 1916, by which time Dobson Schofield was both secretary and treasurer of the firm.[50] Thus we have here a glimpse of a three-cornered interfamily manufacturing network that was grounded in a common history, involved both marriages and production, and spanned generations into the present century.

With regard to the mechanics of production, the Schofields' use of space replicates the Campbell pattern, with variations. That Sevill was forced to refuse McFadden's first offer "on account of his limited means" indicates that the earlier mills were rented rather than held in a fashion that would generate equity. This capital shortage and the first year payment due McFadden account for the initial subdivision of the mill, the partners leasing all but one floor to other manufacturers. The rental income from the two tenant firms, occupying four of the five floors, likely covered the bulk of the sum due, given that the cost of the 45 horsepower delivered by the mill's waterwheel was included in the space rentals.[51] Within four years, the brothers had accumulated sufficiently to dismiss their tenants, purchasing their used machinery in the bargain, and in 1861 they occupied the entire mill. Wartime prosperity enabled Sevill and Charles Schofield to join the scores of Philadelphia textile manufacturers who constructed new factories. Their original mill was enlarged in 1863, the Blantyre Mill was purchased in 1864 and leased to Campbell and Company, and a five-story building was commenced in 1865 and completed the following spring. Repeated constructions and additions brought the total floor space to more than 170,000 square feet by the mid-seventies.[52]

Though not as fully documented, indications of productive flexibility and skill can be gleaned from diverse sources. The original product of the one-room manufactory was evidently woolen carpet yarns,[53] but by 1860 a switch to cotton yarns and some cloths had been made.[54] This is confirmed by a reference in Robson to the fact that "before the war, [they] manufactured largely for the Southern market, his trade [being] wholly suspended during the Rebellion."[55] Having acquired their tenants' wool-spinning machinery, a much larger yarn operation was undertaken, the shift to cottons and back to

---

50 *Davison's Textile Blue Book (1916)*, New York, 1916, p. 372.
51 Freedley, *Philadelphia and Its Manufactures*, pp. 258–61. In 1858, as was proper, the firm was known as M. Schofield; Sevill was operating it in his mother's name as reported in *M&MP*. Of the five Schofield textile firms operating in Philadelphia in 1875, four were in the Manayunk vicinity; all five produced yarn (Freedley, *Philadelphia and Its Manufactures* p. 261; 1860 MCS, Philadelphia Co., p. 474).
52 *M&MP*, p. 186.
53 Goshow, "Mills and Mill Owners," p. 103.
54 1860 MCS, Philadelphia Co., p. 474.
55 *M&MP*, p. 186. Carpet yarn is not a southern market product.

wool showing the flexibility and skill described earlier. This was still a fairly small business, for in 1859 the Schofields worked alongside few employees: "The two brothers worked in every department of the mill, and though they employed but six hands, their progress was so great during the first year, that they were enabled to purchase for cash an entire outfit of new machinery, costing $4,000."[56] But by the summer of 1860 their expanded capacity enabled the firm to report thirty-two workers, half men and boys, likely spinning, and half women, probably weaving mixed goods and cotton cloths for the "Southern market."[57] That they prospered is clear from the purchase of machinery later that year and expansion to the limts of the building, perhaps increasing the work force to more than fifty.

By the summer of 1861, however, the roof caved in with the onset of war. Within a year the Schofields had "begun the manufacture of blankets for the United States government." Although they surely had adequate spinning frames for this trade, they had to expand the building to accommodate additional looms, driven by a new steam engine. The war made the brothers a small fortune. Sevill bought Charles's share for $40,000 in 1864, making the value of the partnership about $80,000 after but five years, a hundred-fold multiplication from the $800 figure given for 1857 before the purchase of the first mill. Here the state as a material factor in accumulation appears mightily, and the contrast with Lowell is direct. Whereas the corporations' rigid production system and managerial "blunders" either closed the great hulks entirely or involved them in experimental debacles with products they had never previously made,[58] the Philadelphia textile mills prospered, their flexibility and government demand for woolens being the keys to state-sponsored accumulation. By 1870 Sevill, as sole proprietor, reported his invested capital as $200,000 and paid wages of $102,049 to a work force of more than 300, composed of 165 men, 112 women, 22 boys, and 15 girls.[59] The building expansion to house these operations has already been noted, but one additional detail is particularly revealing.

The five-story mill constructed in the closing days of the war was fully outfitted with new machinery and ready for production when it burned to the ground in 1867.

> This, being finished in 1866, was filled with the finest imported machinery, and everything was in readiness for operation when it, with its contents, valued at $225,000 was entirely destroyed by fire, March 26th, 1867. The building had been insured for about $80,000, but as he was temporarily using his engine room for drying purposes while his new dry

[56] Ibid.
[57] 1860 MCS, Philadelphia Co., p. 474.
[58] Charles Cowley, *Illustrated History of Lowell*, Boston, 1868, pp. 51, 54.
[59] 1870 MCS, Philadelphia Co., p. 600.

house was being erected, the insurance companies demanded heavy additional premiums; though demurring to their exorbitant rates, he had resolved that on the following day he would renew his policies, the last of which was cancelled on the very day of the fire; the risk ended at 12 M [noon], and before midnight the whole was a heap of smouldering ruins. Thus the delay of a single day, . . . involved a total loss.[60]

Given this disaster, the already dramatic increase in Schofield's personal holdings is even more noteworthy. What did the proprietor do in response to the situation? Three things in sequence. First, he traveled to Britain to "procure new machinery," presumably analogous fine-goods apparatus such as Campbell would soon buy to produce cottons. Second, upon his return in June 1867, he ordered construction of a "fire-proof building," a third larger than the wrecked facility. Third, "until it was completed in 1868, he operated as best he could under the circumstances, having his spinning done by other parties and still running the original mill."[61] His capital resources from war production or commercial credit were solid enough to support this venture, and the network of auxiliary production units was spurred into emergency activity. Without spinners ready to fill his wool yarn needs, Schofield would have had to suspend or secure supplies through commission agents at higher costs. With the supportive manufacturing network in the neighborhood, his firm could recover rapidly and forge ahead. The 1870 Manufacturing Census recorded five wool-yarn spinners in Manayunk, one of which was a mill attached to the J. & J. Dobson complex.[62]

The blankets manufactured during the Civil War, which became a Schofield staple, were supplemented in the seventies by a variety of fine woolens, including "chinchillas, elysians, raze coatings" and yarns for sale. They were marketed directly by the firm, from an outpost at 51 N. Front Street, again central to the wholesale dry-goods district. By 1875, a 150- by 70-foot addition to the new mill had sprung up, and the firm employed "from 500 to 600 hands, consum[ing] annually about 4,368,000 pounds of raw material." By the eighties, yet another mill had been built (the Eagle), the work force had doubled to about 1,200,[63] and beavers and cassimeres had joined the product line.

The Civil War was not only a material bonanza for the Schofields (sales multiplying eightfold, 1862–65); it also triggered two incidents that suggest the cultural dimensions of manufacture. Before his withdrawal from the firm, Charles Schofield twice led contingents of his mill workers in defense of the Union during the mid-war emergencies.

60 *M&MP*, p. 186.
61 Ibid.
62 1870 MCS, Philadelphia Co., pp. 600–8.
63 Lorin Blodget, *Census of Manufactures of Philadelphia (1882)*, Philadelphia, 1883, p. 175.

A Manayunk page from the 1870 Manufacturing Census Schedules, with the entry for Sevill Schofield's woolen mills. (National Archives)

When the Rebels threatened Pennsylvania in 1862 and 1863, moved by the common impulse of patriotism, the proprietors of these mills raised a company of men among their own operatives, continuing their wages during their absence, and sent it out under the command of Charles Schofield, while Sevill assumed the double burden at home.[64]

64 *M&MP*, p. 186.

Both the formation of a military force from the mill and its leadership by one of the partners are noteworthy, but when combined with the payment of absentee wages, they evoke the factory paternalist relationships recently explored by Patrick Joyce for Lancashire and Yorkshire in these same decades.[65] Joyce's claim for the factory as a central defining element of the *culture* of mill communities is here crisply exemplified, as it is the *factory* rather than the neighborhood (or more accurately in addition to the neighborhood) that extrudes a volunteer company for the war. Dobson's mills downstream formed a similar force in 1863, as did the crosstown textile machinery manufactory of Alfred Jenks.[66] In retaining their identities as members of a contingent from a particular manufactory, mill workers reinforced such bonds as were formed in the workplace by sharing their war experiences and their acceptance of the proprietors' authority, now in military discipline. These relationships of obligation were further strengthened by the knowledge that their families would continue to draw their wages in their absence. There is in this configuration an intimation of a capitalist culture whose rationality is distinct from that at Lowell. There workers were dismissed when the mills sold inventory and raw materials in 1861, taking short-run profits in anticipation of a short conflict. Though former mill workers at Lowell undoubtedly enlisted, their patriotism was surely mixed with considerations that their pay and supplementary state benefits would maintain their families. No writer has suggested that the Lowell corporations took any action parallel to that of the Schofields, of mediating workers' engagement in the conflict as a part of a larger paternalistic relationship. The absurdity of imagining Lowell treasurers leading their operatives into battle expresses fully the distance between the two complexes of the material and social relations of production.

Charles Schofield's withdrawal from the firm near the close of 1863, presumably after his return from the Gettysburg emergency, is the second "cultural" element developed in the Civil War context. "[Sevill's] brother, deeming himself sufficiently opulent, and fearing the result of the war, now retired, selling his interest for $40,000 to Sevill, who has since been the sole proprietor."[67] That $40,000 would provide Charles with a comfortable income from interest alone, though he was but 29 years old. A later account of

65 Joyce, *Work, Society and Politics.*
66 Frank Taylor, *Philadelphia in the Civil War*, Philadelphia, 1913, pp. 246–7. An exploration of the participation of such factory volunteer companies in the Civil War, limited to even those from Philadelphia during the emergency periods, would be a project of considerable scope; however, its impact on our understanding of the notions of paternalism, obligation, and community in industrial districts would be equally considerable. Given the vast Civil War literature and documentation, it should be possible to make fruitful inquiries in this area; as I am unfamiliar with the field, starts may have been already made.
67 *M&MP*, p. 186.

the Schofield firm confirms this event, remarking that "Charles Schofield retired with a competency."[68] This marks him as a curious sort of capitalist, one for whom accumulation had a determinate goal, a limit, a moment when one might (and Charles did) say "Enough!" To understand a "competence" and its implications, it will be valuable to call upon Alan Dawley's discussion in *Class and Community:*

> Competence meant the ability to get along well in economic terms – to possess real estate or savings sufficient to house a family, or tide it over during hard times, . . . For working-class families, it was a ticket out of poverty to the regions of minimal security. For middle-class families, the competence was a more liberal endowment of property or savings that generated income through rent or interest to sustain the family through adversity at its accustomed level of prosperity.[69]

Although Charles Schofield bridges several aspects of this working-class/middle-class relation to the competence as the guarantor of security, he fits neatly into neither section. He had been a textile worker from childhood into his twenties, and a capitalist for but five years before his "retirement," part of that time being spent in the military. Finding himself possessed of wealth sufficient for security beyond artisanal dreams, he withdrew, having short-circuited the many years of effort normally necessary to amass a competence. Yet it is in this framework that the full phrase "deeming himself sufficiently opulent, and fearing the result of the war" can be illuminated. Charles had, miraculously, at 29, access to the competence for which others from his background would strive a lifetime in vain. He did not take the chance that reversed fortunes would let it dribble away in debts and canceled contracts. Sevill could double and redouble his business to his heart's content, but Charles had had "Enough." It is, finally, in this sense, that the Schofields' experience underscores the cultural transition to capitalism within a newly capitalist immigrant family. An older, persistent "social ideal" informs Charles's withdrawal from business; Sevill aggressively extends the accumulation process in its "modern" sense, unfolding without end.

Retirements with a competence were hardly confined to Philadelphia, but they were unknown at Lowell, a phenomenon consistent with the accumulation structure of the corporation. How prevalent was this practice? No full study of the "competence" has yet materialized, but an incident from Sevill Schofield's later career suggests both its spread and the potential for non-business activity on the part of the comfortably situated former manufacturer. In 1880–1, a committee of Philadelphia worthies undertook a reform political campaign, designed to unseat the ostensibly corrupt and partisan

68 George Kennedy, *Roxborough, Wissahickon and Manayunk in 1891*, Philadelphia, 1891, p. 112.

69 Alan Dawley, *Class and Community: The Industrial Revolution in Lynn*, Cambridge, Mass., 1976, p. 151.

machine through which Republican bosses and their retainers governed the city. The Committee of One Hundred counted among its members at least eight textile manufacturers, one of whom was Sevill Schofield.[70] Their candidate was a former brush manufacturer, Samuel King, described as follows in a brief sketch of 1888:

> After leaving school, he learned the trade of brush-making with a relative. When he became of age, having established a character for industry, temperance, frugality and probity [ca. 1837], he began business for himself, in which he prospered . . . on Second Street near Callowhill (in Old City), where he continued fourteen years, acquiring by prudent management of his affairs what he considered a competency. He retired from business with an honorable reputation. . . . [ca. 1851]. His prompt and characteristic answer to those who criticized his action in thus early retiring from business was: "I know when I have enough, and I know how to take care of it."[71]

King used his leisure to become involved in Democratic party politics in his home district, the Northern Liberties, first as election inspector, later as a party convention delegate, and finally, in 1861, as an elected member of the Select Council, the upper house of the city legislature, where he served for twenty years. This erstwhile manufacturer was the choice of the businessmen's coalition in the 1881 mayoralty race, his Democratic affiliation and their solid Republicanism being of little import when the issue in this great manufacturing city was reform control of local government. King, like Charles Schofield, knew when he had enough and said so,[72] and in turning his energies to politics he eventually drew the mass support of his fellow manufacturers and was elected narrowly in a tumultuous campaign. King and the committee will reappear in a later chapter in the context of the "labor wars" of the eighties. Here he stands as one example of the liberating possibilities of the competence, at least for the middle-aged capitalist, a phenomenon peculiar to the culture of proprietary and partnership firms.

---

[70] John Thomas Scharf and Thompson Westcott, *History of Philadelphia*, Philadelphia, 1884, p. 850.

[71] George Gordon, "Samuel George King," in *A Biographical Album of Prominent Pennsylvanians, First Series*, Philadelphia, 1888, p. 217.

[72] Though trivial, it may interest readers to know that I drafted the Charles Schofield passages in which the sense of "enough" is put forward about a month before discovering Gordon's attribution of such a sentiment to Samuel King. Historians sufficiently immersed in the lives of past actors *can* develop some notion of their values and intentions, of "what made sense" in another era, a sensitvity that at times will anticipate discovery of confirmation of their suspicions. In no way may the speculations generated in the process of investigation be *substituted* for documented relationships and values, yet such sensibilities form an aspect of history *as art*, to which science, for all its formal reliability, must remain an accessory.

Essentially, private manufacturers could choose the goals of their enterprise. They could sail their firms before the economic winds until age and incapacity halted their supervision of cycles of production and profit. Or, alternatively, they could set a goal, achieve it, and redirect their lives into Christian service, political action, mechanical invention, or leisure in its many forms. On that model, business enterprise became a means toward humanized ends, whether personal or collective, rather than an end in itself. The competence could ease generational succession in family firms, open facilities for fresh entrepreneurial ventures, and, in the best cases, make the skills of able individuals available to their communities. It is one component of a culturally defined alternative to the corporate version of capitalism that was simultaneously taking shape in nineteenth-century America.

Through the experience of these two firms we have had a preliminary look at all the material and most of the cultural and external factors conditioning capitalist accumulation, set in their historical context as examples of the alternative to the Lowell system manifest in nineteenth-century Philadelphia. The question of to what extent these relationships, values, and trajectories are replicated in the aggregate industry will yield only to extensive investigation, the beginnings of which will be exposed here. Yet from these two firms we can derive a fuller appreciation of why skilled textile workers concentrated in Philadelphia. Not only was there an array of small, sophisticated firms, whose specialization "appropriate[d] the talents of the artisans." Suffecent modest housing was available as well, as was easy relocation from firm to firm amid the neighborhood life of immigrant communities, which included to some degree immigrant capitalists. Moreover, there were big mills whose pathway to accumulation called for considerable input of skilled labor and whose social relations retained elements of the familiar craft-centered culture. Finally, there was amid the shifting economic tides "room to move." If the Schofields are not unique, movement was possible not just vertically along some monetary scale but more profoundly into the realm of security, the most systematically elusive goal of workers under capitalism. More modestly, for the immigrant, movement was possible into communities delineated in large measure by the culture of the factory and the workshop. Scores of manufacturers sprouted from the shops of their immigrant predecessors, at least in textiles at Philadelphia.

The Campbell and Schofield cases have served as an introduction to the world of proprietary capitalism in nineteenth-century Philadelphia. To assess the significance of these examples and to document the claim that they represent an alternative format for industrial production, the reconstruction of the moving context in which they functioned is necessary. It is to this task, the description and analysis of the developing Philadelphia textile trades (ca. 1800–5), that we turn in Part II.

PART II

"On their own account": the proprietary textile trades at Philadelphia

4

The Philadelphia textile manufacture in the early republic

I will further observe that my Capital here invested which is the whole recompense for ten years Industry, Economy, Perseverance and Enterprize does not at
present with all my exertions yeald four per centum per annum which I humbly
submit to impartial Legislators to say weather it is fair, weather it is hard or not
that useful industry must thus suffer and thus be rewarded.

> – Remarks by Henry Korn, manufacturer of fringes and trimmings,
> 1820 Census of Manufactures, Eastern District of Pennsylvania,
> Manuscript Schedule No. 587.

In the early nineteenth century, Philadelphia housed the largest population cluster on the North American continent. Old City, a ribbon one by two miles in area stretching between the Delaware docks and the Schuylkill River, housed more than 50,000 souls in 1810. The near "suburbs" north and south (Northern Liberties, Kensington, Southwark, etc.) reported another 43,000 residents to census marshals, and the rural districts (Germantown, Frankford, etc.) swelled the county total to more than 110,000.[1] Two decades later the county population numbered 190,000, the near suburbs having more than doubled in size as the city center neared capacity. (The population in the six downtown wards would increase from 80,000 in 1830 to only 115,000 half a century later as the city total grew to 860,000.) These outlying neighborhoods were the grubby cradles of manufacturing development in leather, brewing and distilling, printing and textiles. Their open spaces sprouted workshops, factories, warehouses, and the long rows of cheap but sturdy worker housing for which the city is still noted. Although Old City retained a significant manufacturing core beyond midcentury, it was in the outer districts that the bulk of immigrants and in-migrants labored, struggled, struck, rioted, and perished as capitalist production took shape in Philadelphia.

Artisanal manufacturing in the city was well established by Revolutionary times, but the first survey of the textile trades appeared with Tench Coxe's tables of manufacturing, the product of the fragmentary 1810 industrial

---

[1] *Hazard's Register of Pennsylvania*, vol. 8 (1831), p. 65; cited hereafter as *Hazard's Register*.

census. Coxe's tables for Pennsylvania indicate the enormous spread and
strength of household weaving, with more than 90% of the wool, flax, and
mixed cloths recorded being produced outside the state's most populous
county. Yet in specialties and mill operations, Philadelphia was already
prominent. More than half the stockings and virtually all the fringe, lace,
carpets, and floor cloths turned out in Pennsylvania were made in Philadelphia. Again with spinning, more than 50% of the mill-generated yarns
came from the metropolis. Nor was the city without "labour-saving machinery," for of its 206 looms, 186 had fly shuttles, for example.[2] As is well
understood generally, the subsequent war with Britain proved a great stimulus to the "domestic manufacture" of textiles. Philadelphia millmen, by
1820, looked back on the midteens as a set of golden years.

The postwar resumption of trade relations with England and the depression of the following years crippled textile production in and around Philadelphia. In cotton and wool, at the height of the boom (1816), more than
3,500 workers spun and wove in the city and surrounding townships. Three
years later a committee of citizens protesting the ravages of "unchecked
importations and a vitiated currency" numbered but 400 "hands" in these
two sectors.[3] These introductory notes suggest three observations. First, at
the time the Boston Associates, merchants-become-manufacturers at Waltham, commenced their quiet accumulation of acreage and canal shares for
the Lowell project, there was in place at Philadelphia an extensive textile
manufacture. Second, the Philadelphia producers were then undergoing a
serious economic crisis shared by other branches of American industry,
granting even that its severity may have been exaggerated by the petitioners.
Third, the structural and operating characteristics of the textile manufacture
in the city at this time rest mysterious. To confront this silence will be the
task of the following pages, wherein an effort will be made to profile the
development of the industry roughly from the turn of the century through
the 1830s. This sketch will provide a base from which to analyze a more
thoroughly documented era (1840–90) and the evolving productive relations
that distinguish the proprietary Philadelphia system from the corporate system at Lowell.

Cloth making in and around Philadelphia can be traced back to the first
decade of the eighteenth century, when the proprietor-governor, William
Penn, encouraged weavers, dyers, and fullers to locate in the new colony.[4]
The household manufacture of coarse woolens and linens became general

[2] Tench Coxe, *Statistical Tables of Manufacture in 1810*, Philadelphia, 1813, pp. 44–8.
[3] *Hazard's Register* vol. 4 (1828), p. 168. The documents reprinted are dated October 2,
   1819.
[4] John Thomas Scharf and Thompson Westcott, *History of Philadelphia*, Philadelphia,
   1884, p. 2300.

by midcentury and continued statewide through the 1850s. Evidence of production for the market dates at least from the 1760s, though sales from artisanal workshops in Old City surely preceded William Smith's 1766 opening of a "market for home-manufactured goods," chiefly fabrics we may presume. That same year a hosier, Daniel Mause, set up shop at The Hat-In-Hand, offering cotton stockings and thread for sale, an effort reminiscent of the informal tavern-centered markets of eighteenth-century English villages.

Of greater interest, suggesting then-current limitations to productive scale in the face of British imports, is a letter by John Penn, dated January 21, 1767, concerning a more ambitious undertaking.

> One [manufactory] was set up about three years ago in this city by private subscription for the making of sail-cloth, ticking, and linens; but the persons concerned have already sunk money by the project, for the high price of labour will not allow any of the articles to be made at so cheap a rate as those of the same quality and goodness made in England are sold for by the retailers here; they have therefore lately resolved to discontinue the undertaking.[5]

The later antagonism between native manufacturers and importing merchants appears here, stifling this early partnership venture. Moreover, the shortage of labor and consequent "high price" that prevailed in many trades into the next century added a further material constraint, despite the firm's technical capacity to produce some cloths of a "quality and goodness" comparable to British fabrics.

Nonetheless, by the time of the Revolution, the city supported a diverse group of textile makers; references surviving attest to the manufacture of yarn, linen, silk, cottons, wools, and hosiery for public consumption.[6] Most noted were the craftsmen of Germantown, whose hosiery and yarns were highly regarded through the end of the century. Household wool weavers in outlying townships could avail themselves of the services of waterpowered fulling mills that shared creek banks with numerous grist, saw, and paper mills throughout the county.[7] However, the Revolutionary decade, with its currency and market confusions, the occupation of the city by the British, and so on, did not prove a propitious time for a repetition of manufacturing

---

5 Ibid., p. 2227.

6 Ibid., pp. 2301–14.

7 See Mildred Goshow, ed., "Mills Along the Wissahickon," typescript, 1970, of a series of newspaper articles from the 1932 *Manayunk Sentinel*, Roxborough Branch, Free Library of Philadelphia. There were 26 millsites along the six miles of the Wissahickon Creek in Philadelphia County and an equal number on the upper branches in neighboring Montgomery County, most dating from the colonial period. Other mills were situated along the Pennypack, Frankford, Mill, and Darby creeks.

experiments such as that noted by Penn. A joint-stock effort, the United Company of Philadelphia for Promoting American Manufactures, was founded in 1775, shares being £10 each, and Benjamin Rush was elected president. For two years, the company sought to manufacture linen, woolen, and cotton cloths, and "it employed some four hundred women in spinning, most of the work being done at home. The Company possessed the first spinning-jenny seen in America, obtained from England in violation of an Act of Parliament forbidding the export of machinery."[8] When the city fell under British control, the United Company folded permanently (1777).

Ten years later a second corporate project appeared, organized by the Pennsylvania Society for the Encouragement of Manufactures and the Useful Arts, with Tench Coxe as the chief promoter. Again shares cost £10 and were transferable. Again the production of cloths with labor-saving machinery was the goal, and leading citizens were again involved in this patriotic capitalist venture. And again the firm folded after two years. Yet there were important differences between this and the earlier company. The state was involved both directly, as the Pennsylvania Assembly subscribed to a block of 100 shares in 1789, and indirectly, as good offices and on occasion specific assistance were provided by Franklin, Jefferson, and Madison in response to Coxe's tireless publicity. To stimulate mechanical inventiveness, the society offered a gold medal for any power-driven machine "by which the ordinary labor of hands in manufacturing cotton, wool, flax or hemp, should be better saved than by any then in use in this State." Finally, the firm sold its own products, realizing a profit of £72 on sales of £448 in the four months from mid-April through mid-August 1788. All this was a healthy augury, but another "external event" brought the curtain down in the spring of 1790, terminating Philadelphia's second corporate textile experiment.

During the night of March 24, 1790, the society's mill, leased from William Bingham, burned to the ground. Raw materials, stock, and machinery, including at least four spinning jennies totaling 224 spindles, were completely destroyed. The reluctance of those possessed of large capitals to risk manufacturing investment surely had conditioned the initial £10-share scheme. After this disaster, that sweep could not be repeated and the enterprise did not resume. However, it may not have been only capital shortages that sealed its fate. The introduction of labor-saving machinery in Britain at this time brought handloom workers out in forceful opposition that materialized both in petitions to Parliament and the king and in threats to en-

8 Harold Hutcheson, *Tench Coxe: A Study in American Economic Development*, Baltimore, 1938, p. 146.

trepreneurs and occasionally in destruction of their factories. The hand spinning that formed a portion of hundreds of Philadelphia household economies in this era was directly threatened by "labour-saving devices." In this context, it should be no surprise that the society believed their facility had been fired by an incendiary.

> On April 13, 1790, a memorial from a committee of the Society was addressed to the Supreme Executive Council of the State [of Pennsylvania], stating that they believed the fire to have been a result of foul play. The Council proclaimed a reward of $300 for the apprehension of the person or persons guilty.[9]

The reward was never collected.

Several comments seem in order. First, however laudable the project of these elite promoters of American industry, their cultural insensitivity and locational strategy were significant blunders. Situating their operations in an urban center that housed hundreds, perhaps thousands, of households engaged in textile handwork and smuggling from Britain machinery that menaced the livelihoods of these families, in an era when political democracy in the city was popular and tumultuous (leading right-thinking gentlemen to redraw the state's Constitution), were errors of an enthusiasm distanced from the laboring poor's daily struggles.[10] How much more shrewd were the Lowell pioneers, planting their brick, mortar, and machines in the vacant realms north of Boston. Second, these two companies were virtually the only corporate undertakings in the Philadelphia textile manufacture before the Civil War. Though merchant capital would later be plentifully invested by Philadelphia grandees in ventures outside commerce, textile manufacturing would not be among them. A closer examination of this phenomenon will appear later. Third, the mill fire makes a regular appearance in the city's textile development. Whereas the huge investments at Lowell were protected by round-the-clock watchmen and the early installation of fire-prevention systems, these precautions appeared much later in Philadelphia, and only in its larger factories. Fires carry a deep ambiguity (accident or arson?) when they occur amid the process of capitalist exploitation and accumulation. Several closely spaced mill burnings triggered cries of "incendiarism" in the 1830s, a decade of intense industrial conflict.[11] Whether workers were torching the mills or not, the operators' public voicing of their fears testifies to both their vulnerability and the sharp labor conflicts of the times. Fires

[9] Ibid., pp. 151–6.
[10] See John Alexander, "Poverty, Fear and Continuity: An Analysis of the Poor in Late Eighteenth Century Philadelphia," in Allen Davis and Mark Haller, eds., *The Peoples of Philadelphia*, Philadelphia, 1973, pp. 13–35.
[11] See J. A. Fowler, *A History of Insurance in Philadelphia*, Philadelphia, 1889.

were "external events" whose impact on accumulation might be direct and throttling.[12,13]

A careful exploration of productive relations in a private Philadelphia textile mill circa 1800–50 will point out the elements of continuity and contrast between the Schofield–Campbell pattern and the factory operations of an earlier generation. For this purpose, developments at Kensington's Globe Mill will serve well, for the Globe both housed several of the city's first factory textile firms and was located in the district where the largest single concentration of the local textile industry would emerge.

The Globe Mill and Craige, Holmes & Co.

Erected near the beginning of the eighteenth century, the Globe Mill was a waterpowered gristmill located several miles north of colonial Philadelphia's central district. About 1796, James Davenport converted it to allow the installation of his patented machinery for spinning sailcloth yarns. Though Davenport enjoyed a visit and favorable comments from President Washington, within a year he was advertising for a partner, likely in need of capital for his fledgling firm. In 1798 Davenport died and his machinery was sold at public auction, ending the first experiment with textiles at the Globe.[14] He was succeeded about 1800 by John Hewson, a famous block printer of calicos. An immigrant, Hewson was intimately connected with the elite merchant and political circles in Philadelphia, having arrived from Great Britain "before the Revolution, having been solicited to do so by Benjamin Franklin."[15]

During the conflict, Hewson served in the Continental Army, was captured at Monmouth, and escaped with a British price on his head (fifty guineas "for his body, dead or alive").[16] Associated with Tench Coxe in the

---

12 For an interesting reading of the threat of incendiarism in a French textile mill, see William Reddy, "The *Batteurs* and the Informer's Eye: A Labour Dispute under the French Second Empire," *History Workshop Journal* 7 (1979):30–44, esp. pp. 34 and 37.

13 Another incident may reinforce the point. An 1830 account of Holmesburg, a district in the northeastern section of the county, reported: "In the same neighborhood are two saw mills —on the scite [sic] of one of them, some 20 years ago or more [before 1810], a saw mill was burnt, as was believed by some evil designing person, because it was employed in sawing mahogany, and thereby was likely to interfere with the demand for labour at manufacturing that article by the whip-saw in the city" (*Hazard's Register*, vol. 5 [1830], p. 138).

14 William Bagnall, *The Textile Industries of the United States*, Cambridge, Mass., 1893, vol. I, pp. 223–6.

15 Ibid., p. 111.

16 Scharf and Westcott, *History of Philadelphia*, pp. 2228–9.

1787 Pennsylvania Society, John Hewson resumed his calico printing, displaying elaborate six-color effects on the society's float in the great procession that followed adoption of the federal Constitution, July 4, 1787.[17] The skill involved in multicolor printing must be underscored; writing of such work, a later observer noted: "What must be the nicety of adjustment . . . can scarcely be conceived, except by those practically engaged in the process."[18] Unlike Davenport, whose coarse sail duck competed with tax-free imported rivals, Hewson's high-quality output brought him extended success. The elder Hewson retired in 1810, turning over the family business to his son, John, Jr. This roughly coincided with their removal from the Globe to other quarters, where the younger Hewson continued calico operations into the 1820s.[19]

Who was next at the Globe Mill? In 1809, a four-man partnership purchased the mill and surrounding land to commence cotton manufacture. Thanks to Bagnall, the background of the partners has been documented: "Adam Seybert was a physician . . . ; Seth Craige was largely engaged in the saddlery and saddlery-hardware business at 110 Market Street; Charles Marquedant was a merchant and Thomas Huston was a journeyman in the employ of Seth Craige."[20] Within three months, Seybert sold his portion to Craige, giving him half ownership and effective control of the firm (as Huston was his employee). With their capital estimated at $80,000, the partners immediately undertook to enlarge the building, adding two stories and erecting an office, salesroom, and warehouse nearby. None of the four original partners had a visible textile background, but narrow textiles (braids, webs, girth tapes) were a regular part of the saddler's stock-in-trade. Huston may well have had a basic knowledge of manufacture and have supervised the mill, as Craige continued his saddlery business on Market Street. John Holmes bought Marquedant's share at the close of 1813, and the firm became Craige, Holmes and Co., the name under which it would operate the Globe Mill for the next four decades. Assembling an adequate capitalization through partnership was one component of this successful accumulation formula. Craige's stable saddlery trade and market connections likely provided some access to sources of working capital and short-term commercial credit, as well as an outlet for part of the output and links to potential buyers for the remainder.

[17] *Hazard's Register* vol. 2 (1828), p. 419. Reprinted from a 1788 newspaper.
[18] Geoffrey Turnbull, *A History of Calico Printing in Great Britain*, Altrincham, England, 1951, p. 58, quoting from an 1884 source, Dodd, *Textile Manufacturing in Great Britain*.
[19] Florence Montgomery, *Printed Textiles: English and American Cottons and Linens, 1700–1850*, New York, 1970, pp. 96–7. The frontispiece in Montgomery's volume depicts a Hewson-printed bedspread in color.
[20] Bagnall, *Textile Industries*, vol. I, pp. 581–2.

In its early years, the firm's manufacturing strategy struck out in three directions. For the saddlery market, the mill produced "saddle-girthing, tapes, and fringes, woven on hand-looms."[21] Cotton yarns were spun, for sale and for the direct production of cloths. One source claims the manufacture of No. 100s, an exceptionally fine embroidery count, then worth a highly profitable $5 per pound (raw cotton generally selling for less than a tenth of that sum per pound).[22] Third, in the same period (1812–16) the partners brought a French immigrant calico printer to a newly constructed outbuilding at the Globe, engaging him to work up part of the cloth output of the mill's handlooms.

> According to Scharf and Westcott, [Francis] Labbe began the [calico] business, on his own account, at 206 Cherry Street [N.B.: a few blocks from Craige's Market Street shop], and discontinued it after four years, becoming then a dancing master . . . It is probable that Labbe was not able to prosecute the business on account of want of capital, and soon transferred to the Globe Mills. The print-cloths [plain goods to be block-printed] were purchased in part, while a considerable quantity was woven on hand-looms, which were operated in several small buildings on the mill-lot, . . . the spooling and warping being done in their lower stories, and the yarns being made in the main mill.[23]

Yet another outbuilding was constructed, for yarn dyeing, and a room for sizing warps was attached to it. A steampowered mill, erected with War of 1812 profits, completed this wave of construction and expansion in 1816.[24]

When one considers, by contrast, the enormous frustrations of the pioneering Slater, Almy and Brown mills in disposing of their machine-made yarns,[25] the scrambling creativity of the Craige firm may be sensed. Rescuing a skilled craftsman from the dancing trade solved one dimension of Craige's output equation, giving the firm attractive calicoes rather than common gray goods to offer in the market. Selling a wide variety of products in the nation's largest urban center and being buttressed by a substantial capital, "this business did not suffer so much as some other textile industries did, on the return of peace,"[26] when the postwar depression bankrupted scores of domestic cotton producers. Another element in the productive relations of Craige, Holmes and Co., which may have insulated the firm

---

21 Ibid., p. 583.
22 Samuel Needles, "The Governor's Mill and the Globe Mill," *Pennsylvania Magazine of History and Biography* 8 (1884):385.
23 Bagnall, *Textile Industries*, vol. I, p. 583.
24 Needles, "Governor's Mill," pp. 383–4.
25 Caroline Ware, *The Early New England Cotton Manufacture*, New York, 1931 (rpt., 1966), pp. 161–6.
26 Bagnall, *Textile Industries*, vol. I, p. 584.

somewhat, was its extensive use of outwork weavers, whose survival needs provided a demand for yarn even in the hardest times.

In their 1820 Manufacturing Census return, the proprietors of the Globe Mill pointed out:

> The remainder of what yarn we spin and do not weave up ourselves is sold to the weavers in the neighborhood and employs about 150 weavers and 80 other hands to weave it up. Formerly employed about three hundred persons when demand for goods was brisk . . . August 24th, 1820.[27]

These weavers were most probably independent immigrant artisans, some of whose kin or neighbors worked in the Globe. At Philadelphia, such families commonly owned a loom, bought yarn, and produced ginghams, checks, and so on for merchant clothiers who set a price at which they would "take" the goods. This introduced a special production sequence. As mill-spun yarn displaced the household spinning wheel and jenny in the city, dispersed handloom weavers served both manufacturing and merchant capitalists, buying from one and selling to the other, making a profit for them but little for themselves. Philadelphia's largest strike of the decade was mounted in 1825 by such weavers, 2,900 of whom demanded "an increase of 25% on their existing prices."[28] The results of this upheaval have not been documented, but the considerable scale of outwork weaving raises a critical issue.

In the 1820s more Philadelphia textile workers toiled in backyard shops than in powered mills. Moreover, as suggested by the Craige comment above, their existence in a nebulous world of relations backward toward yarn spinners and forward to merchants was an essential element in the accumulation matrix *for the factory operators*, in the sense that the millman was relieved of excess capacity. The persistence of thousands of "independent" household and handloom producers into the 1870s may be comprehensible if their auxiliary role in capitalist accumulation is appreciated. To assure use of the tons of yarn the mill produced, the firm could have expended capital to buy looms, hand or power, to "weave it up." Then, however, the firm would have had to dispose of tons of cloth, only displacing the capacity and marketing problems. Yarn might have been placed with commission agents, but that strategy would have brought both a lower return and the potential of loss of control over the firm to the merchants. The existence of hundreds of outwork weavers facilitated the adoption by Craige, Holmes and Co. of a mixed "optimization" strategy analogous to Campbell's later efforts. The firm wove some of its yarn for its own print cloths to be marketed directly, thus avoiding

---

27 1820 MCS, Eastern District, Pa., no. 600.

28 William Sullivan, *The Industrial Worker in Pennsylvania, 1800–1840*, Harrisburg, Pa., 1955, p. 222.

the plain goods trade. It needed looms sufficient only for this sequence, selling the overflow yarn to outworkers whose weaving involved none of the firm's capital. The household workers' marketing relations with merchants were none of Craige's concern; unless the weavers chose to starve or drop the trade entirely, handworkers would continue to purchase yarn, thereby supporting factory-based accumulation. The prices merchants paid for coarse handloom goods (Craige sold No. 14 to No. 20 yarns) were determined by competition in the national market, which was influenced, of course, by the production from mills such as those at Lowell. In due course, the New England production deflated prices.

Craige's direct sales of yarn to weavers represents only one possible format for handloom production. The simplest outwork relationship involved the manufacturer of an intermediary jobber who provided both the raw materials and the loom (or as in Britain at this time, the knitting frame for hosiery) and bought the output periodically at a piece-rate payment. The worker, who contributed only his or her labor power to production, functioned within the confines of the relationship as a proletarian. The piece rates might be chiseled, the machine withdrawn, or fines might be levied for alleged "bad work" – the laborer was at all times vulnerable to the whims of commerce.

If the outworker owned his apparatus, the most common case in Philadelphia, the situation was somewhat different. Like other artisans, this weaver possessed the tools of his craft. The manufacturer, whether a millowner or the proprietor of a handloom workshop, put out yarn and took in cloth, again at a specified price, but options were open to the loom-owning weaver that were denied his propertyless colleagues. If the rates were cut, or other sharp practices appeared, the artisan might undertake to secure yarn from another source. This, to be sure, was utterly dependent on spatial and organizational factors. If there was but one supplier within reach, a weaver could only move elsewhere, a chancy decision that might be beyond his means. Moreover, even if several mills or outwork shops were within easy access, it would be in the owners' interest to set a common price for weaving and thus balk any attempts at "shopping" by outworkers. In times of rising demand for cloth, such collaboration would naturally be imperiled by each manufacturer's desire to maximize output, leading to the pirating of outworkers through short-run rate hikes.[29] Merchants too could enter this picture, offering even Yankee or imported yarns to handloom artisans. Certainly there was more room for workers' positive action in this form of

---

[29] Worse, in such times a power-spinner might invest in power looms which could cut off the handloom outworker entirely, for such looms could quickly devour his yarn output, leaving little or no residue for putting-out.

outwork. In urban areas where clusters of such workers toiled in proximity for a common employer, the potential for collective responses to either millmen or merchant capitalists was theoretically plausible, enhanced by ethnic bonds and craft traditions that facilitated perception of their situation as shared and actionable. It was out of some such conjuncture that the 1825 weavers' strike materialized and spread.

If Craige's remarks are taken as given, the *selling* of yarn defines a third format for outwork in which the handweaver owns both the loom and its product. However, with the need to arrange for the sale of the cloth to a merchant and the minuscule scale of both his yarn demand and cloth output, this worker had little bargaining leverage in either transaction. The general shortage of specie necessitated some credit facilities, with the weaver a debtor in the mill's yarn accounts and a creditor in the cloth merchant's books. A financially adept craftsman could be assured a discount for cash purchases, a small advantage, but was in a poor position to influence whatever pattern of periodic settlements merchants might establish. The choice of output was limited only by his skill and the flexibility of his apparatus. As the Globe Mill ran a dyehouse, neighborhood outworkers who owned multiple-shuttle looms might have had the opportunity to produce more highly valued checks, stripes, and plaids. Though in a somewhat better position than the "primitive" outworker, these craftsmen were still quite exposed. Because accounts at both ends could be finagled, the weaver who was less than vigilant about the figures could be short-changed. If the payments for goods delivered were widely spaced, cash-flow problems could become serious. If glutted markets dropped the cloth price while yarn remained stable, the squeeze could spell ruin. Moreover, sickness, eviction, or a fire at the mill could just as easily wreck this fragile household workshop, which shared the vulnerability of the previous two groups. Under such conditions, survival was a challenge, security an elusive dream. As the dramatic increase in the number of looms in operation in winter suggests, many handworkers, in addition to their use of more familiar economic strategies (e.g., boarders, laboring children), pursued outdoor occupations in good weather (construction labor perhaps).[30] By combining such expedients, handloom weavers endured, contributing with every yard they produced to the profits sought by both merchants and millmen.

In a purely formal sense, outworkers in this third group were "capitalists," though their assets were microscopic, likely less than $100.[31] They bought

---

[30] *Hazard's Register*, vol. 1 (1828), p. 28.
[31] 1820 MCS, Philadelphia Co., no. 676–9. Four handloom shops reported nineteen handlooms, three warping mills, and a total capital of $1,700. The estimate of less than $100 for a handloom may well be high.

raw materials, produced a product, sold it in commodity form, and sought to realize a profit. Yet at the same time, it is unlikely that they hired labor at wages, and the blockades to their accumulation of capital were formidable. It is also presumptuous to assume that accumulation was their goal; "getting a living" from their craft was a task in itself. Yet is it not reasonable to imagine that some of them sought something analogous to the capitalists' "More!" – a workshop perhaps whose row of looms might yield in time a competence? A second loom would be the first step, acquired from a family quitting the trade and moving on, at which an older son schooled in the basics would add to the family output. Perhaps a drop in the yarn price and the arrival of a penniless townsman would lead to both a third loom and offers to make specialties or rush orders for the merchant clothier. With virtually no capital, every step was perilous, yet in 1820, 1850, and 1880 at Philadelphia such modest handloom workshops appear in the Manufacturing Census as one component of the textile manufacture. Most were in no position to survive the smallest economic trauma, yet the handloom manufactory is another element of continuity, like the outworker at home, that spans the century. Whether sprouted in the step-by-step fashion just described, or started by immigrants arriving with a few hundred dollars, the workshop joins the mill and the outworker as a third productive relationship in textiles. Workshops' yarn purchases supported mill capacity, and the larger shops (members of the Society of Weavers in the late 1820s) might have outworkers of their own. Any attempt to understand the operations of the Lowell firms must take into account the links between them, agents sharing information about fractious workers and production costs, treasurers handling the affairs of several firms simultaneously, and so on. Similarly in Philadelphia, the complex of interrelationships between the three methods of production is an essential element in its textile industry, bearing on the uses of capital and space, the structure of production and marketing, and the ways in which a surplus might be accumulated.

It would be an error to dismiss handloom outworkers and handwork shop operators as a "transitional" group, unless the notion of transition be extended radically. As the factory system developed in Philadelphia, their numbers increased, fueled by immigration, to an estimated 7,180 in the 1850s.[32] As the handwork cotton trade eroded, they made wools, knitted specialities, and finally carpets, both rag and ingrain. We know next to nothing about them, and the host of questions their persistence raises cannot even be listed here, much less addressed. Yet they were as meaningful a part of the accumulation process in the city as were the power loom and the networks of merchant connections. Their presence at Lowell, Manchester, or Fall River, however, is simply unimaginable.

[32] Edwin Freedley, *Philadelphia and Its Manufactures*, Philadelphia, 1857, pp. 253–6.

It would be equally inappropriate to view outworkers as hapless victims. They could work at their own schedule, observe St. Monday in an American form if they chose, and avoid the bells and controls of factory toil. At the Globe Mill, "until nearly 1840, the hours of work were . . . from sunrise to sunset in summer, and from 7 A.M. to 8 P.M. in winter, with half an hour for dinner. This averaged 13 hours a day (six days a week); and the present half-holiday (Saturday) was unknown."[33] That the mill's twelve apprentices were assured "one quarter's schooling annually" and that the proprietors showed "much kindness and consideration toward their apprentices and other mill hands"[34] may not have leavened an otherwise hard loaf. The particular dynamics of the Philadelphia textile manufacture enabled thousands of weavers to stay out of the mills and stay out they did.

The role of immigrant textile workers in the Philadelphia industry will be emphasized time and again in these pages. The Globe Mill is no exception. The names of five skilled workers from the period 1810–20 have been preserved. All were immigrants, a French calico printer, an English dyer, and three carders from England and Scotland. In addition, Daniel Large, brought in to construct the first steam engine in 1813, had apprenticed at Boulton and Watt in Birmingham.[35]

Having surveyed the structure, production, labor relations, space, capital, and marketing strategies of Craige, Holmes and Co. before 1820, it is time to carry the chronicle of its development forward. An appreciation of the extent to which accumulation took shape at the Globe Mill in the 1820s can be gained by comparing their 1820 census return with the 1832 materials collected by Matthew Carey and C. C. Biddle for the Treasury Department's *McLane Report*. Starting out with about $80,000 capital in 1810, the firm had increased its capital figure by 1820 to $130,000, which included the original land and mill plus two buildings erected in the teens, along with their machinery. Yet another mill was put up in 1828, housing a 48-horse-power steam engine that was linked by shafting to the 1816 structure. This and the tripled spindlage are reflected in the 1832 capital of $200,000. All the looms in 1820 were powered by hand; only 65 of the 140 looms were in operation, the idle ones had run suspender, tape, and bed lau, which most likely had been overwhelmed by importations. The calico-printing operation of earlier days is absent, suspended as well, it seems, by foreign competition. The firm's product mix in 1820 suggests some scrambling for fractions of an uncertain market. A small number of handlooms for cotton piece goods were placed in one room of the mill about this time, but have disappeared by 1832. All 47 looms listed in the *McLane Report* wove saddle girth, which was

[33] Needles, "Governor's Mill," p. 386.
[34] Ibid.
[35] Ibid., p. 385.

Table 4.1. *Comparison of Globe Mill 1820 census data with the 1832* McLane Report

	Census data 1820	*McLane Report* 1832
Capital	$130,000	$200,000
Machinery		
Spindles	3,250	9,126
Looms	140ᵃ	47
Pounds of cotton used	288,000	ca. 550,000
Pounds of cotton manufactured		518,174
Workers		
Men	70	42
Women	35	72
Boys and girls	95	190ᵇ
Total	200	304
Products	Yarn, sheeting, check, shirting, gingham, diaper, fringes, web, girth, bed lau, millinette, etc.	Yarn, girth, web

ᵃOnly 65 looms were in operation in 1820.
ᵇBoys, 80; girls, 110.
Source: Manuscript Manufacturing Census Schedules, Eastern District, Pa., no. 600, 1820. Louis McLane, *Report of the Secretary of the Treasury, 1832. Documents Relative to the Manufactures in the United States,* 3 vols., 22d Cong., 1st sess., H. Doc. 308 (Washington, D.C., 1833), vol. 3, pp. 214–15.

probably still a hand operation at that date. Although power looms for plain cottons were finally installed on two floors in the 1840s, the distribution of yarn for outwork weaving was continued.[36]

The 1832 figures show two striking shifts at the Globe Mill. With the contraction of handloom production at the mill and the expansion of powered spinning, the proportions of men and women at work have reversed. Likewise with the expanded spindlage, child labor doubled as scores of doffers and piecers were needed. Given that the mill had its own machine shop, engine house, dyehouse, and carding facility, weaving was probably young women's work, with most of the 42 men distributed in the traditional skilled and "heavy labor" jobs. By 1830 there were, most likely, some outwork weaving households in Kensington that included a father who wove

[36] Ibid., pp. 385–8.

Globe yarn at home and children who spun (and perhaps wove) at the mill. By that time Kensington was no longer a remote township. It was rapidly becoming an immigrant destination and a manufacturing district; population had nearly doubled since 1820 to more than 13,000.[37] Although the labor problems of an earlier generation (shortages and a "high price") had vanished, they would soon be replaced by the constraints of resistance and organization.[38]

The second shift is the sharp narrowing of output, from ten or more varieties of cloth plus yarns in 1820 to saddle girth and yarns alone. The production of handloom piece goods within the mill continued at least to the mid-twenties,[39] when it was discontinued to allow the partners to specialize in the yarn and girth trade with which they had begun. The larger spinning capacity could evidently be taken up by the mill looms and outworkers, the balance being advertised for sale at Craige's 110 Market Street salesroom, the same building from which the saddlery business had operated. There are no further mentions of calicoes and handloom sheetings, suggesting that the production of those goods had been an expedient (ca. 1812–25) to allow capacity spinning.

To allow a glimpse of a yarn, a cotton, and a wool mill in the context of their development, we will violate the temporal limits set at the outset of this chapter by tracing Craige, Holmes and Co. over subsequent decades and in so doing will link this early firm with Messrs. Campbell and Schofield. The Globe partnership was redrawn upon the death of Thomas Huston in 1832. His heirs transferred their quarter share to Seth Craige, Jr., bringing three-quarters of the ownership into the saddler's family. The new partnership, Craige, Holmes and Craige, was short-lived. Later in the thirties, most likely upon the father's death, Thomas Craige, a second son, entered the partnership and the original firm name was restored.[40] Thomas traveled with the civic leaders of Old City, an elite group whose considerable fortunes allowed them the leisure to arrange an endless series of fetes, processions, congressional memorials, and charitable functions. On February 1, 1832, young Tom, then in his early thirties, surfaced at a "town meeting" intended to prepare suitable celebrations for the centennial of Washington's birth. Previous association with the "best" people is indicated by his appointment to the group of "gentlemen" constituting the "committee of arrangement,"

[37] *Hazard's Register*, vol. 8 (1831), p. 65.

[38] See Sullivan, *Industrial Worker*, pp. 222–6, for strikes in the 1830s. Philadelphia was *the* center of labor organization in that decade, though only fragmentary references to the textile workers appear in treatments of these movements by John Commons and others.

[39] Needles, "Governor's Mill," pp. 385–6, quoting T. Wilson's *Picture of Philadelphia in 1824*.

[40] Needles, "Governor's Mill," pp. 385–6; Bagnall, *Textile Industries*, vol. I, p. 585.

serving alongside such aristocrats as jurist Benjamin Chew, Thomas Cadwalader, the Penn family's agent, and lawyer and later congressman J. R. Ingersoll. Having met the ensuing week with the mayor, the committee announced their plans, which were subsequently reported in *Hazard's Register* with Craige's name appended. Later in the year, Thomas Craige served on a Committee of Superintendence, which was created to solicit donations to relieve famine conditions in the Cape Verde Islands. Here he worked with a smaller group of fourteen men that included Nicholas Biddle and John Sergeant.[41] Few textile manufacturers in the first half of the century appear on the scores of similar lists of gentlemen taking action on behalf of the public. Perhaps his family's long-standing Old City merchant location provided an opportunity for contacts that were impossible for manufacturers tied to their dispersed waterside mills. The bulk of Philadelphia's textile capitalists, in both factories and workshops, occupied ground outside elite circles; their interests in the success of domestic manufacture were in frequent opposition to those of elite importers and commission traders. The Craiges represent one fraction of the city's textile capitalists, men of commercial standing, well capitalized and conversant with the Philadelphia gentlemen of the age.[42] When he became a full partner in the manufacturing enterprise in the later thirties, Thomas Craige dropped from civic view.

The Panic of 1837 did not collapse the firm, but the disruption of trade it caused may have sparked an attempt at the direct marketing of outwork cottons by the proprietors. One James Lucas began at that time to serve the Craiges: "From about 1838, he had been a 'trader' of cotton goods by means of wagons through Pennsylvania, New Jersey and Delaware; and by this primitive mode was distributed a considerable portion of the Globe Mill handloom piece-goods."[43] This episode reiterates the supportive function of hand production even for a mill as extensive as the Globe, though it cannot be established whether the piece goods came from old looms hauled up from a basement within the factory or from a variant of the yarn-sale putting-out system. In either case, Lucas's wagons peddled cloth made from yarn whose production kept the mill's spinning frames in operation, bringing a measure of profit to the counting room in an uncertain time. The success of this direct marketing effort may well have conditioned the decision to install two floors of power looms for cottons in the early forties. Two observations are in order. First, the Lowell corporations also strove to keep running at or near capacity in hard times, as operations on a partial scale could not hope to cover fixed costs, but to my knowledge such stratagems as Lucas's rural rides

---

[41] *Hazard's Register*, vol. 9 (1832), pp. 80, 102; vol. 10 (1832), p. 256.
[42] See the classic study, E. Digby Baltzell, *Philadelphia Gentlemen: The Making of a National Upper Class*, New York, 1958, chaps. 1 and 5.
[43] Needles, "Governor's Mill," p. 389.

never appeared. Instead, Lowell agents chose either to pile up inventory or to close the mills entirely.[44] Second, it was in this era, 1825–50, as Diane Lindstrom argues effectively, that Philadelphia manufactures squeezed out household production in the regional economy. Though this particular mechanism may have been "primitive," it was an element in the larger process by which the metropolitan core came to establish economic domination over the hinterland.[45] Creation of a regional market for piece goods was a direct stimulus to urban textile expansion before midcentury.

In 1840 Craige, Holmes and Co. expanded its facilities for the fourth time since beginning operations in 1809. Two new mills were erected, a five-story facility (54 by 100 feet) on Germantown Road and a smaller four-story building on St. John Street, along with accessory dyeing and boiler houses, all illuminated by city gas.[46] Some of the capital for this work was provided by the city, which acquired for $12,000 part of the Craiges' nearby land for street construction in 1839. It was into this five-story mill that power looms from two local machinery makers (Alfred Jenks and Thomas Wood) were introduced. They were driven by a third steam engine, bought secondhand from the Smythe distillery in crosstown Fairmount. This last burst of construction seems to have exceeded the firm's needs, for James Lucas resurfaced in 1849 to lease the four-story St. John's Street factory, where he operated, until the advent of the cotton famine, in a fashion now familiar: "obtaining cotton yarn from the Globe mills and elsewhere, and distributing it principally for dyeing and for weaving on outside hand-looms. He also rented for a few years some of the power-looms in the main building."[47] The solutions to excess capacity at the Globe included farming out not only yarn and space but also machinery, a third example of interfirm productive relations characteristic of the special texture of the Philadelphia textile manufacture.

John Holmes died about 1850 and the firm dissolved formally the following year. Absent from the 1850 Manufacturing Census, an unlikely oversight, the mill most likely had suspended operations at the time of the survey. Thomas Craige was at that date spinning yarn at the Star Mills in Kensington, a few blocks north at Howard and Jefferson streets. His substantial enterprise (twelve male and eighty-eight female workers, capital of $75,000) shared the mill with Samuel Needles, who employed eighty-five workers to weave cotton and woolen fabrics.[48]

[44] Paul McGouldrick, *New England Textiles in the Nineteenth Century: Profits and Investments*, Cambridge, Mass., pp. 29–30.

[45] Diane Lindstrom, *Economic Development in the Philadelphia Region, 1810–1850*, New York, 1978, esp. pp. 15–21.

[46] Needles, "Governor's Mill," pp. 387–8.

[47] Ibid., pp. 388–9.

[48] 1850 MCS, Philadelphia Co., p. 67.

Both Seth Craige and Mrs. Holmes emerged from the dissolution with competencies. Craige became a rentier after all the legal agreements were complete, retiring from manufacture to enjoy the income from the Globe leases. Mrs. Holmes's quarter share in the proceeds surely kept her well fed and sheltered in later years.[49] Thomas H. Craige, then a robust 50 years of age, pursued his manufacturing career, as would Sevill Schofield in a similar family situation during the Civil War. The 1852 movements have a delightful balance. A public sale emptied the mill of its cotton machinery, some of the spinning frames perhaps being acquired by Thomas Craige. Into the vacant premises moved Samuel Needles, Thomas's colleague at the Star Mills, now leasing the Globe from his brother. With the capital (and possibly some machinery) from the partition, Thomas Craige evidently occupied the space from which Needles had removed at the Star. By 1860 his spinning operations at the Star Mill employed a work force twice the 1850 total (66 men, 139 women) and listed capital of $150,000.[50] There was thus a spatial dimension to the dissolution, allowing the two manufacturers to expand their facilities in a way that dovetailed with their family relationships and business contacts.

The firm was closed, to the evident profit of all concerned, not as a result of bankruptcy or other calamity. To be sure, the hundreds of workers whose positions evaporated with the suspension of production and the dispersal of the cotton machinery are nowhere mentioned in all the details of the paperwork transactions. The mill stood idle for two years before Needles transferred his activities there. The reformulation of a partnership or relocation of production in the same district might have but little impact on workers. However, a dissolution, particularly one attended by the ragged array of agreements and sales as occurred here,[51] struck them directly. As they were not "interested" in the firm and the machinations of property, partnership, and inheritance law, they were presumably turned out to seek other employment.

With the commencement of woolen production by Needles in 1852, the Globe Mill began to host another generation of textile manufacturing.

---

49 Ibid., p. 389.
50 1860 MCS, Philadelphia Co., p. 411. In 1858 the only other tenant listed at the Star Mills was James Long, a manufacturer of ginghams, checks, diaper, and some woolens, who may have used T. H. Craige's yarns, which were spun in the same building. Long is given by Freedley as a handloom outwork manufacturer, likely having looms in the Star Mill and additional outworkers, as the Craiges did at the Globe a generation earlier. By 1860, Long had entered a partnership with his brothers (capital $60,000) and had set up shop at 1541 N. Second Street where he continued to produce cottons and woolens (see Freedley, *Philadelphia and Its Manufacturers*, p. 253, and 1860 MCS, Philadelphia Co., p. 414).
51 Needles, "Governor's Mill," p. 389.

Though he added two stories to the dyehouse and made other alterations, Samuel Needles remained at the Globe only three years. After his withdrawal in 1855, the mill was recycled, with "rooms in the various buildings . . . rented with power to textile manufacturers, at times exceeding ten in number."[52] Six of these smaller firms can be identified at the Globe complex in 1858: "David Austin, Pantaloon stuffs; Richard Holt, Cotton yarns; James Lucas, Checks, pantaloon stuffs, etc; Thornton and Smith; Apron checks; William Watt, Checks; John Wright, Checks, ginghams, and pantaloon stuffs."[53] Their product overlaps and likely connection to Holt's yarn-spinning operation show that the mill had fully returned to cotton manufacturing and suggest that yet another productive network had jelled temporarily at the Globe Mill. After the death of Seth Craige, Jr., in 1859, his estate sold the mills in two parcels, one to a tenant, the rest to a commercial real-estate entrepreneur who rented "the buildings with power" into the 1880s.[54]

Spanning eight decades, the "lineage" of the Globe Mill displays productive relations rich in their implications for appreciating the structure and dynamics of textile accumulation in Philadelphia. The Craiges were not "typical" of local textile manufacturers in their large starting capital and elite contacts. Still, the sense of movement, flexibility, and scrambling after the main chance that emerges from examination of these three cases is a core element in the accumulation process that distinguishes Philadelphia textile firms from the corporate form.

The British analogy

Those familiar with the development of British textiles, the Lancashire cotton and Yorkshire woolen industries, may have already sensed a structural parallel with the pattern suggested by the three Philadelphia mills just examined. Firm organization was predominantly family partnerships in both British regions, modified into private companies to some degree after mid-century to take advantage of limited liability. Outside partners were brought in frequently once the firm had built a solid trade, as a means of acquiring capital for expansion or for securing particular managerial talents. Such men were selected through community, religious, or trade links, if they were not "blood-relations, in-laws or trusted workmen."[55] The emergence of the

---

52 Ibid., p. 390.
53 Freedley, *Philadelphia and Its Manufactures*, pp. 256–62.
54 Bagnall, *Textile Industries*, vol. I, pp. 587–8.
55 P. L. Cottrell, *Industrial Finance, 1830–1914: The Finance and Organization of English Manufacturing Industry*, London, 1980, pp. 20, 252.

famous Oldham Limiteds in cotton spinning came late in the century (after 1870) and has also been given rather too much emphasis:

> The Oldham mill companies, even taken together with the other private and public converted companies [other incorporations], still in 1886 did not dominate overwhelmingly the cotton industry, only coarse spinning. Fine spinning was still mainly in the hands of private firms, while joint-stock companies were only just appearing as a permanent feature of the weaving branch of the industry in the mid-1880s.[56]

Spatial relations of production also bear comparison to those in Philadelphia. Most British firms started small, commensurate with the more restricted capitals generally available to partnerships. Some mills were built by merchants and landowners and either leased or sold on mortgage to new entrepreneurs. The practice of renting "rooms with power"[57] was quite common, and "as the industry grew, machinery could be rented along with 'room and power.' "[58] Mill expansion by successful firms was "piecemeal, . . . in what were increasingly congested urban areas. . . Consequently, plant layout was seldom if ever rationalized and, instead, new capacity and new technology had to be added in a haphazard manner, which reduced its effectiveness."[59] Furthermore, operating factories "were often sublet – a lucrative way of temporarily reducing the capacity of an existing enterprise."[60]

The high-skill level of a significant portion of British silk, woolen, and worsted workers, along with the long shadow cast by the mule spinners, translates to Philadelphia with ease. British skilled workers migrated to the Quaker City in waves, as virtually every nineteenth-century observer noted. Freedley, writing in 1857 of carpets, hosiery, and fabric printers, stressed the immigrant dominance of the work force in these specialty areas, noting of the factory work force that "the majority of the operatives . . . are English or Anglo-Americans."[61] A quarter century later Lorin Blodget reinforced the point: "The carpet industry in Philadelphia was originally derived directly from the English manufacturing districts, and it has been constantly recruited by a large immigration of English carpet weavers . . . The carpet manufacture has been transplanted in the same manner as the hosiery manufacture and like industries."[62]

The relations and potentials of outwork bore some similarity to the British experience as well. English factory masters knew well that "overall weaving capacity could be regulated by the amount of yarn either put-out or sold to

---

56 Ibid., p. 112.
57 Ibid., p. 251.
58 Ibid., p. 21.
59 Ibid., p. 264.
60 Ibid., p. 21.
61 Freedley, *Philadelphia and Its Manufactures*, pp. 240, 242, 249, 252.
62 Lorin Blodget, *The Textile Industries of Philadelphia*, Philadelphia, 1880, p. ix.

'domestic' weavers."[63] Movement from domestic workshop to factory proprietorship was a common occurrence. "The woolen clothier, certainly in
the Leeds area, by 1800 was essentially a weaver . . . Most clothiers owned
jennies but yarn could be and was obtained either through putting-out or
from a merchant . . . Some domestic clothiers became factory masters by
renting mills built by landowners and merchants."[64]

Philadelphia may well have drawn a substantial share of British textile
migrants, carrying with them both their skills and cultural traditions and
installing elements of the British productive relations in the new city. Writing
of the 1820s, Sullivan noted the English analogy: "Cloth-making in Philadelphia was patterned after the English system. The spinner, the dyer, the
weaver, the printer and finisher were for the most part independent manufacturers, serving the cloth merchants."[65] With this judgment in mind, we
shall move outward from case studies to the industry as a whole in this
period, as reflected in the manufacturing census returns for 1820, the first
substantial survey of the Philadelphia textile trades for which primary
sources have been preserved.

Philadelphia textiles in 1820

The population census of 1820 showed the city and suburbs of Philadelphia
inhabited by 120,000 persons with 17,000 others living in the outlying
county districts.[66] The parallel manufacturing census documented the existence of several hundred productive establishments in the county, thirty-
nine of which worked on textiles and employed more than 1,100 workers.[67]
The census form asked for information under five headings: Raw Materials,
Number of Persons Employed, Machinery, Expenditures, and Production.
Within each category specific queries called for the kinds, quantitites, and
costs of materials, the composition of the work force (men, women, boys,
and girls), the machinery in place and that in operation, the capital invested,
the annual wage bill, "contingent expenses," and a description of products
with their values. The request for information relating to machinery in
operation as well as that in place suggests the depression environment in
which the census took place. A sense of the unsettled times also infects the
final question, an open-ended request for "General Remarks concerning

---

63 Cottrell, *Industrial Finance*, p. 24.
64 Ibid., p. 27.
65 Sullivan, *Industrial Worker*, p. 20.
66 *Hazard's Register*, vol. 8 (1831), p. 65.
67 That the manufacturing returns were incomplete has been generally asserted, and several textile mills known to have been present at that time in the city are indeed absent from
the manuscript schedules.

the Establishment, as to its actual and past condition, the demand for, and sale of, its Manufactures." Full responses to this opportunity for extended comment allow elements of historical process to emerge from notoriously static census data. Their qualitative and subjective character enriches the numerical categories, though caveats must be announced. Not all firms known to have been active in 1820 are included, and no more complete independent list exists. Not every firm surveyed responded to the "General Remarks" section, and of the thirty-four that did, comments range from a single phrase to elaborate discourses on the nature of the trade. Used sensitively, with an awareness of the softness of the statistical data and the subjectivity of the comments, they nonetheless afford a partial glance at the state of the Philadelphia textile manufacture amid depression conditions.

Of the firms recorded, seventeen, or fewer than half, were located in the thickly settled areas of Old City and the near suburbs, Kensington, Northern Liberties, and Moyamensing (Table 4.2). Of that group, sixteen manufactured cottons, Henry Korn's fringe and trimming workshop being the only exception. The other twenty-two manufacturers were rather broadly cast in the outlying townships, the mills with waterpower of course confined to sites with an adequate water-fall. Only five of these scattered firms made cotton goods, with yarn and woolens occupying six and eight manufacturers, respectively. (Five of the six spinners did produce cotton yarn, however.) There were no separate spinning mills or wool manufactories in the older central areas.

Of the thirty-seven firms listed by name on the schedules, thirty appear to be sole proprietorships and seven partnerships. The partnerships employed about 300 of the 1,135 workers reported, not a disproportionately large segment. Moreover, they were spread about evenly over the various textile sectors (three cotton, two wool, one printing, and one linen). The only large factory operation in the area was the Globe Mill, a partnership. At the same time, Crawford and Patterson's handloom cotton workshop was one of the smallest in the survey. Clearly, whereas partnerships could be formed to amass large capitals for mill construction on the Globe scale, they also might represent the joining of quite small sums to commence craftwork production. The two Lewis mills express the family connection directly, and it is possible that the spinning Bairds were kin as well. Henry Whitaker's family successors, who are documented elsewhere,[68] maintained the firm's identity until its dissolution in the 1960s.[69]

<hr>

[68] *Biographical Encyclopedia of Pennsylvania*, Philadelphia, 1874, p. 226; cited hereafter as *BEP*.

[69] Housed in the Hagley Library, Greenville, Del., the Whitaker Papers are the only accessible large collection of records of any Philadelphia textile firm. They have barely been scanned by researchers to this point, their sheer volume necessitating eight single-spaced pages for the brief inventory prepared by the library staff.

Table 4.2. *Textile manufacturers, sector, products, and work force by district, Philadelphia, 1820*

Manufacturer	Sector	Products	Work force			
			Men	Women	Children	Total
Blockley Township						
F. Belmore	Hosiery, knit goods	Stockings	6	5	0	11
Samuel Haydock	Cotton	Sheetings, tape, web, yarn	8	30	22	60
James Kershaw	Wool	Mixed kerseys	13	4	22	39
William Taylor, Jr.	Wool	Satinets	16–20	6	8–10	30–36
J. B. Thomas	Spinning	Wool yarn	2	2	4	8
Bristol Township						
Will G. Hirst	Wool	Broadcloths, cassimeres, shawls, etc.	18	7	10	35
George McCallmont	Mixed goods	Wool: broadcloths, cassimeres, kerseys, satinets; cotton: "a Variety"[a]	25	6	60	91
Thorp & Siddall	Dyeing, finishing	Calico prints	6	0	0	6
Not given	Spinning	Cotton yarn	1	2	8	11
Germantown						
St. Lawrence Adams	Spinning	Cotton yarn	5	3	10	18
Robert H. Baird	Spinning	Cotton yarn	1	5	6	12
Fisher, Gouge & Potts	Wool	Broadcloths, cassimeres, satinets	28	18	20	66
Philip Kelly	Wool	Broadcloths, kerseys, satinets	20	8	3	31
B. Patterson	Wool	White flannel	10	1	5	16

Table 4.2. (*Continued*)

Manufacturer	Sector	Products	Work force			
			Men	Women	Children	Total
Kensington						
Globe Mill (Craige et al.)	Cotton	Checks, ginghams, sheetings, web, yarn	70	35	95	200
Lower Dublin Township						
David Lewis	Cotton	Checks, duck, ginghams, jeans, sheetings, yarn, etc.	7–40	10–30	30–80	47–150
David Lewis' Sons	Cotton	Checks, plaids, sheetings, and "all kinds of plain and twilled goods"	5	6	70	81
Rodman and Morgan	Wool	Broadcloths, cassimeres, satinets	12	6	4	22
Manayunk Canal						
Isaac Baird	Spinning	Cotton yarn	2	3	12	17
Moyamensing						
Crawford and Patterson	Cotton	Checks, ginghams, sheetings, tickings	6	0	0	6
Edward Irwin	Cotton	Checks, plaids, tickings	6	4	0	10
Andrew Kilpatrick	Cotton	Checks, plaids, tickings	4	0	0	4
James Maxwell	Cotton	Checks, ginghams, plaids, sheetings, tickings	19	14	2	35

Alexander Moffet	Cotton	Plaids, sheetings, tickings	11	0	4	7
John Murphy	Cotton	Checks, plaids, tickings	6	0	0	6
James Stranaghan	Cotton	Checks, plaids, sheetings	1	0	0	1
Northern Liberties						
Andrew Morrison	Cotton	Checks, drillings, plaids	29	5	11	13
Joseph Ripka	Cotton	Checks, drillings, plaids, tickings	13	3	3	7
Old City						
James Crosbey	Cotton	Checks, tickings	22	1	9	12
Abraham Cummings	Cotton	Ginghams, sheetings, tickings	16	0	4	12
James Grimes	Cotton	Checks, tickings	22	3	9	10
John Hinshellwood	Cotton	Checks, sheetings, tickings	11	2	2	7
Henry Korn	Mixed goods	Trim, fringes	6	3	2	1
Robert Wilson	Cotton	Checks, tickings	22	0	10	12
Not given	Cotton	Plaids, sheetings, tickings	18	0	7	11
Oxford Township						
Gillingham & Chapman	Linen	Bagging, duck, twine	19	14	0	5
Stephen Sicard	Spinning	Cotton yarn	26	15	6	5
Henry Whitaker	Cotton	Sheetings, yarn	21	17	0	4
Penn Township						
Thomas Ford	Cotton	Checks, plaids	36	0	10	26
Total			1,135–1,244	454–506	252–272	429–466

aCotton mill not in operation.

Source: Manuscript Manufacturing Census Schedules, Eastern District, Pa., Philadelphia County, 1820.

Table 4.3. *Textile firms by sector, capital, and work force, Philadelphia, 1820*

Sector	N	Capital (000)	Work force			
			Men	Women	Children	Total
Wool	8	$178	142 (44)	56 (17)	132 (39)	330 (29)
Spinning	6	44	16 (17)	21 (23)	55 (60)	92 (8)
Cotton	21	335	253 (38)	168 (25)	250 (37)	671 (59)
Other	4	27	18 (43)	7 (17)	17 (40)	42 (4)
Total	39	584	429 (38)	252 (22)	454 (40)	1,135 (100)

Note: Figures in parentheses indicate percentage.
Source: Manuscript Manufacturing Census Schedules, Eastern District, Pa., Philadelphia Couny, 1820.

It is with the work-force figures that the productive relations of 1820 begin to appear. Consolidating the data for wool, spinning, and cotton-goods firms yields Table 4.3.

Three of every five textile workers reported to the census worked on cottons, and women and children comprised more than half the work force in every sector. There was no definition of "Boys and Girls" on the 1820 schedule. However, later manufacturing censuses set the cutoff at 15 or 16 years, and it was quite common for children of 7 or 8 to start on piecing for spinners. Though the Lowell mills ultimately engaged thousands of young women to spin and weave, they were not notorious abusers of child labor, whereas the Philadelphia manufacturers were so charged time and again in the twenties and thirties.[70]

If the cotton firms are sorted into two groups, sixteen in the city and near suburbs and five "out in the country," the central group comes to resemble the wool sector, with adult males comprising about half the work force (Table 4.4). The outlying mills, four of which were powered by water, employed considerable numbers of children. Yet location alone does not reveal the essential linkage between power and child labor. To sort the twenty-one firms again by whether or not they used powered equipment only requires moving one firm from each locational category to the other group (Table 4.5). The Globe Mill in Kensington used both water- and steam-power by 1820, whereas the warping mill and several dye vats at Thomas Ford's Penn Township Mill were hand-tended. Of the child workers count-

[70] Sullivan, *Industrial Worker,* chap. 2.

Table 4.4. *Cotton work force by district, Philadelphia, 1820*

| | Work force | | | |
District	Men	Women	Children	Total
Old City, Kensington, Northern Liberties, Moyamensing	203 (48)	111 (26)	112 (26)	426
County districts	50 (20)	56 (23)	139 (59)	245
Total	253	167	251	671

Note: Figures in parentheses indicate percentage.
Source: Manuscript Manufacturing Census Schedules, Eastern District, Pa., Philadelphia County, 1820.

Table 4.5. *Cotton firms by power source, capital, and work force, Philadelphia, 1820*

| Power source | N | Capital (000) | Work force | | | |
			Men	Women	Children	Total
Hand	16	$ 25	159 (61)	87 (33)	16 (6)	262
Water & steam	5	310	94 (23)	81 (20)	234 (57)	409
Total	21	335	253	168	250	671

Note: Figures in parentheses indicate percentage.
Source: Manuscript Manufacturing Census Schedules, Eastern District, Pa., Philadelphia County, 1820.

ed in 1820, more than half toiled in only five of the thirty-nine reported manufactories in Philadelphia. They were most likely spinners, as the percentages approach those for the separate spinning mills given in Table 4.3. On the other hand, the small size and heavy concentration of men in hand-powered weaving firms strongly suggests that they represented a form of the craft workshop. Some evidence supporting this suggestion may come from an 1827 report on handloom workshops published in *Hazard's Register* by the Society of Weavers. More than fifty craftshop masters were society members, and three of the thirteen signatories to the report were Thomas Ford of Penn Township and Abraham Cummings and Robert Wilson of Old City, who were involved in handloom production in the 1820 enumeration.[71] The capital invested in the handweaving shops ranged from $250 to $4,000, with most clustered between $500 and $1,500.

The five powered cotton mills represented more substantial investments. Samuel Haydock pointed out that "the mill seats, machinery and improvements cost $40,000 being calculated for a greater quantity of machinery than is now on the premises."[72] Haydock, who had operated since 1814 at his West Philadelphia site, had 1,000 spindles in place and sixteen looms, three of which were elaborate contraptions with 10, 12, and 21 shuttles respectively. The mills were temporarily shuttered because of "the great advance [in the price] of the raw material and the depression of prices [of finished products] occasioned by the influx of unusual quantities of foreign goods." When running, the mill turned out "cotton yarn, colored, bleached, and unbleached and thread. Shirtings and sheetings, Suspenders and Boot Webbs, Girth Webbs, Tapes and Furniture Bindings, Cotton Fringes",[73] reflecting the variety of output characteristic of Philadelphia firms.

David Lewis reported $65,000 as his capital figure and his sons reported $70,000 for their establishment. The Globe Mill's $130,000 was the largest sum reported for textile manufacturing investment in the city. Henry Whitaker's factory, the last of the five powered cotton mills, was the smallest of the group with but twenty-one workers and a total investment of $13,550. Of special interest are his machinery and output details. The mill sold both "Twist" (yarn) and "Shirtings, etc.," but reported no looms; only spinning facilities and two warping mills were recorded,[74] indicating a duplication of the Globe Mill arrangement, in which mill-made yarn and warps were put out to household artisans. None of the separate spinning mills in the county reported cloths among their products, but both Isaac Baird and J. B. Thomas noted that their yarns were made for "domestic weavers," presumably a direct-sale transaction with independent outworkers.[75]

The six water-fed spinning mills in Philadelphia were all quite modest ventures, as they each averaged but fifteen workers, three-fifths of whom were children. Four of the six evidently leased their millsites, for their capitals were too small to represent ownership. The much larger sums reported by J. B. Thomas and Stephen Sicard, together with equipment comparable to the smaller spinners, suggest property ownership (Table 4.6). Thomas and Isaac Baird further echo the Globe complex in their mention of looms on the premises (four in each case) but not in operation at the time of

71 *Hazard's Register*, vol. 1 (1828), p. 28.
72 1820 MCS, Eastern District, Pa., no. 665.
73 Ibid.
74 Ibid., no. 604.
75 *Hazard's Register*, vol. 1 (1828), p. 28.

Table 4.6. *Spinning mills, capital, work force, and machinery, Philadelphia, 1820*

Spinning mills	Capital	Work force	Machinery
Stephen Sicard	$20,000	26	816 spindles
J. B. Thomas	12,560	8	picker, 3 cards, fulling mill, 4 "Gennies," 2 billies, doubler, 4 looms
Isaac Baird	5,000	17	picker, 4 cards, 360 spindles, stretcher (72 spindles), 2 reels, 4 looms
St. Lawrence Adams	2,000	18	792 spindles
Robert Baird	1,500	12	310 spindles
Not given (Bristol Township)	2,500	11	320 spindles and preparations

Source: Manuscript Manufacturing Census Schedules, Eastern District, Pa., Philadelphia County, 1820.

the census. Flexible production strategy was not an exclusive property of the Craiges' firm.

The woolen manufacture, so far as it is visible in the returns, was principally carried on in powered mills, and the investment involved was generally greater than that of spinning or handloom cotton production (Table 4.7). The eight woolen mills were integrated, but handlooms were surely also broadly employed in tandem with water-driven preparatory and spinning apparatus. The double task of spinning and weaving commanded a larger work force, comparable to the cotton mills, and their dependence on waterpower placed them outside the central district and its suburbs. Three of the seven firms for which there is information on both capital and equipment may have owned mills, whereas the rest, like most of the spinners, presumably rented space and waterpower rights.

Yet for all their apparent numerical solidity, work-force counts and machine inventories present a portrait that is not only incomplete but unsatisfyingly flat and static. There were certainly two sorts of manufacturers in Philadelphia, as is evident from the preceding data. A sizable group occupied mill sites and carried on factory production. The other, concentrated near the urban center and employing about one-quarter of the recorded textile workers, produced their goods on handlooms. To see them both in motion, confronting the obstacles to accumulation and survival amid depression conditions, it is necessary to probe the remarks and comments that accompanied the tallies of hands and machinery.

Table 4.7. *Woolen firms, capital, work force, and machinery, Philadelphia, 1820*

Woolen firms	Capital	Work force	Machinery
Philip Kelly	$35,000	31	8 cards, 5 spinning jennies, 6 billies, 20 looms, 10 broadlooms
B. Patterson	5,000	16	"woolen machines"
Fisher, Gouge & Potts	—	66	11 cards, 8 jennies, 3 billies, 3 pickers, 22 looms, 3 fulling stocks, 5 shearing frames, 1 "Brewster patent water jenny"
Rodman and Morgan	9,000	22	3 cards, "spinning apparatus," 14 handlooms
William Taylor, Jr.	40,000	30–36	7 cards, 2 jennies, 2 billies, 17 looms
James Kershaw	9,000	39	5 cards, 4 billies, 6 looms, 2 stocks, 2 shearing machines, 2 dyeing kettles
Will G. Hirst	8,000	35	4 cards, 3 jennies, 1 billy, 1 picker, 24 looms, 2 fulling stocks, 21 pair shears, dyeing and finishing machinery
George McCallmont[a]	80,000	91	16 cards, 3 jennies, 9 billies, 2 pickers, 28 looms

[a]McCallmont had both a cotton and a woolen mill but had suspended spinning cotton on the 1,250 spindles in place. When in operation, the cotton mill employed about fifty workers, "principal part Women and Children" (Manuscript Manufacturing Census Schedules, Eastern District, Pa., Philadelphia County, no. 605, 1820).
Note: Dash indicates not available.
Source: Manuscript Manufacturing Census Schedules, Philadelphia County, 1820.

The factory situation in 1820

The 1820 Manufacturing Census was assembled during a depression year, and the impact of that economic instability reverberates throughout the manuscript schedules. Whereas some millmen precisely documented their hard times, others reported running full speed. The wail of the workshop masters was, by contrast, almost uniform, their plight stemming from the deluge of imported British cottons. Large mills, like the Globe, combined factory weaving with outworker yarn sales to more fully employ their machinery. David Lewis's return illustrated a slightly different strategy. While noting that "one-half to two thirds" of the firm's machinery was operating, he continued:

> The demand has so diminished that the prices have been reduced from 25 to 45 per cent in consequence of which a heavy loss has ensued, [while] the price of raw materials has advanced 20 per cent. These circumstances prevent any chance of profit but it is requisite to keep the machinery from damage by using it; even [if] the cost of the raw material and the labour can only be reimbursed.[76]

The elder Lewis evidently rotated work among the frames and other equipment to keep the whole plant in readiness for recovery. His sons were already benefiting from the gradual revival of trade by the time of their census return, dated January 31, 1821. With 1,400 spindles, 14 power looms, and 30 handlooms all running, they observed: "The present state of the manufactory is very good, the demand for the goods is [active?], and at the present time likely to continue."[77] As seventy of their eighty-one workers were "boys and girls," the wages at Lewis' Sons were low enough to facilitate profits at prices that would incur a loss for other manufacturers.

Among the spinners, both Bairds reported yarn demand as steady, but Robert added that the trade was "not so profitable as 3 or 4 years past."[78] Stephen Sicard was blunt: "Nothing done for five years past."[79] The wool men were equally divided, but their replies consistently focused on the glut of British goods and the then-current practice of their sale at dockside auctions to jobbers and wholesalers, thus choking off the market for domestic products.

> George McCallmont: Since [1816] the heavy importations from Europe, and the great sacrifices made at auctions have occasioned considerable distress among the Manufacturers.

> Fisher, Gouge & Potts: In consequence of the excessive importation of British Goods and their sacrifice at auction, it has been necessary to reduce the number of hands by one half and the sale of manufactured goods is at present so uncertain as almost to jeopardize the establishment.

> B. Patterson: This establishment during the late war done well[,] since that has been carried on with much difficulty and not proffitable.[80]

The positive comments are guarded, rather than enthusiastic.

76 1820 MCS, Eastern District, Pa., no. 653.
77 Ibid., no. 654.
78 Ibid., no. 634.
79 Ibid., no. 603.
80 Ibid., nos. 605, 646, 636.

Rodman and Morgan: The Fall of 1820 produced a fair price to the Manufacturers.

Philip Kelly: Sales at present are heavey and present prices do not leave the manufacturer a reasonable profit.

William Taylor: [Products] in good general demand now at a trifling profit, being much injured by sales; checked by the influx of British goods of similar texture.[81]

Although capitalists generally grumble about how impossible it is to make money, thus calling for skepticism in reading their complaints, it must be understood that the auction threat was considerable and long-lasting. Not only were shiploads of cheaper British goods dumped on the American market in 1820, the practice continued for at least a decade. In 1828 a body of Philadelphia merchants and manufacturers finally called on the "General Government" to act to curtail "the existing system of sales by auctions [which] is a great and increasing evil, and highly injurious to the interests of every class of citizens of the United States."[82] Appointed to the committee to pursue this end were two textile manufacturers and the merchant brother of a third. In 1820, however, though comments by Rodman and Morgan and McCallmont suggest that the millmen were aware of one another's situations, there were no calls for action in the census remarks. This silence contrasts dramatically with the pleas for assistance that workshop masters penned on their forms, indicating either that the mill operators had other channels through which to direct their opinions and were thus indifferent to state action or that they had imbibed some version of the classic economics of free trade.

Information of value on material factors of accumulation, in addition to production and marketing strategies, may be gleaned from the remarks of the mill operators. Whereas only a handful of well-capitalized firms were likely to have owned mills and the bulk of the group rented, the census return of Isaac Baird's spinning mill adds another dimension to the rental pattern. Noting the recent launching of his mill, he stated: "The Factory has been only eight months in operation and is rented out in apartments."[83] Here is an early instance of the subdivided mill tenancy noted with the Schofields, "apartments" being floors of the mill let to separate firms. It was rare for a converted grist- or sawmill to be segmented, but buildings erected specifically for textile manufacturing in Philadelphia regularly housed a number of tenants (sometimes including the owner) who shared a common power supply. Baird installed his machinery on the third floor of the Yellow

81 Ibid., nos. 652, 635, 666.
82 *Hazard's Register*, vol. 2 (1828), p. 30.
83 1820 MCS, Eastern District, Pa., no. 623.

Mill at Manayunk, owned by Captain John Towers, who shortly thereafter undertook woolen manufacture on the two lower stories. Baird's success was evident in short order, as he soon occupied two of the houses Tower built near the mill, turning one of them into the mill village's first store.[84]

Turning to the formal organization of the business, J. B. Thomas offers a cheerless example of why Philadelphia manufacturers kept the supervision of their firms within the family or group of "interested" parties. Despite a fair capital, disaster struck Thomas's woolen mill, detailed in these ill-tempered lines:

> It [the mill] was intended for woolen yarn and the weaving of flannels and blankets, But on account of the high wages and the *bad* conduct of the persons to which the proprietor (persuaded from pure patriotic views in contributing his share in promoting domestic manufacture) *entrusted* the management of the mill, the proposed object has not been obtained. The flannels and blankets woven at this mill during the three first years occasioned a heavy loss of about 50 per cent on the capital invested in the purchase of 5000 [lbs.] of wool.

Having abandoned cloth production and thrown out the faithless operators, Thomas was reduced to operating the mill for "the spinning of woolen yarn for the stockings and other weavers and the carding and spinning for the country at large." Because of the severe losses, he could no longer afford to buy the raw materials processed at the factory and operated instead largely on contract. "The production of this mill cannot be correctly stated, owing as it has been stated, that its work is limited to the spinning and carding of wool the greatest proportion of which is sent by customers." Replying to the capital question, Thomas barely contains himself: "Capital, $12,560, including in it the amount of raw materials $3325 of which not one-third has been recovered by the sales of manufactures."[85] Keeping precise accounts allowed Thomas to know the exact extent of his miseries, but as an absentee owner, he lost touch with everyday decisions and awoke one morning to find his "prospects . . . fled," as a Moyamensing shopman aptly put it. Here indeed was justification for the long-held belief that close management by interested parties was the only way to run a mill, a belief that opened, from time to time, partnerships to the most able foremen or skilled workers in Philadelphia firms.

Not only was the output of the millmen spread over a wide range of products (consider the Globe, Haydock, and McCallmont); there was as well considerable sophistication in that production. Patterson's Germantown

---

84 Mildred Goshow, "Mills and Mill Owners of Manayunk in the 19th Century," type-script, 1970, p. 16, Roxborough Branch, Free Library of Philadelphia.

85 1820 MCS, Eastern District, Pa., no. 669.

woolen mill specialized in the production of white flannel, and Will Hirst attempted to make even finer goods.

> I have manufactured a large quantity of shawls of the finest wool with silk warp but at present there is scarcely any article that will pay the expense of the raw material and manufacturing. I should do more than double the business if it would leave a living profit.[86]

Hirst was making Scots Paisley shawls in exactly the fashion then current abroad.[87] Although such production was no mean achievement in 1820 Philadelphia, the sale of "finer goods" was inhibited well into the 1870s by the reputation of the best grades of imported goods. For years to come, the cheaper satinets, rough broadcloths, and cassimeres that Hirst and his fellow wool men produced would be the goods that the market would accept.

James Kershaw represented a different trajectory in textile development at Philadelphia. He operated outside the risks of the market by fulfilling government contracts for "Mixed Kerseys." "Has I have been always employed in making goods for the army alone with an exception of the present year, I do not consider myself competant to say any thing about the general market."[88] Here again the state is a material factor in the accumulation matrix. Were but one firm possessed of such relations, a footnote would be adequate. But the role of government contracts is a persistent feature of the woolen trade in the city. John Towers, proprietor of the first Manayunk factory, had been a naval captain in the War of 1812 and his mill, then in Germantown, "furnished the government with large quantities of Kerseys and woolen goods of various descriptions" during that decade.[89] Samuel Winpenny, as early as 1808, was active in "produc[ing] the first blankets and cloths ever manufactured for the United States Government in this country" at the Kelly mill in Germantown. In the teens, he set up his own works at the Falls of Schuylkill and was "eminently successful with government contracts."[90] His son continued this relationship, managing "the production of kerseys, blankets and blue cloths for the government" in the 1830s and 1840s. Even the Globe Mill got into the act, as their calico printer, Francis Labbe, toiled on government work during the 1812–15 conflict. "Large quantities of heavy woolen felted goods were purchased and printed in imitation of leopard skin, for army use. This printing business was very

---

[86] Ibid., no. 645.
[87] Bagnall, "The Textile Industries of the United States," vol. II, typescript on microfiche, 1970, p. 2654, Merrimack Valley Textile Museum, North Andover, Mass.; transcribed from the handwritten manuscript of Bagnall's draft text; pagination is that of the original manuscript; cited hereafter as "Textile Industries" (fiche).
[88] 1820 MCS, Eastern District, Pa., no. 668.
[89] *BEP*, p. 567.
[90] *M&MP*, p. 463.

profitable for several years, but excessive importations almost ruined it soon after peace was declared."[91] Sevill Schofield's windfalls from the Civil War extended this pattern, but he was only one of many Philadelphia textile manufacturers in that era to reap a bounty from war demands. Guaranteed markets and occasional war profits must have afforded such manufacturers both great satisfaction and the capital to finance additional construction. Such was the case for all those mentioned here.

Technical flexibility, experimentation, and sophistication are evident in a number of mills by 1820. The Globe had introduced steampower a few years earlier, alongside its waterwheels, and Samuel Haydock pointed out that his looms were "all calculated to work by water or by hand."[92] A number of small mills had begun to try power-weaving machines, but they sat idle at the time of the census. The partnership calico printworks of Ishichar Thorp and Joseph Siddal, English immigrants, operated a state-of-the-art plant linked to a suburban cotton factory that was evidently owned by one of Siddal's kinsmen. When they began production in 1810, Thorp and Siddal installed "the first cylinder printing machine ever operated in this country."[93] This represented a significant advance over the hand-block methods used by Hewson and others in the early calico trade, allowing an enormous volume of production that necessitated the employment of only a few skilled men (six in 1820). Their remarks shine with machine boosterism:

> In the year 1812 we printed by Machinery about fifty thousand pieces Calico (viz. one million four hundred thousand yards, which is equal to most of the printing establishments in the neighborhood of Manchester, England) and we do not hesitate to say that with our present machinery double the Amt of yards could be done, and what adds to the Beauty of [the] establishment, they could be Bleached ready on the Premises which is not the case of most of the works in England as there they are generally considered different Branches of Business and are carried on seperately. This concern is connected with those on the Brandywine carried on under the firm of John Siddal and Co., spinners, who have 3,000 spindles in operations and the weaving factory by waterpower, who are manufacturing calicos for printing in this place so that take them all together they have a very large amount of capital invested in the different branches of Spinning, Manufacturing and Calico Printing, *all done by Machinery*.[94]

Here are the mill professionals, whose pride of place and progress exudes from each sentence. The value of their products was kept private, "various"

---

91 Needles, "Governor's Mill," p. 383.
92 1820 MCS, Eastern District, Pa., no. 665.
93 Bagnall, "Textile Industries" (fiche), p. 1782.
94 1820 MCS, Eastern District, Pa., no. 644. Emphasis in original.

being the only comment, and contingent expenses were dismissed as "trifling." By contrast, the chemicals, dyes, and machinery were detailed extensively. The firm carried on past midcentury, Thorp reporting thirty employees and the modest capital of $10,000 in the 1850 Manufacturing Census.[95]

In the late twenties, the firm employed a Belfast immigrant, Thomas Hunter, who later founded a printworks that became one of the city's largest operations.[96] This sequence of advancement, a skilled immigrant worker starting with an established textile firm in Philadelphia and some years later commencing on his own account, is a regular feature of the biographies of successful city textile men. Doubtless many unrecorded ventures along the same path failed to prosper, and others became modest enterprises that did not draw the attention of the publishing entrepreneurs who assembled catalogues of prominent men in later decades. Nevertheless, the material framework of space for rent, agglomerations of skilled labor, a secondhand machinery market, and the cultural ties among immigrants that might blossom into partnership or a strategic marriage facilitated the continuing emergence of worker-entrepreneurs at Philadelphia. Craftshops as well as mills could be the spawning ground for new enterprises, as the case of Henry Korn and Benjamin Bullock will illustrate.

The workshop situation in 1820

Textile millmen were generally not delighted with their situation in 1820, as their grumpy remarks about imports, prices, and untrustworthy managers show. Still, they possessed powered machinery and in some cases sizable capitals that allowed them to take rapid advantage of the recovery in trade that the late-filing Lewis' Sons were already noting. By contrast, the craftshop manufacturers, sorely pressed, expressed their troubles with a rough eloquence that is both arresting and memorable.

Their output of a variety of coarse cottons ran directly into the mountains of British factory goods unloaded weekly at the port. Their dependence backward on yarn producers forced them to absorb the high cost of cotton, and when their merchant buyers cut the purchase price for cloths or refused to take their goods at all, their produce was assigned to the auction rooms as well.

> John Hinshellwood: Formerly made from 7 to [illegible] dollars per week and now not more than 4 per week, owing to the depressed state of the markets. I was obliged to reduce the wages. If the Markets continue

---

95 1850 MCS, Philadelphia Co., p. 18.
96 Bagnall, "Textile Industries" (fiche), pp. 1785–6.

to depres I will be under the necesity to drop it alltogether. As to Sale of our articles we have no other market but Auction Sales as Merchants will not purches privitly.[97]

The situation was indeed bleak.

As historical records rarely allow the voices of handloom operators to be heard with the detail and intensity appearing on the 1820 schedules, their responses will be given here at some length.

> Andrew Kilpatrick – This establishment I commenced about 3 months ago. I invested in it near all my capital [ca. $500]. The expectations I had then are now fled. I am losing every week, therefore determined to give up from present prospect.

> James Crawford and Alexander Patterson in Co. – This establishment we commenced about 3 months ago with the prospect of accumulating a small profit on the above mentioned goods but aless our prosper seems to be fled[.] goods from a foring contry are forced into our market and are sold at such prices as starves the struggling manufacturer of this country without the least eventual hope of suckcess, the Reason is obvious[,] it is but a very few articels of Cotton Manufactrey that we can attempt to make in this contry, if we want fine yarn, say 80s, 90s, 100s, 100&20s to 50s or sixtys for this we must send to *Great* Britton, of the above mentioned numbers are made all the valuable articels of Cotton Manufactury, Books, Muls, Jacknots and fine Cambres, etc. etc. Permit me to suggest one way in which the incouragement of industry and domistick Manufactrey [–] extend from the National funds a certain sum of money to the man or company of men who would put up a proper Cotton Mill with somany spindels and proper machinery for the making of fine yarn[.] this would undoubtedly lay a foundation for future hope.

> James Stranaghan – This business is daily getting worse and now not able to give me a living or pay itself.[98]

James Maxwell barely contained his fury at the situation he faced:

> I have little to say or wish to say little as We unprotected have to contend with Foreigners Protected which is well known to every Man and even Drive us from our own Market unless we can sell Cheaper than they and our goods better than theirs.[99]

The lives of these craftshop proprietors were as different from those of the millmen as was their prose. The discreet professionalism of David Lewis was here replaced by anger, resignation, or earnest petitioning. Crawford and Patterson acknowledged the boundaries imposed by their coarse trade,

---

[97] 1820 MCS, Eastern District, Pa., no. 563.
[98] Ibid., nos. 677, 674, 675.
[99] Ibid., no. 675.

showing perhaps an immigrant's familiarity with fine British spinning in appealing for federal initiatives to supply them with materials to make the quality goods that skilled craftsmen could not then attempt. The low-numbered yarns available from local spinners fundamentally constricted their production options. The yarn itself was a source of trouble to some, as Alexander Moffet's only comment, scrawled in inch-high letters at the foot of the schedule, was "Bad T[h]read."[100]

What strategies could craftworks masters attempt under the circumstances, given restricted raw materials, negligible working capital, clogged markets, and so on? Several mentioned dismissing workers, whereas others listed hands insufficient to operate the looms and related equipment they possessed. Hinshellwood pointed out reluctantly that he "was obliged to reduce the wages." This was not so simple a matter as it might appear to later observers. Handloom weavers spoke in terms of a "price" for loomwork, continuing the eighteenth-century custom and separating themselves from factory operatives who received wages. From this period through the 1870s, handweavers in Philadelphia demanded, negotiated, and struck for the price of work, submitted price lists to shop masters, and resisted all attempts to treat them as, or classify them with, "wage earners." In this context, to reduce the rate paid for weaving was not something craft masters automatically did in response to hard times. It was instead something they were obliged to do, a last resort in contravention of custom and culture.

Two other elements of the early textile manufacture, though not emergency strategies, may have cushioned the impact of the depression and import competition for some of the craftshops. Both the boarding of workers and the employment of close family members and other kinsmen could reduce the actual cash outflow for any firm. The latter certainly played a role in the early accumulation stages for the Schofields, and the former is directly mentioned in 1820 by James Crosbey, an Old City manufacturer of cotton checks and bedtickings. Crosbey, whose twelve looms were principally run by his twelve male workers, complained: "Owing to foreign competition, we are compelled to sell at firm cost. All I make is by boarding my workmen."[101] How prevalent boarding was among 1820 workshops is not revealed by other schedules, but boarding appears with regularity in the 1850 household returns of Philadelphia handloom proprietors, one of whom reported sixteen carpet weavers resident in his enormous household of twenty-nine persons.[102] Boarding might indeed spell the difference between a

---

[100] Ibid., no. 680.

[101] Ibid., no. 571.

[102] 1850 MCS, Philadelphia Co., District 5, p. 47. James Pollock was an Irish immigrant, ca. 1844, as were most of his boarders. His 34-year-old wife had borne him at least eight children, including twins, who were 10 months old at the time of the census.

workshop's survival or collapse, as a visitor to Philadelphia in the late twenties claimed that manufacturers gained "one dollar a week for each hand boarded."[103] The figures Crosbey provided on materials, wages, and value of products indirectly confirm the importance of boarding, showing a net loss of $300 for the year's work without taking into account rent and incidental expenses.

The practice of boarding brings forward the question of the origins of both craftshop workers and manufacturers. Certainly boarders were likely to be single males, but whether they were immigrants or in-migrants from rural districts cannot be established. Neither can kinship relations be demonstrated for this early period. The high proportion of Scots names among this cotton handloom group (Cummings, Crosbey, Stranaghan, Moffet) is suggestive but inconclusive. However, the employment of kinsmen in small workshops during the thirties might be inferred by a close reading of documents pertaining to the Jacksonian bank crisis of 1834.

When President Jackson removed federal deposits from the Second Bank of the United States as a part of his second-term combat with Nicholas Biddle, a series of petition drives for and against Jackson's policies were mounted in Philadelphia. The resolutions and signatures of many of these efforts were published in the volumes of House and Senate documents from the Twenty-third Congress. The most massive of them, House Document No. 86, has appended the names of more than 10,000 Philadelphia endorsers, most of whom noted their occupations. Although the occupational addition was likely designed by the merchant and financial leaders who organized the affair as a way of showing that "every class of citizen" was arrayed against Jackson, the display of people, trades, and politics that resulted remains a rare artifact for historians of the period.

Before this petition was forwarded to Washington, the signature sheets were displayed at a public meeting, which was reported in the local press.[104] In the House of Representatives, the whole bundle was sent to the Ways and Means Committee, which ordered the entirety printed. This required eighty-one double-columned pages of small print, which presumably represented a transcription of the petition's pages in whatever order they were assembled for presentation. Even a casual glance at the contents reveals clusters of occupations throughout. Some of these are clearly manufacturing establishments in which the proprietor's name heads a sequence of his workmen, accompanied by their crafts. Both textile factories and workshops are identifiable. A useful craftshop example is a cluster of twelve weavers

[103] Peter Nielson, *A Six Years' Residence*, Glasgow, 1830, p. 15, cited in Sullivan, *Industrial Worker*, p. 33.

[104] *Hazard's Register*, vol. 13 (1834), pp. 92–3.

headed by William Neely. Four of the eleven names following are Neelys, including William Neely, Jr.[105] Another Neely cluster appears elsewhere in the petition, as do groups of weavers, warpers, and dyers named Galbraith, Hargreaves, Songster, Briggs, Stewart, and Maxwell.[106] If these groups represent neighborhood handwork shops, that the kinship employment pattern is a common feature of such establishments follows directly. Moreover, as all the signers were adult men, the full extent of family employment in both factory and shop was masked to a considerable degree. The 1850 census gives a number of examples of the kinship-core workshop boarding nonkin workers in the household.[107] That such social relations of production were current in 1820 and helped insulate the shop somewhat from the depression seems plausible.[108]

A full example of the combined effects of family labor and boarding on the viability of a tiny firm can be had by crossing into neighboring Delaware County. In Nether Providence Township, Enos Sharpless rented a small spinning mill (408 spindles) to a tenant for whom he prepared the return. The firm employed three men, two women, and eight boys and girls. Sharpless pointed out:

> It will appear by this statement the cost of the raw materials added to the hands wages[,] contingent expenses &c. exceeds the amount of manufactured goods by 224 dollars; to which add 350 for rent and it will appear the tenant looses 574 dollars a year; but as about one half the contingent expenses (100 dollars) has been paid by the owner of the factory, and the tenant and several of his children, for which wages are counted, work in it, and he boards some of the hands, amounting in the whole to 828 dollars[,] it leaves a balance in his favour of 254 dollars a year.[109]

---

105 *Memorial of merchants, mechanics, manufacturers, traders and others . . .* , 23rd Cong., 1st sess., 1834, H. Doc. 86, p. 48.

106 Ibid., pp. 12, 13, 42, 76. Incidentally, an average of 125 signatures appears on each printed page, yielding the 10,000-plus figure claimed by the petitioners. Of these, nearly 800 are textile workers and manufacturers. The frequency of English and Scots surnames among them is quite striking.

107 See Chapter 6, this volume.

108 Paul Johnson has noted that workmen boarded with their workshop owners–employers in this period in his study of Rochester (*A Shopkeeper's Millennium: Society and Revivals in Rochester, New York, 1815–1837*, New York, 1978). He found the number of households "in which labor relations and family life were structurally and emotionally inseparable" on the decline by the thirties, as masters began to "prefer . . . money and privacy to the company of their workmen and the performance of old patriarchal duties" (pp. 47, 106). Although no comparable data set has been developed for the same period at Philadelphia, such close supervision of boarders was surely practiced in small immigrant shops. However, the practice was hardly possible in larger firms that relied on outwork weavers, an independent lot, as suggested by their citywide strike in 1825.

109 1820 MCS, Eastern District, Pa., no. 698.

Although such arrangements may well have extended the economic lives of a number of struggling craftshops, most of them vanish without a trace. It is at present impossible to determine whether the proprietors went bankrupt, left town, died, or prospered quietly; they have simply dropped between the cracks of historical records preservation.

An appreciation of some strategies employed by handloom manufacturers cannot overshadow the complex relations of dependence and vulnerability amid which they undertook to "accumulate a small profit." Costly mill-spun yarn raised their expenses in a falling market, and when it was "bad thread," it lowered the value of their finished goods. Yet they could hardly spin sufficient yarn by hand,[110] nor had they the capital for a waterpowered mill and its machinery. Auction sales only added to the uncertainties of the market for their goods, and merchants who set prices kept them low enough to match the British inflow. Congress had set tariff rates that allowed foreign competition to squeeze them in an international pincer, and their political clout, when visible at all, rarely extended beyond the ward or township. Their boarders, a source of both labor and potential profit, were a dependent group for whom they had to provide work or cease operations.

All together there were eighteen craftshops reported in the 1820 census, sixteen that produced cotton goods, one hosier, and one fringe and trim maker. Of these, only five can be confirmed as still operating later in the decade. As noted earlier, three of the cotton shopmen signed a report on handloom weaving published in 1828. Two of these men were the *only* handloom operators to report at all favorably on their situation in 1820.[111] The other sure survivors were Joseph Ripka, a Silesian immigrant who moved on to become one of the most prominent Manayunk factory operators, and Henry Korn, the fringe and trim maker. Korn's return contained the fullest account of the artisan shopman's plight and the most extensive appeal for state action. His remarks will serve to close this treatment of workshop production.

Henry Korn had been active since the War of 1812, manufacturing "Lace, Fringe, Bindings, Cords and Tassels, Epaulettes . . . wings, wostad Pompoms, and a variety of other milatary articles." He described his equipment in exhausting detail:

> 10 lace and fringe looms, one warping mill, one gimp mill, one twister mill, one scraping mill, five spooling wheels, 50 shuttles, 3,000 bobbins and quills, one pair wool combs, pots, etc. Silvering, Drawing and roving machines, spinning machines containing 36 spindles together, 2

[110] Two handloom shops reported nine and seven manual spinning wheels, respectively; however, these could not supply the total amount of yarn needed for the even larger numbers of looms active in each shop.

[111] 1820 MCS, Eastern District, Pa., nos. 621, 549.

boilers for dyeing, with the appertaining apperattus, Fixtures, etc., one washing machine, one Bullious mill, with many other articles small in nature, too tedious to mention, one Bleaching Box.[112]

With but six workers, only a fraction of this "apperattus" was in operation, and "the large boiler has not been used for 18 months." With equal thoroughness, Korn worked up a table to show his investment, suggesting to what use his profits from the war years were put and the solid property-ownership that allowed him to endure the depression.

Capital invested	–$5600.
Dyestuffs	– 200.
Besides the building in which it is carried on	– 1650.
The dwelling and front shop	– 8000.
	$15450

The valuation of his house, salesroom, and workshop is reasonable, as they were located in the central market district at 82 N. Second Street.

In his assessment of the current state of his trade, this energetic craftsman prepared an essay that is truly extraordinary, imbued with a rhetoric and conviction similar to that of the appeals and petitions of British handworkers in this era.

As respect the actual and past conditions, I would beg to state that in the years 1814 and 1816 the sales was about three times what they are now for since the General Peace in Europe the manufacturers of Tapestries, Milatry article[s], etc. (who wher then employed by the European armies) looseing at once their resources, on finding a market open to them in the United States litterally glutted it so that upholstery trimmings have been for some time sold lower at our Auction Establishments and by Private Sale than they could be manufactured for either in England, France or Germany, to the great Detriment and almost inevitable Ruin of the same class of manufactures in this country. [I]n the year 1814 I had three men four boys and nine women in my employ all with Cheering Countenance Fired with the Stimulus of Business, but now it is quite the reverse, for even what little is done is Reluctantly done because it is hardly wanted.

As respects Coach Trimming, that is very little in demand now owing to the general Depressed State as almost all those who formerly kept Carriages or Gigs now have them to dispose of – Til the year 1817 every Country Merchant that came to Philadelphia to purchase goods wanted Tapestrys also but now they are forgotten.

---

[112] 1820 MCS, Eastern District, Pa., no. 587.

HENRY KORN,

Coach-Lace, Fringe, Cord & Tassel

MANUFACTURER,

No. 82, North Second Street,

BETWEEN RACE AND ARCH STREETS,

PHILADELPHIA:

Where is also kept constantly on hand, a general assortment of Fashionable Trimmings for Ladies' Dresses, &c.; Military Articles; Hatters' Trimmings, and all colours of Worsted and Woollen Yarn, wholesale and retail, on the most reasonable terms.

N. B. Orders from any part of the United States executed with punctuality.

Advertisement for Henry Korn's trimmings manufactory, circa 1820. Note Korn's hope for a national market for his specialty goods. (Historical Society of Pennsylvania)

[I]t will also be remembered that Wool, Cotton, and Flax are staple articles of this Country and we can also manufacture from these same materials all kinds of military Trimmings necessary to be used in the United States and but for that these same articles would have cost enormous prices During the last war with Great Britain, and moreover would have been in all probability manufactured by the very Enemies with whom we where contending.

The little business that is doing at this time is effected by humouring it in every way by sometimes selling lower than can well be aforded and sometimes by effecting Barters, etc; with reasonable protection by Government I am confident all these articles would be manufactured at very low prices the Different Processes of late having been very much improved upon. I will further observe that my Capital here invested which is the whole recompense for ten years Industry, Economy, Perseverance and Enterprize does not at present with all my exertions yeald four per centum per annum which I humbly submit to impartial Legislators to say weather it is fair, weather it is hard or not that useful industry must thus suffer and thus be rewarded. The best proof of a declining system is that in former years a profit would be realized without extraordinary talent or exertions but at present neither nor both will suffice to keep even handed, nay it requires the strictest unremitting attention to ward off the Horrors of Bankruptcy.

It is sincerely hoped that Congress as an enlightened Legislating Body and as the sole guardians of the nation will adopt such measures as in their superior Wisdom will nourish and Protect the manufacturing Interest and useful Industry of this country and not suffer us to be Drained of our last Dollar in support of Foreign monopoly. My humble opinion is that there need be no fear of manufacturers charging too high by being too well protected –the Spirit for embarking into the different Branches is already too well evinced and on the other hand they will prevent Foreign monopolizers from taking the advantage whenever a war or any other circumstance might justify them. All of which is Respectfully submitted by the Government's humble svt. Henry Korn[113]

This skillful and sophisticated tract exhibits a broad awareness of relationships between economics and politics in an international and historical setting. Korn adopts a traditional stance of formal deference not only at the close but also in his hopeful descriptions of legislators as "impartial" and "enlightened." Yet he is persistent in his invocations of nationalist virtues as against foreign "monopolyzers," calling for the simple justice ("weather it is fair") that protection would afford "useful Industry." The value of economic independence is put forward to meet the anticipated criticism of protection as causing a rise in prices, along with the assurance that the "Spirit for embarking" will yield domestic competition preventing "manufacturers charging too high." His explicit reference to a return to capital of a mere 4% reveals a budding capitalist calculating carefully, for all his moralizing claims to "Industry, Economy, Perseverance and Enterprize" and reference to his workers "Cheering Countenance[s]" in better times.

From the text, it is clear that Korn is worried not about raw materials,

113   Ibid.

production, transport, labor supply, or technology but solely about marketing, a process whose complexity he understands and illustrates. Accumulation cannot proceed without realization of the surplus value that inheres in
finished goods. Before the depression, Korn's widely varied output evidently
had four markets: the government (military articles), craftsmen (trim for
upholstery, etc.), country merchants (tapestries), and gentlemen (carriage
accessories). All have deserted him. The end of the war collapsed the military market, the influx of foreign goods sold both at auction and privately has
diverted the craft trade, and the depression led country dealers to drop fancy
items and gentlemen to sell their gigs. Having dismissed two-thirds of his
workers, he is reduced to "Barter" and to claims that "the Horrors of
Bankruptcy" are a daily threat. Shrewdly linking his own fate to that of the
nation, he humbly begs the legislators' attention, believing perhaps that his
essay would influence their deliberations to some degree. Doubtless some-
body read it; but when the 1820 Manufacturing Census returns were finally
tabulated and printed, his appeal appeared condensed, as follows: "Lace,
fringe and binding . . . Much depressed, owing to importations. Wants the
protecting aid of Congress."[114]

Though Korn may have had no impact on the Congress, his workshop did
provide a legacy to the Philadelphia textile manufacture. In 1815, the "one
pair [of] wool combs" in his shop were delegated to an English immigrant,
Benjamin Bullock, giving the latter his start in the new land. Seven years
later, "having accumulated some capital," Bullock

> commenced the business of wool pulling on Front Street, above Poplar.
> In the succeeding year, he removed to the store [at] 32 N. Third Street,
> where he remained thirty-seven years . . . Perceiving a favorable oppor-
> tunity to embark in manufacturing woolen goods, Mr. Bullock, in 1837,
> commenced the business in the "Spruce Street Factory," now [1867]
> owned by Mr. William Divine, who was then foreman at this mill.[115]

Here the successions are elegant. Bullock invested both his savings from
employment with Korn and his comber's skill in the business of raw-materials preparation for wool manufacture. After fifteen years, the Panic of 1837
was for him an "opportunity," likely the chance to take charge of a mill that
had defaulted on debts for his wool, allowing him to integrate forward into
production. His foreman, an Irish immigrant, ultimately replaced Bullock at
the mill after the latter's withdrawal to factories along the Schuylkill near

114 *Census of Manufactures, 1820*, Washington, 1822, Eastern District of Pennsylvania Table,
Philadelphia, unpaged. Korn's return is readily identifiable by the correspondence of
output, worker, raw material, and other figures with his manuscript schedule.
115 J. L. Bishop, *A History of American Manufactures from 1608 to 1860*, Philadelphia, 1868,
vol. II, p. 561.

Conshohocken. By the Civil War, Divine & Sons operated two mills report-ing over $160,000 invested and employing more than 300 workers.[116] Bul-lock's sons continued his operations after his retirement in 1859, the five Bullock brothers reaping a harvest of wartime army cloth contracts from the Quartermaster Corps and by 1867 operating fourteen mills with a total complement of 3,000 workers on various sites.[117] Here are two examples of workers moving into manufacture without visible family links, though both install the family succession (to *their* sons) once they have established them-selves as independent capitalists. No Lowell operative could hope for such openings to materialize in that city's corporate manufacture.

Henry Korn, an unusual character among artisanal producers, was capa-ble of a wider variety of output than were cotton shopmen, was more fully capitalized, and was considerably more refined in his writing. The proprie-tors of two Moyamensing workshops, Edward Irwin and John Murphy, more accurately capture the depression prospects of the majority of their col-leagues. Having filled out their respective census schedules and agreeing on the state of the trade, they penned identical comments at the close, stating memorably: "The weaving business is at present that a man may live but very poorly."[118]

At Philadelphia in 1820, it is evident that there were two distinct but linked manufacturing "systems," neither of which resembled that soon to be established at Lowell by the Boston Associates. The craft-shop manufactur-ers, linked to the mills by their yarn purchases and reaching out to engage household outworkers, could prosper in tandem with factory development. Nonetheless, many of the craft shops and a large proportion of the mills would succumb to the 1820 depression, the downturn of the late twenties, the Panic of '37, or to a death or miscalculation anywhere along the path. Yet as the market for textiles expanded, as the material infrastructure stabilized and expanded (credit, currency, transport), and as thousands of immigrants, British, Irish, and German, continued to arrive in the city, the closed work-shops were replaced by new ventures and the vacant mills were rented to new tenants decade after decade. By 1850 on the same grid of mills, work-shops, and handloom outworkers, Philadelphia would support more than 300 textile firms and 12,000 workers in the industry. It is this structural continuity that gives the Philadelphia textile manufacture its characteristic shape in successive generations.

---

[116] 1860 MCS, Philadelphia Co., p. 175.

[117] Bishop, *History of American Manufactures*, vol. II, p. 560.

[118] The exact texts are: "The waving buisnss is at present that a man may live but very poorly" (Irwin, no. 679); "The weaving buisness is at present that a man may live but weary poorly" (Murphy, no. 678).

Table 4.8. *Textile work force by sector, Philadelphia, 1814–20*

Sector	Work force			
	1814	1816	1819	1820
Cotton	1,761	2,325	149	671
Hosiery	96	48	29	11
Thread (spinning yarn)	444	191	20	92
Floor cloth (carpet)	50	30	25	—a
Wool	1,310	1,226	260	334
Other				31
Total	3,661	3,820	483	1,139

aIsaac Macauley's floor-cloth mill was not tallied in the 1820 Manufacturing Census, though it had been in operation since 1809; it was still in operation in the 1830s.
Source: Hazard's Register of Pennsylvania, vol. 4 (1829), pp. 168–9; Manuscript Manufacturing Census Schedules, Eastern District, Pa., Philadelphia County, 1820.

Outworkers and the handloom trades

Although most textile mills and handloom workshops were included in the 1820 enumeration,[119] outwork households for whom Baird, Craige, and others provided yarn were not considered manufacturers at all. Given their essential connection to the accumulation prospects of the factory operators, it is worthwhile to search for traces of outworkers among some scattered sources to develop a rough idea of the extent of household weaving and its productive relations.

In August 1819, amid the "general decay of business," a committee of citizens undertook an inquiry into conditions among the manufacturers of the city and the county. Their unsigned report has been regularly cited but rarely analyzed to any degree.[120] They assembled information on employment and wages for thirty trades, including five textile sectors, in 1814, 1816, and 1819 (Table 4.8).

Let us take hosiery and spinning first. The Germantown hosiery trade had existed from colonial times but was in decline even at the turn of the century. Stocking hand frames, "but little if at all improved from the frames which

[119] Isaac Macauley's floor-cloth mill, William Horstmann's trimming and fringe workshop, and Dennis Kelly's cotton mills were active in this period but do not appear in the census.

[120] *Hazard's Register*, vol. 4 (1829), pp. 168–9; cited in Scharf and Westcott, *History of Philadelphia*, Bishop, *History of American Manufactures*, and Sullivan, *Industrial Worker*.

had been in use for more than two hundred years,"[121] turned out a product that collapsed before waves of imports. As a local observer pointed out as early as 1804:

> There is yet no other market for the Germantown hosiery but what is brought in three or four baskets to the gutter at the corner of 2d [Second] Street. Formerly an eligible stand was assigned them [in the central market nearby]; but the trade every year getting more and more into insignificance, they were obliged to abandon that situation and give way to the venders of gingerbread, confectionaries and manufactories, which minister more immediately to the wants of agriculture.[122] [The market was the exchange center for farmers and craftsmen until the 1850s when the large sheds on Market Street near the waterfront were leveled.]

The steady decline in hosiery amid the boom, bust, and recovery of 1814–20 is understandable and may indicate fair reliability for the other figures. The precipitous drop in spinners between 1814 and 1816 reflects the establishment in the county of waterpowered yarn mills, which collapsed the hand trade on spinning wheels and jennies, billies, and twisters.[123] That most powered mills closed by 1819 and resumed production in the following year follows directly.

The shutdown of spinning mills and the reductions in work force at cotton factories cited earlier would account for only part of the catastrophic fall in labor in 1814–19 in cottons (Table 4.8). The 1819 survey suggests that in 1814 there was an enormous outwork trade dependent on yarn supplies for its sustenance. The scale of outwork manufacture is not reflected fully in the 1820 manufacturing returns. Nonetheless, with import-glutted markets, high-priced cotton, tight credit, the suspension of production by spinners and integrated mills like the Globe would have had dire consequences for handloom household workers. That they survived, or were replaced by new faces in a few years, is indicated by the 1827 report of the Society of Weavers.[124]

---

121 Bagnall, "Textile Industries" (fiche), p. 1344.

122 Ibid.

123 See Coxe, *Statistical Tables*, pp. 44–7, for information on spinning wheels and related machinery in Philadelphia County about 1810. Coxe also gives hosiery figures: 115 frames (or establishments, the column heading being blank) in the city and county, producing about 54,000 pair of hose in 1810.

124 The parallel dramatic labor reduction in the woolen sector is a topic for further investigation. Handlooms did yield cotton-wool blends in this and other periods, replacing the linsey-woolseys common in colonial times. These looms may have been classed as wool weavers dependent on cotton warps and may have vanished with the cessation of spinning operations. The household production of all-wool goods may have contracted along with that of other marketable items, but the absence of any data on household production in the 1820 *Census of Manufacturers* cripples any evaluation at this point.

Responding to an inquiry from the Pennsylvania Society for Promoting Domestic Manufactures "respecting the number of hand Looms in the city for weaving cotton goods," thirteen members of the weavers association signed the following certificate:

> There are in Philadelphia and its vincinity 104 warping mills at work, each of which is sufficient to employ from 40 to 50 weavers, making the number of weavers about 4500. Dyers over 200, spoolers 3000, bobbin winders 2000.
>
> Wages
> Weavers can now average 5 dollars per week, Dyers 5 do, Warpers 5 do, Spoolers from 50 cents to 1.50 do, Bobbin winders 1 do and found.
>
> Houses occupied
> Manufacturing establishments over 50, average rent 180 dollars per year. Houses occupied by weavers about 1500, average rent 60 to 80 dollars per year. . . .
>
> The above is an estimate for this season – in the winter, when other employment ceases, the number increases considerably, say one-third.
>
> Philad. 25th June 1827.

Thos. Hughes	John Waters	John Steel
John Funston	John Maguire	Thomas Ford
Robert Wilson	Rening & Austin	Patrick McBride
Thomas Laird	Abraham Cumming	Hugh Clark[125]
James Brown Jr.		

Even allowing for overstatement by prideful men, here was an extensive outwork system, engaging thousands of weavers, hundreds of yarn or piece dyers, and the family economies of hundreds of households to facilitate accumulation for the thirteen signatories and their forty or so colleagues in the Society of Weavers. It represents the restoration and further expansion of productive relations interrupted by the crisis of the late teens. (A search for further information on the origins and functions of the Society of Weavers is certainly in order.) If more than 2,300 hands were employed on cottons in 1816, the bulk of them were surely outwork weavers. Scharf and Westcott claimed that 4,000 looms were "put in operation in Philadelphia in 1821, chiefly for weaving cotton goods," and by 1824 "Philadelphia had thirty cotton-mills, which averaged 1400 spindles each, and together employed 5000 looms and 3000 persons."[126] Although these are undifferentiated figures, they give some support to my belief that outwork handloom cotton manufacture and mill spinning and weaving contracted and expanded *in tandem* because of their mutual interdependence in the Philadelphia format of accumulation.

---

[125] *Hazard's Register*, vol. 1 (1828), p. 28. No analogous document has surfaced regarding outwork on wools.

[126] Scharf and Westcott, *History of Philadelphia*, pp. 2234–5.

Other issues related to outwork emerge from the report of the Society of Weavers. Their closing reference to the seasonal variation in employment accords well with a conception of the handloom workers as an immigrant (or in-migrant) group, part of which sought more remunerative work (perhaps construction) in the warm months and then returned to their looms and basic craft skills for family support through the winter. Reference to what sums "Weavers can now average" not only may be inflated but may also gesture toward "preindustrial" work rhythms that lacked the time discipline of the mill and could never be fully controlled by outwork masters.[127] As the society members did not manufacture yarn, adequate sources of this essential material had to be secured from spinning mills (and the excess of integrated mills) and perhaps from the production of New England spinners. Almy and Brown (of Providence) in this period consigned more than 70% of their yarn and cloth output to agents in Philadelphia, one of whom had been cotton-mill owner Samuel Haydock.[128] Finally, as to marketing, Hazard appended a valuable note:

> The gentleman from whom we have obtained the above information further informed us, that these goods are of the denominations called gingham checks, bedtickings and stripes, and are exported in large quantities for the supply as well of the eastern and western, as of the southern states – large quantities being sent to Boston by almost every packet.[129]

The Society of Weavers may well have had its beginning in connection with Philadelphia's largest strike of the decade, an 1825 conflict in which a reported 2,900 handloom weavers stopped work to secure "an increase of 25% on their existing prices."[130] A spontaneous suspension by unorganized workers when their masters lowered the price of work was common enough. But the broad demand for an increase allows the suggestion of a handloom weavers association some plausibility. In shops whose operations combined

---

[127] To earn $5 per week, a weaver would have produced about 120 yards (20 yards per day) at more than 4¢ per yard in a six-day work week (4,500 handloom weavers producing 81,000 yards per day). The Troy Company at Fall River was paying only 3½¢ per yard for handloom shirtings and stripes. In 1827 the Slater firm's rates for the same fabrics averaged 2½¢ per yard for handloom weavers in Rhode Island. It is likely that Philadelphia handloom weavers could reach the $5 level only by working at a rate higher than that current in New England. The 1825 strike was launched to demand a 25% increase in the rate; instead of granting an increase, the shopmasters likely urged workers to produce more and thus earn more. I doubt that the $5 figure was more than society propaganda (see Ware, *New England Cotton Manufacture*, Appendix D).

[128] Ware, *New England Cotton Manufacture*, Appendix F; on Haydock, see Bishop, *History of American Manufactures*, vol. II, p. 129.

[129] *Hazard's Register* vol. 1 (1828), p. 28.

[130] Sullivan, *Industrial Worker*, p. 222.

the labors of boarding weavers with those of "independent" outworkers, the latter were far better situated to associate and press for higher rates. Moreover, if sizable fractions of these workers were immigrants from British handloom districts, carrying their experience of craft activity long matured in the wake of the Combination Acts, the base for collective action would be substantial. Such weavers would represent a formidable challenge to workshop masters, especially insofar as they clustered in neighborhoods like Kensington and Moyamensing. As unions were in 1825 still considered conspiracies before the law, covert activity would be obligatory. The formation of the proprietors' Society of Weavers in this context makes perfect sense, though it may have preceded or followed the strike.[131] Were it demonstrable that a goodly proportion of the workshop masters were British immigrants as well, the restoration of older patterns of labor and conflict and the preservation of a culturally conditioned antagonism would become vivid.

Another glimpse into the situation of handloom outworkers may be secured by examining the results of a recession that developed in the late 1820s. In the summer of 1829 an economic downturn brought immediate crisis to the textile workers of Philadelphia, both factory operatives and handloom weavers.

> It was reported that the Globe Mills situated near Philadelphia had suspended operations entirely and about 400 hands were thrown out of work. Other factories which had continued in operation, had "notified their hands, that a reduction of wages must be submitted to, or the works suspended." Four thousand looms which had been in operation the previous year were said to be idle.[132]

The recession in trade was quite mild, as no later observer accords it much weight. Yet thousands of textile workers were jobless. It is possible either that the cloth trades were particularly affected by this particular contraction or that manufacturers used the business decline as a weapon to discipline

131 That 200 dyers were engaged in work for the masters, as recorded in the 1827 Society of Weavers Report, is supported by other contemporary sources. Working singly or in small groups for craft shops, dyers prepared colored yarn for checks and plaids. Dyeing equipment is present in several of the 1820 shop returns, and a number of the workshoplike groups listed in the 1834 pro-bank petitions include one or more dyers in a cluster of weavers (and perhaps a warper as well). Equally supportive are the reports of the city Watering Committee for 1832 in the northern and southern water districts, areas that included both Moyamensing and Kensington but not old City and Northern Liberties. In these two districts, 120 dyers are present, each paying $10 annually for their supplies of river water. That scores of independent dyers served society members, supplementing the shops' own work forces, provides a parallel productive relationship to the combination of shop weavers and outwork looms here suggested (see Hazard's Register, vol. 9 [1832], p. 95).

132 Sullivan, Industrial Worker, p. 52.

fractious workers. The suffering of domestic weavers was acute in the winter of 1829, as Matthew Carey's investigations illustrated. The number of insolvents applying for court protection jumped from 131 during a week in April to 300 during a similar period in late October. In April only 4 of the applicants were textile workers, whereas in the fall 21 weavers, spinners, and other textile workers went before the courts for relief. Other trades were affected to a lesser degree, the comparable April and October figures for shoemakers being 17 and 24, for carpenters, 7 and 15.[133]

Charitable societies were of some assistance, though never adequate to the need. Discussing one case, Carey reinforces the notion developed earlier that the outwork weaver who possessed his own loom was a key element in the textile manufacture at Philadelphia.

> The family of M'Giffie . . . were actually suffering for want of the common necessaries of life, when their case became known to these excellent women [in one of the charitable societies]. The father was emaciated – the mother lying in a state of insensibility – one child was dead – the other dying! At this crisis . . . a bed was given to replace the straw on which the woman lay – a stove was hired for the use of the family, fuel provided &c. In consequence of the administration of proper nutriment, the physical powers of the parents were renovated; . . . When the man recovered, money was raised to pay for a loom. He diligently sought for, and fortunately found employment. I visited their room lately, and found them cheerful, happy, industrious and likely to continue useful members of society.[134]

Whatever the value of Carey's reading of the mental state of the M'Giffies, the key element in their material prospects was the acquisition of a loom. Finding work was hard, and the declining price for work meant that other family members would also have to work. Spooling, mentioned in the report of the Society of Weavers, was important here, as it was done by women and children. Carey again:

> [Visiting near 11th and Pine Streets, I found] a room fifteen feet long and eleven feet wide, in which there are three beds close together. When I visited it, there were two women at work, one spooling and the other spinning. If they had constant employment, they could each earn only twenty or twenty-five cents a day – but work came in very irregularly.[135]

Contemplating such conditions, Carey briefly turned his fire on the "manufacturers" who profited from it:

---

133 *Hazard*, vol. 3 (1829), p. 224; vol. 4 (1829), p. 336.
134 Matthew Carey, *Miscellaneous Essays*, Philadelphia, 1830, p. 156.
135 Ibid., p. 158.

Every individual industriously employed in a useful occupation, has an indisputable claim to healthful and comfortable support. Those who employ him or her, ought, in honor and justice, to yield that support; and when the remuneration is reduced below that standard, and advantage taken of their distress, or of the competition arising from an excess of numbers, it is flagrant injustice. I venture to assert, that the situation of a spooler, who receives the yarn wet [from dyeing?], and is paid but fifteen or twenty cents per hundred skeins, is as deplorable as almost any of the most oppressed people in any part of Europe.[136]

Such was the cotton manufacture in the 1820s, a complex and shifting set of relationships between powered mills, outworkers, and mediating workshop exploiters who had associated in the Society of Weavers, reaching for a national market while imperiled by domestic and foreign competition. In the dynamics of crisis and growth, we may visualize the handloom outworkers as a variant on Marx's reserve army of labor, though a special low-grade artisanal ornamentation of that theme. Left to starve in the depths of 1819, they helped to facilitate expansion and accumulation in the twenties only to face rate cuts and renewed miseries in the 1829 decline. Exactly what combinations of the outwork relations of production were in place, and in what proportions, cannot be established without additional research. What is clear is that on cottons, both integrated and spinning mills (Globe and Baird) depended on outworkers for yarn distribution, and that by 1827 the cotton workshop masters had organized themselves to operate with both shop-based looms and outworkers.

Tariffs and the role of the state

During the War of 1812, prohibitive tariffs effectively barred British textiles from the domestic marketplace. Upon their expiration in 1816, the conflicting sectional and sectoral interests (North–South, urban–rural, manufacturer–importer) set aside during the war reappeared in the debates over a replacement tariff act. A compromise set of rates was proposed by the secretary of the treasury, Alexander Dallas of Philadelphia. Much modified en route to enactment, the 1816 Tariff Act established an artificial minimum valuation of 25¢ per yard for all imported cottons, on which a 25% tax was assessed (6¼¢ per yard). For fine goods, whose value might be nearly $1 per yard, this was revenue measure. However, coarse cottons of the sort already produced by mill and workshop manufacturers could anticipate full protection. Cheap sheetings, shirtings, and so on would have to be delivered to the

---

[136] Ibid., p. 162.

Philadelphia market at 10¢ or less a yard (plus the duty) in order to compete with the 16¢ price then current in the city for local production. Yet British goods continued to flood the market, "seeking an outlet regardless of price." Weak enforcement apparatus, the auction sacrifice system, and false invoicing all conspired to limit the effectiveness of the act. As woolen manufacturers had to import a considerable portion of their raw material, they "obtained little real relief" under the revised tariff of 1816.[137]

An effort to restrict the auction sales during the winter of 1819–20, though supported in the House of Representatives by most of the Pennsylvania delegation, failed to pass.[138] During the twenties, the state legislature imposed a special tax on import auctioneers, throwing a small rock in their road, but its revenues and impact seem to have been tiny.[139] A revised tariff in 1824 set a 30% duty on imported woolens but increased the rate on raw wool as well, giving on balance only slightly improved terms to woolen manufacturers. An attempt in 1827 to construct a minimum valuation bill analogous to the procedure used on cottons became entangled with the unfolding politics of Jackson's presidential drive and died in the Senate.[140] The next year, the wool minimums went into effect as a part of the strongly protectionist "Tariff of Abominations," though the duty rates for imported woolen goods were set at 40%, whereas almost all other manufactures were taxed on a 50% scale.[141]

Many of Philadelphia's textile manufacturers were pressing wages downward in these same years, and the price of raw cotton trended lower from 1825 to 1832.[142] When in that latter year, Congress upped the minimum valuation of imported cotton goods to 30¢ per yard, producers of coarse cottons could feel increasingly secure. As the auction tide ebbed in Philadelphia, federal tariff provisions helped sustain the city's mill, craft shop, and outwork system, as the state contributed to accumulation in both the Quaker City and Lowell.[143]

---

137 Malcolm Eiselen, "The Rise of Pennsylvania Protectionism," Ph.D. diss., University of Pennsylvania, 1932, p. 41.

138 Ibid., p. 56.

139 *Hazard's Register* gave periodic figures for imports at Philadelphia and auctioneer's tax payments to the State Treasury, 1828–35. Auctioneer records for this era have been preserved at the Historical Society of Pennsylvania.

140 Eiselen, "Rise," pp. 72–3.

141 Ibid., p. 83.

142 H. L. Stettler III, *Growth and Fluctuation in the Ante-Bellum Textile Industry*, New York, 1977, p. 138.

143 A remarkably readable treatment of tariff questions, "Protection . . . Wool and Woolens, Speech of Mr. Slade of Vt. on the Tariff Bill," appears in *The American Laborer* 1, no. 8 (1842):245–56.

Manufacturing capitalists and the Philadelphia elite

To what extent did Philadelphia's 1820 textile manufacturers constitute a "capitalist class"? If we freeze for an instant the accumulation process, we see all of them as owners of capital, employers of labor, and receivers of profits. Even the handloom shopmen of Moyamensing, facing ruin, wrote of their "capital" and their fading prospect of "accumulating a small profit." Individually, on both objective grounds and insofar as we can glimpse their self-perceptions, these men indeed were capitalists. But collectively, their backgrounds and productive relations suggest rather that the manufacturing class in textiles was a set of fractions.

First, the craft-shop proprietors, using hand methods embedded in artisanlike cultures, many of them likely immigrants, had to struggle to install capitalist relationships (the notion of "wages") in their dealings with craftsmen whose resistance might be passive (failures of "time discipline") or active (the 1825 strike). Vulnerable to market shifts or technological developments they could not (or would not) introduce, their individual survival was problematic. Still, the workshop format for production endured. More than fifty such manufactories were claimed by the weavers association in 1827, having extended their reach to thousands of outworkers who appear nowhere in their 1820 returns. Their capacity to absorb a great volume of yarn from local spinners and to provide cheap cottons to a selling market from which foreign competition was gradually being excluded would endure as well. By the 1850s there would be changes (some concentration, the rise of knit and carpet work), but the workshop–outwork system and its handloom capitalists would not fade away. Their labor relations were linked fundamentally with the exploitative measures of their factory cousins, the one welcoming handloom immigrants, the other introducing the factory system to women and children whose labor was keyed to the pace of machinery and the skills of veteran male workers. Even if the Society of Weavers figures for 1827 were considerably inflated, the handloom manufacturers were in charge collectively of the largest segment of textile labor in the city. Evidence for shopmasters' immigrant origins, despite the prevalence of Scots surnames, is frankly, soft.[144]

The small factories of the second group were characterized by modest capitals, powered mills, varied outputs, and virtually complete invisibility in

[144] David Jeremy's recent work does indicate the immigration of thousands of British handloom workers after the War of 1812, many of whom settled in and around Philadelphia, where "specialization in hand loom weaving was apparent by 1820." See David Jeremy, *Transatlantic Industrial Revolution: The Diffusion of Textile Technologies between Britain and America, 1790–1830s*, Cambridge, Mass., 1981, pp. 149, 165.

the political and social affairs of Philadelphia.[145] Located in the city and nearby districts, they had a considerable range of marketing outlets, from yarn sales to domestic weavers to government contracts. Several of the operators may be identified as immigrants.[146] Persistence into later decades was far more likely for their firms than for the craft shops, given the stronger structural position from which they operated. Yet they were hardly secure, as they generally leased rather than owned their facilities and had to obtain credit most likely from raw-materials suppliers and commission agents (borrowing against sales) if they could not market their products directly. Some movement from the craft-shop group into the mill class did take place, as Ripka established himself at Manayunk, first renting and then erecting a factory. William Horstmann, a trim and fringe maker like Korn, also made the leap to mill operations in the twenties. An immigrant craftsman, he was bypassed by the 1820 census though he began his shop in Philadelphia in 1815.

The third and smallest fraction are the five mills (four cotton, one cotton and wool) with the largest capital bases, a group of manufacturers who, connected with the merchant elite of the city, occupied a cultural and social space distinct from other factory operations, a world not dissimilar from that of the Boston Associates. The Globe, the Lewises, Samuel Haydock, and George McCallmont were soon joined by another elite-linked firm, Samuel Comly's Frankford Calico Works. The capitalization of the original five was nearly $400,000 in 1820, more than the combined total of all the other thirty-four firms. Comly's printworks, five years after its founding, provided the *McLane Report* with an investment figure of $75,000 in buildings and $60,000 "cash capital."[147] The scale of these mills alone sets them apart from the rest of the city's manufacturers. The wide variation and sophistication of their output contrasts sharply with the few standard cottons woven by the shopmen; the full integration of their facilities separates their productive reach from all but a few of the smaller mills. Perhaps most important, these men have visible relations with the leading figures of the city's commercial and political elite. In the earlier sketch of the Globe Mill Thomas Craige's activities were noted. George McCallmont and Samuel Comly were promot-

---

145 Stephen Sicard, Henry Whitaker, Gillingham & Chapman, Isaac Baird, St. Lawrence Adams, Robert H. Baird, Philip Kelly, B. Patterson, the Bristol Township proprietor whose identity is unknown, Thorp andSiddal, Will G. Hirst, Rodman and Morgan, William Taylor, Jr., F. Belmore, and J. B. Thomas.

146 Issachar Thorp, Joseph Siddal, and Henry Whitaker.

147 Louis McLane, *Report of the Secretary of the Treasury, 1832. Documents Relative to the Manufactures in the United States*, 3 vols., 22d Cong., 1st sess., H. Doc. 308, Washington, D.C., 1833, vol. III, pp. 200–1; cited hereafter as *McLane Report*.

ers of an 1831 effort to split Philadelphia County and thereby lower the tax rates paid by outlying districts, and Comly surfaced with regularity alongside the Biddle forces in the bank war.[148] His Old City sales- and storerooms were rented from Stephen Girard at $4,000 a year and stood in the same block as the latter's residence. On Girard's death, Comly and Mordecai and Lawrence Lewis joined the mayor of Philadelphia in petitioning the state legislature to charter the magnate's private bank, a matter "of the utmost importance to Merchants, Manufacturers and all others, interested in the trade and prosperity of this city."[149] The only other member of the 1820 cohort to have similar visibility was Joseph Ripka, who appears as a promoter of silk culture on the prize lists for manufactures in Franklin Institute competitions and as a signatory of the pro-bank petitions that Comly and his friends originated.[150]

Their capital, scale of operations, and linkages with both proper Philadelphia and a wider political and business culture give this handful of manufacturers a special character. They represent the closest approximation to the Boston Associates that existed in the Philadelphia textile industry, but are, however, only a pale copy. Rather than being central figures in the churches, clubs, and charities of elite society, they operated on its fringes. None of them formed major corporations to manufacture textiles, and all had ceased operations by the mid-fifties. Two questions arise in this connection. What happened to the major mills of Philadelphia in the 1820s, and, more generally, why did the Philadelphia merchant elite not duplicate the Lowell experiment?

Of the six major mills, five were still in operation in 1832, according to the *McLane Report* or other contemporary sources. Of the five, four vanish somewhere in the mists between 1832 and 1850, though their factory buildings were probably occupied by manufacturing successors. Despite their capital position and other strengths, they remained family firms that could be terminated by the death of a principal. Access to credit may have led them to overextend in a way not available to nonelite millmen. The periodic fire, New England competition, any one of a number of elements in the accumulation matrix could have turned solidly negative long enough to bring down the firms. Or, like the Globe, one or more mills may have simply wound up their affairs after adequate competencies had been acumulated for the proprietors. It is only with the acceptance of the notion of endless

[148] *Hazard's Register*, vol. 8 (1831), pp. 32, 180–1; vol. 13 (1834), pp. 92, 136.
[149] Ibid., vol. 9 (1832), p. 28.
[150] Ibid., vol. 5 (1830), pp. 86–7; vol. 8 (1831), p. 306; vol. 12 (1933), p. 355; *Memorial of Merchants*, p. 17.

accumulation that the survival of a firm in a capitalist society seems natural and its disappearance evidence of catastrophe. This was indeed a transitional era both culturally and conceptually, and we as historians are poorly equipped as yet to comprehend that transition process. Though scholars may see the turnover in firms as a sign of spectacular rates of failure by ineffectual entrepreneurs,[151] the fact remains that such turnover may be imperfectly connected with business success or industry prospects in antebellum Philadelphia. That businessmen quit a trade only when forced out is an assumption distant from the world of the competence.

More relevant to smaller entrepreneurs is the assumption that a firm's disappearance from a particular site implies failure. At Philadelphia it may equally imply success and movement to a larger facility elsewhere in the city or region (e.g., Ripka). Even the county and state lines were breached by mobile factory entrepreneurs with regularity. The disappearance of a firm from a neighborhood or the city itself no more assures us of its failure than the disappearance of a resident implies his or her death. Indeed, relocation was a central motif in the Philadelphia textile format, a spatial movement that most often indicated successful accumulation.

Finally, how may we account for the indifference of the Philadelphia merchant elite to the developing textile industry, a situation so much the reverse of that which spawned Lowell? While the proprietors of the largest Philadelphia mills had links to the city's patriarchs, none of the latter took up the trades or became "interested" in partnerships. There was certainly ample capital in this rich commercial center, and the decline of the foreign component of the commercial base became unmistakable in the twenties with the rapid rise of New York as a port of entry. In Baltzell's study, *Philadelphia Gentlemen*, only two of more than thirty largely merchant families had entered any form of manufacturing by this period (the Wetherills, red lead; the Harrisons, sugar refining).[152] If manufacturing did not draw their capital in the face of trade deterioration, what did?

Those enterprises that might secure the revival and extension of trade, canal and railroad construction, seem the most plausible answer, both structurally and culturally. This explanation was offered in the 1850s by Edwin Freedley, who credited Philadelphia capitalists with providing half the $160 million expended on rail and canal building in the 1820–57 period.[153] The 1830s anthracite speculations opened by canal development and the more substantial and related iron foundries drew additional millions from local fortunes. Freedley rhapsodized:

[151] Bruce Laurie, *Working People of Philadelphia, 1800–1850*, Philadelphia, 1980, p. 17.
[152] Baltzell, *Philadelphia Gentlemen*, pp. 71–7.
[153] Freedley, *Philadelphia and Its Manufactures*, p. 86.

To aid these, her merchants sold their ships; to sustain them, her capitalists declined the profits of Bottomry and Respondentia . . . They have withdrawn their capital largely from prosperous commerce, to invest it in Mines, Railroads, Ironworks and Manufactories.[154]

Thus, by the Civil War descendants of the merchant elite had become ironmasters (Joseph Wharton), coal operators (Eckley Coxe), and railroad presidents (George Roberts), as well as bankers and professionals, but not textile manufacturers.

If iron and coal, however, why not textiles once the door to manufacturing had opened? Two considerations may be relevant here. First, the burgeoning big-mill development in New England may have discouraged city capitalists from undertaking competing enterprises on that scale. Laurie mentions that "local merchants invested in New England mills" rather than founding their own.[155] In fact, it was not a local magnate but a New England in-migrant, David S. Brown, who created the only Lowell-style plantation in the prewar decades.[156] The particular character of textile production in Philadelphia must have been a further discouragement. Rather than generating a base of coarse staples whose production and marketing could be managed from distant offices, the Philadelphia industry developed a specialist dimension that we have seen from Craige to Haydock to Henry Korn. Constant attention at the mill to the complexities of variable output demanded the close involvement of interested parties possessed of a thorough knowledge of the minutiae of production. Whereas rationalized management might work in this early era for the manufacture of staple sheetings by the ton, the elaborate network that was the accumulation path in Philadelphia textiles demanded far greater commitments for potentially precarious returns than did the purchase of coal or canal shares. Thus, the city's merchant capitalists put their funds elsewhere, leaving open spaces in the textile trades into which immigrant entrepreneurs would readily move.

There was, I believe, an overarching logic that unified all this helter-skelter activity: that of the circulation and accumulation of capital under conditions themselves in flux and moved continually by the lagged effects of earlier dynamics of the same process. Thus elite capital drawn off to build transport networks (1) left Philadelphia's textile entrepreneurs chronically capital-short and led to capital-saving expedients that involved output flexibility, outworkers, interfirm linkages, and so on; (2) left the textile manufac-

[154] Ibid., pp. 86–7.

[155] Laurie, *Working People,* p. 16.

[156] Brown's enterprise, created as a mill town across the Delaware from Philadelphia at Gloucester, N.J., was begun in the early 1840s and operative for at least four decades. For additional information, see Bishop, *American Manufactures,* vol. III, pp. 46–7.

ture largely to non-elite immigrants who installed elements of their cultural and business practice in the new environment; yet (3) ultimately erected the transportation infrastructure that enabled the city's textile makers to accumulate by meeting markets that could be reached only through the results of the earlier capital diversion, a diversion that had conditioned the manufacturing expedients in the first place. The groundwork for this unfolding process was in place in Philadelphia textiles in the 1820s. The next two decades, riddled with conflict and economic crisis (and virtually devoid of firm-by-firm data), were a period of erratic expansion upon that base.

5

Interim decades, 1830–1850

The labor for children is not excessive.

– Joseph Ripka, 1837

In the decades between 1830 and 1850, the city and county of Philadelphia more than doubled its population, the census totals soaring from 189,000 to 409,000. With the central Old City area increasingly crowded, the nearby suburbs of Kensington, Northern Liberties, Spring Garden, and Southwark would house by 1850 more residents than had the entire county twenty years earlier.[1] Economic recovery from the 1829 recession had been rapid, but the good years ended suddenly in 1837 as the Panic spawned a depression that lasted through the early forties. The depression brought down both industrial and commercial firms and a vital and successful workers' movement, which had won struggles for higher pay and shorter hours. As Warner has commented: "Not until World War I would the unions of Philadelphia recapture such an effective position in the city."[2] In the wake of the crash, nativism flourished, culminating in the Kensington riots of 1844 in which immigrant handloom weavers and their shop masters were heavily involved. Despite the substantial ethnic and racial antagonisms manifested in these street battles and the political movements that surrounded them, immigrants continued to surge into the city, fleeing European miseries, not least of which was the Irish famine. By 1850 the city, which had but 10% foreign-born two decades earlier (roughly 20,000 people), reported 30% of its inhabitants as immigrants, a sixfold increase (to 120,000).[3]

Dramatic expansion of the city's textile trades corresponded with this influx. Midway through the depression, the 1840 census tallied about 125 textile firms active in Philadelphia, 45 each in cotton and woolen work, and more than 30 engaged in dyeing and finishing cotton goods. The woolen

---

[1] S. B. Warner, *The Private City: Philadelphia in Three Periods of Its Growth*, Philadelphia, 1958, p. 51.

[2] Ibid., p. 74.

[3] John Modell, "A Regional Approach to Urban Growth: The Philadelphia Region in the Early Nineteenth Century," paper, cited in Bruce Laurie, *Working People of Philadelphia, 1800–1850*, Philadelphia, 1980, p. 9; J. D. B. DeBow, *Compendium of the Seventh Census*, Washington, 1854, p. 399.

operations, including 16 fulling mills, which finished handloom yard goods, employed 1,156 workers, most of whom were likely engaged in the carpet and hosiery trades in Kensington and Germantown, respectively. The cotton mills, handloom shops, and print- and dyeworks accounted for 4,727 textile jobs. When 147 workers on silk and flax were added, the industry total for 1840 topped 6,000. Total capital reported was $3,411,000, of which 79% was invested in the cotton manufacture. Product value neared $5.5 million, again, 81% represented by cotton firms.[4] Though the depression worsened after 1840, leading to a major Kensington handloom strike in 1843 against rate cutting, rapid growth clearly followed late in the decade.

The 1850 Manufacturing Census manuscripts showed 326 textile firms in operation, ranging from stockingers running one frame to Joseph Ripka's Manayunk cotton factories, which were staffed by more than 700 workers. Of the total city textile work force of 12,369, 7,141 males and 5,228 females, woolen and carpet production claimed nearly 2,000 workers and cotton-wool blends, another 3,315.[5] Though the number of firms was two and a half times the total reported in 1840, their aggregate capital was only 37% greater than the earlier figure,[6] an indication of the large number of small, new firms that possessed only a few hand-powered fabric looms or knitting frames.

By contrast, Lowell in 1840 had ten textile corporations, the Locks and Canals Company, and a few associated textile firms whose aggregate capital was nearly $11 million. The ten manufacturing majors employed 8,592 workers (1,672 men and 6,920 women), with 500 men in addition working for the canal corporation and 400 undifferentiated "hands" in the other enterprises.[7] In the next ten years, Lowell's population rose from 20,796 to more than 33,000, making it the largest city in sprawling Middlesex County, among whose fifty towns were the Boston suburbs of Cambridge, Somerville, and Medford.[8] By 1850 the textile work force at Lowell numbered 11,976 workers, then distributed among only twelve firms. The sexual breakdown was quite the reverse of that in Philadelphia: 3,702 males and 8,274 females, with 900 of the men employed at the Lowell Bleachery and the Lowell Machine Shop and 2,802 among the ten integrated mill complex-

---

[4] *Compendium of the Enumeration of the Inhabitants and Statistics of the United States . . . from the Returns of the Sixth Census*, Washington, 1842, pp. 135–236.

[5] See Table 6.1.

[6] My total, $4,660,000, is calculated from 1850 Manufacturing Census Schedules, Philadelphia Co., cited hereafter as MCS. Capital figures for all the firms, ranging from a low of $100 to above $100,000, were recorded on the schedules.

[7] *Statistics of Lowell Manufactures, January 1841* and *January 1842*, Lowell, Mass., 1841, 1842.

[8] Ibid., *January 1852.*

es. Only twenty women were reported in textile work outside the ten core mills, all at the Bleachery.[9] Other manufacturing carried on in the city occupied about 1,500 workers; thus nine of every ten manufacturing jobs at Lowell were located in the twelve corporate textile firms.

By 1850 the Lowell majors had increased their public stock to $13,210,000,[10] though this figure understates the total capital engaged, as considerable plant and machinery was acquired through short-term borrowing rather than sales of additional stock. In the period 1846–8, McGouldrick reports a gross new investment in facilities (fixed capital) for seven firms, five of which were Lowell corporations, amounting to $2,327,000, no portion of which involved new stock issues.[11] Though definitions of capital invested at midcentury were just as vague and variable as they had been in 1820, it is nevertheless noteworthy that the 326 Philadelphia firms in the 1850 Manufacturing Census reported capital investments totaling only $4,660,000, one-third the Lowell stock figure for a work force of nearly identical size.[12] If anything, this information reinforces the notion that Philadelphia's textile manufacture successfully used far less capital per worker in an accumulation matrix that included outwork, space rental, and other productive relations foreign to the Lowell system.

In the interim decades between the documentation available from the *McLane Report* of 1832 and the 1850 census, two Philadelphia textile manufacturing districts present in the 1820s experienced substantial if erratic growth, and a third, whose textile specialty had been nearly dormant, was revitalized by the immigrant flow. In Kensington and Manayunk the handloom and factory firms of the twenties were joined or replaced by dozens of new ventures. In Germantown, however, a collapsed hosiery trade that dated to colonial times was revived with the arrival of English craftsmen whose skills would restore the district's reputation for fine knit goods. A brief review of these three neighborhoods during the thirties and forties will introduce a more extended consideration of two pre-1850 firms whose development spans the period and extends forward into later decades.

Anchored by the Globe Mill, handweaver shops multiplied in Kensington

---

9   Ibid., *January 1851*.

10 Ibid.

11 Paul McGouldrick, *New England Textiles in the Nineteenth Century: Profits and Investments*, Cambridge, Mass., 1968, p. 16.

12 My total is from 1850 MCS, Philadelphia Co. These figures are useful as indicators of a great variation in investment in plant and machinery at Lowell and Philadelphia. Just as the Lowell capital figures may be understated, the Philadelphia work force figures may be incomplete, in that outworkers were not consistently reported by the manufacturers for whom they produced goods. Thus errors in the two sets of figures would only increase the disproportion in "ratios" of investment to workers between the two locales.

during the second quarter of the century. A central destination for immigrants, the district grew more crowded year by year, for its population rose from 13,236 in 1830 to 46,774 by 1850. Kensington's two square miles became one of the densest inhabitations on the continent.[13] "In the shadow of the mills were thousands of weavers who turned out cotton cloth on hand frames in tiny red-brick cottages lined up in monotonous rows on grid-like streets." The customary cotton trades were supplemented by carpet shops in the 1830s, but outwork remained "the distinguishing feature" of the neighborhood.[14]

The customs of artisanal life were retained by the immigrant craftsmen. Laurie has documented the spontaneous celebration of St. Monday in August 1828, as workers declared a holiday for drinking and gaming amid the sweltering summer heat.[15] More aggressive actions also appeared when the handloom base of their trades was threatened by the installation of locally constructed power looms for weaving checks at a crosstown Manayunk factory. In 1830 Alfred Jenks's invention was

> introduced . . . into the Kempton Mill at Manayunk, where its success produced such excitement among hand-weavers, and others opposed to labor-saving machinery, as to cause a large number of them to go to the mill, with the avowed purpose of destroying it, from doing which they were only prevented by the presence of an armed force.[16]

Thus the specter of Luddism and its direct-action defense of craft labor surfaced among the community of immigrant weavers.

Craft traditions and that sense of community born of social intercourse in the neighborhood likely conditioned Kensington weavers' participation in the labor organizations of the 1830s. The downward pressure on piece rates from the associated shop masters was met by committees of shop delegates in twice-yearly sessions where the price of work for the next six months was established. Strikes regularly ensued, leading by 1835 to the weavers' affiliation with the General Trades Union of the City and County of Philadelphia, led by weaver John Ferral.[17] Though the weavers received financial assistance from the Trades Union in their 1836 strike, the depression shattered the organization, and subsequent walkouts were increasingly bitter and violent. In a long strike late in 1842, angry weavers "dispersed a meeting of their masters by threatening to tear down the house where it was taking place." Riotous confrontations in January 1843 led to the dispatch of three

13 Warner, *Private City*, p. 57.
14 Bruce Laurie, *Working People of Philadelphia, 1800–1850*, Philadelphia, 1980, p. 11.
15 Ibid., p. 33.
16 Edwin Freedley, *Philadelphia and Its Manufactures*, Philadelphia, 1858, pp. 300–1.
17 David Montgomery, "The Shuttle and the Cross," in Peter Stearns and Daniel Walkowitz, eds., *Workers in the Industrial Revolution*, New Brunswick, N.J., 1974, p. 49.

military companies to the district. Their occupation broke the strike, forcing weavers to accept yet another reduction. With improving markets signaling the end of the depression, Kensington weavers struck twice in 1843, gaining increases that brought their income up from $3 to $5 weekly, the level that some had achieved fifteen years earlier. However, following the nativist riots of 1844, the shop masters successfully reestablished the lower scale, as Philadelphia workers had become deeply divided along ethnic and religious lines and all public meetings had been forbidden.[18]

The later forties were less tumultuous. Hand-frame hosiery shops and dozens of small carpet firms sprouted in the revived economic climate, and several powered spinning mills located in Kensington. Wages rose appreciably, though not to the high-water mark of mid-1843, as shop masters varied their output to include more valuable mixed cotton-wool fabrics. From a survey of the 1850 Manufacturing Census returns for Kensington hand-loomshops, monthly pay for cotton weavers averaged $17.03, for mixed-goods weavers, $17.42, and for carpet weavers, $20.36.[19] Over the next generation, the carpet trades would supplant cotton work as the mainstay of Kensington textile manufacturing, but the artisanal character of hand production would endure: close-knit community, small firms, and the rituals of six-month rate-schedule contracts and shop delegates.

During the thirties and forties, the mills bordering the Manayunk Canal became increasingly occupied by textile firms. In 1828, 1,400 residents clustered about the thirteen mills mentioned in J. A. Elkington's Fourth of July oration. Seven of these were textile factories. By 1834, eleven of sixteen Manayunk mills were devoted to spinning, dyeing, and weaving cottons, and the rail link to Philadelphia had been completed.[20] Between 1830 and 1840,

---

[18] Ibid., pp. 50–1.

[19] Drawn from 1850 MCS, Philadelphia Co., Kensington District. The shops surveyed included those that listed hand power on the schedules.

Hand-powered shops, Kensington District, Philadelphia, 1850

	Shops	Workers	Total wages	Monthly average	Workers per shop
Cotton	15	233	$3,968	$17.03	16
Mixed goods	12	371	6,464	17.42	31
Carpet	14	180	3,666	20.36	13

[20] Mildred Goshow, ed., "Mills and Mill Owners of Manayunk in the 19th Century," typescript, 1970, pp. 4–6, Roxborough Branch, Free Library of Philadelphia; J. S. Miles, *A Historical Sketch of Roxborough, Manayunk and Wissahickon*, Philadelphia, 1940, p. 89.

the population of Roxborough Township had nearly doubled (from 3,334 to 5,797); and in the latter year, Manayunk secured independent political status as a borough, taking with it the bulk of the township's settlers.[21] Its mill workers were active in the union movements of the 1830s, striking in response to cuts in 1828–9 and repeating their generally unsuccessful resistance to additional reductions over the next six years.[22] Though the depression years were a poor time for activism, the late forties brought a revival of the ten-hour movement in which Manayunk operatives were leading figures. Experienced in Methodist Sunday schools and temperance societies, they helped mount a moral crusade for legislation limiting hours of work that resulted in a compromise statute in 1848. When the irascible Joseph Ripka refused compliance, his cotton spinners led a fruitless three week protest strike.[23] Though the economy again stumbled in 1849, the district in 1850 was host to twenty-four textile firms. Of the firms' 1,966 workers, three-quarters labored in the five core cotton mills arrayed along the Schuylkill Canal.[24]

Evidence for the rebirth of Germantown's textile reputation in the 1830s can first be seen in a report of local occupations for 1832. Among 1,024 "taxable inhabitants" are listed 38 weavers, 18 hosiers, 5 spinners, 5 dyers and bleachers, and 4 calico printers.[25] The weavers were engaged by the McCallum brothers, Scots-born carpet manufacturers, who began their Glen Echo mills in 1830 and employed "not more than twenty-five or thirty . . . hands in the first year or two."[26] The dyers and printers were connected with Ishichar Thorp's continuation of the printworks reported in 1820, and the hosiers formed the first installment of a transatlantic migration that would continue for half a century. Aaron Jones of Leicestershire was among the earliest of these, commencing business in 1830. He was soon joined by his son, who traveled to "country stores throughout the State in search of customers."[27] John Button, from the same English district, came to Germantown in 1832 to manufacture children's and men's hosiery, and by 1835 had erected a small building of his own to house his twenty-five knitters. Workers in these early firms, particularly Button's, often departed to form their own hosiery shops.[28]

21 *Hazard's Register of Pennsylvania*, vol. 8 (July 30, 1831), cited hereafter as *Hazard's Register;* Warner, *Private City*, p. 51; Miles, *Historical Sketch*, p. 90.
22 William Sullivan, *The Industrial Worker in Pennsylvania, 1800–1840*, Harrisburg, Pa., 1955, pp. 145–9.
23 Laurie, *Working People*, pp. 143–7.
24 See Tables 6.4 and 6.5.
25 *Hazard's Register*, vol. 9 (January 1832), p. 48.
26 Daniel Robson, ed., *Manufactories and Manufacturers of Pennsylvania of the Nineteenth Century*, Philadelphia, 1875, p. 500, cited hereafter as *M&MP*.
27 Ibid., p. 316.
28 Ibid., p. 255.

Glen Echo Carpet Mills, McCallum, Crease and Sloan, Germantown. A water-powered site, typical of mills along the Wissahickon and its tributaries, these mills contrast sharply with the clustered urban concentrations of firms in Manayunk and Kensington. (Free Library of Philadelphia)

In the next fifteen years, the number of Germantown hosiery firms reached twenty-one, their 771 operatives comprising 70% of all textile workers in the area. Though Button was experimenting with steam, shop and outwork hand methods were still standard at Germantown. Consistent with the Kensington pattern, independent spinners produced the special soft yarns that helped give "Germantown goods" their wide reputation.[29] No evidence of labor conflict for this period has come to light, perhaps in part a result of the dramatically better conditions for hosiers in Germantown than in the beleaguered English knitting districts from which they had come. Further, in contrast to Manayunk, where in 1850 male cotton-mill workers averaged $17.22 per month in wages, Germantown's male knitters received $23.40, over a third more.[30] Steady work at a fair price and the potential for workers to commence on their own account in a small way may have been the keys to labor peace. By midcentury, Charles Spencer, another Leicestershire emigrant to Germantown (1843), had joined Button in the attempt to marry steampower and knit-goods production. In recounting the trajectory

[29] See Tables 6.4 and 6.5.
[30] Calculated from 1850 MCS, Philadelphia Co., Germantown Borough and Township and Manayunk Borough. The returns for all twenty-one hosiers and the five all-cotton Manayunk factories supplied full data on monthly payrolls.

of Spencer's entrepreneurship later, a Germantown example will be added to earlier discussions of Manayunk and Kensington firms.

A few comments on those firms that persisted from 1820 through the 1850 Manufacturing Census will complete this overview. Thirty years after the 1820 manuscript schedules were compiled, at least seven of the original thirty-nine Philadelphia firms remained in business. (A handful of handloom shops in 1850 were run by men with surnames matching those of 1820 operators, but these tenuous links were excluded.) A compressed comparison of their situations reflected in census returns appears in Table 5.1.

This tiny pool of information will not bear extended analysis, to be sure, but several features of the Philadelphia textile manufacture do surface here. The formation and dissolution of partnerships has involved four of the seven firms (Kershaw, Thorp and Siddal, Craige, Maxwell), and three others have moved within the city (Thorp and Siddal, Maxwell, Ripka). The greatest gains were charted not by the two firms that possessed sizable capitals and elite connections in 1820 (Craige and McCallmont) but by two immigrant millmen (Whitaker and Ripka). In three cases, family successions occurred (Craige, Whitaker, and Ripka, the last adding his sons to the firm).[31]

The patterns evident in 1820 persist and extend in later years. The predominance of immigrant capitalists and the retention of handloom production proved to be key material and cultural elements in the structuring of the Philadelphia textile system. Although factory-based manufacture grew steadily, the role of outwork handcraft in the accumulation process in both hosiery and carpets reached forward into the eighties, paralleling its function on cottons in the earlier period. This evolving structure, taken in its unfolding totality, constituted the Philadelphia alternative to Lowell gigantism.

Joseph Ripka: from workshop to factory master

By 1850 Manayunk had become synonymous with factory textile production in the Philadelphia region. About 6,000 residents populated the Upper and Lower wards, political divisions of the borough dating from its 1840 charter. Textile mills shared the canalbank with foundries and paper factories. Seventeen textile firms formed the manufacturing core, drawing daily more than 2,000 workers from the hillside rowhouses and adjacent Penn and Roxborough townships. A third of those workers filed into one complex, the Ripka mills. Most textile factories in nineteenth-century Philadelphia had characteristic names that endured as their occupants changed. In 1820 the

---

31 1850 Population Census Schedules, Philadelphia Co., District 13, p. 24; cited hereafter as PCS.

Table 5.1. *Capital, work force, and district of persistent textile firms, Philadelphia, 1820–50*

Firm 1820	Firm 1850	Capital 1820	Capital 1850	Work force, 1820	Work force, 1850	District 1820	District 1850
Globe mills (Craige)	Multiple mills in dissolution and T. H. Craige	$130,000	$75,000	200	100	Kensington	same
George McCallmont	same	80,000	70,000	91	102	Bristol Township	same
James Kershaw	Jones and Kershaw	9,000	42,000	39	46	Blockley	same
Henry Whitaker	William Whitaker	8,550	50,000	21	54	Oxford Township	same
Thorp & Siddal	Isichar Thorp	8,000	10,000	6	30	Bristol Township	Germantown
James Maxwell	McMakin & Maxwell	3,500	15,000	35	105	Moyamensing	Lombard Ward (12th & South)
Joseph Ripka	Joseph Ripka	3,500	400,000	13	682	Northern Liberties	Manayunk
			90,000		61		Lower Dublin Township

Source: Manuscript Manufacturing Census Schedules, Eastern District, Pa., Philadelphia County, 1820, 1850.

Globe, Wakefield, Crescent, Branchtown, Cedar Dale, and Adelphi were all identified by their mill names in the census schedules. Mill builders used more fanciful and patriotic titles later in the century: Washington, Madison, Arcola, Cohoesink, Frogmore, Lanark, and so forth.[32] Ripka was different, a hard, arrogant, prideful, self-made man whose icy presence dominated Manayunk for a quarter century. There was never a hint of romance about him – his buildings were not christened with names that recalled his Silesian childhood or his later sojourn in France; they were simply No. 1, No. 2, and No. 3.

The career of Joseph Ripka will serve as a useful bridge to connect several aspects of the structure of the industry, insofar as he made a transition from handloom shopman to mill-space renter and thence to the extremity of large-scale factory production achieved in the city before the Civil War. His massive complex by 1850 had reached capital, work-force, and output levels comparable to a number of the Lowell corporations. Yet the fact that Ripka ran aground in the Panic of 1857 and failed completely with the onset of the war suggests the limits to which the Lowell model could be followed at Philadelphia, amid a complex of rather different productive relations. It is just because Ripka was so *un*characteristic in some critical respects that his rise and collapse are especially worthy of review.

Like so many of Philadelphia's textile capitalists, Ripka was an immigrant. Born in Austrian Silesia in 1788 and apprenticed from a farming family to the weaver's trade at age 12, he became a journeyman five years later and worked at his craft until about 1807, when he fled to urban Vienna to evade conscription in his hometown. Two years later, "fearing the vigilance of the military authorities," Ripka moved on to Switzerland, then France, and finally Spain, from which he sailed for America before 1816.[33] While at Lyons, he learned the basics of the silk trade, which he would apply in his new homeland.

Ripka had joined the common man's version of the Grand Tour to avoid, both in Austria and France, the perils of war and long terms of forced service, a trek embarked upon by thousands of Continental Europeans throughout the century. It is easily forgotten that one liberty to which "free-born Englishmen" could point with pride was the absence of conscription in the island kingdom. However, on the mainland, whereas the prosperous, for

---

32 The continuity of factory names facilitates tracing a succession of occupants and documenting space sharing. Of special value is Joyce Post's *Index* to the Hexamer Insurance surveys, a set of more than 2,500 lithographs and engravings of Philadelphia and regional factories made between 1865 and 1900. See Joyce Post, *A Consolidated Name Index to the Hexamer General Surveys*, Free Library of Philadelphia, Philadelphia, 1974.

33 George Kennedy, *Roxborough, Wissachickon and Manayunk in 1891*, Philadelphia, 1891, p. 99.

the most part, could buy exemptions, the lower classes could choose either service with its mortal risks and certainty of blocked expectations, a fugitive life in their native land (such as Ripka led in Vienna), or emigration, itself an illegal act that led to an unknowable future. Ripka had to make this final choice twice, and the extent to which those experiences of vulnerability and powerlessness shaped his later dour acquisitiveness is worth pondering. His ethnic background made Ripka an outsider among textile manufacturers in antebellum Philadelphia. Even by 1850, only four of the fifty or so larger textile manufactories were owned by German-born capitalists.[34] His cultural distance from a principally British and Irish work force was equally considerable and surely fed the tangible bitterness that burst into the open in the 1830s.

In 1816, as a new immigrant, Ripka was alone, but he carried with him the accomplished handcraftsman's traditional skills. Arriving in Philadelphia, he "built a hand-loom" and operated as a solitary weaver, "wheeling his goods in a barrow to the Market Street merchants."[35] Soon, acquiring additional looms, he rented warehouse space in Old City and became an employer of labor. Ripka penned his own account of the years 1816–20 at the foot of his census schedule.

> In 1816 and 17 had 12 Looms in operation and 14 Men, 6 Women and 6 Girls employed, annual wages $6344, the demand moderate. In 1818 and 19 the manufactures were so stagnated that I had only 4 Looms in operation, 4 Men, 2 Women and 2 Girls employed – annual wages amounted to $1200.[36]

The comparable 1820 figures noted elsewhere on the schedule were six looms in operation staffed by seven men, three women, and three "girls," evidence that Ripka was sharing in the gradual recovery mentioned by several other Philadelphia textile men. The wages paid these thirteen workers totaled $1,968 in the census year.

Additional data from the return allow a very rough estimate of Ripka's gross return from the year's production. He used 10,400 pounds of yarn at 35¢ per pound ($3,640) and paid in wages and contingent expenses $2,018, for a total outlay of $5,658. The average value of the four cotton staples woven in his shop was 22¾¢ per yard, with a pound of yarn yielding about three yards of cloth. This somewhat arbitrary calculation would provide a gross value of products of just over $7,000 (31,000 yards), leaving Ripka about $1,400 from which to pay rent, support himself, and add to his capital.

---

[34] The others were Joseph Solms, Martin Landenberger, and William Horstmann. None of them appears to have been of Polish-Austrian background.

[35] Kennedy, *Roxborough*, p. 99.

[36] 1820 MCS, Eastern District, Pa., no. 656.

Even if rent consumed half that figure, the shop master would retain a sum three times larger than the $200 that an adult male weaver could expect as his recompense for a year's effort. Frugal living and diligent accumulation could build the financial reserves for expansion, even starting from the modest base these figures indicate.

Though he may have constructed his first looms himself, Ripka soon enlisted the services of Alfred Jenks, the city's premier textile machinery maker, to produce handlooms for cottonades and cotton lace.[37] It was evidently to meet the expanding demand for the former and to introduce production of a mixed cotton-wool fabric called "rouen Cassimere, an article of pantaloon stuffs,"[38] that he moved his operations into the warehouse on Poplar Street. The twenties proved an enormously prosperous time for Ripka. By 1828 he had rented the third floor of Charles Hagner's Manayunk mill, with its "machinery for spinning worsted yarns,"[39] a component of the cassimere blend. At about the same time he installed powerlooms for cotton production at a waterpowered mill in the far northeast corner of the county, while continuing handloom production at the Old City facility,[40] selling directly from a warehouse recently rented in the Front Street commercial district. In 1829 Ripka leased part of another Manayunk mill, that of Joseph McDowell, bringing handlooms into operation near his spinning plant.[41] This arrangement continued for five years, but the purchase of a millsite in 1830 clearly showed that Ripka regarded erection of his own mill as the next step. For $1,225, he secured from Captain John Towers a lot running three hundred feet along the canalbank.[42] The next year Ripka leased a small amount of waterpower from the Schuylkill Navigation Company; for fifty inches of flow, about 9 horsepower, he was assessed $300 per year.[43] Though some sources give 1828 as its construction date, Mill No. 1, six

---

[37] John Thomas Scharf and Thompson Westcott, *History of Philadelphia*, Philadelphia, 1884, pp. 2253, 2317.

[38] J. L. Bishop, *A History of American Manufactures from 1608 to 1860*, Philadelphia, 1868, vol. II, p. 253.

[39] Charles Hagner, *Early History of Falls of Schuylkill, Manayunk, . . .*, Philadelphia, 1869, p. 71.

[40] Bishop, *History of American Manufactures*, vol. II, p. 253.

[41] *M&MP*, p. 465.

[42] Goshow, "Mills and Mill Owners," p. 20.

[43] Hagner, *Early History*, p. 78. An inch of flow was calculated as the amount of water that would pass through a one-square-inch opening. According to figures given in an 1832 article on Manayunk waterpower (*Hazard's Register*, vol. 9 [1832], p. 158), one horsepower represented 6⅓ inches. The total waterpower available in Manayunk at that date was 332 horsepower, two-thirds of which was rented to cotton factories. One cotton mill listed as "Unknown" in this article may be the Ripka factory under construction. The rate for its 100-inch power, the same as that in the first Ripka agreement, was $6 per inch per year, a rate established in the later twenties for new firms.

stories tall and 94 by 45 feet, was most likely not erected until the above arrangements had been completed, say, 1831–2.[44]

While this Manayunk enterprise was taking wing, Ripka had developed by 1832 an impressive works in the far northeast, adding the Pennypack Print Works to the cotton mill already in operation. The two waterpowered facilities were listed in the *McLane Report* of that year. The Ripka weaving mill at Holmesburg employed 100 workers to produce 750,000 yards of cotton goods annually. It reported capital of $90,000, of which $25,000 was invested in plant and machinery, with the remainder identified as "cash capital," which probably represents some combination of the wage fund, raw materials reserve, and retained earnings. The Pennypack Print Works was the largest in the district, with 80 workers and a capital of $160,000 ($70,000 in plant and machinery, $90,000 "cash").[45] It printed 3 million yards annually, four times the output of Ripka's weaving operation, likely using goods from his Poplar Street and Manayunk mills as well as stuffs purchased from other producers or printed on contract.

No source mentions partners or borrowing; indeed, the exact mechanism by which Ripka rose in twelve years from an investment of $3,500 in a handloom shop to become possessor of at least $100,000 worth of plant and machinery is nowhere given in detail. Several elements in his accumulation strategy may be inferred indirectly. As Ripka was a sole proprietor, with neither partners nor dividend-hungry shareholders to satisfy, he could plow back virtually all his mills' profits into expansion year after year and still live in relative comfort. Second, selling directly from his Front Street warehouse saved commission charges, adding to the profit margins otherwise available. Third, his specialties, cottonades, printed cloths, and cassimeres, were moving into an expanding market in the twenties, and no great economic reversal would strike the economy until 1837. Fourth, from his frequent conflicts with workers, Ripka can be seen as a "grinder," cutting wages at every opportunity, resisting calls for increases with tenacity, fining workers, and withholding pay – all to his own accumulative advantage. Finally, his early heavy use of power looms allowed the employment of women and girls at minimal wages, increasing output and lowering the per-yard labor cost.

One additional "cultural" element that may have fitted Ripka's accumulation strategy remains. About 1823, when his handlooms were still located in Northern Liberties, the 35-year-old manufacturer married. His bride,

[44] *M&MP*, p. 411.

[45] Louis McLane, *Report of the Secretary of the Treasury, 1832. Documents Relative to the Manufactures in the United States*, 3 vols., 22d Cong., 1st sess., H. Doc. 308 (Washington, D.C., 1833), vol. III, p. 196, 200–1. McLane's survey asked for the "capital invested in ground and buildings, and water power, and in machinery" and the average amount in materials, and in cash for the purchase of "materials, and payment of wages."

"Miss Kate Geiger, of Germantown," was the daughter of a family established in Pennsylvania since well before the turn of the century. Marriage for access to capital was hardly unknown and may have entered into this decision. Catherine Ripka, about 30 at the time of their marriage, bore her husband five sons and four daughters, the youngest, Emma, delivered when her mother was 43 (1837).[46]

By 1830 Joseph Ripka had become visible across the city at large, though only in matters pertaining to the textile manufacture. Unlike the Craiges and Samuel Comly, he was not active on even the fringes of elite society, with its charitable traditions. Instead, he may be found involved with the Silk Society, formed in 1829 to promote the domestic culture of silkworms "among the Farmers, whose families can attend to it, . . . without interfering with their usual occupations."[47] Ripka was a member of the Acting Committee whose report of January 1, 1830, revealed early discouragement and frustration. Though the society had offered "more than double the real value of the best cocoons" for locally produced "parcels," the quality of the cocoons submitted was "so bad, that the purchase of them was declined."[48]

The silk craze continued for a few years, and Ripka evidently retained his interest. In 1831 he submitted a sample of black silk to the annual competition held by the Franklin Institute, an exhibition designed to encourage domestic manufacture through awards and publicity for producers who could meet the Board of Managers' exacting standards.[49] Ripka's silk gained an honorable mention rather than a medal, for it fit none of the precise categories announced by the committee. Although Ripka's experience as a Lyons silk weaver no doubt influenced his interest, he never ventured into commercial silk manufacture. The speculative interest in the American production of raw silk faded after the 1837 Panic, and the vision of silk as a second American "grand staple" slipped gradually away.[50] For the next century, until rayon ("artificial silk") destroyed the trade, American silk manufacture would rely on imported raw materials.

During the early thirties, Ripka continued to display his craft virtuosity in the Franklin Institute competitions, winning a silver and a gold medal in 1830 and 1833, respectively. On the first occasion, he drew praise for establishing the "manufacture of Leno in this city," leno being a complex open-

---

46 Kennedy, *Roxborough*, p. 101; 1850 PCS, Philadelphia Co., District 13, p. 24. Kennedy gives the date of the marriage as "about" 1830, but this is implausible, as the 1850 census lists the couple's eldest son as 27 years old. The second and third sons were born in 1826 and 1829 if the ages on the schedules are accurate.
47 *Hazard's Register*, vol. 4 (1829), p. 223.
48 Ibid., vol. 5 (1830), pp. 26–7.
49 Ibid., vol. 6 (1830), p. 321; vol. 8 (1831), p. 307.
50 See L. P. Brockett, *The Silk Industry in America*, New York, 1876, pp. 35–46.

work fabric calling for two sets of warp and "used for dresses."[51] These were fine stuffs, handloom products at the specialty end of the fabric spectrum. In 1833 the institute awarded Ripka a gold medal for his Canton crepe and Cantoon cord, "exceedingly good imitations of the foreign article."[52] Again specialty goods, the Canton crepe was a fabric "having a crinkly surface" with "light cross-ribs, highly finished" and the Cantoons were tough cotton corduroys "used for riding breeches, etc."[53] These entries, exhibiting complex fabrics representing the extremes of delicate and sturdy construction, confirmed Ripka's mastery of the weaving trades. It is likely that his handloom shop was devoted to such fancy work, while the power-loom mills hammered out thousands of yards of staples for printing at the Pennypack works. As noted earlier, power looms for weaving simple checks were just being introduced in 1830, whereas lenos, crepes, and Cantoons surely were still the preserve of craft workers. Ripka of course profited significantly from his combination of the two productive formats.

It should not be imagined that the Franklin Institute competitions were confined to local talent. In 1831 a premium was awarded to the Middlesex Company of Lowell for a cotton-wool cassimere, and the Lowell Company drew a silver medal for its display of ingrain and Brussels carpets. The latter award was not unqualified, however, as the exhibition judges often scolded manufacturers along with commending their efforts. The Lowell Company's carpets were refused the gold medal, and allowed a silver instead, because the raw wool for warps had been imported rather than secured from domestic sources.[54] The contrast between the Lowell pattern and Ripka's awards is significant. The corporations were seeking to perfect the staples that would form the backbone of their output for half a century, whereas Ripka was busily introducing a series of new and sophisticated fabrics as one element in a more complex productive strategy. Both were succeeding.

Though Ripka may have exercised his craft skills and imagination with fabric innovations, he ran his Manayunk mills with a harshness that both revealed his fundamental commitment to profit and sparked repeated protests and strikes in the thirties. Ripka was by no means alone in his tough work rules and sharp wage cuts, as textile factory operators elsewhere in the city (and even at Pittsburgh) had similar reputations.[55] But as his was the largest mill at Manayunk (300 hands and 224 looms in 1834),[56] his actions

51 *Hazard's Register*, vol. 6 (1830), p. 321; Louis Harmuth, *Dictionary of Textiles*, New York, 1924, p. 93.
52 *Hazard's Register*, vol. 12 (1833), p. 355.
53 Harmuth, *Dictionary*, pp. 32, 45.
54 *Hazard's Register*, vol. 8 (1831), p. 306.
55 See *Pennsylvania Senate Journal, 1837–38*, Harrisburg, Pa., 1838, vol. II, pp. 278–359.
56 Scharf and Westcott, *History of Philadelphia*, p. 2236.

likely signaled other operators to follow or risk suffering a competitive disadvantage. Sullivan cites several of the factory rules in force in Ripka's mills about 1833. The hours of work in the summer were from "sunrise to sunset" and in the winter from "sunrise to eight o'clock P.M." six days a week. To allow the machinery to be cleaned, the workday ended on Saturdays "one hour before sunset." A worker who was fifteen minutes late was fined one-fourth of a day's pay; absence beyond this led to a reduction "double in amount of the wages" for the hours or days lost. As elsewhere, smoking and drinking were banned, and it was "forbidden to carry into the factory, nuts, fruits, etc., books or paper."[57] These rules are noteworthy both for their stringency and for their attention to detail. The double-docking of two days' pay for one day's absence reflected Ripka's struggle with prefactory-era time discipline, aiming to crush the old ways without discharging workers. The goal was to make them adhere to the pace of the machinery, not to pack them off into the streets and leave the firm faced with filling their places. The fines system also added its measure to the balance sheet well beyond any effective production loss the offenses given might have occasioned. The specific banning of fruits and nuts may have sprung from an unrecorded incident, but the prohibition of books and paper calls immediately to mind the restrictions faced by contemporaneous Lowell girls who tended power looms.[58]

Long hours were one of the most debilitating conditions of factory labor; resistance to sunrise-to-sunset toil invigorated the two Pennsylvania ten-hour movements of the mid-thirties and late forties. When Ripka and his Manayunk colleagues added to this strain a 20% wage cut in 1833, canalside factory workers responded to their bosses' collusion with a mass turnout. This reduction, the third or fourth since 1828, brought into being the Manayunk Working People's Committee, which issued an appeal to the public on August 23, 1833. The workers decried their thirteen-hour days "at an unhealthy employment, where we never feel a refreshing breeze to cool us, overheated and suffocated as we are, . . . [in] an atmosphere thick with the dust and the small particles of cotton, which we are constantly inhaling to the destruction of our health, our appetite and strength." Along with previous cuts, wages had become so low that workers could save nothing. Thus any serious illness brought "the deepest distress, which often terminates in total ruin, poverty and pauperism." Asking "Are we not worthy of our hire?" the Manayunk strikers observed that rising profits did not bring increased wages and rejected bearing "all the burthen" of a downturn. Divided in the face of

---

[57] Sullivan, *Industrial Worker*, p. 34. The rules were published first in the *Germantown Telegraph*, November 6, 1833.

[58] Caroline Ware, *The Early New England Cotton Manufacture*, New York, 1931 (rpt., 1966). p. 255.

earlier reductions, they were now united, "roused to a sense of our oppressed condition," knowing "full well that the attempted reduction . . . is but the forerunner of greater evils, . . . which would terminate, if not resisted, in slavery."[59]

The strikers' eloquent and sensitive tract rings with the "shall we be slaves?" rhetoric familiar to readers of Dawley's account of Lynn shoemakers and Dublin's Lowell mill girls. Workers' sentiments reached the community through the columns of the weekly *Telegraph*, published in nearby Germantown. Its editors evidently had some doubts about the civic rectitude of the millmen and some sympathy for the operatives, for irate labor did not often have such access to the pages of local papers. Workers announced that "as the poor are sinking, the rich are rising." One letter writer inquired: "Are we so debased as to be afraid to assert our rights, the rights of freemen, to break the shackles of oppression?" Though the Bible taught that "he that will not work, neither let him eat," the lesson at Manayunk was different: "In the present state of society, it happens that many contrive to eat at the expense of those who work."[60] Though the outcome of the strike has not been established, the battle of words continued through the fall of 1833 in the *Telegraph*, with writers favorable and opposed to the factory owners energetically cudgeling one another.[61]

A renewed effort to reduce wages was mounted by Ripka in March 1834, joined this time by other textile men in Manayunk and Blockley Township (West Philadelphia). As might be expected, this conflict was more bitterly fought. Workers' manned picket lines and established relief organizations, and Ripka engaged strikebreakers and attendant "police" to protect them.[62] The planned reduction was 25% (another source gives 30%), but after a month of the turnout, one operator offered to amend it to 15% and was rebuffed. Shortly thereafter, Ripka induced several Protestant clergymen with Manayunk congregations to urge capitulation. At a public rally on May 9, 1834, the strikers, as "free citizens of this republic," condemned the masters and their guards' attempt at "bullying . . . the working people into a reduction of their wages." Ripka's clerical spokesmen were dismissed as those "from whom better might have been expected."[63] The end result was not decisive for either party, as many of the strikers left for jobs elsewhere, perhaps being refused reemployment, and those who returned to Ripka's

[59] John Commons ed., *Documentary History of American Industrial Society*, Cleveland, 1910, vol. V, pp. 330–2.

[60] Sullivan, *Industrial Worker*, p. 146. All quotes are from the *Germantown Telegraph*, August 28, 1833.

[61] Sullivan, *Industrial Worker*, pp. 146–7.

[62] Ibid., p. 147; Laurie, *Working People*, p. 93.

[63] Sullivan, *Industrial Worker*, pp. 147–8.

mill exacted a 5% *increase* over the previous rates.[64] Sources do not specify whether this increase was calculated on the rates prevailing before the announced cut or was merely a rollback of a fraction of the proposed reduction. In either case, to the workers of Manayunk, Joseph Ripka exemplified pitiless capital, grasping for profits by exploiting the poor.

In the Ripka strikes of the thirties, women workers played a public role, mindful of that of their Lowell counterparts. Charles Hagner, a Manayunk drug manufacturer whose mill was not involved in the conflicts, observed in 1837: "On occasions of the 'strikes' it is not an uncommon thing for the women and girls to assemble on the commons in public meeting, pass resolutions, and listen to the harangue of some one, the burthen of whose song is abuse of their unfortunate employer." Women and girls were adopting the forms and exercising the rights of "freemen," rights not theirs by law but instead embedded in that plebeian culture that Edward Thompson has evoked so persuasively for eighteenth-century England. That such events communicated an ethic of resistance to the younger generation also disturbed Hagner, for they were "bad schools" for children, "holding up examples before them which they are . . . too prone to follow."[65] Strikes could have no doubt a dubious effect on the morals of children, at least from a bourgeois viewpoint. Hagner's light touch of irony, "burthen of whose song," does not conceal his deeper disquiet. Turnouts brought into the open the quiet process by which worker antagonisms to their employers were sharpened and transmitted, and the key role of working-class women in this affair was disturbing to gentlemen and manufacturers who cherished other, more passive notions of the characteristics of "true womanhood." In the 1830s labor organizer John Ferral strove to include "women textile operatives" in his Philadelphia General Trades Union. He may well have done so not simply because they were factory workers but because they formed the most vigorous sector of Manayunk working-class resistance.[66]

The combination of rate cutting, use of powered machinery, and the production and direct sale of specialty goods along with staples enabled Ripka to accumulate reserves sufficient to erect a new factory at Manayunk (about 1835), spacious enough to house 600 power looms. This was Mill No. 2, six stories high and 160 by 45 feet,[67] which received a second visitation from outraged Kensington handloom cotton weavers. The "thirty-inch wide" looms installed by Ripka were capable of mass-producing the same varieties of goods generated by workers both inside and outside the shops on a greater scale than ever before undertaken in the city. Realization

---

[64] Ibid., p. 148; Laurie, *Working People*, p. 93.

[65] *Pennsylvania Senate Journal, 1837–38*, vol. II, p. 326.

[66] Laurie, *Working People*, p. 95.

[67] *M&MP*, pp. 411–2; Kennedy, *Roxborough*, p. 100.

of this threat to their livelihood induced "a large mob" to descend on the factory district "to destroy Mr. Ripka's mill and machinery." Informed of the approaching handweavers, the local militia was mobilized and the marchers "were stopped at the Falls of Schuylkill . . . and induced to go back."[68] Shortly thereafter Ripka acquired two additional mills adjacent to his manufacturing site, along with a number of additional houses.[69] He did not, with all this expansion, overextend his resources, for during the Panic of 1837 he laid off much of his work force and was "able to continue the operations of his many industrial establishments"[70] on a reduced scale.

Ripka did confront a different sort of crisis in 1837, however, when the labor practices of his Manayunk mills were questioned during the first investigation of child and factory labor by an American legislature. In response to a petition, the Pennsylvania Senate opened an inquiry to gather factory data relevant to a proposed statute that would have restricted the employment of children under 12. In hearings at Philadelphia and Pittsburgh, nearly fifty witnesses discussed textile manufacturing, the industry in which child labor was most extensive and notorious. The committee chairman observed that "in most occupations the apprenticing system prevails. In our factories there is no such thing; no indenture is executed to secure to the child its trade; no provision is made for its education. . . . Here is the point where legislative interposition seems to be necessary."[71] Testimony taken at Manayunk, and some of that recorded elsewhere in the Philadelphia area, revolved around the practices of the Ripka mills. The proprietor did not appear but forwarded written comments in reply to committee questions, which were printed as the last entry in the official report (1838).

The committee questioned a number of Ripka's employees, immigrant men brought up in the British textile trades. They all certified that the hours of work were too long for children and disputed both their master's calculation of the total hours in a week's work and his claim that "the labor for children is not excessive."[72] They reflected on British practices in their earlier experience and were generally critical of local conditions. Thomas Moseley, a woolen spinner, testified:

> I consider the operation of the factory system upon persons employed, is more oppressive in this country than in England. In the first place, they work longer hours here; in the next place, the climate here is not so congenial to health. I am from Yorkshire.

68 John Kendrick, "The Cotton Goods Industry of Pennsylvania," *Annual Report of the Secretary of Internal Affairs*, Part 3: Industrial Statistics, 1899, Harrisburg, Pa., 1900, p. 37.
69 Ibid., p. 411.
70 Ibid., p. 412.
71 *Pennsylvania Senate Journal, 1837–38*, vol. I, p. 325.
72 Ibid., vol. II, p. 358.

Thomas Siddal, a carder, reported:

> I consider the work of piecers here, at the mule, greater than in England, although here the children attend but one mule; the reason is, that the work in England is much better prepared and requires less piecing.[73]

In his own comments on child workers, Ripka undertook to show that his employment of them derived from a simple benevolence distant from any tinge of profit seeking:

> I employ twenty-five children under twelve years of age, and they are pressed upon me by widows or by mothers of dissipated husbands (sic), and when I employ them it is for mere charity than anything else. Children under twelve years of age are of no profit to the employers in cotton factories, it is the age when they ought to be educated and I have always been against to employ them.[74]

Having shifted the responsibility to the families of child workers, he continued, cooly: "I never heard the parents to ask or wish for any abridgement of any of the hours of labor. . . . If the hours of labor were shortened, the wages would have to be reduced in proportion; but I cannot say what desire the parents may have to that effect."[75] The assertion that small children were "of no profit" was rubbish, as piecers were absolutely essential to the successful operation of spinning mules, and bobbin boys and girls performed necessary throstle tasks at rates cheaper than those of older workers.[76]

In his statement, Ripka also delivered an extended tirade against unions, reflecting on his recent conflicts. The only "evil in the factory system," he asserted, was the "Trades' Union, which has been . . . imported to this country by English and Irish men within a few years." The leaders are "either of low character or designing politicians," who keep the work force stirred up while taking their money to travel about making speeches. Workers did not need unions to find jobs in prosperous years, and "in hard times, the Trades' Union cannot keep up wages or find employment for the working classes. If they could do it, why don't they do it at the present time."[77] Ripka's final comment was timely, for the 1837 Panic crippled the labor movement in Philadelphia as manufacturers cut wages freely while laying off hundreds of workers. His own mills normally operated with a force of more

---

[73] Ibid., p. 316, 313.

[74] Ibid., p. 358.

[75] Ibid.

[76] For production details, see the excellent summary in Anthony F. C. Wallace, *Rockdale*, New York, 1978, pp. 137–47. The higher cost of older workers was confirmed by a number of the witnesses who testified before the committee.

[77] *Pennsylvania Senate Journal, 1837–38*, vol. II, pp. 357–8.

than 400, but in his May 21, 1837, deposition, Jeremiah Wilkinson admitted that "at present, there are not fifty persons employed at Mr. Ripka's mills."[78] The layoffs had been recent, for Ripka in his letter dated May 25 gave an employment total of 409 "when the mills are going on full work, as they have been four weeks ago." Placed in this context, the proprietor's challenge to the unions (Why don't they do it?) voiced the smug self-satisfaction of the powerful regarding a now-floundering antagonist. He had dismissed seven-eighths of his workers; let the Trades Union get them positions now.

Arbitrary firings and manufacturers' abuse of the held-back wages rule were mentioned at several points in the hearings. Ripka was specified as an example of such practices by Samuel Ogden, whose four daughters had worked as power-loom tenders for the Manayunk factory master. All four had been fired without notice, Ripka not having voiced "any real or alleged complaint against . . . any of them." Ogden also related the experience of a neighbor's daughter who had quit her position in the Ripka mills. As she had not provided the proprietor with "notice of her intention," he "withheld the whole of the wages due her, and told her he never would pay her." Though she gained a favorable court judgment through a lawsuit, Ripka had still refused payment, confirming Odgen's assertion "that the work people . . . seldom obtain their withheld wages from arbitrary employers by law means."[79] The Ogden family left Manayunk for work in Kensington's Globe Mill in the wake of these incidents.

Charles Hagner provided the most thoughtful and extensive review of the factory system provoked by the Senate investigation. Beginning with the production of "oil and . . . drugs" about 1820, Hagner commenced the manufacture of satinets (a coarse woolen stuff) in part of his mill three years later, as usual with power looms constructed by Alfred Jenks.[80] By the late twenties, Hagner concentrated his efforts on drug manufacture, renting his upper floors and equipment to a series of entrepreneurs, the last of whom was Joseph Ripka.[81] In the thirties, he was no longer "interested" in any financial way in textile production but was aware of the daily activities of that Manayunk operator around which so much controversy swirled.

An observer of strikes in Manayunk since the early twenties, Hagner offered a review of the manner in which they were spawned, both as wages lagged against prices during inflationary periods and as they were often cut immediately when the demand for goods fell. The end product of this cycle was a deep antagonism:

[78] Ibid., p. 320.
[79] Ibid., p. 297.
[80] Kennedy, *Roxborough*, pp. 26–7; Hagner, *Early History*, p. 70.
[81] Hagner, *Early History*, p. 71.

> The employer, generally speaking, cares little for the workers or their
> welfare; and they have little regard for him or his interests; he contracts
> with them to do a certain amount of work; they do it to the letter of the
> agreement – not one jot more. On pay day, he pays them to the last cent,
> and here ends all communication between them.[82]

Given this, together with the instability of markets and the pace of changing
technology, Hagner concluded that he would not take a cotton mill as a gift.

Clearly sympathetic to factory laborers, Hagner pressed for state action to
control the employment of children and the hours of labor for all. Marketplace competition encouraged individual masters to stretch the workday,
as in large factories "the additional labor of one hour . . . is an important
item, and offers great temptations to the employer, to overwork his hands."[83]
His high regard for mill workers was a sharp contrast to Ripka's vision of a
dumb herd led astray by "designing politicians." The factories held "many
worthy, remarkably intelligent and well-informed workmen" who

> generally understand the exciting causes of the difficulties they often
> labor under, much better than their employers; and in numerous in-
> stances are possessed of far more good sense . . . ; but unfortunately
> they are in humble life and have no power to correct the evils they see
> and feel.[84]

Nothwithstanding the testimony of Hagner, all the workmen, several physi-
cians, and a few manufacturers in favor of regulation, the state inquiry
produced no new statutes. When his mill burned in 1839, Hagner abandoned Manayunk to relocate on Pegg Street in the city.[85]

Joseph Ripka remained dominant. In 1840 his name headed a petition to
the state legislature that secured the incorporation of Manayunk as a borough. Joseph Ripka became the first town burgess the same year, leading the
local government as he did the riverside economy.[86]

The next fifteen years brought Ripka's enterprise to its peak. Between
1840 and 1850, he became reputedly "the largest cotton manufacturer in the
United States,"[87] with more than 1,000 "hands" in his scattered works,
marketing his goods directly "all over the country, especially through Mex-
ico, Texas, and the Southern States."[88] In 1849–50, his mills at Manayunk

---

[82] *Pennsylvania Senate Journal, 1837–38*, vol. II, p. 323.
[83] Ibid., p. 327.
[84] Ibid., p. 328.
[85] Hagner, *Early History*, p. 101.
[86] Miles, *Historical Sketch*, p. 90.
[87] This surely refers to proprietary firms, for the New England corporations of that period
were in some cases more extensive. Ripka's reported capital in 1850 was $490,000; the
investments of several Lowell firms were more than double that figure.
[88] Kennedy, *Roxborough*, pp. 100–1.

alone used just over a million pounds of raw cotton, spinning and dyeing it on the site. The output was a single staple, more than 3 million yards of "Pantiloon stuffs," whose value was 12¢ per yard. Ripka provided precise figures, rather than the rounded approximations so common in census schedules (3,245,732 yards, total value: $389,487), again allowing rough calculation of his costs and surplus. Monthly wages appear as $9,225 for the mill's 682 workers. Though few mills ran year round, if this maximum assumption is made, the annual sum for wages would just top $110,000. Expenses for cotton, dyes, sizing flour, and fuel totaled $179,680, leaving about $100,000 as a residual. From this amount, rent for water power, insurance, any repairs and machinery costs, marketing expenses, and taxes would be deducted. While there are no records to give us these figures, Ripka's annual income was surely enviable.[89] The accumulated result of production on this scale allowed Ripka to report real property of $200,000 to the 1850 Population Census marshal and to include three servants and a coachman in his household.[90]

More important than the figures was the change in productive focus. By 1850 Ripka had evidently abandoned the manufacture of the specialty goods for which he had drawn commendations in the 1830s. Here, again, he approximated the Lowell pattern, narrowing the use of his enormous facilities to produce a single product line, largely for the southern market. This exposed him, as it did the Lowell mills, to later reverses, which were made more serious by the gathering rigidities inherent in such a strategy. Having discarded the flexibility for which he was earlier noted, Ripka created a manufacturing structure ill-suited to rapid modification in the face of the cotton famine.

Like other proprietary entrepreneurs, Joseph Ripka arranged to pass his mills on to family members. By the early fifties, he had taken two of his four sons, Joseph and Albert, into partnership and had welcomed to his household and business a nephew from Silesia, Andreas Hartel. The latter arrived in Philadelphia in 1848, the year Ripka's fourth son, Andrew, was sent off to begin his college career at Princeton University. Andrew Ripka remained there but a single year, returning home to enroll at the University of Pennsylvania.[91] By 1850 Andrew had withdrawn from Penn to become a clerk in his father's factory.[92] Two years later came the first blow; Ripka's eldest son Joseph died at the age of 29. Ripka, then 64, moved his family into the "splendid mansion" young Joseph had constructed and lived there for the

---

[89] 1850 MCS, Philadelphia Co., p. 85.
[90] 1850 PCS, Philadelphia Co., District 13, p. 24.
[91] Goshow, "Mills and Mill Owners," p. 28. Although Andrew did not graduate, his death was reported in the alumni register.
[92] 1850 PCS, Philadelphia Co., District 13, p. 24.

rest of his life.[93] In the same year (1852), Ripka transferred the operation of his Pennypack Print Works to Hartel (then 24) and Andrew (22).[94] After Andrew's return to the Manayunk firm in 1857, Hartel continued to run the works, first as a partnership (Williams and Hartel, 1860) and later as sole proprietor into the 1880s.[95] Ripka's succession was thus arranged, with his surviving sons Albert, Robert, and Andrew at Manayunk and his nephew Hartel at Holmesburg.

Though Hartel prospered, Ripka lived to witness the collapse of his Manayunk plans. Marketing his own goods, he had long been in the position of extending sizable credit to purchasers. No commission house guaranteed the payment of these notes, as was the common practice at the large New England mills. When the 1857 Panic broke, Ripka was pressed hard by defaults, as his operations of sales "agencies" in "all the principal cities" meant that bad news arrived from every direction.[96] Robson stated simply that Ripka "was ruined by non-payment of debts due to him."[97] Stunned perhaps, but not yet ruined. Reorganizing his affairs, he commenced again after a time. By 1860 the firm had recovered its momentum, reporting to the census 900 looms, 100 carding machines, 21,000 spindles, and 696 workers at the Manayunk mills. The capital had been reduced from the 1850 figure of $400,000 to $350,000, perhaps reflecting no new investment and some depreciation. Output was almost identical to 1850, a bit over 3 million yards.[98]

The 1860 Population Schedules reveal that the patriarch still reported real and personal property of $200,000, had a retinue that included a coachman, gardener, clerk, and four Irish servants and that his three partner-sons still resided unmarried (aged 34, 30, and 28) under his roof.[99] Another nephew, Francis Ripka (45), and his wife and six children had migrated from Austria to join the clan in 1857 and were housed nearby. Toward them Joseph held a special obligation, for it was Francis's father (and Joseph's brother), Franz, who had been taken instead by the military after Ripka's flight from conscription fifty years earlier.[100] Three lodgers boarded with the new arrivals, a weaver and two factory operatives, and both Francis and his eldest son were likewise listed as "Fac'y op."[101] It is possible that they all

93 Kennedy, *Roxborough*, p. 101.
94 *M&MP*, p. 103.
95 1860 MCS, Philadelphia Co., p. 497; Lorin Blodget, *The Textile Industries of Philadelphia*, Philadelphia, 1880, p. 17.
96 Bishop, *History of American Manufactures*, vol. II, p. 283 (note).
97 *M&MP*, pp. 411–2.
98 1860 MCS, Philadelphia Co., p. 474.
99 1860 PCS, Philadelphia Co., Ward 21, p. 82.
100 Goshow, "Mills and Mill Owners," pp. 24–5.
101 1860 PCS, Philadelphia Co., Ward 21, p. 82.

worked in the Ripka mills; another source places the 16-year-old Francis Ripka, Jr., there as he "learned the business of cotton manufacturing in the mills of his great-uncle Joseph Ripka."[102] He had but little time to develop his skills, for the Civil War intervened and destroyed the firm.

Ripka had long depended heavily on southern markets for the sale of his cotton goods and on southern producers for his raw materials. The threat of war left him doubly imperiled. Perception of the imminent disaster perhaps accounts for Ripka's appearance on December 13, 1860, at a huge rally in the city aimed at staving off the coming division. He was named one of perhaps two hundred vice-presidents for the day and was accompanied by four other major cotton factory masters who must have shared his apprehensions (Archibald Campbell, David F. Brown, William Divine, and General Robert Patterson).[103]

With war came the end of the Ripka mills, a second major shock in four years: "The war having caused the ruin of his southern customers and entail[ing] a loss upon him of a quarter of a million dollars, he was forced into bankruptcy, and the mills closed."[104]

He died in January 1864 at the age of 75. Francis Ripka, Jr., went on to the mills of Archibald Campbell, where he became superintendent.[105] Andrew served in the 119th Pennsylvania Infantry as an officer during the war and was discharged "for disability" in 1863. He left the textile trades, and Manayunk too, turning "to mining and manufacture of iron, in which he was engaged for many years."[106] He died in Massachusetts just after the turn of the century. General Patterson, who was active in cotton production in Delaware and Chester counties, acquired the Ripka mills and reopened them. He evidently also sought Ripka's old markets, as Bishop notes: "After the close of the war, . . . General Patterson made another important contribution to the nation's prosperity by loaning freely to Southern planters on liberal credits to enable them in developing their shattered resources."[107] Patterson, an immigrant like his predecessor (born County Tyrone, Ireland, 1792), carried on the mills into his eighties, and his "Estate" was still running them in 1882 at the time of Blodget's citywide industrial census.[108]

[102] Horace Platt and William Lawton, *Freemasonry in Roxborough . . . , 1813–1913*, Philadelphia, 1913, p. 208. Francis Ripka, Jr., was later master of Lodge No. 135. The second son in this family was named for his great uncle and the youngest daughter (2 years old in 1850 and born after the family's arrival), Catherine, was named for her great-aunt, Joseph Ripka's American wife of nearly forty years.

[103] Scharf and Westcott, *History of Philadelphia*, pp. 28, 739.

[104] Kennedy, *Roxborough*, p. 101.

[105] Goshow, "Mills and Mill Owners," p. 58.

[106] Ibid., p. 28.

[107] Bishop, *History of American Manufactures*, vol. III, p. 52.

[108] Lorin Blodget, *Census of Manufactures of Philadelphia (1882)*, Philadelphia, 1883, p. 168.

Between his periods of military service in the 1812, Mexican, and Civil wars, Patterson amassed a sizable fortune from his mills and merchant connections.[109] His purchase of what remained of the Ripka assets likely set Andrew up in his mining ventures and provided for other heirs as well. As so often at Philadelphia, the entrepreneurs came and went, but the mills endured.

Ripka's Manayunk cotton factories were the closest approximation to the Lowell system undertaken in antebellum Philadelphia. They resembled the Massachusetts firms in the scale on which space and machinery was employed (multiple six-story mills, tens of thousands of spindles, etc.) and in the integration of all functions within the same firm's control. Their cotton staples were standardized products for a national market, their work force enormous, heavily female and increasingly immigrant in origin. When on strike in the thirties, their workers used the language of republican freemen and -women. The Civil War brought crisis both to Ripka and to Lowell, though ultimately with different results.

The contrasting fates of the Manayunk proprietor and the Massachusetts corporations in the war era are linked with the differences between Ripka and the Lowell firms. Direct marketing twice forced the Manayunk concern to absorb significant losses, ultimately leading to collapse. The family form of proprietorship, while it enabled the concentration of profits for many years, did not embrace outside managerial "expertise" with ease. Ripka's response to the 1857 debacle was simply to bring Andrew back from Holmesburg. Moreover, however closely knit, the family staff must have been strained to its limits in handling crises in an establishment of that scale. Having started as an immigrant with few financial resources or contacts, Ripka remained outside the merchant and banking elite, which played such a critical role in the fortunes of the Lowell corporations.

While both the corporations and the aging factory master were powerful in their communities, the former acted through agents from a distance, cushioning to some degree the weight of their influence. Ripka was personally visible, antagonistic, the center of sharp and repeated conflicts, triggered by his acts and embodying his power. The Lowell firms, by contrast, enjoyed relative labor peace, perhaps in part because their material force was combined with a managerial facelessness. The "modern" pattern, familiar in later labor–corporate struggles, was early established, as the agent acted on

---

[109] Before 1812, Patterson was trained "in the counting house of Edward Thompson, a leading merchant in Philadelphia" (*M&MP*, p. 413). His mills in Manayunk alone reported capital of $800,000 in 1870 (MCS, Philadelphia Co., p. 600). The collections of the Historical Society of Pennsylvania occupy a building on the site of Patterson's city mansion, at the corner of 13th and Locust streets, though no trace of his mills' operations are preserved among the wealth of materials in its collections.

orders of the treasurer, who was the servant of board, and the board was responsible after all to the shareholders. With power so bureaucratized and abstract, who was there to hate, to mobilize against, once Kirk Boott had passed from the Lowell scene?

A few years after the Civil War, Charles Hagner produced an account of early Manayunk, reviewing the men and women, mills and machines that had structured that industrial district. Near its close, Hagner penned a poignant paragraph on Joseph Ripka's funeral.

> Having but recently died, there are so many living in Manayunk familiar with his excellent qualities, that it seems superfluous to mention them. He was public spirited, liberal, and generous in everything tending to the improvement and good of the village, universally loved and respected by its citizens. The respect paid to his memory on the occasion of his funeral was a beautiful evidence of it, and will not soon be forgotten. All the mills, stores and shops were closed; the factory bells tolled, and hundreds of operatives, male and female, lined the street through which the melancholy procession passed. He left a host of friends and admirers to mourn his loss, and the termination of his valuable and useful life.[110]

Hagner may have been sincere in his effusions and fellow entrepreneurs may have mourned Ripka's passing, but facing the shuttered and bankrupt mills and reflecting on years of thirteen-hour days, the workers in Manayunk's streets may well have turned out with rather different emotions.

Charles Spencer and the Germantown hosiery trade

The narrative of Joseph Ripka's career has served both to exemplify ante-bellum factory textile production at Philadelphia and to bridge the gap between the manufacturing world of the 1820s and that of midcentury. Chronicling the development of Charles Spencer's Germantown hosiery mill will reinforce some elements of the accumulation matrix visible in the Ripka case and develop a number of contrasts to balance and extend our introduction to the patterns of textile production in the fifties. Whereas Manayunk showed the factory system in its Philadelphia incarnation, Germantown, like Kensington a center of outwork and handloom manufacture, was experiencing a revival of the eighteenth-century hosiery trade through the arrival of hundreds of British craftsmen. Whereas Ripka's story closed with the Civil War, Spencer's reaches beyond it into the eighties, with his wartime experience providing a key contrast to Ripka's collapse and Lowell's

---

[110] Hagner, *Early History*, pp. 71–2.

Charles Spencer, proprietor, Leicester Knitting Mills. (Free Library of Philadelphia)

suspension. Lacking the drama that accompanied Ripka's quest for dominion and his ultimate decline, Spencer's quiet accumulation process more adequately captures the experience and success of the city's textile capitalists.

Charles Spencer was brought up in a stockinger's world. Born June 21, 1821, in the Leicestershire village of Enderby, he moved with his father and family to Loughborough, in the same district, as they followed the erratic handwork trade. During the thirties, the family migrated to Nottingham, where William Spencer took up lace weaving. In 1835 Charles was "indentured . . . to a hosier," concluding his apprenticeship about 1840, only a year before his "master failed." As he had spent most of his learning years in the mercantile, rather than mechanical, end of the business, he soon found commercial employment where "he attained a knowledge of book-keeping."[111]

By 1842 his father had decided to emigrate. Charles dutifully joined the family; his brother William, Jr., arrived in America the following year. Like countless other English travelers, the family landed at New York and "the next day" proceeded to Philadelphia.[112] Charles obtained his first position as a bookkeeper to a downtown hat finisher, "at five dollars per week."[113]

[111] William Bagnall, "Textile Industries of the United States," vol. II typescript on microfiche, 1970, pp. 1346–8, Merrimack Valley Textile Museum, North Andover, Mass.; volume II of Bagnall's classic study; cited hereafter as "Textile Industries" (fiche).

[112] Ibid., p. 1351; *M&MP*, p. 33.

[113] *Biographical Encyclopedia of Pennsylvania*, Philadelphia, 1874, p. 165.

Table 5.2. *Charles Spencer's hosiery mill, Germantown, 1850–70*

	1850	1860	1870
Capital	$15,000	$175,000	$375,000
Work force	140	278	350
Value of products	$50,000	$250,000	$420,000
Total wages	$21,120[a]	$59,808	$90,000[b]
	(19,360)	(54,824)	
Wages as % of product value	42.2	23.9	21.4
	(38.7)	(21.9)	
Cost of raw cotton and wool yarn	$14,000	$102,000	$250,600
Cotton and wool as a % of product value	28.0	40.8	59.7

[a]The 1850 and 1860 Manufacturing Census Schedules give monthly wage figures, whereas the 1870 schedules give a yearly total. The upper figure represents twelve times the monthly wage; the lower figure in parentheses equals eleven times that number.
[b]In operation eleven months.
Source: Manuscript Manufacturing Census Schedules, Philadelphia County, 1850, 1860, 1870 (Germantown, 1850 MCS; Ward 22, 1860 and 1870 MCS).

After a year of this work, he took the $50 he had saved and commenced hosiery manufacture in a very small way, renting an upper floor in a Germantown building.[114]

The dimensions of his ultimate success may be roughly gauged from Table 5.2.[115] Here is accumulation fully as impressive as that mastered by Ripka a generation earlier, and from as humble beginnings. Yet, impressive as Spencer's 1870 capital may be, the tabular data cannot tell much about *how* he moved from assets of $50 in 1843 to $15,000 seven years later and thence to $175,000 in another decade's time. However, by relating "literary" materials to the matrix conception of accumulation, the elements of his strategy may be teased out of the data. Spencer, along with other Germantown hosiers, adapted the outwork system familiar to them from their English training to the task of generating capital for the erection of factories and gradually introduced powered manufacture in those brickworks, shifting to complex hand-knit goods that were not amenable to machine production. More than technology, of course, was involved; although Spencer and Ripka were different in time frame, notoriety, and conflict, in elements of firm organization, marketing, and the sequential use of space, they were both

[114] *M&MP*, p. 32.
[115] 1850 MCS, Philadelphia Co., p. 20; 1860 MCS, Philadelphia Co., p. 482; 1870 MCS, Philadelphia Co., p. 616.

participants in the broader Philadelphia format for capital accumulation in textiles.

In the 1840s Spencer traversed the now familiar path from rented rooms to mill construction. In October 1843 he "commenced operations" at Germantown, moving six months later to a building on Church Street in Franklinville. Late in 1844, the second site "having proved too small," he returned to his original Germantown location. Over the next four years, Spencer moved twice more, the second time to a former "flour mill," where he may have experimented with powered spinning. In 1850 he took the big step, buying a plot of land and erecting "a mill 75 × 35 feet."[116]

With five moves in seven years, Spencer qualifies as a classic peripatetic Philadelphia manufacturer, one of a group whose locational decisions, as Freedley noted, "have not generally been governed by any other than reasons of convenience and economy."[117] I suspect his first location was too large for his fledgling budget, leading him to other quarters that within a year proved too confining; the return to his first location was probably the initial step in spatial expansion. The mill built in 1850 was small; if four-storied, it would have enclosed but 10,000 square feet of floor space.[118]

Once having constructed his own building, Spencer remained at that site for the rest of his long manufacturing career. Over the next quarter century, regular additions to the plant eventually covered "about two acres." The first mill was taken out of service and recycled as a wool warehouse and two additional warehouses were erected, one for wool and another for yarn. Manufacturing by 1875 was carried on in two mills, four and five floors, respectively, and in "dye and bleaching houses, trim shops and all the necessary outbuildings."[119] Gradually, Spencer fully integrated production; having commenced with a few hand frames, he introduced spinning (500 spindles) in 1850 and by 1860 he was dyeing and finishing his own goods.[120] These developmental steps are analogous to the pattern apparent in the actions of other Philadelphia textile men and are the result of profits accumulated and reinvested over an extended period, a strategy to which the proprietary or partnership firm was admirably suited.

How was Spencer's production organized in 1850? What relations of production enabled him to amass sufficient capital to build his own mill at

---

[116] *M&MP*, pp. 32–3.

[117] Freedley, *Philadelphia and Its Manufactures*, pp. 250–1.

[118] 1850 MCS, Philadelphia Co., p. 20. See also stockingers' returns on page 21, which report yarn in small quantities at nearly $1 per pound and raw wool at from 35¢ to 60¢ per pound. Because of variations in grade of both wool and yarn these figures are only rough estimates.

[119] *M&MP*, p. 33.

[120] 1850 MCS, Philadelphia Co., p. 20; 1860 MCS, Philadelphia Co., p. 482.

The Germantown mills of Charles Spencer and Co., circa 1875. (Collection of Patricia O'Donnell)

the age of 29? Clues to the answers to these questions originate with the disproportion between Spencer's 1850 capital and the size of his work force. With only $15,000 invested, he employed 40 men and 100 women in the production of woolen hosiery, cravats, and "Fancy Goods." The connecting link is the mingling of hand-frame work in and out of the factory, saving capital while facilitating large-scale production. The out work system was standard in Nottingham where Spencer learned the hosiery manufacture. At 14, he was indentured to a warehouse-based hosier who put out yarn to independent knitters, men who worked "their frames at their homes," frequently miles from the warehouse. A master hosier's skills might be "wholly mercantile," as his commercial transactions necessitated but a sparse knowledge of the manufacturing techniques involved in stocking work. Spencer, trained in the warehouse, became a tradesman "without having learned the mechanical part of the business."[121]

Spencer's chances for success locally were quite limited, however, as the Nottingham hosiers seemed to have formed a closed fraternity that sought to block new entrants. Subcontract work from the masters was available to new firms, but the old core controlled the marketing channels. These subcontractors were widely despised, for they were prone to grind and cheat their workers. They provided frames to poor cottagers, the middlemen's income being derived from a host of charges deducted from the customary

[121] Bagnall, "Textile Industries" (fiche), pp. 1346–7.

compensation paid for stocking work. Owen Osborne, a Philadelphia hosiery manufacturer and English emigrant, later explained:

> The warehouse would supply the middleman with yarn, and it was the duty of these middlemen to get the work made and take it back to the warehouse, and yet pay [the stockinger] the same price for making as he [the middleman] received from the so-called manufacturer. This necessitated the iniquitous system of frame-rents and charges. . . . These charges were itemized as follows: Frame-rent, standing room, light and fuel, winding, taking-in, deductions for bad work, etc.[122]

In such an "iniquitous" situation, it is no surprise to discover an outmigration of both young hosiers like Spencer and frame workers with sufficient resources to pay their passage abroad.

As Spencer was not trained to make stockings but to handle the process of getting them made and sold, it is likely that his efforts in the 1840s involved a partial re-creation of the British "inside" and "outside" warehouse system. Purchasing frames worked in his rented shop and supplying yarn to outworkers who owned their own frames provided him with a flow of goods that could not have been generated from his own equipment alone. Like the Globe Mill, Spencer could accumulate from two sources and had the mercantile training to minimize slippage in that process. These relationships avoided the iniquities of the middleman frame-rent model, as outworkers in Philadelphia seem generally to have owned their hand-powered machines.[123] As Spencer sold his goods directly, he was not in the position of being "middled" himself. Installing spinning apparatus in the 1850 mill gave him better control over raw materials, both in terms of quality and price. He may also have encouraged immigrant frameworkers to lodge their machines in his facility in exchange for a nominal rent, expanding capacity without additional capital outlay. Whatever variants on the English base were put into play, they took shape within a field of shared cultural and even regional backgrounds of hosiers (manufacturers) and stockingers (workers) alike. That outwork was solidly entrenched is indicated by Freedley's observation regarding the Germantown knit trades of the fifties:

> The distinctive feature of the business is its hand-looms and domesticity. Fully one-half of the persons engaged in the production have no concern with the ten-hour system, or the factory system, or even the solar system. They work at such hours as they choose, and their industry is mainly regulated by the state of their larder.[124]

---

[122] Owen Osborne, *The Story of the Stocking*, Philadelphia, 1927, pp. 24–5.

[123] Freedley, *Philadelphia and Its Manufactures*, p. 253. There is no specific mention of knitters' owning their frames, but both cotton and carpet handloom workers are specified, the latter in George Wallis, *Special Report on the New York Exposition, House of Commons* Westminster, 1855, p. 31.

[124] Freedley, *Philadelphia and Its Manufactures*, pp. 240–2.

Noting that the knitters were "largely Leicester and Nottingham men," Freedley pointed out the indifference of Germantown workers to the political movement that mobilized other labor sectors in this era. This should not be presumed to indicate that Germantown stockingers were hapless losers, refugees from British mechanization whose docility could be assumed to flow from having absorbed a generation of setbacks. Rather, their indifference to political action came from their strong and flexible structural position amid relations of production that allowed them to use their craft skills while retaining a measure of independence from the factory system. There are at least four elements of this structural position to consider.

First, the factory mechanization of hosiery production was a haphazard and piecemeal process that continued from the early 1800s to the close of the century. As on cottons, only the simplest techniques were brought under power at first, and in Philadelphia, this application was only beginning in the 1850s. Second, unlike simple cotton handlooms, the stocking frame could be converted to knitting goods of many varieties. The lace industry of Nottingham was a product of the conversion of stocking frames, and fancy knit goods were long produced on hand frames after common hosiery became the province of power knitters. Third, the stockingers themselves were most often the technical innovators, regaining ground lost to machinery by exercising mechanical inventiveness in conjunction with frame makers. Osborne writes of the British situation that the hand-frame worker "held his own" until 1880 by adapting his devices to "the making of fancy fabrics." In creating these "contrivances which were rarely patented," knitters and framesmiths collaborated to produce on the frame patterns that "had been made previously by laying of the threads by hand."[125] Finally, these high levels of skill were integrated into a proud and sustained culture that clearly perplexed Freedley, for stockingers were neither lazy nor ambitious, falling outside the convenient continuum of Victorian economic moralizing.[126]

Although the hand production of knit goods was extensive in 1850 Germantown, Charles Spencer did in subsequent decades introduce powered knitting machines whose output was enormous. To fully understand the advances and limitations of this machinery, it is important to grasp the basics of knitwear technology in this period. Two sorts of frames were operated by

---

125 Osborne, *Story*, p. 31.
126 For a comprehensive investigation of the British hand-frame trades, see *Report from the Select Committee on Stoppage of Wages (Hosiery), Together with the Proceedings of the Committee, Minutes of Evidence, Appendix and Index, House of Commons, 1855*, Westminster (?), 1855. This House of Commons document, which is more than 600 pages, is a thorough examination of the relations of production in knit goods and of the conflicting notions about work and economics held by hosiers, workers, and parliamentarians. The testimony frequently echoes the descriptions given by Osborne of stockingers' independent dispositions (see *Report from the Select Committee*, pp. 73, 82, and Osborne, *Story*, pp. 25, 29).

Knitting hand frame from the early nineteenth century. Variants of this flat knitter were in general use in Philadelphia through the Civil War. (Philadelphia College of Textiles and Science)

handworkers at midcentury, a flat frame, which yielded yard goods very much like that produced by shuttle looms, and a circular or rotary frame, which produced a continuous tube of knitted fiber. The flat frame was the elder of the two, having been introduced in the late sixteenth century, its essential principles unmodified over the next three hundred years. The rotary frame was new, with practical models dating from the 1830s and in general use only from about 1850–60. The classic stocking frame was a flat-knitter, called the narrow frame, whose product was from 15 to 18 inches wide. When fitted with devices for narrowing the width of the fabric as it was being knitted, the stocking frame could turn out a tapered flat piece of silk, wool, or cotton that, when seamed, approximated the shape of the leg. These products were known as fashioned or full-fashioned hosiery. They were not finished when taken from the frame, as seaming, heeling, and footing had to be done, the heel and foot also knitted by hand. These latter tasks were generally done by women and children, as was the winding of the large bobbin whose single thread was continuously knitted on the frame. This was an exacting and skilled production, with an able stockinger generally producing three dozen pairs (seventy-two individual stockings) a week. Women and boys who worked frames might turn out one or two dozen a week. The hand frame was propelled by a foot treadle. Though it was certainly feasible to power these devices in rows on factory floors, this was not yet done. The necessary attention of the stockinger to the narrowing of the knit and the delicacy of the single thread were factors that resisted speedup.

To increase production, the cut-hose trade, which employed flat frames wider than the traditional 15-inch, or narrow, frame, was developed. Knitting a plain fabric up to 50 inches in breadth, wide frames did not create individual stocking-legs. Thus, the wide frames were not stopped after every stocking body was completed for the setup of another, as was the narrow frame. Like warp looms, wide frames could yield continuous runs of fabric and were amenable to powered drive. Yet that fabric had to be *cut* to stocking shapes and then seamed and finished, wherein lay new problems. Cutting the single fiber from which knitted goods were fashioned immediately made it possible for the whole fabric to begin unraveling. This was not a problem for the narrow-frame stockings whose knit integrity was not disturbed by seaming, as they came directly from the loom ready for finishing. Cut hose from wide-frame knitters rapidly gained a reputation as shoddy goods, for with use, the stockings fell apart. (It was the introduction of wide frames and the cut-hose trade that helped trigger the stockingers' portion of the Luddite riots.) Variations in knit technology gradually alleviated this limitation, and the versatility of the wider fabric's uses reinforced the wide frame's importance. Not only was its output potentially greater, but underwear, cravats, shirts, and pantaloons could all be cut from 30- to 50-inch knit goods.

Rotary or circular head frames, which were first built in the late eighteenth century, came into general use in France, England, and the United States a half century later. The seamless tube that emerged from these machines was almost automatically a stocking, and the device was easily adapted to powered motion to maximize output. Rotary frames were, however, much more expensive than the flat variety. (British figures for 1855 give the following comparisons: rebuilt narrow frame, £5; rebuilt wide frame, £10 to £20; new rotary frame, £30 or more.) Further, although the tube only had to be cut, stitched at the bottom, and hemmed at the top to resemble a stocking, the fit such a product gave its wearer was so shabby that seamless stockings were quickly dubbed "leg bags." There was no heel to this item, no foot, no taper. Given the limitations of both wide frames and rotary mechanisms, it is understandable that for generations fine stockings, stockings that fit and were durable, were the province of the narrow-frame craftsmen. Still, the output and standardization characteristics of the other two and the variability of end uses for wide-frame fabrics contributed to their spread, particularly in factory settings.[127]

How did Spencer tie into this technological network? He used the old flat frames modeled on the originals invented by William Lee in 1589 until about 1850, when, in his newly completed factory, "he adopted the circular or rotary knitting machines." He recycled the reciprocating frames to produce heel webs, which was not possible on the rotaries, and "devoted them to the manufacture of fancy knit goods, which soon became an important part of

---

[127] Osborne, *Story*, pp. 19–37; *Report from the Select Committee*, pp. 208, 570; and Maurice Daumas, ed., *A History of Technology and Invention, Volume III: The Expansion of Mechanization, 1725–1860*, New York, 1979, pp. 619–32. Because the terms "circular" and "rotating" were imprecisely used in the nineteenth-century knitting trades, attribution of machine types and work processes is difficult without extremely detailed information. Basically, the needles of machines that produced flat fabrics might be arranged in either a straight line or a moving circular track, which was sometimes called a rotary frame. A tube fabric could be produced on either a circular-head frame or a flat frame. On a circular-head frame the fixed needles were arranged in a circle, the threads moving around them and thus generating an endless column of fabric. (One such machine is currently in operating condition at the Slater Mill Historic Site, Pawtucket, R.I., to whose staff I owe thanks for demonstrating its operation.) On a flat frame, or Lamb machine, two sets of needles are employed, with proper adjustment, to produce a tubular fabric (leg bags). To further blur the picture, the Lamb machine can also be prepared to generate flat goods. British and American usage seems to have differed as well in describing these processes. In both locations the standard narrow frame was labeled "reciprocating," referring to the pumping pedal motion that activated the machine. A "Balmoral" knitter refers, however, to a specific tube-knitting machine, forty-five of which were present in Spencer's 1880 mill, along with 280 "circular" frames, which I believe also produced tubes. See also, Max C. Miller, *Principles of Knitting*, New York, 1931.

his business."[128] Integrating the circular knitters with his hand frames by converting some of the latter to making heels allowed Spencer to assemble a composite stocking, the upper section rotary-knit, the heel (and foot?) produced by hand, and the pieces sewn together by women in or out of the factory. The fancy goods operation, which occupied the other hand frames Spencer owned or contracted for with outworkers, was significant indeed. In 1850 the firm reported the manufacture of 15,000 dozen fancy goods and cravats to the manufacturing census,[129] as well as 16,000 dozen wool hose.

Although no equipment details appear in the 1860 returns, by 1870 Spencer had expanded his machinery to include 65 knitters (rotary heads) and 11 looms (wide frames), all likely powered by this point.[130] The 1880 information Blodget gathered is most complete. With more than 500 workers and mills worth perhaps a half million, Spencer's Leicester Knitting Mills were powered by four steam engines totaling 150 horsepower and had five sets of cards and 4,000 spindles. Knitting machinery included 280 circular heads, 45 Balmorals (a particular model of rotary frame), 25 rib and heeling frames, 84 wide frames, and 100 sewing machines for assembly. Production soared to 6,500 dozen hose and fancies per week, the mill making in one month more goods than had been turned out in the year 1850.[131] No hand-powered frames remained in Spencer's productive array, but nearly 600 were still in operation in the city, according to Blodget, who in the 1880 study passed over many of the smallest firms that were later reported when he compiled the citywide industrial census in 1882. This development suggests two themes. First, Spencer, like Ripka, made the transition from craft-shop master to factory industrialist gradually, retooling and combining hand and powered production bit by bit to optimize the advantages of each format. Steam power did not march in and replace handwork, rolling like some technical juggernaut. It was, rather, one element in a larger complex of options, to be considered alongside the potential for changing output mix, modifying outwork relations, seeking government contracts, or opening direct sales outlets. Second, according to Blodget's figures, it is clear that hundreds of hand knitters were still plying their specialty trades (Cardigan jackets, gloves, fine hose) in Philadelphia in 1880. An enormous knitting industry had grown up around them but had not displaced them. Even outwork persisted into the eighties, its capital-saving contribution to accumulation a still potent component of the Philadelphia textile manufacture.

The variation and extension of output that Spencer undertook was a

---

128 Bagnall, "Textile Industries" (fiche), p. 1350.
129 1850 MCS, Philadelphia Co., p. 20.
130 1870 MCS, Philadelphia Co., p. 20.
131 Blodget, *Textile Industries*, p. 58.

general feature of the knit-goods trades. Stockings might be produced in many colors, with stripes, ribs, diamond patterns, and so on. Cravats and fancy goods were articles of fashion whose character changed with the wind. By the seventies, the Leicester Knitting Mills offered shawls and scarfs as well, and in 1880 Blodget noted fifty-four broadlooms in place, as the successful mill broke new ground into woven goods. These, along with narrow looms, had been introduced in 1875 for the manufacture of quality cassimeres, according to Bagnall.[132] As Archibald Campbell and Company had produced varied specialty cottons, Spencer followed the same track in hosiery and woolens, both knit and woven. Specialization without flexibility speeded Ripka's downfall, but specialization along with flexibility gave Campbell and Spencer a resiliency that compensated for the enhanced market risks.

Two elements of Spencer's marketing strategy are worth special attention: selling direct (like Ripka) and securing government contracts (unlike him). By 1875 Spencer's firm sold a "great variety of goods, . . . without the use of agents, from their own warehouses in Philadelphia, New York, Boston, Chicago and Baltimore."[133] Establishment of a New York office coincided with Spencer's erection of his own mill and installation of more productive circular-head frames, suggesting a coordination of manufacturing and marketing strategies. Bagnall noted that direct selling had been the firm's policy "from the beginning," and though "difficult at the outset when he had to contend with the embarrassment of a small capital, [it] has no doubt been a large element in his success."[134] Arguably, a related element was the steadily rising demand for hosiery among an expanding population and the absence of the numerous and huge New England concerns with which Ripka had to contend for the staple cotton market.

The Civil War channeled a good deal of the nation's hosiery demand into the hands of the Quartermaster Corps of the army, which maintained a central eastern depot at the Schuylkill Arsenal in Philadelphia. Contracts were let for millions of pairs of woolen half-hose during the war, and Charles Spencer secured his share of the flow. Although many of the contracts were acquired by merchants who subcontracted to manufacturers, Spencer and a number of other Philadelphia textile makers eliminated this middleman and bid directly and successfully. Spencer's first award, in April 1863 for 30,000 pairs, was followed that November by another order for 100,000 pairs. He received his third wartime contract for 100,000 pairs in February 1864 and a final order for 11,100 pairs at war's end, April 17,

---

132 Ibid., p. 32; Bagnall, "Textile Industries" (fiche), p. 1350; *M&MP*, p. 33.
133 *M&MP*, p. 33.
134 Bagnall, "Textile Industries" (fiche), pp. 1352–3.

1865.[135] The lateness of the first contract may indicate that Spencer was at first a subcontractor to one of the speculative entrepreneurs, seeking work on his own only in 1863.

The total of goods provided, nearly 250,000 pairs, is a bit less awesome than first appears. Hosiery output was counted generally in dozen pairs, which reduces the figure to 20,000 dozen pairs, or about two months' production for the expanded mill as it stood in 1870. When the value of the contracts is considered ($80,981), it bulks a bit larger, representing about one-third of the product value reported by the Leicester mills in 1860. Clearly, the government awards were not overwhelming in scale, but they did represent a sizable sale to a single customer in an emergency market. It is Spencer's direct entry into the competition and his capacity to match precise arsenal samples for the goods desired that shows the twin characteristics of Philadelphia manufacturing strategies, market sensitivity and productive flexibility.

Charles Spencer headed a family firm, in which his father, elder brother, and sons were involved in various capacities. From probably about 1850 until his death in 1863, William Spencer, the father, "superintend[ed] the works" on Mill Street. Spencer's brother, William G., started a small stocking workshop of his own in the mid-forties but "relinquished the business" in the 1847 recession. His activities over the next decade are undocumented, but in 1857, Charles took him into the knitting firm as a partner. William G. "retired from the firm" at the beginning of 1869, presumably to an appropriate competence. The principal's elder son, 21-year-old Robert, had joined as a partner on January 1, 1868, and his second son, Charles H., replaced William G. Spencer in January 1870, likewise in his twenty-first year. One nonfamily member also was admitted to the firm, Charles Poulson, who had been for many years in "charge of the New York warehouse." His partnership began in 1867 and lasted until his retirement in the mid-seventies. Charles and his two sons shared the responsibilities of directing the firm, the founder handling its "mercantile relations," Robert taking charge of the weaving division, and young Charles supervising knit-goods production.[136]

Charles Spencer married twice; Robert and Charles H. were the sons of his first wife, Priscilla Smethurst, "a native of Lancashire, England, where her father had been a leading manufacturer." The extent to which capital was raised by this marriage and by the admission of Charles's brother and

---

[135] *Abstracts of Contracts, 1861–65, Quartermaster Corps*, National Archives, Record Group 92, Entry No. 1239. Contract dates were April 24 and November 23, 1863, February 16, 1864, and April 17, 1865 (vol. 1, pp. 221-22; vol. II, pp. 42, 263).

[136] *M&MP*, p. 33; Bagnall "Textile Industries" (fiche), pp. 1350-3.

the New York agent to the firm has not been established, but it is possible that capital was involved in all three cases. In 1880 Charles Spencer was in residence on Mill Street near his factory with his second wife, Elizabeth, 29 and Virginia-born and their 11-month-old son, Lindsay. Robert and Charles A. also lived with their wives, children, and servants as neighbors on Germantown's Locust Street,[137] a block from their father's home.

Politically, Spencer was first a Whig and then a Republican, "though never an aspirant for political honors." He reportedly was generous in contributing "to the maintenance of soldiers' families" during the war and to the charities related to the Episcopal Church. In the considerable labor turmoil of the late seventies and early eighties, Spencer surfaced as a member of various reform and manufacturers associations. His own mills, and indeed those of Germantown generally, were not touched by strikes in the era. Nor were the Labor parties of the period able to find response there, as the pages of the *Public Ledger*, crammed with organizing and political news of Kensington, Manayunk, Frankford, and the southern wards, have only the most occasional mention of Germantown activity.

Spencer's close contacts with his fellow Philadelphia textile capitalists stemmed most likely from their common direct-marketing salesrooms located centrally in the wholesale districts (Front, Water, and Market streets) and the commercial blocks of Chestnut Street nearby. Two groups crystallized in 1880, the Textile Manufacturers Association of Philadelphia and the political reform Committee of One Hundred. The first was headed by Thomas Dolan, a wartime textile millionaire whose woolen mills at Frankford were among the city's largest establishments. Intended to be a permanent organization, the TMA announced at this January session its concern with tariffs, publicity for the industry, and the like. Its creation would also ultimately help provide a forum in which manufacturers could forge common policies toward workers who themselves were banding together in the Knights of Labor. Both Charles Spencer and Sevill Schofield attended this organizational meeting, each contributing $500 toward the costs of a display and reception held for General Grant; in addition, both men accepted appointments to the Board of Managers of the new association.[138]

In November a collection of Republican merchants and manufacturers calling themselves the Committee of One Hundred moved to gain control of the city's political apparatus. Pledged to end bossism and corruption and to establish a policy of administering local offices "regardless of partisanship," they challenged the leaders of their own party, nominating independent candidates for mayor and receiver of taxes. Of the eight readily identifiable

---

[137] 1880 PCS, Philadelphia Co., District 439, pp. 9–10, 14, 15.
[138] *Public Ledger*, January 28, 1880.

textile men on the committee, five, including both Spencer and Schofield, were present at the founding meeting of the TMA.[139] Their mayoralty nominee, Samuel G. King, was a former brush manufacturer who had retired at 35 with a competence and thereafter devoted his energies to local politics. Elected after a fierce three-way campaign, he proved "essentially a safe man to be at the head of the municipal government."[140]

Subsequently, the manufacturing relations of Spencer and Schofield diverged dramatically. In the next five years wage cuts and strikes were repeated features of life at the Economy Mills as Schofield claimed he was responding to slack markets. By contrast, reports on the Germantown hosiery mills referred to full running, season after season, and turnouts were nonexistent.[141] Though the Knights of Labor held an 1885 organization meeting at the edge of the district, with an address by R. F. Trevellick of Detroit that drew "80 to 90 hosiery weavers and knitting trade workers," the pledge to form a Hosiery and Knit Goods Assembly was stillborn.[142] Indeed, the only occasion during these years on which Germantown hosiery manufacturers organized themselves was *not* to deal with uprising labor but to protest royalty charges that were attached to a patented trimming machine they sought to purchase for their mills, a protest in which Charles Spencer joined.[143] So long as demand was steady or rising and work was plentiful at adequate wages, accumulation proceeded steadily, a situation Germantown hosiers enjoyed into the nineties.[144]

There may well be a generational life cycle to the family firm that is as potent a threat to its continuation in the same line as any of the market or productive elements that might affect its fate. As with other firms already examined, Spencer had arranged for his sons to succeed him, had erected a massive complex that employed more than 500 workers by 1880, and had wide-ranging market outlets and state-of-the-art equipment. Yet a generation later, while the Leicester mills stood solidly on their Germantown acreage, no Spencer family member was present to operate them. Instead, two long-standing city textile manufacturers were in possession of the mills,

---

[139] Scharf and Westcott, *History of Philadelphia*, pp. 849–50.

[140] George Gordon, "Samuel George King," in *A Biographical Album of Prominent Pennsylvanians, First Series*, Philadelphia, 1888, pp. 217–22.

[141] *Public Ledger*, August 30, 1880; January 4, 1883; January 22, 1884; February 2, 7, 25, 28, March 2, 3, 17, June 4, 1885; March 16, April 22, 1886.

[142] Ibid., March 27, 1885.

[143] Ibid., March 15, 1881.

[144] There were apparently seasonal layoffs in the Germantown mills as elsewhere, but the only strikes noted in the *Public Ledger* between 1876 and 1886 in that district were two flurries over the dismissal of Knights of Labor activists in 1886, neither of which generated any noteworthy followups.

incorporated as the Leicester and Continental Mill Co. N. T. Folwell, president, and James Dobson, vice-president,[145] were wool men, Folwell from Kensington and Dobson one of the partners in the enormous Falls of Schuylkill mills. The production was changed slightly, to knit goods and wool yarns, because the cloths formerly produced conflicted with those made by both men in their other mills, but the scale had not: 10,000 spindles, 10 sets of wool cards, 150 knitters, and dyeing facilities intact.

Whether the brothers sold out to enjoy their competencies or whether the old firm went down in the mid-nineties depression will require additional inquiry. But another element in the pattern of Philadelphia textile development is suggested: One intergenerational succession is fairly standard for the persistent firm, but in the swirling tides of capitalist development, there is a second generation burnout. To trace the careers of a set of native-born sons of immigrant manufacturers after they succeed to ownership of the inherited firm might reveal a cultural fragility to the family firm that was of more weight than corporate competiton. Whereas Charles Spencer was reared as a hosier in the warehouses of Nottingham, his younger son was an 1869 graduate of Princeton.[146] The difference in the cultural baggage and expectations derived from these polar experiences may be of considerable moment for our understanding of the long-range fate of proprietary manufacture.

Of course, Joseph Ripka and Charles Spencer were only two of more than 300 textile manufacturers active in Philadelphia in 1850. They represent large-and medium-scale production in two of the formats that were prevalent in the period, the factory complex and the mixed mode of hand and power, in- and outwork. Yet there were hundreds of others and thousands of workers from whom they sought to extract products and profits. We shall indeed have a closer look at the small, even tiny, textile makers and their workers in a more extended analysis of Kensington, Manayunk, and Germantown about 1850. But first, an effort will be made to present the characteristics of the industry as an aggregate, as was done for 1820, drawing on the 1850 manuscript manufacturing census data for Philadelphia. Having moved from the personal to the general, we will then return to the neighborhoods where Ripka, Spencer, and their colleagues engaged thousands of their fellow immigrants in the production of yarn and fabric.[147]

---

[145] *Textile World Official Directory of the Textile Mills and Buyers of Textile Fabrics, 1900*, Boston, 1900, pp. 216–7.

[146] Bagnall, "Textile Industries" (fiche), p. 1351.

[147] Though thousands of textile workers inhabited Kensington, the sources for probing their experience are nowhere near as plentiful as those available for a comparable examination of Germantown or Manayunk residents. Though nearly complete collections of the *Germantown Telegraph* and several Manayunk weeklies have been preserved at the Historical Society of Pennsylvania, a similar file of nineteenth-century Kensington newspapers is, unfortuantely, absent.

6

Proprietary textiles at midcentury: Kensington

Carpet Manufactory – Cresheim, foot of Chestnut Hill
CARPETS VERY CHEAP FOR CASH
The subscribers beg to announce that they manufacture and always have on hand for sale a handsome assortment of Superior List Carpeting from 45 to 50 cts; and Rag Carpeting of the best quality, from 25 to 37½ cts.

Carpets woven to order at the shortest notice and at as low rates as at any other establishment.

Also Cotton Laps, wholesale and retail, cheap for Cash. Building stone, of a good quality, for sale

J & E France

Advertisement, *Germantown Telegraph*, July 7, 1847

The brothers France, John and Edwin, with their tiny carpet mill, will introduce the world beyond the considerable enterprises of Ripka, Campbell, and Schofield, the world of small manufacture inhabited by at least four-fifths of Philadelphia's textile producers in 1850. With a diminutive capital ($5,000), a few workers (thirteen), and negligible powered equipment (twenty-one spindles and a card), the proprietors of this Germantown firm nonetheless shared significant elements of the Philadelphia accumulation format with their more substantial colleagues. Their production was both specialized and flexible, offering a sturdy wool and flax carpet (List), a cheaper rag variety, carded cotton laps ready for spinning or use in quilts, and an ability to produce goods for special orders. They marketed their products directly, though locally, their classified advertisement a weekly feature of the *Telegraph* for years. A family partnership, they had emigrated from Britain and shared the same Germantown household with their elderly mother. Her presence (at 66) with her unmarried sons (46 and 43 in 1850) indicates the blending of capitalist entrepreneurship with cultural traditions visible elsewhere at Philadelphia. Their concern for cash speaks directly to the credit puzzles that plagued textile firms lacking access to financial networks.[1]

---

[1] 1850 Manufacturing Census Schedules, Philadelphia Co., p. 18, cited hereafter as MCS; 1850 Population Census Schedules, Philadelphia Co., District 9, p. 81, cited hereafter as PCS.

J & E France introduce, rather than typify, the smaller manufacturers of Philadelphia textiles. Given that the capitalization of "small" firms ranged from $150 to $10,000, that their numbers of employees ranged from one to several hundreds, and that their products and services varied widely, no measure of typicality is available. Investment does not necessarily co-vary with employment, even within specific sectors (cottons, hosiery). Facing this situation, a central purpose of Chapters 6 and 7 will be to examine the multiple, discrete formats of production current in the 1850s in all their variety, suggesting their interconnections and situating them in manufacturing districts of widely differing character. A second goal will be to examine in some detail the firms from each of these formats and to explore the elements of continuity and contrast with the larger manufactories. Finally, we shall labor to distill pattern from the chaos of independent producers, through an aggregate and sectoral analysis of the Philadelphia textile industry in 1850 and 1860 and, ultimately, through a discussion of its partial transformation in the war decade (Chapter 8).

Overview: the Philadelphia textile manufacture, 1850

The starting point for this presentation will be a review of the textile industry as a totality in 1850 Philadelphia, turning the whole like a prism to view it from a variety of angles. Basic contrasts with Lowell having been established, the whole will be disaggregated and dissected, again along several dimensions, to reveal the overlapping formats of production that coexisted in the industrial city. More than 300 textile firms reported their activity in Philadelphia on the 1850 Manufacturers Census Schedules. The distribution of firms and workers citywide by productive sector indicates that two-thirds (65%) of Philadelphia's textile workers were employed in the traditional cotton and woolen fabric trades (Table 6.1). However, it may be equally remarkable that one-third, or more than 4,000, of the workers were engaged in "specialty" sectors, about equally divided among knits, carpets, and services (dyeing and spinning). At Lowell in 1850 only 220 workers at the Bleachery functioned outside the major integrated mills. The Lowell Manufacturing Company had 124 power carpet looms in operation, the only departure from the staple track at that date,[2] occupying perhaps a hundred operatives. Together they represented less than 3% of the 12,000 textile workers in corporate service. The second simple work-force contrast with Lowell is the high proportion of male workers in Philadelphia, 58% citywide and about the same in the cotton, wool, and mixed-fabric sectors. Other

---

[2] *Statistics of Lowell Manufactures, January, 1851*, Lowell, Mass., 1851; Ewing, John and Norton, Nancy, *Broadlooms and Businessmen*, Cambridge, Mass., 1955, p. 25.

Table 6.1. *Textile firms by sector and workers by sector and sex, Philadelphia, 1850*

Sector	No. of firms	Male workers	Female workers	Total workers	% of sector workers to total textile work force	Average no. of workers per firm
Cotton	63	2,372 (56)	1,835 (44)	4,207	34.0	67
Cotton-wool	52	1,884 (57)	1,431 (43)	3,315	26.8	64
Wool	14	273 (54)	229 (46)	502	4.0	36
Silk	6	81 (36)	146 (64)	227	1.8	—[a]
Dyeing, finishing	32	908 (81)	207 (19)	1,115	9.0	35
Spinning	25	185 (53)	167 (47)	352	2.9	14
Hosiery, knit goods	51	416 (34)	800 (66)	1,216	9.8	24
Carpet	71	951 (75)	318 (25)	1,269	10.3	18
Other	12	71 (43)	95 (57)	166	1.3	14
Total	326	7,141 (58)	5,228 (42)	12,369	99.9	38

[a] Omitted because of the small number of silk firms, one large and five small.

Note: Figures in parentheses indicate percentage. Sector definitions: cotton: woven goods, including integrated and "weaving only" operations; cotton-wool: woven mixed goods, usually cotton warp and wool filling (jeans), although sometimes output included all-cotton or all-wool fabrics; wool: woven all-wool goods; silk: woven silks and narrow goods (ribbon and trim); dyeing and finishing: separate dyeing, finishing, and printing establishments, no weaving; spinning: cotton and wool yarn production only, no weaving; hosiery and knit goods: included knitted shawls, jackets, gloves, and so on, in addition to hosiery; carpet: woven carpets, principally wool; other: flax, cotton laps, elastic web, and so on.

Source: Manuscript Manufacturing Census Schedules, Philadelphia County, 1850.

Table 6.2. *Textile firms by sector and work-force size, Philadelphia, 1850*

Sector	Work-force size					
	1–5 workers	6–25 workers	26–50 workers	51–100 workers	100+ workers	Total firms
Cotton	13	13	11	14	12	63
Cotton-wool	2	13	20	7	10	52
Wool	1	6	2	4	1	14
Silk	4	1	0	0	1	6
Dyeing, finishing	11	11	2	5	3	32
Spinning	11	12	0	2	0	25
Hosiery, knit goods	22	20	4	1	4	51
Carpet	29	29	5	6	2	71
Other	6	3	3	0	0	12
Total	99	108	47	39	33	326

Source: Manuscript Manufacturing Census Schedules, Philadelphia County, 1850.

textile sectors at Philadelphia diverge widely, however, carpet weaving and dyeing heavily male, knit goods the reverse. In 1850 Lowell, only 31% of the operatives were male.

Statistics of average firm size suggest the great differential between the textile firms at Philadelphia and those at Lowell, and the unusual position of Joseph Ripka, whose Manayunk mills employed more than ten times the average city work force on cottons. Breakdowns of the aggregate work-force data indicate that "big" firms were important in Philadelphia, as thirty-three of them engaged more than half the city's textile workers (Tables 6.2 and 6.3). Has the era of factory concentration appeared already? Is Philadelphia just a step behind the New England mills on the growth track? Several bits of additional information suggest otherwise. First, if an additional column was added to the table to express Lowell-scale bigness, "500+ workers," only *three* Philadelphia cotton mills would meet that standard, two in Manayunk and one in Kensington, together drawing 15% of the city's textile workers (Ripka, 682; Kempton, 624; Peter Hickey, 520). Second, all three firms closed within the next dozen years (Kempton in 1851, Hickey by 1857, and Ripka was bankrupt at the start of the Civil War). Given the constraints of competition, proprietary management, and so on, there was perhaps an upper limit to the effective size of an antebellum textile firm in the city. Third, if the imaginary additional column was "250+," only one more firm

Table 6.3. *Textile workers by sector and work-force size, Philadelphia, 1850*

| | Work-force size | | | | | |
Sector	1–5 workers	6–25 workers	26–50 workers	51–100 workers	100+ workers	Total workers
Cotton	51	171	432	984	2,569	4,207
Cotton-wool	8	202	725	461	1,919	3,315
Wool	4	86	87	223	102	502
Silk	16	11	0	0	200	227
Dyeing, finishing	37	115	80	362	521	1,115
Spinning	51	149	0	152	0	352
Hosiery, knit goods	63	240	128	75	710	1,216
Carpet	85	321	161	436	266	1,269
Other	18	49	99	0	0	166
Total	333	1,344	1,712	2,693	6,287	12,369

Source: Manuscript Manufacturing Census Schedules, Philadelphia County, 1850.

would be added to the three above, Aaron and Thomas Jones of German-town, hand-frame stocking outwork contractors whose 265 workers were set in motion by a capital of $7,000. Clearly, large agglomerations of workers at Philadelphia do not necessarily indicate progress along a linear pathway toward "modern" business forms and functions, nor do they even indicate that the workers were gathering in factories for their day's labor. This reality dictates our use of "firms" as the central term of reference for manufacturing enterprises, as "mills" and "factories" are variables, not assumable even when large groups of workers have been engaged. Twenty-eight of the thirty-two largest firms producing textiles had between 102 and 225 workers, and many of these firms, like Jones, were handloom and outwork operations. This is a point to which we shall return.

Of those firms active in 1850, two-thirds were small (207 of 326 had twenty-five or fewer workers) and were present in all sectors of production. These family and proprietary workshops employed about one-seventh of the city's textile workers but accounted for a fourth of the knit-goods workers and a third of carpet operatives. The firms of independent spinners were generally quite small, as were those of contract dyers. The large dyeing and finishing firms were uniformly outlying printworks, principally engaged in producing calicoes, whereas smaller yarn and specialty cloth dyers tended to locate near other textile firms to service their needs. To gain some appreciation of the patterns of agglomeration and dispersion that existed in 1850 textile manufacturing, a spatial dimension must be added to these general breakdowns (Tables 6.4 and 6.5).

The geographical distribution illustrates the wide variation and specialization of the city's textile districts. Kensington held a third of the firms and workers operating in Philadelphia at midcentury. As David Montgomery has pointed out, the district's total 1840 work force numbered about 3,000, of whom 39% were "classified in manufacturing and trades."[3] By 1850 nearly 4,000 Kensington workers functioned in textiles alone, their handloom crafts still the dominant presence in the neighborhood. Half the city's carpet weavers, the largest spinning and silk mills, and a dozen small dyehouses were crowded alongside the thousands of cotton and mixed-goods handworkers in sheds and workshops. (Kensington occupied less than three square miles, about 2% of the land in Philadelphia County.)[4] An immediate contrast to its concentration was the Northern Liberties district directly to the south along the Delaware between Kensington and Old City, where only a few hundred textile workers occupied an equally built-up neighborhood, whose tight streets had long been filled with the leather and clothing trades. Such occupational clustering of craftworkers suggests that immigrants' urban location decisions may have stemmed from occupational, as well as ethnic or religious, influences.

Germantown was far and away the premier hosiery district, embracing two-thirds of the city's frame workers and twenty-one knitting firms. The other outlying areas, West and Northeast Philadelphia, held most of the area's scattered creek- or riverside printworks. As most of the land in those townships was still farm or forest, the noxious discharges from large-scale dyeing caused few of the problems that would have accompanied a more central location. These sites also satisfied dyers' demand for water and, for those on the Schuylkill or Delaware, provided ready access to central markets for their goods. Manayunk was the preeminent waterpowered factory district, with 90% of its textile workers producing cotton and woolen fabrics, both in mill complexes and factories divided into rented "apartments."

Closer to the central commercial area was Spring Garden, where 1,200 operatives generated almost as wide an array of goods and services as those of Kensington. In Spring Garden, the overlap of productive formats was extensive, as fifteen steam-powered mills coexisted with eight fair-sized handwork shops and eleven tiny firms, the last chiefly stockingers, carpet

---

3 David Montgomery, "The Shuttle and the Cross," in Peter Stearns and Daniel Walkowitz, eds., *Workers in the Industrial Revolution*, New Brunswick, N.J., 1974, p. 45.

4 John Thomas Scharf and Thompson Westcott, *History of Philadelphia*, Philadelphia, 1884, p. 1742.

Table 6.4. *Textile firms by district and sector, Philadelphia, 1850*

District	Cotton	Cotton-wool	Wool	Silk	Dyeing, finishing	Spinning	Hosiery, knit goods	Carpet	Other	Total all sectors
Kensington	16	31	4	2	12	3	14	42	2	126
Germantown	0	1	1	0	2	7	21	2	1	35
West Philadelphia	0	4	3	0	2	3	2	1	0	15
South Philadelphia	16	1	0	0	0	0	1	2	1	21
Manayunk	5	5	2	0	1	8	0	0	3	24
Spring Garden	8	1	3	0	5	3	7	7	0	34
Northeast Philadelphia	3	1	0	0	8	0	0	0	0	12
Northern Liberties	2	4	1	0	1	1	4	8	2	23
Old City	13	4	0	4	1	0	2	9	3	36
Total	63	52	14	6	32	25	51	71	12	326

Note: Kensington: Kensington District (8 wards); Germantown: Germantown Borough and Township, Bristol Township; West Philadelphia: Blockley Township, West Philadelphia District; South Philadelphia: Passyunk, Moyamensing, Southwark, Kingsessing; Manayunk: Manayunk Borough, Roxborough Township; Spring Garden: Spring Garden, Penn District and Township; Northeast Philadelphia: Northern Liberties Township, Bridesburg, Frankford, Aramingo, Lower Dublin, Oxford, Richmond, Whitehall, Moreland, Byberry; Northern Liberties; Old City: City of Philadelphia (17 districts).

Source: Manuscript Manufacturing Census Schedules, Philadelphia County, 1850.

Table 6.5. *Textile workers by district and sector, Philadelphia, 1850*

District	Cotton	Cotton-wool	Wool	Silk	Dyeing, finishing	Spinning	Hosiery, knit goods	Carpet	Other	Total
							Sector			
Kensington	654	2,094	92	203	56	119	103	650	6	3,977
Germantown	0	15	102	0	34	59	771	173	5	1,159
West Philadelphia	0	132	31	0	248	15	27	6	0	459
South Philadelphia	791	60	0	0	0	0	6	48	29	934
Manayunk	1,474	196	115	0	3	139	0	0	39	1,966
Spring Garden	467	32	145	0	251	15	80	226	0	1,216
Northeast Philadelphia	163	36	0	0	505	0	0	0	0	704
Northern Liberties	8	154	17	0	11	5	176	28	18	417
Old City	650	596	0	24	7	0	53	138	69	1,537
Total	4,207	3,315	502	227	1,115	352	1,216	1,269	166	12,369

Note: Kensington: Kensington District (8 wards); Germantown: Germantown Borough and Township, Bristol Township; West Philadelphia: Blockley Township, West Philadelphia District; South Philadelphia: Moyamensing and Southwark, Kingsessing; Manayunk: Manayunk Borough, Roxborough Township; Northeast Philadelphia: Northern Liberties Township, Bridesburg, Frankford, Aramingo, Lower Dublin, Oxford, Richmond, Whitehall, Moreland, Byberry; Northern Liberties; Old City: City of Philadelphia (17 districts).
Source: Manuscript Manufacturing Census Schedules, Philadelphia County, 1850.

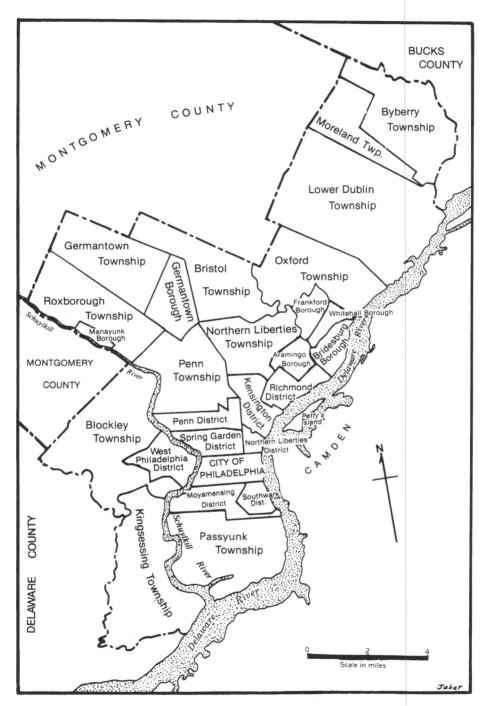

Map 2. The city and county of Philadelphia, 1850. (Adapted from John Daley and Allen Weinberg, *Genealogy of Philadelphia County Subdivisions*, Philadelphia, 1966, p. 43.)

weavers, and spinners. No one sector dominated, and the largest firm was a calico printer with but 134 workers.[5] In South Philadelphia, principally the Moyamensing District, diversity was not in evidence. There, 85% of the textile workers wove cottons, and the same handloom production of checks and plaids reported in 1820 continued a generation later.

A little over 10% of the city's textile firms and workers remained in Old City, two square miles between the rivers, bounded by Vine Street at the north and Cedar (later South) Street. Three-quarters of the 1,200 hands in the cotton and mixed-fabric sectors, however, were concentrated in the southwest corner of Old City (Cedar Ward). The area along the Delaware to the east was by 1850 crammed with commercial and residential buildings, dockside facilities, aging workshops and warehouses. As a result, the few textile factory builders in Old City found adequate space available only on the western fringes of downtown Philadelphia.

Of the nine districts into which we have divided Philadelphia, three– Old City, Spring Garden, and Kensington –show a wide diversity of textile manufacturing. In all three, at least seven of the nine textile sectors are present and no single one characterizes the district's textile output. (Just over half of Kensington's workers did weave mixed goods, making it a borderline case in this respect.) There is little textile activity in Northern Liberties, but the other five districts each sport a leading sector occupying generally two-thirds or more of its workers (dyeing in West and Northeast Philadelphia, hosiery at Germantown, factory cottons in Manayunk, and handloom cottons in South Philadelphia).

Both material and cultural elements in accumulation conditioned the layout of textile production at Philadelphia. The presence of a developed waterpower at Manayunk and the availability of mill floors for rent facilitated the early establishment of almost exclusive factory relations of production there. The extent to which it became an immigrant destination for workers with factory skills and backgrounds cannot be precisely established, but all the Manayunk workers testifying at the 1837 Pennsylvania Senate hearings spoke of mill experience in Britain. Moreover, no carpet or knit-goods handloom craftshops were set up in 1850 Manayunk, as handworkers knew the character of the district and located elsewhere. The handloom tradition of Moyamensing was solidly in place by 1820, providing a neighborhood base for aspiring shop masters and work opportunities for cotton weavers who sought an alternative to Kensington's legendary rowdiness. No ambiguity surrounds Kensington's position as a haven for immigrant weavers, nearly 80% of whom were Irish-born.[6] The Kensington workshop masters and

5 1850 MCS, Philadelphia Co., p. 22.
6 Montgomery, "Shuttle," p. 48.

outwork contractors were also largely Irish, a cultural parallel that reinforced Old Country work practices and relationships in an otherwise strange setting. The agglomeration of thousands of craftsmen in the district made for a ready labor supply and an ease of outwork management not found in rural areas. For shop masters, there was no struggle to find hands; for weavers, work could usually be had without long searching. The proximity of Kensington to both rail and water transport and to the central wholesale district facilitated a full flow of goods and information. Its political independence (until 1854) allowed master weavers a measure of local power and prominence, though the very visibility of master weaver Hugh Clark and proprietor Michael Keenan led to Clark's villification and the firing of Keenan's workshops in the nativist riots of the forties.[7]

Germantown experienced a symbiotic migration of English hosiers and framework knitters to a district once famous for that production. Its rural hills and vales recalled the cottager's environs, as did the village center, but the daily trains to the urban center enabled its hosiery producers to reach central markets in Old City without difficulty. As suggested earlier, dyers' water requirements and foul byproducts determined the establishment of their works along the Schuylkill and Delaware, forming villagelike clusters in otherwise open lands. We may imagine that incoming printers and finishers were quickly made aware of the location of the Horrocks, Martin, Hunter, or Ripka plants, which were themselves established by immigrant capitalists. Recently developed, Spring Garden was the "progressive" center of the textile manufacture insofar as mill expansion there involved both "modernization" and exclusively economic considerations. Although the factory format was introduced to Philadelphia through Manayunk's 1820s waterpower development, that power source was itself a constraint on its users. The mills were stopped frequently by low water, ice, and the annual canal repairs. At Spring Garden, steampower became the mill norm, for no waterpower was available. The location, along the Schuylkill just north of Old City, was ideal for delivery of anthracite by the canal system and lay astride the main lines of the Philadelphia and Reading railroads, which connected north to the coal regions and east and south to other rail lines.[8] Despite the presence of several sizable mills in Cedar Ward, center city Philadelphia was in decline as a textile manufacturing district as fashionable residences, banks, clubs, and shops gradually filled the blocks west of the old market, dock, and workshop areas. Bucking the trend toward outlying mill and shop sites, the Horstmann silk and trimmings firm, during the fifties, relocated from Ken-

[7] Ibid., p. 45; *Daily Chronicle*, September 25, 1841.

[8] Jeffrey Roberts, "Railroads and the Downtown: Philadelphia, 1830–1900," in H. Gillette, ed., *The Divided Metropolis*, Westport, Conn., 1980, p. 30.

sington to Fifth and Cherry, carrying on production, warehousing, and sales in two buildings near the commercial center. No other major firm copied Horstmann's venture.[9]

The form of organization adopted by textile firms is not given directly by census or other data, but the names used by the operators for their enterprises allow a rough estimate of the proportion of sole proprietorships and partnerships active in 1850 Philadelphia. Where two names or "and Brother," "and Son(s)," "and Co." appear, a partnership is clearly in operation. Single names likely refer to sole ownership, though in some cases they may conceal silent partners or sons taken into the firm but not acknowledged by a name change (e.g., Ripka). What appears in Table 6.6. is a base line for the minimum number of partnerships visible in census returns, given by district.

Of all firms, at least one in six were partnerships, though they were more common in districts of factory manufacture and printing (7 of 24 in Manayunk, 11 of 27 in the West and Northeast). When firms having about 100 workers are examined, ten of the thirty-three are definite partnerships, suggesting the capital assembly function often a rationale for the teaming-up of prospective mill operators. This relationship is emphasized by noting that ten of the twenty-one individually owned firms in this group were handloom enterprises, able to employ large numbers of workers with an investment of fairly small capital. The two remaining firms were Germantown's incorporated Wakefield Mills, a descendant of the 1820 Fisher, Gouge, and Potts,[10] and Spring Garden's Madison Company, for which little information is available. More important, if all four firms identified by a company name were presumed corporate in form, less than 3% of Philadelphia's textile workers would have been involved.[11] The contrast with Lowell could hardly be more complete.

Before we focus on individual districts and firms, it is important to note how female labor varied from district to district, by firm size, and in the various textile sectors. At Lowell the employment of "unskilled" women proceeded in tandem with the early expansion of powered spinning and weaving capacity. As immigrant men could be hired for identical piece rates in later years, women's employment ceased to be an indicator of the extent to which low-skilled operative jobs had been created there. Given the far greater complexity of the textile manufacturing structure emerging at Philadelphia, an understanding of women's employment must consider the par-

---

[9] Edwin Freedley, *Philadelphia and Its Manufactures*, Philadelphia, 1858, pp. 245–7.

[10] Scharf and Westcott, *History of Philadelphia*, p. 2307.

[11] The four mills lacking family names are Madison (134 workers), Wakefield (180), West Philadelphia's Rose Mills (22), and the Moyamensing House of Industry (45), the district's poorhouse where paupers wove rag carpets, 1850 MCS, Philadelphia Co., pp. 6, 95, 222, 256.

Table 6.6. *Textile firms by district and form of organization, Philadelphia, 1850*

District	N	Form of organization				
		One name	Two partners	Three partners	"& Co." "& Bros."	No family name
Kensington	126	116	8	1	1	0
Germantown	35	28	4	0	2	1
West Philadelphia	15	9	5	0	0	1
South Philadelphia	21	16	3	0	1	1
Manayunk	24	17	6	0	1	0
Spring Garden	34	28	1	0	4	1
Northeast Philadelphia	12	6	3	0	3	0
Northern Liberties	23	22	0	0	1	0
Old City	36	30	5	1	0	0
Total	326	272	35	2	13	4

Source: Manuscript Manufacturing Census Schedules, Philadelphia County, 1850.

ticular formats of production in which they were involved. (As there was no category in the manufacturing census for child workers until 1870, the figures mask the extent to which "boys and girls" formed a part of the shop and mill labor pool.) The distribution of women workers is broadly reflective of the dominant productive sector in several districts (Table 6.7). The lowest proportions (19% and 32%) appear in the two areas possessing large dyeing and calico printing establishments. Higher concentrations of women appear in those areas with water- and steampowered factories, principally on cottons and mixed goods (Manayunk, Spring Garden, and Old City), and in Germantown, whose knit-goods operations had a large female component. Close to the citywide average were those areas of handwork operations, Kensington, South Philadelphia, and Northern Liberties.

To see the very different positions occupied by women in the relations of production, consider first the tiny handwork shop, reporting perhaps a half dozen workers to the census marshals (Table 6.8). About a hundred such firms were tabulated in the 1850 Philadelphia textile trades, weaving cottons, mixed fabrics, and carpets and knitting hose and gloves. Generally family-based, such shops traditionally engaged the wives and children of the small master, along with a handful of countrymen or kinsmen who boarded with the family and worked in a shed at the rear of the house. Family members would be called upon to spool, prepare warp, and repair flaws in finished goods. In time, sons would be "called" to the loom to learn the craft. Women's work in this setting supported the structure and operation of the

Table 6.7. *Textile workers by district and sex, Philadelphia,*
1850

District	Textile workers	
	Male	Female
Kensington	2,386 (60)	1,591 (40)
Germantown	575 (50)	584 (50)
West Philadelphia	311 (68)	148 (32)
South Philadelphia	615 (66)	319 (34)
Manayunk	1,026 (52)	940 (48)
Spring Garden	656 (54)	560 (46)
Northeast Philadelphia	573 (81)	131 (19)
Northern Liberties	224 (54)	193 (46)
Old City	775 (50)	762 (50)
Total	7,141 (58)	5,228 (42)

Note: Figures in parentheses indicate percentages.
Source: Manuscript Manufacturing Census Schedules, Philadelphia County, 1850.

artisanal workshop, and few such firms could have functioned without it. Yet
when the reports from 103 handloom shops with seven or fewer workers are
surveyed, two-thirds (65) of them show *no* women workers. Why?

That women contributed labor to the output of handwork shops is certain;
that they were not considered "employees" in family shops, that is, they were
not paid, may account for the discrepancy.[12] The uncompensated labor of

---

[12] The census schedules contributed to what I believe was a failure to record these women
as workers by asking in parallel columns for numbers of male and female workers and
the monthly wages paid each group. In a small shop family members sometimes did not
receive wages and thus they might well not have been listed as workers, given the
structure of the census form. The example of Sevill Schofield's long years without wages
(Chapter 3, this volume) should further suggest that this disparity between census
counts and the labor pool was not confined to women. Such a divergence may not be
statistically significant on the aggregate, but it is historically significant in any search for
productive relationships. Whatever else it may imply, this questioning of the "accuracy"
of small-shop census data should encourage researchers to acknowledge the difficulties
of extracting an understanding of the transitional processes through the use of data
sources that *presumed* the existence of capitalist relations of production, particularly in
the presence of a narrow economic rationality that finds no problem in specifying who
the "workers" are in a firm. The same transitional ambiguity is evident in the listing of
small-shop masters as workers. In some cases, five looms and four workers were given,
the fifth loom presumably run by the proprietor who excluded himself from the group

Table 6.8. *Textile handworkers at firms of 7 or fewer workers by sector and sex, Philadelphia, 1850–70*

Sector	No. of firms	Male workers	Female workers
Cotton	17	62	10
Cotton-wool	4	19	3
Wool	4	18	3
Silk	4	8	8
Hosiery, knit goods	30	81	32
Carpet	38	125	17
Other	6	17	3
Total	103[a]	330	76

Note: Dyeing, finishing omitted because it was almost exclusively "men's work"; spinning omitted because it was powered.

[a] The 38 shops reporting female workers also reported 114 male workers. The 65 shops "without" female workers reported 216 male workers.

Source: Manuscript Manufacturing Census Schedules, Philadelphia County, 1850.

women and children was likely confined to the master's family, boarding kin, or women connected with male weavers. Some may indeed have been members of the master's family for whom wages were calculated (and perhaps even paid), a symbolic step into the transactional economics of the marketplace. In any case, shop masters failing to report family members as employees were incompletely socialized to capitalism, their returns masking the labor of women and children, which was necessary to the preservation of an artisanal workshop format.

If women in smaller shops were immured in a productive format that generally did not classify them as workers, despite their role in manufacture, what was the position of women in larger enterprises? Turning to the other extreme of scale, firms with 100 or more workers in 1850 segregated by power source (Table 6.9), we may examine the twenty-one large cotton and

earning wages. In other cases, loom and worker counts match, though the production was hardly sufficient to permit the master to limit himself to keeping the books. Such examples illustrate the contrasting conceptions of who was and who was not a "worker," an important element in the gradual development of capitalist notions about society and production (for examples of this last pattern, see 1850 MCS, Philadelphia Co., pp. 47, 48, 67).

Table 6.9. *District, sector, capital, and work force of cotton and mixed-goods firms of 100 or more workers by power source, Philadelphia, 1850*

Power source	District	Sector	Capital	Male workers	Female workers
Steam					
William Brady	Kensington	Cotton	$22,000	50	80
George Clark	Kensington	Cotton-wool	12,000	70	56
William, Thomas & Stephen Douthwitt	Old City	Cotton	40,000	65	65
Thomas Drake	Old City	Cotton-wool	250,000	80	130
William Dunn	Old City	Cotton-wool	57,000	63	65
Peter Hickey	Kensington	Cotton-wool	80,000	320	200
Robert Selfridge	South Philadelphia	Cotton	30,000	66	60
William Watt	Old City	Cotton-wool	85,000	41	160
Wilson & Allen	Kensington	Cotton	70,000	50	100
Water					
Joseph Ripka	Manayunk	Cotton	400,000	366	316
Stephens & Whitakers	Manayunk	Cotton	75,000	57	50
Steam & water					
J. C. Kempton	Manayunk	Cotton	250,000	290	334
Subtotal			1,371,000	1,518 (48%)	1,616 (52%)
Hand					
Blair & Bannister	Kensington	Cotton-wool	10,000	80	35
Thomas Harkness	Kensington	Cotton-wool	4,000	76	56
Daniel Hickey	Kensington	Cotton-wool	8,000	150	75
George McCrate	South Philadelphia	Cotton	25,000	75	30
McMakin & Maxwell	Old City	Cotton	15,000	75	30
Thomas Mulcahey	Kensington	Cotton-wool	6,000	60	42
Dominick Murphy	Kensington	Cotton	3,000	80	40

Table 6.9. (*Continued*)

Power source	District	Sector	Capital	Male workers	Female workers
Granleeb Norris	South Philadelphia	Cotton	12,000	100	40
Wright, McCall	South Philadelphia	Cotton	25,000	150	0
Subtotal			108,000	846 (71%)	348 (29%)
Total			1,479,000	2,344	1,984

Source: Manufacturing Census Schedules, Philadelphia County, 1850.

mixed-fabric firms, which employed a third of the city's textile workers. Of these firms, twelve were steam- and waterpowered mills and nine were handloom workshop and outwork enterprises. (There were actually twenty-two firms in this category, but that of Michael Keenan, a Kensington hand-loom master weaver in the 1840s, is unclassifiable, as the space on the schedule for "motive power" was left blank.) The contrasting proportions of women at work in the powered and hand formats is obvious.

The large handloom shops employed proportionally fewer women by far than did the powered mills. This is consistent with both the outwork charac-ter (of uncertain dimensions) of handloom work and the preservation of the male weaver's craft within the shops. All the shops bought yarn, lacking the power to spin their own, indicating that women spooled, warped, inspected, and repaired for these firms as they did in the tiny household shops. That men were weavers and women aides is shown in the returns for George McCrate and Granleeb Norris in which the number of male workers and looms are identical.[13] Interestingly enough, the no-women feature reported by many small workshops reappears with Wright, McCall and Co. This may not, however, reflect an extension of the artisanal perception of women; rather, a comparison of wage data with other firms in the same area suggests that the total wages of $2,400 paid per month might well have been allocated to 100 men at $20 and 50 women at $8, rates prevailing in the district.[14] If

[13] The census marshals were quite inconsistent in gathering machinery data; however, their handloom counts and male worker figures match consistently in several wards of Moyamensing. Machinery information elsewhere is quite scattered, principally appear-ing in the returns of powered mills.

[14] 1850 MCS, Philadelphia Co., pp. 42–70.

this adjustment is allowed, the proportion of male and female workers at the large handloom firms would be two-thirds and one-third, respectively, a balance consistent with workshops of middling (25–99 workers) and small (under 25) size as well.

The much more substantial presence of women workers in powered mills reflects their positions as loom tenders in addition to the standard service functions (in the mill, bobbin changing in throstle frames, warp dressing and drawing-in, and cloth inspection). Women power-loom operators posed a direct threat to male handloom weavers in districts like Kensington and Moyamensing. There is some evidence that, for 1850 at least, power looms were not standard equipment in steam mills in those two areas, whereas more than a thousand of them were running in Old City and Manayunk, areas where handloom operations were virtually nil. Of the five cotton and mixed-goods steampowered factories in handloom districts, three seem largely to have operated with handlooms, using power chiefly for spinning. George Clark listed only eight power looms in his Kensington mill, though he manufactured more than 350,000 yards of woolen and cotton goods in 1849–50, engaging 126 workers.[15] Thomas Selfridge of South Philadelphia, who had 66 male workers and 66 "looms," was cited as a handloom proprietor in an 1857 survey published by Freedley.[16] Peter Hickey, Kensington's largest textile employer, ran 350 looms; but their products included shawls and carpets, as well as staple cottons, indicating that some, perhaps most, of the looms were hand-operated.[17] Sixty "power looms" were in place at Brady's mill, and there were 120 "looms" in the Wilson & Allen factory, with 100 women and 50 men workers. As this latter facility did its own spinning and dyeing, it is reasonable to visualize the looms as powered and tended by the bulk of the female work force. The cautious introduction of power looms at Kensington and their standard use at other factory sites (Kempton had 250, Ripka over 600) deserves closer attention. What might account for the differential in development?

The Kensington steampowered mills were established in a community that already had a complex set of manufacturing and social relations centered on handloom weaving. This material and cultural environment acted as a constraint on the use of power looms and women tenders on the scale common at Manayunk. The Schuylkill waterpowered mills were the core edifices around which Manayunk was constructed. No prior social network operated there to restrain technological innovation, though its impact on local workers was resisted in strikes and its threat to the livelihood of handworkers precipitated the 1830s marches on Manayunk by Kensington textile

[15] Ibid, p. 43.
[16] Ibid., p. 96; Freedley, *Philadelphia and Its Manufactures*, p. 254.
[17] 1850 MCS, Philadelphia Co., p. 42.

men. Given their history of riotous activity, Kensington weavers had to be
taken into account by prospective factory operators who would undertake
mass production in their district. The mixing of hand- and power looms by
Clark and Hickey, perhaps combined with outwork contracts, suggests an
accommodation to the neighborhood cultural and political environment similar to the earlier practices of the Globe Mill proprietors. Rather than challenge the handwork format frontally, they sought to integrate it into a partially powered system. Spinning, as at the Globe, was the key, for the
production of bulk yarn kept both handshop and millweaving in business. A
staged introduction of power looms to "take up the overflow" from spinning,
to be run by kinswomen of handworkers, would have been tactically
reasonable.

This gradualist pattern may also have been dictated by the chronic shortage of capital experienced by immigrant manufacturers. Piecemeal machinery extension was the rule, going hand in hand with the spatial sequence
illustrated by the Ripka and Schofield experiences. Profits from handloom
operations must have enabled several of the Kensington entrepreneurs to
take the first steps toward powered production, though in 1850 most of
Kensington's textile workers were situated outside the mills. The craft workshop was a man's dominion, the weaver's prowess an element in the constitution of patriarchal family relationships. The manufacturer at Kensington
who entered upon female-staffed power-loom production would threaten
not just handweavers' jobs but the social fabric of the community. Ambitious
shopmen, seeking to move into factory settings, were well advised to abandon Kensington in earlier years, as Ripka did (even though steam engines
were available had he chosen to remain there). This cultural brake had
evidently lost some of its force by 1850, with two mills running power looms
exclusively; the others' mixed formats indicate, however, that textile capitalists, in seeking profits, had taken steps based to some degree on recognition
of the non-economic factors that could facilitate or impede the accumulation
process. Just as the Lowell corporations felt obliged to provide a chaste and
secure environment to secure the services of Yankee farm girls, a cultural
dimension of capitalist development, so too at Kensington, manufacturers
who participated in, yet sought to transcend, the culture of handweaving
either moved with caution in introducing women as powerweavers or moved
out of the district entirely.

The handwork trades in Kensington

In 1850 Kensington was divided into eight wards, all of which had some
textile manufacturing within their borders. However, three-quarters of the
firms and workers were counted in the central and adjacent Third and Sixth

wards. With 1,600 workers and forty-nine firms, the Sixth Ward was the most heavily packed textile neighborhood in Kensington, a rough square bounded by Frankford Avenue and Second, Oxford, and Franklin streets. Linking manufacturers to the 1850 Population Census for the Sixth Ward provides an assessment of the ethnicity, wealth, and age distribution of a sizable group of handshop masters and a base from which to specify aspects of the relations of production visible through the census returns.

Of the forty-nine firms in the Sixth Ward, good links to the 1850 Population Census were obtained for forty-five; in all but one case links were to heads of households (first name listed in a household).[18] The first conclusion from the linkage effort is that the overwhelming majority of Kensington's Sixth Ward manufacturers lived either close to or at their workshop sites. Forty-four of the forty-six local handloom masters were successfully identified as Sixth Ward residents. One of the two steammill owners who did not reside nearby was Thomas H. Craige, who lived in Old City.

Located at the Star Mill, which was shared with Needles and Evans, Craige's spinning firm was the largest in the city, producing more than 160 tons of yarn annually.[19] Much of it was surely directed to the handloom workshops on adjoining streets, as had been the output of his father's spinning frames at the Globe. Yet Thomas Craige had little in common with his fellow Kensington manufacturers. Native-born, living among and circulating with the city's economic gentry, and linked to them by marriage, he operated amid a collection of immigrant shop masters, most of whom were Irish.

Of the forty-five manufacturers linked, thirty-three (73%) were Irish-born, eight English, two Scots, and one, William Hogg, Jr., was a Pennsylvania native, born in 1830 to an Irish immigrant carpet weaver. One of the "English"-born, James Douglas, was from an Irish family that settled in Britain for a few years before reaching the United States in the early thir-

---

[18] Linkage rules used, which were employed also in the Philadelphia Social History Project, sought a match for first and last names *and* occupation. Small variations in last name proved insignificant (Wallace, Wallice), occupation appeared generally as "manufacturer" or "weaver," sometimes prefaced by "cot." or "stocking." Though many of the surnames seem common, in only four cases were there two or more ward residents with identical first and last names, and the occupational column segregated them immediately. The possibility of false matches, with the "real" manufacturer residing across a ward line, is present but of small moment, given the probable overlap of residence and workshop for numerous small firms. The only manufacturer linked to the population schedules who was not a household head was James Douglas, 23, who lived with his widowed (?) mother, four brothers and sisters, and three weavers who boarded with the family. His occupation was "manufacturer" and the James Douglas firm employed three male workers, the complementary firm and household data confirming what might otherwise have been a questionable link.

[19] 1850 MCS, Philadelphia Co., p. 67.

Table 6.10. *Manufacturers by trade, ethnicity, and age, Kensington, Ward 6,*
1850

| | | Age of manufacturers | | | | |
Trade	Ethnicity	29 or less	30–39	40–49	50+	Total
Carpet	Irish	3	9	3	1	16
Cotton and cotton-wool	Irish	4	6	5	2	17
Hosiery, knit goods	English, Scots	2	2	1	0	5
Others	English, Scots, U.S.	3	0	3	1	7
Total		12	17	12	4	45

Source: Manuscript Manufacturing Census Schedules and Population Census Schedules, Philadelphia County, Kensington, Ward 6, 1850.

ties.[20] All five hosiers in the Sixth Ward were English or Scots; the Irish
masters ran handlooms on cottons, mixed goods, and carpets (Table 6.10).
The proportion of Irish manufacturers matches Montgomery's calculation
for weavers in Kensington and confirms his inference that "both masters
and workmen in the weaving business were predominantly Irish."[21]

The tabular information gestures toward an aging cotton handloom group
with younger shop masters taking up carpet manufacture, a hand trade that
showed a long-term rise from the forties through the seventies. The small
number of older masters may indicate both the mortality risks of craftsmen
in congested urban areas and the withdrawal of those shopmen who had
achieved a competence. There are throughout the Sixth Ward Census returns middle-aged men with families who list their occupation as "None,"[22]

20 1850 PCS, Philadelphia Co., Kensington, Ward 6, p. 65. James and his 21-year-old
   brother were born in England, placing the family there in the late 1820s. His sister, 16 in
   1850, was born in Pennsylvania circa 1834, thus establishing a rough estimate of the
   period of transatlantic migration.
21 Using the 1850 Population Census Schedules, Montgomery established the proportion
   for weavers but did not link manufacturers from the Manufacturing Schedules to the
   Population Census to confirm the parallel for masters (see, Montgomery, "Shuttle," p.
   48 and note 20, p. 69).
22 For example, Frank Farley, 45 and Irish, listed no occupation but recorded $1,800 in
   real estate (1850 PCS, Philadelphia Co., Kensington, Ward 6, p. 43); four others are
   similarly recorded on adjacent pages. There are also moderate numbers of propertyless
   younger men who give "none" for occupation, perhaps indicating unemployment. Such
   data allow no close reading, but the possibility should be entertained that the older men
   listing no occupations had retired to competencies.

though whether in pride at having retired in security or in desperation at being worn out and unemployable cannot be known.[23] No correlation appears between age and the size of the work force or capital employed. Both young and middle-aged masters can be found in the ranks of small and large employers.

Reviewing household entries in the 1850 Population Census allows some estimation of the dates by which manufacturers were residents of Pennsylvania or other states as the birthplaces of children indicate the dates by which American settlement had taken place. This is of particular interest in a heavily Irish community at the close of the famine period, during which blocks of Kensington were filled with new immigrants. When such an examination is conducted for the thirty-three Irish masters shown in Table 6.10, at least twenty of them had children born before 1844 in the United States.[24] Two had no children, and of the remaining eleven, six were under 30 with new families. Thus it seems that the bulk of the Irish textile employers in 1850 Kensington were present to welcome the famine-era immigrants to their workshops, rather than being new arrivals themselves. The accumulation of capital at Kensington at this time, and citywide over a longer period, was consequently made possible by the exploitation of immigrants by immigrants, countrymen who welcomed their brethren to communities whose very embrace impeded the development of a critical awareness of the economic processes taking place.

A salient characteristic of the handloom shopmen's economic profiles was the small capital necessary in both the city and the outlying districts for their basic functions (Table 6.9). More than 1,100 workers were employed in the largest cotton and mixed-goods shops with less than half the capital used by Thomas Drake alone in operations involving 210 workers. The difference is fundamental to the structures of the two formats, as handloom proprietors had but to rent a workshop or build a shed for their looms, the cost of which was a fraction of the powered variety. Without spinning frames, usually without dyeing facilities, and frequently with even the looms owned by their operators, handloom masters averaged but $90 per worker in capital invested (Table 6.9). With their mixed modes of operations, the five large Kensington and Moyamensing cotton and mixed-goods mills registered $203 invested per worker, whereas the fully integrated and powered mills of Manayunk and Old City averaged a rather grand $555 in plant and machinery for each

---

[23] That the path toward the competence was widely traveled, at least in Kensington, I will undertake to show shortly.

[24] Douglas's presence in Pennsylvania in 1836 is indicated earlier. The birthplaces of the children of the other nineteen men indicated that they had immigrated before the famine. Totals were calculated from work sheets drawn from Ward 6 schedules.

worker. The handloom shops in the Sixth Ward included in Table 6.10 reported capital totaling $124,150 and a work force of 1,443,[25] a gross average of $86 per worker, suggesting a fairly constant level of per worker investment, whatever the size of the handloom shop. Movement to powered manufacture increased the ante considerably, first in the partial form, to which a mill and spinning apparatus was basic, and then enormously when the full range of integrated and powered equipment was established in a factory built for the purpose.

The potential for, in modern terms, quite satisfactory returns to capital on an annual basis from handloom operations should be clear, even facing the depressed price of goods generated by the New England mills' mammoth output. With but $4,000 invested, 30-year-old Thomas Harkness was able to claim the services of 126 workers in the census year. He reported expenses of $29,200 for yarn, dyeing, wood, and coal (presumably to heat the workshop), whereas the goods he offered to the market – cotton checks, wool and cotton pantaloon stuffs, shawls, and cotton "table diaper" – were worth $51,575. Though demand was variable, and labor seasonal, if the monthly figures given are simply multiplied by twelve, the annual wage cost would maximize at $20,016, leaving the proprietor at least $2,300 gross profit. Although only 4.5% on sales, this represents more than a 50% gross return to capital, from which even sizable deductions for rent and other charges would still leave enough for a life far more comfortable than that afforded his workers, whose income averaged about $216 per year for men, $72 for women.[26] A comfortable life, perhaps, but here is not a pathway to rapid accumulation or great riches. The retained profit of most handloom shopmen could not finance the quantum leap to factory-based production. Moreover, in 1850 Kensington, powered mills with rental space were scarce. Finally, handloom masters likely did not possess any great familiarity with, or affection for, the steam engine and its power-driven frames and looms. If most of them did not seek to "modernize," what did they do, what could they do with their profits?

A review of the 1850 Population Census entries for the forty-five linked manufacturers in Kensington's Sixth Ward suggests that those with a surplus to invest bought real estate, most likely accumulating a number of four- to six-room houses for rental. Small frame homes in Kensington could be purchased for as little as $150, old brick structures for about $300, and brand-new, six-room buildings for about $1,000.[27] Of the forty-five manu-

[25] Calculated from work sheets from Ward 6 schedules.

[26] 1850 MCS, Philadelphia Co., p. 68.

[27] Dennis Clark, *The Irish in Philadelphia*, Philadelphia, 1973, p. 50 and note 52; Montgomery, "Shuttle," p. 48.

facturers, twenty listed "Value of Real Estate owned" of $1,000 or more. More important, in fifteen of these twenty cases the real-estate value was equal to, or greater than, the capital invested in their firms. A house in fair condition worth perhaps $500 rented for $50 or $60 a year; a half dozen such buildings would establish the base for a competence. It is this pathway that is indicated by the pattern of real-estate holdings by small manufacturers. Generally older than average, only three of these property owners were under 35, and twelve were over 40 years of age. Fifty-year-old James Mitchell owned $4,000 in real estate. If his investment represented eight $500 houses, one of which he lived in, he might receive in rents from the other seven more than $350 per year. His security in old age was achieved.[28] Few might reach the level of comfort enjoyed by Charles Hill, an English dyer whose real-estate holdings, excluding his shop, were valued at $15,000, but most could hope for a competence like Mitchell's if no disaster struck. After all, of the sixteen masters over 40 in Table 6.10, twelve were property holders. Excluding Hill, the average for the other eleven was a substantial $2,850, easily four houses for rental and one for occupancy at 1850 values.

That the competence was in fact a part of Kensington shop culture is illustrated by the experience of William Hogg, Sr., whose son expanded the family firm into the Oxford Carpet Mills, active into the 1880s. The elder Hogg began his carpet handshop in 1832 "in a small way," meeting gradual success until in 1846, "having amassed a competency, he withdrew, entrusting it to his eldest son."[29] In fourteen years, the founder had set aside sufficient revenue to retire from the trade. It seems plausible that he enjoyed the income from housing investments, perhaps renting to carpet weavers who toiled in the family's workshop. Although his exemplary success may have stimulated both envy and admiration in the neighborhood, it also reveals the persistence of an attitude toward capitalist entrepreneurship that was far removed from the philosophy that guided entrepreneurs at Lowell. Like Charles Schofield somewhat later, Hogg participated in a manufacturing culture that saw an end to gain in personal and familial security. Once that goal was achieved, it was appropriate to "withdraw."

[28] These figures are of course arbitrary, but the return in rentals on home values, conservatively, seems to have been about 10%, that is, a four- to six-room house priced at from $400 to $800 returned about $1 to $1.50 a week. The rent for houses, selling at $1,000 or a bit more, was $8 to $10 per month (see Clark, *Irish*, pp. 50–5). Incidentally, shopmen may have counted the value of their residences as part of their business capital *and* as real estate if weaving was done there or in backyard sheds. This in no way would affect the conclusions presented here, as I have included a house occupied by the manufacturer in the real-estate package. If house values were commonly included in manufacturing capital figures, it would only underscore the minimal financial requirements for handwork-shop and outwork production.

[29] Daniel Robson, ed., *Manufactories and Manufacturers of Pennsylvania of the Nineteenth Century*, Philadelphia, 1875, p. 38.

The role of boarding

Whereas the competence was an element in the long-term structure of productive relations, the boarding of workers with their masters' families was part of the day-to-day workshop system. Such boarding has long been associated with the apprenticeship-journeyman system, which involved close familylike relations of power and control along with the transmission and exercise of artisanal skill, as Paul Johnson has shown for the Rochester hand trades. In such workshops, the master was responsible for his workers' moral welfare as well as their craftsmanship. However, at least in Johnson's Rochester, these relationships were fading by the mid-1830s as masters withdrew into distanced private households and journeymen became employees who worked for a wage. There, between 1827 and 1834, the proportion of live-in workers dropped from 25% of all shoemakers to 5%, and overall, the proportion of "small-shop craftsmen" with boarders fell from one-half to one-third. Yet in the textile handcrafts of midcentury Kensington, boarding was still solidly in place, as half the handshop proprietors in the Sixth Ward reported weavers or dyers living in. As the masters were largely pre-famine immigrants to Philadelphia and as their boarding workers were much younger men (60% age 25 or under), Kensington craft-shop boarding likely represents a relationship by which new immigrants became situated in the work community of the metropolis.[30]

Of the forty-five linked Sixth Ward households, thirty-two held persons readily classifiable as boarders; in six cases the single boarder was a young Irish female, four of whom lived in property-owning manufacturers' households. These women were most probably servants and/or kin. In two cases, nontextile boarders, one "Protestant Clergyman" and one "Saxton" (Sexton?), were the only additions to the family, which was Irish. This gently reinforces the notion that Protestant and Catholic Irishmen coexisted in Kensington, the decline of the Ulster handloom linen trade having generated an immigration parallel to that of southern Irish cottagers. Twenty-four households contained boarders identified as "weavers" or "dyers," strongly suggesting the presence of a work shed on the premises. We shall consider

---

[30] Boarders are those persons living in the household whose names are different from the family surname. All but one household (Douglas) contained such a core grouping. Though the 1850 census did not specify relationships within each household, allowing, for example, a 9-year-old niece to appear to be a daughter, some surname "relatives" do regularly appear appended to the age-descending cluster of the head of household's immediate family. This hardly interferes with the main point of this discussion, however, which is concerned with the frequent practice of weavers and dyers living in the shop master's household, occasionally in prodigious numbers. For Rochester, New York, see Paul Johnson, *A Shopkeeper's Millennium: Society and Revivals in Rochester, New York, 1815–1837*, New York, 1978, pp. 44–8, 106–7.

these shortly at greater length. The thirteen remaining families with no boarders include seven property owners, one stockinger whose two sons were listed as working in the trade, and a half-dozen families either quite young (the father 30 or under) or so large as to limit the possibility of taking boarders (e.g., seven children).

Owners of substantial amounts of property hardly needed to board their handloom workers in order to enjoy an annual surplus. Indeed, they quite likely rented their properties to employees to encourage stability in the work force, to cut cash flow (rent could be deducted from wages due), to have some leverage over workmen in wage disputes, and to have influence over the condition in which their properties were maintained. Masters with boarding workmen had not advanced so far along the road to a competence; two-thirds of them listed no real estate at all.

The functions of boarding may be construed in several overlapping senses. First, the practice continued the relationships once based on apprenticeship and journeyman labor common in artisanal shops of the early nineteenth century. Though many of the training functions had atrophied, cultural residues may have continued to foster its retention. Second, the economic gains to be made by boarding were quite real, in the deductions from wages that could be made for bed and board, the appropriation of family women's labor to the firm's profit goals even if they neither warped nor mended, and the closer control over labor and life that was possible in this expanded patriarchal network. Third, boarding may be considered as a way station in the life cycle of a handloom firm, insofar as the accumulation made possible by the many small exploitations could fund the purchase of property, leading first to the reduction and then the final conversion of boarders into tenants and ultimately to the assumption of a competence. Table 6.11 presents the outlines of boarding by shop masters, including work-force composition and capital to indicate the extent to which boarders formed only a part of the firm's complement and the prevalence of small capitals among shops with boarders. Though firms with boarders are largely Irish (twenty of twenty-four), the incidence of boarding is only slightly higher than the overall prevalence of Irish firms (83% vs. 76%). Women boarders, who were present in small numbers, likely contributed to the work flow or household labor, but the occupational information requested in the 1850 Population Schedule impedes a determination of their activity. It asked for "Profession, Occupation, or Trade of each Male Person over 15 years of age." Census marshals sometimes noted single-women household heads as having "no occupation" but otherwise ignored thousands of working women in accordance with their instructions. In only one of the boarding cases, the household of William Young, are three women listed as weavers.[31] However,

---

[31] 1850 PCS, Philadelphia Co., Kensington, Ward 6, p. 60.

Table 6.11. *Textile workshop/households with boarders by sector, Kensington, Ward 6, 1850*

| Shop master/ household head | Workers | | | Household head | | Boarders | | Family | | Total[a] | Value of real estate |
	Capital	Male	Female	Nativity	Age	Textile workers	Other	Wife & children	Kin		
Carpet											
Joseph Allen	$3,000	24	4	Irish	44	13	0	6	0	20	—
John Graham	4,000	13	5	Irish	38	9	2F	5	1[b]	18	$2,000
Robert L. Graham	2,500	12	4	Irish	29	8	1F	3	0	13	—
Stuart Hyndman	1,000	7	4	Irish	30	10	2F	2	1[b]	16	2,000
William Hyndman	800	6	3	Irish	35	4	0	4	0	9	2,200
James McCauley	12,000	60	20	Irish	28	14	2F	2	0	19	—
Andrew McGill	1,300	8	4	Irish	27	5[c]	1F	4	0	11	—
David Moffitt	1,200	8	4	Irish	56	7	1M	8	0	17	—
James Moffitt	1,500	4	1	Irish	37	3	1M	1	0	6	1,400
William Steel	6,000	20	8	Irish	38	7	1F	6	0	15	—
Robert Steenson	3,000	50	16	Irish	34	4	1F	2	0	8	7,000
William Young	1,000	8	4	Irish	40	8	4F	3	0	16	3,000
Cotton											
John Dallas	500	3	0	Irish	50	3	0	6	1[d]	11	3,000
Robert Dallas	1,000	8	4	Irish	45	2	0	3	0	6	1,600
James Dickson	1,200	4	0	Irish	35	2	0	4	0	7	—
James Douglas	850	3	1	English	23	3	0	0	5[c]	9	—
Thomas Roaney	200	4	2	Irish	28	3	0	2	0	6	—
William Stephenson	400	8	1	Irish	40	3	1M	6	0	11	—

Table 6.11. (*Continued*)

| Shop master/ household head | Capital | Workers | | Household head | | Boarders | | Family | | Total[a] | Value of real estate |
		Male	Female	Nativity	Age	Textile workers	Other	Wife & children	Kin		
Cotton–wool											
George McDade	1,500	16	8	Irish	28	5	0	2	0	8	—
John McKinstrey	400	6	0	Irish	29	4	1F	2	0	8	—
Thomas Mulcahey	6,000	60	42	Irish	39	2[f]	1F	4	0	8	—
Dyeing											
Charles Hill	1,000	5	0	English	53	1[f]	1M/1F	6	0	10	15,000
Hosiery											
John Goold	250	2	5	Scots	41	2	0	6	0	9	—
Oliver Scott	150	3	10	Scots	31	2	1F	1	0	5	—

[a]Includes household head.
[b]Father.
[c]One dyer, four weavers.
[d]Mother.
[e]Mother and siblings.
[f]Dyer(s).

Note: Dash indicates none given.

Source: 1850 Manufacturing Census Schedules and 1850 Population Schedules, Philadelphia County, Kensington, Ward 6.

they are at the foot of a column of eight male weavers, and one of the three was only eleven years old, indicating not an occupational attribution but a case of runaway ditto marks.

A number of interesting patterns emerge from the tabular data. Carpet weavers tended to have households considerably larger than manufacturers in other sectors, averaging fourteen residents, nine of whom were boarders. The twelve carpet firms accounted for 92 (75%) of the 124 textile workers boarding in twenty-four households. The nine cotton firms averaged eight members to a household, four of whom were boarders. A good deal of the difference might be related to the much smaller size of the cotton firms, both in capital and work force. Nine of the sixteen firms with fewer than ten male workers boarded the whole male staff, if the master is included in the work force in several instances. Larger shops, particularly the five with twelve to twenty-four male employees, probably combined a backyard shed with out-work, as a sizable space would be needed for fifteen or twenty carpet looms. The three very large handloom enterprises may have operated from a sepa-rate building, rented or owned, or have had extensive outwork agreements in the neighborhood with weavers who possessed their own looms. The capital reported by McCauley and Mulcahey could well reflect ownership of a manufacturing site (a converted warehouse), whereas Steenson's $3,000 seems inadequate to cover ownership of a facility sufficient for fifty weavers.

The four pairs of surnames that appear in the group do not necessarily imply family relationships. However, the Hyndmans, Dallases, and Grahams each surface on the same page of a population schedule sequence, strength-ening the possibility. In each case, one of the pair had an elderly parent in his household, the only incidence other than Douglas in the group. Moreover, these presumptive brother-sets were close enough in age to suggest a blood relationship. Stuart Hyndman was the only manufacturer to board more weavers than he employed, perhaps indicating possession of a larger house in which several of his brother's workers could be sheltered. The ages and birthplaces of the Hyndmans' children show that both men had been in Pennsylvania before 1842, making plausible a weaving family migration, with two sons who followed their father's craft setting up their own workshops side by side. In all three cases, the residence of a parent with one of his or her sons shows the failure to amass a competence in the previous generation. This makes it all the more interesting and reasonable that the three pairs count five of the nine boarding masters who have invested in real estate, which for both the Dallases and the Hyndmans represented considerably more than the business capitals.

An additional "cultural" element in these productive arrangements is the ethnic unity between master and boarder that prevailed across the group. With only one exception, every boarding textile worker in the house of an

Irish master was born in Ireland. There were no Scots or British, no Americans. The four boarding stockingers were Scotland-bred as were their bosses; Charles Hill's single resident dyer was an Englishman. Douglas, as before, is a partial variant; English-born, he housed three Irish weavers, but he had an Irish mother, dissolving the confusion.

As might well be expected, boarder-workers were much younger than their masters. Overall, whereas three-quarters of the proprietors had passed their thirtieth year, 60% of their co-resident weavers were 25 or under (75 of 124). Young boarders were more prevalent in the cotton handshops than in the carpet households, with a third of them under 20 (vs. 15% in carpets). This may indicate some retention of an apprenticeship relation in the older craft. Only six of the boarding group were over 40, four of whom were found again in cotton households. Aging single weavers might well be expected to dot the venerable handloom cotton sector; but in the newer carpet trades, dating from the thirties, there was but one boarder over 40 in the group of 92 workers residing with Sixth Ward proprietary households.[32]

Boarding weavers were predominantly young, single Irishmen, clustered in both the households of manufacturers and weavers who were not recorded as manufacturers on the industrial schedules. These secondary groupings may represent subcontractors whose shops ran up goods for the larger proprietors and whose workers were included in their reports. Dependent bosses might work alongside their boarders at the same piece rates, making their profits largely from boarding charges and other fees. Twenty-three Irish-headed households of such a character appear in the Sixth Ward population schedules, a few of whose heads listed themselves as "manufacturers." These subordinate shops add another dimension to the portrait of handloom productive relations, bringing the ward total to forty-seven weaver-boarding households, comprising 21% of the work force listed on the industrial schedules. This incidence of boarding is four times greater than the 5% established by Johnson for 1834 Rochester shoemakers. If only those workers who resided with proprietors are considered, the total for Kensington still more than doubles the earlier proportion (12.5%). The reason for the persistence of an artisanal practice is not difficult to divine, for in the thirties this customary format for production was declining in Rochester, whereas it remained vital at Philadelphia until well after the Civil War. Boarding was a constituent element in the life cycle of the handshop family firm, providing both control and income (or a reduction in cash needs for wage payments) and allowing the proprietor to build both his productive

---

[32] Calculated from 1850 MCS work sheets. Some of these men may have immigrated without their wives and children, planning to bring their families over later with the earnings from their labor. There is no way to detect the incidence of this practice from census data.

capacity and his competence. The influx of famine-era emigrants adds another dimension to the practice at Kensington. If most young boarding weavers were fairly recent immigrants, it is reasonable to imagine their use of the workshop as a stopping place, perhaps their first in America, before seeking more promising situations. Making a connection with a master from one's own county, living within a household that shared common local experience, must have eased the transition. Workers seeking to bring kinsmen "across" may have stayed several years in these shops before seeking a house and loom of their own.

However, most Sixth Ward handworkers did not live in, even with subcontractors. Of the 700 weavers and dyers located in the 1850 Population Schedules, 495 lived in family residences intermingled with residences of manufacturers and nontextile workers and operators. Every standard configuration was evident: "nuclear" families with young children, elderly couples with sons at home working the trade, a few widows supported by their weaver sons and so forth. The tally does indicate that some 250 male workers cited by Sixth Ward manufacturers were not residents of the ward. Though a good deal of weaving was done "at home," the larger workshops drew workers from areas that crossed the artificial boundaries within which records were generated. It is also probable that some of the Sixth Ward residents traveled to work in the adjacent Third, as we have examined only one-half of the Kensington weaving district here. Yet even with these limitations, we have developed a rough sense of the structure of handloom manufacture in one neighborhood of 1850 Philadelphia. Given the heavy Irish presence in the rest of Kensington and in the handloom enclave of Moyamensing and the similar characteristics of size, capital, and output spread of the firms there, we might expect comparable production relations to have existed throughout Kensington and South Philadelphia.

Moving from the Sixth Ward back to Kensington as a whole, a number of additional elements in the process of textile manufacture may be exposed. As noted earlier, cotton yarn was readily available from the Craige spinning plant, enough to sustain hundreds of handlooms even if part of it was marketed to the powered mills. The source of woolen yarns, however, is not clear. Both carpet weaving and the mixed-goods trade called for woolen yarns, with heavier, coarser yarns required for the former than for the latter. The census returns tell nothing of the source of raw materials or the means by which products were marketed. Firm biographies showing direct sales practices exist chiefly for factory-based enterprises, operations that were larger than those in place in Kensington.

It is probable that the supply and market connections of handloom shops, both small and substantial, passed through the nexus of cloth and yarn merchants concentrated near the Old City docks. Merchants extended credit on woolen yarns to handloom masters, who in turn put out part of that yarn to outwork weavers, ran up the rest in their workshops, and sent the total output back to Front Street for sale. This implies a two-level putting-out system that fits the available resources for raw materials and sales.

What is clear from the manufacturing returns is that most Kensington shops did not do their own dyeing. Even the sizable Craige spinning mill showed no dyeing expenses. There were, appropriately, a cluster of independent dyehouses in the district, Charles Hill, Caudwell and Craige, and others, whose returns show their work as yarn dyeing. They did not purchase the yarns but were paid a fee for the service they rendered. Every large workshop listed expenses for dyeing among their materials costs, not expenses for dyestuffs. Thus we may reconstruct the flow of mutually sustaining materials and services in this urban neighborhood, involving a number of separate steps and separate firms. Yarns from several sources passed into and through the hands of shop masters, were dyed in the scattered vat shops, were returned to the masters for distribution as warp and filling to inside and outside looms, some of which were manned by subcontractors and their boarders. The finished products, returned to the shop, were likely sent to the downtown wholesale district, with accounts being periodically settled all around. That most shopmen resided in the ward where their work was done reinforces the contention that their goods were sold by middlemen to the jobbers and country merchants who frequented the central business houses. The complexity of this production process was its greatest hazard, for though dis-integration allowed specialization of function and the entry of shopmen with small capitals, it also set up the conditions for a spreading crisis should any party to the process fail in his responsibilities. Of such a character were the opportunities and contingencies of textile manufacture in 1850 Kensington.

Firm persistence

The fifties were an era of widely acclaimed expansion for domestic manufacture, of which Freedley's trumpeting is but one sign. Moreover, the 1857 Panic tested the strength of those firms whose fortunes were built on a decade of rising demand. The growing railroad network and the increasing sophistication of mechanically driven production on a national scale were supplemented by the local consolidation of the city of Philadelphia with its surrounding county districts and by continuing waves of immigration, which swelled the population past half a million.

To survey the persistence of individual firms through this decade, we shall have to leave Kensington temporarily. City directories, the most valuable source for assessing the survival of antebellum firms and the continued residence of individuals, do not cover Kensington with any consistency until after the consolidation of city and county districts, which is first evident in the 1855 Directory. However, in the Old City area, the official City of Philadelphia until 1854, McElroy's directories provide annual information of considerable value. Since there were thirty-six textile firms in the Old City area in 1850 (11% of the city total) and 1,537 workers (12%), involving seven of the nine textile sectors, tracing the persistence of these firms will be both possible and useful. Using the 1850 and 1860 manufacturing returns as brackets and selecting directories from four intermediate years (1852, 1854, 1857, 1859), the fates of these firms may be sketched and assessed.

The two largest concerns active in 1850 in Old City were the steam powered cotton and mixed-goods mills of Thomas Drake (210 workers) and William Watt (201), involving capital of $250,000 and $85,000, respectively. Both were immigrants, and Watt with his kinsman John operated a second downtown firm, a cotton handshop with 45 workers, to take up the excess yarn from his spinning frames. William Dunn's mixed-goods factory and John Sidney Jones's carpet mill completed the set of powered firms in Old City. Jones, with capital of but $10,000, likely spun carpet yarns for hand-loom weaving and marketed the result from his showroom, Carpet Hall. Eighteen handwork shops with from 14 to 130 workers turned out cottons, carpets, hosiery, and specialty goods in the central district, Cedar (later South) Street north to Vine between the two rivers. Finally, fourteen tiny shops (fewer than 10 workers) plied special trades like silk-trim manufacture or silk dyeing or wove carpets and cottons by hand on a much smaller scale.[33] Old City thus provides an interesting mix of all the formats for production evident citywide in 1850: factory integration, factory spinning for handweaving, outwork and manufactory shops, and tiny household firms. How did these firms fare during the fifties?

Linking the census reports to the 1850 *McElroy's Directory* to provide a starting pool produced twenty-seven connections. (A sample of thirty Kensington firms brought only seven links, indicating the unreliability of the *Directory* for outlying districts.)[34] One additional name can be added retrospectively, John Campion, a hosier who moved to Germantown after the 1850 manufacturing survey and reappeared there in the enlarged McElroy tallies later in the decade.[35] Thus we have twenty-eight linked firms (78%) with which to work. The absent eight included five tiny shopmen, two larger shop masters, William Perry and Adam Beatty, and Dunn, whose residence was perhaps outside the central area. Of the core group, only one departed

---

[33] Drawn from 1850 MCS, Philadelphia Co., City of Philadelphia.

[34] *McElroy's Philadelphia Directory for 1850*, Philadelphia, 1850.

[35] *McElroy's Philadelphia Directory for 1854*, Philadelphia, 1854, p. 652.

from the city directory in 1852, a carpet weaver whose marginal shop had reported only $300 capital in 1850. The remaining twenty-seven were all still active in 1854, but two had changed their occupations. Charles Sharratt, who reported his occupation as "silk reeler" in 1850, had given up his small silk handshop by 1854 to operate a tavern at 173 S. Front Street. A proprietor of a cotton handshop with forty-five workers in 1850, Robert Beatty had become a merchant, changing his occupational listing in the directory. Sharratt's tavern may have been the silk reeler's version of a competence, but it did not last long. By 1859 he had moved farther south on Front Street to number 309, where he plied the grocer's trade.[36]

The 1857 *Directory* was compiled before the Panic could work its effects on the city trades, so that such attrition evident from its listing reflects the three pre-crisis years. Of the twenty-five textile firms in operation in 1854, seventeen continued to operate in 1857. Two men had evidently retired, as they appear in the *Directory* at the same address but with no occupation. Yet another had dropped handshop manufacture to list himself as a merchant. The transition from outwork and shop proprietor to small merchant, which was possible in the central commercial district, was far more difficult for outlying handcraft masters. Three Irish brothers who had managed a firm with 130 millworkers in 1850 were now gone, either to death (one was still active in 1854) or relocation.[37] Three other small cotton weave shops and one fringe and trim maker just dropped from sight.

The Panic had surprisingly little impact on the residual proprietors. Between 1857 and 1859 only one of the seventeen, a small carpet firm, disappeared from the *Directory*. Thus in 1859 sixteen of the twenty-eight linked 1850 Old City firms were still active, while the proprietors of two others had moved into the purely commercial end of the business.[38] In the 1860 Manufacturing Census, fourteen of these are present, the two missing firms having ceased active manufacturing to pursue the distribution of their specialties, carpets and small wares (fringe, coach lace, etc.). Exactly half the 1850 links were still in the manufacturing business in 1860, with four others merchandising textiles. Together they represent nearly two-thirds of the original group. Table 6.12 gives the comparable data for 1850 and 1860 for the fourteen persistent manufacturing firms.

36 Ibid., pp. 29, 472; *McElroy's Philadelphia Directory for 1859*, Philadelphia, 1859, p. 637. There was only one person named Sharratt in the Philadelphia directories during the 1850s.

37 *McElroy's Philadelphia Directory for 1857*, Philadelphia, 1857, pp. 460 (James Maxwell), 527 (Robert Paul). The brothers were William, Thomas, and Steven Douthwitt; see *McElroy's Philadelphia Directory for 1852*, Philadelphia, 1852, p. 115.

38 They were John Sidney Jones of Carpet Hall and William Mintzer, who handled regalia, trim, and fancy openwork goods, including netting; see *McElroy's Directory 1859*, pp. 360, 501.

Table 6.12. *Capital, work force, and power source of persistent textile firms by sector, Old City, 1850–60*

Sector	Capital 1850	Capital 1860	Workers 1850	Workers 1860	Power 1850	Power 1860
Cotton						
Thomas Drake	$250,000	$230,000	210	234	Steam	Steam
Robert Guy[a]	4,000	50,000	40	150	Hand	Steam
William & James Watt	8,000	20,000	45	100	Hand	Steam
William Watt[b]	85,000	166,000	201	324	Steam	Steam
Cotton-wool						
Bernard McNutt[c]	6,000	37,000	57	75	Hand	Steam
Hosiery, knit goods						
John Campion[d]	2,000	3,000	14	15	Hand	Hand
John Gadsby[e]	9,000	10,000	39	100	Hand	Steam
Dyeing, finishing						
William F. Hansell	1,000	2,500	7	2	Hand	Hand
Carpet						
George Albrecht	1,000	600	2	4	Hand	Hand
George Cleeton	300	700	2	2	Hand	Hand
William Lancaster	1,000	1,000	2	2	Hand	Hand
James Pollock[f]	800	10,000	4	35	Hand	Hand

Table 6.12. (*Continued*)

Sector	Capital 1850	Capital 1860	Workers 1850	Workers 1860	Power 1850	Power 1860
Other						
Henry Conkle	5,000	10,000	17	12	Hand	Hand
Henry Duhring[g]	10,000	5,000	25	14	Hand	Steam
Total	383,100	545,800	665	1,069	12 Hand 2 Steam	7 Hand 7 Steam

[a]Became RG & Co. by 1860.
[b]Became Divine & Co. by 1860.
[c]Moved to Spring Garden by 1860.
[d]Moved to Germantown by 1860.
[e]Became John Gadsby & Sons by 1860.
[f]Moved to Northern Liberties by 1860.
[g]Became Henry Duhring & Co. and moved to Northern Liberties by 1860.
Source: Manuscript Manufacturing Census Schedules, Philadelphia County, 1850, 1860.

Both the changes that occurred and in some cases their absence are important. Five of the persisters relocated outside the Old City district as rents increased with crowding and as satellite textile areas gained strength. Campion's move to Germantown was natural, given its rising hosiery reputation, and McNutt's relocation to Spring Garden goes hand in hand with his conversion to steampower and probable construction of a factory. Three smaller firms moved just north of the old commercial center to Northern Liberties, but one of them, Henry Duhring and Co., was edging out of manufacturing toward the merchant path chosen by others. During the fifties, Duhring brought two kinsmen, Casper Duhring and his son William T., and two outsiders into the firm. All five partners listed their 1859 occupations as "merchant."[39]

Other firms brought in new blood to facilitate expansion and succession. John Gadsby's three sons joined his growing knitwear firm, and Robert Guy took on a marketing partner, Robert C. Taylor, who resided next door to his Spruce Street home in 1859 and had previously worked as a clerk in a commercial house at 37 Market Street. Though his firm remained in the Old City district, Thomas Drake had relocated his residence to suburban Darby in adjoining Delaware County. John Sidney Jones, nearing 50, both discontinued manufacturing and removed to Penn Grove Farm in the Olney region of north-central Philadelphia. Meanwhile, William Watt sold one of his two operations and converted the other to steampower.[40]

As much as these changes reflect the dynamic growth of the fifties, the quiet continuity of the handworkers must not be overlooked. Four of the small carpet shops endured; only James Pollock relocated and then substantially increased the scale of his production. Hansell's silk-goods dyeshop and Conkle's cord and small-ware trade grew modestly without steam engines, and Campion settled firmly in Germantown's handcraft knit center. Though these specialty craft operations were rather delicate economic institutions, they were not being swept aside by a tide of modernization. Indeed, across the board, the character of the persisters' growth illustrates Philadelphia's distinctive path toward accumulation and expanded production. Consistent with a broadening labor and skill-intensive approach to textile production, the work force engaged by the fourteen firms in Table 6.12 grew at a rate nearly half again as large as that of the reported capital investment in plant and machinery. Between 1850 and 1860, whereas investment increased by 43%, the number of operatives jumped 61%.

If the four merchant shifts are counted, eighteen of the thirty-six textile

---

[39] 1860 MCS, Philadelphia Co., p. 333, and *McElroy's Philadelphia Directory for 1859*, p. 189.

[40] *McElroy's Philadelphia Directory for 1859*, pp. 243, 279.

Table 6.13. *Textile firms by sector and ward, Kensington, 1850 and 1860*

			Kensington firms, 1860		
Sector	Total firms 1850	Total firms 1860	Wards 16, 18[a]	Ward 17[b]	Ward 19[c]
Cotton	16	34	8	1	25
Cotton-wool	31	21	4	13	4
Wool	4	3	1	0	2
Silk	2	0	0	0	0
Dyeing, finishing	12[d]	14	4	6	4
Spinning	3	10	2	4	4
Hosiery, knit goods	14	22	4	1	17
Carpet	42	86	20	26	40
Other	2	12	8	1	3
Total	126	202	51	52	99

[a]Formerly Wards 1, 2, 4, 5.
[b]Formerly Wards 3 and 6.
[c]Formerly Wards 7 and 8 and Richmond.
[d]Includes one firm recorded in Richmond.
Source: Manuscript Manufacturing Census Schedules, Philadelphia County, 1850, 1860.

proprietors counted in the 1850 census were active in Philadelphia a decade later. Some had moved out from the central area, others had built where they stood, and half had sold out, retired, or failed. Such high levels of persistence for unincorporated firms will not be found in the Kensington district, whose distance from the central docks made the transition to merchant operations difficult and whose numerous small firms were more exposed to the vagaries of the economy than was the mix of powered and shop-based downtown enterprises.

While the ordinary shifts in the market might threaten handshop livelihoods even in steady times, the Panic of 1857 cut a swath through the Kensington textile trades. Suffering was severe, unemployment high, charities driven to the limits of their resources to supply the poor.[41] Of 126 firms in 1850 Kensington, only 23 could be located in the 1860 Manufacturing Census. Yet the firms that closed, through failure, retirement, death, or removal to other locations, were rapidly replaced by firms whose character and sectoral distribution was little altered from the 1850 profile. The four

41 Clark, *Irish*, pp. 47–8.

wards of 1860 Philadelphia that included all of Kensington (and some additional acreage that was almost barren of textile firms in 1850) reported more than 200 textile firms active, 76 more shops and a 1,000 more workers than in 1850 (Table 6.13).

The sectoral distribution was preserved between 1850 and 1860, with a noticeable increase in both independent spinners and the handloom carpet firms they supplied, as well as in those so employed in the outlying districts (Table 6.14).[42] Small shops also persisted in lower, central, and upper Kensington over the decade (Table 6.15).

By 1860, 180 new textile firms were operating in Kensington. These shops were overwhelmingly small, the proportion of firms with 25 or fewer workers in 1860 almost exactly what it had been ten years before (72% and 71%). Despite an increase of over 25% in the number of textile workers in the district, there was no concentration of labor in ever-larger establishments. Indeed, the reverse was the case, as the number of firms with over 100 workers declined absolutely (from 12 to 8), with the large 1860 firms employing a smaller percentage of the total work force than did their 1850 predecessors. The eight large firms of 1860 engaged 1,629 workers, 32% of these in the four wards; the twelve corresponding firms in 1850 had had 2,069 workers, 52% of all those in Kensington. The average number of workers in the big mills had risen to above 200, and six of the eight present in 1860 were new to the district. Only Thomas Craige's spinning mill and Wilson and Allen's cotton factory (reformed by 1860 as Allen and Witte) had lasted the decade. Of the ten large firms that had disappeared, one had moved (Horstmann), two had shrunk, and seven had vanished (five of which were the largest handshop operations in 1850).

Some of these departures may simply have been retirements to the enjoyment of real-estate revenues, bearing no relation to the Panic. An 1857 survey, prepared before the crisis, noted twenty-five Kensington handloom proprietors with more than twenty looms on cottons and mixed goods. Fourteen of these firms were present in the 1850 Manufacturing schedules.[43] Of the six handloom firms with more than 100 workers in 1850, only one, Dominick Murphy, continued operations. The other large masters all seem to have withdrawn from the trade before the economic contraction. Whatever the fate of the largest shops and however deeply the ranks of small

---

[42] Wards 1, 2, 4, and 5 of the old district (Lower Kensington) were consolidated in 1854 into Wards 16 and 18. Ward 17 was formed out of the central textile area (Wards 3 and 6). Ward 19 of the City and County of Philadelphia encompassed Wards 7 and 8 of Kensington and the adjoining Richmond District along the Delaware River. In the 1850s two-thirds of Kensington's textile firms and three-quarters of its workers were reported from the old Wards 3 and 6.

[43] Freedley, *Philadelphia and Its Manufactures*, p. 253.

Table 6.14. *Textile workers by sector, sex, and ward, Kensington, 1850 and 1860*

Sector	Total workers				Wards 16, 18[a]		Ward 17[b]		Ward 19[c]	
	Male 1850	Female 1850	Male 1860	Female 1860	Male 1860	Female 1860	Male 1860	Female 1860	Male 1860	Female 1860
Cotton	354	300	567	558	149	93	50	25	368	440
Cotton-wool	1,287	807	708	410	155	227	494	151	59	32
Wool	52	40	190	103	36	28	0	0	154	75
Silk	72	131	0	0	0	0	0	0	0	0
Dyeing, finishing	55[d]	1[d]	63	4	12	0	23	4	28	0
Spinning	28	91	158	247	14	32	107	177	37	38
Hosiery, knit goods	42	61	220	418	144	360	20	6	56	52
Carpet	490	160	1,116	284	230	67	346	62	540	155
Other	6	0	47	13	36	11	2	0	9	2
Total	2,386 (60%)	1,591 (40%)	3,069 (60%)	2,037 (40%)	776	818	1,042	425	1,251	794

[a]Formerly Wards 1, 2, 4, 5.
[b]Formerly Wards 3 and 6.
[c]Formerly Wards 7 and 8 and Richmond.
[d]Includes eight workers recorded in Richmond.
Source: Manuscript Manufacturing Census Schedules, Philadelphia County, 1850, 1860.

Table 6.15. *Textile firms by work-force size and ward, Kensington, 1850 and 1860*

			Textile firms, 1860		
Work-force size	Total firms 1850	Total firms 1860	Wards 16, 18[c]	Ward 17[a]	Ward 19[b]
Workers					
1–5	41	75	25	14	36
6–25	50[d]	69	11	19	39
26–50	13	30	7	9	14
51–100	10	20	5	8	7
100+	12	8	3	2	3
Total	126	202	51	52	99

[a]Formerly Wards 3 and 6.
[b]Formerly Wards 7 and 8 and Richmond.
[c]Formerly Wards 1, 2, 4, 5.
[d]Includes one textile firm recorded in Richmond.
Source: Manuscript Manufacturing Census Schedules, Philadelphia County, 1850, 1860.

shopmen were thinned by death, retirement, or reverses, handloom weaving in Kensington was still widespread in 1860, and in carpets, growing.

Both in number of firms and total employment, the greatest expansion in Kensington textiles during the decade was in the carpet manufacture. More than 1,400 workers pounded out ingrain, Brussels, and cheaper rag carpets by 1860, half of them in the newly infiltrated Nineteenth Ward. Paralleling this development, the number of spinning mills rose quickly, with the first wool spinners making their debut to supply the demand for carpet yarns. Craige hummed along, doubling his capital and more than doubling his work force to remain the largest spinning plant in the city. The relocation of Martin Landenberger's hosiery mill from Northern Liberties to Kensington accounts for the bulk of the knit-goods increase. With 430 workers in 1860, down a bit from the "nearly five hundred" reported in 1857,[44] Landenberger was far and away the largest single textile employer in the area.

The increase in the number of cotton and mixed-goods firms went along with a decline in the work force for the two sectors taken together. The increase in cottons may be illusory, as switching from wool to cotton filling was a simple matter for skilled weavers. Many workshops in 1850 had

[44] Ibid., p. 243.

outputs that included all-cotton, mixed, and even some all-wool goods, the balance of their production likely varying with the season and the perceived demand for any number of fabrics and weaves. Some all-cotton damask and "Table Diaper" fine-goods weaving was practiced in Kensington in the fifties, notably by Patrick Quin's shop.[45]

The increase in the number of firms reflects the reconstitution of the large groups of weavers managed by departed "big-shop" masters into smaller clusters. The overall decline in work-force numbers does not show, I suspect, any significant incidence of transfer from cotton to carpet weaving. Minimally, a completely different loom was needed for carpet work; much greater physical strength and a slightly different set of skills were also involved. (Among persistent firms, 1850–60, none had switched from fabrics to carpets.) Rather, the slippage in this quarter indicates that workers who left the cotton trade or the district were replaced by immigrants who started out on carpets, many of whom occupied the newly built-up streets of the Nineteenth Ward.

This suggestion is strengthened by the relative and absolute decline of the district's 1850 manufacturing center, the Third and Sixth wards. Whereas the two old wards hosted thirty-eight of Kensington's forty-seven cotton and mixed-goods firms in 1850, only fourteen of fifty-five such firms in 1860 Kensington were located in the center area. In the fifties both handshops and steam mills generally located outside the old core area. By 1860, 958 workers on cottons and mixed goods labored in powered mills (though some still operated handlooms) in Wards 16, 18, and 19, whereas only 61 labored in a single steam mill in the old Ward 17.

In the fifties Kensington experienced in miniature a rapid case of core stagnation and peripheral development. There were, for example, twenty-five carpet shops with 545 workers in the Third and Sixth wards of 1850 and twenty-six carpet firms in 1860 in the same territory with only 401 employees. Whereas the old Seventh and Eighth wards and all of Richmond supported 449 textile workers and eight firms in 1850 (one of which, Horstmann's, was soon to move to Old City), a decade later more than 2,000 workers and just short of 100 firms had established themselves there. As the old handloom fabric trades drifted slowly toward the total eclipse that the cotton famine would seal, the rising handloom carpet trades and the new steam mills continued to locate in Kensington, exploiting its pool of skilled workers and its reputation as an immigrant destination. However, the newcomers situated their shops and mills outside the old fabric center, reaching out along the long rows of housing to the north and east. By 1880 the Nineteenth Ward would become the worksite for nearly 20,000 textile oper-

45 Ibid., p. 254.

atives, comparable to the total Lowell work force, but still only a third of the city of Philadelphia's textile workers.

The output flexibility of Kensington textile firms was consistent with that previously shown for the Globe Mill and the Manayunk factories. Handloom shops wove a variety of cotton and blended stuffs; in 1850 Daniel Hickey alone reported 500,000 yards of wool plaids from his handlooms, 200,000 yards of wool tweeds, thousands of loom-fashioned shawls, and significant quantities of Cassimeres and all-cotton pantaloon goods.[46] Thomas Harkness shipped out a mix of checks, wool and cotton pantaloon stuffs, table diaper, and shawls in the same census year.[47] Carpet patterns were varied with the season, with new weaves introduced periodically to keep the market alive with novelty. While some small shops turned out checks or plaids only, the gross yardage figures conceal the variety of designs that were standard in the trade. Specialization extended into the service sectors, as the district sported not only yarn dyers in 1850 but a stocking finisher, a flannel carder, a carpet-loom rigger, and another craftsman who built and repaired carpet looms.[48] One carpet manufacturer, George McDade, sold linseys as well as ingrains, evidently, like Harkness and Hickey, involved in a combination of shop and outwork manufacture.

However, the prize for flexibility and variation goes to Martin Landenberger, who arrived in the district after 1850, planting his enormous knit-goods works at the corner of Frankford Road and Wildey Street. A fully integrated mill with its own carding, spinning, and dyeing, the factory had "2560 spindles" and "upward of fifteen different kinds of looms." The *Public Ledger* made special note of "a new loom, the invention of the proprietor, for weaving . . . four neck-comforts of a double fabric, and each of a different pattern." This design flexibility was due to Landenberger's adaptation of Jacquard principles to narrow weaves. Given his mechanical aptitude, it is no surprise that "all the new machinery used" was "made on the premises."[49] Though he commenced in 1842 with "about twelve hands," Landenberger was by 1857 the proprietor of a five-story, 200- by 38-foot mill that manufactured "eight hundred different styles of goods, of all sizes, every season," including "hoods, talmas, opera-cloaks, neck-comforts, scarfs and hosiery of every conceivable description and variety.[50]

The expansion of the handloom carpet manufacture in Kensington between 1850 and 1860 extended and deepened the complex artisanal network that had characterized the district in earlier decades. Yet that very expansion

[46] 1850 MCS, Philadelphia Co., p. 66.
[47] Ibid., p. 68.
[48] Ibid., pp. 37–40, 64–5.
[49] Quoted in Freedley, *Philadelphia and Its Manufactures*, pp. 242–3.
[50] Ibid.

made possible the parallel development of steampowered firms, most particularly the more than twenty spinners and dyers directly connected with the hand trades. Larger steam mills also had sprouted in the outlying districts, some retaining handlooms to weave the yarns spun by power. By 1860, just under half the textile work force (2,499 of 5,106) in the four Kensington wards were employed in steampowered firms.[51] Nearly a fifth of them (430) assembled daily at Landenberger's plant, and the other forty-five powered firms employed an average of 46 workers each. Even the Landenberger plant seems to have relied on handweaving, for its steam engine was only a 15-horsepower model, placed so as to run the cards and spinning frames, but hardly adequate to drive a five-story mill full of power knitters.[52] Power looms for weaving carpets were installed in 1850 by one Kensington firm, whether Bigelow machines or models of local design is not clear. John Markley of Kensington reported using twelve power looms to produce 60,000 yards of carpets, probably ingrains, the earliest effort with that technology in the region.[53] Markley's firm did not survive the decade, though ten of his neighboring handloom competitors did reappear in the 1860 Manufacturing Census Schedules. Progressive technology, as ever, was only one element in the elaborate matrix of factors that facilitated accumulation. Whether fire, feud, or poor accounting spelled failure for the Markley firm, the acquisition of power looms held no guarantee of their profitable employment.

The continuing strength of the handloom shops in the late fifties was documented, even trumpeted, by Edwin Freedley in his 1857 account of manufacturing in the city. As his remarks recapitulate a number of the points documented here, they will serve well in summing up this discussion of Kensington and the handloom productive format.

> It is a remarkable fact, that notwithstanding the rapid substitution of power for the production of textile fabrics, and the growth of large establishments from the results of accumulated capital, there is no actual decline in the number of handlooms in operation . . . There are now, within our knowledge, 4,760 hand looms in operation [in Philadelphia] in the production of Checks and other cotton goods; Carpetings, Hosiery, &c; and it is probable that the true number approximates six thousand.
>
> The material is furnished by the manufacturers and the weavers are paid by the yard. The weaving is done in the houses of the operatives; or in some cases a manufacturer, as he may be termed, has ten or twelve looms in a wooden building attached to his dwelling, and employs jour-

---

[51] Calculated from 1860 MCS, Philadelphia Co., Ward 16 to 19.
[52] Freedley, *Philadelphia and Its Manufactures*, p. 242.
[53] 1850 MCS, Philadelphia Co., p. 41.

neymen weavers – the employed in some instances boarding or lodging in the same house as their employer. Throughout parts of the city, especially that formerly known as Kensington, the sound of these looms may be heard at all hours – in garrets, cellars, and out-houses, as well as in the weavers' apartments. Among the weavers, there are many very intelligent men, and some that have been employed in weaving those magnificent damasks, and other cloths, that Europe occasionally produces to gratify the pride of her rulers.[54]

To this statement was appended a report on handweaving by Edward Young, which listed the twenty-five Kensington shopmen previously mentioned. That group was credited with running a total of 1,250 looms, principally on outwork, as Young stressed that "the manufacturers do not own the looms."[55] Despite the Panic of 1857, eighteen of the twenty-five were still operating their shops in 1860, and eight had been present as well in the 1850 schedules. A more detailed glance at one of them, Dominick Murphy, will bring us back to individuals and families and close the analysis of midcentury Kensington with a glimpse of the next generation.

Like so many of his handloom colleagues, Dominick Murphy was an Irish immigrant. He landed at New York with his wife and 2-year-old son about 1835, when he was 26. A year later his eldest daughter was born to the family in New York State. By 1838 they had settled in Philadelphia where "for forty years" Murphy would be a cotton-goods manufacturer. In 1850 Murphy reported to the census eight children, $1,400 in real estate, $3,000 invested in his business, and 120 workers employed, evidence of modest success. Dominick Murphy reappears in the manufacturing schedules for Kensington in both 1860 and 1870, each time with fewer employees, 60 and 45, respectively, and each time as well with only handlooms as the means to produce a changing mix of cotton and woolen goods. The proportion of men to women employed (2:1) is constant in all three reports, suggesting the unchanging nature of the productive relations in place. With $10,000 capital in his 1870 firm, Murphy at 61 was certainly able financially to retire. That he seems not to have done so may have resulted from a commitment to assist his sons' entry into the textile manufacture.[56] An 1888 biographical sketch of one of them, Joseph P., shows the family connection.

Joseph Murphy was born in Philadelphia in 1845, the fourth of six sons living in the 1850 household. Having attended public schools, he entered an apprenticeship with his father before the Civil War. In 1866, "shortly after he had attained his majority," he began a weaving shop of his own, most

---

[54] Freedley, *Philadelphia and Its Manufactures*, pp. 252–3.

[55] Ibid., p. 253.

[56] 1850 MCS, Philadelphia Co., p. 63; 1850 PCS, Philadelphia Co., Kensington, Ward 6, p. 137; 1860 MCS, Philadelphia Co., p. 404; 1870 MCS, Philadelphia Co., p. 470.

likely with financial backing from his father. Three years later Joseph was running nine looms with about twenty-five workers. The manufacturing schedules in 1870 list Joseph P. Murphy as a cotton and woolen manufacturer in the Nineteenth Ward, occupying a mill at 249 Oxford Street. Though only 25, he had $15,000 invested and was spinning his own yarns, using a 5-horsepower engine. Weaving, however, was still done on handlooms, with a total of nineteen men and twenty women employed by the firm. Dominick Murphy's workshop remained where it had been for a generation, on Palethorp Street in the old Seventeenth Ward.

After a few years on Oxford Street, Joseph Murphy relocated to two small mills at 531 East York Street, at the eastern edge of the Nineteenth Ward. By 1879 he had twenty-two power and seventy-five handlooms in operation. The York Street mills were a spatial constraint, being four stories high but only 54 by 30 and 54 by 37 feet. There was no spinning or preparatory machinery at this mill, for the development of independent spinners and dyers visible already in 1860 Kensington had continued through the following decades, making such expenditures unnecessary for the accumulating manufacturer. In 1879 Murphy made his exit from the handloom trade. He purchased a lot at Fourth and Cumberland at the western edge of the Nineteenth Ward and erected a five-story factory, 200 by 45 feet. On its completion in December 1879 Murphy installed 400 power looms. By 1882 he employed 546 workers, which was consistent with a two-loom system on fancy goods (shawls, spreads, and worsteds) or even a single-loom arrangement, given that no spinning or dyeing was set up in this facility. By the late eighties, Murphy had purchased a second mill across Cumberland Street and had over 500 looms and 900 workers who produced "cotton, wool and worsted goods of all descriptions to the value of $1,500,000 annually."[57]

This tale provides a later Kensington variant of the proprietary firm sequence we have examined in other configurations for the Craiges, Schofields, and Ripkas. Here a handloom shopman provided his son with the skills and means to pursue the traditional craft, but the son reached gradually outward to engage the technology and productive structures that promised larger-scale profit and accumulation. Joseph Murphy, like Sevill Schofield, seems to have stepped out of the capitalism of competence into that of ceaseless expansion. That transition was not a matter of one decision but the project of a lifetime and the product of a long string of linked choices, which he evidently made with an accuracy that eluded many others. To move to larger quarters, to bring in that first set of power looms, to buy land and build a mill, to abandon spinning his own yarn, to specialize in woolens and

[57] *Biographical Album of Prominent Pennsylvanians, Third Series*, Philadelphia, 1890, p. 221; 1870 MCS, Philadelphia Co., p. 566.

high-ticket worsteds, each of these decisions took Joseph Murphy another step away from the social and productive relations of the workshops in which he had been schooled. In the fifties, sixties, and seventies, handloom production in Philadelphia was a vital element in the larger network of textile manufacturing. The eighties would bring the end. Textile workers immigrating to Philadelphia by then were no longer handloom journeymen but factory veterans seeking factory jobs. The spinning mills and dyehouses whose rise had been linked to the needs of handloom masters and their shops now served independent weave sheds like the mill Murphy erected on Cumberland. In the nativist riots of the 1840s one Kensington shop master, fresh from bitter conflicts with weavers over the price of work, distributed arms to his men in the face of external threat.[58] The complex and tenacious bonds exemplified by that incident were by the eighties being replaced by the transactional motif so basic to "modern" capitalism, which Charles Hagner had assailed as an element of the factory system at Manayunk in the thirties. Scrapping his handlooms in December 1879, Murphy symbolically signaled that the last stages in a transition fifty years in the making had arrived.

[58] *Biographical Album, Third Series,* p. 221; Lorin Blodget, *The Textile Industries of Philadelphia,* Philadelphia, 1880, p. 25; Lorin Blodget, *Census of Manufactures of Philadelphia (1882),* Philadelphia, 1883, p. 178.

7

Proprietary textiles at midcentury: Germantown and Manayunk

Distressing Death – Hannah McDonald, aged 14 or 15, . . . came to a shocking death on Wednesday morning last, in the woolen mill of Jacob Mehl, Esq., of this borough. She was attending a picker in a room by herself, and the picker becoming foul[ed], she took her hand, instead of an implement provided for that purpose, to clean it out, when the hand was caught by it and the arm was drawn in up to the shoulder, stripping the flesh amost entirely off and breaking the arm in several places. She made no outcry, and was not discovered for some time after, when she was found lying on the floor. She complained of little pain and related all particulars of the accident. She died in four hours after.

– Germantown Telegraph, November 7, 1849

Steam Versus Water – We notice that our manufacturers are determined to be troubled no longer with the interruptions of low and high water. Heretofore in the spring season, they were greatly annoyed with too much water, compelling them to stop, and during the dry summer months, vice versa, too little water to allow them to run . . . But now we observe our enterprising friend, Mr. A. Campbell, is about introducing a new engine of about 200 horsepower and will hereafter do away with water altogether.

– Manayunk Star and Roxborough Gazette, May 21, 1859

In the northwestern quarter of the city, separated by perhaps a mile of hilly terrain, lay two other centers of textile manufacture in antebellum Philadelphia, Germantown and Manayunk. Their production characteristics and the contrasts between them and crosstown Kensington will be explored next. While the distinctiveness of each district will be exposed, their coexistence within a common urban framework should not be lost to sight. They shared not only the larger spatial and market environment of the metropolis but also common forms of firm organization and common trajectories of development; their proprietors and workers were immigrants as was the case in other city textile districts.

Germantown and the knit-goods trade

Germantown Borough and Township and adjacent Bristol Township were still largely rural districts in 1850, about 18 square miles of farms and creekside mills, at the center of which was the village of Germantown, first settled a century and a half before. Its weekly four-page newspaper had a full complement of helpful articles for farmers, advertisements for implements, beasts, and land, weather notes and the like. Germantown too had developed a summer trade, becoming early in the nineteenth century a hilly refuge from the city's summer heat and occasional plagues and fevers. With the construction of the rail line to the central district in the thirties, a prosperous commuting population settled there year round.

Yet in 1850 its three rural jurisdictions, soon to be consolidated into the Twenty-second Ward, housed more than 1,000 textile workers who produced more than $600,000 worth of manufactured goods, including yarns, calicoes, carpets, and most widely, hosiery.[1] The thirty-five textile firms in the borough and townships included all the largest manufacturing employers in the area; only one nontextile firm, a saw and spring-making works, had more than forty employees. Four large hosiery firms employed more than 600 workers, of whom two-thirds were women. Seventeen other hosiers, most of whom were clustered near the village center, plied their hand-frame trade. Thirteen of them, as in the small Kensington shops, reported no women engaged in production. Two firms active in 1820 still churned along: George McCallmont's woolen mill, now run by the founder's son, and Ishichar Thorp's printworks. Andrew McCallum's carpet factory was fully integrated, with spinning and dyeing facilities, 160 workers, and a downtown salesroom. Of McCallum's employees, 140 were male; most of them operated the 105 carpet handlooms reported in the decennial census. Thus McCallum's integration was of that special character, power spinning together with hand operations, which was found elsewhere in midcentury Philadelphia. Seven separate spinning mills, a yarn dyer, the France brothers' carpet works, a small manufacturer of Kentucky jeans, and a cotton-lap operation completed the local textile complex. The wealth of detail in the manufacturing schedules combined with the small number of firms and their physical distance from other textile districts allows an examination of the intersectoral relationships among spinners, dyers, handshops, and mills in midcentury Germantown.

Wool was the fiber of record in most Germantown textile manufacturing.

---

[1] Calculated from 1850 Manufacturing Census Schedules, Philadelphia Co., pp. 5–6, 15–21, cited hereafter as MCS.

Weavers' housing, Germantown. An example of the modest scale of housing erected by several factory operators in outlying districts, the houses are roughly similar to those of nearby Delaware County depicted in Anthony Wallace's *Rockdale*. (Free Library of Philadelphia)

In addition to McCallmont's woolen fabric mill, all hosiery was woolen as was all carpet filling (warps were flax). These yarns were evidently obtained from the five wool-spinning firms lodged in the district, which together produced 126,800 pounds of yarn for sale in the census year.[2] McCallmont spun his own yarns and had sufficient overflow and demand to offer 50,000 pounds to the market. Purchases of raw wool and spindle figures show that five other mills spun for their own needs but did not sell yarn (Spencer, Button and Smith, and Wakefield on hosiery, McCallum's carpet, and Kelly's jeans mills). However, none of the handshops, including A&T Jones's extensive outwork firm (265 workers), did any spinning. Together they bought 89,100 pounds of yarn for hosiery. The France brothers' twenty-one spindles were probably used for flax spinning, for that firm purchased 50,000 pounds of woolen yarn for its carpets. These nineteen yarn buyers accounted for three-quarters of the 176,000 pounds of wool yarns spun by independents and McCallmont. It is probable that the independents satisfied local needs and that the city-connected McCallmont disposed of his surplus to Kensington carpet firms through downtown merchants.

[2] Ibid.

The wool yarns locally produced had to be dyed before they could be used in hosiery manufacture. It is satisfying to discover that the one independent dyer in Germantown, John Dawson, processed 124,000 pounds of woolen yarns in the census year,[3] just a hair under the output reported from the five independent spinners. (McCallmont had his own dyehouse.) Dawson performed his magic on contract, noting an income of $10,000 and expenses only for dyestuffs; the purchase and resale of the yarns would have produced much larger figures. Among the spinners, two worked up carpet yarns only, in quantities consistent with the France brothers' purchases. The other three probably spun for the hosiery shops. All the independent spinners were small firms, averaging about 500 spindles and five workers each. The integrated mills carried on spinning on about the same scale, suggesting a cautious backward integration as their production expanded.

It is this dispersal of function among small firms coexistent with tentative and incomplete integration among the larger firms that gives the Germantown textile makers a distinctive character, one that encapsulates a pattern that would become general in Philadelphia in subsequent decades. Spinners and dyers are structurally critical in a manufacturing array that features both integrated mills that attempt to meet specialized and variable demands and scores of independent weaving firms, whether shop- or mill-based, that must rely on the skills of other craftsmen in order for their production to proceed. Integrated firms may need additional yarn supplies, special dyeing and finishing techniques, or, as with Manayunk's Campbell and Co., more looms than they have on hand in order to adjust production to heightened demand. They may spin but not dye, as did Spencer, Button and Smith, and Kelly at Germantown. The capital savings accomplished by weavesheds (e.g., J. P. Murphy) carried a structural dependency that encouraged the establishment of stable and long-term relationships with outside contractors. All this is part and parcel of the format for textile manufacture established in Philadelphia, fragility combined with flexibility involving the necessary linkage of textile capitalists in related sectors of the industry.

As in Kensington, Germantown textile manufacturers in 1850 were overwhelmingly immigrants, though in this case from England rather than Ireland. An effort was made to link the operators of the twenty-eight firms in Germantown Borough and Township manufacturing schedules with the 1850 Population Census. Of the thirty-four individuals involved, taking partnerships into account, thirty links were secured. Twenty-two of the linked manufacturers were born in England, two in Scotland, and three in Ireland, and of the three born in the United States, two were a father and

---

[3] 1850 MCS, Philadelphia Co., p. 5.

son in the same firm.[4] None of those for whom links were not made was a major manufacturer, the four (three hosiers and a spinner) having only twenty-six employees among them. Evidently they were either missed by the census marshals or their names were sufficiently butchered by census takers to make linkage impossible.

That this was probable is indicated by the case of George Fling, alias George Flynn. Fling was a British immigrant hosier who ultimately became prominent in the Germantown trade, taking the backyard-shed, build-a-mill pathway traveled by so many others. The short biography of him that appeared in Robson's *Manufactories and Manufacturers of Pennsylvania* (1875) establishes him as a small hosiery maker in Germantown as of 1848.[5] No one named George Fling appeared in either the population or manufacturing manuscripts, but a George Flynn was in both, where he was described as a stocking weaver.[6] That Flynn was Fling is clear from a comparison of the composition of his household with the information of Robson's account. In Robson, Fling's marriage to Ann Maria Harris in 1840 is described, a marriage from which five children issued before the wife's death in 1853. In the 1850 Population Schedule, George Flynn is living with wife Ann and four children, the oldest of whom is 8. To tie the knot, boarding with the family is 20-year-old Maria Harris, his wife's sister most likely. Thus Flynn was Fling, and both manufacturing and population marshals got it wrong in the same fashion. (Doubtless, a fair proportion of missed links in research efforts stem from similar inaccuracies in the original data, few of which are as easily resolved as was this one.)

The Germantown textile makers were an appreciably older group than their Kensington counterparts. Only four of the thirty linked were under 30 years of age, two of these being partner-sons of proprietors. Eighteen of the group were 40 or older, fourteen of them English immigrants. Six manufacturers, all mill operators, had substantial real-estate holdings. Three of these were spinners, each of whom had as much or more invested in land as in their mills. Joseph Carr, 48, a Pennsylvania native, was the most propertied of the 1850 manufacturers. His real estate was reported at $30,000, whereas his manufacturing enterprise, the Pleasant Mills, a Cresheim Creek spinning plant, was capitalized at only $5,000. Carr had bought the mill and "five lots" adjoining in 1839 for a total of $6,000, converting it from papermaking

---

[4] 1850 Population Census Schedules, Philadelphia Co., Districts 8 and 9 (Germantown Borough and Township), cited hereafter as PCS.

[5] Daniel Robson, ed., *Manufactories and Manufacturers of Pennsylvania of the Nineteenth Century*, Philadelphia, 1875, p. 406, cited hereafter as M&MP.

[6] 1850 PCS, Philadelphia Co., District 9, p. 42; 1850 MCS, Philadelphia Co., p. 15.

shortly thereafter.[7] Handwork shopmen were distinctly small operators, with the exception of A&T Jones, who showed a capital of $7,000 and property valued at $2,000 in 1850. Of the other twelve stocking masters linked, only three had real estate; they each averaged five workers and less than $1,000 capital.

The pathway to a competence at Germantown may have been obstructed by two elements in the local environment. First, boarding large numbers of workers, a practice that was frequent at Kensington and contributed a measure toward accumulation, was rare in Germantown. None of the group boarded more than three stocking weavers, a total of but fifteen boarding workers appearing in the twelve linked households. However, all seven hosiers over 40 reported sons at home in the trade, suggesting the passing on of traditional skills to the next generation from an artisanal family core rather than the immigrant workshop destination common at Kensington. Second, if real estate and land purchases were an important element in building a competence, Germantown hosiers were poorly situated to make acquisitions consistent with their resources. The real estate offered for sale in the pages of the *Telegraph* year after year consisted overwhelmingly of farms and country estates, far beyond the reach of craftsmen but attractive to city merchants for residence or summer retreat.[8]

This hardly meant that hand-frame shopmen were doomed to failure. Their survival rate in the fifties was far better than that shown by their Kensington colleagues. Of the seventeen hand-frame operators in the 1850 Manufacturing Schedules for northwest Philadelphia, ten reappear in 1860, indicating that a solid economic base for their work persisted throughout the decade. They divide readily into two groups, one of which seems to have focused simply on "getting a living" from their trade and whose 1860 circumstances were little different from those previously documented, and a second group that accumulated sizable capitals, acquired mill space, and introduced powered spinning, making the transition from workshop to factory as did Murphy rather later across town. It may be that this division was related to the competence blockages, with some shopmen expecting family support in old age and others moving toward expansion beyond the work-

---

[7] James Magee, "Mills in the Wissahickon Creek Valley," edited by M. Goshow, typescript, 1967, p. 40, Roxborough Branch, Free Library of Philadelphia.

[8] This is, of course, hardly conclusive, as small houses might well have been bought on a private market, which only extensive deed research would uncover. However, Germantown was by no means the locus of vast housing construction for working-class families, and the resale of older row houses was common, as was the case at Kensington in the same period. Small homes in Kensington *were* advertised in the press, as Dennis Clark has pointed out (*The Irish in Philadelphia*, Philadelphia, 1973, pp. 50–1, esp. note 52).

shop toward the factory settings that were already visible with Spencer and others at the time. Certainly, the expanding market for "Germantown goods" helps account for the high persistence rate across the board, a market that brought considerable growth to the two hosiery factories running at midcentury as well as opportunities for either stability or expansion for the shopmen. Table 7.1 gives a brief look at the 1850 workshops whose operators were still in the trade at Germantown ten years later.

Jones's huge outwork operations have vanished, as did most of the analogous large cotton and mixed-goods shops in Kensington, replaced by steam-powered knitters whose output exceeded that of the corps of handworkers a decade earlier. The small steam engines in the factories of both Allen and Wade were for spinning only, and their sizable workforces may include some of the outworkers dropped by Jones. The five shops retaining handwork exclusively registered modest increases in investment and work force. (The considerable increase in Graham's capital, combined with a shrinking labor force and the retention of hand power, strongly suggests that one of the three 1860 data bits is in error.) Thurman stayed in business and spun off a small shop for his son, who continued the family craft, and Twiss entered a partnership with a new arrival. Of the seven handshops that did not last the decade, three were not linked to the 1850 Population Schedules, one was in 1850 being run by a 71-year-old hosier, and two of the remaining three were operated by Irish immigrants who may have relocated at Kensington.[9]

The proprietors who died or departed were hardly missed, for the hand-frame hosiery trade in Germantown expanded dramatically in the fifties. Where seventeen handshops had operated in 1850, forty shops stood in 1860 in the consolidated Twenty-second Ward. Of the forty, thirty-five were new (the hold-overs are given in Table 7.1). The handshops in 1860 were larger than those in 1850, averaging a dozen workers (only four of the forty having fewer than five) and reporting a total capital of nearly $140,000 (only five firms showed figures under $1,000). Apparently, as the national distribution network developed with the surge of railroad construction and as the local market swelled with the population of Philadelphia and other eastern cities, the tide of demand rose, carrying with it both shopmen and factory masters. The wool tariff afforded protection; the continued migration of "Nottingham and Leicester men" kept the skills pool brimming. As at Kensington, there was no simple replacement of "old-fashioned" handworkers

---

[9] These last two were John Henry and James Boyd. In 1860 Kensington there were in operation two small hosiery workshops run by a John Henry and a William Boyd, capital $1,300 and $600, respectively. In the household of James Boyd at Germantown in 1850 was a probable kinsman, William Boyd, also Irish-born (see 1850 PCS, Philadelphia Co., District 9, p. 3; 1860 MCS, Philadelphia Co., pp. 428, 543).

Table 7.1. *Capital, work force, and power source of persistent hosiers, Germantown, 1850–60*

Hosiers	Capital		Work force, 1850		Work force, 1860		Power source	
	1850	1860	Male	Female	Male	Female	1850	1860
William Allen	$2,000	20,000	9	10	20	110	Hand	Steam[a]
Elias Birchall	600	25,000	4	0	36	70	Hand	Steam
Amos Cowell	100	400	1	0	2	0	Hand	Hand
George Fling	1,000	—[b]	6	0			Hand	
William Graham	3,000	15,600	5	22	9	5	Hand	Hand
A&T Jones	7,000	25,000	65	200	35	30	Hand	Steam
Isaac Morrell	400	1,000	1	0	2	2	Hand	Hand
Joseph Thurman	3,000	4,100	6	0	5	4	Hand	Hand
Joseph Thurman, Jr.		2,100			4	6		
John Twiss[c]	1,800	3,000	6	0	7	7	Hand	Hand
Edward Wade	100	15,000	4	0	15	50	Hand	Steam[a]

[a] The power source provided 4 HP.

[b] Closed because Fling was in Britain purchasing new machinery. By 1870 he had $20,000 capital, twenty-five workers, and a 9-HP steam engine (Manufacturing Census Schedules, Philadelphia County, 1870, p. 927; Daniel Robson, ed., *Manufactories and Manufactures of Pennsylvania of the Nineteenth Century* [Philadelphia, 1875], p. 406).

[c] The firm had become Twiss & Markham by 1860.

Source: Manuscript Manufacturing Census Schedules, Philadelphia County, 1850, 1860.

The Wakefield Mills, Germantown. Operating as Fisher, Gouge and Potts, this firm involved the brother of the famous Philadelphia diarist Henry George Fisher. It was one of the few incorporated mills in antebellum Pennsylvania. (Free Library of Philadelphia)

by "modern" factory enterprise. The Panic of 1857 may have wrecked the fortunes of many Kensington shopmen, but larger mills submerged as well, owing at least in part to their much heavier credit demands. In Germantown, the incorporated Wakefield Manufacturing Company, with both steam- and waterpower and 180 workers in 1850, failed to survive the decade. The two large proprietary hosiery mills active in 1850 did rather better, as the firm of Button and Smith quadrupled its capital investment to $40,000 and Charles Spencer's success made him one of the region's largest millmen. In 1850 Spencer reported 140 workers and $15,000 capital; by 1860, he employed 278 workers and reported a massive capital of $175,000. The close personal supervision of the manufacture of specialized goods that was fundamental to proprietary firms may have been better suited to the market structure of the hosiery trade than was Wakefield's incorporated form of organization and management.[10]

---

[10] The Wakefield firm, formerly Fisher, Gouge and Potts, was active in Germantown in 1820; when its production was altered from woolens to hosiery in the 1830s (*M&MP*, p. 316; John Thomas Scharf and Thompson Westcott, *History of Philadelphia*, Phila-

Biographical information gathered by Robson on three of the hosiery firms active in 1850 Germantown shows the fairly standard development pattern of the city's textile districts traced back into the 1830s. Aaron Jones, born in Leicestershire (1807), followed his hosier father to Germantown in 1832. His father, who had migrated two years earlier, had established a shop, and Aaron worked there for a time. Soon, however, he assumed responsibility for sales, "visiting country stores throughout the State in search of customers." In 1834, the elder Jones sold his frames to Thomas Fisher, proprietor of the Wakefield mills, and arranged to superintend their operation. When he died before this agreement could be consummated, Aaron took his place. For six years, he managed Wakefield, expanding its capacity by purchasing "all the knitting machines he could." In 1840, Jones started on his own enterprise, "with two knitting machines, in a small mill and house combined." On that property, he ultimately erected the steam factory he occupied in 1860, "gradually increasing the number of machines and products." By 1875, Jones's firm, the Hinckley Knitting Mills, which stood on a lot 400 by 180 feet, employed more than 200 workers; all three of the founder's sons had been taken into partnership, as Aaron Jones had retired from the "active details of the business."[11]

George Fling, the son of a London silk dyer, left school at 15 to learn the trade in the shop where his father was employed. Shortly thereafter (ca. 1835), the father and son repeated the sequence experienced by Aaron Jones and his father; Fling, Sr., emigrated to Philadelphia, and two years later young George followed and joined his father at work. The shortage of skilled dyers in the textile trades at this time is emphasized by George Fling's appointment at the age of 20 "to take charge of Mr. Hale's silk dyeing and printing establishment, in Rahway, New Jersey." After two years, he returned to Germantown with his bride of a few months and opened a shop for the dyeing and finishing of hosiery. For the next three years Fling worked on contract for Aaron Jones, Charles Spencer, and Martin Landenberger, among others, but his health failed in 1844 and he was obliged to quit the dyer's trade. William Allen took him on as a stocking maker, but "he met with a strong opposition from the Stocking Makers' Trade Union," presumably as he had not served an apprenticeship.[12] He was able somehow to remain with Allen for four years and then set out on his own "in a one story

delphia, 1884, p. 2307), Thomas Fisher was "proprietor of the Wakefield Mills." As he secured a government contract for army hosiery in 1848, the firm may have been closely held when incorporated and dissolved in the fifties for unknown reasons (*Register of Contracts, QMGC*, vol. II, 1847–51, National Archives Record Group 92, Entry No. 1238, p. 61).

[11] *M&MP*, pp. 316–17.

[12] No other reference to this evidently transplanted stockingers union surfaced in my research.

frame shop, 18 by 14 feet, situated in the rear of his residence." Employing at first one man and a boy, he had six workers by 1850, "increas[ing his trade] from time to time" through the fifties. Having accumulated sufficient reserves, Fling traveled to Britain in 1860 to purchase new machinery capable of producing "Super stouts, half hose . . . equal in every respect to the imported article." During the Civil War, he secured government contracts for hosiery on three occasions, though in the Gettysburg summer he closed the mill and joined the emergency forces. The next year "his son, Thomas Fling, together with other of the hands employed at the mill, enlisted in the army, and after faithful service, were honorably discharged." By the seventies, Fling occupied his own small factory, with an adjoining engine and dyehouse, erected on the same lot as his original residence and shop. About 1875, twenty workers were employed in the mill and, extending the long-established outwork practice, "from twenty to fifty hands – according to the state of the trade [were] supplied with work to be performed at home." Fling's son, Thomas, managed the factory.[13]

The founder of Button and Smith, John Button, was another Leicester-shire hosier. The son of a lace maker, he arrived in Philadelphia in 1830 with "two small machines for knitting hosiery" and began the manufacture of children's socks in 1831, moving to Germantown the next year. There Button rented a small building and set up his machines, soon adding eight more and extending his output to men's hose. Robson credits him with being the first hosier to revive the trade, having a local "monopoly . . . for a number of years" in children's hosiery. By 1835 Button's resources enabled him to buy three acres of land and put up his own mill, sufficient to "accommodate his machinery" and "about twenty-five hands." Enlargements were consistently made over the next thirty years. Some part of this expansion was facilitated by Button's partnership with Conyers Smith, which can be roughly dated as forming before 1835, for on the birth of his second son the following year, Button named him Conyers. Smith and Button were brothers-in-law, but whether Smith married Button's sister or Button married Smith's sister is impossible to tell, for the two couples and Button's children all shared the same household in the 1850 Population Census. Here the business partnership and family connection overlapped to a remarkable degree.

The following year Smith withdrew from the firm, "possessed of an ample fortune," and returned to his native England with his wife and his competence to retire at the age of 51. He was replaced by Button's eldest son, Joseph, who was later joined by Conyers before their father's retirement in

---

13 *M&MP*, p. 406; *Abstracts of Contracts, QMGC*, National Archives, Record Group 92, Entry No. 1239, vol. I, p. 223; vol. II, pp. 42, 263.

Left: John Button, credited with reestablishing the Germantown knitting trades in the 1830s. *Right:* Conyers Button, son of John and his successor in the family firm. (Free Library of Philadelphia)

1861 to "a substantial old-fashioned house fronting the mill property," where he continued to reside in 1875, retaining "a lively interest in the business." In 1865 Joseph Button also withdrew, whether to other ventures or to retire at 37 on the strength of wartime profits is not recorded. Conyers continued the manufacture into the 1880s, taking on a partner himself in 1869, his nephew Theodore Fleu. John Button had been the first Philadelphia hosier to attempt steampowered knitting, making the transition from handshop to engines and shafting during the 1840s. In subsequent years, "under his instruction many of those now at the head of similar industries learned the art of making knit goods by steam power."[14]

These three hosiery manufacturing firms display strikingly similar profiles, even though Fling got a late start and did not apprentice in the knitting trades. All were family-centered enterprises and each was passed along to the next generation. Each followed the pathway from shop rental to mill ownership, and the open spaces of Germantown enabled them to expand their plants without relocation. All ultimately undertook steam manufacture, but gradualism was the rule, a steplike process consistent with the economics of small capitals and their immersion in handcraft experience. Machinery was extended from retained profits, a few frames at a time, though a judicious partnership might ease the path to mill construction or expansion. This

[14] *M&MP*, p. 255; 1850 PCS, Philadelphia Co., District 8, p. 85.

gradualism, steampowered-spinning added to hand frames, a few power frames added later, and so forth, makes sense in terms of the cultural relations of production as well. Hosiers reared at the hand frame, or even converted dyers, with years of experience on it (Fling), would not shed their notion of the right and proper ways to make their goods all at a stroke, particularly if they were functioning in a community in which handwork was not only alive but expanding. Early power knitters were not only expensive, newfangled, and of uncertain capacity and reliability; they were linked with the degradation of the craft and thus involved a morally equivocal decision. Consequently, there were no sudden plantations of giant hosiery mills at Germantown, no mergers of shopmen to venture ahead on the path of industrial progress. Instead, there were cautious, individual experiments, with the capitalism of "more" and "bigger" contained within the context of family legacies and punctuated by occasional quiet statements of "Enough!" as men like Conyers Smith withdrew from manufacture entirely.[15]

The textile workers of Germantown

What of the midcentury textile workers in Germantown? Here again the 1850 Population Census Schedules are both crucial and frustrating sources. We may extract material on the age and ethnic structure of the adult male group in the district, but the female portion of the work force remains as invisible as it was at Kensington. Household structures allow some speculations about women's employment, but little more can be gleaned with presently available sources. Table 7.2 illustrates the ethnic distribution of male textile workers in Germantown Borough and Township.

Three-quarters of the textile workmen and 80% of the weavers were immigrants, the largest block of whom were, like the shop- and millmen, English-born. They clustered residentially in the village center, the borough, but were only a fraction of the smaller work group living in the rural township. Of the textile men in Germantown Borough, 63% were British; in both the borough and the township the percentage was 58, but in the township alone, where native-born and Irish textile households were sprinkled in proportions greater than their percentage of the district total, only 19% of

---

[15] *M&MP*, p. 255. Conyers Smith's brother may also have lived in 1850 Germantown, for a 44-year-old English-born weaver named Joseph Smith appears in the Germantown Borough Schedules (1850 PCS, Philadelphia Co., District 8, p. 71) with his wife and five children, including a 10-year-old Conyers and a 5-year-old daughter, Sarah Ann, the first American-born children in Joseph's family. Conyers Smith's wife was Sarah; John Button's wife, Ann (1850 PCS, Philadelphia Co., District 8, p. 85). Joseph Smith reported no real property and was not otherwise visible.

Table 7.2. Male weavers and skilled workers by nativity, Germantown Borough and Township, 1850

	U.S.-born	English-born	Scots-born	Irish-born	German-born	French-born	Total
Weavers							
Germantown Borough	55	228	15	33	15	2	348
Germantown Township	30	11	8	15	3	0	67
Subtotal	85	239	23	48	18	2	415
Skilled workers							
Germantown Borough	20	16	0	1	2	0	39
Germantown Township	7	4	1	0	0	0	12
Subtotal	27	20	1	1	2	0	51
Total	112	259	24	49	20	2	466

Note: Weaver was the term used in the census schedules to describe most textile operatives, including knit-goods and fabric workers. *Skilled workers* refers only to men specifically designated as carders, spinners, dyers, and wool sorters, and does not imply that weavers were unskilled.

Source: Manuscript Population Census Schedules, Philadelphia County, Districts 8 and 9 (Germantown), 1850.

the workers were British. Skilled workers were almost exclusively native or British, a number of the native-born calico printers and dyers stemming probably from families long associated with Thorp's venerable printworks, then in its fourth decade of operation.

The 466 male textile workers tallied from the 1850 Population Schedules surpass by 60 the total reported for Germantown Borough and Township on the manufacturing returns. These figures underscore the cottage basis of handwork, for a handful of small home-workshops were likely missed by the industrial survey but reached by population marshals who visited every dwelling. In general, this discontinuity would imply an undercount of hand-shops and a slight overstatement thereby of the proportions of textile workers employed in larger establishments and unlikely to be overlooked. These 466 men represented 13% of the male population in the borough and 7% in the township if all ages are included. Of those listing occupations, however, they totaled 26% of the economically active men in the borough and 14% of those in the outer areas, where farming was still the most frequently cited profession. In the shuttle-clacking Sixth Ward of Kensington, textile work was the livelihood of 39% of males whose occupations were noted, a comparison that shows the considerable significance of textile labor in the borough economy. Table 7.3 shows the age distribution of this population, indicating that immigrant weavers were on balance older than their native-born fellow workers. The average age of British workers was just over 36, that of Pennsylvanians, 31.

That the British group is noticeably older than the other Germantown contingents is consistent with a migration that began gradually twenty years before the 1850 census and continued over the decades through the Civil War. The bulge in the U.S. column for men aged 20–29 suggests the immigration of rural males and the probable adoption of factory work by a few sons of local farmers who were striving to remain near the family center. Three Germantown farmer-headed households had adult sons living in and reported as weavers; others may have been resident elsewhere in the district but descended from farm parents. These men were predominantly single, unlike those in the two other groups. While 56% of English and other foreign-born weavers were married heads of households, only 36% of the U.S. natives across all ages were so classified. This fits with the age differentials and is not inconsistent with the inference about the local rural origins of many native-born weavers. The "Other" group was more than half Irish-born, and its pattern of age distribution fits closely with that of the sample from heavily Irish Kensington, both factors indicating the recent influx of famine-era emigrants. Kensington was, however, an older Irish settlement where more than 80% of the sample was Irish-born, which partly accounts for its higher percentage of over-40 weavers.

Table 7.3. *Nativity of weavers by age, Germantown, 1850 (in percentage)*

Nativity	Age						Total %	N
	Under 20	20–29	30–39	40–49	50–59	60+		
U.S.-born	16	43	21	9	4	6	99	85
English-born	13	26	27	21	8	6	101	239
All other	4	42	31	14	9	0	100	91
Germantown overall	12	33	26	17	7	5	100	466
Kensington, Ward 6[a]	5	39	26	21	5	5	101	131

[a]A 20% sample.
Source: Manuscript Population Census Schedules, Philadelphia County, Districts 8, 9, and 10, 1850.

Although manufacturers boarded few Germantown textile workers, boarders were not unusual in the households of weavers themselves. In the borough and township, seventy-six households appeared with more than one weaver present. Two of these were inns in which eight textile workers resided alongside other single laborers. The rest were family groups composed of every imaginable combination of sons, kinsmen, and outsiders (residents with noncore family surnames). Some of the putative "outsiders" may have been kin, but not until 1880 were the relationships within census households reported on the schedules explicitly. The family craft succession was quite strong among this group, as thirty of sixty-one households headed by weavers had some combination of father and sons resident and working the trade. Eight of these held working boarders in addition. Of the other thirty-one households, six showed a probable kinsman sharing home and work, their age proximity suggesting a pair of co-resident brothers. The other twenty-five had boarders whose relationship to the head of the household remains uncertain. Of course, younger weavers were heavily represented in the boarding group, and in four of the six brother pairs both were under 30.[16]

There is a rough pattern to this array of fathers, sons, kinsmen, and boarders that fits well with the cottage and outwork character of much of the Germantown textile manufacture in 1850. The complex subcontractor shop system present in Kensington does not surface in Germantown. Instead, the

[16] Calculated from work sheets drawn from 1850 PCS, Philadelphia Co., Districts 8 and 9.

family basis of cottage production was retained, with younger workers taking in immigrant boarders, usually from their own home countries, and rearing their sons to learn the trade. Although the population returns omit reference to women's and children's work, winding and sewing were essential tasks in hand-frame hosiery making, and their importance at Germantown is confirmed by the sizable number of women workers recorded in the manufacturing manuscripts.

The total workers in these seventy-six households comprise nearly half the male textile work force in Germantown Borough and Township (217 of 466) and more than half that of the weavers (217 of 415). The family economy is linked to the family life cycle, for boarders, whether independent frame workers or factory weavers, add income to the household, at a time when children are too young to contribute. Gradually, as sons are able to operate a frame themselves and become steady producers, the family is enabled to dispense with boarders and to attempt the accumulation of property toward a competence. This is indicated by the age breakdown of households with weaver sons only, as contrasted with that of the group having both sons and boarding weavers. All twenty-two households in the first group were headed by a male over 40, while four of the eight in the latter group had a father 40 or younger atop the census group. Further, while four families in the first group owned real estate valued at over $1,000, none of those in the second did so.[17]

That the family production center involved powerful bonds of obligation can be seen from examining the four households in which working weavers over 70 years of age were present. In all four cases, one or more sons lived with the father, two with their own wives and children as well. The other two cases were striking. John Buddy, 77 and a native Pennsylvanian, worked with his two unmarried sons, 38 and 32, in a household kept by a spinster daughter, 40. Similarly, 76-year-old George Betts knitted stockings alongside his three sons, 42, 30, and 27, aided by three single daughters, 25 and older.[18] Six single "children" toiling alongside their widowed father mark an extreme case, to be sure. However, not one of the weavers over 60 in midcentury Germantown lived alone, outside a family productive context, underscoring culturally based relationships that were a pillar of hand-frame manufacture there.

The placid labor relations of Germantown's textile trades contrast immediately with the boisterous history of strikes and riots that can be seen at both Kensington and early Manayunk. At this point, only a few general thoughts might be relevant. First, the conditions faced by immigrant frame workers in

17 Ibid.
18 1850 PCS, Philadelphia Co., District 8, p. 15; District 9, p. 43.

Germantown were paradiasical compared with the brutal suffering then being endured in the British trades. The 1855 Blue Book, *Stoppage of Wages (Hosiery)*, offers a catalogue of abuses and exploitive practices current in the knit-goods trades,[19] few of which are mentioned in any American context. That contrast, freshened by the tales of new arrivals, may have induced an acceptance of unequal power relations. Second, the demand for German-town goods in the fifties was strong enough to effect the simultaneous expansion of hand and powered manufacture, allowing dozens of skilled knitters to open their own workshops. In such a "work-for-all" environment, labor struggle might seem hardly necessary. Third, there was an enormous gap between small shops and the few large Germantown mills and no evidence of collaboration or cooperation among their various masters, as was clearly the case with the price-list controversies at Kensington.[20] Little clear evidence of union organizing in the hosiery manufacture comes until a generation later (Chapter 6). Fourth, the handcraft workers of Germantown were plying their trade in a familiar and culturally comfortable environment, in village and rural shops, surrounded by farms, with space for gardens easily had, the whole complex mindful of the county districts wherein they were reared and a brisk contrast to the daily miseries of Leicester or Nottingham, through which they had likely passed. Finally, the family-centeredness of much of Germantown's production surely masked an exploitation that was somewhat more visible in Kensington's warehouse weaving rooms and boarding workshops, the latter populated with hundreds of single immigrants whose family financial obligations were less restraining than those of Germantown households. These elements, some historical, some economic, some cultural, likely all contributed to the peaceful character of capitalist development in Germantown textiles. With the prospect of opening one's own shop ahead for the ambitious young workers (at least four of the new handshops present in 1860 were started by knitters who had labored in 1850 Germantown),[21] the emergence of class consciousness and class conflict was obstructed profoundly. There was, of course, a fair silence at Manayunk in the 1850s as well, but there labor's quiescence was the product of a developing factory culture, the context for which we shall explore next.

---

[19] *Report from the Select Committee on Stoppage of Wages (Hosiery), Together with the Proceedings of the Committee, Minutes of Evidence, Appendix and Index, House of Commons, 1855,* Westminister (?), 1855.

[20] David Montgomery, "The Shuttle and the Cross," in P. Stearns and D. Walkowitz, eds., *Workers in the Industrial Revolution,* New Brunswick, N.J., 1974, pp. 49–50.

[21] There may have been more such cases, as the four here mentioned were noticed among a cluster of 1850 households for which full data was transferred to work sheets because boarders or kinsmen in the same trade as the head of household were present. No attempt was made to link all new starts back into the 1850 Population Schedules.

Manayunk: factories and fabrics

Late in 1847 the *Germantown Telegraph* published a brief survey of the "statistics of Manayunk," reprinted from the *Public Ledger*, the downtown daily that periodically issued reports of the state of various Philadelphia neighborhoods. The ethnic diversity of the district was visible in the array of established churches: two Methodist and one each from "Dutch" Reformed, Presbyterian, Episcopal, and Roman Catholic denominations.[22] The Catholic Church was erected in 1830 on land donated by an early cotton manufacturer, Jerome Keating, who also "defrayed most of the cost of the building."[23] The ground on which the Episcopal Church was erected had been provided by Joseph Ripka;[24] the birth of the Presbyterian congregation was assisted by James Darragh, who opened "a small room in the dye-house" of his mill for services during its first year.[25] Other millowners served as Trustees and Sunday-school masters, a practice that extended into the 1880s.[26]

The *Telegraph* also reviewed the manufacturing scene, counting "five woolen cloth factories, three Kentucky jean factories, two woolen yarn factories, [and] eleven cotton cloth and cotton yarn factories." Together they processed more than 3 million pounds of raw cotton and 1.3 million pounds of raw wool annually, "the whole giving constant employment to 1880 hands, including 1026 females, among whom many are young, handsome and intelligent, and 285 boys."[27] These figures closely resemble the returns from the 1850 Manufacturing Census, which showed twenty-four textile firms in the area and 1,966 workers, 940 females and 1,026 males, their production valued at more than $1.6 million.[28] Ten years later, fifteen of those firms were still functioning in Manayunk's textile industry, the highest rate of persistence in the three districts examined closely here.[29] Two of the firms closed upon the retirement of the principal; James Kempton leased his several mills to Sevill Schofield and Archibald Campbell, and James Shaw withdrew in 1856 to interest himself in local public affairs. Shaw had been

---

[22] *Germantown Telegraph*, November 24, 1847.

[23] Mildred Goshow, ed., "Mills and Mill Owners of Manayunk in the 19th Century," typescript, 1970, pp. 53–4, Roxborough Branch, Free Library of Philadelphia; *Hazard's Register*, vol. 5 (1830), p. 335.

[24] Goshow, "Mills and Mill Owners," p. 25.

[25] Ibid., p. 74.

[26] *Manayunk, Roxborough and Falls of Schuylkill Directory for 1883*, Philadelphia, 1883, pp. 44–63, only known copy available at Falls of Schuylkill Branch, Free Library of Philadelphia.

[27] *Germantown Telegraph*, November 24, 1847.

[28] 1850 MCS, Philadelphia Co., pp. 84–7, 184.

[29] 1860 MCS, Philadelphia Co., pp. 470–4.

burgess of Manayunk for five years in the 1840s as well as a woolen manufacturer, and he remained active in school matters until his death in 1885.[30]

The structure of the Manayunk cluster of textile firms shows both the options available to factory-sited producers and the importance of the larger urban textile complex to the prosperity of Manayunk capitalists. All twenty-four firms active in 1850 were powered by water or steam: twenty-one water, two steam, one with both; no handloom firms appeared at all as the factory system was fully planted. A generation earlier, Ripka had installed handlooms in his first Manayunk mill, but by 1850 the power loom was standard. Further, at that date no hosiery or carpet manufacturer located in Manayunk. Indeed, the agglomeration of hosiery and carpet firms in Germantown and Kensington visible in 1850 would continue to function as a magnet for new enterprises throughout the century. The direct marketing of goods common in Philadelphia firms and the clustering of appropriately skilled workers made it sensible to undertake new knit-goods or carpet mills alongside those already operating.[31] About 90% of the district's textile workers in 1850 labored in fabric mills, with the balance scattered among a dozen small spinning, dyeing, and carding firms.[32]

The fabric plants were either partially or fully integrated. All five mixed-goods firms spun their own woolen yarns and bought cotton warp, a total of 123,000 pounds among them. The seven single-fiber firms spun all the yarns for their own needs, and one marketed an overflow of 30,000 pounds in the census year. Both groups had weaving and dyeing facilities on their premises. As in Germantown, the yarn purchased by the mixed-goods manufacturers was probably the product of local spinners, five of whom ran cotton fabric and carpet yarns. The largest of these was Daniel Arbuckle's plant, which produced 350,000 pounds of spun cotton. The other four firms generated another 600,000 pounds of cotton yarns for fabrics and carpets, the grand total vastly in excess of the quantities bought by Manayunk millmen. When the 150,000 pounds of woolen yarns from three small wool spinners are added to the total, Manayunk spinners show a yarn output of

---

[30] Goshow, "Mills and Mill Owners," pp. 55, 76.

[31] This locational advantage (agglomeration effect) was well known to manufacturers in the textile trades. John Hayes, head of the National Association of Wool Manufacturers, would later put it simply: "Practical men say that the best place to plant a new mill is by the very side of those which have been long established" (*Awards and Claims of Exhibitors at the International Exhibition, 1876*, Boston, 1877, p. 450).

[32] Agglomeration increased the possibility of being visited by wholesalers, jobbers, and country merchants who traveled about in the hosiery and carpet districts. Although the use of commission houses, road agents, and preproduction sales agents by Philadelphia hosiery manufacturers has been documented, little detail about early marketing efforts has been discovered. The larger firms (McCallum) had downtown salesrooms (Chestnut Street), but shopmen's selling channels are not at all clear.

500 tons in excess of local demand.[33] Where was this vast overflow directed? The obvious choice is Kensington, where the Craige mill could supply only part of the handloom demand for cotton yarns and where no carpet yarns were then being spun. Again, the absence of firm stock books and records makes it impossible to confirm this inference, though in the 1880s Manayunk spinner John Wilde was running carpet yarns and his customers were exclusively Kensington shopmen.[34]

If this relationship was operative in the fifties, the interlock between hand and powered manufacture deepens, with Manayunk spinners and Kensington handshops mutually dependent within the larger urban economic system. Factory fabric producers at Manayunk were within reach of the city's commercial nexus at Front Street, able to market directly and to gain up-to-date information on the vagaries of specialty demand in a way difficult for rural mills, which were compelled by spatial and informational constraints to run staples.

Similarly, Manayunk factory yarn producers were able to function with some confidence because of the steady demand for their products within the same urban network, though their target was Kensington rather than the dockside marketplace. As handwork expanded in the fifties, so did the production of Manayunk's spinners. The total value of production in 1850 for the nine firms offering yarn was $212,000; in 1860, thirteen mills in the district generated yarn for direct sale worth more than $475,000. The changing proportions of this output also reflect an expanding carpet manufacture in the city. In 1850 Manayunk produced $112,000 worth of cotton yarn, $60,000 of wool, and $32,000 of cotton carpet yarns. The 1860 cotton valuation reports showed virtually no change, remaining steady at $113,000, whereas wool climbed to $245,000 and cotton carpet yarns to $104,000.[35] This accords well with the relative stagnation of handloom cottons as contrasted with the rapid development of the carpet trade.

The neighborhood market for cotton yarn had not expanded with fabric production, for by 1860 only four of the twelve firms running mixed goods were still buying cotton warps, the value accounting for about a third of Manayunk fabric cotton yarn production. The other eight were now spinning both cotton and wool, itself another suggestion of the mechanical gradualism noticeable at Kensington and Germantown. Woolen yarn showed a slightly different picture, for Daniel Arbuckle had added looms to his 1850

---

[33] 1850 MCS, Philadelphia Co., pp. 84–7, 184.

[34] *Mill Production Book, 1886–93, John Wilde and Brother Carpet Yarns*, Manayunk; in possession of Russel Fawley, a descendant of the founders and the current proprietor of the firm, which is operating at the same site as in 1880.

[35] 1850 MCS, Philadelphia Co., pp. 84–7; 1860 MCS, Philadelphia Co., pp. 470–4.

spinning mill and by 1860 was able to weave a million yards of cassimeres in his expanded facilities. For these blended fabrics he purchased $90,000 of woolen yarn in the census year, more than a third of the Manayunk total output.[36] If these five mills bought Manayunk yarn, as seems plausible, nearly $350,000 worth of goods still remained to be sold elsewhere.

One Manayunk firm did buy a variety of yarn not available in 1860 from riverside spinners. James Lord, Jr., a spinner of woolen and cotton yarns, who also manufactured carpets with part of his production, purchased 50,000 pounds of worsted yarn, valued at $20,000, for fine all-wool ingrains. Lord's worsted yarn was probably imported from beyond the region, for only one small Philadelphia firm was then spinning worsted. Peter Erben, a wool manufacturer in the Spring Garden area, would later undertake worsted spinning on a considerable scale, leading Philadelphia toward its ultimate prominence in fine woolens.

The Lord firm appears in both the 1850 and 1860 censuses, with the contrast between the two reports providing an insight into the pathway taken by an expanding small factory. In 1850 James Lord operated two small spinning mills along the Wissahickon, one making cotton carpet yarn and the other a smaller quantity of ordinary cotton yarn. His raw materials were the waste from the large Manayunk mills, for he paid but $16,000 for 350,000 pounds of raw cotton and had a loss in carding and spinning of nearly a third of that weight (a 10% loss was expected for baled new cotton). He was probably also a partner in the wool-spinning firm of Lord and Kitchen that appears on the same schedule page, which reprocessed woolen rags into carpet yarn.[37] Lord thus was integrated both into the larger network of Manayunk textile production, providing the canal mills with an outlet for their sweepings and a bit of quiet income that did not appear on their schedules, and into the urban complex toward whose handlooms he directed his low-grade yarns.

In 1853 he purchased a larger mill and surrounding acreage on the Wissahickon, consolidated his operations, and installed steampower. By 1860, his son was spinning cotton and woolen yarns and had added fifty-two carpet looms to weave part of the product of the 2,200 spindles in place. From the prices given for raw materials on the 1860 schedule it appears that the firm had stepped up from the shoddy trade to buying fresh wool and cotton, a move toward quality output that is also indicated by its purchase of worsted yarns.[38] The looms were probably power-driven, as 60 horsepower was available from the steam engine and only fifty workers were employed

---

36 1850 MCS, Philadelphia Co., p. 473.
37 Ibid., p. 184.
38 1860 MCS, Philadelphia Co., p. 470; Magee, "Mills in Wissahickon, " p. 20.

for carding, spinning, and running more than fifty looms. This would have been a more risky move in handloom Kensington; but in Manayunk, far from that source of potential resistance, it opened the door to rapid accumulation. In the 1859–60 census year, James Lord, Jr., reported materials costing $97,900, wages of a bit more than $11,000 if the mill ran twelve months, and products worth $145,000.[39] During the Civil War, it is possible that Lord, like the Germantown McCallum carpet firm, converted to the manufacture of heavy woolens and blankets. This surmise is more probable given that in 1864 Lord sold out to a New York entrepreneur, Holmes Ammidown (for $75,000), and that in 1870 one Charles Ammidown was running the mill and producing woolen blankets exclusively.[40] The factory was shuttered in 1872, its site purchased for inclusion in the Fairmount Park system, but by that time Lord had long since withdrawn from textile manufacture in comfort. The firm's career shows the flexibility, movement, gradualism in integration, and ultimate withdrawal from capitalist manufacture that the generation of a competence permitted. The factory could facilitate that accumulation; the Civil War added an "external" impetus of considerable force.

All the fabric firms at Manayunk in both years did their own dyeing, with the result that only one dyer, Robert Haly, appears in the 1850 census. By the 1860 tally, Haly had added spinning frames to his mill, offering both dyed woolen yarn and the service of dyeing yarns for other spinners.[41] This double function is present in seven firms in 1860 Manayunk, indicating just that set of relationships described by Bishop as "calling into service the equipment of other manufacturers." Besides Lord and Haly, of five mixed-goods firms, three offered yarn for sale and two dyeing services. The range of woven goods was generically broad – tweeds, jeans, plaids, blankets, shawls, zephyrs, and cottonades – with each mill having a capacity for variety akin to that displayed by A. Campbell and Co. (Chapter 3). Despite the slipping fortunes of the Ripka Mill, which had been surpassed by Campbell in both output and work force, the textile manufacture in Manayunk had grown virtually to the limits of the space available along the Schuylkill, and new mills now clung to the steep hills that defined the district.

Where twenty-four firms had operated in 1850, thirty-eight were in place on the eve of the war, and more significant, eleven of the new arrivals each produced more than $50,000 in goods during the census year. The scale of manufacture was certainly rising – more workers, more firms, more value produced – yet the relationships among these increases are more significant than any of them taken individually. Between 1850 and 1860 the Manayunk

---

39 1860 MCS, Philadelphia Co., p. 470.
40 Magee, "Mills in Wissahickon," p. 20; 1870 MCS, Philadelphia Co., p. 608.
41 1860 MCS, Philadelphia Co., p. 470.

work force increased by 66% (1,966 to 3,255), capital invested rose a roughly parallel 72% ($1.1 million to $1.8 million), and the value of output
surpassed both, growing 93% ($1.6 million to $3.1 million).[42] Indeed, what
is striking about these figures is the modest gap between added work force
and investment and the resultant productive increases. When it is recognized
that one main element of change in the productive arrays represented by new
investment was the installation of steam engines, the increase in production
seems to have resulted from technology rather than from any speedup or
stretch-out policies. Mills generally could rely on losing one to two weeks of
production annually when the canal was shut down for repairs and, on
average, another two weeks or more when high or low water prevailed. Being
able to run twelve months, if demand was sufficient of course, was the great
benefit of steampower. Thus, most of the additional production was not
facilitated by the introduction of the Lowell-style four-loom operation,
which spread the same work force over more equipment. Instead, one part of
the surplus at Manayunk came from the dozen firms that added steampower
to waterpower or substituted it entirely. Another element in the added value
of production came from the upgrading of the quality and variety of goods
being made. Like Lord in the fifties, other manufacturers moved from low-
grade outputs to more sophisticated and valuable goods. For example,
Joseph Solms began to run all-wool tweeds alongside his usual production of
cotton and woolen Kentucky jeans. Though his total yardage increased a bit
more than 60% during the decade, its total value doubled.[43]

The question of paternalism

The conditions for labor exploitation and struggle at Manayunk were little
changed in 1860 from those in 1850 and the changes were not the sort to
induce labor militancy. There were more jobs in the district than a decade
before, and steampower made payless weeks less likely in a number of the
larger mills. If the markets contracted, as they did with the threat of war in
1860, the mills shut down and the local *Star & Gazette* called for charity and
patience, but the external source of such crises rarely brought opprobrium
down on the millowners' heads.[44] If Manayunk was a tiresome place to live
and work in 1850, with the 1848 strike lost and revivalist and temperance
orators preaching salvation and abstinence, it was not an appreciably worse
place in 1860. Most of the mills had remained fairly small, the two giants,

---

[42] Calculated from 1850 and 1860 MCS, Philadelphia Co. (Manayunk).
[43] 1860 MCS, Philadelphia Co., p. 473.
[44] *Manayunk Star and Roxborough Gazette,* April 6, 1861.

Ripka and Campbell (succeeding Kempton), having together only 155 more workers than in 1850, or 12% of the increase in the district work force. Moreover, the religious leadership and political activity displayed by Manayunk millowners, should not be seen only as the grasping of whatever sources of local power and influence were to be had by a group of self-conscious hegemonists. To be concerned about education, to provide land and leadership for churches, to commit one's energies after retirement to public service in politics and associational activities, these were duties as much as opportunities to extend the networks of dominion. Whereas such paternalist actions ceased at Lowell after the departure of the founding generation and with the solidification of a bureaucratized and economistic managerial system, they continued to appear in the family-firm context of factory Manayunk.

In his discussion of Victorian Lancashire and Yorkshire's textile industries, Patrick Joyce has recently documented the emergence of a parallel system of factory paternalism that transcended the harsh laissez-faire notion that "the relations between employer and worker were to be merely those of the cash nexus."[45] In the wake of several bitter decades, factory owners undertook to reconstitute relations of community, centered on the mill, that both confirmed the new order of things and recognized the delicate interdependence of master and man. By hiring increased numbers of adult male workers, employers transformed their mills into centers of family employment, rather than pure exploiters of women and children. As a substitute for class-based antagonism, manufacturers offered factory canteens, the occasional picnic, and funding for church construction and temperance clubs. Such actions both reinforced their sense of superiority and responded to a religiously derived notion of duty and service. Parallel with these overt actions were a host of tiny practices that "placed" the operator and the workers in relationships that were centered on neither the transactions of the market nor the authoritarianism of the father role. Circulating through the mill, the master knew his workers by name and talked shop with them from his knowledge of the trade. He hired their offspring or kin (or let them do so) and elevated model operatives to positions of increasing responsibility. This was the paternalism that was "largely unknown to historical record . . . the stream of social life that characterized all factories."[46] Operatives responded to this personalism with "testimonials, which were almost as frequent as the benefactions which were their cause."[47] Although the setting was new, these

---

[45] Patrick Joyce, *Work, Society and Politics: The Culture of the Factory in Later Victorian England* Brighton, England, 1980, p. 136.

[46] Ibid., p. 140.

[47] Ibid., p. 149.

relationships were rooted in a complex of cultural traditions that reformulated older material and religious notions of mutualism and hierarchy.

What of Manayunk? Situated in its close valley, packed with mills and rows of tiny houses, Manayunk bore a physical resemblance to the classic, if mythical, industrial town of the nineteenth century. It had experienced in the bitter thirties conflicts whose intensity resonates with that of British events. Moreover, its workers and mill operators themselves were in large part veterans of the British factory system. The coexistence of large firms and those leasing "rooms with power" was equally suggestive of a parallel development, as was the solidity of family ownership and succession. Likewise, after a tumultuous era, the relations of production at Manayunk settled into a quieter pattern. Those factory owners who can be linked to religious denominations consistently surfaced in the same sects whose moral tenets underlay the emerging patterns of factory paternalism in Britain. Finally, like their English counterparts, Manayunk proprietors had often moved from craft to mill, carrying with them elements of the artisanal obligations denounced as irrational by the standard-bearers of political economy. With these overlaps, did a Manayunk analogy to the British paternalist relations appear in the midcentury decades?

No unequivocal answer can be derived from available sources. Certainly manufacturers were the focal points of the political, religious, and cultural life of the canalside community, just as their mills were its spatial backbone. Enterprising skilled workers did receive assistance in starting on their own account, and in the McFadden/Schofield case on terms that were fairly generous. The personal quality of work relations in the smaller mills and the importance of skill in flexible production likely encouraged the sort of "fellow feeling" to which Joyce refers. On the other hand, Manayunk proprietors did not erect canteens, sponsor workers' libraries, excursions, and the like. Ritualized festivals on the occasion of proprietors' sons joining the family firm are nowhere reported in the surviving fragments of the local weeklies. The interior dynamics of the factory floor are rarely glimpsed. Nonetheless, several incidents from the Civil War era may indicate that a rough approximation of the British pattern was present at a number of Manayunk factories. Each involved the blending of war patriotism with paternalist relations, adding to the ambiguities of their meanings.

The winter of 1860–1 was both cold and depressed in the textile districts. The prospect of war had contributed to a general "derangement of trade," which the *Star and Gazette* summarized in its snippets column as "A notorious fact – that the times are hard in Manayunk."[48] A later article, which discussed the March 1861 closing of the mills for canal repair, singled out

[48] *Manayunk Star and Roxborough Gazette*, February 2, 1861.

the firms of Stephens and Whitaker and Sutton and Son as those in the community that had "run constant all winter," a feat made possible by their steampower. Later in the spring a remarkable ceremony took place at the Stephens and Whitaker factory. Within a week after the commencement of hostilities at Fort Sumter, the operatives at the firm's Arkwright Mills, in a burst of gratitude for full employment through the winter and patriotic sentiment, presented the partners with a 15- by 18-foot version of the national flag "made by the young ladies of the establishment."[49]

The ceremony was repeated at another Manayunk factory the following winter. William Simpson, a calico printer with a large establishment just downriver, had taken over John Maxon's mill and kept it running, evidently with the same labor force. In February 1862 the workers "prepared a large and beautiful American flag," which was presented to Simpson on the steps of the mill. In reply to their gesture of patriotism and respect, the *Star and Gazette* reported: "Mr. Simpson has had a supper gotten up for their benefit at Morris' Hotel, where, we have no doubt, they will spend a merry hour."[50] Both the personal manufacture of the two flags and the reciprocal feast match British patterns and illustrate a mix of patriotism and expression of esteem and respect for the master, which is acknowledged graciously by him. Both Simpson and Stephens were British immigrants, the first Manchester-born, and Whitaker was a first-generation American, the offspring of the English Whitaker clan that was present in the 1820 census and active in Philadelphia textiles well into the twentieth century. The Schofield and Dobson mills that mobilized emergency companies later in the war, units led by proprietors, were likewise headed by English-born entrepreneurs. Schofield's contribution of wages to the families of workers who volunteered for military service seems to be an extension of the same compound of mutualism and hierarchy evident in the flag incidents.

Aspects of Joseph Ripka's later years also reflect elements of the paternalist dimension of proprietary manufacture. Extension of partnerships and employment to distant relations (Hartel, Francis Ripka) was a patriarch's privilege, but Ripka also fought to keep his mills running and his workers employed even as his business suffered successive crises. Responding to losses from the 1857 Panic, he borrowed heavily from city bankers at usurious rates that reflected their reluctance to handle industrial clients. At the same time, the *Star and Gazette* observed, "the stock broker who produced no wealth and the importer of foreign finery we could do without were each accustomed to large sums at the customary bank rate."[51] Ripka was long a

---

49 Ibid., March 3, April 27, 1861.
50 Ibid., February 22, 1862.
51 Ibid., March 29, 1862.

pillar of the Espiscopal Church, a man credited with being "public spirited" and "generous" in matters of benefit to the village by his old antagonist Charles Hagner. Even his funeral evokes the British model – all the mills closed, the streets lined with observers, the factory bells tolling on all sides.[52]

The factory paternalism that developed in midcentury Manayunk derived from the factory culture of clustered proprietary firms. The lives of immigrant entrepreneurs revolved around their firms, families, and churches. From the set of obligations necessitated by business, blood, and belief flowed a variety of practices and gestures that seem to mirror the patterns developed in contemporary Britain. Each represented an independent, though culturally linked, solution to problems of the social relations of production beyond the realm of classical political economy. On the available evidence, the Manayunk version was paler than the British formulation, but its boundaries were similar, as we shall soon see.

Textile proprietors and textile workers in Manayunk

Ethnically, the manufacturers of Manayunk were a somewhat more heterogeneous lot than were those of Germantown. A search of the Manayunk and Roxborough 1850 Population Schedules located thirty-three of thirty-nine proprietors or partners then active, indicating that residential proximity to the mill or shop was a constant across the city. More than half those linked were English-born (17), with one Scots, two Irish, and four German millmen bringing the immigrant proportion to 76% (twenty-five of thirty-three). Moreover, five of the nine native-born textile capitalists were sons of immigrants. By 1860, the balance had shifted somewhat. Of fifty-two millmen linked in that year (fifty-seven possible links), twenty-one were British, five Irish, one Scots, and one German (54%). The remainder were native-born, though half of that crew were again immigrant offspring (eight English, three German, one Irish).[53] The increase in first-generation Americans represents the settling of family successions by aging firm founders. A number of such transfers had been made during the fifties (James Lord, Sr., William Kitchen, and Edward Preston) and others were shortly anticipated. Though Joseph Ripka would be balked in his plans, by 1860 George Sutton and John

---

52 Gashow, "Mills and Mill Owners of Manayunk," p. 21; *Manayunk Star and Roxborough Gazette*, March 29, 1862.

53 Even the increase from four to twelve probable NBNP manufacturers is slightly misleading, for a pair of brother trios accounted for six members of this group, their two small firms totaling $7,500 in capital and eighteen workers. Meanwhile, the two largest firms in the district were in the hands of immigrant families.

Maxon were both past 65 with sons for partners, and James Lord, Jr., then 45, had brought his son, James, into the firm to learn manufacture.[54]

The figures given in the census for property holding may not be thoroughly trustworthy, but comparing the group of linked manufacturers in the two census years shows an interesting overall pattern. In 1850 only six of the thirty-three linked listed any real-estate holdings. Though many must have owned the homes in which they lived, they were evidently not generally the possessors of blocks of housing rented to workers in the district. Their capital was likely tied up in their manufacturing enterprises. Ripka was surely the exception, for he was known to have "tenements" as early as the 1830s for favored workers. Of the other five, only Preston and John Winpenny held sufficient property ($16,000 and $40,000, respectively), to readily include a sizable group of small houses.

By 1860, however, substantial real-estate holdings are the norm rather than the exception among Manayunk textile men. Of fifty-one linked, thirty-nine owned such property, and in twenty-three cases it was valued at more than $5,000. As the plants and work force expanded, the housing problem became a nagging constant in the local manufacturing equation. It is reasonable to expect that some manufacturers realized both the necessity of, and the profit potential inherent in, throwing up rows of cheaply constructed homes. Census evidence is, however, ambiguous, for real estate figures may reflect combinations of vacant land, housing, and mill property. Research in county deed records is needed to reveal the sources of workers' housing at Manayunk. Nevertheless, between 1850 and 1860, the total real estate held by the linked manufacturers rose from $275,000 to more than $630,000[55]; the holdings of Joseph Ripka fell from $200,000 to $150,000, reflecting both his troubles and the spread of property holding by the other textile men.

Local folklore has it that Manayunk was dominated by British and Scots-Irish ethnic groups, a place where the Irish Catholics were both pitied and maligned. The weekly neighborhood newspaper advocated temperance, but abstained from any direct attacks on religious beliefs or institutions. Whereas the activities of the Catholic parish were not reported, however, the sessions of the interdenominational Protestant Sunday School Association received

---

54 Compiled from Manayunk PCS work sheets, as previously. For the brother trios, see 1860 PCS, Philadelphia Co., Ward 21, pt. 1, pp. 78, 80, 88; pt. 2, pp. 63–4. For Sutton and Maxon, see ibid., pt. 1, pp. 96, 191, 246.

55 The personal property data from 1860 were excluded from consideration; for the linked group it totaled another $605,000, showing the effects of a decade of accumulation despite the intervention of the 1857 Panic. For a subgroup of thirteen persistent (1850–60) manufacturers, the real-estate totals are $245,500 for 1850 and $488,000 for 1860, with an additional $309,000 in personal property reported in 1860. Their work force increased by almost half (1,004 to 1,449).

lengthly reviews.[56] Nor should the presence of Irish manufacturers allow us to imagine that those at Manayunk were anything other than Orangemen, unlike the Kensington mix. Born in County Monaghan (Ulster), David Wallace not only possessed a classic Scots surname but also named his youngest son Robert Burns. His second marriage, to Mary Preston, the eldest daughter of a British-born Manayunk millman, preceded by a year the formation of the firm of Preston and Wallace (1854).[57] John Campbell, another of the Irish clan, named his daughter Elizabeth, for the Plantation queen, and George Sutton dubbed his mills Perseverance, an appropriately uplifting choice.[58] Campbell's brother Archibald superintended the Sunday school at the First Presbyterian Church, his "complete control and good management" of which drew extended praise from the Roxborough gentleman lawyer Horatio Gates Jones.[59] Even the Austrian Ripka was a practicing Episcopalian of long standing, despite his Catholic homeland. The masters of Manayunk were Greater British or Protestant or both, and the bulk of their workers shared part or all of that heritage, attending the schools and churches they managed, voting for them in local elections, living in their tenements. The Irish Catholics had their church, their jobs, and each other, but broke the surface of local affairs only when accounts of barroom brawls were used as points of departure for lectures on dissolute behavior in the weekly newspaper.

The *Manayunk Star and Roxborough Gazette* made its debut on February 5, 1859, eleven years after the district's first newspaper, the *Courier*, had succumbed with but ten issues to its credit. The paper, like so many of the mills, was a partnership, twice reorganized in the first two years. Featuring moral tales on its first page, editorials, local news, letters, and advertising on the inside, and advice to farmers on the last page, it mirrored the format of the successful *Telegraph* of Germantown.

In their second issue, the editors took it upon themselves to assess the state of the community, revealing its shabby physical state, the stature ascribed to the textile men and the broader social responsibilities that such status carried. Observing that Manayunk was "directly or indirectly dependent upon the business of the Mills," the *Star* deplored the state of the district's factory housing. "Roofs may leak, doors be almost off their hinges, plastering fall from the walls, . . . pumps be out of order," yet little was done by the factory proprietors. "They are THE men of the place," who too often

---

[56] *Manayunk Star and Roxborough Gazette*, April 2, 1859, and monthly thereafter.

[57] Goshow, "Mills and Mill Owners," pp. 139–40; 1860 PCS, Philadelphia Co., Ward 21, pp. 1, 163.

[58] 1860 PCS, Philadelphia Co., Ward 21, pt. 1, pp. 244–5; Edwin Freedley, *Philadelphia and Its Manufactures*, Philadelphia, 1857, p. 262.

[59] *Manayunk Star and Roxborough Gazette*, April 2, 1859.

look solely "to the amount of work and how it is done, . . . without any concern as to how the people live at home."[60]

The exploitation of mill workers' labor on the job had its counterpart in the subtler exploitation of the housing market. Of course, better built and maintained houses could not command appropriately higher rents unless wages went up, whether the landlords were millowners or shopkeepers. The closed economic circle of cheap construction, low rent, slender wages, and wretched living conditions passed over the heads of the editorial writers, who were better at exhortation than analysis. The unpaved streets on the hillsides became mud wallows spring and fall and dust filled the air all summer. When the *Star* and the "operatives" looked to the manufacturers for action (and funding) to improve "the appearance of the town," they were disappointed.

The tension between individual gain and its social consequences runs through Manayunk. The manufacturers had controlled its political life at least since 1840, yet after two decades Manayunk had "not the advantages of cheap gas from the city works, no provision for water, . . . miserably muddy and ungraded streets, and though professedly lighted with gas, in many places there are poor flickering fluid-lamps."[61] Although manufacturers were concerned with education, temperance, and church building for their workers, their paternalistic gestures had stopped short of using the tax power to meet the health and safety requirements of that population whose labor added daily to their capital. With these issues we may spy the borders of paternalism. Improvement was an individual affair, to be fostered rather than forced. Individuals' decisions in these matters might be deplored, but must be respected. The *Star* dared not call for tax levies to bring pure water or safe streets to Manayunk, for those with taxable property were its audience, its first few hundred subscribers. (The paper was not sold singly and carried no cover price.) Indeed, the consolidation of Manayunk with the city (1854) relieved whatever pressure there had been for the borough to tax itself (or for the prosperous to tax themselves), deflecting comfortably the responsibility for local wants to the Council members and the mayor, who were unlikely to act to improve the situation but who might be discreetly chided for their inattention. Joyce, observing the contemporaneous British situation, commented: "The operatives' education and religion always took precedence over their bodily needs. The general failure to provide adequate housing, or to investigate the social conditions of the operative, again indicates the limits to paternalism."[62] As previously argued, a similar ideological and cultural

---

[60] Ibid., February 12, 1859.
[61] Ibid., February 5, 1859.
[62] Joyce, *Work, Society and Politics*, p. 138.

context unfolded at Manayunk, with boundaries that are properly congruent with those of its Midlands counterpart. In subsequent years, the *Star* would continue to grumble about oozing streets and decaying houses, and the manufacturers would continue to tend their mills and keep good order in the Sunday schools.[63]

If the living conditions for Manayunk textile workers were squalid, their working conditions were fraught with danger. Scarcely a month went by without the *Star*'s reporting a mill accident, often with the full and grisly detail so beloved by those readers who never had to face a carding engine in full thunder. For example, at Arbuckle's mill, "a young man, named Joseph Adams, living on Washington Street above Hipple's Lane, had his right hand fearfully lacerated."[64] Or, "Mr. Benjamin Riley, boss-weaver in Mr. Ripka's factory, had his hand injured, on Thursday last, by being caught in the wheels. He had it dressed at Dr. Morrison's Drug Store."[65] Most of the injuries reported were to hands, though scalds from steam leaks and broken bones from tangles in power belts also appeared. The carding rooms were most frequently mentioned, their wire-teethed rollers destroying hands with some regularity. What is particularly interesting about these reports is the surrounding silence. None was followed up with later accounts of the fate of the injured, and, more interesting, none was accompanied by invocations to care and caution in the mills. Such warnings regularly closed the analogous reports in the *Telegraph*,[66] suggesting that its readers included laborers, whereas the *Star* was merely reminding the bourgeoisie to reflect appreciatively on the relative safety of their shops and offices. After a week in which five accidents were discussed, no accident reports appeared in the *Star* for more than four months, perhaps the result of a few well-placed words from mill operators.

Most mill accidents surely were not documented in the press, though the occasional fatality could not be ignored. Spinners and weavers rarely suffered injuries, though unguarded power belts were a definite hazard. The preparation and engine rooms were the most dangerous areas in the mills, and the most grisly death in the period took place in a calico works where a printer was crushed by a giant cylinder machine. When one considers the

---

63 Both the *Star and Gazette* and the *Telegraph* are replete with lively details of contemporary hangings, murders, and disasters, which rest uneasily beside the constant homilies to family and virtue run on the front pages and the tedious theological disputes carried in the letters column. Taken together, however, they evoke a bourgeois mentality of God, duty, and the consequences of sin that meshes well with the industrial tandem of bounded individualism and factory paternalism.

64 *Manayunk Star*, August 13, 1859.

65 Ibid., October 1, 1859.

66 *Germantown Telegraph*, November 7, December 19, 1849.

day-to-day health risks entailed by the lack of sewerage and the crowded living quarters, Manayunk's unsavory reputation in the larger community seems fully justified, however much the *Star* labored to demonstrate the contrary. It need hardly be stressed that few of these threats faced the handloom shopworkers of Germantown and Kensington. Their machines were handmade and hand-controlled, familiar rather than infernal. The healthful and spacious Germantown environment contrasted sharply with the dense packing of mills, homes, and people along the Schuylkill. Though Kensington too was closely settled, sewer lines were laid as the brick row houses extended outward, and paved streets were no rarity.

To look more closely at Manayunk's workers, and to place them beside those of Kensington and Germantown, the 1850 Population Census is again invaluable. Sifting the census schedules for Manayunk in 1850 and 1860 will permit some assessment of the structure of the factory work force in textiles and the extent of change in its composition during the fifties. The 1850 Manufacturing Census for the district showed 1,966 textile workers, though the adult male bias of occupation data in the population schedules made tracing women and young workers impossible. Nonetheless, 517 male textile workers were located:[67] their craft and nativity breakdowns are displayed in Table 7.4, representing the bulk of the adult men employed in the mills.

Fewer than a third of the male workers in the Manayunk factories were weavers, a job that on power looms had been largely assigned to young women, as at Lowell. The most highly skilled craft, dyeing, was almost completely staffed by immigrants, predominantly German and British; carding, which required heavy labor, claimed a much higher proportion of native and Irish-born workers. Two-thirds of these were teen-agers (thirty-six of fifty-six U.S. and Irish carders), whereas half the British carders were over 30, some listed as "boss carder" on the schedules. Similarly, though a third of Manayunk's spinners were native born, three of every five in that subgroup were teen-agers as well. Clearly, the experienced and skilled positions in the Manayunk mills were generally filled by British (and some German) workers, whereas the native and Irish groups were more commonly present in lower-skilled jobs, which was due, in part, to their youthful profile.

A closer look at the young American-born spinners and carders gives some depth to this outline. Of fifty spinners and carders age 15 to 19, forty-five were living with one or both parents, and five were boarding with other

---

67 The obvious undercount is attributable to the data recorded. The occupations of women, who comprised half the work force, were generally not recorded. Nor were the 300-odd "boys" who formed part of the mill complement a few years before the census (*Germantown Telegraph*, November 24, 1847). Of the 1,966 reported workers, more than 1,250 may have been women and boys. Thus the 517 adult men discovered represent in all likelihood 75% to 85% of those engaged in mill labor.

Table 7.4. *Ethnicity of male textile workers by skill, Manayunk, 1850*

| | Ethnicity | | | | | |
Skill	U.S.	England	Ireland	Germany	Other[a]	Total
Weavers	23	42	30	39	9	143
Warpers and beamers	8	11	12	14	2	47
Carders	34	22	22	5	5	88
Dyers and finishers	6	33	15	22	3	79
Spinners	43	61	23	1	7	135
Miscellaneous[b]	3	15	5	1	1	25
Total	117	184	107	82	27	517

[a]Scots, 15; French, 7; Swiss, 4; and unknown, 1.
[b]Fullers, 4; sizers, 4; textile machinery mechanics, 5; and wool sorters, 12.
Source: Manuscript Population Census Schedules, Philadelphia County, Manayunk, 1850.

families. The parents of twenty-five U.S.-born teen-age carders and spinners were native-born; only six of their fathers were working in the textile trades (four of whom were spinners with spinner sons). Seven fathers were shoemakers. The passing on of spinning skills was standard; the cluster of six shoemakers' sons in the carding rooms perhaps betokened the fading future of their fathers' craft. Seven American youths worked to support a single parent, presumably widowed mothers in six cases and a father who had "no business," according to the census marshal. Thus, though a few of the native-born teen-agers of native parents were from textile families, the majority were either abandoning a traditional craft or assisting a single parent.

Of the twenty U.S. teen-agers of foreign-born parents, fifteen were Irish and five were British. In eight of the Irish households, only the mother was present, though, as with the American-born mothers, the possibility of a father being absent to engage in construction or other casual labor must be considered. Of the other seven, whose fathers were resident, six gave his occupation as "Laborer" and one as a stonemason. None had any visible textile background. For those of British descent, two fathers were in textiles (a spinner and a dyer), one father was an iron roller, and two fathers were absent. By contrast, of the fourteen teen-agers *born* in England and working in spinning and carding rooms, ten lived with families headed by a Manayunk textile worker, reinforcing the notion of family craft succession among the British workers, a phenomenon much less prevalent among native families. Of the twenty-three young spinners and carders born in Ireland, twenty were living with their families; of eighteen fathers present, eleven were laborers, only three having any textile occupation. Given that a factory textile industry had developed only around Belfast by this time, and that handloom carftsmen were welcome at Kensington, it is reasonable to find that the young Irish textile workers came principally from families outside the trade.

British workers, the numerically largest group among adult textile men at Manayunk, occupied strategic, skilled positions to an even larger degree. For example, three-quarters of the spinners over 30 were English-born, many of them with long experiences in factory labor. The likely leaders of the 1848 spinners' strike, they were just as likely to be responsive to the subsequent elaboration of paternalistic relations that mirrored those of their native countries. To the extent that factory culture in Manayunk was a recapitulation of that present in Victorian Britain, the overlapping and shared backgrounds of transplanted British manufacturers and skilled workers conditioned that resemblance. Nothing so simple as the relocation of already paternalist employers and employees took place. Instead, a more complex pattern of devising similar solutions to similar dilemmas was experienced by Manayunk manufacturers and workers whose cultural and industrial "tools" were those of their Lancashire and Yorkshire counterparts. Just as the presence of Nottingham and Leicestershire men in Germantown facilitated the reconstruction of cottage and small-factory relations on knit goods akin to those current in their homelands, so too elements of Midlands factory culture were reconstituted at Manayunk, where many of the manufacturers were Manchester or Oldham men whose mills welcomed factory immigrants from those same districts. In both cases the physical environment – the proximity of the urban nexus, and the larger economic structure of tariff protection and swelling demand allowed the establishment of shop and factory cultures distinct from those at Lowell.

The much larger differentiation of occupations in Manayunk textiles contrasts immediately with both Germantown and Kensington, where the vast majority of textile workers were weavers. At Manayunk, the siting of work in the factory, supplemented by the specialized character of both some mills and their products, led to the use of women as power-loom weavers. Indeed, only 28% of the male workers were "weavers" in 1850 Manayunk, with the rest of the male work force scattered in carding rooms and the skilled crafts. Though it is presently impossible to document, I suspect that the male weavers in factories were engaged in setting up and operating power looms for steadily changing varieties of cottonades, plaids, and so forth.

The more formalized division of labor at Manayunk did not result in the creation of a property-holding cluster of labor aristocrats, however. Of the 517 men listed in the 1850 Population Census as identifiable textile workers, only 19 possessed any real estate, averaging about $1,250 ($125 to $3,000).

As might be expected, the majority (fourteen) were over 40, but otherwise the group reflected almost exactly the proportions of the overall occupational distribution (five weavers, fourteen skilled craftsmen, but no carders). English workers were overrepresented (ten), which was to be expected as they were as a group the oldest sector of the work force.

When these findings are compared with the property held by Germantown workers, the more vulnerable position of factory workers becomes clearer. Though the hosiery revival at Germantown followed by a decade the establishment of factory production on the Schuylkill, by 1850 Germantown textile workers were twice as likely to have property as their Manayunk colleagues. Of 466 Germantown workers, 35 had real estate given in the schedules, again averaging about $1,250 ($90 to $5,000), and the age distribution showed more younger workers with land and/or a house than at Manayunk (thirteen, or 37%, under 40, vs. five, or 26%, at Manayunk). As a group, Germantown workers were a bit older than Manayunkers (36 vs. 32), but that gap seems inadequate by itself to account for the scale of the difference. Both the family production unit and the competence goal of handshop work were more easily translated into property holding at Germantown than were mill wages, however reinforced by the multiple-worker families present in Manayunk. (It is further possible that those few Manayunk workers who were able to accumulate savings sought to leave the crowded hillsides altogether or to invest their surplus in shops or taverns. The presence of savings derived from mill employment in the property figures given by store- and inkeepers is plausible both at Germantown and Manayunk. The craft tradition of hosiers and Germantown's scattered population might have constrained such shifts there, whereas the concentration of demand and the rigors of life in the mills could have enhanced them at riverside. In either case, surviving sources conceal career changes at mid-life most effectively.)

The age distribution of male textile workers is given in Table 7.5, along with a breakdown for weavers to allow comparison with Germantown weavers (Table 7.3).

British workers constitute more than half of the entire group over 40 years of age (64 of 123), which is consistent with their presence as experienced and skilled spinners, dyers, boss carders, wool sorters, and so forth. Totaling 36% of the overall work force, they were underrepresented at both age extremes (14% of teen-agers, 25% of workers over 60), whereas Irish workers were overrepresented (20% overall, 56% of the group over 60, 24% of teen-agers, and the bulk of the native-born teen-age workers whose parents were foreign-born). The very small proportion of older native-born American workers in the group confirms either recent arrival in the mills or reluctance to remain there. The total preponderance of immigrant workers –

Table 7.5. *Ethnicity of male textile workers and weavers by age, Manayunk, 1850*

| | Age | | | | | | |
Ethnicity	15–19	20–29	30–39	40–49	50–59	60+	Total
All workers							
U.S.-born	65[a]	32	14	3	2	1	117
English-born	19	56	45	40	20	4	184
Irish-born	32	25	19	13	9	9	107
German-born	11	36	19	11	4	1	82
Other	5	11	5	2	3	1	27
Total	132	160	102	69	38	16	517
Percentage	(25)	(31)	(20)	(13)	(7)	(3)	(99)
Weavers							
U.S.-born	8	7	3	2	2	1	23
English-born	5	13	11	7	5	1	42
Other	16	27	10	13	5	7	78
Total	29	47	24	22	12	9	143
Percentage	(20)	(33)	(17)	(15)	(8)	(6)	(99)

[a]About half were native-born of immigrant parents.
Source: Manuscript Population Census Schedules, Philadelphia County, Manayunk, 1850.

77% of the adult males were foreign-born – is almost as striking as at Kensington or Germantown. If the teen-age workers of immigrant families are deducted from the U.S. column, that proportion of native workers falls to 16%, bearing out recent assertions by Herbert Gutman that the manufacturing class in industrializing America was an immigrant class to a degree hitherto unappreciated. What is particularly striking in Philadelphia textiles is that this is true regardless of the manufacturing format in place and that the owning class was principally foreign-born as well.

The factory's taste for youthful workers appears when the age distribution for Manayunk is contrasted with that for Germantown. For weavers alone, teen-age workers were 20% of the Manayunk total but 12% at Germantown, where workshops and cottages coexisted with a half-dozen mills. When the full work forces, including all occupational titles, are examined, the contrast intensifies, as workers 15 to 19 years of age formed a quarter of the males reported from Manayunk but 11% of those found at Germantown. At the other end of the age cycle, workers over 40 were a third of the Germantown textile force but only 23% of those laboring the Manayunk factories. These figures, of course, do not reflect the hundreds of "boys" earlier mentioned as being in the Manayunk mills and the larger group of young women and girls requisite for throstle spinning and power weaving. In Germantown, young women and boys were surely a part of the family workshops and the larger mills, though at least in the family environment their efforts were not driven to the pace of powered machinery.

By 1860 there are noticeable movements within the work force in Manayunk factories. Census marshals in the First District exceeded their instructions and gathered details on all persons employed, including small children, thus providing a rare census look at factory labor in its totality. In that area a total of 2,358 textile workers were located, 72% of all those reported for the ward in the 1860 Manufacturing Census.[68] Unfortunately, skill distinctions were not made by the population marshals; instead, the generic term "operative" was used to designate more than 90% of the textile workers, flattening the otherwise comprehensive data in this respect.[69] Table 7.6 presents Manayunk's 1860 First District textile workers, arrayed by sex and ethnicity.

The most obvious conclusion to be drawn from these statistics concerns the large role in factory textiles played by Irish immigrants, who comprised more than a third of the whole force and 40% of its female component. The contrast with the German immigrants is quite crisp as well, for where more than half the Irish workers in Manayunk were women, less than a third of German-born operatives were female.[70] The very small number of American-born sons and daughters of German-born parents relative to the Irish totals is also suggestive of different familial structures, which may be checked against the full-scale age, sex, and ethnic breakdowns in Table 7.7. If the attitudes toward child labor were the same and the Germans were

---

[68] The Second District marshals seem to have omitted women's and children's occupations quite generally, making a total reconstitution impossible. However, a survey of identifiable Second District textile workers showed no radical departure from the age and ethnic distribution of the comparable group (males over 15) in the First District; consequently, we will allow the far richer data of the First District to stand for the whole.

[69] "Operative," like "manufacturer," was a term that unmodified referred to textile production, differentiating textile labor from that in other factory occupations. At Manayunk, factory work was available outside textiles only in foundries and paper mills, whose employees were labeled in the census specifically as "roller," "paper-maker" and whose ordinary hands were identified as "rolling mill laborer," and so on. "Operatives" totaled almost half the 4,600 occupational entries in the First District schedules, with "laborers" the second most numerous group at 9%, which is consistent with the overarching presence of textile work as the district's main productive activity.

[70] Attempting to account for this will lead us shortly to search for female-headed households among each group.

Table 7.6. *Textile workers by ethnicity and sex,*
Manayunk, First District, 1860

Ethnicity	Male workers		Female workers		Total	
U.S.-born	238	(19)	308	(28)	546	(23)
English-born	227	(18)	94	(9)	321	(14)
English parents	52	(4)	70	(6)	112	(5)
Subtotal	279		164		443	
Irish-born	257	(20)	298	(28)	555	(24)
Irish parents	119	(9)	134	(12)	253	(11)
Subtotal	376		432		808	
German-born	271	(21)	103	(10)	374	(16)
German parents	17	(1)	32	(3)	49	(2)
Subtotal	288		135		423	
Other	76	(6)	29	(3)	105	(4)
Other parents	19	(1)	14	(1)	33	(1)
Subtotal	95		43		138	
Total	1,276	(99)	1,082	(100)	2,358	(100)

Note: Figures in parentheses indicate percentages. All U.S.-born offspring of foreign-born parents were living in parental households. NBFP who lived in other than the parental household (e.g., as a boarder in another household) cannot be distinguished in the 1860 census. These are included in the U.S.-born entry.
Source: Manuscript Population Census Schedule, Philadelphia County, First District, Ward 21, 1860.

simply recent arrivals, then German-born children should appear in large numbers there.

As in 1850, the overwhelming majority of the workers were immigrants or their children. It should be further understood that additional immigrant offspring are concealed within the U.S. category, for scores of U.S.-born workers under the age of 20 boarded in homes not occupied by their parents. In some cases children with common surnames and clustered ages were scattered among several families on the same block, probably orphaned and taken in by neighbors, working in the mills for their keep and living within reach of one another. That some of these were native-born children of foreign-born parents is indubitable; thus the U.S. total is a maximum, the

Table 7.7. *Textile workers by ethnicity, age, and sex, Manayunk, First District, 1860*

Ethnicity	Age							Total
	14 or less	15–19	20–29	30–39	40–49	50–59	60+	
Males								
U.S.-born	51	83	60	23	8	11	2	238
English-born	8	27	60	59	39	24	10	227
English parents	16	24	12					52
Irish-born	42	63	58	43	27	14	10	257
Irish parents	62	51	6					119
German-born	36	43	69	73	33	15	2	271
German parents	9	8						17
Other	8	20	13	12	15	5	3	76
Other parents	9	9	1					19
Subtotal	241	328	279	210	122	69	27	1,276
Females								
U.S.-born	54	119	93	21	15	6	0	308
English-born	13	30	30	17	3	1	0	94
English parents	24	28	16	2				70
Irish-born	38	85	126	31	8	8	2	298
Irish parents	38	64	30	0	2			134
German-born	26	40	29	5	1	1	1	103
German parents	15	13	3	1				32
Other	6	11	9	1	1	1	0	29
Other parents	3	7	4					14
Subtotal	217	397	340	78	30	17	3	1,082
Total	458	725	619	288	152	86	30	2,358

Source: Manuscript Population Census Schedules, Philadelphia County, First District, Ward 21, 1860.

native-born/foreign-born-parent subtotals are all minimums, incapable of further refinement given the database. Consequently, it is fair to estimate that about four-fifths of the total textile factory force were immigrants or the children of immigrants. With some adjustment of the information in Table 7.7, a comparison can be made of at least the male workers over the age of 15 in 1850 and 1860 to assess the extent of any significant shifts in the composition of the factory population.

The importance of child labor to the operation of the Manayunk mills is here revealed at a stroke. Nearly 20% of the workers were 14 or under and half were under 20. The largest group of the youngest workers were Irish, in a proportion somewhat larger than their overall presence (39% of those under 14 vs. 35% overall). When women workers are considered separately, the youthful profile of factory textile workers sharpens, for less than 12% of the women workers at Manayunk were over 30. The age distribution of male workers was more scattered, with 34% over the age of 30, a cluster encompassing the bulk of the skilled workers engaged in textile manufacture.

British-born men in the older ranks (31% of those over 30) were closely trailed by German natives (29%). Although this proportional gap between older British and German male workers had closed since 1850 (48% vs. 16% in 1850), both groups were numerically larger.[71] There was virtually no change in the representation of native-American or Irish-born men in the older pool during the fifties, being about 10% and 22% of the total, respectively, at both census dates.

These rough estimates of a shifting ethnic balance may be refined by contrasting the male work force of 1850 with that of 1860 (Table 7.8). Combining all native-born workers of foreign-born parents allows comparable categories for analysis. The increase of the German segment is here confirmed across all ages, as is the relative British decline, though it should be stressed that all groups had increased absolutely by 1860. The sizable rise in the proportion of U.S.-born workers is largely due to the factory employment of foreign-stock youth. Nor should the "Other" line be ignored, for when its small augmentations are combined with the Germans, it indicates that almost 30% of the textile work force by 1860 was not English-speaking.

When the increasing cultural heterogeneity of Manayunk is taken into account – a Continental influx, two sorts of Irish, mill-district British, and in-migrating natives – another element in the long silence of labor begins to coalesce. I refer not to a simple ethnicity of divided and ruled workers, though mutual antagonism and mistrust – rooted in diverse religions, languages, and cultures and reinforced by the ethnic residential clustering so frequent in factory towns – were certainly of value to the mill masters. Instead, or in addition, the shop-floor role of the skilled British and Ulster workers should be imaginatively reconsidered. The boss carders, master weavers, spinners, and dyers were not only the natural leaders in resistance

---

[71] Interestingly, with more than 400 Germans working in 1860 Manayunk, no reports of their fraternal or other associational activity appeared in the *Star and Gazette*, which regularly covered the picnics and parades of the Odd Fellows and the nativist Order of the United American Mechanics. Like the Catholic Irish community, the Manayunk Germans were virtually invisible, despite their expanding industrial and neighborhood presence.

Table 7.8. *Nativity of male textile*
workers, 15 and over,
Manayunk, 1850 and 1860
(in percentage)

Nativity	1850	1860
U.S.-born	23	29
U.S.-born parents	(16)	(18)
Foreign-born parents	(7)	(11)
England	36	21
Ireland	21	21
Germany	16	23
Other	4	7
Total	100	101
N	517	1,035

Source: Tables 7.5, 7.6, and 7.7.

or accommodation; they also shared a common origin and factory experience with the immigrant millowners. It was they who spoke the language of the bosses, the dialects of machinery and trade, they who trained the owners' sons as they moved through the mill "learning manufacture," they too who attended the Sunday schools in the church or chapel built and/or managed by factory masters. It was finally they who mediated the elaboration of "the culture of the factory," sharing daily in the creation of that version of factory paternalism that, with all its limits, still drew forth presentations and testimonials in the Civil War era. By 1860, German arrivals were filling many of the new slots opened by mill expansion, doubtless learning the routines and language of the factory largely from British, Irish, and Scots "superintendents" and "boss weavers" (and from countrymen who had been similarly introduced). Yet their cultural and religious separateness left them outside the core of factory social relations, where Anglo-American males held sway.

A brief glance at the households and property-owning patterns among Manayunk workers will bring this account to a close. The First District's 2,358 textile workers were members of a total of 1,056 households in the 1860 Population Census. About one-fifth of these households were headed by single women (207), most of whom had children working in the mills. Three-quarters of them had property valued at $100 or less, with forty-nine listing no real or personal property at all. The largest group among them were Irish-born (ninety-four), Americans were second (sixty), and British and German mothers trailed (thirty and seventeen). Their advanced age (averaging 49) suggests that most were widows. Women whose spouses were absent, working on construction gangs, for example, might be expected to be somewhat younger. Their considerable numbers and general poverty suggest the migration of widows and their families to that mill district in Philadelphia where young workers were an important part of the labor force. Although the wages of children allowed for little more than subsistence living in most cases, only 18% of the widows themselves reported occupations, being either too elderly for mill work or restricted to caring for younger children in the home. Of those who were employed, three-quarters worked in the textile factories. Daniel Walkowitz discovered a similar high incidence of female-headed households at the Harmony Mills in Cohoes, New York,[72] confirming this linkage of factory textile production and the exploitation of widows and orphans. The children of these women comprised 19% of the entire Manayunk First District work force. Their daughters were 26% of all women textile workers reported in 1860.

The presence of hundreds of orphans in the Manayunk mills was but one aspect of the family economy in the textile manufacture. The typical textile worker was but one member of a household in which several textile workers could be found. Of the 1,056 textile-worker households, more than 600 included two or more operatives, most commonly a parent and children (256 cases and one-third of the First District total of textile workers). Laborers headed seventy-six households with two or more children in the mills, two-thirds of whom were Irish-born. The mills also beckoned to some skilled workers and men in commercial occupations, as more than 100 such families had two or more mill operatives among their resident children. Skilled trades included the paper and foundry workers engaged in factory production elsewhere in Manayunk, along with shoemakers (9), construction workers, millers, bakers, and stonecutters, for a total of 57 households and 173 textile factory workers. The trade and transport group contributed another 143 household members to the mills, the offspring and kin of storekeepers, teamsters, boatmen, and one cook. Mill labor thus was a part of the family economy not just of an isolated class of trudging operatives and their descendants. It supported widows (and nineteen elderly widowers), allowed craftsmen supplementary income in slack periods, and brought cash into the coffers of shopmen and carters throughout the district. These relations add yet another weight to the scales of passivity in the relations of labor and capital at Manayunk. The employment of workers from every sector of the local social structure, the youth and dependence of the bulk of the work force, functioning as subordinates in both the factories and the households throughout the community, fragmented whatever potential existed for op-

[72] Daniel Walkowitz, *Worker City, Company Town*, Urbana, Ill., 1978, pp. 112–13.

position, much less militancy. The furies who had opposed Ripka in the thirties were both gone and forgotten.

Finally, when the property held by male textile workers in Manayunk in 1860 is compared to the holdings of their 1850 counterparts, another dimension of industrial calm appears. Whereas only 3.7% of the workers owned any real property in 1850, the First District proportion for 1860 had nearly doubled, rising to 6.8% (70 of 1,035 males over 15). When age, ethnicity, and the size of holdings are considered, the distribution conforms with expectations. None of the 328 males 15 to 19 years of age held real estate, and only 7 of the 279 in their twenties did so. Many of these teenagers still lived with their parents, were boarders, or rented some of the district's dilapidated small houses. However, of the 428 men 30 or more years of age working in textile factories, 63 (15%) owned property valued at nearly $78,000, or an average of more than $1,200 per worker. Although 13 of this group owned only their own houses (valued at $500 or less), 36 had several properties, as is indicated by valuations of $1,000 or more, and were likely drawing rental income from other workers and building toward the elusive competence.

English-born workers were the most numerous group among those with real estate (26 of 70; 24 of the 63 over 30). Nearly 1 in 5 of the 132 English workers over 30 in the First District owned one or more houses, and almost 1 in 3 of those over 50 (10 of 34) did so. These ten had nearly a quarter of the total holdings ($18,800) of the over-30 group, attesting to the early arrival of English-born workers in the canalside district. The Irish, both Catholic and Protestant, had fared nearly as well, with 17% of those over 30 being homeowners, although their holdings were somewhat smaller than those of the English, averaging about $950. German-born workers, many of whom had reached the United States in the fifties, ranked lower (17 of 123 over 30, or 12%, with real estate), and the transience of native-born workers is suggested by their place at the bottom of the ladder (5 of 44 over 30, or 11%).

Even if 15% of mature male textile workers were homeowners, their colleagues were far less fortunate. When a 30% sample was taken of all First District male textile workers 30 or over, not possessed of real estate, only 18% (24 of 130) reported *personal* property worth over $100, and 16% (21) had virtually no possessions at all.[73] Though skilled workers and those fortunate enough to have steady work and/or head families with multiple wage-earners might become homeowners, the largest proportion of operatives lived from week to week in rented quarters.

One additional comment is in order. A small portion (about 10%) of the

[73] All drawn from 1860 PCS, Philadelphia Co., Ward 21, District 1.

residents in households with two or more textile workers were probably boarders, that is, residents with different surnames, some of whom may have been the kin of household members. These cluster in two ways. First, widows often had both children and boarders in the mills, and a handful of innkeepers reported groups of resident textile workers who joined some of their own children in the factories of Arbuckle or Campbell. Their dependence on steady work was, if anything, greater than that of family members, though they surely had greater latitude for departure to seek work elsewhere than did the 16-year-old daughters of Irish laborers. Second, the households that reported a single textile worker (454) were predominantly young married couples whose children were too young for mill employment. German workers were overrepresented in this category, again indicating a relatively recent immigration consistent with their age profile, which averaged about five years younger than British-born textile workers (31 vs. 36).

The textile situation in 1860

Manayunk's midcentury textile operatives share many characteristics with stereotypical textile factory work forces of nineteenth-century America. Predominantly immigrants operating from family economies, they were poor and subordinate, the young to their elders, the machine tenders to their overseers, the skilled to their bosses, the Sunday schools to their superintendents. Beneath these interlaced dominions lay the divided foundations of language, culture, and religion, though at Manayunk the most skilled segment of the work force was linked in all three dimensions to the mill masters, thus further diminishing the potential for challenge or resistance. Small wonder that Manayunk labor was virtually silent throughout the long middle decades of the century.

Antebellum Philadelphia, as we have seen, supported three coexisting and partially interdependent formats for textile production. In crowded Kensington, handloom workshops were the vital center of cotton and carpet manufacture. Germantown's village hosiers and few mills were an equally vigorous nexus of hand-frame production, principally immigrant British in contrast with Kensington's Irish majority, and were situated among spatially and culturally familiar conditions. Manayunk served as the city's mill town, a heterogeneous factory district whose inhabitants were disciplined by both the powered machines they tended and the dependent social relations into which they were drawn. All three formats expanded on their bases in the fifties, though by 1860 some of the lines of longer-term transitions were becoming visible. Handloom carpet manufacture was rising in Kensington, whereas cotton handshops stagnated. Handloom hosiers in Germantown

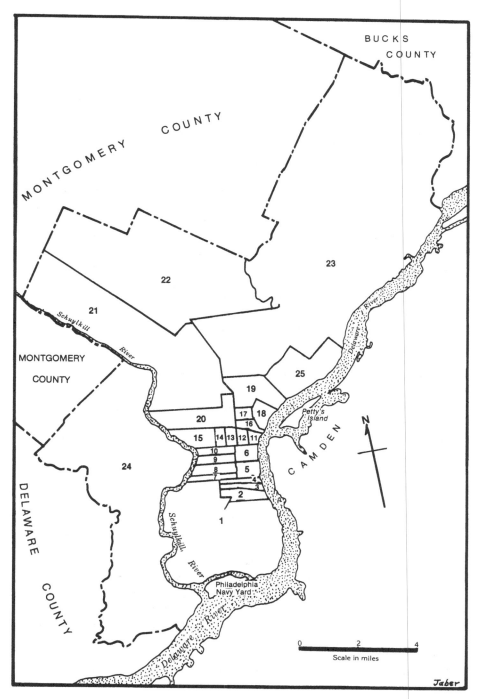

Map 3. The wards of Philadelphia, 1860. (Adapted from John Daley and Allen Weinberg, *Genealogy of Philadelphia County Subdivisions*, Philadelphia, 1966, p. 65.)

had begun to introduce powered spinning and to locate their operations in mill buildings. At Manayunk, by 1860, more mills had integrated functions than a decade earlier, and, more critical to the overall pattern of the Philadelphia textile manufacture, the variety of goods produced had increased noticeably. In all three centers, capital invested was up and the work force, number of firms, and output had increased, as whatever check had been incurred by the 1857 Panic was overcome by the end of the decade.

Despite their many contrasts, the three formats shared essential structural characteristics. All were predominantly owned and run by immigrants, the manufacturers reared in the textile trades having built their enterprises through a succession of small steps (along different paths), a tactic conditioned by their small capitals, the difficulties of securing bank finance, and the constraints of craft and neighborhood culture, though Manayunk might be exempted from this last consideration. The form of operation was proprietary, the management personal, the production flexible, and the marketing direct. The urban milieu within which all were located brought flows of information and buyers readily to hand and allowed crosstown links between producers of yarn and weavers, each sustaining the other's growth or viability. Although formally all the manufacturers were capitalists, there existed a set of complex bonds between owners and laborers, a network of ethnicity, religion, and custom that, although different in each format, was present in visible forms throughout the city. In all three locations, manufacturers rented premises before buying or finally building their own. The family succession was a common goal of the owning class, and the desire to commence business on one's own account was not at all uncommon among the workers.

By 1860, citywide, both the numbers of textile workers and the firms engaging them had increased by half over the 1850 totals, reaching nearly 18,000 workers and more than 450 establishments. The sexual composition of the work force was nearly equally divided between men and women, a sign of the increased factory cloth production at Manayunk and elsewhere. (The proportion of cotton and mixed-goods women workers rose from 43% in 1850 to 55% at the close of the decade.) At Lowell in the same decade the changes had been minimal. Whereas 12,000 workers had been employed in 1850, 12,400 toiled in 1860. The sexual balance was little altered as well (69% female in 1850, 68% in 1860).[74] The stretch-out was clearly apparent, however, in that 2,000 looms and four mills had been added to the Lowell complex, with no appreciable increase in the number of operatives to run them. All the Lowell corporations were still functioning, though the Middlesex mill had undergone a thorough reorganization in 1858, after "the

---

[74] *Statistics of Lowell Manufactures, January 1851, January 1861* (for previous years).

entire capital of the company was lost" through mismanagement.[75] Interestingly enough, the changes at the Middlesex mill included the termina-
tion of marketing through commission houses; it was replaced by a plan
whereby the treasurer of the company handled sales directly, his compensation being a share of the profits so realized. Cowley observed:

> By this arrangement, the business of selling was kept directly under the
> Company's control, and the interests of the selling agent made identical
> with those of the Company. Since their reorganization, they have been
> remarkably successful – their percentage of profits exceeding those of
> any other company in Lowell.[76]

This "arrangement" approached the format for marketing by interested
parties so fruitfully used at Philadelphia. In addition, The Middlesex Company, as a woolen mill, was able to keep running during the ensuring war,
adding surely to the profitability to which Cowley alludes.

If during the years before the Civil War there are sharp contrasts between
the formats for accumulation at Lowell and Philadelphia and the patterns of
growth they engendered, the war itself formed the single greatest "external"
event that affected the two complexes during the generations addressed by
this study. The rigidities of corporate Lowell and the entrepreneurial aggressiveness and flexibility of Philadelphia crystallize in the war years.
Whereas the Massachusetts cotton mills closed or stumbled, the Philadelphia textile manufacture became an essential part of war production. To
examine more closely these diametrically opposed responses to the same
"stimulus" is the task next undertaken.

[75] Charles Cowley, *Illustrated History of Lowell*, Boston, 1868, p. 53.
[76] Ibid., p. 54.

8

The sixties: war and prosperity

During the late War, however, the Merrimack Company showed great "lack of sagacity and forethought" – in stopping their mills – in dismissing their operatives – in discontinuing the purchase of cotton . . . The blunders of this company were naturally copied by the others . . . in this instance, . . . exaggerated and intensified to a fatal degree. The other cotton companies actually sold out their cotton, and several of them made experiments in other branches of manufacture, by which they incurred losses, direct and indirect, exceeding the amount of their entire capital.

– Charles Cowley, *Illustrated History of Lowell*

In Philadelphia, which was perhaps the largest center of manufacturing in the country, 58 new factories were erected in 1862, 57 in 1863, and 65 in 1864; and the building inspectors reported that those erected in the last-named year were generally very large.

– Emerson Fite, *Social and Industrial Conditions in the North During the Civil War*

McCallum, Crease and Sloan, Carpet Manufacturers, Philadelphia . . . During the War of the Rebellion, the firm was extensively engaged in the manufacture of army blankets, at first under a sub-contract with those supplying that article to the government, and afterwards under a direct contract. For some portion of this time, the mill ran night and day, and was worked by two sets of hands.

– Daniel Robson, ed., *Manufactories and Manufacturers of Pennsylvania of the Nineteenth Century*

The panoply, confusion, corruption, and high tragedy of the Civil War retain a dramatic power to this day. The hordes of genealogists sifting regiment and pension records at the National Archives, the platoons of military devotees re-creating its engagements on playing boards and, in their meticulous uniforms, on the battlegrounds themselves, and the scores of academics assessing and debating its fine points and great decisions, all testify to the continuing magnetism of the national schism. Here, however, somewhat dryly, the Civil War appears as the "Great Externality," that "outside" influence whose impact on the textile accumulation matrix illuminates the different capacities of Lowell's corporations and Philadelphia's entrepre-

272

neurs to handle the complex of opportunities and constraints that emerged on a hitherto unprecedented scale. The war proved an object lesson in manufacturing economics for both the Lowell and Philadelphia capitalists and was the first instance of massive state expenditure in the war economy of American industrial society. Lowell missed its chance to sup at the public trough, to seek war contracts and the high profits inherent in intensified demand. Philadelphia's textile men drank deeply, if not uniformly, running "night and day," expanding and building apace, accumulating in great gulps, and, ultimately, both effecting a partial transformation of the city's manufacturing network and sowing the seeds for the florid labor–capital eruptions of the following decades. Both patterns are comprehensible when arrayed against the systems of accumulation in place in the two productive centers, the task undertaken in this chapter.

As previously, an introduction to the Philadelphia experience will be afforded by examining a proprietary firm in some depth. The wider incidence of its involvement with government contracts will be demonstrated through reference to firm biographies and its wartime textile contracts, which were managed by the Quartermaster Corps. Comparisons of 1860 and 1870 Manufacturing Census profiles for those firms identified as federal suppliers will suggest the importance of war demand for rapid accumulation. Finally, the aggregate development of the Philadelphia textile manufacture in the sixties will be surveyed and the Lowell experience considered, both settings viewed through the matrix of accumulation. This will allow a tentative evaluation of the structural elements that conditioned the divergent experiences of textile manufacturers at Lowell and Philadelphia in the war decade and their implications for later developments.

The Winpennys: family firms and government contracts

The Winpenny family manufactured woolens in Philadelphia for three generations. From the arrival of the first family member, Samuel Winpenny, in Germantown in 1808 to the retirement of his son James B. about 1884 and grandson Bolton in 1872 (at age 36), members of the clan plied the craft that had been a part of the family's heritage from the early years of the eighteenth century. Through the seven decades of their activity at Philadelphia, the Winpennys, in a succession of partnerships, ran broadcloths, kerseys, blankets, woolen and later cotton yarns and consistently secured government contracts for military goods. Pioneers both in the wool trade and as federal suppliers, they are of particular interest as we focus on the war era and the relationships between proprietary firms and the state.

Born about 1777 in Wike, England, Samuel Winpenny was a Yorkshireman, the son of a "well-known manufacturer of broadcloth," and the grand-son of a Flemish cloth manufacturer active before 1750. Trained in his father's business, upon reaching his majority (ca. 1798) he married "Ellen, daughter of James Bolton, a member of the Royal Academy at Edinburgh and an artist of some distinction." In 1805, leaving behind his wife and first two sons, Samuel sailed to America. After spending three years in North Carolina, he relocated to Germantown where he "operated the mills now known as Kelly's Mills and . . . produced the first blankets and cloths ever manufactured for the United States Government in this country."[1] In 1810 he brought his family across "in the vessel of Captain Towers," who later would become the entrepreneur largely responsible for the opening of man-ufacturing at Manayunk. The following spring Samuel removed from Ger-mantown "to the works now occupied by William Simpson and Sons, at the Falls of Schuylkill, where he was eminently successful with Government Contracts [during the War of 1812], and continued till 1815."[2] While at the Falls, he employed his two elder sons, age 12 and 8 in 1812, and fathered two more. At war's end, Samuel returned for three years to Germantown, but his business failed in the postwar depression and he trekked back to the falls to work for other manufacturers.

Birth of a fifth son (1817) completed the second generation of the man-ufacturing Winpennys. Samuel's successors were John (1800, Yorkshire), Samuel (1804, Yorkshire), William (1811, Falls of Schuylkill), Joseph (1815, Falls of Schuylkill), and James Bolton (1817, Germantown). All became textile manufacturers. Their father never again had a mill of his own after the 1818 collapse. He worked through the next decade "setting up machin-ery and promoting the interests of other manufacturers" until his death at about "fifty-two years" of age in 1829. His widow opened a shop at the Falls of Schuylkill, which was operated from 1834 to 1841 by her youngest son, James. In the latter year, he departed for Virginia, where he worked for three years as a "contractor for railroads and bridges." Though Samuel and Ellen Bolton Winpenny had had respectable, even august, origins in Britain, they were surely disappointed at their fates in the new land. Despite early success, Samuel had not the resources to withstand the three-year slide that followed the return of British competition and the diminution of government demand (echoes of Henry Korn and the "horrors of bankruptcy"). A decade later, he died near the edge of poverty, leaving his wife, "a woman of unusual culture [who] carefully instructed her children," to spin out her remaining years keeping shop. His sons fared far better, probably rendering some assistance to their mother as their fortunes improved.

---

[1] Daniel Robson, ed., *Manufactories and Manufacturers of Pennsylvania of the Nineteenth Century*, Philadelphia, 1875, pp. 463, cited hereafter as *M&MP*.
[2] Ibid.

By the time of his father's death, John, Samuel's eldest son, had commenced textile manufacture in a small way on his own account in rented space at a Falls of Schuylkill mill. In 1828, with sixteen years of factory experience behind him, John, "by the assistance of Frederick Stoever," the mill's owner, began weaving woolen goods as his father had done twenty years before. His younger brother Samuel had learned dyeing in his mill apprenticeship, becoming "one of the best blue dyers in the United States." This skill was of particular relevance in making government-grade woolens, which were uniformly to be indigo-dyed in several shades of blue, the continuity of color over successive batches necessitating the application of considerable skill. After six years in the leased mill, John brought Samuel into partnership "and continued to operate, for the production of kerseys, blankets and blue cloths for the Government, at Stoever's mill for some years [1834–39], and though twice burned out, their energy triumphed over every misfortune."[3] In 1839 the brothers Winpenny purchased the mill of Charles Hagner, who was departing Manayunk to relocate his drug business in the city. Having converted the mill to wool production and having erected an additional building on the site, the partnership was ready to commence in their own facility when fire again struck, destroying the original building. The mill was "immediately rebuilt," and manufacturing began "early in 1840" with fifty workers engaged in weaving and finishing broadcloths and kerseys, a thousand yards of which were turned out weekly. A third Winpenny brother, Joseph, served as superintendent of one department of the factory and was later elevated to a partnership role. William Winpenny had left Manayunk for Millersville, Indiana, date uncertain, where he manufactured textiles until his death in 1861.

The brothers' firm was dissolved in 1847 at the withdrawal of Samuel Winpenny, who shortly left for Ohio with his share of the accumulated capital. There "he was engaged in various speculations until 1850, when he returned [to Philadelphia] and lived in retirement until 1861." With Samuel's departure, Joseph became the replacement partner for the next five years, when he too retired from active manufacture. Although John Winpenny had become a locally prominent figure, serving as chief burgess of Manayunk "for many years" and being a close associate of Pennsylvania Governor John Bigler, he continued his manufacturing career until his death in September 1856,[4] when the mills passed to his widow, Esther, and son, Bolton.

The sequence of government contracts had continued into the fifties. In January 1854 the Quartermaster Corps notified John Winpenny that he was the successful applicant for the opportunity to weave 30,000 yards of "6/4

---

[3] Ibid.
[4] Ibid., p. 498–500.

Sky Blue indigo-dyed twilled woolen cloth" at the price of $1.35 per yard.[5] In 1850 the Winpenny firm reported an annual output of 70,000 yards of woolens worth $100,000.[6] This contract alone meant nearly half a year's work for the factory and was a prize well worth the seeking. The next year the firm again scored a major contract, this time one that would test their skills and versatility. The citation called for the manufacture of

> 5,000 yards sky-blue twilled cloth, 22 oz/yd. at $1.16/yard, 5,000 yards dark-blue twilled cloth, 21 oz/yd, at $1.55/yard, 10,000 army blankets, woolen, gray, with the letters U.S. in black four inches long (in the center), to be seven feet long, five feet wide, to weigh five pounds each, for $2.48 per blanket.[7]

The total value of this 1855 contract ($38,350) was comparable to that of the previous year, though its production was certainly more of a challenge than its predecessor. (To set this immediately in a larger context, only thirty cloth or hosiery contracts were processed by the Quartermaster Corps between 1853 and 1856. Twenty of these were secured by firms in the Philadelphia region, setting the stage for the city's important role in Civil War textile manufacture.)[8]

Bolton Winpenny, the third generation, had not been reared in the mills. Instead, he had been sent to a private school in Wilmington, Delaware, and at 16 had entered the drug trade, perhaps through the Hagner connection, with Samuel Grant and Co., whose mill he superintended at the time of his father's death. By the close of 1858, he had completed execution of his father's estate,

> when he was induced to engage in manufacturing in the mills previously occupied by his father. As he was without practical experience in manufacturing, he had objected to taking the mills, but yielded to the advice of James Dearie, and engaged in business with a few looms and $100 capital.[9]

Bolton rapidly took as a partner Edward Preston, Jr., the offspring of another Manayunk textile family. After two years, Preston pulled out of the firm, but Bolton was shortly able to persuade his uncle, the retired Samuel Winpenny, to join him in 1861. Samuel's experience with government work was especially valuable, and the new firm was once again "engaged in the execu-

---

[5] *Abstracts of Contracts, QMGC,* National Archives, Record Group 92, Entry No. 1238, vol. XII, p. 113; 6/4 indicated six quarter yards, or 54 inches, the width of the cloth.

[6] 1850 Manufacturing Census Schedules, Philadelphia Co., p. 84, cited hereafter as MCS.

[7] *Abstracts of Contracts,* vol. XII, p. 197.

[8] Ibid., pp. 61–78, 113–4, 196–8, 282–5.

[9] *M&MP,* p. 464.

tion of Government contracts." After two years Samuel removed a second time to his competence, which he continued to enjoy in his seventies at the time Robson amassed his biographical collection of manufacturers.

Bolton continued as sole proprietor until 1872, when he sold out to the partnership of James Preston and Alexander Irwin. Bolton Winpenny had become a wealthy man, his interests broadening to include half ownership of the Arch Street Opera House in Philadelphia and a special partnership in a New York textile commission house, William Yelland and Co. (1868). His 1867 marriage to the daughter of "the Hon. Pierre A. Sutton of Danbury, Connecticut," further suggests the distance from the mill floor traversed by this youngest manufacturing Winpenny.

James B. Winpenny, Bolton's uncle and the immigrant Samuel's youngest son, also entered into the textile trades upon his return in 1844 from his three-year sojourn in Virginia. James B. joined in partnership with one George Moyer for the purpose of spinning cotton yarns, moving to larger quarters after three years. In 1852, Moyer having left the firm, James moved a second time, leasing the mills formerly occupied by James Shaw, who had retired to his competence and the pleasures of politics and school direction. With an entire building at his disposal, James Winpenny doubled his work force to sixty and by 1860 was running twenty cards and 3,500 spindles to yield more than 400,000 pounds of yarn in the census year.[10] During the war he secured looms and contracts for the manufacture of blankets, his elder brother Samuel (Bolton's partner) co-signing the surety bonds necessary for confirmation of the federal agreements[11] and likely providing needed expertise on the fine points of blanket making. Though he may have made blankets for agents who had secured contracts early in the war, between April 1863 and December 1864, James B. Winpenny bid successfully three times for blanket orders on his own behalf.[12] The total value of the three contracts (70,000 blankets, $344,825) was four times his mill's 1860 yarn output ($84,000) and thus provided the wherewithal to purchase the old Shaw mill, which he had been leasing for eleven years, and the funds to erect, in addition, a new three-story building. Family skills had allowed him to "seize the time," but at the close of the war he "resumed the spinning of cotton yarns," returning to his earlier speciality.[13]

By 1870 the effects of his wartime activities were clear in his census report. The firm was capitalized at $100,000, more than double the 1860

[10] *M&MP*, pp. 464, 500; 1860 MCS, Philadelphia Co., p. 473.

[11] *Bonds and Agreements, Philadelphia, QMGC*, National Archives, Record Group 92, Entry No. 2227, pp. 15, 31.

[12] *Abstracts of Contracts, QMGC*, National Archives, Record Group 92, Entry No. 1239, vol. I, p. 229; vol. II, pp. 50, 283.

[13] *M&MP*, p. 500.

total. The looms previously devoted to blankets now wove cottonades, the production of which neared 800,000 yards and was valued at more than $150,000.[14] Profitability had hardly lagged, for in 1871 he "enlarged and raised the main building," adding both a fourth floor and an attached four-story structure, thus doubling the mill floor space.[15] In the next four years James Winpenny added 3,000 spindles to his machinery and commenced again selling yarns, this time for "cotton hosiery and counterpanes," expanding his work force from 86 (1870) to 120 workers (1875).[16] Over the course of his Manayunk career, he had served, like so many other millmen, on the Borough Council (before 1854) and had been by 1875 "nearly twenty years a school director."

James B. Winpenny was the last of the clan to manufacture textiles in the city. Though his mill was listed by Blodget in 1880 as J. B. Winpenny and Son, two years later the city manufacturing census noted that it was in operation for "six months only," and by 1885 it had disappeared from directory listings. Whatever the final fate of Winpenny's Arcola Mills, it is clear that the expansion continued nearly to the point of the founder's withdrawal (in 1882 James B. was 65 years old). The 1880 report noted 6,000 spindles and twenty-six cards, an advance over all earlier figures, though the work force had dropped to 100 when weaving was replaced by a straightforward specialization in the cotton yarns with which the enterprise had commenced in 1844.[17] As in other cases, continuity between the first and second generations might be maintained on the basis of financial success and mill upbringing, but third generation succession was evidently a more difficult transition, despite the aggregate vitality of the textile industry in the Philadelphia of the 1880s. Bolton Winpenny transferred his energies from manufacture to commerce shortly after his considerable wartime successes. James B. Winpenny's son seems never to have embarked on his own as a mill operator.

Both their extended involvement with government work and their network of family skills and support mark the Winpennys as a special case among the city's immigrant textile capitalists. Their productive flexibility, involvement in local politics, pattern of spatial use and expansion, and gradual accumulation are all characteristic of many Philadelphia firms. Yet in the hothouse of the Civil War, they took special advantage and the results were visible both in the contract records and in the clustered mill and machinery additions

---

[14] 1870 MCS, Philadelphia Co., p. 606.
[15] *M&MP*, p. 464.
[16] Ibid., p. 500.
[17] Lorin Blodget, *The Textile Industries of Philadelphia*, Philadelphia, 1880, p. 38; Lorin Blodget, *Census of Manufactures of Philadelphia (1882)*, Philadelphia, 1883, p. 170.

that crowd the war years. Samuel Winpenny's two-year emergence from retirement (1861–3) was not only timely; it assured the success of his nephew who "after a short but remarkably successful career, . . . became sole proprietor."[18] Clearly, the intensification of opportunities for accumulation during the war was met by the Winpennys with a full family mobilization whose outcome interestingly parallels the experience of the Schofields. Whereas Charles Schofield retired "sufficiently opulent," Samuel Winpenny withdrew a second time from manufacturing and was followed in a few years by Bolton, who was still a relatively young man. Sevill Schofield, like James B. Winpenny, remained a manufacturing capitalist for two more decades and undertook to pass on his firm to his sons. The Civil War accumulations in both cases highlight a cultural crossroads in the development of textile capitalism.

Were the Civil War manufacturing experiences of the Winpennys common among Philadelphia millmen? Did other firms have prewar relations with the Quartermaster Corps? How important a part of overall production was the manufacturing carried out for federal needs in the wartime Philadelphia textile industry? How much benefit did contractors derive from their government income and what other federal actions might have assisted or retarded accumulation in the sixties? These key questions are impossible to answer with precision, though a preliminary sketch in response to each will be attempted. The first point to underscore is the connection of the Civil War experiences to national economic development, as articulated by historians Alfred Chandler, Thomas Cochran, Hunter Dupree, Louis Hartz, and others. If any consensus might be extracted from their diverse commentaries, it would focus on the contrast between the narrow effects of war spending and the longer term impact of structural shifts in the national economic framework brought about through war legislation. On the aggregate level, the hundreds of millions spent for war goods produced no wave of technical innovation, no fundamental alteration of production or managerial systems, no revolution in finance or marketing. To be sure, fortunes were made by those strategically placed, and some industrial sectors enjoyed particular prosperity, but no great acceleration of economic development occurred at the national level. (Thomas Cochran has indeed argued, though not without opposition, that the war retarded an industrialization process heartily under way from the forties.)[19] However, war statutes did alter the conditions for accumulation in the longer term, but how decisively only exacting future research will illuminate. Most prominent surely are the

---

[18] *M&MP*, p. 498.
[19] See articles by Cochran and Stephen Salsbury in R. Andreano, ed., *The Economic Impact of the Civil War*, Cambridge, Mass., 1962, pp. 148–68.

Homestead and federal Banking acts, but equally long term in their establishment of industrial relationships were the war Tariffs of 1861, 1862, and
1864, revised and extended in 1867, acts that created the tariff walls that
persisted into the eighties.

The Morrill Tariff of 1861 was in part the product of an extended agitation by Philadelphia manufacturers who sought to block the competition of
British woolens in the American market. Their object was achieved before
the outbreak of hostilities, in time both to choke off a long-established trade
in English blankets[20] and to reserve for themselves access to much of the
later war demand. Indeed, later tariff actions with reference to the woolen
trade, which Taussig argues did little for the industry as a whole, were of
particular value to the speciality elements of woolen production, which were
centered in Philadelphia (carpets and worsteds, most especially),[21] a point to
which we shall return in time. The wartime demand for wool was nearly
treble that of the late fifties,[22] leading scores of Philadelphia mills to use
their flexible capacity to best advantage by dropping cotton work in the face
of short supplies and astronomical prices to run wool in unprecedented
quantities. McCallum's shift from carpets and Winpenny's move from cotton yarn to blankets are only the tip of an iceberg. From a variety of sources,
we may hope to derive a rough idea of its dimensions.

The Quartermaster Corps at the commencement of the war faced stag-
gering problems. The peacetime army had numbered about 13,000 men,
whose material and equipage needs had been supplied through annual, or
occasionally biennial, contracts. By the summer of 1861 more than 300,000
Union men were under arms and Congress had authorized a three-year
force of half a million. "First in priority among the problems of supply . . .
was that of uniforming the new troops who came to join McClellan's and the
other growing armies."[23] Philadelphia had long been the center for military
clothing manufacture, all uniforms having been made at the Schuylkill Arsenal. (This alone helps account for the earlier presence of military contracts
throughout the Philadelphia area.) Yet early in the war mass confusion
reigned. There had been no contingency plans for a war on such scale,
"nothing resembling an office of industrial mobilization to ensure that the

20 Frederick Glover, "Philadelphia Merchants and the Yorkshire Blanket Trade, 1820–
    1860," *Pennsylvania History* 28, no. 2 (1961): 142–55. Imports continued to be impor-
    tant in the early war years but were subsequently superseded by domestic production.
21 F. W. Taussig, *The Tariff History of the United States*, 8th ed., New York, 1931 (rpt.,
    1964), pp. 155–70, 194–218.
22 Emerson Fite, *Social and Industrial Conditions in the North during the Civil War*, New
    York, 1913 (rpt., 1963), p. 84.
23 Ibid., p. 83; R. G. Weigley, *Quartermaster General of the Union Army*, New York, 1959, p.
    183.

national economy would be able to satisfy the requirements of supply."[24] The army bought cloth of all descriptions at first, of questionable quality and at prices that more than hinted of "jobbing" and fraud. With the exposure of corruption in the St. Louis district, the dismissal of General Frémont and his clique, the accession of Secretary of War Stanton to replace the ineffectual Simon Cameron, and the routinization of supply techniques, Quartermaster General Montgomery Meigs, of Philadelphia and West Point, settled into the business of keeping half a million men under arms fed and clothed, horsed and shod. After the first year of the conflict, outright theft from public coffers diminished rapidly. This did not mean, however, that scrupulous attention to the terms of federal contracts could be expected, as we shall see.

To provide uniforms for a portion of the vast forces arrayed in defense of the Union, Meigs secured from the government of France in 1861 full outfits for 10,000 troops, sufficient for ten regiments, "material [which] proved to be of excellent quality, . . . its cost differ[ing] little from that of American goods."[25] This skillful move brought a storm of opposition from New England wool manufacturers calling for the employment of domestic mills to provide military cloths. While the quartermaster general well knew that desperate demand far outstripped existing capacity, he made no further foreign contracts, the practice being formally barred by Secretary Stanton early in 1862. If existing wool mills could hardly supply sufficient volume of kersey and broadcloth, not to speak of blankets and hosiery, where was the War Department and the army to turn? A significant portion of the solution to that dilemma was provided by the flexible capacity of the Philadelphia textile manufacture. To comprehend the challenges involved in wartime supply necessitates an appreciation of the structure of military contracting and of the Quartermaster Corps in that era.

First, from the sheer bulk of the operations necessary to supply clothing, fuel, horses and forage, and transportation to the Union armies, the Quartermaster general was obliged to function in a planning and supervisory role from the outset. As regards cloth contracting, the regional supply depots and their respective quartermasters were the operative units for decision making. Although the Washington headquarters was responsible for inspection and regulation of contractual fulfillment, only six inspectors were available to undertake these tasks nationally. Thus the depot commanders, on the basis of estimates drawn up in Washington, announced their needs and awarded contracts, often in great haste, given the emergency situation. Indeed, under special circumstances, awards might be made without bidding, a practice

---

[24] Weigley, *Quartermaster General*, p. 218.
[25] Ibid., pp. 200–1.

that was widely abused in the St. Louis cases. Whether or not the awards were competitive, those mills with experience that were located near the depots and perhaps close to their personnel were well placed to secure federal contracts.[26]

Second, the successful contractor was by no means necessarily a manufacturer of the goods he had been selected to deliver. Experienced cloth merchants, including some importers, outright speculators, mill proprietors, and agents, all bid and won contracts during the war. This hopelessly complicates any effort to determine precisely how much of what goods were produced in any particular mill, much less any particular city. Nevertheless, on the contract lists, both Philadelphia merchants and millmen are consistently present, not only in those contracts let at Philadelphia but also in lists of awards for Cincinnati and New York, the other two major clothing depots of the Civil War. Although Philadelphia mills were running full speed in the early part of the war, it appears that the bulk of their contracts were actually held by merchant capitalists. Later in the war, Philadelphia proprietors bypassed those middlemen, securing awards in their own names and supporting one another in providing the bonds required to assure the timely delivery of the goods as designated in their contracts.

Third, the federal forces supplied by the Quartermaster Corps were not the only source of demand for military cloths. Until President Lincoln drafted the state militia, those organizations contracted independently for uniform cloths, often fashioned into the outlandish uniforms that decorate volumes of Civil War "fashion" history. Privately raised volunteer companies also secured their cloth and clothing independently, adding yet more buyers to the marketplace. The makers of private uniforms, whether running sweatshops or converted shirt factories, sewed a company's worth of suitings at a time, the cloth for which was secured from merchants or mills directly. Thus, in retrospect, particularly in the first two years of the war, vast supplies of woolen goods, hosiery, blankets, and trimmings were sought from merchants and manufactured for an array of competing buyers only one of which was the Quartermaster Corps of the Union Army. That Philadelphia mills operated first on subcontracts and later on their own initiative is confirmed by the McCallum, Crease and Sloan reference that headed this chapter, as well as by an 1865 investigation of contracting practices at the Philadelphia depot that was ordered by General Meigs.[27] Yet the assessment of the total

---

[26] Large firms, including some Philadelphia mills, evidently sent representatives to the major depot cities to bid whenever contracts were offered. Thus New York merchants secured some Philadelphia and Cincinnati awards, then subcontracted the production to manufacturers, some of whom were likely Philadelphians.

[27] "Report of a Special Investigation at the Philadelphia Depot," 1865–6, National Archives, Record Group 92.

volume and ultimate end use of these goods would demand perfect preservation of a variety of firm, state, and private records, supplementary to those retained by federal authorities. This has not taken place, but at least for later war years (1863–5), Quartermaster contracts were the vehicle by which nearly all the cloth needs of the Union armies were met. We shall focus more carefully on them in short order.

Fourth, a secondary and related external event directly linked to the opening of the Civil War, the cotton famine, had considerable importance for the vigor of the Philadelphia textile manufacture during the war years. With cotton in short supply, nongovernmental demand for substitute goods soared. Fite estimated that of the more than 200 million pounds of wool annually consumed during the war, almost two-thirds was for private consumption (135 million pounds), which was 60% above annual total wool consumption in the late fifties. Philadelphia firms, handloom and mill-based, had a long history of producing mixed goods, an obvious means to stretch short cotton supplies. Moreover, Philadelphia firms had heavily produced for a southern market (slave goods known as Negro cloths) that had evaporated. Both their experience with mixed goods and flexible capacity served to prepare Philadelphia textile manufacturers to adapt to rapidly changing market and supply conditions and allowed them to continue production even in the absence of federal contracts. Indeed, even spinners accustomed to reprocessing cotton and woolen waste and rags contributed to the ability of the Philadelphia group, as an aggregate, to meet the crisis and profit thereby.

By mid-1862 the Philadelphia depot had accumulated 3.2 million yards of army cloths, sufficient for a half million uniforms. Although the worst scrambling had ended, regular contracts were awarded throughout the next three years to meet replacement needs. The level of waste of military clothing shocked the quartermasters. On one occasion, during a long march, 800 men in 1,000-man regiment discarded their overcoats along the road, yet replacements had to be provided "whether the regulation clothing allowance called for them or not."[28] In such circumstances, and to combat the gross profiteering that emergency procurement brought, quartermasters were instructed to keep clothing reserves high. "Eventually each of the three depots was to accumulate full equipment for 100,000 men, plus the supplies necessary to meet the ordinary wear and tear of an army of 200,000."[29]

If Philadelphia's textile manufacturers were poised to respond to the needs of the Quartermaster Corps, other city industries also benefited from the demand for military hardware. At the Baldwin locomotive shops early in the war "matters were near a standstill"; but "unexpectedly, . . . the Na-

[28] Weigley, *Quartermaster General*, p. 254.
[29] Ibid., p. 252.

tional Government ordered many engines," pushing Baldwin's output to record levels.[30] Between 1858 and 1861, the works had completed 226 locomotives, but in the four years of war contracting (1862–5), 416 engines were assembled, "many of them the heaviest and most powerful ever constructed."[31] Similarly, the Cramp Shipyards, on a subcontract from "Merrick and Co., Philadelphia engine builders," built the hull of the battleship New Ironsides, using the occasion to "make the switch from wood to iron construction."[32] As Frank Taylor later noted: "At the shipyards, machine shops, textile mills and in factories of many lines, Government contracts soon afforded abundant employment. Our workmen were able to provide heavy and light artillery, swords, rifles, camp equipage, uniforms and blankets in great quantities."[33]

Brief accounts of the development of a number of Philadelphia textile firms, assembled in the 1870s, refer directly to their proprietors' engagement with these contracts. The experience of Sevill Schofield and McCallum, along with the Winpennys, has already been reviewed. A few other examples will lead us toward the more meaty materials present in the Quartermaster Corps contract books. The Dobson mills, woolen manufacturers at Falls of Schuylkill and closely connected with Sevill Schofield's firm and family, were called "to supply immense quantities of their superior blankets, etc., to the Army and Navy Hospitals and other public and private institutions." They expanded their factory capacity in 1862, 1864, and 1867, continuing on that base into the seventies to become one of the largest woolen firms in the nation. Before the war the two small Dobson partnerships, one making carpets, the other shawls and blankets, had had a total capital of $38,000; having discarded his partners, James Dobson alone reported an investment of $250,000 in 1870.[34]

Two venerable Philadelphia manufacturers, William Horstmann and Sons and William Whitaker, active since the 1820s, were engaged in wartime contracting. The Horstmann firm had been a regular federal supplier for many years, military trimmings being the firm's specialty, though its market extended to scores of militia companies and fraternal associations as well. Between 1853 and 1856 Horstmann twice secured awards from the Quartermaster Depot (totaling about $10,000) for an array of trimmings (in six

30 Frank H. Taylor, *Philadelphia in the Civil War, 1861–1865*, Philadelphia, 1913, p. 14.
31 *History of the Baldwin Locomotive Works, 1831–1920*, Philadelphia, 1920, pp. 55, 57; Taylor, *Philadelphia*, p. 14.
32 David B. Tyler, *The American Clyde: A History of Iron and Steel Shipbuilding on the Delaware from 1840 to World War I*, Newark, Del., 1958, pp. 19–23.
33 Taylor, *Philadelphia*, p. 14.
34 *M&MP*, p. 52; 1860 MCS, Philadelphia Co., pp. 470, 477; 1860 MCS, Philadelphia Co., p. 608.

colors), sashes, buntings, and the like. During the war, their awards were frequent and much larger, with five direct contracts in the first eight months of 1864 totaling more than $65,000.[35] The Whitaker firm, cotton manufacturers, converted their plant to meet the new opportunities. Departing from their practice of "the weaving of tickings," the Whitakers ran blankets to supply "the unusual demand created by government contracts."[36] No contracts were recorded in Whitaker's name, indicating that, like McCallum, this work has handled through subcontracting. Also like McCallum, this firm returned to its customary trade after the war.

In hosiery, the newly formed partnership of Schofield and Branson quickly became stocking suppliers to the Philadelphia depot. In business just three years and having erected a new mill in Kensington, the partners secured enough of the profitable trade to facilitate further expansion, for they put up a second factory near the first site in 1863.[37] Clearly, war-generated accumulation brought quick prosperity to the partners. After 1863, however, they withdrew from supplying the army, being underbid by other mills whose use of shoddy and waste as raw material allowed them to produce "an inferior article," which was nevertheless accepted by inspectors. Schofield and Branson sought to market their goods in "the channel of regular trade, which was then reviving." By 1875 the firm employed "300 operatives, besides nearly an equal number engaged without the walls in various processes of manufacture,"[38] continuing the hand- and outwork relations customary in the antebellum knitting trades at Philadelphia.

A somewhat grisly spinoff of one aspect of the war's textile demand fueled the expansion of William Simpson's Washington Print Works, located on the west bank of the Schuylkill opposite the falls. Simpson for many years had been "noted for the superiority of its mourning goods, upon which they [had] been principally engaged." Their market too extended sharply during the conflict, allowing not only the erection of new buildings at the falls and the acquisition of new machinery but also a backward integration into the production of cloths for dyeing and printing. In June 1865 the Simpson firm invested its war profits in the purchase of the Wyoming Cotton Mills, upstream at Norristown, two waterpowered mills driven by Leffel turbines, together with "over seventy comfortable tenant houses."[39] Although the war brought boom years to Philadelphia's textile trades, government contracts were not the only means to accelerated accumulation. Simpson's funereal

[35] *Abstracts of Contracts, QMGC.* vol. XII, Entry No. 1238, pp. 61, 285; *Abstracts of Contracts QMGC,* vol. II, pp. 86, 307.
[36] *Biographical Encyclopedia of Pennsylvania,* Philadelphia, 1874, p. 226.
[37] *M&MP,* p. 368.
[38] Ibid.
[39] Ibid., p. 323.

success works an unnerving counterpoint to the savagery on the battle-grounds, as mass death provided the base for expanding an enterprise that continued textile production well into the following century.[40]

The Quartermaster Corps contract registers give a more detailed look at the work done by dozens of additional firms that bid successfully under their own names for textile awards. Though the records are incomplete (pages are missing for part of 1863), they indicate the minimum scale and value of direct contracting to Philadelphia firms and, with some sifting, some of the linkages between merchant bidders and local millmen. Hosiery was a local specialty and a military necessity. During the five war years, the Quartermaster records contain contracts for nearly 15.5 million pairs of woolen stockings, with individual contracts ranging from 1,500 to 500,000 pairs. The three principal depots, New York, Philadelphia, and Cincinnati, awarded all but a handful of the contracts, the two eastern centers drawing 36% each of the total, the western outpost, 27%. Fifteen Philadelphia firms secured direct awards for 2.25 million pairs, the total value of which was $765,000, about 15% of the aggregate. Of that group, only Aaron Jones and Martin Landenberger bid successfully at depots other than the Schuylkill Arsenal, with Jones netting orders for 165,000 pairs at New York and Landenberger (probably through an agent), 350,000 pairs at Cincinnati.[41]

Although large, these figures form only a small proportion of the national total. Commercial houses received most of the remaining contracts, which were then subcontracted to the mills for manufacture. The most developed center of hosiery manufacture in the nation was at Philadelphia. One of the earliest textile directories, *Dockham's Dry Goods Trade* (1868), lists 112 hosiery firms active a few years after the war's end. Of these, 42 were concentrated in Philadelphia, the only district in the nation to have a separate hosiery and knit-goods category in the directory's headings. New York State and Massachusetts trailed with 24 and 20 firms, respectively, and the five other New England states were represented by 21 knitting manufacturers.[42] Although these figures are terribly soft, they do suggest that manufacture of another 2 million to 3 million pairs locally through subcontracts would not be an unreasonable estimate if Philadelphia firms received contracts roughly proportionate to their presence in the pool of knitting mills. Most of the hosiery awards at Philadelphia were made to local merchant houses, which had not far to look for productive facilities. Indeed, in several of these cases, the surety bonds for performance were signed by Germantown hosiers (Elias

---

[40] Some of the Simpson firm records are held at the Eleutherian Mills/Hagley Foundation Library, Greenville, Del. See *Guide to Manuscripts*, EM/HF Library, 1970, p. 709.

[41] Calculated from *Abstracts of Contracts*, QMGC, Entry No. 1239, vols. I and II. The Jones and Landenberger contracts are in vol. I, pp. 210–11.

[42] C. A. Dockham and Co., *The Dry Goods Trade . . . : A Directory*, Boston, 1868.

Birchall, William Allen, and Thomas Branson), though the bids had been won by wholesale traders.[43]

Heavy-duty military blankets proved the one commodity that the nation's woolen manufacturers could not generate in sufficient quantities. As late as 1864, Cronin, Huxthal and Sears were commissioned to secure 100,000 "English woolen blankets" to fill the supply/demand gap.[44] (Though expanded domestic blanket capacity contracted after the war, the English trade did not revive.) Philadelphia woolen mills churned out blankets throughout the conflict, winning twenty-five direct awards for delivery of 894,000 units.[45] The roster of contractors was filled with familiar names: John Dobson, James Winpenny, Sevil Schofield, James Lord, Jr., William Divine, Orlando Crease (of McCallum, Crease and Sloan), and Benjamin Bullock's Sons. These seven firms grossed $4,156,837 for direct production alone, revenues from any subcontracts they or others might have received being additional. Again, some of the contracts were secured at other depots, but the direct awards by the Philadelphia depot to local mills accounted for more than 40% of the blankets ordered, about double the proportion in hosiery, where much smaller firms might be expected to respond more readily to middlemen's initiatives. With the income from these (and other) operations, Schofield, Winpenny, and Dobson expanded their mills methodically; Lord sold out to the Ammidown firm near the war's end and retired, and the Bullocks erected a local woolen empire centered on the Norristown works to which they had removed from the city in the late fifties. The Bullocks, sons of Henry Korn's immigrant wool comber, were the most aggressive and successful of all the Philadelphia war textile contractors, garnering eighteen separate awards that involved more than $5 million in military supplies.

The largest portion of the harvest reaped by Bullock's Sons lay in the standard uniform cloths, kerseys and broadcloths, of which they were the country's largest producer. Though 1863 records are missing, in the other four years of the war, the Bullocks collected ten contracts for 2.25 million yards of blue woolens. Their 1862 contract for 400,000 yards of broadcloth, alone worth $1,392,000, was the only sizable agreement for broadcloth manufacture in that year. Their wartime purchases of mills throughout the district, discussed in Chapter 4, encompassed thirteen factories and more than 3,000 workers at their peak. The Bullocks also ran flannels during the war for the Quartermaster Corps, signed sureties for other woolen contracts not directly let to them, and became an integral part of the downtown merchant community in a fashion unimaginable a generation before. Midway through the war, the brothers were the recipients of an elaborate silver service pur-

---

[43] *Bonds and Agreements*, pp. 10, 15.

[44] Weigley, *Quartermaster General*, p. 253; *Bonds and Agreements*, p. 34.

[45] Calculated from *Abstracts of Contracts QMGC*, Entry No. 1239.

chased in their honor by the workers in the Norristown mills, in recognition of their provision of full work and fair wages. In 1871 George Bullock withdrew from the operating partnership to specialize in commercial matters for a time and then began the production of doeskins on a large scale. His brothers continued their manufacturing on a reduced scale into the 1880s.[46]

Beneath the extremity of the Bullocks' accumulation were the dozens of firms for whom the war was a more modest bonanza. Only the fringes of this production can be viewed through the Quartermaster registers, and yet those portions attributable to millmen's direct contracts total $12 million of war business for about thirty firms in the district. By contrast, the total value of woolens and woolen hosiery produced in Philadelphia in the 1859–60 census year was $2.7 million.[47] Whatever imprecision must remain concerning the actual total yardage, dollars, and number of firms affected, it seems reasonable to conclude that war demand sustained the factory manufacture of textiles in Philadelphia and allowed a sizable group of firms to expand their facilities, some dramatically.[48]

Despite occasional pious claims of selflessness regarding profits, the margins enjoyed by wool manufacturers during the war were decidedly favorable. Those firms that had the funds to purchase large stocks of raw materials were able to sell their goods in a rising market, with profitability increasing month by month as warehoused stock was run off. As Cole observed, "whether the source of profits was merely inflated wool prices or not, their realization unquestionably provided a direct stimulus to the enlargement of old plants and the establishment of new enterprises in this field."[49]

As Philadelphia would ultimately become best known as a wool city (hosiery, carpets, and worsteds leading the way), the implication of war-spurred woolen manufacture is of special importance to the long-term structuring of the textile manufacture there. Statewide comparisons of Massachusetts and Pennsylvania may be extracted from later government documents to illustrate the enormous burst of the latter's woolen industry in the sixties, the largest portion of which was planted in Philadelphia. In 1860 Massachusetts reported producing woolen goods of all varieties (including carpets) in 136 firms, involving 14,277 workers and a capital of just over $11 million. Ten

---

[46] See Blodget, *Textile Industries*, p. 61.

[47] J. L. Bishop, *History of American Manufactures from 1608 to 1860*, Philadelphia, 1866, vol. 2, pp. 530–3.

[48] No full-scale study of Civil War Quartermaster contracting has been completed, much less any attempt to assess the demand of state and private regiments. Only a massive linkage of military and merchant records with manufacturing firms would allow any analysis reaching beyond the direct contracting discussed here.

[49] Bishop, *History of American Manufacturers*, vol. 2, p. 563; A. H. Cole, *The American Wool Manufacture*, Cambridge, Mass., 1925, vol. 1, pp. 380–1.

years later the state showed 220 firms, 25,825 employees, and a capital of a little more than double the prewar figure, $23.5 million. In Pennsylvania, 270 much smaller firms employed only 6,088 workers in 1860 with the total investment but $4.3 million. By the end of the war decade, the number of producers had risen to 488, the work force had tripled to 16,632, and the investment engaged multiplied more than four times to $17.6 million.[50] Whatever segment of this growth may be accounted for by government contracts, the war years and the sixties as a whole were evidently much more stimulating to the Quaker state than to the New England cradle of the textile industry. By the eighties, Pennsylvania's wool mills would hold considerably more workers than those of Massachusetts, as capital invested again doubled in the seventies, with the work force nearly tripling a second time to more than 42,000. Philadelphia's share of the statewide totals rose from about half in 1860 to more than three-quarters by 1880, as the city's textile manufacturing base extended in all directions.

Part of the profit from government contracts was secured by using low-grade raw materials, including waste and shoddy, and thus submitting to the depots goods whose quality was lower than the standards set in contracts. Manayunk folklore to this day includes references to the indictment (or investigation) by federal authorities of Sevill Schofield for defrauding the government on his blanket contracts.[51] More substantial is the "Report of a Special Investigation at the Philadelphia Depot" conducted in 1865 by Col. George Rutherford on orders of Quartermaster General Meigs. The inquiry was triggered by allegations of irregularities both in the acceptance of low-grade cloths and in the setting of quality standards for government goods.

> In short, the statement is that the Department's standard was known to the public bidders, and yet goods contracted for as "Army Standards" of inferior quality were received, and further that there was a trick in the manufacture of the sample of March 1864 from Philadelphia [used in setting the standard], the benefit of which trick those interested in getting up the sample have been enjoying.[52]

The crux of the problem rested on standards set in 1864 specifying the strength of materials, which were modified by officials at the Philadelphia Depot without clear authorization. The kerseys purchased by the government, according to the official standard, were acceptable only if they with-

---

[50] Worthington Ford, *Wool and Manufactures of Wool*, Washington, D.C., 1894, pp. 52–3.
[51] Interview with Thomas McMaster, March 12, 1982. Mr. McMaster, who was born in Manayunk in 1903, was the son of a boss spinner at the Platt Mill. Federal records do not refer to such an inquiry.
[52] "Report of a Special Investigation at the Philadelphia Depot," 1865–6, National Archives, Record Group 92, letter from M. C. Meigs, p. 3.

stood a lengthwise strain of 90 pounds and a lateral strain of 55 pounds. Curiously, the standards adopted at Philadelphia "require[d] only a strain of 75 to 85 pounds lengthwise and 37 to 50 pounds crosswise."[53] The colonel in charge claimed no knowledge of the official standards, certifying delivery of large but unspecified quantities of kerseys under the lower "local" specifications. Rumors reached Washington that goods rejected for failing tests at other depots had been forwarded to Philadelphia, where they were passed.

Colonel Rutherford was extremely cautious in his evaluation of the situation. On the submission of goods rejected elsewhere, he wrote: "It does not appear from any information *accessible* that any of the Francis' kerseys have been received or even offered on any of the existing contracts at Philadelphia." (Emphasis added.) On the "trick" of lowered standards, he wrote that "any trick in the preparation of the original [local] standards does not appear. It was not possible unless connived at by the Chief Inspector – an imputation Col. McKim and others are confident would not apply."[54] Nonetheless, he is precise in demonstrating that *none* of the goods accepted on four enormous kersey contracts under the lower standard, once tested directly, met even their reduced requirements. Rutherford sampled twenty pieces from each of twelve batches of kersey in the depots' stores, tested them exhaustively (including six pages of detailed tables in his report), and commented:

> It will be seen by the foregoing that none of the sky blue Kerseys received on the contracts hereinbefore enumerated, conform even to the modified specifications.
>
> There is so little difference in the samples that it would seem that the machine tests had not been applied when the goods were received and inspected at the Schuylkill Arsenal.[55]

As official prose goes, this is a fairly damning assessment. Not only had the standards been cut, without plausible explanation, but volumes of goods inferior to the revised standards had been accepted without being tested against even their lower requirements. Whatever the confusion about the proper strength levels for kersey, the depot had accepted goods that should have been rejected, under contracts that totaled more than 2.1 million yards. What chicanery or carelessness had allowed this to happen during the last year of the war, Rutherford did not pursue.

Two observations are in order. First and most obvious, the failure of goods to meet the specifications implies the use of yarns weaker than those mandated by contract obligations. A healthy dose of shoddy added to new

---

[53] Ibid., Col. Rutherford letter, p. 4.
[54] Ibid., pp. 4, 6–7.
[55] Ibid., p. 9.

wools before spinning would save considerably on production costs while yielding a product of inferior strength and durability whose appearance would vary little from all-new goods. Federal contracts also specified the fineness of the weaves (number of threads per inch) to be used in cloth making, but Rutherford admitted that he did not go so far as to check conformity to these requirements. By using coarse wools and coarser yarns than required, additional savings could be made by the manufacturers, at a cost of further departure from federal standards. Thus might profitability be enhanced.

Second, all four of the kersey contracts investigated by Rutherford were awarded to merchant houses in Philadelphia, namely, John B. Hughes (500,000 yards, two awards), Lewis, Boardman and Wharton (605,000 yards), and W. C. Houston (1 million yards). It would be especially useful to be able to trace the slipshod goods back to their manufacturers, in order to link the practice of substandard manufacture to particular firms. Thanks to the detail provided by Rutherford on the samples from one of the four contracts, Houston, the largest, this is feasible. Nine samples of the twelve tested came from the Houston lots, each of which was separately identified in the "Report." Eight mills were involved, along with the especially shabby goods "purchased" by Houston to complete his order, possibly goods rejected elsewhere but not identifiable as such. Of the eight firms listed by mill name, seven are Philadelphia area manufacturers and the last (Kymensing) has a familiar ring (Moyamensing). Included were the Norristown Mills of Benjamin Bullock's Sons and the Gulf Mills of George McFarland in neighboring Montgomery County, along with five city firms, three of which were sited in Manayunk. Though the Haydock Street Mills were one of the last center-city operations, S. J. Solms' Pekin Mills, John Maxon's mills, and those of J. B. Winpenny were all part of the Manayunk complex where Schofield, Dobson, and, nearby, Lord operated. (Solomon Wilde, the fifth, ran a factory in Northeast Philadelphia.) Solms and, interestingly enough, Charles Spencer of Germantown signed the surety bond for the Houston contract, widening the network of Philadelphia textile capitalists engaged in discreet war profiteering.[56]

This rare look behind the merchant contractors to *their* suppliers suggests that even those local manufacturers not directly awarded war contracts (Solms, Maxon, Wilde) nevertheless were involved in the networks of subcontracting. Further, this example may just skim the surface of the mechanisms whereby accumulation, aided by state necessities, was accelerated through sophisticated evasion of contractual requirements and, arguably, through suborning inspectors who should otherwise have rejected goods of

[56] Ibid., pp. 8–9; *Bonds and Agreements*, p. 41.

inferior quality. The plausibility of corruption is underscored by Weigley's discussion of Quartermaster staff problems: "The Quartermaster's Department frequently received as officers persons whose principal qualification was their ability to endear themselves to the politicos in their state capital . . . [men] who failed to take their responsibilities seriously, who were almost totally unacquainted with their duties."[57]

If such practices were widespread, and if other Schuylkill Arsenal contracts were run at local mills, as in the Houston case, the vitality of capitalist accumulation in wartime Philadelphia factory firms is yet more vivid. The four contracts here investigated brought to their holders a total of $3.4 million, of which $1.6 million was involved in the Houston bundle alone.[58] The profits from a goodly chunk of any of these would have helped refit a mill, add an extension, or if several such subcontracts could be strung together, construct a new facility outright.

In the wake of the Civil War, state action again assisted the burgeoning wool sector of the Philadelphia textile industry through the special legislation of 1867, the Wool and Woolens Act. Though federal contracts came to an abrupt halt in the spring of 1865, the elevated rates on woolens made abroad and the complex system of compensatory duties established in 1861 was extended, offering protection against any repetition of the collapse of the late teens. The Morrill Tariff Act laid the foundations for a set of wool duties that would endure for the next generation. Taussig explained:

> In that act . . . [t]he cheaper kinds of wool, costing eighteen cents or less per pound, were still admitted at the nominal rate of five percent. But wool costing between eighteen and twenty-four cents per pound was charged three cents per pound; that costing more than twenty-four cents was charged nine cents per pound. The duties on [manufactured] woolens were increased correspondingly. An *ad-valorem rate* of twenty-five percent was levied on them; in addition they paid a specific duty of twelve cents for each pound of cloth. This specific duty was intended merely to compensate the [domestic] manufacturers for the duty on [imported] wool, while the *ad-valorem* rate alone was to yield them any protection. This is the first appearance in our tariff history of exact compensating duties.[59]

It was expected that forcing up the price of imported wools would increase the return domestic wool producers could command as well. Thus to prevent foreign weavers from ducking under the tariff barrier, goods manufac-

---

[57] Weigley, *Quartermaster General*, p. 230.
[58] *Abstracts of Contracts QMGC, Entry No. 1239*, p. 136.
[59] Taussig, *Tariff History*, p. 195.

tured abroad were subject to a double woolens levy, the compensating tariff on the wool they contained, leveling upward the materials cost, and the 25% protectionist rate added to it, based on the value of the products.

During the war, the compensating and *ad valorem* tandem was retained, and the rates were adjusted upward sharply to further compensate manufacturers for related duties on dyestuffs and internal revenue taxes on finished products. In the second revision (1864), the charge for the most commonly used grades of imported wools (those costing from 12¢ to 24¢ per lb.) was hiked to 6¢ and the compensatory duty on foreign woolens to 24¢ per pound, to which was attached a 40% *ad valorem* charge.[60] This was serious protection, but the fear of postwar depression led a handful of major New England manufacturers to demand, and get, yet more. Organized as the National Association of Wool Manufacturers, these makers of carpets, blankets, and worsteds collaborated with a cluster of domestic wool producers, the National Wool-Growers Association, and devised a "scheme" of wool and woolens duties calculated to preserve them from outside competition. The schedule of rates, reviewed and "approved by the United States Revenue Commission," was inserted in the proposed 1867 tariff bill. When this failed to pass, the wool and woolens section was plucked out, resubmitted as a separate bill, and became law without a murmur. Taussig was appalled:

> The whole course of events forms the most striking example – and such examples are numerous – of the manner in which in recent tariff legislation, regard has been exclusively to the producer. Here was an intricate and detailed scheme of duties, prepared by producers of the articles to be protected, openly and avowedly with the intention of giving themselves aid; and yet this scheme was accepted and enacted by the National Legislature without any appreciable change.[61]

The Wool and Woolens Act reclassified the grades of imported wools in accordance with the needs of the sponsoring manufacturers and their associated sheepmen. Coarse raw wool of the sort used heavily in the carpet manufacture was lightly taxed; but the duties on all finer grades of wool, those most widely grown in the United States, were roughly doubled, "the increase concealed under a change in classification." Beyond this ruse was a maze of valuations and levies on finished goods that in their turn increased further the level of protection afforded to domestic manufacturers.

> The whole cumbrous and intricate system – of ad-valorem and specific duties, of duties varying according to the weight and the value and the square yard – was adopted largely because it concealed the degree of

---

[60] Ibid., p. 198.
[61] Ibid., p. 200.

protection which in fact the act of 1867 gave. Duties that plainly levied taxes of 60, 80 and 100 per cent. would hardly have been suffered by public opinion or enacted by the legislature.[62]

If the shenanigans at the Philadelphia Quartermaster Depot concerning the acceptance of substandard goods represented a profitable corruption of state functions in miniature, the 1867 Tariff Act replicated that action on a grand scale. The sectors in which its sponsors operated, carpets, blankets, and worsted goods, "were highly profitable for some years."

Though they had not the clout of their New England counterparts, the Philadelphia manufacturers in the same trades enjoyed the same advantages once the 1867 rates went into force. The wartime glow in wool and blanket production that brought profit and expansion was sustained over the next half-dozen years. The long-term development of the Philadelphia carpet manufacture was thus abetted, despite the small-shop basis of its activity and the consequent invisibility of its proprietors at the national level. The results of both wartime accumulation and postwar intensification of protection appear in the returns of the 1870 Manufacturing Census, revealing a partial transformation of the aggregate format and a few striking changes at the level of the neighborhood and the individual firm.

By linking firms that secured war contracts with the manufacturing censuses of 1860 and 1870, a rough illustration of the effects of federal spending and the tariff wall on the accumulation process in Philadelphia textiles may be assembled. About forty firms could be identified as direct or subcontractors during the war, and complete information in both censuses was available for twenty-five. (The largest part of the residual were firms that got their start after the 1860 enumeration; a few others were sited outside Philadelphia County.) Table 8.1 presents these manufacturers in two groups, sixteen direct contractors and nine subcontractors. The latter were identified from firm biographies, the Rutherford documents, and the surety registers. Several manufacturers held both direct contracts and subcontracts (McCallum), and, of course, many mills that ran government goods are omitted because of incomplete sources and the dead ends encountered with most of the merchant awards. Here then is a group of firms that likely reflects the pattern of accumulation achieved under war and postwar conditions by Philadelphia's textile capitalists. As it is a thoroughly nonrandom

---

62 Ibid., p. 215–6. Taussig shows convincingly how one aspect after another of the "scheme masked advances in the tariff not evident on the surface." For example, he notes that the standard ratio of 4 pounds of wool to 1 pound of finished cloth was an overstatement of the actual conditions of manufacture, in which close to 1½ pounds of goods were derived from 4 pounds of raw wool. Had a 3-to-1 ratio been used, the compensatory duty on foreign cloths would have been lowered by a third (from 24¢ to 18¢ per pound).

sample, their experience will be later assessed against aggregate figures for capital and work force by sector in 1860 and 1870.

First, consider the paired characteristics of flexibility and specialization that mark much of the activity of Philadelphia textile firms before the war. None of the six blanket contractors with direct awards was running blankets in 1860; indeed two were operating cotton mills and Winpenny was engaged in spinning exclusively. All were able to adapt their facilities to meet federal demand successfully. Two of the firms (Schofield and Lord/Ammidown) continued blanket manufacture thereafter, but the other four dropped it, either to return to their old output mix or, as did Dobson and Divine, to proceed to yet other productive options. Whereas the increase in capital for Divine and Winpenny is modest, the other four registered sharp gains. (The Divine firm, in 1869, appears to have sold off one of its two mills; the 1870 capital figure reflects the remaining mill only.) Lord retired comfortably late in the conflict; Charles Schofield took his competence, leaving Sevill the sole owner of the $200,000 firm in 1870. Dobson's path is equally impressive, as he discarded both partners and looms to erect one of the largest spinning operations in the region, processing 1.2 million pounds of raw wool in 1869–70.[63]

If the flexibility of the fabric mills allowed them to move into and out of war production, the specialty trade did equally well in responding to the need for goods for which they had become widely known. (Both Landenberger and Horstmann rated special and extensive individual treatment in Freedley's 1857 *Philadelphia and Its Manufactures*.) Both the knitters and the braid-and-trim firms plied their craft to good advantage in the sixties, with only J&A Kemper experiencing a decline, which was perhaps less attributable to competition from the immense Horstmann mills than to their retention of hand-powered production while others had gone on to steam. No firm shifted completely away from its 1860 output, though several firms added additional lines to their knit basics by 1870. Even the very tiny operations grew apace; Hansell, for example, plowed his profits into a new factory and retained some handworkers at the Old City shop location. As a group, the direct contractors saw their capital invested in manufacture rise 145% in ten years and their collective work forces increase 46%. If the aggregate city total approached these proportions, the case here argued for an acceleration of accumulation in the war decade will be strengthened, particularly as comparisons may be made with the preceding decade's growth.

Following this pattern closely, subcontractors experienced expansion ranging from creditable to spectacular (Schofield and Branson), with only one case of slippage. Again, none of the blankets and kerseys were woven by

---

[63] 1870 MCS, Philadelphia Co., p. 608.

Table 8.1. *Capital, workers, and domestic and war-contract products of contractors and subcontractors by district, Philadelphia, 1860–70*

District	Capital		Workers		Products		
	1860	1870	1860	1870	Domestic 1860	War contract 1861–65	Domestic 1870
Contractors							
Germantown							
Elias Birchall	$25,000	$100,000	106	124	Comforts, hoods, hosiery	Hosiery	Hoods, scarfs, shawls
Aaron Jones	25,000	75,000	65	85	Hosiery	Hosiery	Hosiery
McCallum, Crease & Sloan	100,000	250,000	160	297	Carpets	Blankets	Carpets
Thomas Mottram	3,000	7,000	14	20	Hosiery	Hosiery	Hosiery
Charles Spencer	175,000	375,000	278	350	Hosiery	Hosiery	Hosiery, fancy knits
Kensington							
Martin Landenberger	130,000	400,000	430	750	Knit goods	Hosiery	Knit goods
Manayunk							
James Dobson[a]	38,000	250,000	153	156	Carpets, woolens	Blankets	Wool yarn
Edward Holt	50,000	75,000	95	162	Knitted underwear	Knitted underwear	Knit and woven mixed goods
James Lord, Jr.	20,000	250,000	50	225	Carpets	Blankets	Blankets
Sevill Schofield[a]	15,000	200,000	32	314	Carpet, yarn, jeans	Blankets	Woolens
J. B. Winpenny[a]	48,000	65,000	60	100	Cotton yarn	Blankets	Cotton yarn
Old City							
William Divine & Sons	166,000	200,000	304	205	Cottons	Blankets	Cotton, woolens
John Goldthorp[b]	1,000	10,000	4	39	Trim	Trim	Trim
William Hansell[b]	2,500	55,000	2	52	Trim	Trim	Trim

					Subcontractors		
William Horstmann & Sons	450,000	800,000	450	400	Trim	Trim	Braid, trim
J&A Kemper	30,000	20,000	76	40	Trim	Trim	Trim
Germantown							
Joseph Fling	14,000	25,000	6	20	Hosiery	Hosiery	Wool yarn
Kensington							
Schofield & Branson	10,000	240,000	26	218	Hosiery	Hosiery	Hosiery
Manayunk							
Jacob Heft[c]	32,000	50,000	42	75	Mixed goods, dyeing	Kersey	Mixed goods
S. J. Solms	70,000	200,000	80	125	Jeans, tweeds	Kersey	Cassimeres
Bolton Winpenny	80,000	100,000	80	85	Mixed goods	Blankets	Cottons
Northeast Philadelphia							
William Whitaker & Sons	25,000	150,000	70	158	Cottons	Blankets	Cottons
Solomon Wilde	40,000	30,000	150	61	Mixed goods	Kersey	Woolens
Old City							
Greer & McCreight	75,000	100,000	180	106	Cottons	Flannel	Cottons
Milne Bros.	100,000	200,000	260	212	Mixed goods	Kersey, blankets	Mixed goods

[a] A partnership in 1860 that had become a sole proprietorship by 1870.

[b] Hansell and Goldthorp secured war contracts as a partnership; Hansell erected a steam-powered mill north of Spring Garden in addition to his Old City shop.

[c] A sole proprietor in 1860, Heft had added a partner by 1870; he was the only proprietor to do so.

Source: Manuscript Manufacturing Census Schedules, Philadelphia County, 1860, 1870; *Abstracts of Contracts*, QMGC, National Archives, Record Group 92, Entry No. 1239; *Bonds and Sureties*, QMGC, National Archives, Record Group 92, Entry No. 2227; Daniel Robson, ed., *Manufactories and Manufacturers of Pennsylvania of the Nineteenth Century* (Philadelphia, 1875); *Biographical Encyclopedia of Pennsylvania* (Philadelphia, 1874).

firms that had been running those goods in 1860, and none continued to manufacture the same goods after the war's end. Although Joseph Fling's involvement may have been little more than the production of yarn for others' contracts, Schofield and Branson evidently made no mistakes, pulling out of the government trade as secular demand revived and thus multiplying their wealth geometrically by 1870. There is no clear evidence that the two Schofield proprietors in Table 7.8 were related, though both were Lancashire men. Benjamin Schofield, Branson's partner, seemingly had a more tortuous road to entrepreneurial success than did Sevill. Orphaned at age 5, he was swiftly sent into the Lancashire woolen mills from which he escaped twenty-one years later, having saved enough to cover his transatlantic passage. Working as a laborer in Philadelphia (ca. 1847), he landed a textile mill position with W. L. Crook, a wool manufacturer for whom he had been digging a cellar. After seven years with Crook, Schofield bought land with the intention of becoming a farmer. He abandoning this prospect, however, when an uncle offered him a partnership in his wool-spinning business in the Spring Garden district. After three years, the 1857 Panic brought down the firm. Schofield's uncle died at the year's close, and after running the mill long enough to liquidate their debts, Benjamin shut it down in 1858. His partnership with Thomas Branson, a Nottingham-born hosier to whom he had sold yarns, brought spinner and knitter together just in time for the Civil War.[64]

Other firms whose formation was timed too late to be recorded in the 1860 census also played a role in war contracting and appear unannounced and huge in the 1870 schedules. Campbell and Pollock, who provided flannels to the Quartermaster, reported 164 workers on mixed goods and a plant valued at $150,000 in South Philadelphia. Near Spring Garden, Nichols, Whittle and Co. established a hosiery works worth $75,000, financed no doubt by the largess derived from their 1864 contract for 275,000 pairs of army stockings. Most impressive was the appearance of two firms in the burgeoning nineteenth Ward, upper Kensington. Maurice Raleigh and Co., a complex of mills at Sixth and Columbia that specialized in worsted goods and webbings (both cotton and wool), estimated production at over $1.6 million in the census year.[65] This accumulation appears to be based more on postwar demand (and the tariff) than on the two modest contracts Raleigh secured during the conflict. Raleigh's capitalization ($950,000) and work force (976) was surpassed by only one firm in Philadelphia, that of the shadowy Thomas Dolan.

Dolan was only 27 in 1861 when he left the Philadelphia knit-goods

---

[64] *M&MP*, pp. 368–9.
[65] 1870 MCS, Philadelphia Co., pp. 568, 658, 903.

Thomas Dolan, proprietor of a Frankford woolen firm, supporter of the textile school project, leader of the Philadelphia Textile Manufacturers Association, and ultimately the first president of the National Association of Manufacturers. (Free Library of Philadelphia)

commission house where he had learned the dry-goods trade to begin manufacturing "Germantown goods" on his own. Though his name does not appear on war contracts, Dolan built a prosperous business during the war, either by subcontracting through his old firm or in the regular channels of marketing. In 1866 he shifted from knits to worsted shawls, running up his own yarns in a spinning mill near the Delaware County line. In 1870 that facility reported 115 workers and an output of 600,000 pounds of worsted yarns, the whole of which was consumed by Dolan's weaving and knitting mills at Oxford and Hancock streets. There 1,250 workers dyed yarns and ran 650 looms and knitting frames, producing half a million shawls, opera hoods, and scarfs a year. The Raleigh and Dolan firms attest to the rapid rise of the worsted trades in the city, consequent on both the wartime demand for woolens and the special provisions of the postwar tariff extensions.

Dolan, like so many Philadelphia textile manufacturers, varied his output continuously. In 1872 he added the weaving of men's suiting worsteds and three years later fancy cassimeres and ladies' cloakings.[66] President of the Philadelphia Textile Manufacturers Association in the eighties, he became the first president of the National Association of Manufacturers at its forma-

---

[66] Ibid., p. 520; John Thomas Scharf and Thompson Westcott, *History of Philadelphia*, Philadelphia, 1884, pp. 2306–7.

tion in 1895, nominated as, among other things, "a staunch Republican and a straight-forward protectionist."[67] Little wonder. Dolan ultimately associated with the Widener group in promoting street-railway manipulations, and by 1900 he had abandoned textile manufacture for the green fields of high finance.[68] (Neither firm records nor personal papers have been preserved, and Robson was evidently refused an interview, for only one pathetic paragraph on the Dolan empire appeared in his 1875 compendium.) The remarkable element in Dolan's triumphant accumulation is its consistency with the Philadelphia pattern. With Lowell-scale mills, his flexibility and specialization are rooted in the local production strategies present for half a century; further, Dolan started as and remained a sole proprietor until his outside interests led him to accept several partners about 1880.

From these particulars, we cycle back to the aggregate. However substantial were the rising fortunes of individual firms, they were only fragments of a manufacturing totality that cannot be fully assessed by biographical means alone. Thus Tables 8.2 and 8.3 are offered to indicate the distribution of textile firms and workers by district and productive sector in 1870 Philadelphia (the format duplicates that of Tables 6.4 and 6.5 for easy comparison with the situation in 1850).

Kensington, prominent in the textile manufacture in 1850, had by 1870 more than doubled its complement of firms and increased its proportion of the total citywide work force from 32% to 40%. This does not, however, represent concentration in any simple sense. The mean firm size rose only from 32 to 38 workers, an increase that can be attributed in good measure to the emergence of the two giant mills just discussed. Rather, the pattern of development, evident already in 1860, was a gradual northward spread of small, new firms, which filled in the open reaches of the old Kensington District, now the Nineteenth Ward. Whereas the number of fabric firms had changed little in twenty years, the handloom cotton and mixed-goods component virtually collapsed in the cotton famine. In 1870, thirteen handshops continued their craft, employing 264 workers, while 90% of Kensington's fabric workers plodded off to steampowered mills. The expiring handloom fabric shops, however, never held as many Kensington workers at their peak as did their successors, the handloom carpet shops of 1870. More than 3,000 of the district's carpet workers were shop-centered, reversing the fabric proportions, with but 384 employed at three factories that had introduced the power loom.[69] The density of textile workers in Kensington's four

[67] Albert Steigerwalt, *The National Association of Manufacturers, 1895–1914*, Ann Arbor, Mich., 1964, pp. 31, 203.

[68] *Financiers of Philadelphia, 1900*, Philadelphia, 1900.

[69] These were the two Bromley family firms, John Bromley and Son and James Bromley and Brothers, along with James Doak.

Table 8.2. *Textile firms by district and sector, Philadelphia, 1870*

District	Cotton	Cotton-wool	Wool	Silk	Dyeing, finishing	Spinning	Hosiery, knit goods	Carpet	Other	Total
Kensington	6	26	3	0	23	18	20	172	6	274
Germantown	0	0	6	0	2	9	41	3	0	61
West Philadelphia	3	3	6	0	0	5	0	6	1	24
South Philadelphia	8	6	2	0	1	2	0	11	0	30
Manayunk	5	4	4	0	0	5	0	0	2	20
Spring Garden	0	12	10	3	8	4	3	16	3	59
Northeast Philadelphia	4	1	2	0	10	2	3	6	0	28
Northern Liberties	0	1	1	0	4	0	3	7	1	18
Old City	4	7	0	14	17	2	1	10	10	65
Total	30	60	34	17	65	47	72	231	23	579

Note: Districts are drawn to ward boundaries: Kensington, Wards 16, 17, 18, and 19; Germantown, Ward 22; West Philadelphia, Wards 24 and 27; South Philadelphia, Wards 1, 2, 3, 4, and 26; Manayunk, Ward 21; Spring Garden, Wards 15, 20, and 28; Northeast Philadelphia, Wards 23 and 25; Northern Liberties, Wards 11, 12, 13, and 14; Old City, Wards 5, 6, 7, 8, 9, and 10.
Source: Manuscript Manufacturing Census Schedules, Philadelphia County, 1870.

Table 8.3. *Textile workers by district and sector, Philadelphia, 1870*

					Sector					
District	Cotton	Cotton-wool	Wool	Silk	Dyeing, finishing	Spinning	Hosiery, knit goods	Carpet	Other	Total
Kensington	243	2,584	26	0	165	799	3,213	3,402	111	10,543
Germantown	0	0	395	0	7	113	1,450	386	0	2,351
West Philadelphia	302	299	214	0	0	195	0	15	4	1,029
South Philadelphia	294	631	154	0	1	65	0	34	0	1,179
Manayunk	1,810	418	718	0	0	308	0	0	31	3,285
Spring Garden	0	1,208	862	160	85	395	212	403	8	3,333
Northeast Philadelphia	429	110	279	0	333	295	230	21	0	1,697
Northern Liberties	0	9	10	0	11	0	20	59	11	120
Old City	558	472	0	1,116	58	123	2	393	127	2,849
Total	3,636	5,731	2,658	1,276	660	2,293	5,127	4,713	292	26,386

Note: Districts are drawn to ward boundaries: Kensington, Wards 16, 17, 18, and 19; Germantown, Ward 22; West Philadelphia, Wards 24 and 27; South Philadelphia, Wards 1, 2, 3, 4, and 26; Manayunk, Ward 21; Spring Garden, Wards 15, 20, and 28; Northeast Philadelphia, Wards 23 and 25; Northern Liberties, Wards 11, 12, 13, and 14; Old City, Wards 5, 6, 7, 8, 9, and 10.
Source: Manuscript Manufacturing Census Schedules, Philadelphia County, 1870.

small wards (2.6 square miles) was more than 4,000 per square mile, treble that of the second densest agglomeration, Old City.[70]

Germantown remained a wool center, doubling its overall textile population and its hosiery workers in two decades. However, the skyrocketing increase of Kensington's knitting mills eclipsed Germantown's early domination of the local manufacture. Other older phenomena persisted: Manayunk continued as a factory fabric district with neither a hosiery nor a carpet presence; Spring Garden, which included the largest group of dyehouse workers in outlying areas, still offered a wide variety of functional units; and the silk trade that developed during the fifties in Old City still clustered in the Sixth Ward. Although South Philadelphia's handloom fabric operations were replaced by mid-size factory firms, the size of the neighborhood textile work force changed little between 1850 and 1870.

Yet there were substantial alterations in the structure of the Philadelphia textile manufacture that the emergence of the few Kensington giants and the explosive rise of a handloom carpet sector only begin to tally. The cotton shortage brought grief to the calico printworks in the northeast and western

[70] Though such density data are of limited use, the figures for textile workers in 1860 are given here, against the total population density for each district. By these calculations, of the three most congested (and oldest) districts, Kensington housed the largest number of textile workers, though a slightly larger proportion of the Germantown total population worked in the trade. The Manayunk textile population concentrated in about a 2-square-mile area adjacent to the canal, was more clustered than these figures reveal. As suggested in Chapter 8, manufacture was far less differentiated at Manayunk than elsewhere, as one of four residents of all ages worked in mills.

Density of textile population, Philadelphia, 1870

	Square miles	Textile workers per square mile	Total population per square mile	Percentage of textile workers to total population
Kensington	2.6	4,055	43,150	9
Germantown	18.1	130	1,248	10
West Philadelphia	21.4	48	2,070	2
South Philadelphia	14.3	82	9,275	1
Manayunk	7.1	463	1,952	24
Spring Garden	8.1	411	13,785	3
Northeast Philadelphia	54.5	31	725	4
Northern Liberties	0.9	133	80,683	0
Old City	2.3	1,239	54,167	2
Total	129.3	205	5,212	4
Total population 1870: 674,022				

Source: Manuscript Manufacturing Census Schedules, 1870; John Thomas Scharf and Thompson Westcott, *History of Philadelphia*, Philadelphia, 1884, pp. 1752, 1762.

Table 8.4. *Textile firms and workers by sector, 1860 and 1870, and workers by sector, sex, and age, Philadelphia, 1870*

Sector	Firms 1860	Firms 1870	Workers 1860	Workers 1870	Workers, 1870 Male	Female	Youth[a]
Cotton	72	30	5,118	3,636	1,141	1,957	538
Cotton-wool	45	60	3,967	5,731	1,827	3,104	800
Wool	19	34	1,345	2,658	1,104	1,112	442
Silk	14	17	1,034	1,276	305	905	66
Dyeing, finishing	51	65	1,253	660	575	31	54
Spinning	28	47	728	2,293	991	709	593
Hosiery, knit goods	90	72	2,412	5,127	1,344	2,734	1,049
Carpet	123	231	2,382	4,713	3,463	918	332
Other	22	23	282	292	97	140	55
Total	464	579	18,521	26,386	10,847	11,610	3,929

[a]Females 16 or under; males 15 or under.
Source: Manuscript Manufacturing Census Schedules, Philadelphia County, 1860, 1870.

areas of the city. Those that survived cut back their functions to dyeing and finishing, appearing in the 1870 census as smaller firms across the board. Factory cotton producers generally shifted production to other lines or mixed goods. When raw cotton again became available, some manufacturers resumed their customary trade, as did General Robert Patterson, for example, who reopened the Ripka Mills at Manayunk. Others held to their new courses, the total employment on cottons by 1870 not recovering to even the level present in 1850 (3,636 vs. 4,207) and cotton manufacture declining as a proportion of total textile employment (1850, 34%; 1860, 28%; 1870, 14%). Tables 8.4 and 8.5 illustrate the shifts by sector and district between 1860 and 1870 in firms and workers and provide male, female, and child labor breakdowns. With these in hand, other elements of movement in the manufacturing structure will be exposed.

Whereas the Old City silk firms accumulated substantially during the sixties, their work force changed hardly at all. Investment in new machinery and plant appears in the manuscript schedules for many of these firms, though the retention of hand processes on fancy goods was common. The other two fabric sectors, mixed goods and wools, showed the effects of the war era directly. Many 1870 "Cotton-wool" firms had shifted sectors by changing production from all-cotton manufacture, although the total number of cotton and mixed-goods firms and the size of their work forces had changed little by 1870. Underneath this apparent stasis lay the replacement

Table 8.5. *Textile firms and workers by district, 1860 and 1870, and workers by district, sex, and age, Philadelphia, 1870*

District	Firms 1860	Firms 1870	Workers 1860	Workers 1870	Workers, 1870 Male	Workers, 1870 Female	Workers, 1870 Youth[a]
Kensington	202	274	5,106	10,543	4,868	4,194	1,481
Germantown	62	61	2,052	2,351	962	897	492
West Philadelphia	17	24	1,284	1,029	478	335	216
South Philadelphia	20	30	1,172	1,179	357	661	161
Manayunk	38	20	3,255	3,285	1,241	1,505	539
Spring Garden	30	59	1,165	3,333	1,067	1,786	480
Northeast Philadelphia	21	28	1,364	1,697	793	634	270
Northern Liberties	26	18	143	120	79	27	14
Old City	48	65	2,980	2,849	1,002	1,571	276
Total	464	579	18,521	26,386	10,847	11,610	3,929

[a]Females 16 or under; males 15 or under.
Source: Manuscript Manufacturing Census Schedules, Philadelphia County, 1860, 1870.

of handshops by new powered mills, as already noted. Wool, by contrast, doubled, with the two wool speciality sectors, hosiery and carpets, more than doubling. Though the power-loom weaving of wool fabrics was now reaching perfection, the skills involved in the variable production of quality wools and worsteds helped to keep the participation rates of male workers higher than in any other fabric sector.

The general increase in women's presence in the Philadelphia textile industry is, however, unmistakable. In 1850 the sexual breakdown was men, 58%, women, 42%. The blurring caused by the addition of the "Youth" classification in 1870 can be adjusted by using 1860 Manayunk as a proxy for apportioning these young workers (52% male, 48% female) or their numbers can simply be divided in half. The extent of the increase in the employment of women is still striking.[71] By 1870 the corner had turned; women now constituted about 51% of the pool, males about 49%, with the end of the bastion of male workshop labor in the cotton and mixed-goods sectors being the largest contribution to this situation. Male workers on cottons and mixed goods declined by a third (1,300) between 1850 and 1870, whereas

[71] There seems to be no reason to presume that the youth group was either overwhelmingly male or female. Even if one or the other sex constituted as much as two-thirds of the total work force, the percentage balances would shift only two points in either direction and thus in no way seriously alter the aggregate rise of women's proportion of textile labor.

the number of women workers rose by more than half (up 1,800). In no other sector was there a comparable shift in the proportions of male and female workers; women's share rose in silk and woolens, remained about steady in knit goods, and declined in dyeing (their inspection and packing jobs were eliminated by the closing of the printworks) and carpets (where male-dominated handshops opened by the score). The extension of wool spinning on jacks (similar to mules for cotton) in independent mills raised the number of adult male workers to five times the 1850 level but also drew forth the highest proportion of child laborers of all sectors (26%). Young workers formed about a fifth of the knit-goods work force, where looping and sewing tasks commanded their attention.

The rising proportion of women's textile employment should not however be presumed to indicate a necessary dilution of skill within the Philadelphia textile manufacture. As the city's textile firms began to reach for the quality end of the marketplace, the skills necessary for a number of customary women's jobs (e.g., inspection and repair) became crucial to an enterprise's profit strategy. With finer and more complex weaves and knitting patterns, an intimate knowledge of the details of production was necessary for most workers. If women were frequently excluded from male-dominated crafts (dyeing), many nonetheless developed skills that were central to flexible manufacturing.

The most portentous development, linked to the rising woolen manufacture, was the rapid development of dozens of independent spinners to provide woolen and worsted yarns for weavers, knitters, and carpet firms. Independent spinners were a pivotal segment of the overall productive matrix at Philadelphia, for they allowed the extension of the specialty linkage pattern previously encountered. Both handshops and powered weave sheds were able to function to advantage by saving capital, needing less space, and so on, insofar as the yarn mills met their needs for raw materials. The internal market for "producers' goods" in Philadelphia textiles matured in the sixties, the tandem growth of all the wool-using sectors calling forth and being facilitated by a correlate expansion of yarn manufacture. Between 1860 and 1870 the number of yarn mills nearly doubled and their workforce tripled, outstripping all other sectors of textile production in their rate of expansion. It should be stressed that these firms and workers do not include those spinners or mills attached to integrated operations (Dolan), some of which also marketed yarns in addition to their woven or knitted output. By 1870 the capital engaged in segregated yarn manufacturing neared $2.5 million, more than four times the 1860 figures for that sector.

The geographical distribution (Table 8.5) merits only a brief addendum. Half the city's male workers operated in Kensington, the great bulwark of handloom work, now penetrated by factory operations in knit goods and fabric weaving. Though Kensington doubled its textile work force in ten years, its achievement was, in a sense, bested by that of Spring Garden, where the number of textile workers had tripled since 1860. The spatial comparison rightly should be between Spring Garden and Manayunk, for powered factory production had long prevailed in both districts. The riverside confines of Manayunk allowed little expansion of the work force during the sixties, though capitalizations of the firms rose with the tide. Manayunk experienced genuine concentration, as a handful of large institutions, each with hundreds of workers, replaced a larger number of smaller mills and workshops. (Some of its antebellum small proprietors moved crosstown to Kensington, among them, George Noone's hosiery business.) By 1870 the "typical" Manayunk mill had several hundred workers, though none reached the scale of Dolan and Raleigh.

By contrast, Spring Garden grew through the replication of middling-sized firms in all sectors, firms that were larger than their 1860 counterparts but still showed a mean work force a third the size of the Manayunk cluster. Spring Garden, like Kensington, did not have the geographical constraints that bounded Manayunk, and thus the same spread pattern can be plotted there as obtained in the eastern district. Elsewhere in the city, the sixties did not witness significant enlargement in the textile work force. Of the other six districts in Table 8.4, two showed small gains, one was virtually static, and three reported small declines in their numbers of textile workers. The sectoral and spatial data merge with the larger war and tariff analysis when it is understood that those areas experiencing modest and significant growth were all connected already with the woolen trades or were newly invaded by woolen producers (the northeast).

The sectoral patterns of capital accumulation in Philadelphia textiles may be gauged through a review of census data for 1850, 1860, and 1870 (Table 8.6). Given the shift of some fifties cotton firms into mixed fabric production, the "Cotton" and "Cotton-wool" lines may be combined. Together, their 1870 reports show a tripling of capital invested in twenty years, the bulk of the increase coming in the war decade.

With peace restored, some cotton mills that had survived the famine by converting to mixed goods returned to the production of the cottonades and other specialties that had supported their accumulation in earlier decades and once again sought their old southern markets (Campbell and Company). General Patterson, having reactivated the Ripka factories, "loan[ed] freely to Southern planters on liberal credits"[72] once the war was ended. However, the consolidation of cotton manufacture into fewer larger facilities brought accumulation far less impressive than that realized in all sectors associated with woolen production. In carpets, knit goods, and woolen fabrics, the

---

[72] Mildred Goshow, ed., "Mills and Mill Owners of Manayunk in the 19th Century," typescript, p. 29, 1970, Roxborough Branch, Free Library of Philadelphia.

Table 8.6. *Textile capital by sector, Philadelphia, 1850–70*

Sector	1850 Capital (000)	N	1860 Capital (000)	N	1870 Capital (000)	N
Cotton	$1,747	63	$2,355	72	$4,331	30
Cotton-wool	925	52	1,797	45	4,488	60
Wool	448	14	684	19	1,811	34
Silk	211	6	767	14	1,105	17
Dyeing, finishing	723	32	1,182	51	846	65
Spinning	184	25	577	28	2,446	47
Hosiery, knit goods	171	51	767	90	3,577	72
Carpet	206	71	899	123	2,983	231
Other	41	12	105	22	532	23
Total	4,656	326	9,123	464	22,119	579

Source: Manuscript Manufacturing Census Schedules, Philadelphia County, 1850, 1860, 1870.

reported capitals rose to about triple their 1860 levels, spinning more than quadrupled, and the mixed-goods sector more than doubled. The great gains in silk during the fifties tailed off slightly, and the closing and cutback of printworks brought contraction in the dyeing and finishing group. Even the handful of miscellaneous Old City specialty firms, making webbing, tassels, tape, and fringes, showed growth rates well above those of the cotton firms.[73]

[73] Changes in the number of firms, work force, and capital by sector, 1860–70, drawn from figures in Tables 8.6 and 8.7, may be of interest in this regard. Capital figures were adjusted for both the Hoover Retail Index and Wholesale Textile Index to drain off inflation effects.

Changes in capital, work force size, and number of firms, selected sectors, 1860–70, in percent

	Capital (HRI)	Capital (WTI)	Work force	Firms
Cotton	+30	+45	−29	−59
Cotton-wool	+78	+98	+45	+33
Wool	+88	+108	+98	+79
Dyeing, finishing	−49	−44	−47	+27
Spinning	+200	+234	+215	+68
Hosiery, knit goods	+231	+267	+125	−20
Carpet	+135	+161	+98	+87

Table 8.7. *Adjusted manufacturing capital totals, Philadelphia, 1850–70*

	1850	1860	1870	% Change 1850–60	% Change 1860–70
Philadelphia textile capital (000)	$4,656	$9,123	$22,119	+96	+142
Hoover Retail Index (U.S.)	92[a]	100	141		
Adjusted for HRI	5,061	9,123	15,682	+80	+72
Wholesale Textile Index (Philadelphia)	89[b]	100	127		
Adjusted for WTI	5,261	9,123	17,407	+73	+91
Manufacturing capital other than textiles (000)	27,300	63,900	151,900	+130	+138
Adjusted for HRI	29,700	63,900	107,800	+115	+68

Note: The Wholesale Textile Index is an unweighted composite of annually averaged monthly prices for raw wool (full blood), cotton yarn (Nos. 14, 15, and 16), sheeting, and calico prints. Derived from locally gathered data, the wholesale base of the WTI is more directly relevant to manufacturers' affairs than is the retail series. "All Items" aggregate used here.

[a]1851.

[b]1852.

Source: Ethel D. Hoover, "Retail Prices after 1850," in *Trends in the American Economy in the Nineteenth Century,* vol. 24: *Studies in Income and Wealth* (Princeton, N.J., 1960), p. 142; Anne Bezanson, *Wholesale Prices in Philadelphia, 1852–1896* (Philadelphia, 1954), pp. 436, 475, 483, and 506.

If the capital figures present in the census manuscripts are adjusted to reflect price changes (Table 8.7), that part of the increase caused by inflation may be removed. When this is done, a third (on the wholesale scale) to a half of the war-era gain disappears. Yet when considered against the changes in capital involved in all other manufacturing at Philadelphia, the textile industry, which had lagged behind other trades in investment growth during the fifties, moderately exceeded the aggregate performance in the next decade. On the whole, even adjusted capital rose faster than either the number of firms or workers in both periods. Between 1850 and 1860, capital rose 73% (WTI), whereas the number of manufacturers was up by 42% and the work force increased by half (from 12,369 to 18,521). This disparity accelerated in the sixties. By 1870, adjusted capital had nearly doubled (WTI); the number of firms and workers increased 25% and 42%, respectively.

Although the burst of mill construction noted by Fite and in biographical sources was surely fueled by war-era profits, not all the capital shown in 1870 was the product of plowbacks. New capital was recruited for start-up funds and, at times, expansion, through an increasing number of partnerships. To be sure, once running, such firms relied largely on their own resources for further development. Nevertheless, the proportion of textile firms that had more than one "interested party" increased sharply between 1850 and 1870. Both the increasing scale of production and marketing and the practice of family succession in persistent firms contributed to this development. By the seventies, firms like Campbell and Company, with partners handling separate but complementary tasks in the accumulation project (production, sales, accounts, and finance), were not uncommon.

Table 8.8 stands as a final companion to the series in Chapter 6, in this case replicating the information from Table 6.6 on form of organization for 1870.

When compared with the 1850 profile, it is evident that the proportion of partnership firms has doubled, from 16.5% in 1850 to just over 32% by 1870. Moreover, the sole proprietorships are heavily concentrated in Kensington, the center of handloom carpet workshops, which rarely involved multiple partners. More than half the putative one-owner firms are sited in the Kensington wards, with fully two-thirds (142) of those being carpet firms. Outside Kensington, the proportion of partnerships among textile manufacturers averaged 39%, with the highest percentage at Spring Garden (46%), the district that early on supported steampowered mills and had ample room for their expansion, to which both profits and new partners contributed. (Two of the three "no family name" firms in West Philadelphia were pauper workshops operated by the city Almshouse and thus were neither proprietary nor partnerships.)

Thus by 1870 Philadelphia textile proprietors were continuing to develop a sophisticated strategic alternative to Lowell-style manufacture. Larger firms with greater marketing and production challenges added partners, exercised options to generate new lines of goods, built additions or entirely new mills, opened sales offices in New York, and so forth. Handloom operators took advantage of the boom in woolens to buy the buildings they had leased, add looms, and experiment with more complex and valuable products (Brussels, Venetians). Independent spinners prospered in their specialty, supplying both the hundreds of handshops and the growing numbers of powered weaving firms that could dispense with spinning their own yarns. It is in this sense that there was a "partial transformation" of the Philadelphia textile manufacture in the sixties. The external interventions of the war and tariff created conditions for accumulation to which the antebellum accumulation matrix was well suited. The flexibility and specialization that

Table 8.8. *Textile firms by district and form of organization, Philadelphia, 1870*

		Form of organization				
District	N	One name	Two partners	Three partners	"& Co." "& Bros."	No family name
Kensington	274	205	28	1	39	1
Germantown	61	41	9	2	9	0
West Philadelphia	24	12	0	0	9	3
South Philadelphia	30	21	6	0	3	0
Manayunk	20	12	4	0	4	0
Spring Garden	59	32	13	1	12	1
Northeast Philadelphia	28	16	3	0	9	0
Northern Liberties	18	14	3	0	1	0
Old City	65	39	12	1	12	1
Total	579	392	78	5	98	6

Source: Manuscript Manufacturing Census Schedules, Philadelphia County, 1870.

characterized its productive capacity, the skills of its workers, the personal supervision and direct approach to marketing that long had been common at Philadelphia, all were moments in the continuing process of industrial structuring, a process accelerated by the Civil War and its legislative aftermath. Yet within this tide of capitalist development, there surely were elements of undertow, contradictions, and founts for antagonism and conflict. Just as the reach of the railroad brought rural textile mills in the forties access to both outside marketing possibilities and an influx of competition for their local markets, so too the rapid expansion of the Philadelphia textile trades held a range of potentials for disaster. The struggles among local capitalists, between owners and workers, and between the Philadelphia mills and rival manufacturers elsewhere in the nation that crowd the next two decades were the offspring of success, unwanted children, perhaps, but fathered by the same set of events, decisions, and commitments that brought the Philadelphia textile manufacture to increasing prominence in the sixties. The closing portion of this study will be devoted to chronicling and assessing the "further adventures" of the accumulators whose pathways we have traced from the early years of the century. Before moving ahead to that task, however, a glance at Lowell in the sixties will serve to reinforce the distinctive character of the Philadelphia experience and help us anticipate the sorts of trials that lay ahead for both formats of capitalist manufacture.

The Lowell mills that were closed during the war suffered no lasting injuries, regardless of the harm they may have caused their workers and the city tradesmen who were dependent on supplying the operatives' daily needs. None of the corporations went bankrupt; indeed, several added spindlage shortly after resuming production in 1864–5. Those that experimented with manufacturing goods outside their traditional staples were stung with losses, however. Both the Suffolk and Tremont mills, having the same treasurer, embarked on the manufacture of woolen cassimeres during the war, a project that "aborted, leaving them depleted of their capital."[74] The Lawrence mill undertook to make hosiery, accumulating "a loss of half a million dollars." The Hamilton Company,

> when the war was drawing to a close, . . . threw out a large portion of their cotton machinery, and put in a lot with which to manufacture woolen goods, and purchased a large stock of fine wool, paying for this machinery and wool the ruinous prices which the War had entailed. Thus they superadded to their losses by the war, a new category of losses caused by the collapse of prices on the return of peace.[75]

Withdrawal from these ventures was gradual, and not total. Both Suffolk and Tremont ceased running cassimeres after 1866, and the Hamilton turned to the production of worsted yarns in that year. By 1870, Hamilton had stopped weaving delaines, cut its weekly consumption of wool from 10,000 to 6,000 pounds, and increased its cotton use from 50,000 to 70,000 pounds weekly. The Lawrence company continued to turn out hosiery, though the use of wool dropped from a modest 2,000 pounds weekly in 1866 to only 1,000 pounds by 1870. On the other hand, the Lowell Manufacturing Company, long experienced with handling wool in its carpet manufacture, virtually withdrew from the cotton trade. In 1860 the Lowell company had woven cotton osnaburgs and shirtings along with carpets, averaging 40,000 pounds of cotton weekly. In the late sixties the firm used only a tenth of this volume, replacing its earlier lines with woolen serges.[76] Having invested in facilities for woolen manufacture, several firms seem to have pursued profits in the woolen sector for a few years after the war before admitting defeat. The Lowell company was the only major corporation to shift decisively away from cotton goods, a move for which it was uniquely prepared, given its twenty years of powered-carpet experience.

The boom in woolens did generate other changes in the Lowell manufacturing landscape, however. The burst of new starts referred to in Chapter 2 involved wool manufacturing almost exclusively. Of the dozen or more smaller firms (reporting from 30 to 200 workers) not present in 1860, only one ran cottons, the incorporated Lowell Hosiery Company, according to

---

74 Charles Cowley, *Illustrated History of Lowell*, Boston, 1868, p. 54.
75 Ibid., pp. 51, 55.
76 *Statistics of Lowell Manufactures*, 1861, 1866–71.

the 1871 Lowell *Statistics of Manufactures*. Though half the new firms copied the format of the majors (being incorporated and listing agents in the Lowell *Statistics*), a number of the others seem to bear at least a surface resemblance to the form common at Philadelphia. James Dugdale specialized in making woolen braids, and John Walsh was an independent spinner of worsted yarns. Several firm names evoke the family and partnership format common in the metropolis (Livingston, Carter and Co., H. S. Hale and Son, L. W. Faulkner and Son).[77] Even at Lowell, a few proprietary firms began to lodge themselves during the sixties in the interstices of the manufacturing structure left vacant by the rigidities of the majors.

The great corporations at Lowell continued their expansion along proven lines into the 1870s. Spindlage rose by 50,000 in 1869 alone, topping half a million for the first time. By 1878 the "founding" corporations reported 745,000 spindles and had passed prewar levels of cotton consumption. They crushed the few embers of worker resistance with their unified and resolute action in the spinners' strikes. If the Lowell corporations could not adjust their production with ease and skill to changing circumstances, as the war experiences showed, they could at least do one thing well. They were experts at running mountains of staples and exercising control over the relations of production entailed by that formulation of the accumulation matrix. Having survived the strains of the sixties, the Lowell treasurers must have looked with no small satisfaction at the tumult that bubbled in the seventies and exploded in the eighties at Philadelphia, where textile labor and textile capitalists fought an extended battle whose combatants and context were radically different from those in the Lowell conflicts.

[77] Ibid., 1871.

9

Flexibility and specialization: Philadelphia as the "paradise of the skilled workman," 1870–1885

Mr. Kingsbury stated that he had visited Philadelphia, with great distrust, as he was aware that the manufacturers of Pennsylvania, as a class, had, so far, manifested but little interest in our association. There were peculiarities in the system of manufacture in Philadelphia which make it difficult to reach the manufacturers, and especially to obtain statistics of their mills. There are many establishments which simply card and spin, while the work is carried to another factory to be completed.

"Proceedings," *Bulletin of the National Association of Wool Manufacturers, 1869*

Mr. Kingsbury's train ride south from Boston in 1869 was a necessary if unpleasant venture. It was necessary because the Philadelphia woolen manufacture had become the largest concentration of active firms in the nation, a group whose presence in the National Association of Wool Manufacturers was crucial to the association's viability. But it was also unpleasant, because both the men and their system seemed "peculiar" to their New England colleagues, who were accustomed to the integrated and corporate production format. Kingsbury noticed immediately the structural contrast, the functional linkages among separate firms. For him the bale-to-package mill was natural, and deviations from it, curious. More important perhaps, for one used to the published accounts and reports of Massachusetts corporations and to a way of industrial life conditioned by these public measuring tools, was the close-to-the-chest style of Philadelphia operators. Such privacy was the privilege of proprietary manufacture, a fact noted by others and one that made it, for Kingsbury, "difficult . . . to obtain statistics of their mills."[1]

---

[1] In later surveys of the NAWM and the Pennsylvania Bureau of Industrial Statistics, most Philadelphia textile men simply refused to return the forms with the requested information. However, the confidentality of the Industrial Census, much trumpeted by Lorin Blodget, did produce wide compliance, aided no doubt by the personal visits of census

If Kingsbury was uncomfortable with these odd fellows, his pitch nevertheless brought a gratifying response. From his solicitation journey to Philadelphia, he reaped fifty-two new members for the NAWM, forty-four in the city and eight from nearby towns. Not only did the Philadelphia contingent represent half the year's increase in membership, the list of names read like a chronicle of the city's Civil War contractors. George Bullock and Charles Spencer had been involved with the founding Boston aggregation, but Kingsbury also brought in Elias Birchall, George Fling, Schofield and Branson, the Dobsons, Sevill Schofield, and a host of others.[2] They were valuable recruits, having already developed a sense of the importance of the federal government to their prosperity, for defense of the protectionist tariff was the association's first priority. When the advance of protection was joined with a second commitment toward "the perfecting of our manufactures," upgrading quality and reliability, the argument for enrollment was clinched.

Although many of the class of 1869 may have remained members of the association during the seventies, few of the Philadelphia men were active participants in its tariff propagandizing and banquet-table speechifying. Archibald Campbell and Martin Landenberger served as the first two vice-presidents of the NAWM, 1869–71,[3] yet some stagnation of concern on the

marshals and reminders of the legal obligation to respond. For Kingsbury's full remarks see *Bulletin of the National Association of Wool Manufacturers* 1 (1869): 186; cited hereafter as *Bulletin, NAWM*.

[2] *Bulletin, NAWM* 1 (1869): 187–8. Forty of these manufacturers were located in the 1870 Manufacturing Census Schedules, Philadelphia County, cited hereafter as MCS. The following breakdowns for 1870 are derived from work sheets, 1870 MCS, Philadelphia Co.

Sector		District		Capital		Workers	
Wool	9	Germantown	16	$30,000 or less	15	50 or fewer	15
Cotton, mixed goods	6	Manayunk	8	30,000 to 99,000	7	51–100	8
Spinning	12	West Philadelphia	2	100,000 or more	18	101–250	14
Hosiery, knit goods	10	Northeast	1	Total	40	251 or more	3
Carpet	3	Kensington	7			Total	40
Total	40	Spring Garden	2				
		South Philadelphia	2				
		Old City	2				
		Total	40				

[3] *Bulletin, NAWM* 1 (1869): i, 306. In addition, John Dobson and George Evans were named "Directors" for the state of Pennsylvania, and Benjamin Bullock and S. J. Solms served on NAWM committees. Campbell was not active after the first year and died in 1874.

View of the city looking southeast from the Spring Garden district, circa 1875, where Star Braid's mill was situated. (Free Library of Philadelphia)

part of the Quaker City manufacturers is indicated by their complete absence from the top offices until Thomas Dolan was chosen to be one of five vice-presidents in 1879 at sessions hosted in Philadelphia by the local Textile Manufacturers Association, which Dolan headed.[4]

[4] *Bulletin, NAWM* 9 (1879): 273–6.

Philadelphia's creation of an industrywide but local association is particularly intriguing, as it suggests an awareness on the part of the city's textile capitalists that they were indeed a different breed. To some degree at least, the structure of textile production in Philadelphia made lateral cooperation within the region a matter of considerable moment and of tangibly more interest than activism within a national organization that was defined along sectoral lines and dominated by integrated mills whose problems and interests differed markedly from theirs. The banquet at which they hosted the rest of the industry proved to be both a symbolic and a practical turning point, confirming the breadth and power the Philadelphia manufacture had developed and opening an era in which its proprietors played a constant and provocative role in the affairs of the association and by extension in those of the entire industry and the nation.

John Hayes, the association's secretary and editor of its quarterly *Bulletin*, in celebrating the rekindling of relations with Philadelphia, observed that "there has been no recent event in the . . . wool industry more interesting and important" than the November 1879 meetings in the Quaker City. The banquet invitation served to prepare the way for the reentry of the Philadelphia hosts by acknowledging the latter's growing stature. "The officers of the Association . . . have selected Philadelphia, the most important wool-manufacturing city in this country, as the most suitable place" for their annual gathering. They urged the presence of both NAWM members and "all others engaged in wool manufacturing who can conveniently attend."[5]

Of course, those most "conveniently" located for attendance were the scores of Philadelphia operators whose seduction into the association was the core design. More than 150 woolen manufacturers and merchants from the city were present at the meeting, supplemented by 40 or so others from nearby Pennsylvania and South Jersey mills, their participation solicited by an organizing committee composed in part of manufacturers Thomas Dolan, James Dobson, and Theodore Search and merchants W. C. Houston and W. H. Coates. The setting was magnificent, including floral displays in which rosebuds, carnations, and the like were formed into representations of a bobbin and a spinning wheel.[6]

More impressive yet were the tributes awarded by the Bostonians to the ways of doing business common at Philadelphia, a format that earlier (and among historians later) had been regarded as "peculiar." Reviewing the general development of the industry since the Civil War, Hayes observed that, along with improvements in manufacturing, firms had become more commercially independent, moving away from commission houses toward direct selling. He also noted:

5 Ibid., pp. 273–4.
6 Ibid., p. 293.

> Another important change in the system of manufacture is a greater
> specialization in our industry of distinct branches of the same general
> manufacture, such as wool-scouring, spinning, weaving, finishing, as
> separate branches of industry, – a system insuring greater perfection of
> work, and permitting the embarking in manufacture of workmen with
> moderate capital and whose success is nowhere in this country so well
> illustrated as in Philadelphia.[7]

For his part, Dolan gently apologized for the inactivity of Philadelphia
manufacturers in the association's projects, from the success of which they
so clearly had benefited: "Now for years, New England has been called
upon, when necessity required, to do all or nearly all the work for the support
of this Association, and I cannot see, . . . what right we have to ask New
England to do our fighting in this conflict."[8] Yet the most telling comments
were those offered by James Dobson, proprietor by 1879 of "the largest
individual woolen enterprise in this country," the mills at Falls of Schuylkill.
Though historically inaccurate in their retrospective detail and rhetorically
excessive to the edge of discomfort, Dobson's remarks capture a sense of
personal triumph that was all the richer for having overwhelmed generations
of disregard and contemptuous "distrust" emanating from the New England
grandees. If the immigrant Philadelphia millmen had not brought the
Yankees to their knees, they *had* at least brought them to their tables, to
suffer through Dobson's gruff boasting. He began bluntly:

> It is fitting that the annual meeting of the National Association of Wool
> Manufacturers should have been held here today. We are exceedingly
> glad, as merchants and manufacturers, to tender to them the right hand
> of fellowship, while we, as Philadelphia manufacturers and wool-mer-
> chants, have great cause to rejoice over the material progress made in
> the leading branch of the industry of this great city. For I can well
> remember, sir, when Philadelphia-made goods had an unenviable repu-
> tation. The articles made were [considered] something cheap and com-
> mon. There was no branch, Mr. Chairman, unless it was the knit goods
> of Germantown, . . . which Philadelphia could be proud of. Hence it is
> pleasant for me to note the progress made during the last decade.
>
> Why sir, there is scarcely a known branch of textile manufacture that
> is not in full operation in this city. . . . We here to-night represent
> industry centered in this city of nearly sixty millions of dollars; giving
> employment to tens of thousands of workpeople, and I am happy to say
> that I know of neither a spindle nor a loom that is now standing for want
> of work.[9]

7 Ibid., p. 281.
8 Ibid., p. 294–5.
9 Ibid., pp. 313–4.

And so on, until Dobson "sat down, amidst great applause," doubtless principally from his fellow Philadelphians.

The city's textile manufacturers may have lacked restraint and polish, but they were possessed of a format for the successful prosecution of textile manufacture, elements of which others might now undertake to copy. The explosive growth of the Philadelphia trade in the seventies, a decade plagued by panic and depression, worked a delicate counterpoint to the overall nervous state of the rest of the textile industry, in which staple overproduction had flattened profit margins and threatened wide ruin. If the Philadelphia textile manufacture had "come of age," the remarks of northern capitalists make it clear that it had done so without approximating to the Lowell model. Quite the contrary, its success was due in large part to the extent to which as a totality it had departed from that format, though, to be sure, the Philadelphia trajectory was not without its own contradictions, limits, and dilemmas, as we have suggested. The closing sections of this study will outline the context and dimensions of the rapid extension of the textile industry at Philadelphia, 1870–85, and will assess the crescendo of labor struggles that attended that process. The cultural bases for strike rituals, the associational activity of workers and manufacturers and the latter's effort to found an institute for technical education in textiles will be reviewed as we probe for elements of continuity and change linking the Philadelphia format of the eighties back to the antebellum trades and forward into the current century.

Structure and strategy

> The manufacturers of our city have suffered much less during the past year [1876] than those of New England, and . . . there has been a very great amount of employment, though wages and profits are both low. Some branches of textile manufactures have been exceptionally busy; others have increased their machinery, and in those which are depressed – such as the carpet manufacture – there has been a great advance in the production of fine qualities, which is of good omen for the future.[10]

To gauge the extent to which the textile industry of Philadelphia blossomed in the 1870s, no better source exists than the *Census of Manufactures of Philadelphia (1882)*, an officially sponsored city survey (police officers were used as census marshals) directed by the indefatigable Lorin Blodget.[11]

---

[10] *Penn Monthly* 8 (March 1877): 176.

[11] The study was triggered by the preliminary figures of the 1880 federal census, which showed a preposterous error, in a net decline in Philadelphia industry, 1870–80. Though the Census Bureau juggled its figures and released an upward revision, the city

Tables consistent in form with those drawn earlier from the 1850 and 1870 Manufacturing Census Schedules will serve to illustrate the aggregate development and its spatial, sectoral, and work-force distributions. Links with the 1880 Population Census manuscripts will ultimately add background data on the ethnicity and households of manufacturers once we have examined the production and marketing characteristics that worked to the advantage of the city textile trades in the wake of the Civil War.

In 1883 the *Census of Manufactures of Philadelphia* offered the public a special chapter focused on the textile firms active in the city, containing both a full listing of firms, products, locations, and work force at each and an introductory attack on the inadequacies of the 1880 federal treatment of the city's fabric, carpet, and hosiery trades. Tables 9.1 and 9.2 are derived from these printed lists, as the original schedules have not been preserved.[12] In twelve years, the number of reported firms had increased by two-thirds, the total work force more than doubling from 26,600 to nearly 58,000. The distribution of these gains may be seen from an examination of the tables and a comparison with their 1870 counterparts (Tables 8.2 and 8.3).

Both long-term continuities and substantial changes from the situation evident in 1850 to 1870 are readily apparent. Kensington remained the largest textile district in the region, but its leading sectors of 1870, carpets and knits, were now joined by a substantial factory-based woolen production, the most sizable component of which was Dolan's Keystone works. The number of carpet firms rose minimally, but the work force doubled, the result of the demand-fueled addition of handlooms in the workshop firms and the installation of power weaving and some spinning facilities in the steampowered mills (Bromley, J. Kitchenman).[13] Persistence for carpet shops, 1870–82, was far higher than for their cotton-goods predecessors, 1850–60, as 59 of 113 carpet firms operating in the Nineteenth Ward in 1870 were still in business a dozen years later. Fifty of them employed more workers at the later date, with both steampowered and hand-powered mills showing striking increases.[14] Nonetheless, the proportion of the total Ken-

---

was determined to redo the entire survey at its own expense and set Blodget to the task. For historians, this has proved especially fortuitous, as part of the 1880 Philadelphia federal schedules have since been lost, making the city census the only full survey of local manufacturing in the eighties.

12 When the 1870 Manufacturing Census of Philadelphia was attacked as inadequate as well, a set of supplementary schedules was generated. As the supervisor of this supplementary effort, Lorin Blodget's signature tops every page. This thoroughness makes comparison with the 1882 survey less vulnerable, as both were handled by the city's resident industrial statistician.

13 Lorin Blodget, *The Textile Industries of Philadelphia*, Philadelphia, 1880, pp. 5, 21.

14 Calculated from 1870 MCS, Philadelphia County, Ward 19, and Lorin Blodget, *Census of Manufactures of Philadelphia (1882)*, Philadelphia, 1883, pp. 159–63.

Table 9.1. *Textile firms by district and sector, Philadelphia, 1882*

District	Sector									
	Cotton	Cotton-wool	Wool	Silk	Dyeing, finishing	Spinning	Hosiery, knit goods	Carpet	Other	Total
Kensington	11	13	25	21	44	27	59	192	18	410
Germantown	1	1	1	1	3	21	55	15	3	101
West Philadelphia	3	5	4	4	2	5	0	3	0	26
South Philadelphia	10	7	3	1	0	3	4	10	5	43
Manayunk	4	4	11	0	5	18	0	0	0	42
Spring Garden	6	7	2	3	5	8	9	16	2	58
Northeast Philadelphia	14	3	0	5	23	11	14	55	4	129
Northern Liberties	0	0	1	5	3	0	7	13	0	29
Old City	1	1	2	24	10	3	19	12	0	72
Total	50	41	49	64	95 (144)[a]	96	167	316 (330)[a]	32	910 (973)[a]

[a]Includes 49 small dyeing and finishing firms (134 workers) and 14 small carpet firms (31 workers) for which locations could not be established.

Source: Lorin Blodget, *Census of Manufactures of Philadelphia (1882)* (Philadelphia, 1883), pp. 159–78.

Table 9.2. *Textile workers by district and sector, Philadelphia, 1882*

District	Cotton	Cotton-wool	Wool	Silk	Dyeing, finishing	Spinning	Hosiery, knit goods	Carpet	Other	Total
Kensington	669	1,768	4,463	1,329	1,074	999	6,101	7,044	512	23,959
Germantown	70	25	110	13	66	553	3,088	436	77	4,438
West Philadelphia	359	844	407	162	138	252	0	12	0	2,174
South Philadelphia	567	1,007	1,052	73	0	549	36	65	0	3,349
Manayunk	1,359	743	2,195	0	86	517	0	0	11	4,911
Spring Garden	398	1,719	53	975	192	1,095	635	2,092	190	7,349
Northeast Philadelphia	883	473	0	162	931	258	1,036	835	108	4,686
Northern Liberties	0	0	105	420	33	0	155	24	0	737
Old City	365	228	115	2,531	109	898	1,580	186	0	6,012
Total	4,670	6,807	8,500	5,665	2,629 (2,763)a	5,121	12,631	10,694 (10,725)a	898	57,615 (57,780)a

aIncludes 134 workers from small dyeing and finishing firms (49) and 31 workers from small carpet firms (14) for which locations could not be established.

Source: Lorin Blodget, *Census of Manufactures of Philadelphia (1882)* (Philadelphia, 1883), pp. 159–78.

sington work force on carpets and knits had declined (from 63% to 55%) with the introduction of steampowered fabric mills, now that the last generation of handloom cotton masters and workers had passed from the scene. The recovery of dyeing and the introduction of silk manufacture are also worth noting, as Kensington by 1882 showed a significant number of firms in all nine textile sectors.

Germantown remained devoted to the knitted goods for which it had become famous, both doubling the work force in that sector and increasing the knit-goods proportion of the total textile mill population (from 62% to 70%). If differentiation was gradually taking place at Kensington, specialization was becoming yet more deeply rooted in Germantown. Likewise, Manayunk's cloth factories stood solidly entrenched, joined by neither knit or carpet firms nor by any of the rapidly rising elements of the silk manufacture. There was a sharp increase in the numbers of independent spinners at Manayunk, who chiefly ran carpet yarns for the Kensington trade, perched in small mills on the hillsides and sometimes sharing mill floors powered by steam engines. With the mills no longer dependent on waterpower, Manayunk experienced its last bit of crowding. In the sixties, the number of Manayunk textile firms had declined, as war prosperity had led proprietors such as Schofield to expel tenants and expand their own capacity to the limits of their structures. By the seventies, new mills for rental had been erected and small proprietors flourished once again, as the presence of eighteen independent spinners in 1882 indicates. South Philadelphia too continued to hold its character as a locus of the traditional fabric manufacture, its growth quite substantial after 1870, although undisturbed by any significant plantings of silk, hosiery, or carpet ventures.

Comprehension of these long-term continuities must condition our understanding of what "growth" means. It does not represent a simple action of the market or of technological innovation upon a passive social landscape that is thereby reshaped. Instead, there are complex and reciprocal interactions between moments and initiatives for expansion and the environment – physical, political, ethnic, and more broadly cultural – which pushes back in some cases (resistance) or, like stony ground, simply denies nourishment to the seedlings of "progress," disappointing those foolish enough to have failed to assess the total terrain before planting. In a sense, the strength of the handloom tradition at Kensington is most visible not in the strikes and violence of the thirties and forties but in the fact that capitalists favoring steampower had largely to wait until that generation had passed, laid low by the cotton famine, before they could build themselves into the neighborhood productive system in the 1870s. Few Philadelphia manufacturers were in a position to emulate the Belgian Scheppers brothers, who brought their ma-

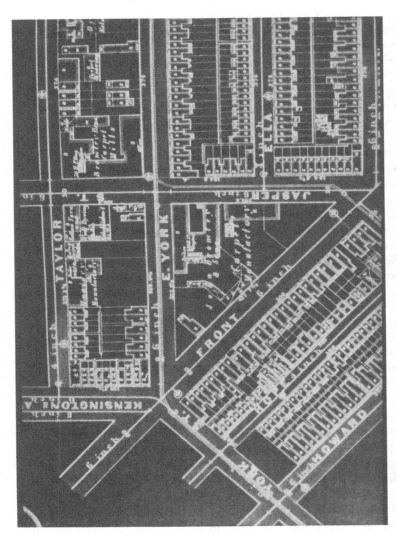

Kensington, the neighborhood of John Bromley's carpetworks, circa 1875. Note the nearby Bromley Brothers firm and the small handwork shops tucked along side streets and in backyards. (Philadelphia Social History Project)

chinery and workers with them to the city.[15] Most had instead to set up operations where the workers with appropriate skills already were, where there was open space for building, and so on, that is, through a process that took into account the cultural and environmental constraints on accumulation, the non-economic elements in economic decision making. By entering the stream of these historical continuities, shrewd capitalists might hope to divert a part of it to their own advantage, whether at Kensington, Germantown, or Manayunk.

Spring Garden continued its pattern of widely diversified firms, its several large worsted spinning plants using fine combing wools to fuel the newest wrinkle in the city's textile array, the production of worsted "dress goods" for both men's and women's apparel. Theodore Search, a partner in one of them, would become active in the NAWM throughout the eighties, arguing consistently for positive actions to upgrade quality rather than an excessive and negative focus on the tariff as a means of limiting competition. His commitment to the role of skill in manufacture led him to found the Philadelphia Textile School in 1884, and his effective advocacy of manufacturers' interests made him a knowledgeable successor to Thomas Dolan as the second president of the National Association of Manufacturers in the nineties. One anomaly does appear in the Spring Garden returns; whereas 862 workers and ten firms had worked woolens in 1870, only two small operations with 53 employees were recorded in the 1882 tally. The explanation comes in classic Philadelphia fashion. Although one large firm had closed (by 1880 its mill was partly occupied by a successor engaged on other goods), two of the other 1870 Spring Garden wool firms had altered their output, thereby leaving the woolen fabric column. One, S. B. & M. Fleischer, had moved heavily into worsted spinning, and the other, Kaufman, Lipper (Keystone Braid), had transferred its manufacture from woolen to silk trimmings.[16] This pattern of lateral productive mobility was widespread, a point that we will reinforce shortly.

The upsurge in silk operations was most visible in Old City's northeast quarter (Sixth Ward) where a constellation of smaller firms arrayed themselves, in a classic agglomeration pattern, around the three local giants, Hensel, Colladay, and Co., Kauffman, Strouse, and the pioneering W. H. Horstmann and Sons, who had been active since the century's second decade. In the seventies, a specialty silk district had emerged in the Sixth Ward, gradually spilling over into the adjacent Northern Liberties, where for the

---

15 *Bulletin, NAWM* 1 (1869): 186–7, 290–1.
16 Blodget, *Textile Industries*, p. 60; Blodget, *Industrial Census*, p. 172. Kaufman, Lipper seems to have dissolved into two firms, M. W. Lipper and Kaufman, Strouse, and moved into Ward 6. The remaining five firms likely failed, as their total 1870 capital was but $44,000; together they employed only 91 workers.

first time in a generation there was increased textile activity. More than half the city's silk workers were engaged in this confined area, spinning tram and organzine and running braids and upholstery trim for a cluster of interrelated firms and supported by specialty silk dyers and yarn printers.[17] Of equal interest were a set of knitting outwork firms located in several neighboring shops on Market Street. Though stockings were by this time largely knitted on circular heads and Balmorals, to which power had delicately been applied, the finest fancy knits were still produced by hand. The Market Street firms were both brand new and quite traditional. The combined work force of four of them totaled more than 1,000 workers,[18] though it is likely that few of them resided nearby. The goods themselves were delivered (or gathered in by travelers to Kensington and Germantown) for storage and sale to the main street shops, which were ideal for marketing the fancies to jobbers. Consequently, the sharp rise in Old City textile employment should be tempered by an awareness that the silk component was real, the knit goods, illusory. The preservation of classic outwork relations of production in combination with a central-district marketing site had just that quality of strategic opportunism that has so often surfaced in this extended review of the Philadelphia format for capitalist accumulation.

The sudden appearance of hosts of hosiery and carpet firms in the northeast indicates the continued northward surge of the Kensington complex. By the eighties, the Nineteenth Ward (which had been split down the middle to form the Thirty-first Ward) was "built"; housing, workshops, and mills next sprouted in the lower northeast (Frankford, the Twenty-fifth Ward). All but five of the sixty-nine hosiery and carpet firms in the northeast occupied sites in the Twenty-fifth Ward, as did the bulk of the spinners and dyers. The older cotton firms (Whitaker, Hartel) were situated in the country but were steammills now at their original waterpower sites. Thus, as with the Northern Liberties developments, spillover from burgeoning adjacent districts accounts for a portion of the area's "growth." In a larger sense, this phenomenon begins to indicate that the districts themselves, both as analytical units and as productively discrete locales, were gradually melding into the metropolitan complex. Though the cultural base for neighborhood identification (and antagonism) has persisted to this day, the material functions that once were inseparable from that neighborhood consciousness had begun to blur, at least in textiles, by the eighties.

To emphasize the rising importance of both wool-related production and the specialized services of independent spinners over the long term, Table 9.3 shows the proportions of the city textile work force engaged in each of

17 Blodget, *Census of Manufactures*, pp. 172–3.
18 Ibid., pp. 38, 164.

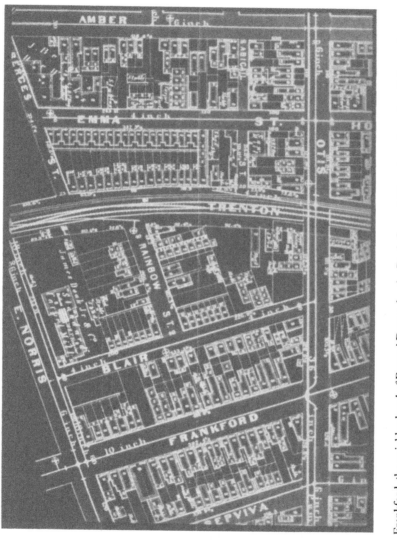

Frankford, the neighborhood of Berges' Dyeworks, the Doak Carpet Mill, and a variety of small shops, circa 1875. (Philadelphia Social History Project)

Table 9.3. *Textile work force by sector, Philadelphia, 1850–82 (in percentage)*

| Sector | Work force | | | |
	1850	1860	1870	1882
Traditional fabrics				
Cotton	34.0	27.6	13.7	8.1
Cotton-wool	26.8	21.4	21.7	11.8
Wool	4.0	7.3	10.1	14.7
Subtotal	64.8	56.3	45.5	34.6
Specialty products				
Silk	1.8	5.6	4.8	9.8
Hosiery, knit goods	9.8	13.0	19.4	21.9
Carpet	10.3	12.9	17.9	18.5
Subtotal	21.9	31.5	42.1	50.2
Service functions				
Dyeing, finishing	9.0	6.8	2.5	4.8
Spinning	2.9	3.9	8.7	8.9
Other	1.3	1.5	1.1	1.6
Subtotal	13.2	12.2	12.3	15.3
Total	99.9	100.0	99.9	100.1
Total workers	12,369	18,521	26,386	57,780

Source: Manuscript Manufacturing Census Schedules, Philadelphia County, 1850, 1860, 1870; Lorin Blodget, *Census of Manufactures of Philadelphia (1882)* (Philadelphia, 1883).

the nine sectors for the four census years, 1850–82. To dramatize the acceleration of specialized production, three sets of subtotals are also offered, for the traditional fabric sectors (cotton, mixed goods, and woolens), the specialty products (silks, largely trimmings; hosiery and knit goods, and carpets), and service functions (dyeing, spinning, and other – wool pulling, cotton laps, and so forth).

Overall, the relative decline of standard fabric forms and the upswing of the more specialized sectors is quite evident, though these figures conceal the wide variations in fabric output that the wool and cotton mills featured. Within the traditional sectors, woolen manufacture steadily increased its proportion of both the sectoral and the total work force. After a very modest absolute increase in the sixties, the silk manufacture reached major proportions in the seventies, the numbers employed increasing nearly fivefold between 1870 and 1882. Independent spinners had multiplied in the war decade, likely encouraged to set up their modest operations by the huge yarn demand that accompanied the boom in woolens. In absolute terms, the number of spinning firms and workers shot up impressively in the seventies as well, appropriately at a rate nearly identical with the overall growth rate of the industry in the city. The long slide in dyeworks fractions represents the absence of new printworks in the fifties and the failure or shrinkage of most of them during the cotton famine. With industrywide demand for their services in the 1870s, however, independent dyers set up shop at a rapid pace, the 2,763 workers active in 1882 being more than four times the 1870 total and double that reported for 1860.

In a context of rising demand from a national market, the steady upward trend of hosiery and carpet operations was fueled, in the one case, by the adaptation of hand frames to power, with output soaring under the protection of the tariff, and, in the other, by a swelling migration of English handloom carpet makers, particularly in the period 1862–70.[19] In 1880 more than 4,000 handlooms were each turning out an average of 130 yards of carpet per week in Philadelphia, with yet another thousand power looms located in several dozen factories.

> The most rapid growth was in 1873 to 1880, at the time most disastrous to business generally; the hosiery interest then growing up to take the place of the previous heavy importations from Germany and England; and the carpet manufacture even more decisively filling the local market to the exclusion of importations, and supplying the large new demand from the interior and the west.[20]

"At the time most disastrous to business generally" – what was true for the knit and carpet sectors singled out here was equally the case for the silk, dyeing, woolen, and spinning sectors.

It remains to state and respond to the key question: What elements of the structure of its manufacture and of the strategies of its proprietors fitted the Philadelphia textile industry to achieve such "decisive" expansion while others looked uneasily at the tariff to protect them from the twin perils of depression and competitive overproduction? By this time, much of the answer will be fairly obvious, for in a way, this entire study has worked to prepare the answer to that question and to stimulate a host of others that flow from it.

In stressing both historical continuity and the importance of the proprietary form of organization as elements in the seventies' surge, Blodget's description of the wool-using sectors could be applied to silk, cotton, and dyeworks as well.

---

[19] Ibid., p. 156.
[20] Lorin Blodget, "The Woolen Industry of Philadelphia," *Bulletin, NAWM* 10 (1880): 31; Blodget, *Textile Industries*, pp. vi, vii.

> The woollen industries of Philadelphia are remarkable for the direct-
> ness of their derivation from English original types, and for their fixed
> relation to the occupations and interests of large numbers of people.
> They could not be removed [to other locations] or discontinued, and,
> though the introduction of improvements is easy, the leading charac-
> teristics do not change. They have generally been prosperous, and with-
> out any aid from corporate organizations have in some instances devel-
> oped proportions second to none in magnitude and in continued
> success. They have suffered less in periods of business depression than
> other industries, due perhaps to the fact that proprietors own their
> establishments, and have acquired land, buildings, and machinery as
> they were able to pay for them from the profits of their business during a
> period often of many years.[21]

Firms in full possession of their facilities need not make decisions to run full
or shut down based on a set of debt and overhead calculations that haunt
others, mounted on elaborate structures of credit and dividend outlay. If
buildings are erected for cash, rather than through borrowing, if stocks are
purchased as needed, rather than a year in advance (with more loan activity),
if sales are handled directly from the office, rather than through agents who
take from 7% to 15% of the profits, the financial health of firms will be
conserved. In times of financial panic, the obligations of such firms will be
modest, while their cash reserves will allow them to snap up bargains (Bullock, 1837; William Hogg, Jr., 1857).[22] There are certainly different definitions as to what constitutes "conservative" financial management, but the
"cash"-style of Philadelphia firms and their steady profit-plowback were
both the children of necessity (remembering their distance from elite financial circles) and the keys to product aggressiveness, the decisive taking of
risks with varied outputs stemming from a base that was secured in proprietary ownership and family control.

What other segments of the Philadelphia textile system came to bear
crucially on the viability of the industry in the trough of the seventies?
Consider first the manifold aspects of productive flexibility. First, it was a
consistent feature of the fabric mills to possess looms capable of running
cotton, wool, or mixed goods. "Almost every mill and every weaver or knitter
works cotton and wool both, and changes from one to the other with the
season."[23] This capacity was directly, and in a cost-saving manner, linked

---

21 Blodget, "Woolen Industry," p. 33.
22 Daniel Robson, *Manufactories and Manufacturers of Pennsylvania of the Nineteenth Century*,
Philadelphia, 1875, p. 39, cited hereafter as *M&MP*; J. L. Bishop, *History of American
Manufactures from 1608 to 1860*, Philadelphia, 1866, vol. 2, p. 561. On commission
charges, see R. A. Robinson, "Questions of the Day for Woolen Manufacturers,"
Bulletin, NAWM 3 (1872): 353–65.
23 Blodget, "Woolen Industry," p. 17.

with marketing. Mills ran a wide variety of samples of the goods they were capable of making for the upcoming season, circulated them to their regular customers, and booked the orders in advance of production, insofar as was possible.

> Woolen and mixed fabrics characteristic of Philadelphia . . . are very rarely made up in stocks, depending on an entire season to be disposed of. The habit from the beginning has been to deal with orders chiefly, and while this practice has not favored founding large establishments, it has kept the manufacturers in position to turn their production frequently and to profit by a brisk demand without much risk of loss.[24]

Blodget's discussion of the totality of the changeovers is so striking as to merit full citation.

> These patterns [samples] are run upon worsted and cotton, or upon all cotton at will in the same looms, and large mills which have usually made cotton goods are now [Winter, 1879–80] in some cases changing to all-wool goods, while others are making the reverse change; conspicuous instances of both might be cited. The present or winter season shows cotton fabrics generally leading; and checks, ginghams, shirtings, drills, cottonades, and osnaburgs, all cotton are occupying the machinery. Large quantities . . . of cotton and worsted dress goods are made at this season, the same mills in the summer running on goods of mixed wool or worsted, and on all-wool goods.[25]

In all, Blodget counted "about fifty mills" holding 7,500 looms run on such a flexible pattern at Philadelphia.

There are two additional elements that buttressed this accumulation strategy. First, these mills did not tie up their working capital in warehoused finished goods or in raw cotton and wool. Instead, they stocked yarns, which could be rapidly dyed and run up and which could be readily supplemented by supplies from the scores of independent spinners who, as a generation before, prospered in tandem with the mill-based weaving firms. Second, this set of arrangements for production allowed for extremely rapid response to either orders or perceived demands for a particular fabric, a time function that may have been as critical as price in competitive markets. For woven fabrics, as well as carpets and knit goods, the manufacturer needed "not more than thirty days . . . from the purchase of yarns to the delivery of finished goods on his orders, which may be for cash if he chooses."[26]

The last phrase is significant, for the rapidity with which Philadelphia manufacturers could adjust their production gave them power to demand

[24] Ibid., p. 18.
[25] Ibid., p. 19.
[26] Ibid., p. 18.

cash for their goods, an enormous advantage over granting the three- to six-month credit that was usual for sellers of textile products, a source of cash-flow problems that brought grumbling comment in the NAWM *Bulletin* from time to time. Of course, a mill's steady and favored customers were offered credit as a favor; but the decision lay with the manufacturer and was not governed by the customs of the staple trade (whose bulk products were substitutable in the market) or the whims and charges of commission agents.

If flexibility was an enduring hallmark of the Philadelphia textile manufacturer, the gradual spread of high quality production was a more recent development. Dobson's touchiness about the "reputation" of Philadelphia goods was largely based, I suspect, on the experience of the Civil War years. Though it dates to earlier times, the still-common reference to inferior products as "shoddy goods" links directly to the widespread war time use of reprocessed rags to spin woolen yarns that looked good but wore badly. More generally, the practices of false labeling (Philadelphia fabrics were on occasion sold as "imported") and skimping on the requirements of federal contracts were well known. Early handloom ingrains and rag carpets from Philadelphia were fairly plain goods as well. Yet antebellum Philadelphia already had sectors of high quality production: Germantown hosiery and knits, which Dobson acknowledged, handloom damasks and silk and worsted trimmings (Horstmann), which he did not. What took place in the decade after the war was the elevation of fine work in the fabric and carpet sectors to the standards already current among knit and silk manufacturers. For fabric mills, the emergence of scores of independent spinners was a blessing, as these firms began the manufacture of finely drawn and finished yarns, particularly worsteds, which were the basis for the coatings and dress goods of which Dobson was so proud. Not only did the spinners bear the capital expense for combs and frames; their location in the same neighborhood as the mills allowed manufacturers who possessed spinning equipment to contract with nearby spinners for standard yarns while using their own facilities for experimental counts and mixtures.

In carpets, innovation toward upgrading the quality of output came not from the introduction of the power loom but from the attachment of an eighteenth-century device, the Jacquard mechanism, to the handlooms. "About 4,000 hand-looms are still employed on carpets, shawls and wool fancy articles. The Jacquard attachment is used with most of these, and particularly with the hand-looms on carpets. This change is recent, or rather the extent to which the ingrains are so modified from the earlier plain patterns."[27] Power looms were brought into production on some ingrains and on new types of carpets, particularly Brussels and Wiltons; but through

---

[27] Ibid., p. 26.

Venetian carpet handlooms with Jacquard attachments (top) in James Pollock's weave room. (J. R. Kendrick, "The Carpet Industry of Philadelphia," Seventeenth Report [1889], Pennsylvania Bureau of Industrial Statistics, p. D-10.)

the eighties, firms venturing into the manufacture of Smyrna and Turkish rugs purchased handlooms for these novel and skill-intensive items.[28] The technical requirements for powered machinery that could handle complex weaves or fine yarns and have the flexibility to vary their outputs across a broad range were considerably different from the requirements for machinery whose task was the ever-faster running of staples (the Draper loom). It is thus plausible that there were multiple trajectories in textile machinery building that have yet to be explored.

The functional "dis-integration" of the Philadelphia trades was a third element in their rapid expansion in the seventies, structurally related to both the mills' flexible capacity and the progress toward finer goods. The demand for yarns by small shops that had not the capital to spin their own helped trigger the deployment of dozens of separate spinning plants in the sixties and seventies, along with their companion dyeworks. The skills of these master spinners could be directed toward the manufacture of a variety of yarns, enhancing the capacity of weaving mills to vary their product lines and, in time, to run fine and fancy fabrics. By the eighties there was considerable differentiation among spinners, given the enormous yarn usage in the

---

[28] J. R. Kendrick, "The Carpet Industry of Philadelphia," *Seventeenth Report (1889)*, Pennsylvania Bureau of Industrial Statistics, Harrisburg, Pa., 1890, pp. D-43–4.

hundreds of diverse weaving operations in the city. About one-third of the yarns consumed, the worsteds and blends and the finer counts, were drawn from Philadelphia spinners. Regional spinning mills in suburban counties were kept busy supplying part of the coarse carpet and somewhat finer hosiery yarn market, while "immense quantities of cotton yarns" were secured from North Carolina, Georgia, and New Jersey, chiefly for mixed fabrics and carpets.[29] That early southern mills commenced their operations quite often with coarse yarn spinning has been widely appreciated; that the Philadelphia trades exercised a demand-pull that contributed to their viability is less well recognized.

By the late seventies, local wool spinners' flexible productive capacities contributed to the upgrading of quality in both fabrics and knitwear. Several weaving firms specialized in top-of-the-line worsteds. Their yarns came from a set of city worsted spinning plants that did "no weaving," ten of which held 119 combs and 65,000 spindles.[30] Yet other mills ran a range of "full and soft" yarns for fancy knitting, loosely known as "zephyrs," which were used in shawls, scarfs, hoods, and opera cloths.

The relations between spinners and fabric firms, predicated on a system of flexible cloth output, were arranged through batch contracting. Neither running yarns for stock nor the taking of contracts "of any magnitude" was common, "because of the frequent changes in the character of the demand."[31] Dyeing too was varied, "according to the styles at the moment required." Thus the millmen were able to draw on the machinery of other manufacturers in a fashion that extended their capacity to innovate and allowed them to use their capital directly in altering or adding to their weaving apparatus.

Manufacturers understood the special advantages this structure offered. Some years later Clarence Whitman explained why it was "impracticable" for firms with varied cloth output to engage in spinning. Weaving mills that sought to spin "a large variety of yarns, must, inevitably, either in equipment or cost of product, and probably in both, fall behind the mills which specialize on similar yarns."[32] With standardized outputs, economies of scale favored integrated manufacturing; but in flexible production the advantage lay with linked separate specialists, that dis-integration of function so evident at Philadelphia. Thus the skills of each sector of the city's textile industry interlocked, each contributing to the success of all.

---

[29] Blodget, "Woolen Industries," p. 18.

[30] Ibid., p. 20.

[31] Ibid., p. 30.

[32] Clarence Whitman, "The Field for Textile Graduates in the General Textile Industry," *Fourth Annual Report (1905)*, Alumni Association of the Philadelphia Textile School, Philadelphia, 1905, pp. 21–2, Philadelphia College of Textiles and Science.

The fourth and often overlooked element in the special set of factors present at Philadelphia was its work force, particularly the thousands of skilled adult male immigrants who had for generations succeeded one another in the textile districts and, in not a few cases, as proprietary occupants of factory or workshop space. It need hardly be stressed that the skill requirements of every phase of this manufacuring format were qualitatively higher than those needed in the mass production of staple goods. There were still thousands of loom-tending and bobbin-changing jobs in the city's mills, and women and children were largely assigned to them. But the simple fact remains that in 1882 Philadelphia over 20,000 adult men worked in the textile trades, more than double the number reported in 1870. Small wonder that in writing of the carpet trades, John Hayes penned a line that could apply across the spectrum, dubbing Philadelphia "the paradise of the skilled workman."[33] The textile factories of the city were perhaps a paradise insofar as they challenged skilled workers to use their talents to the maximum. In other respects, however, conflict was rising along with the tides of success, a phenomenon with which we shall contend shortly.

If all these factors were not enough to set the mill counting rooms humming at Philadelphia, there was finally a parallel manufacturing and marketing development in the postwar era that formed a part of the larger economic context, the rise of the ready-made clothing manufacture and the department stores and wholesale clothing houses that distributed finished apparel. There had long been a custom-tailoring trade in the city, but the massive manufacture of ill-fitting clothes must be laid to the accounts of the Schuylkill Arsenal during the Civil War. There mountains of woolens collected from contractors were fashioned into coats, trousers, and other articles by a force of in- and outworkers that reportedly topped 8,000 at its peak.[34] Individually, Strawbridge and Clothier, dry-goods merchants, and John Wanamaker opened department stores, a central feature of which was clothing made in bulk rather than to order.[35] Higher quality goods, particularly men's suitings, were worked up by firms such as Jacob Reed's Sons. Similar clothing enterprises and department store outlets appeared in New York (Macy's) and Chicago (Marshall Field) in the same period. Philadelphia firms attempted to reach the New York markets by opening offices there or by engaging commission agents to act for them. At home, direct

[33] John Hayes, ed., *Awards and Claims of Exhibitors at the International Exhibition, 1876,* Boston, 1877, p. 371.

[34] Interview with Jerry Coates, National Archives, Washington, D.C., January 21, 1981. Mr. Coates, a most knowledgeable student of contracting practices, is researching the operations of the Quartermaster Corps during the Civil War.

[35] Alfred Chandler, *The Visible Hand: The Managerial Revolution in American Business,* Cambridge, Mass., 1977, p. 226.

contacts were available, for by 1882 nearly 17,000 workers were employed by seventy-nine clothiers in the Sixth Ward (Old City) alone, many of course on outwork.[36] Changes in fashion were the lifeblood of the Philadelphia trades, and their success in responding to clothiers' orders was a constant factor through the century's later decades.[37] John Wanamaker was the largest of the Philadelphia clothing manufacturers in 1882, reporting 2,485 workers in three city locations. His woolens supplier was Thomas Dolan, and upon that relationship Dolan's fortune was confirmed.[38] (Dolan also placed his fabrics with Strawbridge and Clothier.) To complete the advantages, the wholesale and department store clothing network in Philadelphia further extended the conservative financial solidity of the fabric makers, for the cloth purchases clothiers made were paid for promptly in cash.[39]

With all this in mind, the comments of a New England spokesman for the wool interest, writing in 1872, sharpen the contrast between Philadelphia's skilled specialization and Lowell-style (or more properly with wool, Lawrence-style) bulk staple manufacture. Commenting on the failure of prices to rise despite increases in the cost of raw materials and a great warehouse fire in Boston that destroyed tons of backstocked fabrics, R. A. Robinson argued that "the only way to bring goods to a remunerative figure is for the woolen mills, generally, . . . to produce a less quantity." If only a few mills cut production, others "drive the harder," negating the effect of diminished output. Moreover, glutted markets had "exploded" the standard tactic "of driving machinery as hard as possible, in order to produce the greatest quantity of goods and keep the prices up."[40] Bewailing the overproduction generated by the strategies of big mills, Robinson appealed for unified cutbacks. In Philadelphia, however, where variety in output was the norm, manufacturers would have asked a simple question: "Why not make something different?" But the northern staple mills had few such options, for every element in their system of production conspired against precisely that flexibility and specialization without which no escape from the wars of bulk competition could be managed. They had neither the machinery nor the skilled work force to hop from wools to cottons with the shifts of fashion, nor

---

36 Blodget, *Census of Manufactures*, pp. 188–9.
37 It did, however, produce a nagging aggravation, with clothiers' canceling contracts for fabrics because of changes in market conditions. This was more common with commission agent sales than with direct marketing; see R. T. Francis, "Marketing Textiles," *First Annual Report (1902)*, Alumni Association of the Philadelphia Textile School, Philadelphia, 1902, pp. 44–52.
38 Blodget, *Census of Manufactures* pp. 188–90; Dennis Clark, "Philadelphia, 1876: Celebration and Illusion," in D. Clark, ed., *Philadelphia: 1777–2076*, Port Washington, N.Y., 1975, p. 52.
39 Chandler, *Visible Hand*, p. 227.
40 R. A. Robinson, "Question," *Bulletin, NAWM* 3 (1872): 362–3.

did their managers have the personal decision-making power inherent in proprietary ownership that allowed decisive action with regard to markets and risks. The operations of New England companies were governed by vast networks of credit, overhead, and indebtedness, whereas Philadelphia firms, geared to cash and custom trade, could run profitably at two-thirds capacity, unburdened by overloads of interest, dividend demands, and commission house charges. "Driving machinery" for "the greatest quantity" aptly summarizes the big-mill strategy,[41] a format for textile manufacture that promised ruin. Thus, in the end, it was "fitting" that the New England textile men trekked south to meet their Philadelphia colleagues in 1879 and endure Dobson's strutting. Like it or not, they had a good deal still to learn.

Immigrant proprietors: the textile manufacturers of 1880

The war having come to an end, the people turned eagerly to commercial pursuits. Its contracts had resulted in the establishment of large private fortunes, many of them corruptly gained. Families which had counted for nothing in the community before this time were elevated to wealth through hay, mules, gun barrels and army uniforms.[42]

Squinting down his nose at Philadelphia's postwar capitalists, Ellis Oberholtzer barely concealed his disgust for the unseemly manner in which fortunes were amassed in the sixties and seventies. Textile manufacturers, like most other industrial figures, "counted for nothing" among the city's elite either before or after the war, the prosperous heights reached by a few industrialists affording little more than a view of the clubs and social circles through which their betters circulated. This cultural situation differed little from that half a century earlier, and, as we shall see, the composition of the textile manufacturing class was little altered as well over that span. As in 1820 and 1850, few gentlemen investors were "interested" in the textile trades; as before, Philadelphia's textile men were principally immigrants and their offspring, operating in a sphere distanced from the Philadelphia Club, with whose patrons they had little in common.[43] Many had traveled a path

---

[41] Omitting to mention, of course, the "driving" of those workers who had to handle that machinery.

[42] Ellis Oberholtzer, *Philadelphia: A History of the City and Its People*, Philadelphia, 1912, vol. II, p. 388.

[43] Only two of the city's textile manufacturers, Search and Dolan, were profiled in Oberholtzer's four-volume study. Both native-born, they were likely included as a consequence of their presidencies of the National Association of Manufacturers. Only Dolan figured in E. Digby Baltzell's later study of city patricians, *Philadelphia Gentlemen: The Making of a National Upper Class* (New York, 1958).

from child labor to skilled work, and thence to proprietorship, a mahogany desk, and a home on Mount Vernon Street. By 1880 most millmen had advanced only partway along that road, and still others, small dyers and handloom shopmen, remained attentive only to the process of getting a living.

In the following pages the ethnic background of Philadelphia's textile manufacturers circa 1880 will be profiled and their trade experience emphasized. Their associational activity will be briefly reviewed, along with evidence for some continuity in the patterns of neighborhood factory paternalism. Finally, a closer look will be taken at the political activism in which some were engaged, nationally in defense of the wool tariff and locally in municipal reform efforts.

The ethnic dimension of textile capitalism at Philadelphia will be approached from two directions, a citywide survey of middling and large firms and an in-depth pursuit of smaller operators in that district where they were most concentrated, Kensington. The first effort will address as an aggregate those firms with fifty or more workers, enterprises that by 1882 accounted for four-fifths of textile employment in the city. The second approach will isolate a fraction of the 650 smaller firms for which locations could be ascribed,[44] allowing a comparison in Kensington across time and adding depth to the first analysis. Tables 9.4 and 9.5 represent the results of an effort to link the larger firms given in the 1882 city industrial census with the 1880 Population Census Schedules. Because many wool, cotton, and mixed-goods producers varied their "fabrics" production widely by this date, the three sectors are grouped together as in Table 9.4.

As no linkage effort is effectively random, these distributions must be cautiously viewed. For example, the very large incidence of English manufacturers may partly be due to the unusual success in matching Germantown workplaces and residences (18 of 19 possibles). Nevertheless, the enduring British dominance of the Germantown knit trades can be clearly seen, the power of the migratory magnet and the practice of family successions continuing. Overall, the 163 firms linked employed 34,462 workers, or 60% of those active in the city in 1882. Within those firms having more than fifty workers (249), the linked firms represented 65% of the enterprises but 73% of the workers so employed, suggesting that the owners of smaller firms were more likely to have been missed. Consequently, the existence of any significant suburban (Main Line) resident cluster of native-born elite textile manufacturers seems doubtful. The two-year gap in gathering the data sources also allows missed links, resulting from in-migrating new starts, and 1882 manufacturers who were not present in the city for the 1880 population survey (probably firms at the smaller end of the range).

[44] Sixty-three small firms could not be geographically placed; see Table 8.8.

Table 9.4. *Ethnicity of linked textile manufacturers in mills of 50 or more workers by sector, Philadelphia, 1882*

Ethnicity of manufacturers	Sector						Total all sectors	%
	Fabrics[a]	Silk	Carpet	Hosiery, knit goods	Dyeing, finishing	Spinning		
English-born	12	3	8	35	6	12	76	27
English-stock	5	0	2	15	3	2	27	10
Irish-born	26	0	20	1	3	0	50	18
Irish-stock	11	0	7	3	0	0	21	7
Scots-born	3	1	2	2	1	0	9	3
Scots-stock	2	0	1	0	0	0	3	1
German-born	4	8	1	5	2	3	23	8
German-stock	2	3	0	5	0	2	12	4
American-stock	22	10	5	13	2	11	63	22
Total manufacturers	87	25	46	79	17	30	284	100
Total firms	89	24	42	63	10	21	249	
Firms linked	52	12	30	44	9	16	163	65

[a]Cotton, wool, and mixed goods.

Source: Lorin Blodget, *Census of Manufactures of Philadelphia (1882)* (Philadelphia, 1833); Philadelphia Social History Project, Manufacturing Households File, 1880 Population Census, Philadelphia County.

Table 9.5. *Ethnicity of linked textile manufacturers in mills of 50 or more workers by district, Philadelphia, 1882*

District	Ethnicity					Total manufacturers	Firms linked	Total firms
	English-stock	Irish-stock	Scots-stock	German-stock	American-stock[a]			
Kensington[b]	34	40	5	13	27	119	70	112
Ward 16–18	6	14	0	10	8	38		
Ward 19	5	17	2	2	17	43		
Ward 31	23	9	3	1	2	38		
Germantown	30	1	2	0	1	34	18	19
West Philadelphia	3	2	1	0	4	10	7	12
South Philadelphia	0	8	0	2	7	17	9	19
Manayunk	6	4	0	1	0	11	9	17
Spring Garden	9	12	3	2	8	34	16	21
Northeast Philadelphia	18	2	0	3	4	27	18	22
Northern Liberties	1	0	0	0	2	3	2	5
Old City	2	2	1	14	10	29	14	22
Total	103	71	12	35	63	284	163	249

Note: The foreign-stock category includes foreign-born.

[a] Of American parents.

[b] Wards 16–18 comprise most of 1850 Kensington. Ward 19 of 1870 was split down the middle by 1882, with the eastern half designated Ward 31 and the western half retaining the Ward 19 label.

Source: Lorin Blodget, *Census of Manufactures of Philadelphia (1882)* (Philadelphia, 1883); Philadelphia Social History Project, Manufacturing Households File, 1880 Population Census, Philadelphia County.

These caveats having been offered, the continuing preponderance of immigrant capitalists and their children in the Philadelphia textile manufacture remains striking. Only 22% of the linked millmen had American parentage, whereas 56% were foreign-born and the rest (22%) came from immigrant families. The characteristics of the participation of millmen who were native-born of native parents (NBNP) may be refined through a closer look at the firms in which they functioned. Of the thirty-nine linked firms with NBNP proprietors or partners, only twenty-four were run exclusively by "Americans"; the other fifteen firms were partnerships that included immigrants and one or more of the NBNP group, who were likely brought in for either their capital or their marketing and financial skills. If Thomas Dolan was at all typical in his route, the entry of NBNP men into Philadelphia textiles was more often preceded by training in commission houses or the wholesale trades than by the mill-experience progression common among immigrants.[45] This "management" rather than shop-floor track was followed by a few immigrant proprietors, though Charles Spencer was reared in the hosiery trade and Benjamin Bullock was a wool worker before becoming a merchant and (after 1837) manufacturer.

In 1880, as in 1850, capitalists from particular ethnic groups clustered in sectors and neighborhoods. Three-fifths of the linked carpet manufacturers were Irish; half the spinners and dyers and fifty of the seventy-nine knit-goods operators were English. Germans were most visible in the newly rising silk trades concentrated in Old City. At Kensington, there was a refinement, with English knitters bunched in the eastern part of the old Nineteenth Ward (the Thirty-first in 1882) and Irish carpet firms a large presence in the western half and the three southern wards that constituted Kensington District in 1850. English immigrants formed the largest proportion of linked manufacturers in Northeast Philadelphia, indicating both the spread of knit-goods firms from Kensington into Frankford's Twenty-fifth Ward and the preservation of older and scattered dyeworks, several of which had been mentioned in the 1832 *McLane Report* (Ripka/Hartel, Horrocks). NBNP operators were noticeable in silk and spinning, which showed quite rapid growth in the seventies, and least important in the dyeing and handloom-centered carpet sectors, which demanded considerable craft skill.

Other customary elements of the Philadelphia format had endured. The partnership and proprietary form of ownership was still dominant, as Blodget

---

[45] For Dolan, see Ellis Oberholtzer, *Philadelphia: A History of the City and Its People*, Philadelphia, 1912, vol. III, pp. 18–23; John Thomas Scharf and Thompson Westcott, *History of Philadelphia*, Philadelphia, 1884, p. 2306. The Midnight Yarn Co. was similarly founded by a veteran of the "retail hosiery business" (*M&MP*, pp. 50–1), and NBNP partners listed in the 1880 Population Census as "Merchant" were members of Edward Heald and Co. (cottons), T. J. Mustin and Co. (hosiery), and the Horstmann silk firm.

noted in his review of the wool-related industry. A few firms had embraced the forms of incorporation by the eighties (e.g., Archibald Campbell's heirs), but the separable functions of production, marketing, and accounts were embodied in persons, family members and partners, not congealed into bureaucratic structures. As might be expected in larger enterprises, nearly two-thirds (105) of the linked firms were partnerships in 1882, the remainder (58) sole proprietorships. The family base for partnerships was still standard; 54 firms showed partners with the same surname, and 13 others had two or more like-named partners and additional outside members.

As ever, the children of immigrant manufacturers were learning the business in the shops. In hosiery, the two teen-aged sons of John Blood worked in his Kensington mill, as did Joseph Boulter's four sons, whose ages ranged from 24 to 14 in 1880.[46] Older sons who had not yet been made partners but who had graduated from the mill to the office were described as "clerks" or "salesmen" on the census schedules.[47] Though working daughters of manufacturers were rarely if ever brought into partnerships, on occasion they remained in the mills in a position of some authority. A case in point was Annie Fling, 27, who worked as a "forewoman" in her father's Germantown hosiery operation in 1880 and lived at home with her parents and three younger brothers, none of whom were then associated with the firm.[48] More routine was the engagement of William Leech's daughters, aged 20, 19, and 15, to work in his Manayunk cotton factory,[49] presumably until such time as they could be properly wed. All these mill operators were immigrants whose assumptions about what was the reasonable course for the next generation are dimly visible through these and similar "placements." Sons should be schooled, but not too much, for mill apprenticeship was the best experience for succession. For daughters, generally, marriage was the alternative to indefinite service in the parental household. That outside handloom shop-culture manufacturer's daughters remained on occasion candidates for mill-work indicates the distance between those families and those of more stereo-typed industrialists, whose daughters' "marriage chances" were to be improved by learning French and taking lessons in walking and piano. The fate of the firm and that of the family were inextricably linked within a capitalist family economy that had deep roots in the Philadelphia textile trades.[50]

---

46 "1880 Manufacturing Households," printout, Philadelphia Social History Project, 1979, pp. 44–1; hereafter PSHP, *1880 MH*.

47 For examples see Ibid., pp. 423, 430, 434.

48 Ibid., p. 449.

49 Ibid., p. 340.

50 As with Malley Schofield in the fifties, manufacturers' widows also appear as firm partners or proprietors in the eighties; of the four women in the linked group, three were in partnership with sons and one, Sarah Yewdall, was independent. Additional detail as to their roles in manufacturing are regrettably lacking.

The antebellum practice of workers' boarding in manufacturers' homes had not vanished by the eighties. Its incidence in smaller firms will be examined shortly when the focus narrows to Kensington's wards. Yet it is not a little surprising to find a number of proprietors of mid-size firms housing workers with their families. Thomas Flavell's household included a father and son pair of stocking weavers, but their presence is accounted for when the Relationship-to-Head-of-Household column is scanned. Enoch Holland was Flavell's stepfather and his son was the hosiery manufacturer's stepbrother by way of his deceased mother's earlier remarriage. Other groups of boarding workers are not kinship-connected. John Priestly, an Englishman, had both hand and power looms in his carpet mills on Susquehanna Avenue. In his Kensington home, four blocks from the factory, he sheltered four young weavers: two Englishmen, a Scot, and a lad from Connecticut.[51] Another carpet operator, Irish-born Daniel Jackson, boarded ten Irish weavers half a square away, his household totaling seventeen residents. Four other linked manufacturers each had one boarder. None of the six millmen employed more than 125 workers.[52] However, nonkin coresident with a proprietary textile family were far more likely to be servants, as more than half the 284 households were beneficiaries of live-in help, the number of which was covariant with the size of the mill work force.

The modest capitals with which many Philadelphia textile firms began their operations made the availability of rental factory space a critical feature of the Philadelphia format. Manayunk millowners had leased quarters to fledgling manufacturers before the Civil War (Hagner, Schofield), and similar arrangements were made in Spring Garden and South Philadelphia. Amid the accentuated specialization of function that developed during the sixties and seventies, one city textile partner emerged as a specialist in the erection of mills for tenants' use. William Arrott was the "financial partner" of a mill veteran, James Doak, Jr., in a carpet firm that converted to worsted manufacture between 1876 and 1880. Arrott had followed "various occupations" for eight years after his arrival in Philadelphia (1851), settling in an insurance business, which he purchased at the close of the war. The following year, after Doak had been employed briefly as a clerk by Arrott, the two entrepreneurs, both Orangemen, joined forces. The demand for "floors" led scores of new textile millmen to lease any available space in the factory districts, regardless of condition. When such buildings subsequently burned down with regularity, drawing sharp comment in the NAWM *Bulletin*,[53] the need for specialized new construction was obvious. Arrott, attuned to the

---

[51] PSHP, *1880 MH*, p. 418–22, 426–7, 449.

[52] Two of the millmen operated spinning establishments, one produced hosiery, and the fourth manufactured silk trimming. Three were English and one was German; their boarders included a weaver, a spinner, and two operatives.

[53] *M&MP*, pp. 82–3; *Bulletin*, NAWM (1869): 205–6.

situation from his insurance activities, had five fireproof mills constructed between roughly 1875 and 1885, which were leased to tenants duly recorded on the regular Hexamer-Locker Insurance Surveys. Arrott, both a shrewd businessman and an "interested" manufacturer, was thus able to offer prospective occupants rooms with power and insurance at reasonable rates in buildings erected with their accumulation opportunities and risks in mind.[54]

Through a second effort to link the manufacturers of the Nineteenth Ward with the 1880 Population Census, we may gain a closer look at Kensington's most concentrated textile area and at the households and ethnicity of smaller manufacturers. Some of them were Arrott's tenants and others were proprietors of handshops, which held their own elements of continuity with the patterns of an earlier time.

The 1882 *Census of Manufactures of Philadelphia* listed ninety-two textile manufacturers in the Nineteenth Ward with fewer than fifty employees. Of these, forty were carpet firms, fourteen knitworks, and the rest scattered among the other sectors. Scanning the 1880 Population Census Schedules produced forty-one links (46%). Missed links fell largely among the smallest firms, as only thirteen of thirty-seven operations with fewer than fifteen workers could be found in the 1880 manuscripts, whereas more than half the mid-size firms (15–49 workers) were linked.[55] The distribution of links by ethnicity and sector is given in Table 9.6. Though the limitations of such a partial linkage success are evident, the almost complete absence of NBNP entrepreneurs among the smallest manufacturers is both striking and consistent with the Kensington pattern of 1850. It is surely plausible that a small group of such proprietors did operate in the district, residing elsewhere, as did most of the NBNP owners of larger Kensington firms. Yet this surmise would only reinforce the district's continuing character as an immigrant neighborhood whose factory and street culture had a distinctly "foreign" tone. Moreover, most Americans who joined or started textile firms had either factory-based experience or commercial backgrounds that led them in the case of larger firms (Table 9.3) preponderantly toward fabric, silk, or

---

54 Arrott's mills are depicted on the following Hexamer-Locker engravings: 1034, 1353, 1362, 1454–5, 1632, 1844, 1886, 1889, 2056, 2272–3, 2720, 2744 (missing from set at the Free Library of Philadelphia). These plates cover the period 1875–93, with several views of some of the structures over time, showing the succession of tenants.

55 This relatively low rate of linkage is due, in part, to the two-year gap between the two sources. Small new starts would not have been present in the 1880 survey. Perhaps more important is the artificial boundary that cut Ward 19 in half to form two divisions in the seventies, which created a smaller Ward 19 and the new Ward 31. Manufacturers residing south and east of the line could not be linked. The shops and mills of about forty textile manufacturers living in Ward 19 (1880) were located elsewhere in Kensington.

Table 9.6. *Ethnicity of linked textile manufacturers in mills of 50 or fewer workers by sector, Philadelphia, Ward 19, 1880*

Ethnicity of manufacturers	Sector						
	Fabrics[a]	Silk	Carpet	Hosiery, knit goods	Dyeing, finishing	Spinning	Total all sectors
English	1	2	1	3	3	0	10
Irish	0	0	18	0	1	1	20
Irish-stock	1	0	7	0	0	0	8
Scots	0	0	1	0	0	0	1
German	3	0	8	0	1	0	12
American	0	0	0	0	0	1	1
Total manufacturers	5	2	35	3	5	2	52
Total firms	13	7	40	14	11	7	92
Firms linked	5	1	27	3	3	2	41

[a]Cotton, wool, and mixed goods.

Source: Lorin Blodget, *Census of Manufactures of Philadelphia (1882)* (Philadelphia, 1883), pp. 159–78; Manuscript Population Census Schedules, Philadelphia County, Ward 19, 1880.

spinning operations rather than the craftshop-based carpet, knit, or dyeing trades, where more than two-thirds of the Nineteenth Ward's smallest firms were situated.

Several other interesting inferences may be tentatively offered on the basis of the links achieved. The most successful sector for linkages was the carpet manufacture (twenty-seven of forty possible), indicating that the masters of small shops tended to live near, and in some cases still *at*, their worksites. Yet the practice of boarding workmen was not as widespread as it had been a generation before. Of the thirty-five carpet manufacturers, only four boarded weavers in their households, and five others listed children as workers.[56] One explanation for the decline lies in the appearance of numerous boardinghouses run by unmarried women or widows, which often hosted a dozen or more textile workers.[57] As earlier, Irish (and, with surnames like Gilmore, Gould, and Winchester, perhaps Scots-Irish) proprietors were especially visible among the small carpet firms and continued to pass along their trades to offspring. Four McDade brothers carried on their father's craft, their widowed mother living with the youngest partner. Two firms listed father and son partnerships in which the fathers themselves may have been brothers (the fathers, James and John Winchester, had their shops on the same block of North Front Street). The 76-year-old father of James Gilmore lived with his manufacturer son on Howard Street, still giving his occupation as "carpet weaver."[58] Even among small shops, the legacy dimension of family firm operations persisted into the eighties, though the extended household of master and workers had faded.

Few owners of hosiery firms with fewer than fifty workers were found in the Nineteenth Ward schedules, though, as elsewhere in the city, the three linked were English-born. If the pattern evident in Table 9.5 continued for small mills, the missing proprietors would be found a few blocks east in the

---

56 Boarding masters included were James Bole, W. T. Cunningham, William McDade, and Thomas Winchester; see, respectively, 1880 Population Census Schedules (cited hereafter as PCS), Philadelphia Co., Enumeration District 371, p. 19; 369, p. 9 (for Cunningham and McDade), and 369, p.2. The five men whose children worked were John Buchanan, Cunningham, Daniel Currie, Theodore Metius, and David Sheard; see, respectively, 1880 PCS, Philadelphia Co., Enumeration District 352, p. 30; 369, p. 9; 371, p. 18; 356, p. 4; and 380, p. 27.

57 Two examples among many are the residences detailed in the 1880 PCS, Philadelphia Co., Enumeration Districts 350, p. 17, and 351, p. 16. The latter, managed by Mary Peacock, an Irish widow, housed seventeen boarders, of whom thirteen were textile workers.

58 For McDade, see 1880 PCS, Philadelphia Co., Enumeration District 369, pp. 6, 9, 19. For Winchester, see Blodget, *Census of Manufactures*, p. 161. For Gilmore, see 1880 PCS, Philadelphia Co., Enumeration District 359, p. 13. W. T. Cunningham's son David, 26, who lived at home and may have been the "and Son" of the firm's name, listed no occupation (Enumeration District 369, p. 9).

Thirty-first Ward, where a number of "British" hosiery firms had developed, with the spillover spreading into the Frankford district (Twenty-fifth Ward). A thorough search might also turn up some of the absent spinners and dyers, among whom English origins were quite common. Such informal clustering would not be remarkable; even in the small pool of linked German carpet manufacturers, seven of the eight lived and/or worked within a few square blocks between Front and Third streets in one corner of the Nineteenth Ward.[59]

When the ethnic composition of the linked Nineteenth Ward manufacturers and that of the larger firms are set alongside the distribution of the city's total work force, the immigrant character of Philadelphia's textile proprietors is reinforced. Table 9.7 presents this comparison. In a city in which two-thirds of the population was native-born, British proprietors are present among textile firms of all sizes in proportions four to six times their occurrence in the working population; and among small firms, Irish and German masters surface at a rate double that of their countrymen in the aggregate. Though the Nineteenth Ward linkage is incomplete, when taken together with the citywide survey of larger firms and when contrasted with the ethnic distribution of the general population, it appears that an immigrant base was common in the textile trades regardless of firm size, perhaps nearing exclusivity at the level of the smallest enterprises. Family "schooling" in the skills central to the firm's survival was as general as in the antebellum era, though workshop boarding had ebbed to a considerable degree. The residential proximity of manufacturers to the workplace was eroding slowly, but even weak evidence of some ethnic clustering suggests that the shop and the broader cultural relations between operators and workers had not yet become a wasteland that linked work with the cash nexus and little else.

The struggles between textile workers and owners during the seventies and eighties nonetheless had a cash component. In "playing out" the conflicts, which were usually generated by attempts to advance or reduce the rates of work in carpet and cotton production, the cultural bonds that enmeshed both manufacturers and laborers became apparent. As the instabilities of capitalist production and realization threatened to rend the social fabric, carpet workers and proprietors (among others) organized themselves first separately in mutual opposition and later in collaboration with one another to ameliorate the threat. We shall detail these machinations shortly, after a brief detour to depict the composition of the city's textile work force in 1882, breaking down the data from Table 9.4 by sector into adult men and women and (unfortunately undifferentiated) youngsters, then peer-

[59] Four were located on Front Street, two on Third, and the last in between on Hope Street, all between the 2100 and 2400 blocks (Ward 19 work sheets, 1880 Population Census Schedules).

Table 9.7. Linked Philadelphia textile manufacturers and total Philadelphia work force by nativity, 1880 (in percentage)

	Nativity						
	England, Scotland	Ireland	Germany	Other	United States	Total	N
Linked manufacturers							
50 or more workers	30	18	8	0	44	100	163
50 or fewer workers	21	38	23	0	17	99	52
Total Philadelphia work force	5	16	9	2	68	100	348,900

Source: Tables 9.5 and 9.6; *Statistics of the Population of the United States at the Tenth Census* (Washington, D.C., 1883), Table XXXVI, p. 895.

ing more closely at Kensington, the district where strike activity was most widespread. As we gear up to discuss the context and forms of labor struggle, it must be reemphasized that whole regions of the city's textile industry were barely touched by the problems besetting the carpet and cotton sectors. This contrast will be explored as the analysis develops.

The textile work force, 1870 and 1882

The dramatic expansion of the Philadelphia textile industry in the dozen years between the two surveys (Table 9.8) is immediately apparent. Most sectors more than doubled their work forces, with the grouped fabric cluster lagging only a bit. The inclusion of cotton, woolen, and mixed fabrics under one heading has concealed the rapid development of the woolen and worsted trades and the near-stagnation of the older cotton sector, which was partially relieved by ventures into variable output. With the enormous increase in the total work force, there was but a small aggregate rise in the overall proportion of women workers (up 3.5%). Indeed, that the adult male work force had increased by 12,500 by 1882 suggests the continuing importance of immigration (and perhaps some in-migration from other U.S. areas) to satisfy the needs of the specialized trades.

Consistent with the increased demands for skilled workers in the fabric mills and the silk manufacture, these two sectors showed a *rising* proportion of adult male workers along with a relative decline in women's employment. Male dominance of dyeing and finishing continued, the small proportional slippage traceable to the introduction of several sizable printing establishments that replaced some of the capacity that folded with the cotton famine. A third of the women and youths in this sector (1882) were engaged at six printworks, with the rest scattered among nearly 150 other firms. In spinning and carpet weaving, though male employment increased absolutely, women's share increased substantially. The rise in the female share of spinning work was perhaps due to the tremendous expansion of carpet yarn production, in which a few standard counts were used widely. The introduction of power-loom ingrains triggered the carpet shift, as women tended the new machinery. By 1882, working women represented two-thirds of the hosiery and knit-goods force. Although no single influence led to *any* of the changes summarized here, on knits several specific movements can be discerned. First, almost all the knitworks in Old City were new outwork firms that engaged women to knit specialty items by hand, having virtually no male or child employees. Their appearance accounts for about a third of the new positions for women in the knit sector. Second, the expanded capacity of powered knitters on hosiery substantially increased the numbers of women needed for seaming and finishing tasks. Third, with some years of experience running

Table 9.8. *Textile workers by sector, sex, and age, Philadelphia, 1870 and 1882*

Sector/year	Textile workers			
	Male	Female	Youth	Total
Fabrics				
1870	4,072 (33.8)	6,173 (51.3)	1,780 (14.8)	12,025
1882	8,733 (39.2)	10,554 (47.4)	2,998 (13.4)	22,285
Silk				
1870	305 (23.9)	905 (70.9)	66 (5.2)	1,276
1882	1,754 (29.4)	3,628 (60.7)	593 (9.9)	5,975
Carpet				
1870	3,463 (73.5)	918 (19.5)	332 (7.0)	4,713
1882	6,571 (58.5)	3,632 (32.3)	1,027 (9.1)	11,230
Hosiery, knit goods				
1870	1,344 (26.2)	2,734 (53.3)	1,049 (20.4)	5,127
1882	2,297 (18.1)	8,361 (66.0)	2,009 (15.9)	12,667
Dyeing, finishing				
1870	575 (87.1)	31 (4.7)	54 (8.2)	660
1882	2,177 (82.7)	191 (7.2)	263 (10.0)	2,631
Spinning				
1870	991 (43.2)	709 (30.9)	593 (25.9)	2,293
1882	1,693 (31.2)	2,123 (39.2)	1,605 (29.6)	5,421
Other				
1870	97 (33.2)	140 (47.9)	55 (18.8)	292
1882	113 (17.0)	417 (62.7)	135 (20.3)	665
Total				
1870	10,847 (41.1)	11,610 (44.0)	3,929 (14.9)	26,386
1882	23,338 (38.3)	28,906 (47.5)	8,630 (14.2)	60,874

Note: Figures in parentheses indicate percentages. Given the movement of many firms from cotton to mixed or wool fabrics in a year's time, the three sectors are here combined.

Source: For 1870: see Table 8.3; for 1882: Lorin Blodget, *Census of Manufactures of Philadelphia (1882)* (Philadelphia, 1883), "Summary Tabular Statement," pp. 112–29. The tabular totals for 1882 from the "Summary Tabular Statement" exceed by about 5% the totals drawn from the accompanying list of individual firms, "Manufacturers of Textile Fabrics" (pp. 156–78), which was used in constructing Tables 9.1 and 9.2, this volume. Resort to the "Summary" statement was necessary to provide a breakdown by sex. The total number of textile establishments in the "Summary" statement exceeds the total in the individual firm list by about eighty firms, principally fabric manufacturers. It is possible that some firms declined to release their "personal" information at an individual level but did not object to contributing anonymously to the sectoral summaries. Extensive notes to the "Summary" statement indicate considerable care in its preparation.

Table 9.9. *Textile workers by sector, sex, and age, Kensington, 1870 and 1882*

Sector/year	Textile workers			
	Male	Female	Youth	Total
Fabrics				
1870	897 (31.4)	1,472 (51.6)	484 (17.0)	2,853
1882	2,756 (37.8)	3,644 (50.1)	878 (12.1)	7,278
Silk				
1870	0	0	0	0
1882	739 (51.4)	521 (36.2)	179 (12.4)	1,439
Carpet				
1870	2,605 (76.6)	589 (17.3)	208 (6.1)	3,402
1882	4,658 (62.1)	2,279 (30.4)	565 (7.5)	7,502
Hosiery, knit goods				
1870	765 (23.8)	1,848 (57.5)	600 (18.7)	3,213
1882	1,254 (19.1)	4,307 (65.5)	1,015 (15.4)	6,576
Dyeing, finishing				
1870	164 (99.4)	1 (0.6)	0	165
1882	976 (87.3)	42 (3.8)	100 (8.9)	1,118
Spinning				
1870	406 (50.8)	208 (26.0)	185 (23.2)	799
1882	438 (37.6)	383 (32.9)	343 (29.5)	1,164
Other				
1870	31 (27.9)	76 (68.5)	4 (3.6)	111
1882	93 (20.6)	286 (63.4)	72 (16.0)	451
Total				
1870	4,868 (46.2)	4,194 (39.8)	1,481 (14.0)	10,543
1882	10,914 (42.8)	11,462 (44.9)	3,152 (12.3)	25,528

Note: Figures in parentheses indicate percentages.
Source: Manuscript Manufacturing Census Schedules, Philadelphia County, Wards 16, 17, 18, and 19, 1870; Lorin Blodget, *Census of Manufactures of Philadelphia (1882)* (Philadelphia, 1883), pp. 64–85. The 1882 figures are drawn from the special district tables in the first part of Blodget's volume. For Kensington, Blodget added Ward 20, west of Kensington proper between Sixth and Broad streets. This was a largely residential area, with a handful of mills strung along Germantown Avenue as it proceeded northwest from Kensington. From the list of individual firms, it appears that twelve textile firms with just under 1,000 workers were located in this ward. As they were spread among all sectors except silk, and as there is no way to extract them from the composite tables, the 1882 Kensington data are not perfectly congruent with the area from which the 1870 distributions were taken. Given the small numbers involved and the spread of the firms among most sectors, the "extra" ward does not substantially distort the comparison, but it does reinforce the frustrations of not having access to data on an individual level such as those presented in the original

varied work on power-knitters, women could surely operate these machines with dexterity and skill and/or serve as "foreladies," as did Annie Fling.[60]

However cautious we must be in evaluating these figures, it seems fair to state that by the early eighties the size and skill of the textile labor force in Philadelphia was unequaled elsewhere in the nation. Though the base for expansion had been laid in the prewar era, solidified with war contracts, and protected by the tariff, the "crucial decade" for rapid development of these resources and capacities was surely the 1870s. If the textile manufacture was present in nearly every quarter of the city by the eighties, Kensington remained the productive hub. For this reason, and as it was the stage on which the strikes and reconciliations of the era were most frequently mounted, we will use the format of Table 9.8 to zero in on its textile operations as presented in the 1882 city report and contrast them with the figures from the 1870 Manufacturing Census Schedules (Table 9.9).

With the arrival of the silk business and the trebled powered production of fabrics in the nineteenth and thirty-first wards, textile expansion in Philadelphia's oldest weaving district matched the pace achieved throughout the metropolis (Table 9.8). At both dates, Kensington showed slightly higher percentages of male workers and lower shares for women and children than the citywide data, a situation likely related to its large numbers of small workshops and to the presence of more than two-thirds of the carpet trade. Though the expansion of independent spinners was modest, about half the new dyehouse positions that materialized in the seventies were located in Kensington, and both knitting and carpet sectors more than doubled their employment figures. Over the thirty years since the 1850 Manufacturing Census, the district and the city as a whole witnessed a five- to sixfold multiplication of industrial textile work. Jobs for women developed more rapidly than those for men, most dramatically in the knitting sector, but the skill demands of Philadelphia's specialized and flexible-output trades drew thousands of British, Irish, and German factory and craft veterans to its shops and mills. In Kensington, their work and that of their sisters, daughters, and kin became rooted amid overlapping networks of factory culture, community life, and family economies. Something of the substance of these generally invisible contextual elements is revealed in times of strain and conflict, which we shall next consider in reviewing the associations and interactions of manufacturers and workers in the seventies and early eighties.

60 If adequate sources could be assembled, a study on women's work in knit goods might provide a fascinating companion piece to Susan Levine's "Their Own Sphere: Women's Work, The Knights of Labor and The Transformation of the Carpet Trades, 1870–1890" (Ph.D. diss., City University of New York, 1979). Interestingly, in knits, unlike all but one other sector, the proportion of child workers dropped substantially as women's roles extended. Whether this is a statistical accident or a shift of some significance can be determined only after further research.

10

Continuity and crisis: the early 1880s

The constitution stated that the object of the organization is to . . . effect a more sympathetic feeling between employer and employe, and to discourage all injustice. The name of the organization was fixed as the "Damask Carpet Weavers and Manufacturers Protective Association of Philadelphia." Admission fee – 25¢ for weavers and $1.00 for manufacturers.

Public Ledger, June 19, 1880

There has been no simple linear unfolding of the structure of Philadelphia's textile manufacture. So too, an account of the postwar emergence of proprietors associations, employees unions and organizations in which they joined hands appears chaotic on the surface. However, a closer examination of the complex of material and cultural relationships that underlay events will reveal elements of pattern and process more clearly. In the following pages, we shall undertake to link two varieties of manufacturers associations to the contexts in which their members operated. In the first section, we will expose a developing "crisis" in one major sector (carpets) and will discuss the proprietors (and workers) associations that responded to it. In turn, the activities and aims of a second organization, the Philadelphia Textile Manufacturers Association (PTMA), will be related to the productive orientations of its founders, the group to whom Dobson delivered his oration at the beginning of Chapter 9.

If in general, ethnic, family, and organizational characteristics were elements of continuity in the vast expansion of the Philadelphia textile industry, the associations initiated by operators in the seventies and eighties also had roots in earlier contacts and connections. In the thirties, the Manayunk cluster of fabric manufacturers, led by Joseph Ripka, had collaborated in confronting the resistance of workers to wage cuts and oppressive working conditions. This ephemeral collusion likely faded with the end of the activist period and the market scramble accompanying the 1837 Panic. More definite were both the earlier Society of Weavers, the 1820s grouping of master shopmen of which so little is known, and the concurrent convocations of handloom masters in Kensington, which were assembled twice annually into the 1840s to determine the "bill of prices" for cotton and carpet weaving for the ensuing six months.

In addition to these production-oriented relations, their participation in church management and neighborhood politics brought manufacturers into close and regular contact with one another, as did other community and individual projects, such as the creation of local banks, in which at least at Manayunk millmen figured prominently. Finally, the network of interactions included societies and associations operated by manufacturers and their sons that were of interest and possible benefit to a larger constituency, such as the Manayunk Bachelors' Library and the Debate Society at whose public sessions millowners discussed slavery, women's suffrage, and so on.[1] Hence, the Civil War connections among city textile manufacturers, visible in overlapping signatures on surety bonds for federal contracts, were based on contacts of long standing.

Most of these links were, it must be stressed, constructed on a neighborhood or a productive-sector base, which in much of the city were one and the same (Manayunk-powered fabric and yarn mills, Germantown knit goods, etc.). They did not automatically lead toward either a citywide association of textile manufacturers nor toward participation in such national organizations as the National Association of Wool Manufacturers (NAWM). Though the Civil War may have brought a heightened awareness of the role of the state in capitalist prosperity to a fraction of the city's millowners, it was not until the end of the next decade that the old boundaries of trade and district were tentatively dissolved with the formation of the Philadelphia Textile Manufacturers Association. The early sallies of the NAWM, a classic halls and hearing-rooms pressure group, enrolled in 1869 a number of "war veteran" Philadelphia firms, members who were distinguished over the next decade only for their passivity with regard to the NAWM's persistent tariff crusades. Yet ten years later, the PTMA hosted and lectured the NAWM's New England stalwarts, commenced sending its own delegations to Washington, secured "quarters" for meetings, and entered upon the publication of its own position papers. In the moving context for its formation, both the continuities and contradictions of the postwar manufacturing environment in Philadelphia played important roles. The activities of episodic manufacturers' associations in the carpet sector and their replication in other textile areas are the element of continuity here. The rising rhythm of labor struggles, provoked chiefly by rate cuts that were consequent on depression and interregional competition, was central to the creation of these associations,

---

[1] The ledger of the antebellum Bachelors' Library is in the possession of Russell Fawley of John Wilde and Brother, Manayunk. J. B. Winpenny and other manufacturing men were principal members. The meetings of the Debate Society were regularly reported in the *Manayunk Star and Roxborough Gazette*, 1859–61.

reflecting in turn several layers of emerging contradictions in capitalist manufacture. In the most flexible and specialized sectors, manufacturers and workers eluded the competitive squeeze that forced confrontations at carpet firms and staple-based fabric mills. In reviewing the sectors in which conflicts abounded, as well as those quiet throughout the era, and in detailing the patterns of strikes and labor organizing, we shall see again reflected the strengths and vulnerabilities of the diverse components of the Philadelphia textile manufacture.

With expanding capacity, some manufacturers made the sequential decisions that led toward bulk production, principally in carpets and what remained of the cotton industry. They found themselves tested by the rigors of overproduction and constrained by the technical and skill-related choices that facilitated bulk output but forced a cut in wages as prices dropped. The cultural and urban context in which rates were slashed, however, was not that of a single-mill or a single-industry company town. It was instead a metropolitan context in which neighborhood support, artisan traditions, and a burgeoning labor movement in iron, shoes, clothing, and transport provided workers with the tools of resistance – material, moral, and rhetorical. Workers who struck might be replaced by learners, who, because of the lower skills required by narrowed production, could, within a month or two, become effective workers. Yet during the strike, such new employees were hooted through the streets, and the legacy of bitterness that remained afterward could hardly be calculated. Once the struggle was over, the circle had merely been closed, for the conditions for more bulk manufacture, more overproduction, and further price drops and wage cuts had been restored. One season's scabs might well become the next season's strikers, with heavy costs to family, community, and the fabric of social relations in these firms. Although this scenario flattens the differences between cotton and carpet struggles, the contrast between them and the other textile sectors is sharp.

There are times when silence is inordinately informative. Of the several hundred textile strikes in Philadelphia during the two decades after the Civil War, only a handful occurred in the sectors that showed a maximum commitment to flexibility and innovation: knit goods, wool and worsted, silks, and the related independent dyeing and spinning operations. Functioning with highly skilled workers, working short runs of "better grade" goods, extending their capacity to respond to subtle market shifts, these firms faced few risks of overproduction, though they were not immune to general depression or the cancellation of orders that accompanied panics. Able to provide steady work at "fair wages" over the long term, they were not involved in rounds of reductions and turnouts. When bad times led them to propose a reduction, the reasons were given, and a pledge to restore the cut was made and kept. None of this is meant to suggest that all was sweetness and light in these mills; accumulation was the pervasive goal of production, the cards and looms rumbled no more softly on worsted, than they did in cotton factories. Nevertheless, the extended quiet in these sectors indicates that the accumulation process was successfully managed through the complementary efforts of skilled labor and equally skilled entrepreneurs who held a measure of respect for one another's capacities. This was not the labor peace of magnates and benumbed operatives but a fairly durable expression of the mutual competence of workers and proprietors, each of whose obligations the other understood. To be sure, if one or the other of the parties betrayed these largely unspoken commitments, tumult could well result. Yet without our appreciation of these social relations of production, the occasional conflicts that appeared in these sectors will remain opaque, for they resist homogenization into standard categories.

From this initial review, it seems that textile trade associations in Philadelphia took shape along two tracks. The "crisis" associations appeared with some regularity in those sectors whose productive strategy fell afoul of national market competition. Their members leagued together to cut rates or to attempt output controls. Resistance by their work forces and countervailing initiatives from the shop floors led to struggles, several of which will be treated in this chapter. The "progressive" associations, for want of a better term, were spawned in the most technically advanced and functionally flexible sectors, where rate cuts were infrequent. These groups were concerned with sharpening their prowess, lobbying for protection, and, in time, encouraging technical education. Together, these efforts went far beyond the crisis defensiveness of carpet and cotton masters, for the "progressives" were concerned with reaching beyond the mill and the salesroom to gain influence over long-term factors affecting their accumulation projects.

In this chapter we shall encounter both the "crisis" and the "progressive" forms of association. First, in detailing the carpet conflicts of the late seventies and mid-eighties, the "crisis" associations will be situated within a neighborhood and factory culture, where the violation of customary "rules" makes visible both the elements and the ritual patterns of labor–capital antagonism that the culture functioned to contain. A glance at Manayunk will indicate that such relations were not confined to Kensington and, by extension, may have been general in mills where overt struggle was absent because the canons of mutual respect and steady work were observed. Second, in closing, we shall visit the PTMA, whose activities were described at the beginning of Chapter 9, examining its constituency and exposing the context of its ultimate support for technical education as an example of yet another pathway opened by Philadelphia's "peculiar" textile entrepreneurs.

The crisis in carpets and echoes elsewhere

The past twenty years has brought forward many methods of weaving ingrain carpets and the field of design has shown a wonderful growth, . . . [Yet] the outlook for the industry in the United States is not a very bright one . . . The major portion of the output of the Eastern [ingrain] plants is shipped to the South and Middle West, [to] the small towns and farming districts of these localities.[2]

From the Civil War well into the twentieth century, more textile workers wove carpets in Philadelphia than in any other locale in the nation. In the 1870s the industry became fiercely competitive, as hundreds of Quaker City firms scrambled for shares of a market sought as well by a small number of huge northeastern firms. To understand the character of that competition, and the options available in Philadelphia to respond to the crises it regularly generated, requires a brief review of the carpet manufacture, both in the city and at its eastern sites. With the technical and historical context sketched, the difficulties besetting Philadelphia's carpet firms may be delineated in short order.

In terms of their structure and the processes that attended their manufacture, four sorts of commercial carpets were manufactured in nineteenth-century America. The simplest and cheapest were rag carpets, flat constructions in which "strips of woven wool, cotton, or linen were sewn together and inserted as weft"[3] between stout, generally cotton or linen warps. Also flat, but woven of yarns for both warp and filling were ingrain and venetian carpets, "which dominated carpet production throughout the nineteenth century." The standard ingrain was a double-cloth, meaning that two sets of warps and two of fillings were simultaneously woven together into patterns that were identical on both sides of the product, known as a "two-ply." Three-ply ingrains were yet more complex, sturdier, and more expensive than the standards. With sophisticated loom mechanisms, elaborate patterns were possible; in addition the carpet could be built on cotton or wool warps, with wool or worsted fillings varying the output, along with the price, even further. The name "ingrain" is most commonly thought to refer to the fact that the pattern was woven into the fabric rather than printed on its surface.[4] These carpets were the core of the Philadelphia trade, from the handshops of the 1830s to the factories of the early 1900s.

Pile carpets, in which filling yarns are drawn up in loops above the woven

[2] Robert J. Carson, "Ingrain Carpet Industry," *Second Annual Report (1903)*, Alumni Association of the Philadelphia Textile School, pp. 54–5.

[3] Anthony Landreau, *America Underfoot*, Washington, D.C., 1976, p. 36.

[4] Ibid., p. 43; Louis Harmuth, *Dictionary of Textiles*, New York, 1924, p. 53.

surface, were produced in two basic forms. Those in which the pattern was constructed through the weaving were called Brussels or Wiltons, the latter having the tops of the loops clipped off "to provide a more velvety surface and more precise design." A cheaper means to the same effect were pile carpets on which designs were achieved by printing the colors in intervals on the filling yarns. When accurately woven (on a much simpler loom), "a single set of yarns . . . supplie[d] the place of the four or five sets of yarns [or 'frames'] required by the more elegant Brussels or Wiltons."[5] With uncut loops these were known as tapestry carpets; with cut pile, velvets. Two variations of these pile basics involved the insertion of filling pile into pre- viously woven jute or cotton backing; the more elaborate style was known as Axminster and a cheaper, similar "two-faced version" was called Smyrna. Other forms might be added, but the four basics, two flat (rag and ingrain) and two pile carpets (woven and yarn-printed designs), account for well over 90% of commercial production in this period.

The competitive structure can be visualized along three dimensions: in- ternally at Philadelphia, the ingrain center; between Philadelphia ingrains and those mass-produced at Lowell, Hartford, and elsewhere; and between all ingrains and the forms of pile carpet manufactured on power looms principally at three New York sites, Amsterdam, Yonkers, and Manhattan, each of which had a single large firm with huge output capacity. Power looms were available by the mid-seventies for all the main pile varieties, as well as ingrains, but the key rival for the mid-price ingrain trade seems to have been the yarn-printed tapestry (and cut-pile velvet) line, heavily produced by Amsterdam's Sanford and Sons and E. S. Higgins and Co. of New York City.[6] The market segmentation and price movements in the seventies and eighties are illustrated in Table 10.1.

Clearly, Brussels carpets, unlike the other four given in the table, were oriented toward an up-scale market; and the tapestry carpet provided an alternative for buyers who might also be ingrain consumers. Because enor- mous printing drums were required to prepare the yarns, tapestry manufac- ture was a big-mill rather than workshop operation. The market attractions of a figured pile carpet, priced below the best-grade ingrains and just a tad above the standard flat extra-supers, led ultimately to a long-term decline in the ingrains trade as a whole, as described by Carson at the beginning of this section. Both ingrain handshops and powered mills were in the seventies at the beginning of a structural squeeze.

---

5 Landreau, *America Underfoot*, pp. 54, 58.
6 Susan Levine, "Their Own Sphere: Women's Work, the Knights of Labor and the Transformation of the Carpet Trade, 1870–1890," Ph.D. diss. City University of New York, 1979, pp. 35–7.

Table 10.1. *Retail prices of carpets, 1870–85 (per yard)*

	Five-frame Brussels	Tapestry	Three-ply ingrain	Two-ply extra-super ingrain	Two-ply medium-super ingrain
1870	$2.00	$1.20	$1.42½	$1.15	$1.00
1872	2.10	1.30	1.60	1.35	1.20
1875	1.95	1.20	1.25	1.00	.90
1877	1.50	1.05	1.10	.90	.82½
1878	1.45	.85	1.05	.85	.77½
1879	1.35	.80	.90	.72½	.67½
1880	1.50	.95	1.15	.95	.87½
1881	1.45	1.00	1.05	.82½	.75
1882	1.40	.90	1.05	.85	.75
1883	1.40	.90	1.05	.85	.75
1884	1.32½	.80	.90	.72½	.67½
1885	1.25	.82½	.85	.67½	—

Note: Dash indicates not available.
Source: J. R. Kendrick, "The Carpet Industry of Philadelphia," in *Seventeenth Report (1889)*, Pennsylvania Bureau of Industrial Statistics (Harrisburg, Pa., 1890), pp. D-34–5.

Along with the threat of substitution, the internal mechanics of the sub-sector contributed to the depression in ingrain prices. Bigelow's original carpet power loom had been an ingrain machine and had by this time long been present at the Lowell Manufacturing Company as well as at the inventor's own Hartford works. The expiration of the early patents and the development of other ingrain looms (the Murkland was adopted in Philadelphia) indicated that expanding capacity would intensify the effects of tapestry rivalry. As Levine observes:

> While production soared and the new machines promised reduced costs, increased production and high profits, prices in the industry began to decline sharply . . . As early as 1875 the trade journals began to call for regulation of the competition in the industry and an organized cutback in production. Production, they feared, had exceeded the "national demand."[7]

With falling market prices, the differences between the situations at the "eastern" ingrain mills and the Philadelphia firms sharpened, as it was

[7] Ibid., pp. 38–9.

everywhere admitted that labor rates for manufacture were appreciably higher in Philadelphia than elsewhere.[8] Savings that Philadelphians made on other cost factors (shipping, interest, commission charges, patent fees) might well allow a living profit even with payment of decent rates for handloom manufacture. But when depression and expanded aggregate capacity coincided, as they did by 1873–4, a crisis confronted scores of small firms in Kensington. It is this situation that leads us to examine the internal character of the Philadelphia carpet trade, the options available to, and exercised by, manufacturers, and the resistance they met.

In the early seventies, carpets were almost exclusively a handloom product in Philadelphia. The first major powered operation was launched in 1873 by James Dobson, who produced fancy all-wool Brussels carpets at his Falls of Schuylkill mills, well away from the Kensington core.[9] In the old handwork district, workshops predominated, few with more than a hundred workers, most with less than a score. For such operators, as they recognized the troubles ahead, a range of responses were theoretically possible. That some took each of a number of paths is understandable, that a few tried to cluster together for common action equally so, and that the whole picture seems fairly chaotic is perhaps a necessary corollary. Kensington's carpet workers were at this point, as later, predominantly immigrants from Greater Britain, whose arrivals had surged in the war decade.[10] They melted into the immigrant community readily and would act to defend its values and customs against violations. Many manufacturers had themselves been shop-trained and were reluctant to abandon traditional skills and relationships for the calculator's role. Others, at the smaller end of the spectrum, plied their looms alongside their fellows, as had the antebellum shop masters. Overlapping allegiances, the economics of capitalist survival, community status, and shop autonomy all intersected in the conflicts that dotted the next decade. The ritual theatricality of the struggles and the search for a customary means to restore stability indicate that the culturally based bonds between masters and workers were threatened by the cumulative anarchy of capitalist market relations.

---

[8] In 1872 Bromley Brothers paid its male handloom carpet weavers an average of $3.83 per day, whereas the Lowell Company offered female power-loom operators $1.17. By 1874, with Bromley's introduction of power looms, handworkers' rates dropped to $3.33, with the new women workers receiving $1.33, compared with $1.02 at the Lowell Company in that year. By the end of the decade, Bromley's remaining handweavers earned but $2 a day, but the gap in the rate for power weavers had widened: $1.41 at Bromley, 90¢ at Lowell. Wages paid other classes of workers were uniformly higher at Philadelphia; for details, see Joseph Weeks, *Report on the Statistics of Wages in Manufacturing Industries*, Washington, D.C., 1886, pp. 324–5.

[9] Lorin Blodget, *Census of Manufactures of Philadelphia (1882)*, Philadelphia, 1883, p. 56.

[10] Ibid., p. 156.

Given that gradualism and proprietary organization were basic to textile development in Philadelphia, no sudden merger of a half-dozen firms for corporate manufacture with powered equipment could be expected and none materialized. Instead, shopmen individually shouldered the costs of change, associating with one another only in crisis. All alterations involved expenses: material if new equipment and shifted product lines were adopted, cultural if the social relations of production were involved, and in many cases both. The smallest firms, with little in the way of capital or credit capacity, had roughly three possible tracks from which to select a strategy. They might continue to pay the trade schedule of prices for work, accept reduced or no profits in hope of better times, work their children, and hope to get a living somehow. Failure would mean seeking work for another firm, a hard but not dishonorable fate. As an alternative, they could shave the rates – easily done if others would lead but difficult as a solitary act. A depression emergency would mediate such reductions, but continued over a longer term, they would erode shop-floor mutuality into antagonism. Or the small-shop proprietors might elect to produce less costly grades of carpet whose market cheapness did not justify the commitment of powered facilities to their manufacture. Because power-loom ingrain mills concentrated on the better grades of woolen carpets, for which the return per yard was potentially higher, a vulnerable yet visible opening was available at the lower end of the trade. In the mid-eighties, shops that exercised this last option continued to be active in the city.[11]

For mid-size firms, more positive steps could be imagined, given modest capital for expenditure. With less than a thousand dollars, shop proprietors could move sideways into handwork on carpets to which machine skills had not yet been applied. This was most widely done in the case of Smyrna rugs, to the extent that Kendrick reported about 2,000 handlooms working Smyrnas in the late eighties.[12] Securing several power looms for ingrain work involved both a significant investment and, of course, power, either rented at a new site or added to the present workshop. If these obstacles were surmounted, women, possibly workmen's kin, could be hired to run the new looms at rates well below the cost per yard of handwork. Though a family connection might ease the introduction of new machinery, there was another problem. This strategy would in no way address the potential for oversupply in ingrain markets; indeed, it would only aggravate it. But at the level of the firm, this perception was uncommon. By 1880, at least thirty-one shops had added ingrain power looms to their handloom base, a dozen of them having

---

[11] *Public Ledger*, November 4, 1884; cited hereafter as *PL*.

[12] J. R. Kendrick, "The Carpet Industry of Philadelphia," *Seventh Report (1889)*, Pennsylvania Bureau of Industrial Statistics, Harrisburg, Pa., p. D-52.

ten or fewer of the new machines. Alternately, mid-size firms, with, say, twenty, thirty, or forty hand and power looms, might attempt to vary their production within the grades of ingrains seeking the best margins, work to develop new patterns or variations on those that had seen success in the market, or propose reductions, perhaps in concert with other maneuvers. Unimaginative "bad masters" would adopt but one strategy: cut the price of work; stoic "honorable" shopmen would stand fast, take their losses, and hope for a change in the economic wind.

Power was hardly the automatic choice for ingrain proprietors, as the 1880 survey just cited listed an additional thirty shops operating twenty or more handlooms, a group that had not chosen to mix hand and powered weaving. One clue to yet another strategic option for this cluster comes from annotations to the list, which point out that eight of the thirty shops ran outwork looms at workers' homes, a continuation of the antebellum practice.[13] Thus, as we reconstruct a number of alternative survival strategies for carpet firms, individually chosen, none inherently fatal (other than passivity in the long run), we begin to appreciate the complexities of the manufacturing context that are invisible at the level of price series or total output. Differing firm sizes, resources, skills, and different evaluations of the calculus of personal interest and communal obligation, as well as variations in information about costs and margins and in the concern for such bookkeeping detail, all combined to generate a wide range of responses (and nonresponses) to the larger movements of the ingrain market. Against this context, it is little wonder that carpet manufacturers had great difficulty in sustaining united action through the troubled decades.

The handful of large firms had the widest options.[14] With deeper pockets, they could envisage direct competition with the eastern giants on ingrains or pile carpets, could engage designers full time to reproduce or originate patterns, and could mix their output among the various lines. In the long run, they accumulated the resources to build new plants, add other textile prod-

---

13 Lorin Blodget, *The Textile Industries of Philadelphia*, Philadelphia, 1880, pp. 45–50. Two of the mixed-goods firms had also retained outworkers on handlooms.

14 Of the eleven firms in 1880 with more than 100 looms, nine were in Kensington: Bromley Brothers (164 looms) produced ingrain, damask, and tapestry; John Bromley and Sons (206 looms), ingrain, Smyrna, and Brussels; Boggs and White (130 looms), ingrain; James Gay (107 looms), ingrain and damask; Wm. Hogg, Jr. and Son (104 looms), ingrain, damask, and Brussels; Horner Bros. (125 looms), damask and Brussels; Ivins, Dietz and Magee (150 looms), ingrain, damask, and tapestry; Judge Bros. (170 looms), ingrain and damask; and Thomas Leedom & Co. (203 looms), ingrain, damask, and Brussels. Dobson had 330 looms on ingrains, tapestry, and Brussels, the largest operation in the city. The eleventh firm was Alex Crow and Son, Spring Garden, with 165 looms that produced ingrain and Brussels carpets. All but Dobson had substantial numbers of handlooms in place, generally more than half the total.

Table 10.2. *Philadelphia capital, work force, and product value as percentage of national totals, 1880*

Sector	Capital	Work force	Product value
Wool	12	13	13
Worsted	22	23	25
Knit goods	22	29	28
Carpet	33	43	45

Source: Report on the Manufactures of the United States at the Tenth Census (Washington, D.C., 1883), pp. 9–14, 421–4; George Bond, "Report on Wool Manufacture in All Its Branches," in ibid., p. 2.

ucts, and adopt or create innovations in machinery or processing. The bigger firms were "natural" leaders in movements to press wages downward and equally crucial targets for resistance; yet they remained competitors with one another and with the smaller operators as well as with "the East"; they did not all make the same goods, so that changes in markets or the price of work affected them differently. Should a group conspire to lower rates and trigger a strike, other mills (and unaffected firms of any size) might fill the vacated market spaces. Again, capitalist solidarity was a defensive phenomenon, born of crisis and fragile even in those circumstances, as we shall see.

Two additional bits of background information are important. First, as an 1876 survey illustrated, the city's carpet sector was thoroughly committed to ingrain production. In the summer of that year the *Ledger* reported that the industry boasted 180 carpet manufacturing firms, 7,325 workers, and 3,517 hand and 592 power looms. The year's output was estimated at a little over 21 million yards, valued at $14 million. Of this total, more than three-quarters was ingrain carpet, chiefly wool filling on cotton warps (11,990,000 yards, or 56%). All wool ingrains constituted 22% of the whole, trailed by damask and Venetians (8% each) and the varieties of pile carpet (tapestry and Brussels, 6%). Thus 94% of the local output was flat carpeting, all producers of which were pressured by the massive eastern mills' tapestry output. Further, most Philadelphia firms were weavers only, as there were only 61 spinning sets in the carpet sector as a whole.

Moreover, it was in carpets that Philadelphia's firms bulked largest in the national textile industry. This is evident from Table 10.2 which shows the 1880 proportion of national investment, work force, and product values for four of the city's most prominent textile trades. The gap between the capital and product value figures indicates again the wide use of rented space and the presence of specialized weave sheds. It does not reflect heavy production of the most expensive grades of carpet, although the proportion of pile carpets had risen to 12.6%, double the 1876 percentage despite a slightly larger yardage total (22.6 million vs. 21 million yards), which is consistent with the observation from *Penn Monthly* cited earlier. Nationally, in 1880 the city manufactured three-quarters of all ingrains, all the reported Venetian carpet, but only a quarter of the Brussels and a fifth of the tapestry varieties.[15]

Second, as the "scale" or "bill of prices" was a recurrent subject of controversy in the shops, the details of this artisanal term are worth relating. As in the 1820s, craftshop workers did not accept "wages." Instead, they retained the notion of setting the price for their skilled labor at the handlooms in a table of rates. The schedule was organized by "pairs," the number of doubled filling threads per inch of fabric woven. Coarse yarns (7 or 8 to the inch) paid less than finer work (13 or 14), which took more throws of the shuttle to produce an equivalent yardage. The "bill of prices" was thus a table prepared to show each gradation of fineness and the corresponding number of cents per yard required for each sort of carpet manufactured (ingrain, damask, etc.). These were complicated schedules, whose intricacies were fully understood by both manufacturers and shop craftsmen. In practice, a weaver on coarse goods would expect to receive about the same recompense for a month's work as one on finer varieties, given his faster output at lower rates and his colleague's slower but better rewarded toil. Further, movement of weavers from one to another grade would little alter their return for labor in a properly adjusted rate schedule. We shall return to this point later.

Adjustments to the bill of prices were a customary source of contention between manufacturers and workers in Kensington. It was clearly in the workers' interest to have a uniform schedule to which all operators conformed, thereby preserving the standards of the trade. Craft solidarity, apparent throughout the conflicts in this period, focused on the "bill" but was reinforced by ethnic and community relationships of the immigrant neighborhood. Manufacturers with different strategies could not accept a common schedule so readily, though appeals to devise one surfaced repeatedly. Firms with power looms already in place might well afford to subscribe to a rate level for their handloom work that would be high enough to preserve *their* overall profitability but squeeze competing shopmen who had not installed the cost-saving powered machinery. Handwork manufacturers trying

---

[15] *PL*, July 27, 1876; George Bond, "Report on the Wool Manufacture in All Its Branches," in *Report on the Manufactures of the United States at the Tenth Census*, Washington, D.C., 1883, pp. 16–17.

to accumulate sufficient profits to purchase power looms would seek to establish lower rates than those who intended to rely on tinkering with their hand-operated equipment. Marginal, tiny shops, aiming to expand even on handlooms, would be tempted to press for lower rates than those who were content with just "getting a living" or who felt more acutely their duty as masters to pay fair wages for good work. Thus both the formation of associations and their effectiveness were constrained by the competitive structure of the trade and the wide variation in goals and strategies of its component firms.

In the early seventies, carpet manufacturers' groups had neither formal names, stable memberships, nor headquarters. Like the parallel workers' associations, they were fluid and reciprocally convoked, the one calling forth the other to deal with a particular situation. Before becoming formalized in 1879, when the antebellum custom of reviewing the price of work twice yearly was renewed, the relationships among manufacturers and with workers were fairly haphazard. A group of ingrain shopmen might meet to discuss the troubled markets, the falling prices amid stable costs, and determine that the "scale of prices" for work had to be adjusted downward. Preparing a new schedule to which they pledged themselves, the manufacturers would post notice in their shops of the new rates, to take effect to a date stated, and either await workers' response or, at times, circulate "papers" among the operatives for their assent to the alteration. Individual firms that did seek to change their schedules on their own risked standing alone if workers resisted, called for community and trade support and declined to work at the proposed terms. Under such circumstances a single firm might see its looms idle, its striking workers receiving donations from working comrades, and its competition continuing to function, filling its place in the market. This grim prospect made reasonable the association of like-situated firms for common action, but structural constraints prevented total unanimity or institutionalization of the provisional alliances thus formed.

The entire process could be, and was, initiated from the shop floor as well. Carpet workers in the seventies frequently elected delegates by shops who assembled to discuss adjusting the bill of prices upward or standardizing rates. Subsequently, the delegates prepared *their* schedules and presented them to manufacturers for approval. Individual shops here too acted on occasion independently but, given the supporting network in which they were located, with fewer risks than firm owners. A success at a prominent shop would trigger parallel activity throughout the district. There was then at Kensington, before the creation of permanent organizations of capital and labor, something like a customary process for channeling market-induced conflicts between immigrant operators and immigrant workers in the carpet trade. Together, the rituals of workers' activity (shop elections, consultations, "visiting committees") and those of the manufacturers' association (discussion, public notice in advance of changes, acceptance of workers' right to refuse rates) constitute a loose shop culture engaged in by those on both sides. The informal rules of this relationship become at least partly visible in the conflicts reviewed in the following sections. Violations of the rules that threatened the integrity of either party were met with resolute opposition, as happened when manufacturers offered divisive work rules along with a reduction in 1873 and when workers brought outsiders (the Knights of Labor leadership) into a major conflict a decade later. This "system" of the social relations of production in shops and small factories, erected on the common experiences of workers and masters, was aimed at stabilizing the human aspects of perpetually uncertain economic relations. The larger movements of the industrial economy made this unvoiced project hopeless in the long run, but in the extremities of the eighties' struggles, the Kensington carpet trade reaffirmed its commitments to customary forms, narrowly sidestepping the gateway to class war.

The Kensington "troubles" in the generation after the Civil War deserve a full-scale monographic study in their own right. Here we will only dip into the reservoir sufficiently often to illustrate the relationships posited above, to detail the theatrical and ritual qualities of conflict, and to suggest the character of the crisis that brought the great strikes of the mid-eighties.

Conflict in the carpet trades, 1873–1880

In fall 1873, both Jay Gould and the railway boom went smash, setting off a depression whose effects hovered over the economy for most of the decade. The ingrain carpet manufacture quickly felt the effects of the shock, for its market placement was perilous. Carpeting is a "consumer durable," a necessity in no basic budget. Ingrains were sold heavily to working-class householders and the middling shop and farm populations of towns and rural districts. A pleasant acquisition for families with a modest surplus, they were unlikely purchases in strained times, quickly dropped from consideration as thousands recalculated their finances toward meeting subsistence needs. With the contraction, and its attendant market price declines, at least ten Kensington carpet firms sought in December 1873 to reduce the bill of prices.[16] Their price list was accompanied by a standard contract, to which workers were expected to consent.

16 No formal association was named, but the ten firms involved were: John Boggs, Thomas Devlin, George McDade and Sons, James Doak, Henry Holmes, Thomas Caves, John Bromley and Sons, Thomas Baker, William Hunter and Sons, and James Bromley and Brothers. Nine were present in Blodget's 1880 survey of the textile industry, eight still running carpets (Doak had converted to woolen fabrics but retained 18 carpet hand-

Smyrna carpet handlooms and handweavers at the Bromley mills. (J. R. Kendrick. "The Carpet Industry of Philadelphia," Seventeenth Report [1889], Pennsylvania Bureau of Industrial Statistics, p. D-43.)

In the context of depressed trade, some shops accepted both the reduction and the contract, and others refused the "paper" but took the rate cut. Gradually, as the implications of the contract were appreciated, daily meetings were called in Kensington, at which shop delegates called for resistance to both the manufacturers' initiatives. At a mass gathering on December 6, the "paper" was denounced as a "coolie contract," rhetoric drawn from the then-current anti-Chinese agitations that were steadily covered in the Philadelphia press. The offending document was published in full by the *Public Ledger* on December 15, as strikes were in process at a score of carpet firms:

> Whereas, we, the undersigned, each of us, have accepted employment from——, as a competent and skillful carpet weaver, we do hereby personally covenant and agree with them, the said employers, to comply with all factory regulations and to finish in good and workmanlike man-

looms). Of the 550 looms (395 handlooms and 155 power) in operation in 1880, 138 were owned by the two Bromley firms (Blodget, *Textile Industries*, pp. 45–50). In his conversion to woolen fabrics, James Doak acquired spinning machinery, but this did not indicate acquiescence to any imperative to integrate production. Instead, it represented an experiment by a hard-pressed carpet manufacturer seeking to shift his options. Ultimately, Doak chose to follow the specialty track by discarding all weaving operations, focusing on spinning high quality worsted yarns exclusively. This strategic flexibility preserved the family firm well into the following century. See Charles Doak Papers, Pastore Library, Philadelphia College of Textiles and Science.

ner, every piece of carpet we each begin, at such price as is being paid at the time of beginning the piece, and that if we or any of us, quit or discontinue on a piece of carpet in loom, whether by reason of combination (commonly called "strike") or for any other reason (continued sickness excepted) we each discharge ourselves and quit claim to loom, to employment and to the payment for any and all weaving we each may have done on such unfinished piece of carpet so left in loom, hereby forfeiting to our employers all pay for the same. This agreement is not to be violated by change of loom or style of work, and relinquishing or by suspension and resumption of work.[17]

The contract not only threatened to deprive workers of earnings if they failed to complete a full piece, it also menaced the potential for united action on the part of the shop force. Handloom ingrain workers produced from 14 to 20 yards of carpet in a day's work, a full piece accumulating on the roll at the back of the loom in a week or ten days of weaving. In any shop, pieces were always at different stages of completion; should all the looms run out of warp at once, warpers and beamers would be overwhelmed and the shop paralyzed. Thus the forfeiture of pay provision, which was the heart of the manufacturers' contract, would in turn have crippled workers' ability to turn out over grievances or rate changes, for all would lose income in widely differing amounts. Though manufacturers softened the impact of cuts by pledging to pay the same rate throughout the weaving of any roll, it might be noted that any upward adjustment would thereby also occur only when workers started a new warp. In sum, the "coolie contract" was a device aimed at dividing the workers against one another, reducing them from a united shop force to individual employees. As such, the contract was far more a threat to the weaving community than any single wage adjustment and, once so perceived, was condemned and successfully opposed along with the cut.

The winter strikes were successful in blocking the manufacturers' efforts. Though twenty mid-size shops, which together had had 622 workers in 1870,[18] were stopped completely, a hundred competitors were unaffected. By January 1 only seven manufacturers were still trying to enforce the lowered rates and the contract had become a dead letter. Three of these gave up in subsequent weeks and no more was heard from the others.[19] Commercial distress had led to a clustered response by proprietors seeking to reduce costs. Yet by tying oppressive terms of work to the reduction, by attacking the base of workers' shop solidarity, they overreached themselves and stimulated organized opposition that led to defeat on both fronts.

---

17 *PL*, December 15, 1873.
18 Worksheets, Ward 17 and Ward 19, 1870 Manufacturing Census Schedules, Philadelphia Co., cited hereafter as MCS.
19 *PL*, December 4, 6, 8, 10, 18, 1873; January, 1, 6, 10, 16, 31, 1874.

Events the following year suggest that the ingrain proprietors had learned from their winter setback. Gathering into the fold the vast majority of Kensington carpet firms, they confined their attentions to the price schedule and turned back a thrust by workers for improved conditions. In the early spring, united action having failed them, individual proprietors attempted to shave the rates that workers had defended a few months before. In response, shop delegates were called to a meeting on March 19, amid a scattering of turnouts against firms failing to pay the standard prices. Of those gathered to compare their situations, 48 delegates reported departures from the fall bill of prices, and widespread stoppages followed their resolution "that we unitedly stand together for the present standard prices."[20] The workers' "paper" called for uniform prices, weekly payment of wages, restrictions on the width of fabrics, and the ten-hour day.[21]

Each side showed considerable sophistication in the ensuing conflict, though the results this time favored the masters. Workers distributed their handbill citywide, and Spring Garden carpet weavers promptly asserted that they would "stand firm on the strike until we receive the standard prices according to the printed list, of which each employer received a copy."[22] Strikers responded to "unfair" press coverage by appointing a committee of five to correct newsmen's misconceptions. Efforts were made to reach outwork weavers and bring them into the strike; individuals representing 120 such operations (with about three looms each) were reported in attendance at a mid-April Kensington meeting. Internally, the weavers' strike committee exercised some centralized power, as an early resolution (March 27) to entrust "guidance of the strike . . . to the delegates from the various shops" was rejected at a general meeting of the carpet workers.[23]

This reluctance to decentralize decision making may have been related to the vigor shown by the carpet manufacturers, seventy-five of whom issued their common bill of prices on March 26. That day an operators' delegation had waited upon Mayor Stokeley to complain of the many "annoyances" strikers were causing, eliciting a pledge of police assistance if laws were being violated.[24] By the end of March the weavers reported 112 shops on strike, having again made contact with "German weavers," whose separate informal organization had supported the winter turnouts. Though some of the manufacturers broke ranks and acquiesced to the standard list, most held out, and eight weeks later, with a dignified statement, the workers' committee conceded the strike had been lost.

[20] *PL*, March 24, 1874.
[21] *PL*, March 26, 1874.
[22] *PL*, March 25, 1874.
[23] *PL*, March 26, 28, April 15, 1874.
[24] *PL*, March 27, 1874.

> After resolving to invite those weavers who have contributed to the
> support of the strike to examine the books of the Executive Committee
> and thanking Messrs. Mussleman and Lyons, Bromley and Bros., James
> Kitchenman, and Dornan, Maybin and Co. for not interfering with their
> men in their efforts to aid the strikers, the meeting adjourned, subject to
> the call of the Executive Committee.[25]

The vote of thanks at the close is particularly interesting. During the turnout, workers at shops that had accepted or were already paying the specified
prices donated portions of their pay to support those on strike. At Mussle-
men and Lyons, weavers pledged half of their earnings,[26] others contributing lesser amounts. In defeat, the vote of thanks to firms whose neutrality
toward the manufacturers' association aided the strike effort shows a gap in
the operators' front. Several of the district's largest firms[27] did not support
the efforts of the majority to chisel down the rates the weavers had defended
in the winter struggle. The weavers' expression of appreciation may have
been as well a discrete appeal to them to refrain from following the current
debacle with reductions in their own mills.

The associated carpet firms were triumphant, savoring their success in a
June 2 announcement that they planned to make permanent the organization
formed during the strike. Yet getting back to production seems to have been
more important than solidifying their gains, for it took two months before a
meeting could be arranged for the election of officers. Though the Carpet
Manufacturers' Association announced that its membership total had
reached eighty-eight, including firms with 1,750 looms and about 2,100
workers, attendance at the meeting was slim. No business was transacted
other than the election of officers and the issuance of a statement that "The
object of the Association is to adopt an unanimity of prices."[28] If the four
officers were representative of the membership, the association consisted of
middle-sized firms, with both the very small and the fairly substantial
(Bromley) outside the fold. The member firms averaged 24 workers each,
and the four officers (James Judge, Lewis Stremmel, James Pollock, and
Joseph Dittie) had but 114 workers among them in 1870.[29] Each of the firms
thanked by the defeated strikers had employed more than 100 workers at
that earlier date, indicating that Kensington's most substantial firms, better
able to endure the economic strain, had not made common cause with their

---

25 *PL*, May 30, 1874. The strikers' attention to financial responsibility also testifies to the
    sophistication of their autonomous organizations.
26 *PL*, May 5, 1874. Kitchenman's workers pledged $1 per week, from 10% to 12% of
    their estimated earnings.
27 Each of the three firms active in 1870 (Bromley, Dornan, Kitchenman) had more than
    100 workers.
28 *PL*, August 6, 1874.
29 Work sheets, Ward 17 and Ward 19, 1870 MCS, Philadelphia Co.

smaller competitors. The bigger firms had probably done well in a shrunken market by paying the workers' scale throughout the strike weeks. On other occasions when all were involved together, the smaller operations would succumb to workers' demands more quickly, setting the pattern for capitulation and getting back into the market first. Striking weavers were not unaware of these matters, as their 1874 thanks and later tactics illustrate. The mid-size shopmen's commitment to permanent organization faded rapidly. After one December 1874 meeting, the association sank from view.[30]

For several years after the 1874 strike, there were no serious outbursts in the Kensington carpet trade. Demand still lagged; reductions followed one another; some mills undertook the installation of power looms, operated at half the rates per yard paid for handwork, and employed a growing corps of young women, immigrant or first-generation daughters of Kensington workers, whose fathers for the most part were also textile-connected.[31] When the demand for their products stirred again in late 1876, the carpet workers of Kensington stirred with their demands as well. The year 1877 was one of strikes and victories for carpet workers, 1878 a year of strikes and defeat, and 1879 brought yet more strikes and an effective means to stabilize the tattered relations of labor and capital with the resuscitation of a customary ritual at least two generations old. Nonetheless, the pageantry of these busy years should not be allowed to create an image of "quiet times" for the period 1874–7. While the manufacturers held sway in carpets, sustained challenges were mounted to reductions of wages in Manayunk and in cotton mills

[30] Other ephemeral manufacturers' groups appeared in the early seventies in other sectors of the industry. In 1872 the cotton quilt (coverlet) producers leagued together to cut the piece rate from 22 ½¢ to 17 ½¢. The shops promptly went out, and though the manufacturers modified the reduction to 20¢, workers convened a "Weavers Union" to oppose any reduction. The weavers association may have been operating underground before the reduction, for it immediately offered to pay strike benefits of $8 per week for married men and $6 for single men. Whatever the source of these funds, the sudden crystallization of the union's character is apparent in its simple declaration of purpose: to assist "journeymen weavers out of work and to resist a reduction from 22 ½¢ to 20¢." Like the carpet workers later, the quilt workers met with separately organized German colleagues, who welcomed the "English society" and pledged that they would not take strikers' places. The results of the strike are not clear, but delegates from the Kensington quilt weavers, along with shawl and Venetian carpet shop delegates, were present at a mass meeting of ingrain workers during the 1873–4 strike. The shawl weavers followed up on their pledge to gain "a fair compensation for their labor," spinning off a bill of prices and successful strikes at seven firms at the conclusion of the carpet turnout. These cooperative endeavors indicate a neighborhood solidarity across craft lines that antedated any effective similar movement by manufacturers (see *PL*, November 14, 19, 1872; December 18, 1873, February 2, 10, 12, 19, 1874).

[31] Levine, "Their Own Sphere," pp. 69, 74. Of the women workers on carpets in Ward 19 in 1880, 92% were foreign-born or foreign-stock; 49% of their fathers were textile workers and 31% were skilled workers in other trades or laborers.

throughout the city. Labor associations in other industries were cautious during the worst of the depression, and strikes outside textiles were fairly rare in Philadelphia.[32]

An incident in the carpet district in 1876 provides evidence that the infrastructure for workers' mobilization remained solid. In May of that year, a carpet shop master proposed another reduction in the price of work, several such cuts having been enacted after the failure of the spring 1874 strike. Workers from the shop selected delegates, who in turn published a call for an assembly of shop delegates at a Mascher and Columbia Avenue hall, in the heart of the Kensington district. At this session, the general problem of lowered rates was aired, but action on a wider strike was deferred for forty-eight hours, at which time the delegates would return, presumably after consulting their shopmates. Under this pressure, the following day the proprietors withdrew the reduction and restored the previous schedule. When this settlement was announced to the second delegates' meeting, they agreed that further action was "unnecessary" but took care to have the acceptable schedule published, noting that not all shops were paying even these rates.[33]

This sequence is intriguing for several reasons. First, it was clearly difficult for any single shop to stand against the weight of collective response from craft workers, the memories of lost business in the earlier strikes being more durable than the elation provoked by victory. Second, no call went out to millowners to assemble to force through the cut, the Carpet Manufacturers' Association having been stillborn. Third, the full apparatus of shop meetings, delegates, calls for districtwide selection and gathering of representatives, back-to-the-shop consultation, and the publication of schedules had survived intact without the existence of formal institutions. It is phenomena such as these that are the core elements of working-class shop culture. Strikes might be lost, but a general acquiescence to the masters was unimaginable. Finally, the printing of the price list for ingrains not only publicized the successful resistance but also allow a measure to be taken of the erosion of work rates between 1874 and 1876.

The schedule of prices the Carpet Manufacturers' Association hammered into place in the 1874 conflict appeared in the *Public Ledger* an March 26, 1874. Table 10.3 sets these figures, grade by grade, alongside those successfully defended in the 1876 affair. As price cuts most often were a cent (or a cent and a half) at a time, it seems reasonable to estimate that the protest-inspiring reduction was the third or fourth announced to the weavers in two

---

[32] See *PL*, July 10, December 15, 1874; November 11, 1875, for strikes and strike threats by goldbeaters, sailors, and oystermen.

[33] *PL*, May 18, 23, 25, 1876.

Table 10.3. *Ingrain carpet handloom rates, Kensington, 1874 and 1876 (cents per yard)*

Ingrain carpets	Handloom rates		Reduction	% 1874–76
	1874	1876		
Extra-supers (13 pr.)	23, 24	18½, 19½	4½	24, 23
Supers (12½ pr.)	21½, 23	17½, 18½	4, 4½	23, 24
Regular (9 pr.)	14, 15	12, 13½	2, 2½	17, 11
Regular (8½ pr.)	13, 14	11	2, 3	18, 27

Note: The double figures indicate the differential paid for plain vs. figured work, though this had disappeared on the coarser grade by 1876.
Source: Public Ledger, March 26, 1874; May 25, 1876.

years. Workers were being paid, on balance, about 20% less than the rates in force after the failed strike of 1874. The rather greater absolute reduction in the higher grades kept the difference per yard between weaving coarse yarns faster, and weaving finer yarns more slowly at about 70% (the constant ratio between 8½ and 13 pair). This equalized the reductions so that variations from loom to loom in the quality of goods at any time did not lead to variations in the workers' pay packets.[34] As before, a fully competent weaver could be assigned to any grade of goods without necessarily adding to or subtracting from his income, a craft tradition whose preservation both kept peace in the shop and made difficult the sort of favoritism that might fracture workers' solidarity.[35]

[34] This is to say that at both dates workers producing fine goods (13 pair) received nearly the same pay packet as workers who produced coarser goods (8 ½ pair). It is also worth noting in this connection that the price of extra-supers had fallen only 11% in the same two years ($1 per yard in 1874 vs. 90¢ in the summer of 1876). For medium-supers, which may be comparable to the 12 ½ pair of Table 10.3, the drop was only 6% (87 ½¢ to 82 ½¢); this suggests that handloom rate cuts beyond market necessities may have been set in place partly to fund power loom purchases.

[35] As labor historians have begun to appreciate, there are many varieties of defeat in unsuccessful strikes. Regardless of the loss in earnings initiated by reductions, for manufacturers to have presented a scale of prices that broke the ratios between the piece rates for coarse and fine work and then to permanently assign some weavers to work that generated widely differing pay at month's end would have struck directly at the heart of shop traditions. Close readings of "price of work" scales can potentially unmask both such managerial strategies, on which "literary" sources are silent, and can (if a series of such scales survives) allow the timing of movements to be charted and placed in context. See William Reddy, "Decoding Wage Demands: The *Tariff* and the Life Cycle in the Linen Mills of Armentières (1889–1904)," paper delivered at the Social Science History Association sessions, Philadelphia, October 1976.

The 1877 events opened with a strike in February at the mill of Thomas Leedom and Co., one of the district's worst rate cutters. Leedom, a native of Bucks County, had come to the carpet manufacture from a background in a Cincinnati commission house. He returned to Philadelphia in 1865 with Aaron Shaw, an Ohio furniture manufacturer who became his partner in the Kensington mill. Because neither partner had experience in manufacturing carpets, two Scots millmen, Robert and Arthur Stewart, were included (1870).[36] Despite the acquisition of veteran carpet-shop skills (and with them, the raw material for factory paternalism), Leedom ruled the firm in a fashion that made it a frequent flash point for all-out confrontations through the mid-eighties. By the winter of 1876–7, he had reduced the rates so drastically that on the highest grades of ingrains his workers were earning only 13/14¢ per yard, clear of winding.[37] Leedom's weavers struck in February 1877 for an increase of 2¢ per yard, which was understandable given the low base from which they sought to advance. On the February 22, the "Committee" announced their success, noted the price to which their compensation had risen, and calmly "request[ed] all on the same grade to come out and seek for living prices."[38] As if the tocsin had sounded, strikes for advances and, in time, notices of advances gained without standouts filled the papers. Twenty-three individual firms were named, the increases of generally 1¢ per yard testifying to the unusually low rates previously prevailing at the Leedom firm.[39] The firms specifically mentioned in the newspaper ran 1,060 handlooms (1880) and included three of the district's largest employers.[40] If this strike wave was at all similar to others before and after, the remaining ingrain firms adjusted their rates upward quietly in the ensuing weeks, though the smallest employers and outwork contractors may have resisted the tide.

In the fall of 1877 the issue was joined again. Though the reports are sketchy, it appears that a dozen or more carpet manufacturers united to effect a reduction as the mills entered the winter season. When price cuts were announced, the workers' network geared up and launched a bevy of

36 Daniel Robson, *Manufactories and Manufacturers of Pennsylvania of the Nineteenth Century*, Philadelphia, 1875, pp. 96–7.

37 Carpet rates were quoted either with winding included or "clear of winding." Winding was the fee paid to weavers' young assistants for preparing bobbins for their looms, usually 1¢ to 2¢ per yard. The figures in Table 10.3 include winding, which was customarily paid by the weavers directly to their helpers, who were at times their own children. Thus Leedom's 13¢ to 14¢ translates for comparison to 14/15¢ to 15/16¢, about 4¢ per yard less than the 1876 rates for 13-pair extra-supers.

38 *PL*, February 22, 1877.

39 *PL*, February 27, 28, March 1, 2, 5, 6, 8, 13, 1877.

40 Blodget, *Textile Industries*, pp. 45–50. The three large firms were Leedom, Boggs and White, and Judge Brothers, each of which had 120 or more handlooms in 1880.

strikes during November. By mid-December, the "Executive Committee" announced that only two shops were still out in an effort to restore the spring rates; the "Employer's Union" had broken up as a result of competition. This time it was the weavers who pledged to form a permanent organization, electing the head of the emergency Executive Committee as president of the Weavers Union. Consistent with the resources of workers who had lost economic ground in earlier years, the union's initiation fee was 25¢, weekly dues 5¢.[41] Like the complementary manufacturers' association, once the crisis was past, it vanished from sight.

A month later the attempt of Judge Bros. to institute a ½¢ reduction triggered an eleven-day strike that forced the firm to resume the old rates. In the summer James Gay ventured a penny drop but changed his mind after a weeklong walkout.[42] The classic scenario was being replayed; in rising markets, workers, even one firm at a time, have leverage. Consistently, however, when the economic signals reverse, as they did in 1878, the initiative passes across the table. As Susan Levine has so well observed, "the 1878 spring season was an unmitigated disaster for Philadelphia carpet firms."[43] The manufacturers, suffering in silence for a time, went back on the offensive that fall. The leading firms first proclaimed a 1¢ per yard reduction in handloom work in October, and when that was accepted with protest, they turned next to their newest work force, the power-loom weavers. A parallel reduction of 1¢ per yard was effected on powered ingrains,[44] producing a dramatic three-month strike. One reason for the turnout of hundreds of women power weavers lay in the fact that a penny's cut to them represented a far more severe loss than it did to handloom weavers. Power-loom weavers were paid 6¢ per yard in 1878,[45] roughly $10 a week; a cent off their rate would reduce their earnings to less than $8.50. For male handloom workers earning, say 11¢ per yard, the weekly total earnings might come to about $13, which a penny's reduction would bring down about 10%. A penny's loss to power-loom weavers was more than half again as large as to handloom workers (16%). They walked out.

Most of the firms involved in the power-loom strike are familiar: the Bromleys, Leedom, Judge Bros., Gay, John Dornan, Ivins, Dietz and Magee, and James Kitchenman leading the way. Some mills closed completely (Leedom); others ran their handlooms (Bromley) while seeking "learners" for the power machines. Yet the key point regarding the 1878

[41] PL, December 17, 22, 1877.
[42] PL, January 7, 11, July 13, 19, 1878.
[43] Levine, "Their Own Sphere," p. 87.
[44] PL, October 23, November 13, 1878.
[45] PL, November 14, 1878.

strike is that it affected *only* nine firms with power looms,[46] a fraction of the total Kensington complement. The strike lasted eleven weeks, its extraordinary duration linked to the continued labors of the kinsmen or fraternal supporters of power-loom resisters.

The women strikers were resilient and articulate. When manufacturers asserted that they were paying appreciably more than their "eastern" rivals, offering a table of comparative rates, their antagonists immediately countered with facts and figures to show that the cost of living was higher in Philadelphia than in Amsterdam, New York, or Lowell.[47] A month later the manufacturers addressed a condescending threat to their female belligerents; the women politely reasserted their determination.[48] Nonetheless, when some broke ranks and returned at the close of the year, outrage took palpable form at the Bromley mills. A "girl" strikebreaker was assailed by a crowd on her way home from work, her mother was "abused" (probably more verbally than physically), and police were called to handle the situation.[49] Street gatherings on subsequent days were broken up by squads of bluecoats. Four weeks later the strike ended. The workers who were rehired were taken back on the "employers' terms," and a hundred or so activists were refused entrance as the learners had taken their places.[50]

Several observations are in order. First, the solid resistance of the firms was partly due to the large stocks of carpets they possessed, having adopted a bulk-run strategy with their new power looms. As the strike wound on, they were still in the marketplace to offer warehoused rolls, 4,000 or 5,000 of which were sold while the mills were either idle or partly staffed.[51] Despite this unity, no sectorwide coalition was attempted once the crisis had passed. Second, the engagement of learners was a potent tactic in manufacturers' hands, as it provoked both divisions in the community and tumultuous street demonstrations that triggered police involvement. This sequence may have

---

[46] *PL*, December 4, 1878.

[47] *PL*, November 14, 16, 1878.

[48] "With the kindliest feelings toward our employees, we give them to understand that we shall not re-employ them until they comply with the terms offered, and in the event of their continued refusal to accept the proposed terms, it is our purpose to bring the unemployed skilled Eastern labor to take their places, and to educate others to fill the gap occasioned by their continued refusal" (*PL*, December 19, 1878).

"Resolved, that we are compelled to accept of no reduction, in order to sustain life honestly, as it is impossible for us or Eastern weavers to do so at the proposed reduction. Resolved that we stand as a united body, and will not go to work . . . at the proposed reduction. Resolved, that we will help any weaver who may be in need, to stay out with us" (*PL*, December 20, 1878).

[49] *PL*, December 28, 30, 1878.

[50] *PL*, January 23, 1879.

[51] Ibid.

been a key to breaking the strike, for as state intervention inhibited the direct intimidation of scabs, it is nevertheless likely that women who were not a part of larger supportive networks (widows, shopkeepers' daughters) slipped back to work, fearing permanent loss of one of the "honorable" means of employment in the neighborhood. Nonetheless, women workers had shown that they were not as a body subservient and passive, a lesson manufacturers would learn yet again through an even longer struggle in 1884–5. And third, the operators' triumph was short-lived, as handloom carpet workers resumed the fray within weeks of the January 1879 defeat in a series of March and May challenges that produced the first durable settlement of labor–capital relations within memory.

In the first week of March the traditional call went out for handloom shop delegates to assemble to deal with the question of the price of work. In a few days in the wake of a flurry of strike calls, advances were granted and the workers' enduring resilience demonstrated. Few carpet manufacturers were evidently willing to settle into another round of conflicts, as three of the seven firms involved in both winter and spring engagements rapidly granted handloom increases to avoid further trouble.[52] (The strike results at the other firms were not mentioned in published reports.) Some shop delegates, as if to remind the masters of their presence, attended convocations only to report that they had not yet demanded adjustments. In April another fledgling union was announced, the Kensington Factory Operatives Association,[53] and in the following month a delicate sequence of thrusts and parries produced a means to handle "the whole question of the remuneration for labor."[54]

The March increases had generally been ½¢ per yard; the May resolution was sparked by the attempts of some manufacturers to get back what they had given. A number (unspecified) of shop masters had announced a ½¢ drop in the price of handwork, to which handweavers responded by appointing a visiting committee to make the rounds of manufacturers and assess the general situation. On May 23, a general meeting was convened at which a Committee of 12 was selected to meet with employers to attempt "to determine a schedule of prices satisfactory to all." Invitations went out immediately, but only nine manufacturers appeared at the first joint session on May 24. After some discussion, the weavers urged the manufacturers to create their own committee "to confer" with their hands and "draw up a schedule of prices." Three days later, the workers published their proposed bill of prices, the modest rates indicating why they at least were interested in

[52] *PL*, March 3, 5, 6, 1879.
[53] *PL*, April 25, 1879.
[54] *PL*, May 23, 1879.

stabilizing the general situation. Since the Leedom settlement in 1877 had established a price for 13 pair at 15¢–16¢ per yard, there had been reverses. By midway through 1879 the weavers proposed a slate of prices headed by 13 pair rates of 14¢–15¢, which presumably involved rejection of the ½¢ reduction that had started this round of jockeying.[55]

The next day workers at the mill of John Boggs struck against his determination to reduce the rates ½¢, despite attempts to resolve the conflict by what was then termed "arbitration." Within the week, Boggs had succumbed and accepted an increase of ½¢–1¢ in place of the reduction he had intended. In the wake of this setback, a cluster of thirteen manufacturers met on June 2 to review the proposal offered by the Committee of 12. Though clearly divided in their sentiments,[56] they ultimately resolved to accept the workers' bill, which was to run for six months, and to meet with the committee to discuss what to do about firms that might reject the uniform rates.[57] On the June 5, the two groups again met, agreeing that weavers would send visiting committees to present the terms to recalcitrant firms and observing that those who remained opposed to the general list were "nearly all proprietors of small shops."[58] This reference seems to suggest that the larger firms, having refused to attend the initial meetings, adopted the policy of those with whom they had collaborated in the earlier power-loom conflict.

Both the tactics workers proposed to use to bring reluctant shops into line and the principal reason that lay behind the operators' willingness to sign the agreement appeared at the sessions on June 7, when the weavers' committee presented the price list for their constituents' approval. It was announced that a survey would be made of all shops not conforming to the accepted rates but that they would not all be struck at once. Instead, the walkouts would proceed one firm at a time, stopping work in each violator "as it received a large order." For their part, consenting manufacturers would have, first, six months of guaranteed labor peace, no small item, given their recent experiences. But perhaps more crucial, as one speaker noted, was that "the object in adopting the new scale of rates for six months was to have them [in effect] during the time that buyers came around." Strikes mounted when orders waited filling could heavily damage a firm's trade; the agreement thus neutralized a tactical lever with which both parties were familiar.

---

55 *PL*, May 23, 24, 27, 1879.

56 Those reported in favor of acceptance included Judge, Robert Carson, Samuel Magee (of Ivins, Dietz and Magee), Samuel White (Boggs and White), and the recently defeated John Boggs (a different firm). Opposed were Thomas Burns, James Graham, and Andrew Givens. Conspicuously absent were several major firms from the power-loom strike, the Bromleys, Leedom, Dornan, and Gay, though both Judge and Ivins, Dietz and Magee had been involved.

57 *PL*, June 3, 1879.

58 *PL*, June 6, 1879.

John Bromley, patriarch of the Bromley family; a number of Bromley firms in carpets and lace derived from his original Kensington enterprise. (Free Library of Philadelphia)

The agreement reached far beyond the 600 workers and thirteen firms that had initially accepted the Committee of 12's bill. A week after the ratification of the "arbitration rates," 1600 ingrain weavers were reported receiving full prices in Kensington. At the same time, the traditional manifestations of workers' displeasure were under way at the shops that had rejected the proposal: Dornan Bros., William Hogg, and Gay among others. By the first of July, more than 2,300 looms were reported engaged on the schedule, with but seventy-five weavers still striking their stubborn employers. Success was general, the desirability of having a permanent organization was again voiced, and everybody went back to work. Yet underneath the euphoria that issued from having "solved" a chronic antagonism, some, most, or even all of the workers and manufacturers looked toward December, wondering what unanticipated and confounding events lay in store.

Although one of the provisions of the June agreement forbade strikes for the next six months without permission of the workers' executive committee, shop autonomy was not so quickly reined in. At the end of September, the ingrain weavers at John Bromley and Sons called for a 1¢ advance, and when refused, stopped work. Their delegates rushed to Dornan's mill nearby to call out the workers there and were infuriated when, respecting the agreement, their comrades remained at their looms. A number of the Bromley strikers "remained for some time around the building, shouting epithets at the hands at work."[59] Though the workers of Dornan, Judge, and other shops joined the Bromley workers the next day, the initial reluctance of

[59] *PL*, September 30, 1879.

Dornan workers suggests that workers' solidarity was complex. Respect for hard-won agreements coexisted uneasily with the obligation to support fellow workers seeking improved rates during the busy season. Equally important, as a joint committee of workers and masters had been formed in August, adopting articles of federation only a week before the Bromley scuffle, a mechanism was at hand to deal with the walkouts. On October 1, Kensington's handloom manufacturers met in general session, agreed to offer a compromise advance of ½¢ per yard, and posted notices of their offered schedule. The next day, in all but a few shops,[60] the conflict had ended and normal work resumed.[61]

This confrontation is significant along another dimension of the labor–capital relationship. It is not certain that the Bromleys or their workers had signed the June pact; but in joining the dispute, the Judge weavers clearly violated their pledge. Yet the manufacturers did not assemble in full wrath to condemn their employees and the fledgling effort to regulate the price of work on a general basis. Instead, their discussions led to a quick settlement, halfway between the 1¢ demanded and the "no advance" that had been the proprietors' first response. Both operators and workers were learning (or relearning) how to handle the details, the mechanics of negotiation.[62]

---

60 The reports are not terribly clear on the extent to which the strike spread after the initial rebuff at Dornan's. Judge and "a number of small shops" were reported out; my guess is that a dozen or so shops were stopped by the second day, energizing the manufacturers to compromise during the busy season.

61 *PL*, October 1, 2, 1879.

62 A revealing contrast with the conflict-spawned carpet groups may be gained by looking at the only documented activity of the spinners association, the preparation of a yarn exhibit for the 1876 Centennial Exposition. Because there were no recorded strikes in independent spinning firms from 1870 through the time of the exposition, it is doubtful that the impetus for their association came from shop-floor difficulties. Listed in the *Official Catalogue* as the Philadelphia Worsted Spinners Association, the prowess of these eight firms, "all exclusively devoted to making merino combing-wool worsteds," drew applause from John Hayes, chief judge and secretary of the NAWM. "The perfection of the yarns was fully recognized by the experts in the group of judges," he wrote in summary. This display likely reopened contacts between Hayes and one of the partners in a major Philadelphia worsted-yarn firm, Theodore Search of Fiss, Banes, Erben and Co. Search later referred to the Centennial exhibition as the source of his determination to found a textile school; its spinners association may also have been the seed that germinated under his care as the Philadelphia Textile Manufacturers Association (January 28, 1880). Just as their "separate establishments" were the pivots around which the most aggressive portion of the Philadelphia industry spun, the worsted spinners and their manufacturing clients became the core of the first citywide textile association (see *Official Catalogue of the International Exhibition of 1876*, Philadelphia, 1876, p. 119; John L. Hayes, ed., *Awards and Claims of Exhibitors at the International Exhibition, 1876*, Boston, 1877, p. 333; *PL*, January 28, 1880).

The creation of a standard list for the trade was hardly new, but the process by which the list was developed was changing. Prior to 1879, the two bodies, however constituted, drew themselves together and offered one another "take-it-or-leave-it" propositions. Compromises were few, generated when both sides neared exhaustion. By contrast, in the weeks that followed the October 1879 wildcat strikes, orderly proposals and counterproposals were shuffled back and forth between committees of weavers and owners, resulting in a sophisticated December compromise that renewed the agreement and satisfied both parties. The Weavers' Committee first forwarded a request for a penny advance to the Manufacturers' Committee, who called their constituents into meeting and returned an offer of ½¢. When the workers rejected this proposal, the Manufacturers' Committee met a second time. James Judge presided over the discussions, which produced an offer of ½¢ now and another ½¢ in three months, the agreement to run for six months, until June 9, 1880. At a general meeting of carpet workers the evening before the 1879 contract was to expire, the half-and-half was accepted and the new schedule ordered published in three daily newspapers.[63] The names of those firms not complying with the settlement were "to be furnished to the society for publication," evidently by the Manufacturers' Committee.[64] Two days later the price schedules appeared in the press. In early January a reporter visited the district and found workers satisfied with their increase and proprietors pleased that they no longer had to fear sudden strikes and that their labor costs were a known quantity for a definite period.[65] To complete the sequence, the list of resisting firms (six in all) was printed in the *Ledger* on January 21, 1880, and the March increase went into effect without incident.[66]

For nearly five years, no major strikes on ingrain carpets occurred in Philadelphia. The committees met in their appointed cycles, agreed on schedules that either maintained or increased the price of work, and, after ratifications, proclaimed their mutual satisfaction with the price schedule and hearty fellow feeling to the public.[67] A reporter covering the ingrain

63 This indicates, I think, that manufacturers and workers did not patronize the same daily newspapers, so that for full notification multiple insertions were necessary. The *Public Ledger* was the closest thing to a "labor" paper in Philadelphia, its usually fair coverage of strikes making it the paper in which workers associations published their meeting and shop-action notices. Manufacturers were more likely to read the *North American*, the *Inquirer*, and the *Press*.

64 *PL*, November 22, 26, December 3, 5, 9, 1879.

65 *PL*, December 11, 1879; January 6, 1880.

66 *PL*, January 21, March 11, 1880.

67 *PL*, May 21, November 10, 1880; on the working-class use of ingrains, see *Bulletin, NAWM* 14 (1884):74.

discussions in 1880 summarized the remarks by James Judge, head of the manufacturers' delegation:

> Mr. Judge spoke of the difficulty that had existed in the district before the bill of prices had been amicably arranged, and said that there had been no breach of contract between the employers and the employed. He thought that it was nothing but fair to readopt the bill of prices, as the weaver was only making a fair living now and they were [sic] worthy of that much. He also said that it would be a sorry day for Kensington when the present arrangement fell through.[68]

He was accurate on every point, including the last, as we shall see.[69]

Manayunk and Kensington: strikes, rituals, and the Knights in the early eighties

With the affairs of the carpet district "settled" for a time, we may turn to look toward another arena, factory Manayunk, where one of the infrequent conflicts that appeared in the less troubled, versatile sectors of the Philadelphia industry took shape at the woolen mills of a familiar figure, Sevill Schofield. The strikes at the Economy Mills, first in 1882 and later in 1884–5, will illustrate the continuity of customary relations in Kensington and the crosstown Schuylkill factories and the importance of ritual activities in the world of proprietary manufacture. We will then return to Kensington for the mid-eighties confrontations that will close this section.

Along with his fellow Manayunk operators, Sevill Schofield cut wages in the wake of the 1873 collapse and experienced several strikes that evidently failed to block the reductions.[70] On the whole, Schofield's operations were in far better shape than those of his cotton cousins. Archibald Campbell's firm, for example, never departed from the all-cotton base. After his death in 1874, it alternated between running full and being closed,[71] following a track

---

68 *PL*, May 23, 1880.
69 A handful of major carpet firms were connected with a regional association of eastern power-loom mills and were generally outside the groupings set by mid-size firms. Thomas Leedom, the Dobson brothers, and the Bromleys were a part of this aggregation, which resolved in 1878 to limit production after the depressed sales of the spring season. Whether their plan for a four-day-week operation was ill observed or simply not sufficient to deal with an overstocked market is unknown; the subsequent power-loom rate cut and strike followed within months (Levine, "Their Own Sphere," p. 89). The frequent turnouts at Dobson's carpet mills were related to both his heavy involvement in mass production and his abrasive personal style, of which we had a taste at the beginning of Chapter 9.
70 *PL*, June 2, November 24, 28, 1874.
71 *PL*, December 1, 1874. The firm's operations were also likely hampered by the two years required to execute Campbell's estate.

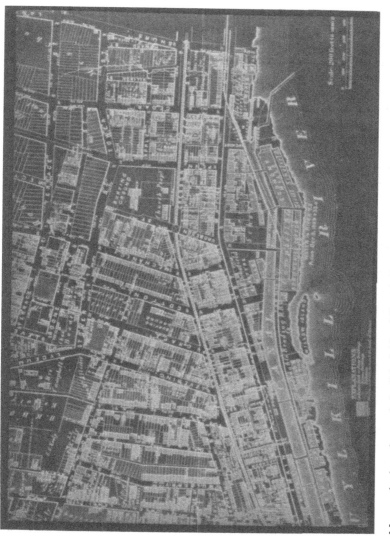

Manayunk, along the canal; the Schofield and Campbell mills are right of center and the Ripka factories are at the lower left, circa 1875. Housing has filled all the relatively level areas, and lots are marked out on the steep inclines for additional development. (Philadelphia Social History Project)

peppered with reductions and strikes, until the mills burned down in a pair of massive fires late in the eighties. The demise of the Campbell mill signaled the end to "the last but one exclusive cotton manufactory in Manayunk."[72] Although Schofield mirrored the productive strategies of other wool men in running fashionable patterns, he also persisted after the war in the blanket trade, a specialty that was becoming increasingly crowded and competitive. Whether this staple commitment was a source of difficulties cannot be known without additional data. In any case, Schofield's attempt to cut rates on at least four occasions between 1882 and 1885 provide a glimpse of factory social relations that parallel those at Kensington.

In April 1882 Schofield notified his work force that the state of his trade necessitated a reduction in wage rates. In response, the workers selected a committee that "visited" him to offer a counterproposal. The mill force, through its representatives, indicated a preference for selective layoffs rather than a general rate cut. With this, Schofield altered his plans and dropped 40 of the 1,000 workers on his payroll.[73] This brief exchange points both toward an openness and flexibility in the relations between the proprietor and his hands and to the family economy of mill district households. As many families had multiple workers in the textile mills, it was clearly preferable that one earner be dismissed to seek other employment, rather than that all should experience a loss of income. Whereas such exchanges make a good deal of sense in the personalized environment of the Philadelphia textile manufacture, they would be something of a surprise if discovered at Lowell.

The spring compromise held through the summer and fall production seasons, but during the week after Christmas, 1882, workers at the Economy Mills were notified that a 15% reduction was to take effect in the new year. Winter was the slow period for woolen mills, as buyers placed orders in the spring months for goods to be retailed in the following winter's markets. Production then was its busiest through the summer into early fall. Schofield did not run mixed goods or cottons, which were ordered in the fall, produced in the winter and spring, and distributed thereafter. As a result, during the slack winter months, samples, blankets, and some staple woolens might be run, keeping a sizable part of the work force active in anticipation of next season's orders. Those mills that shifted production from woolens to mixed goods and cottons could expect to run year round, but seasonal variations in the size of the work force (or in rates) were present at firms, like Schofield's,

---

72 *PL*, March 2, April 4, 5, 7, 9, 1883; January 21, April 27, October 14, 1885; Mildred Goshow, ed., "Mills and Mill Owners of Manayunk in the 19th Century," typescript, 1970, p. 58, Roxborough Branch, Free Library of Philadelphia.

73 *PL*, April 24, 1882.

that had a narrower range of variable output. Schofield's 1882 reduction may have been an attempt to keep the bulk of his force intact and at work in anticipation of the coming season, while cutting the risk involved in running goods without orders by lowering labor costs. Whatever the proprietor's precise situation, his workers resisted the change. Some quit upon learning of the proposed cut, and after the New Year passed and it took effect, "the card room boys struck work, followed by about 250 weavers," effectively shutting the plant. Schofield accepted their refusal with equanimity, telling a reporter that trade was so dull that he didn't "mind closing for a while."[74] Spring orders surely reopened the facility, but whether or not the reduction was effected was not recorded.[75]

Almost two years later, in the fall of 1884, Schofield put forward a reduction of 10%, again at the close of the season. This time it was accepted without incident. However, after Christmas, the failing state of the economy having rendered the slack season more depressed than usual, he closed the mills for five weeks. Late in January 1885, notices signalling the reopening of the mill the first Monday in February also announced a second 10% cut. On the appointed day, Schofield's weavers gathered inside the factory and "discussed the situation," the proprietor arriving to present his case. Though market conditions remained poor, he offered the hands the chance to weave up the materials on hand "more for their sake than his." Asked if wages would be increased when prices recovered, Schofield cautiously averred that they would be "when conditions warrant it." Departing the mill, the weavers, who were for the most part women, met formally in a nearby hall. After some discussion, they decided to "refuse the reduction" and "resolv[ed] to join the Knights of Labor."[76] The mills stayed shuttered, and the district remained quiet for almost four weeks.

At the end of February, Schofield announced again that his mills would reopen, with the reduction in effect. Twelve workers showed up to accept his terms. They were met at the close of the day by a crowd of 600 or 700, who hurled insults, and eventually snowballs, at the scabs and their twenty police escorts. Both the proprietor and the police agreed that the striking weavers were not among that unruly gathering. The strikers issued a notice rich with disingenuous simplicity:

> To the Public – We the undersigned, do respectfully request the law-abiding citizens of the town to stay away from the Economy Mills, and not to encourage mob law or violence, for innocent persons may get hurt.

[74] *PL*, January 4, 1883.
[75] I suspect that it was dropped, for to reduce wages at the *start* of the busy season would invite a turnout that could ruin the year's trade.
[76] *PL*, February 4, 1885.

> We, the striking weavers, discountenance all disturbance, and will do all in our power to discourage any acts of violence. Also, we hope every person will remain away off the streets until the present difficulty is over; for if these scabs that are working can stand last night's trouble, we are sure we can, and we sincerely hope all business men and citizens will boycott them. We are on our strike and intend to stay out until we receive fair compensation for our labor.
>
> Yours, respectfully, The Committee of Weavers.[77]

Notwithstanding this appeal, 500 Manayunkers congregated at the mills the next afternoon, but Schofield had dismissed his strikebreakers at an early hour to avoid a repetition of the events of the previous day. Later, when Schofield claimed that weavers would make $8 or $9 a week even with the reduction, H. B. Behan, "chairman of the Weavers' meeting," said the strikers would jump at such an offer if it was guaranteed. Schofield did not respond.

Three weeks later, however, the proprietor succumbed, reopening the mills for the spring season without the reduction but refusing at first to hire Behan, the spokesman. At a meeting of the Schofield workers, James Wright, a master workman of the local Knights of Labor, encouraged them to "stand by Behan," and they resolved to stay out until the "chairman was reinstated at the mill." He was, and work commenced at noon the following day.[78] Six months later, facing the slack winter season, Schofield "increased the wages of all employees 5%, without being asked."[79] Given the context, this step appears to be a fairly transparent attempt by the proprietor to soften the effects of several harsh years and to reassert the aura of paternal consideration that had once informed factory relations.

The personal character of the relationships and the formal structure of the interactions involved in the Schofield strike (shop meeting, the proprietor explaining his situation, processions and deliberations, even the language of "refusal") were constituent elements in a factory culture that was quite similar to those relationships played out in the carpet shops of Kensington and at fabric mills in South Philadelphia and Spring Garden.[80] The offering of a reduction and its subsequent refusal and the customary means by which each was handled emphasized the autonomy of each party to a transaction that was at once economic and cultural. The personal quality of the exchanges, codified in standardized expressions, allowed a path to be charted between the twin rocks of individually embodied arrogance (Ripka)

---

[77] *PL*, February 28, 1885.

[78] *PL*, March 17, 18, 1885.

[79] *PL*, September 10, 1885.

[80] For examples at Schofield's, see *PL*, February 28, 1885; in South Philadelphia, *PL*, April 21, 1882. Others abound.

and cooly distanced economizers (Lowell), preserving the dignity of the opponents while confirming their respective social and productive roles. Neither a reduction nor its refusal demeaned or belittled either party. Subjectively, there could be within the rules of the system neither "exploiter" nor "exploited," for the intensions of such designations would explode the entire cultural network of autonomous and dignified contracting parties disagreeing about the terms of work.

The assertion that such relationships were rooted in both shop and factory culture in Philadelphia textiles denies neither that the parties were unequally placed with respect to resources and power in the social and economic system nor that, objectively, capital was using labor in order to accumulate. The point is that it was precisely through these rituals that those objective conditions were experientially translated into formal conflicts of reliable shape rather than class war. Without some appreciation of the cultural roots of such practices, the seriousness with which carpet workers regarded signing the "manufacturer's paper" can hardly be comprehended. Without this understanding, interviews with Manayunk strikers that found them bearing "no hard feelings" toward rate-cutting mill masters will seem to be arrant nonsense.

Through an awareness of these cultural relations of production, other activities take on new meaning. The hooting and jeering of scabs reflects neither fear for the loss of jobs nor wild mob rule. It was, instead, part of a scenario that materialized "according to the rules." In a strike, it was possible for manufacturers to offer their terms to other workers; what was incorrect was workers' acceptance of these terms, the penalty for which was the shaming and neighborhood outrage directed at such workers, not the millmen. Consistently in the textile districts, those arrested in strike disturbances were not strikers, indicating yet another plausible layer of differentiation. Strikers time and again undertook to persuade scabs of the error of their decisions; it was for others not individually involved in the strike to administer the social punishment for obstinacy. We may thus imagine street dramas of fair sophistication being played out in strike situations, all parties living their roles.

If there were informal rules of conflict such as those sketched here, breaking those rules threatened the viability of the system, threatened to add social incoherence to the anarchy of capitalist industrialization. What might such transgressions include? The manufacturers, for example, might enlist the power of the state to spoil the show. The position of the police in these manifestations was important and equivocal. Drawn from the same ethnic and neighborhood roots as the strikers and as some of the manufacturers, they were sworn to preserve order and protect property. Rarely did strikers concern themselves with the manufacturers' property; after the wave of incendiary fears in the thirties, mills burned down regularly but without any assistance from striking workers. Order was a different matter. When scabs went to work, police frequently were entrusted with escorting them to and from the shops. This was a particularly volatile situation, but there were roles in it as well. So long as the police did not interfere with the jeering procession that accompanied scabs to their door, all went smoothly. So long as the crooning locals did not throw stones, ice, or potatoes[81] or physically assault the working few, order was being preserved, albeit under an unusual construction of the term. However, when zealous officers attacked a crowd that was only playing its part, or when members of the crowd precipitated police violence by lobbing rocks, melees ensued. Mayoral proclamations that banned assembly following such a collapse of the "orderly" process of intimidation were bitterly resented precisely because they represented an intervention that, however lawful, was simply unjust. That strikers' assemblies pledged to disown any of their party who engaged in violence makes perfect sense. Persuasion was their task, shaming and intimidation were a community responsibility, and assault lay just outside the pale.

What else shook this framework of ritualized conflict? To bring in outsiders was a major offense, for the threat to replace strikers with workers "from the East" was a serious breach of trust. On their arrival they were enveloped by the cultural networks, which would likely provoke one of three responses. First, if they shared what we here call "factory culture," they rapidly comprehended what was afoot, claimed they had been lured to the district by trickery, and departed, sometimes voicing support for the strikers. Second, were they strangers to the scenes that confronted them, as some Lowell carpet weavers evidently were, their fear and bewilderment at the "mobs" produced either panicky flight or, alternatively, a grim determination not to be cowed. This last behavior escalated the struggle, for an influx of outsiders who bent to management rather than to the community could fracture the whole system. It was, significantly, native-born Thomas Leedom, whose background involved commercial interests rather than mill training, who most defiantly recruited at large, generating "riotous" exchanges in the long power-loom strike of 1884–5. As a compromise settlement to that affray was being hammered out, Leedom's untenable position in the district materialized in an announcement that he was beginning construction of a carpet mill in Bristol, Pennsylvania, twenty miles upriver on the Delaware. His comment, paraphrased by a reporter: "When a mill was isolated, there was generally less trouble experienced with its employees than when there were a number of them together, as in Philadelphia."[82]

---

[81] The peculiar meaning of potatoes hardly needs emphasis. All these objects and others *were* thrown when things fell apart.

[82] *PL*, February 22, 27, 28, March 4, May 18, 1885; quote is from March 4.

In a somewhat subtler way, the development of institutional vessels for these fluid relations was another threat to the rituals of conflict. Though activists on both sides regularly invoked the value of "permanent organization," perhaps drawing on their experiences in political parties and religious and social associations and the example of the building trades, neither manufacturers nor workers were able to sustain the groups convoked in crises. Certainly, competition made manufacturers' unity a temporary thing, for, other than shared misery making common action reasonable, to what purpose would they gather? Shop autonomy was a centerpost of workers' culture in big mill and small; that delegates returned to their co-workers for instruction involved both democracy and direct accountability, embedded in a wider craft solidarity of which the Visitation Committee and mutual support were only the most obvious signs. To hand over executive power to a small group in any permanent way was to destroy the system. Even in districtwide strikes such authority was not granted without dissent. And once the crisis had ended and the "leaders" called for permanent organization, their constituency melted back into the shops, to summon up the whole apparatus at the next crisis. Both manufacturers' independence and workers' shop autonomy were compromised by the five-year cycle of six-month contracts, which was agreed to by both sides only after two years of guerrilla warfare. As impressive as their "harmony" was, the consultations of committees could only lessen, not prevent, the impact of slack times on the price of work. The manufacturers' association (PTMA), which was permanent, was formed by men who occupied the least strife-torn sections of the industry. It focused its attention away from the shops and was drawn into the struggles of the mid-eighties only by a major "violation" of the rules on the workers' part, their enlistment in the Knights of Labor.

The extreme antagonism felt by Philadelphia textile manufacturers regarding the Knights may become comprehensible when placed in the context of the social relations of proprietary manufacture as here outlined. By the mid-eighties, the Knights had all the fearsome characteristics of a juggernaut; they were enormous, spanned dozens of trades, and were moving toward a collective vision that chilled the proprietary hearts of the city's millmen. Textile manufacturers, and only some of them, had managed to league together in extremis or to banquet and talk of tariffs and education. By contrast, "Labor" was massing, building nationally the kind of transindustrial coalition that bid fair to destroy society, society being that set of relationships whereby mill-boys like Sevill Schofield had managed to accumulate capital, status, and authority. Objectively, it must be allowed that manufacturers in the trades had contributed to the fate that confronted them. Those who committed their mills to the bulk output of blankets, ingrains, and cottons felt the whiplash of the larger capitalist economy in falling margins and prices and in depressions for which they could hardly feel individually responsible.

The Knights well fit, from the manufacturers' perspective, the definition of labor's outsiders. They "organized" workers, a claim preposterous on its face, given how well the workers organized themselves. They "authorized" strikes, an action that soon would create internal battles among the textile troops who had enlisted. But perhaps worst of all, they "negotiated" settlements, shattering the direct social relations between proprietor and work force with the intervention of foreign parties. When one added to this the promises of financial support for strikers (promises that were more in the air than in the bank) and the fact that the Knights were a "secret society," it was but half a step to the conclusion that they had to be opposed, stopped, rooted out. It mattered little to manufacturers that they had provoked their employees to embrace the Knights. "Outsiders" knew little of the textile manufacture, knew personally neither their members nor the millowners with whom they proposed to treat, and yet, claimed to "represent" strikers and offered to "intercede" and discuss a settlement. Something had gone horribly wrong.

As should be expected, the textile manufacturers of Philadelphia responded in a variety of ways to the enrollment of their workers in District Assembly No. 1 of the Knights of Labor. Sevill Schofield seems to have ignored the whole matter until the end of the 1885 strike, at which time he briefly attempted to exclude their most vocal spokesman. When workers united around the issue of H. B. Behan's reinstatement, Schofield acquiesced. Moving later in the year to repair his standing vis-à-vis the operatives, he granted a nominal, but unsolicited, wage increase. Other masters, intent on destroying the intruders, engaged the Knights in frontal confrontations, even at the cost of mass dismissals and bitter legacies. Still others sought ultimately and collectively to reestablish the direct relationships that antedated the emergence of the Knights, groping for a way out of the "sorry day" that the great carpet strike of 1885 had brought to Kensington.

The first salvo in the Kensington carpet struggles of 1884–6 came from the Brussels division, where committees of manufacturers and workers met in May 1884 to discuss the proprietors' proposal of a 1¢ per yard reduction. The weavers, promising an answer in a few days, returned to their shopmates for consultation. When the workers rejected this proposal, the millmen "offered" a compromise ½¢ cut. However, before the workers could reject or ratify the offer, five of the eight principal Brussels firms broke faith by posting this figure as the official rate. The five firms were struck, the remaining three were not. One of the struck mills broke ranks within a week and rescinded the reduction. The others (Horner Bros., Schofield Mason and Co., John Bromley and Sons, and Hogg & Metzger) stood firm, withdrew their ½¢ compromise offer as of June 1 and began to hire learners, claiming that they would not take back members of the "Weavers Association."[83] The Power Loom Brussels Carpet Weavers Association of the U.S. was another local operation with an ambitious title, but faced with exclusion from the mills, the membership voted to join the Knights after a month on strike.[84] Two days after the initiations, Horner Bros. folded. Though the Knights did not pay a dollar in strike benefits, contributions from other weavers, including Brussels workers at "Eastern mills," supported the strikers well into August.[85]

On the eighth of August, in the thirteenth week of the strike, a committee from the District Assembly of the Knights intervened "to try to adjust the difficulty with the employers."[86] Though they pledged to either support the strikers or find work for them if no settlement could be reached, none of the three committeemen were carpet weavers. The intercession of the Knights leadership,[87] however well intended, was a thorough disaster. At the end of August, the best the Knights' negotiators could recommend was the acceptance of the ½¢ compromise reduction offered in May. The weavers approved and returned to their shops only to find that the three manufacturers had agreed neither to the compromise settlement with the Knights nor to the reinstatement of their former workers. This shocking result was reinforced a few days later when the few learners solicited to replace them were granted permanent berths.[88]

Meanwhile, at the Kensington workshop of Stinson Brothers & Kurlbaum, another Brussels struggle produced an equally discouraging outcome. During the last week of August, a weaver returning from an extended illness found that the shop superintendent had failed to ready a loom for him to resume work. Several co-workers, individually members of the Knights, lodged a protest with the owners. On September 1, when they arrived for work, the protesters were "called to the office and notified that unless each one severed his connections with all labor organizations, he was discharged." Learning of this ultimatum, the entire shop walked out, leading the proprietors to fire the whole work force. The Stinson mill masters issued a resolute statement:

83 *PL*, May 7, 9, 12, 13, 20, 21, 27, 1884.
84 *PL*, June 10, 12, 14, 1885.
85 *PL*, June 16, July 23, 1884.
86 *PL*, August 8, 1884.
87 The committee included the current district master workman, the recording secretary, and the past master workman.
88 *PL*, August 29, 30, September 2, 1884.

> Being owners of our establishment, we have made up our minds that we
> are the proper persons to say in what way it shall be run, and to make
> such rules and regulations as suit us best, although we have always and
> under all circumstances avoided, for the sake of harmony, all such rules
> as might be deemed arbitrary or oppressive to our employees. The
> source of the whole trouble arose from the fact that our weavers be-
> longed to a weavers' union, and that this union was through our weavers
> endorsing to dictate to us how and in what way we should conduct our
> business. This of course we could not submit to, and on Friday morning
> before dinner we discharged the entire force and will not re-employ any
> of them until they have left the various associations.[89]

What is especially telling about this exchange is that the Stinson weavers
were members of the fledgling independent Tapestry Brussels union. When
their boldness in the shop resulted in a mass firing, a few quickly capitulated
and went back to work, discarding the organization; the rest voted formally
to join the Knights as a body, for only some had been members individually
before the walkout–dismissal.[90] Some manufacturers had developed a hair
trigger in response to "unions," which threatened to replace the "committees" whose right to voice shop grievances was long established. Whether the
Knights members were precipitate in walking out, whether management was
overreacting in firing the lot, or whether the superindendent in question was
swinish or a misunderstood functionary, what is critical about this sequence
is the volatile and explosive context. Management mistakenly believed that
banning the "organization" would restore their traditional prerogatives, for-
getting that it was their own abuse of those prerogatives that had led workers
to just such a combative redefinition of the rules of conflict. For their part,
the workers erred in expecting the Knights to negotiate peace with the
proprietors, failing to realize that the customary pattern of opposition was
shattered once the Knights were involved.

The Knights leadership may not have fully comprehended either the
textile "factory culture" or the convulsions that their acceptance of textile
workers into the organization was triggering at its foundations. They were,
however, by no means insensitive to the effects of their intercessions on
many mill operators. While Schofield tried to recover his initiative, the
Kensington ingrain carpet manufacturers, digesting the same economic slippage as their Brussels colleagues, put forward their reductions in the fall of
1884. Rejected by handloom craftsmen, the cuts were similarly refused by
power-loom women workers, who struck, joined the Knights, and faced an

---

[89] *PL*, September 2, 1884.
[90] Ibid.

all-out "damn their eyes" response from the ingrain proprietors (Leedom, Bromley, and others).

The intricacies of the five-month strike that bracketed the winter months of 1884–5 can barely be summarized here. A few particulars are important, however. The ingrain trade was at its lowest state since 1873, according to the weaver-secretary of the joint manufacturer and weavers Protective Association, who reported that he had had but three weeks' full work in the last three months. The November reduction offered by the masters' delegates was, then, no surprise, and its rejection by the handloom workers was handled in standard fashion. The handlooms soon stood silent, though one mill operator pledged to start again "with new men."[91] A week later, on November 19, after a secret meeting and with no regard for the usual formal procedures invoked to process a reduction, more than thirty power-loom ingrain firms posted notices of immediate reductions for their largely female power weavers, setting off the second phase of the long struggle. When the manufacturers blustered that they would take back no worker connected with a secret society, weavers of both sexes joined the Knights by the hundreds. When the manufacturers brought in scabs from outside the community, the Knights distributed a leaflet that urged them to join the union, and the street theater of direct intimidation was mounted daily. By January, the cadence quickened. The proprietors' threat to deny work to the whole body of strikers cut into the vitals of the community; crowd violence became a daily riposte. At mid-month, Thomas Dolan appealed to the mayor for a major police intervention, at the same time affirming that "he did not believe the striking weavers were at fault."[92] With hundreds of police circulating throughout the district, by the end of January the struck firms claimed to have reactivated about a third of their power looms, though 125 of them were at mills that had broken ranks and brought their weavers back at the old rates.

Leedom's Lowell imports blew the lid off at the end of February, with a week of howling street scenes. And then, as if all the parties came to recognize the precarious brink at whose edge they teetered, the district quieted. Over the next month, the strikers, the manufacturers, and the Knights each contributed to a scenario that allowed them to backpedal from a fight to the finish. The first step, as was often the case, was a matter of rumor. As the scuttlebutt had it, the Knights were seeking to enlist as an intermediary the Universal Peace Society, a group committed to amicable relations between labor and capital. The next week Master Workman James Wright offered a

[91] *PL*, November 12, 1884.
[92] *PL*, January 16, 1885.

conciliatory move that showed some appreciation of the system of social relations whose breakdown was imminent.

> I will be perfectly satisfied to see the weavers go back to work at the old wages without forcing our order upon the manufacturers, providing the weavers hold to their organization. I want to see the manufacturers deal with their people directly, and if the former do not want to see the Knights of Labor, they should not be forced upon them.[93]

The next day manufacturers announced they would meet with workers from their own mills. After a week of visiting the mills where they had worked, individual committees reported no concessions had been offered by the masters. This would soon change.

Workers at Bromley Brothers reached a settlement on April 4, but neither other workers nor other firms followed, as the Bromley compromise was distasteful. The firm agreed to halve the reduction to ½¢, but demanded returnees' signatures on "a paper renouncing the Knights of Labor."[94] For hard-line manufacturers, this concession on the price of work seemed too expensive; for most strikers, such renunciation was too bitter to accept. But two weeks later the strike was settled, in the old and tried way, after a series of meetings between committees of delegates from each side. Bromley's rate compromise was accepted widely but careful language was used to evade a direct call for abandonment of the Knights. Indeed, the one modification in practice adopted, the use of a "disinterested" arbitrator to resolve an impasse, had been put forward by the Knights in Philadelphia's shoe trades before its introduction to the carpet industry. The agreement read, in part:

> And we also agree that we will not, as weavers or employers, cause to be introduced into any workshop any system or organization that will in any manner interefere with the conduct or manner in which they shall conduct their business affairs, and that our works shall be conducted in the same manner as heretofore, and all disputes that may arise hereafter as to the price of weaving shall be referred to a Board of Arbitration, the said Board to consist of an equal number of manufacturers and weavers not to exceed five . . . of each, and if they cannot agree, they shall have power to call in a disinterested person or persons as agreed upon, and to abide by the result of said arbitration.[95]

Both weavers and owners were bound not to alter the customs of the trade; there was no mention of "papers." The two constituencies met separately to ratify these terms, the manufacturers, as agreed, confirming and signing first, then reporting to the strikers their affirmation, upon which notice, the

93 *PL*, March 20, 23, 1885.
94 *PL*, April 4, 1885.
95 *PL*, April 18, 1885.

weavers enthusiastically declared the strike at an end. They reminded the millmen of the compromise with regard to membership in the Knights (the heart of which had been presented in Wright's March statement): "It was said that the [workers] would regard the presentation of any paper renouncing the Knights of Labor as a violation of the terms of the agreement."[96] Consistent with this vigilance, the shop delegates assembled to report on "papers" two days later. Though some millmen grumbled about accepting members of the Knights, the agreement had generally been observed.

The conditions that led to a settlement that revitalized customary forms of factory social relations were not simply the fruit of economic attrition. Indeed, the new manufacturing season was upon the carpet masters, and after five months without pay, the workers were surely straining family economies throughout the district. These were substantial considerations, of course, but no less crucial was the perception that the escalation of the struggle by March was threatening the social and cultural foundations of both factory and community. The Knights withdrew gracefully from the spotlight, an older script was dusted off, modified to handle impasses via a "disinterested" party, and catastrophe was averted.

If there was an attempt to rescue the cultural relations of production in the carpet trades, some evidence for the retention of its forms and styles should be advanced. The week after Christmas 1885, the power-loom shop delegates assembled to elect three Arbitration Committee members to present a request for an advance to the millmen. The delegates circularized the manufacturers, notifying them of the "dissatisfaction with the present scale" and prompting their selection of three delegates to attend a New Year's Day convocation. The agreement of April 17, 1885, was reaffirmed in all details, and the price of work was advanced ½¢ per yard, restoring the pre-strike rates. At two meetings on the fourth and sixth, shop delegates reported the new scales in effect in forty-six of forty-eight power-loom mills, reports lacking from the other two. With satisfaction general, the new agreement was ratified.[97] The next day handloom ingrain carpet weavers convened their delegates, announced a request for an advance of from 1 to 1½¢ per yard, nominated members to an arbitration committee, and published *their* circular. When the manufacturers reported that their association had dissolved, the weavers resolved to deal with individual firms, and by the end of January they voted to strike. If they were a pitiful residue of a dying craft, toward which Kendrick and others would direct polite concern, they were not aware of it. Twelve hundred handloom ingrain weavers struck seventy-five shops and won. Some shops gave up quickly; Ivins, Dietz, and Magee held out

---

[96] *PL*, April 20, 21, 1885.

[97] *PL*, December 29, 31, 1885; January 2, 5, 7, 1886.

until February 24, by which time the rates on 1,500 handlooms had been advanced.[98] On the first of March Brussels carpet weavers presented their new bill of prices to manufacturers, and so it continued.

The conflicts and customs here reviewed provide a partial sketch of a fairly complex system of shop and factory social relations, durable yet capable of modification. Its forms and rituals were most evident in crises, and were broadly rooted in the textile trades of nineteenth-century Philadelphia. Whereas the general prosperity of silk, woolen, and other sectors based on specialization and flexible capacity led to few conflicts, the Schofield case sheds some light on the extension of shop practice into the factories. Other firms sailed along without incident. For example, William Emsley, one of the PTMA's founders, could report at the close of the seventies that no reductions had been posted at his yarn mills since 1866. Briggs and Brothers, fancy cottonade manufacturers with forty workers in 1870 and seventy in 1882, reported no reductions in any grade of work for twenty years.[99] Such stability does not generate the illumination offered by great strikes and the means devised to deal with them. Yet it may well be reasonable to suggest that analogies to the cultural relations at the carpet manufactories and the Economy Mills were present generally in other quarters of the industry. They too were populated by proprietary firms of immigrant origin that shared the same neighborhood spaces and community networks as those examined more closely here. If the associations and unions spawned by economic dilemmas proved ephemeral, the cultural elements in the matrix of accumulation that led to their formation and their capacity to deal with one another were both durable and historically consistent with the social and material relations of production that made the Philadelphia textile manufacture distinctive and successful.

The Philadelphia Textile Manufacturers Association: protection, politics, and education

The conjunction of two events in the first month of 1880 will set us to our final task, a review and assessment of the Philadelphia Textile Manufacturers Association and the establishment of a technical school for textile education. Shortly after the turn of the year, following the announcement of a

---

98 *PL*, January 8, 19, 23, 29, February 2, 5, 12, 15, 16, 19, 23, 25, 1886. Kendrick, the editor of the *Philadelphia Carpet Trade*, prepared a much-cited, but not wholly reliable, survey of the Philadelphia carpet industry for the 1889 report of the Pennsylvania Bureau of Industrial Statistics. Levine also takes the handloom workers rather too lightly (see "Their Own Sphere," pp. 54–6, 103–7).

99 *PL*, August 1, 1878; Weeks, *Report on the Statistics of Wages*, p. 384.

round of advances in the carpet trades, workers at the major cotton mills of Manayunk requested increases in rates, which had been steadily eroded since the early seventies. When refused, thousands of textile workers struck five cotton firms, two yarn mills, and a dyehouse. By the tenth of January, weavers at Patterson and C. S. Jones had achieved their goals, an 11% increase. Both the spinners and the dyehouse workers had also agreed to advances, the latter a flat 50¢ per week as dyers did not work on piece rates. As the news traveled across the city, cotton factories in Spring Garden and South Philadelphia turned out in close order.[100]

Two weeks later, encouraged by the auspicious beginning made in hosting the fall 1879 NAWM sessions, the Philadelphia Textile Manufacturers Association met at another splendid banquet to formalize their association. That the establishment of a "permanent organization" followed the NAWM visitation strongly suggests that the PMTA was first pulled together for the occasion of the November convention, the successful results of which prompted Thomas Dolan, James Dobson, and others to convert a temporary expedient into a lasting association. Press coverage summarized the addresses given and named individually thirty manufacturers in attendance. From their remarks, it is evident that the concerns of these men were not riveted to the shop floor.[101] They planned a reception for former President Grant, discussed the tariff situation, and selected a committee to visit Washington to express their concern. The promotion of Philadelphia as a "textile center" was encouraged, and Theodore Search's pet project, a school of design and weaving, was broached.

Perhaps equally interesting was the absence of the recently struck Manayunk, Spring Garden, and South Philadelphia cotton proprietors. This was not just a reflection of cotton versus wool but of diverging approaches to manufacturing, a question of pathways, the bulk staple option versus the skill-intensive flexibility of which Hayes and Blodget wrote warmly.[102] Those cotton producers who faced strikes repeatedly were both the agents and victims of their own accumulation strategy. The sequential decisions they had made about mass production brought them within the orbit of competition with the New England mills whose postwar thrusts toward high quality cottons (earlier a standard at Philadelphia) were in turn launched partly in response to the beginnings of cheaper southern coarse staple manufacture. All turned to victimize their workers within the narrowed options allowed by their commitments, but at Philadelphia (and Fall

---

[100] *PL*, January 10, 15, 17, 1880.

[101] Only a handful of those present – Dobson, Sevill Schofield, and several carpet manufacturers – had experienced any strike activity in the seventies.

[102] Lorin Blodget attended the PTMA banquet, an invited guest most likely, for his interest in the textile industry was statistical rather than financial.

River),[103] unlike other sites, the cultural base for resistance was deep and ever-renewed by the exemplary acts of workers in other sectors and districts of the metropolis.

Facing this situation, it is not surprising that cotton manufacturers (first carpet warp spinning firms and later weaving and integrated mills) gathered together in associations of their own. Survival topped their agenda, not the establishment of schools to foster greater flexibility and novel designs. The negative effects of agglomeration were pressing upon them: the easy communicability of the strike virus and the increased community support for workers' outrage against the rounds of wage cuts. Their discussions revolved around limiting production, agreements to common output quotas or reduced workweeks (three days a week in spinning),[104] not receptions for aging warriors. Those cotton firms that had moved aggressively toward mixed goods and a seasonal variation of cottons and wools prospered, as Blodget observed. Those that had taken a different path scrambled to stay afloat.

Also underrepresented at the PTMA's January banquet were the carpet firms. Only three such proprietors were among the attendees named, and only one of them, James Judge, was connected with the Kensington manufacturers association of 1879–80.[105] Judge headed the carpet group in 1880 and was present at the dinner more as an observer than as a recruit, I suspect. Silk manufacturers too were absent as they already had their own organization,[106] based in New York; F. O. Horstmann was a director and other local firms were members. Silk trim, braid, ribbon, and fabric manufacture was virtually by definition flexible, and the production mix responded rapidly to shifts in the styles of hats, clothing, and upholstered furniture. (Two silk manufacturers did later make modest pledges toward

---

103 See John Cumbler, *Working Class Community in Industrial America*, Westport, Conn., 1979.

104 *PL*, June 7, 14, 1880; March 18, 22, 1881; May 11, 1882; for New England, see Louis Galambos, *Competition and Cooperation*, Baltimore, 1966, chap. 1.

105 Spring Garden's Alexander Crow, well known as a "good master," was also present. The following notice from his workers to their fellow weavers appeared in *PL*, July 27, 1880: "At a meeting of the employes of the Caledonia Carpet Mills, held this day [July 26], it was resolved, that the sincere thanks of all are due and are hereby heartily tendered to our respected employers, Messrs. Alexander Crow and Son, for their uniform and continued kindness, especially for their great liberality in providing an Excursion and Dinner at Cape May [N.J. seaside resort] on Saturday July 24, free for us all. Resolved, that as a slight token of our appreciation, these resolutions be published in the Ledger, and the Evening Bulletin."

106 I am aware of no study of the Silk Manufacturers Association, but its minute book (available at the Paley House, Philadelphia College of Textiles and Science), indicates that its members' interests were similar to those of the PTMA, with tariffs of major concern.

the PTMA's school project in 1884.) The rough parallels between the cotton and carpet sectors, whose manufacturers' alliances had similar goals, and their general absence from the PTMA, serve to reinforce the contention that a production-centered division can be spotted in the city's postwar textile industry. Shop-floor and output-restriction issues dominated the discussions of the cotton and carpet associations, and tariffs and state policy, education, and publicity were of interest to those manufacturers committed to continuing innovations and the preservation and extension of high-skill flexibility.

Armed with this information, an observer of Philadelphia in the mid-eighties, if called upon to predict which portions of the textile industry would prosper and which would expire over the coming quarter century, might well have ventured that cotton and carpet firms would face a grim future unless they could reverse their commitments to the bulk manufacture of staple goods. The specializations and flexibility apparent in other sectors, the spreading of risk and the retention of skill, were by contrast a sound base for future development, provided that the innovations of one decade were supplemented by others in the next. (Of course, in individual cases, the recovery of initiative by a cotton firm would not prevent the collapse of a neighboring wool mill.) On the whole, the Philadelphia system was far better suited to market-sensitive entrepreneurship than to the mass production of staples.

Such an analysis, as historians can now confirm, would have captured the large outlines of what materialized in the city textile trades over the next generation. Indeed, a study of manufacturing in Philadelphia issued just before World War I pointed out the decline in production of ingrain carpets: "During the last ten years there has been a great decrease in the quantity of ingrain carpets, so that less than one half as much was made in 1909 as in 1899 . . . There had been a large increase in the manufacture of Axminster, Wilton, Brussels and velvet carpets." On cottons, the contrast with New England was stressed.

> In the New England cities, the mills confine themselves to the manufacture of cotton piece goods and yarns. Very little white piece goods, which form a large part of the New England product, are made in Philadelphia.
>
> It was Philadelphia manufacturers who discovered the value of cotton as a decorative adjunct, and conceived and made into beautiful textures a vegetable fibre formerly unknown in decoration. It was from 1880 to 1890 that cotton chenille was found applicable to window curtains. Later the manufacture of tapestries and covers for pianos and tables and other minimum light fabrics was developed.[107]

[107] John J. Macfarlane, *Manufacturing in Philadelphia, 1683–1912*, Philadelphia, 1912, pp. 24, 27.

Advertisements, circa 1895, for two specialty firms whose names illustrate family succession. The Woll firm is still active in the same sector of the trade. (Philadelphia College of Textiles and Science)

In hosiery, knit goods, woolens, worsted, and felted goods, the city retained its national prominence. Though the silk manufacture in part removed to suburban sites, the Horstmann family firm retained its preeminence in the city's trade, its diverse skills undiminished. "When the Government asked for bids to supply the army with national and regimental flags at the opening of the Spanish War, they were the only bidders, no other company being able to meet the requirements of the Government as to time and quality."[108] Despite the fact that the manufacturing census by 1909 had ceased to include "all establishments not operated on the factory system and all the so-called neighborhood . . . industries," more than 65,000 textile workers could be found in its Philadelphia summary tables.[109] With unknown numbers of small proprietors eliminated from the totals, a remarkable 679 establishments were active in the city textile industry in 1909.

[108] Ibid., p. 30.
[109] Ibid., pp. 6, 98–9. No separate category for yarn spinners was included in the summaries, their workers were perhaps dumped into the "other industries" category, an undifferentiated pool of 41,000 workers, or 16% of the total workers in the city. The omission of neighborhood firms ("all the little weaving shops" Kendrick called them in 1889) will make reconstitution of the later manufacturing environment a difficult task. Tiny firms were last included in the manufacturing census of 1899, the original schedules of which seem not to have been preserved.

Though a full study of this later era will be necessary to chart the movements within the mass, we may at this point at least tentatively concur with Lorin Blodget's 1880 observation that "though the introduction of improvements is easy, the leading characteristics do not change." Upon foundations laid in the antebellum era, a considerable system of manufacture had been erected in Philadelphia textiles by the 1880s, and upon that system, improvements and refinements continued to be made.

That the whole operation was conducted by hundreds of individual proprietors and that their separate establishments intersected, overlapped, and competed in crazy-quilt patterns was one of its great strengths. The actions (or inaction) of "a few great fools" could not wreck the whole, as elsewhere. Indeed, the errors made by some manufacturers, and the gluts and labor crises that followed, could serve to reinforce for others at Philadelphia their distinctive commitments to quality, specialization, and flexibility, to personal management of production and marketing, and to the engagement of skilled workers to an extent unmatched elsewhere in the industry.[110]

The founders of the Philadelphia Textile Manufacturers Association were the city's most effective practitioners of the accumulation strategy just described. Their firms were among not only the largest in the trade but also the oldest, with most in operation for fifteen or twenty years and a few tracing back into the 1840s. With a review of their later actions, as an organization and as individuals concerned with reform politics, this extended exposition of post–Civil War developments in the Philadelphia textile industry will draw to a close.

Representing about twenty firms, the thirty men who attended the January 1880 organizational banquet employed more than 9,900 workers, ranging from more than 2,000 in the Dobson brothers' carpet and cloth factories to 50 at Shaffner and Stringfellow's South Philadelphia yarn mill. They were drawn from all parts of the city: Button, Allen, and Spencer from Germantown; William Wood, Alex Crow, and the Search worsted-spinning contingent from Spring Garden; Sevill Schofield of Manayunk, and so forth. The chief officers elected[111] represented the same balance of neighborhood and productive sectors that appeared in the nominations for a Board of Managers, which included two proprietors with fewer than 100 workers.[112]

Their first task was the enlistment of members who supported the tariff

---

[110] An 1882 statewide survey by the Pennsylvania Bureau of Internal Affairs reported nearly 14,000 skilled workmen in textiles, most of whom, given the unsophisticated products of outlying mills, can be "placed" at Philadelphia (*Report of the Secretary of Internal Affairs, Part 3, Industrial Statistics*, Harrisburg, Pa., 1883, p. 97).

[111] Dolan (president), Kensington, woolens; Dobson, Schuylkill Falls, carpets and woolens; Button, Germantown, hosiery; Arrott, Kensington, worsteds and yarns.

[112] *PL*, January 28, 1880.

and other concerns of the core group. By early spring the secretary of the association reported more than 100 enrollments, a dozen or more in the week preceding the April 5 meeting.[113] This effect may have been assisted by the political storm that accompanied yet another effort to revise the tariff on imported raw wool and woolens. The NAWM had begun a petition drive to defend the current protective levels, calling for a special commission of "expert" opinion to replace the unpredictable horse trading common in congressional committees. Given the close relations of the national and local organizations (Dolan was vice-president of the NAWM), it may be assumed that activist members of the PTMA sought both members and endorsements of the petition simultaneously. Thus the printed list of firms supporting the NAWM position that appeared in the fall 1880 issue of its *Bulletin* may serve as a rough proxy for that community of interest in Philadelphia supportive of the PTMA. The April membership claim and the number of Philadelphia signatories (91) are close enough to suggest[114] some connection, in lieu of a PTMA membership list, which has yet to be located.

Of those backing the tariff effort, the largest fractions were spinning and knitting firms (25 and 19), with a sizable representation of carpet manufacturers (17). Fourteen woolen and mixed-goods mills, three small specialty shops, and James Lord's cotton works complete the roster of seventy-nine firms that could be linked with manufacturing census entries.[115] The wide sectoral distribution was matched by a considerable geographical spread, indicating fair success for this first effort to build a citywide coalition.

The PTMA soon settled into the dull routine of regular meetings, including sector meetings, and speeches on the tariff and the state of the trades. Meanwhile, some of the more prominent members of the association became politically active in another coalition drive, the governmental reform campaign of the Committee of 100. Briefly, corruption in city politics had reached new and outrageous dimensions, as Mayor William Stokeley, elected in 1871 on a reformist clean-up platform,[116] entrenched himself through the same tactics honored by his predecessors. By the late seventies, the Stokeley administration was rocked with scandal, bribery, and fraud, partic-

---

113 *PL*, April 6, 1880.

114 Some of the largest founding PTMA firms are not on the printed list, including Dobson and Dolan. This may have been an NAWM publicity feint.

115 *Bulletin, NAWM* 10 (1880); 364–6. The 79 linked firms had just over 9,000 workers in 1882 according to Blodget's city census. But those leaders of the association who were not on the printed NAWM list employed yet another 6,500, or about 28% of the cotton work force and 37% of the wool, mixed-goods, carpet, knit-goods, and spinning work force.

116 Ellis Oberholtzer, *Philadelphia: A History of the City and Its People*, Philadelphia, 1912, vol. II, p. 400.

ularly in relation to the city gasworks and the office of the Receiver of Taxes.[117] When Stokeley geared up for a fourth-term campaign, a group of downtown merchants mobilized to form an independent opposition, the bulwark of which was the Committee of 100.

Amos Little, a dry-goods dealer, who presided at the first preliminary meeting, was authorized to select "not less than one hundred business men" to carry the banners of good government. He chose 108, among whom were 8 textile manufacturers[118] who were also active or interested in the PTMA: William Arrott, Rudolph Blankenburg, James Dobson, F. Oden Horstmann, Charles Spencer, Sevill Schofield, J. C. Watt, and William Wood.[119] Blankenburg, a finisher and knitter of Germantown yarns, played a leading role in pressing the reformers toward the nomination of an alternative slate, stalking out dramatically from a December 1880 meeting at which the committee offered the mayor its support if he would pledge a thorough cleanup of his administration.[120] When Stokeley delayed, offering polite words but declining to break with the gas-trust boss James McManus, the Committee withdrew its "nomination" of the incumbent on January 15. Two days later, Blankenburg rejoined the committee "amid a vigorous clapping of hands," though the irascible Dobson, who had hoped to retool Stokeley, resigned in disappointment.[121]

After a good deal of jockeying, the reformers selected as their mayoral candidate Democrat Samuel King, a manufacturer who had retired with his competence several decades earlier to devote himself to city politics. None ventured to call King dynamic ("a sturdy figure," "retiring and seclusive"), but his honesty was unquestioned and his commitment to run the government "upon a purely business basis" was welcome.[122] To fill the most corrupt office under Stokeley, that of Receiver of Taxes, the committee supported John Hunter, a Republican councilman and a West Philadelphia

[117] Ibid., pp. 416–7.

[118] Ibid., pp. 418–9.

[119] The final committee was composed of 39 merchants, 37 manufacturers, 7 bankers, 5 lawyers, 4 coal operators, 2 doctors, 2 "gentlemen," and a dozen others. John Wanamaker, Justus Strawbridge, and A. J. Drexel, among other luminaries, were included in the membership.

[120] George Vickers, *The Fall of Bossism: A History of the Committee of One Hundred . . .*, Philadelphia, 1883, pp. 109–15. Readers will find in Vickers's breathless account of the reformers' successes a virtuoso display of rhetorical pacing and polemical fervor that lives in the intensity of the moment. It deserves a place alongside Plunkitt (William Riordan, *Plunkitt of Tammany Hall*, New York, 1963) in the primary literature of machine politics and reform and is well worth reprinting.

[121] Ibid., p. 143.

[122] *A Biographical Album of Prominent Pennsylvanians, First Series*, Philadelphia, 1888, pp. 217–22; Oberholtzer, *Philadelphia*, vol. II, p. 419.

printworks proprietor. A Belfast native, Hunter had succeeded his father in 1848 in a textile firm founded twenty years before and subsequently operated it in partnership with his brother James, "a practical chemist" credited by Bagnall with introducing alizarin/madder dyeing to this country.[123] With the entry of three younger brothers into the firm in the seventies, John Hunter was freed to pursue a political vocation. As the family mills prospered, the brothers purchased a cotton mill to supply them cloths for printing (1873).[124] After election to City Council, John became the city's most persistent critic of official corruption.

Cheered at his appearance, and belatedly nominated by the opportunist Democratic committee to replace a faceless loyalist first put forward, Hunter led the reform ticket in the mid-February election, his winning margin three times greater than that of the drab but dignified Samuel King. Though both were veteran manufacturers, it would be an error to visualize them simply as extensions of an owning class, seeking, for example, to use police to break strikes. Stokeley had long dispatched officers to disperse factory district crowds and to escort scabs to their residences. If anything, King disrupted the police force by appointing the first black patrolmen in its history. Instead, the mayor was, as he had advertised himself, a plain Quaker who expected good work and honest dealings from those with whom he was associated. Aided by Hunter, King cleaned up scandals that haunted the tax office, reduced the city debt by nearly $3 million, and authorized the 1882 city manufacturing census.[125,126]

The three years of King's mayoralty were quiet and properous for Philadelphia's textile manufacturers.[127] With the economy between convulsions, the PTMA could turn its attention to other matters. Keeping an eye on the tariff, the association began to publish its own *Bulletin* in 1883–4, a slim periodical that the NAWM "welcome[d] to the fold of protective journals of

---

123 William Bagnall, "The Textile Industries of the United States," vol. II, typescript on microfiche, 1970, pp. 1785–96, Merrimack Valley Textile Museum, North Andover, Mass.; transcribed from the handwritten manuscript of Bagnall's draft text; pagination is that of the original manuscript.

124 Ibid., pp. 1800–1.

125 *Biographical Album, First Series*, pp. 219–20.

126 Although each of these efforts was of value to manufacturers, King's calm, predictable probity was likely even more important, though the extent to which it influenced behavior at lower levels of administration awaits investigation. I, for one, am enormously grateful for the 1882 *Census of Manufactures* (Blodget), without which this entire section would have been vastly more difficult to prepare.

127 The *Public Ledger* reported only twenty-one textile strikes during King's three-year term; more than half the strikes were concerned with yet another reduction effort by the plagued cotton manufacturers in 1882 (see *PL*, March 3, 13, 19, 20, 29, April 2, 4, 5, 6, 7, 10, 12, 13, 16, 17, 23, 24, 30, 1883).

the country."[128] Of more lasting significance was the effort of the association to sponsor the creation of a school for textile education at Philadelphia. It was a positive step toward a capacity for continued innovation, which its originator, Theodore Search, would later contrast with the essential negativism of tariff defense.[129]

The textile school project

At the 1876 Centennial Exposition, Theodore Search had been impressed with the virtuosity of design present in the displays of European textile manufacturers. The superiority of British and French design had long been recognized; indeed, the practice of copying the leading patterns had become commonplace in American mills. As Sevill Schofield admitted in the "Claim" accompanying the Economy Mills exhibit at the exposition:

> We claim for all our varieties of goods, not so much originality in design and construction, as an adaptation in both these particulars of the leading styles of the market, to general consumption. In this direction, that of furnishing the multitude with *facsimiles* of high-cost goods, at low prices, yet of good materials, we have led the manufactures of the country for many years. (Emphasis in original.)[130]

Although this summed up neatly an essential element of Philadelphia's textile prowess, Search and others realized the limitations of depending on others' creative successes. As a French manufacturer boasted a few years later to an American visitor:

> We claim to furnish the brains for the world in the matter of manufacturing. We mean to lead in the invention and composition of designs and styles. We expect you [Americans] and the English to use them after we have thrown them aside. You are welcome to them, as we shall have made our profit out of them before you can introduce them. Our profits will be greater, because novelties pay better than second-hand patterns. While you are weaving and printing one-year-old figures, we are bringing into market new combinations.[131]

The American commissioner at the 1878 Paris Exposition, where the above remarks were recorded, was forced to admit their accuracy. He saw that the potential for further extension of European supremacy in design was already present in "their system of special education."

---

[128] *Bulletin, NAWM* 14 (1884):183.
[129] T. C. Search, "Textile Education in America," *Bulletin, NAWM* 25 (1895):2–5.
[130] Hayes, *Awards and Claims,* p. 44.
[131] *Bulletin, NAWM* 11 (1881):269.

> Throughout Germany, Austria, Switzerland, Russia and France, weav-
> ing schools have long been exerting a powerful influence on the man-
> ufacturing industry; several have been established in England, . . . I
> desire, . . . to place upon record my unhesitating conviction that special
> trade and art schools have become one of the paramount necessities in
> nations whose prosperity is largely dependent upon handicraft. . . The
> American may not need the incentive of school discipline, but he does
> require, and the near future will demonstrate that he must have, the
> thorough knowledge and methods of systematic training. Even now our
> textile industries are suffering by reason of our lack in this respect. In
> mechanical expedients to cheapen production no nation is so fertile as
> ours, but in the higher and more intellectual elements, we are sadly
> wanting . . . [W]here beauty and gracefulness unite in the formation of
> attractive and alluring wares, it is our highest ambition to *steal*. (Empha-
> sis in original.)[132]

Recommending that their members give "special attention" to the necessity
of technical education in textiles, the NAWM concurred with his evaluation.
Search's campaign to begin such an institution in Philadelphia drew upon
both a rising concern in the larger manufacturing environment and the
particular character of the city's textile establishment.

There were in Philadelphia a number of creative designers whose support
he could seek. Most prominent among them was John Dornan, whose ingrain and damask designs were patented, along with the machine innovations he had devised at his Kensington mills.[133] Such men were few, however; far more common was the design process described later by New York
commission merchant Edward Page.

> The designers we found were mostly men of some years and experi-
> ence; perhaps mill superintendents or bright boss weavers who had
> picked up ideas in weaves and fabrics, or perhaps trained designers
> brought over from France, England and Germany . . . These men were
> necessarily located at the mills; their work was ineffective unless trans-
> muted at once and before their eyes into patterns that they could look at
> as they wove them on the loom, and their inspiration came from bought
> or stolen samples.[134]

Search aimed to create an institution, modeled on the European schools,
that would replace copying with originality and thereby further deepen the
productive foundations of the city's textile industry. The money would come

---

132 Ibid., pp. 268–9.
133 For a color illustration of one of Dornan's patented designs, see Landreau, *America Underfoot*, p. 51. On his mechanical work, see Kendrick, "Carpet Industry," p. D-15.
134 Edward Page, "Textile Graduates in the Selling Agency," *Second Annual Report (1903)*, Alumni Association of the Philadelphia Textile School, Philadelphia, 1903, p. 20.

from the PTMA manufacturers and the students from the mills, both skilled workmen ("bright boss weavers") and the sons of manufacturers.[135] Search reasoned that their creative capacities could be released only by a systematic departure from the traditional haphazardness of shop learning. Boss weavers and loomfixers who moved from mill to mill eventually acquired a working knowledge of a wide variety of machinery and weave formations and in this respect were better trained than family firm members whose experience was limited to a single factory. Yet neither had had the opportunity, standard in the European schools, of learning the principles alongside the practices, comparing the capacities and operations of a half-dozen varieties of looms, and running experimental mixes and numbers of yarns to test their suitability for a range of end uses. From 1882 well into the new century, Search devoted his best energies to realizing that vision.

By the early 1880s, Theodore Search had been connected with the woolen trades for more than fifteen years. Before his association with the wool merchant house of Davis, Fiss, and Banes in 1866, he had served as a teacher in rural schools and private academies for a half-dozen years, finishing his first educational career with two positions at Philadelphia commercial schools in 1865–6. In 1872 he joined in partnership with several merchants for whom he had worked as head bookkeeper, commencing the production of worsted and woolen yarns. The worsted industry was then "in its infancy," fostered by the tariff but terribly short of experienced workers, much less of innovative designers. Thus his firsthand experience of the trade's current boundaries, the revelations of the Centennial Exposition, the publicity given to European schools, and his own teaching background channeled Search toward the formal proposal he presented to the PTMA in 1883, that a fund of $50,000 be subscribed for creation of a textile school at Philadelphia.[136]

The association endorsed the plan and authorized Search to seek pledges, with the provision that if the whole amount could not be subscribed, the project would be dropped. The cost of the proposed machinery and facilities necessitated the full amount, the association "fearing that failure would follow with any less sum." Search, however, was to be disappointed. "After long and tedious work and considerable opposition from many very successful manufacturers, who could not fully appreciate what could be done for a young man in a school that would be of advantage in his practical life, he

---

[135] Finding and keeping a faculty proved the knottiest problem, though the quest for seed money preceded these difficulties. Before the school was established, individual courses in fabric design were offered occasionally at both Lowell and Philadelphia. The Lowell Textile School, now the University of Lowell, was first proposed in 1891 and opened its doors in 1897 (*Bulletin of the Lowell Textile Institute – 1936*, Lowell, 1936, p. 6).

[136] Oberholtzer, *Philadelphia*, vol. III, pp. 107–10.

finally was able to secure [subscriptions totaling] thirty-five thousand dollars."[137] The project was thus abandoned by the association. Search kept the subscription book, inscribed with the names of those who had supported the project and the sums they had pledged (Table 10.4).[138]

Though the core group of the PTMA clearly provided the bulk of his pledges ($22,500), Search convinced three machinery manufacturers and the proprietors of several leased Spring Garden mills to add substantially to that total ($4,250). Though the geographical and sectoral spread was considerable, Search was able to raise only $5,750 from the rest of the industry. Only three of the core firms present at the January 1880 meeting had failed to contribute (two small spinners and James Judge), but the response outside that group was surely unimpressive. Why did Search not reap a richer harvest?

Four somewhat related answers may be offered. First, the timing of this campaign proved unfortunate, as the downturn of the economy in the 1883–4 production season caught the city's textile trades head on. As had previously been the case, the cotton mills were the first victims of the decline; but by January 1884, as a *Ledger* review of the state of the textile business pointed out, only the knit-goods mills were in full production. The rest of the industry was running at three-quarter speed, with layoffs and short time reported in all districts.[139] By February 1884 carpet manufacturers were complaining that winter orders had been "less than expected,"[140] and the subsequent rate cuts that fall set off the monumental 1884–5 Kensington strikes. Second, the most rapidly growing textile specialty in Philadelphia, Search's own worsted trade, was badly shaken by a reduction in the tariff on worsted goods. He summarized the problems caused by this 1883 lowering of the protective barrier in an article evidently written in the fall of the year and published early in 1884. The debate over alteration of the rates "unsettled the foundations of the trade," causing prices to "droop." Once the cuts went into effect, the situation grew worse as "many orders for woolen cloths were cancelled by the purchasers because of the change of duty which now enabled them to purchase at greater advantage, and the manufacturers were compelled to sustain another serious loss."[141]

All the wool-using trades were thus "unsettled" in the period before the

137 Ibid., vol. III, p. 110; also, *Second Report (1903)*, Alumni Association of the Philadelphia Textile School, pp. 17–8.
138 This notebook is available at the Archive Room, Pastore Library, Philadelphia College of Textiles and Science, along with other materials on the college's history.
139 *PL*, November 14, December 23, 1883; January 22, 1884.
140 *PL*, February 5, 1884.
141 *Report of the Secretary of Internal Affairs, Part 3: Industrial Statistics, 1882–83*, Harrisburg, Pa., 1884, p. 39.

Table 10.4. *Philadelphia Textile School subscribers, 1883*

Subscribers	Pledge	Sector	District
Thomas Dolan & Co.[a]	$5,000	Wool	Kensington
John & James Dobson[a]	5,000	Carpet, wool	Falls of Schuylkill
William Wood & Co.[a]	2,500	Cotton-wool	Spring Garden
James Doak & Co.[a]	2,500	Wool	Kensington
Fiss, Banes, Erben & Co.[a]	2,000	Spinning	Spring Garden
John Yewdall	2,000	Mill realtor	Spring Garden
George Campbell[a]	1,000	Cotton-wool	South Philadelphia
Conyers Button and Co.[a]	1,000	Knit goods	Germantown
Sevill Schofield[a]	1,000	Wool	Manayunk
Alex Crow and Son[a]	1,000	Carpet	Spring Garden
Thomas Smith	1,000	Shoddy	Kensington
James and George Bromley	1,000	Carpet	Kensington
James Smith	1,000	Textile machinery	Germantown
Merrill A. Furbush & Son	1,000	Textile machinery, wool	South Philadelphia
John Bromley & Sons	1,000	Carpet	Kensington
James Pollock[a]	500	Carpet	Kensington
Charles Spencer & Co.[a]	500	Knit goods	Germantown
Thomas A. Harris	500	Dyeing, finishing	Kensington
Robert Beatty	500	Cotton-wool	Kensington
Henry Becker and Co.	500	Knit goods	Kensington
James Long[a]	500	Cotton	Kensington
Andreas Hartel	250	Dyeing, finishing	Northeast Philadelphia
William Hall and Co.	250	Spinning	Pattonville (Delaware Co.)
H. W. Butterworth & Co.	250	Textile machinery	Kensington
S. B. & M. Fleischer	250	Spinning, braids	Spring Garden
Joseph P. Murphy	250	Wool	Kensington
Grundy Bros. Campion	250	Spinning	Bristol (Bucks Co.)

Note: Six $100 pledges were penciled inside the back cover: Firth, Firth and Brothers (dyers), Davenport, Hinsell (both silk), Boyd (carpet), and Wheller (not linked).
[a] Attended the first PTMA meeting in 1880.
Source: Subscription Book, Philadelphia Textile School, Archives, Pastore Library, Philadelphia College of Textiles and Science; Lorin Blodget, *Census of Manufactures of Philadelphia (1882)* (Philadelphia, 1883); *Public Ledger,* January 28, 1880.

results of the political process were known, with a second round of miseries following for those firms whose customers canceled orders either to buy imported worsted, now cheapened by the reduction, or simply to sit out the falling market for a while, so as not to be in possession of goods whose market value fell between the time of their acquisition and their sale. These were not auspicious months during which to be out and about raising funds for a newfangled idea.

Oberholtzer's reference to "considerable opposition from many very successful manufacturers" is a clue to another obstacle. As their biographers repeated with tedious precision, most of the Philadelphia textile veterans were "self-made men." They had come up through the mill to win their success; and though they bore a measure of respect for the skilled workmen essential to that progress, they expressed little interest in "book-learning." It is noteworthy that three of the most prominent figures in the school campaign, and those who ultimately rescued the notion from abandonment, were Dolan, Arrott, and Search, all of whom had come to the mill from the countinghouse. Outside the core group, they won few converts to the cause of technical education, for their whole project departed from, criticized, and even threatened a mill-based culture shared by the majority of Philadelphia textile proprietors. The conviction that the trade was learned in the mill situated such manufacturers far closer culturally to their workers than to banquet-going gentlemen. Finally, the roots of their project among the wool-related firms of the PTMA blocked access to another potential source of funds, which might have been tapped had their vision been yet broader. Whereas the cotton sector was threatened with decline, the silk manufacture at Philadelphia was enjoying a new burst of prosperity. As Search and his colleagues knew nothing of the requirements and problems of silk operations, their plans for instruction bypassed silk skills entirely. The silk proprietors spoke a different language (one "throws" silk; it is not "spun") and traveled in different circles. Predominantly German, they had their own association. Yet there were more than sixty silk manufacturers in the city in the eighties, some employing hundreds of workers. However understandable on both technical and cultural grounds, the failure to provide for the participation of silk manufacturers narrowed the constituency from which support for the project might have been drawn.[142]

By the fall of 1884 the results were evident. Having failed to reach the $50,000 funding level, the project was abandoned by the association and all

---

[142] This oversight was eventually remedied, and by the turn of the century the "silk course" had joined the other two- and three-year courses (wool, dyeing, and cotton). It is also interesting to note as a sign of the loose and tentative structure of the PTMA that it did not assess its members to fund the school project but simply gave Search permission to badger the membership for whatever amounts he could raise.

the pledges were nullified. If Search was distanced from the mill culture embraced by most of the city's textile proprietors, he soon showed that he shared something essential to their whole approach to business. The day following the association's decision to drop the plan, he commenced operations on his own account. With virtually no capital, Search "rented a room, opened an evening school with an attendance of five pupils, whom he personally taught three evenings in a week, and attended to his . . . business interests during the day."[143] His solitary venture, after an unspecified period, came to the attention of Thomas Dolan and William Arrott, who "offered at once to share the expense of the further conduct of the school." They in turn secured the assent of the association for a "recanvassing" of the subscribers, whose promises if renewed would be called in to fund Search's fait accompli.

> The recanvassing of these individual subscriptions procured the consent of thirty-seven thousand five hundred dollars to be donated to this purpose and twenty-five per cent of this sum was immediately collected and placed in banks subject to drafts upon it for school purposes, and thus was inaugurated the first textile school in the United States.[144]

If this chronicle has a fairy-tale, too-good-to-be-true quality to it, Search's pencil notes in the margins of his subscription book lend an air of authenticity to the recanvassing element. Next to the names and pledges of four original backers, he noted "Refd," which indicates "refused" on the second appeal to confirm their support. The only cotton proprietor who offered funds initially, James Long, was one of these men, which testifies to the financial trouble besetting that sector. George Campbell and Joseph Murphy also "Refd"; both had reduced their workers' rates and experienced strikes in 1884–5. Strikes and the depressed market also were likely to have prompted the enigmatic note alongside the Bromley brothers' pledge, "not bound." Thomas Smith, in the interim between the two efforts, had "died."[145,146]

The later development of the school and technical education in textiles may deserve separate attention on its own;[147] only one further incident will be recounted here. Financing the school was certainly a serious problem, as

---

[143] Oberholtzer, *Philadelphia*, vol. III, p. 110.

[144] Ibid.

[145] *Subscription Book, Philadelphia Textile School* (ca. 1883–4), unpaged.

[146] The out-of-town William Hall and Co. also refused, bringing the total lost from these six cases to $4,000. As the six $100 pledges are also inscribed in pencil, they may have been acquired on the second round. What other new moneys were secured to arrive at Oberholtzer's total of $37,500 is not known.

[147] David Noble's *America by Design: Science, Technology, and the Rise of Corporate Capitalism*, New York, 1977, would provide a good theoretical and comparative point of departure, particularly chaps. 2 and 3.

the struggles to get even the first commitments to its opening showed. However, at least one part of the budget was shortly provided by the state, in this case the State of Pennsylvania, as the 1892 report of the federal Commission of Labor observed: "Since 1887 the school has received assistance from the state to the extent of $10,000 a year, in return for which the school grants free scholarships, one for each county, to be filled by appointment of the governor."[148] A more elegant solution to cash-flow dilemmas could hardly be imagined. The school received both assured funding and students to fill a number of its places; the governor of Pennsylvania received the benefits accorded to a dispenser of political patronage.

The mid-eighties were no stopping place for the textile capitalists of Philadelphia, nor for their workers, their families, their suppliers and salesmen. Yet they will be a stopping place for this study, the major points of which have been asserted and documented, I hope, to a satisfactory degree. The millmen of the Quaker City in the mid-eighties were independent proprietors of family or partnership enterprises, as they had been a half century before. They largely operated through personal supervision of their works, buying carefully, manufacturing to match the vagaries of the market, stealing their designs from foreign sources, selling direct to a considerable degree, and expanding their operations by plowing back their profits. They were aided in their endeavors by the skilled efforts of thousands of immigrant workers and the less-skilled labor of their kinsmen and children. The saga of the textile school project suggests the nodal point that had been reached in the middle eighties. A handful of manufacturers had become sharply conscious of the global nature of the economic environment within which their enterprises were mounted. The sense that ever yet more had to be done imbued their educational visions; somehow, it was no longer possible for these men to conceive of their mills as merely a way of getting a living or gathering a legacy for the next generation. That others retained these values and the habits of mind and production that accompanied them is suggested by the indifference and opposition the school project inspired.

As if the manufacture of textiles under the conditions prevalent at Philadelphia were not disaggregated and complex enough, new layers and dimensions of complexity presented themselves for attention. Politics and the state had to be confronted, controlled, and turned to their ends if possible, at the level of city reform, state funding, and federal tariffs. The flexibility of the manufacturing system alone might not be enough to sustain it; rather, it had

---

[148] *Eighth Annual Report of the Commissioner of Labor, 1892: Industrial Education*, Washington, D.C., 1893, p. 107. The director's salary, the highest at the school, was $1,800 in 1891. The state appropriation surely covered the bulk of the faculty budget and perhaps some other expenses as well.

to be supplemented by yet additional skill. The city had imported its textile capitalists and workers for more than a century; it now had to generate them in particular forms to preserve that "faculty, which it seems to possess above all other cities of appropriating the talents of . . . the skilled workman."[149] To top it off, workingmen and -women were expressing their strength in unmistakable terms in the 1880s. In the last great strike, as the networks of factory relations seemed on the verge of collapse, the need for harmony in the mill and the neighborhood was voiced on all sides. What was to be done?

There was no single answer to any of these dilemmas, structured as they were within a manufacturing and community array invested by overlapping and contradictory loyalties, customs, and intentions. Although objectively there were owning and laboring classes in the Philadelphia textile industry, and although the boundaries between them were clear enough to most, consciousness of that relationship as one of exploitation and degradation was at most partial and potential rather than actual in the early eighties. Yet the materials for class coalitions and fully conscious class conflicts were just as surely present, and an intense examination of the antagonism between the Knights and the all-industry Manufacturers' Club of Philadelphia[150] might well show them blossoming in both rhetoric and action. The research necessary to probe these issues lies beyond the limits of this study, but the vitality of the participants and the utter lack of easy homogeneity on the "two sides" will make the effort both exciting and daunting. For all its deep continuities, at levels of technique, association, and labor–capital relations, it seems that Theodore Search was correct when in 1883 he noted: "The textile industry of Philadelphia is passing through a transition period."[151] To document and analyze the character of that transition and to explore its twentieth-century results are tasks flowing out of the work begun here.

---

[149] Hayes, *Awards and Claims*, p. 371.

[150] Formed in 1886–7 around the core of the PTMA, the Manufacturers' Club invited manufacturers from all industries to join an effort to discipline both the unruly work force *and* their fellow capitalists who refused to cooperate in attempts to form a collective policy (see *Business Classification of the Members of the Manufacturers Club of Philadelphia*, 1895, Grundy Library, Bristol, Pa., which contains a brief account of the founding of the club).

[151] *Report of the Secretary of Internal Affairs, Part 3: Industrial Statistics, 1882–83*, Harrisburg, Pa., 1884, p. 42.

11

Conclusion: separate establishments

This study opened with a set of questions about industrial development, questions concerning the conditions and strategies that facilitated capitalist accumulation in the Philadelphia and Lowell textile industries during the nineteenth century. As an organizing tool, the theoretical notion of a "matrix" of accumulation factors, material, cultural, and external, was employed to permit a clearer sense of the complex, moving context in which the contrasting trajectories of the Lowell and Philadelphia industries were inscribed. Now, at the close, we shall review briefly the principal points of contrast, the issues generated and addressed in establishing them, and the elements of continuity and transformation that attended the gradual deployment of an enormous textile assemblage in the city of Philadelphia.

To speak of corporate versus proprietary, big versus small firms risks radically distorting the contrasting constellations of institutions and actions at Lowell and Philadelphia for which these paired terms are a woefully inadequate shorthand. Scale and form of organization were but two of the multiplicity of elements that combined to delineate divergent approaches to manufacture in the two locales. Recapitulating the main elements of each matrix will thus both stress their differences and check any tendency to collapse them into a single-issue dichotomy. Consider first the areas of firm organization, finance, materials purchases, and output marketing. The Lowell companies were limited-liability corporations owned by shareholders who could expect dividends without either activity on their part or knowledge of the manufacture their investment had set in motion. Though the spread of ownership hardly approached twentieth-century dispersion, the group was far larger than any partnership discovered at Philadelphia. Further, both expertise and action were expected of interested parties in proprietary firms in all but a few cases. Whereas proprietors directed the affairs of the firm at the shop and dock level, corporations generated in time a standard hierarchy of responsibility and authority whose slots were filled by treasurers, agents, and the like. Though talented overseers in Philadelphia might gain a partnership through marriage or merit, or start on their own account after a time, the blocks to such entrepreneurial initiative at Lowell were sufficiently well known that Cowley could readily list a score of its ablest men who had had to depart the city to open their own plants.[1]

The Lowell corporations bought a year's raw material at a time and warehoused it in ample storerooms; the Massachusetts entrepreneurs sold the products of their mills through commission agents who took charge of the entire mill output. These agencies were available as one source for working capital, demands for which were heavy, given the rhythms of huge purchases of materials and machinery, seasonal markets, and the steady payouts of wages and other expenses. Considerable borrowing activity was standard in corporate circles, with a wide variety of institutional and private suppliers being recruited for short or longer term notes.[2] Philadelphia firms were plugged into no network of merchants and bankers, a separate elite whose capital and social life circulated outside their environs. Their acquisition of materials and equipment usually depended on trade credit and was characterized by lot buys and a gradual accumulation of frames and looms. Cash purchase was preferred when funds from profitable operations could be plowed back. Many sold their output directly, bypassing middlemen's commissions and improving thereby both their market sensitivity and their profit position.[3] (The smallest producers of piece goods, carpet, and hosiery most likely operated through merchant houses, though on a standing very different from that of the Lowell giants.) The much smaller debt loads carried by many Philadelphia firms made credit crises on occasion a source of opportunity for those whose husbanded cash resources allowed the purchase of materials, machinery, or even plants at panic prices. Proprietors or harmonious partners could act decisively in such circumstances, though decisive errors were surely possible as well.

If their organization and financial operations were substantially at variance, the physical contexts within which the Lowell and Philadelphia industries took shape were equally distinct. The textile corporations fashioned Lowell, channeling the Merrimack, erecting huge edifices, creating a city around a power supply that was linked to Boston first by canal and later by a rail line, which they sponsored. People, houses, and shops filled in the

---

[1] Charles Cowley, *Illustrated History of Lowell*, Boston, 1868, p. 61.

[2] Lance Davis, " The New England Textile Mills and the Capital Markets: A study of Industrial Borrowing, 1840–1860," in A. W. Coats and R. M. Robertson, eds., *Essays in American Economic History*, London, 1969, pp. 62–86.

[3] By the postwar era at least one Lowell corporation had begun selling directly, and in the eighties roughly a sixth of the Philadelphia firms listed in annual textile directories were using agencies to sell part or all of their goods. These latter relationships were, however, of the sample and order variety rather than the advance production of warehoused stock common among corporate staple mills.

spaces left by the mills, reinforcing the latter's economic and psychological centrality. Culturally, the old residents of Chelmsford rightly saw Kirk Boott, Luther Lawrence, and their associates as invaders, fought them politically, but were vanquished. The Philadelphia experience was quite different. A sizable city half a century before the early nineteenth-century shop and mill developments, Philadelphia and its manufacturing industries grew symbiotically. The commercial nexus drew both ships and carts laden with raw materials and country merchants to haul away that portion of the finished goods not consumed by the substantial resident population. The textile industry was but one part, albeit an increasingly prominent part, of a highly diversified manufacturing array. Thus the city did not tremble with every shift of raw cotton prices. Rather than a single focal point for textile production dictated by a river's fall, shops and factories appeared in all quarters of Philadelphia, agglomerating in Kensington, Spring Garden, Manayunk, and Germantown and sprinkled as well for a variety of reasons almost everywhere else. There were few big mills at the outset. Instead, the industry was populated by scores, then hundreds of small shops and factories whose proprietors frequently moved from rental to purchase to construction on their own resources over a generation's time. Though most of the Philadelphia textile entrepreneurs were new not only to the locality but also to the country, they merged with the city's growing populace with little stir. (When nativists damned the foreign-born in the 1840s, landlords, proprietors, dockers, and artisans of all crafts were their object, though Irish textile masters and workers were at the center of the Kensington riots.) Until the tumultuous eighties, Philadelphia's textile operators were generally preoccupied with the demands of their businesses. A few sought neighborhood influence as aldermen or council members, but only Joseph Ripka dominated a single district for any extended period. If Lowell was a not-quite-blank slate upon which the Boston Associates could sketch their great enterprises, Philadelphia might be seen as an arena within which more modest firms could attempt to situate themselves so as to draw upon existing resources for accumulation (markets, labor, rental space, etc.).

In approaching the strategies and processes of production, some of the most striking contrasts between the two formats emerged. The Lowell corporations commenced as integrated mills, devoted to the bulk manufacture of coarse staples. From this base there was some variation over the next half century, most notably the introduction of carpets at the Lowell Company. Specialized manufacture was added at Lowell after the Civil War, principally by the appearance of new firms, some proprietary, rather than by ventures on the part of the veteran companies. The corporations were successful in their quest to introduce technology that would speed manufacture and increase bulk output while lowering unit costs. Their efforts to produce new products were a defensive response to externally imposed crises (the Civil War, the rise of coarse cotton manufacture in the South), not an extension of a basic moment in their accumulation strategy. The financial relations surrounding production maximized profitability at near-capacity levels of operation, pressuring managers in troubled times to choose between running full and total shutdown, as corporate mills running at half speed generally lost money. Although the firms spent millions on updated, "state-of-the-art" machinery, it should be noted that their commitments to the rapid and reliable manufacture of staples helped define a particular segment of machinery demand that valued durability, speed, and low skills above flexibility of function. Innovations along the latter pathway of machinery building would hardly be regarded as progressive by Lowell standards; they were, however, of considerable interest to Philadelphia manufacturers.

The production system in the Quaker City varied at every point of comparison. Its technology was directed at flexible output, from the multiple box-looms and Jacquard attachments on carpet handlooms in craftshops to the dozens of specialized knitting frames, braiding machines, and so on in Landenberger's and Horstmann's mills to the widespread practice of alternating woolen and cotton manufacture on machinery fitted for such variation. To the extent that manufacturers owned their enterprises and were immune from the dividend demands of shareholders, they could afford to run their plants at a level of capacity proportional to demand and still make money. The generation of new product lines was endemic and was gradually sophisticated in the postbellum era through the reproduction of European fashions, attempts at innovative designing, and the practice of running samples for the solicitation of orders before putting an item into full production.

Perhaps most visibly, the Philadelphia firms were characterized by their maintenance of "separate establishments." Although some integrated mills operated in the city, most Philadelphia textile producers performed one specialized fraction of the total production sequence, links among them leading to the appearance of completed goods. Weave sheds were connected backward to spinners and dyers and forward to finishing plants. Woolpullers, shoddy manufacturers, cotton-lap makers serviced the yarn mills. Similar relations obtained in silk and carpet manufacture. This intersecting activity was not confined within neighborhood clusters, as crosstown supply relations were common, particularly in yarns. Nor was this a fading system, for the expansion after midcentury showed no displacement of dis-integrated relationships by integrated firms. Instead, a further degree of specialization appeared with commercial realtors (Arrott) who bought and erected mills designed for occupancy by separate, mid-size, specialized firms. Setting these two arrays side by side, their production orientations might be summarized by observing that whereas the Lowell corporations charted a course toward accumulation that was capital intensive and labor saving, the Philadelphia firms sought a similar result through strategies that were skill intensive and capital saving. A closer look at the capitalists and workers at each site and at their social relations of production may add some depth to this seductively tidy formulation.

Two characteristics of the Philadelphia manufacturers are initially salient: They were largely brought up in shops and mills and were immigrants, and thus shared a cultural framework with their work forces. Until the eighties, most lived near the mills, above or in front of their workshops; many were active in churches and neighborhood associations, elaborating community-based bonds between owner and employee. Networks of customary relations in the mill were constituted out of these personal and cultural "makings," which at their most developed appeared in both factory paternalism and the theater of strike activity. Such relationships did not prevent conflict, but they bounded and channeled it, humanized it, and obstructed that abstraction and generalization from experience that could constitute class consciousness. The diversity of goals evident among Philadelphia proprietors further hindered their self-realization as a class and their being perceived as such by workers. Small shopmen (dyers, handloom carpet masters) went about getting a living from their craft on the same streets occupied by Thomas Dolan's vast aggrandizing enterprises. In between were hundreds of firms whose operators regarded them at least in part as a family legacy, rather than as an engine for maximum exploitation. It was these men who shared the craftsmen's goal of a competence for old age, and they who withdrew from manufacture once it had been achieved, turning over the works to kinsmen or able workers (McFadden to Schofield) who then "commenced on their own account." Even Dolan, aggressively seeking the best return, did so by engaging skilled workers whose talents could be rapidly turned from one branch of production to another; and to protect both them and his investment, he operated one of the safest mills in the city.[4] (This differentiation itself had a personal dimension, for operators at all three "levels" were known as good masters, such as Bromley and Dolan, or hard men, such as Ripka and Spencer, which further obscured their objective commonality as owners of capital and employers of labor.)

Lowell's founders and shareholders were distanced both physically and culturally from those engaged by their agents for work in the factories. Their interests were from the outset uniformly focused on the delivery of divi-

---

[4] When a tragic mill fire killed a number of Kensington workers in 1881, Dolan both spoke at an indignation meeting and contributed $500 for relief of the victims' families. He drew warm praise from workers at that time for the safety provisions in place at his factory; *Public Ledger*, October 14, 19, 1881.

dends, an expectation usually met by managers over long decades of operation. Although resident agents had both power over hiring and a considerable presence in the city, their autonomy was limited. Absentee boards and visiting treasurers made the fundamental decisions about investment, marketing, and the future of the corporation. Even the calculating paternalism of boardinghouses and church attendance sprang from a cool appreciation of the cultural requirements for collecting an adequate work force and was discarded after a generation, once the cost–benefit ratios turned downward. Whereas the corporations' united actions in cutting rates and firing striking mule spinners offered the raw materials for a developing critical awareness among workers, the sheer power of the firms crushed sparks of resistance as they flared. Finally, the corporations refused to supply steampower to new firms not created from their template. Taken together, these details suggest that Lowell lacked the overlapping cultural and community relationships among workers and owners that smoothed accumulation at Philadelphia, though corporate strength sufficed to block serious interference. Another factor in the Lowell pattern was its narrow entrepreneurial frontier. Although dissident workers could hardly expect a ready welcome at the next mill down the canal, neither could prospective manufacturers readily locate a site in the district for their modest beginnings.[5] At Philadelphia there was no such formalized system of power; casualties of failing strikes could expect work at hand, if not in the neighborhood, at worst across town.[6] Other than at Manayunk, no central body controlled access to space or power, and even there it was common practice to accommodate small operators.

A good deal more could be done here in extending and recapitulating the contrasts in structure and process of the textile industries in Lowell and Philadelphia, but the systematic divergence of the two formats is apparent. Each aimed at success within a capitalist economy, but their approaches to the matrix elements differed radically, as did their operating definitions of "success" and "capitalism," each of which surely had several constructions in Philadelphia alone. The Philadelphia manufacture was indeed distinctive in its creation of an interlocked set of "separate establishments." But in addition, the textile manufactures of Philadelphia and Lowell as entireties represented "separate" ways of "establishing" capitalist industry, each of which was prodigiously successful and each of which had separate strengths, vulnerabilities, and identifiable trajectories of development.

---

[5] It should be noted that there were a handful of independent water- and steampowered mills south of the main canal district in the antebellum period, and a number of new starts after the war. Only in the later era did they engage as much as 10% of the city's textile workers.

[6] During the strikes of the 1880s, reports circulated of carpet workers' taking employment in hosiery mills while standing out over grievances in the carpet shops.

At Lowell, over six decades, what changes and continuities stand out? Certainly management was professionalized to a considerable degree, with decision making routinized well before the Civil War. In response to the price declines that attended mass production, both the technology and social relations of speedup and stretch-out were engineered. The company boardinghouses and their vital Yankee sisterhoods gave way to private boarding and slum-housing construction that embraced thousands of Irish and Quebecois migrants. Periodically, the corporate mills continued their expansion, constructing new buildings or erecting replacements for the early mills, adding hundreds of thousands of spindles. After the war, the major firms attempted to produce a higher grade output to deal with the looming glut and the onset of southern production. In addition, they watched local yarn and worsted firms pop up, at last liberated from dependence on waterpower by the spread of coal-fired steam mills. Yet beneath the moving surface was the deep continuity of dominion. Lowell was hardly a simple company town, but it was from the thirties through the eighties a multicorporate city, never escaping the defining influence of the mills along the Merrimack even into the present century, as they one by one fell silent. The strategy of bulk staple production remained, and the reliance on easily replaceable low-skill labor was only enhanced by the immigrant influx. And, of course, the firms remained; after the founders were interred, after generations of managers and workers had departed, married, or died, the complement of companies, of massive integrated establishments, endured: Massachusetts, Hamilton, Lowell, Appleton, Tremont and Suffolk, Lawrence, Middlesex, Boott, and the originator, the Merrimack. If, as Batchelder observed, some were running much the same goods in the 1870s that they had been making a half century before, the extraordinary achievement that their collective survival represented cannot be minimized.

When the question of transformation and continuity is addressed in Philadelphia, a rich tapestry of quite different movements and stabilities emerges. The numbers of firms and workers soared from the fifties to the eighties. In fabric manufacture the early cotton predominance was surpassed by woolens and worsteds. Having taken root in the thirties, the knit-goods and carpet trades exploded to national prominence. Silk producers sprouted around Horstmann's founding effort; yarn mills and dye shops of all sizes appeared in rapid succession in the later decades. Yet in all this growth, there was considerable turnover. Firms chronically short of capital and credit failed, principals died, retired, or argued their partners into dissolution. New men replaced them, applying their craft or commercial skills to the array of opportunities that flexible and specialized manufacture afforded in Philadelphia, indicating the deeper strengths of that approach to production. After the war, new products and designs reached toward fashion in clothing, upholstery, trimmings, and carpets and by the eighties in curtains and lace. Blocks of samples were run to test these waters, showing the firms' productive capacities. Powered weaving grew alongside the venerable handloom crafts, the latter fading as their masters and workmen aged. (This process was hastened on cottons by the cotton famine during the Civil War, but carpet handworkers were resilient into the late eighties when 2,000 handlooms on Smyrnas were reported active.) With the increasing importance of powered weaving and knitting came a rising proportion of women workers, though the considerable skill demands of the Philadelphia trades kept the absolute numbers of adult male workers increasing as well. By the close of the period, manufacturers and workers in several sectors were engaged in erratic and ambiguous conflict, both reaching for citywide support and forming ostensibly permanent organizations for mutual aid and defense. The most visible manufacturers association was in addition concerned with influencing federal tariff policy and, after prodding, with undertaking a venture into technical education.

Still, there were elements in the 1885 Philadelphia trades that would have been recognizable to manufacturers and workers of earlier generations. Shops and mills of all sizes and from all sectors were to be found in the textile districts of Kensington, Germantown, and Manayunk. Selling offices at the factory or near the docks were staffed by interested parties from the firms, whose private proprietary operations echoed those of days gone by. Sons were being groomed for inheritance, working their way through the factory to the counting rooms. Immigrants and their children and kin predominated on rosters of both owners and workers. Firms still started up in rented rooms (with or without power), skill was still central, machinery was flexible rather than fast, and production shifted with the markets. If hundreds of new firms had supplanted scores of older ones, the mill buildings themselves stood fast, hosting new occupants. The Globe, the Manayunk canal row, and the hundred wartime additions were now joined by newer plants, buildings to be rented or owned and operated by rising stars like Wood, Dolan, Dobson, and Doak. Finally, the city in which this industry had bloomed remained the greatest center of diversified manufacturing in the nation, with a quarter million production workers in hundreds of trades among its 1880 population of more than 800,000. The Philadelphia textile industry could seem "peculiar" only to those who were mesmerized by the Lowell experiment and its successors. What they failed to see, and what we have here demonstrated, was that Philadelphia exhibited a fully realized alternative format for capitalist industrial development, a proprietary matrix different from the Lowell system at every point of analysis.

Overall, the exploration of Philadelphia's textile industry presented in these pages seeks to contribute to historical understanding along three lines.

Conceptually, the use of the matrix notion as a means to appreciate complex social and economic processes may prove of some value elsewhere for researchers formulating approaches to other dimensions of economic history.[7] More concretely, the reconstruction and analysis of the Philadelphia format for textile production exposes the dynamics of proprietary capitalist manufacturing in a manner that may stimulate comparison with other sectors and other eras.[8] If, in economic history, studies of the capitalist "rank and file" begin to accumulate along lines symmetrical with the exciting work in labor history over the last decade, we may collectively build in time a synthetic account of industrial development in America that both integrates the corporate and proprietary dynamics and presents the industrialization process as a historical totality. Finally, in a time of persistent economic crisis, refining our sense of historical alternatives should indicate some of the questions we must ask in the future and alert us to both the human costs of progress and profit and the capacities and limitations of capitalism as a system of power and production. If through such work, we begin anew to acknowledge the potency of human agency, the contingency of the given, and the importance of culture and accident in historical processes, we may further the effort to imagine alternatives within, and to, capitalism, as a systematic reconstruction of the past may provide us raw material for the struggles that lie ahead.

[7] An analogous notion, that of the "social structure of accumulation," has been introduced by David Gordon, Richard Edwards, and Michael Reich in *Segmented Work, Divided Workers: The Historical Transformation of Labor in the United States*, New York, 1982, pp. 22–6.

[8] For a collection of stimulating perspectives on this issue, see Stuart Bruchey, ed., *Small Business in American Life*, New York, 1980. Though concerned with a later period, James Soltow's contribution to this volume, "Origins of Small Business and the Relationships Between Large and Small Firms: Metal Fabricating and Machinery Making in New England, 1890–1957," parallels my reconstruction of proprietary capitalism in nineteenth-century Philadelphia at a number of points, indicating the persistence of flexible, skill-intensive firms well into the present era.

Index